Volume I

AMERICA

THE COVENANT NATION

A Christian Perspective

From America's Foundations in the Early 1600s
To the Great Depression of the 1930s

Miles Huntley Hodges

Copyright © 2021 Miles Huntley Hodges

All right reserved. No part of this book may be used or reproduced by any means, graphic, electronic, or mechanical, including photocopying, recording, taping or by any information storage retrieval system without the written permission of the author except in the case of brief quotations embodied in critical articles and reviews.

ISBN: 978-1-7376413-8-4 (soft copy)
ISBN: 978-1-7376413-9-1 (hard copy)
ISBN: 979-8-9851074-0-1 (laminate copy)
ISBN: 979-8-9851074-1-8 (e-copy)

Library of Congress Control Number: 2021921153

thecovenantnation.com

CONTENTS

PREFACE: AMERICA – THE COVENANT NATION   1
    THE PARABLE OF THE FOUR GENERATIONS
    THE PURPOSE AND NATURE OF THIS STUDY
    THE PERSONAL BACKGROUND TO THIS STUDY
    ABOUT THIS STUDY

INTRODUCTION: ON BEING A COVENANT PEOPLE   15
    JOHN WINTHROP AND THE PURITAN COVENANT
    AND HOW DO THINGS STAND TODAY WITH THAT COVENANT?

1. COLONIAL FOUNDATIONS   20
    THE TWO DISTINCT CULTURAL MOTIFS
    THE ORIGINS OF THE WESTERN OR CHRISTIAN SOCIAL LEGACY
    THE FIRST YEARS OF EUROPEAN COLONIZATION OF AMERICA
    VIRGINIA - AND ITS ENGLISH ARISTOCRATIC (OR FEUDAL) TRADITION
    PURITAN NEW ENGLAND (EARLY 1600s)

2. THE COLONIES MATURE   72
    THE VARIETY AND NATURE OF THE AMERICAN COLONIES
    MARYLAND: THE PROPRIETARY CATHOLIC COLONY
    THE ENGLISH CIVIL WAR, COMMONWEALTH AND RESTORATION
    THE CAROLINAS
    NEW YORK
    NEW JERSEY
    PENNSYLVANIA AND DELAWARE
    THE GLORIOUS REVOLUTION (1688–1689)
    THE COLONIES' EVER-EVOLVING SPIRITUAL CHARACTER
    COLONIAL SOCIETY IN THE 1700s
    GEORGIA – THE LAST OF THE THIRTEEN COLONIES
    THE "GREAT AWAKENING" RESTORES THE CHRISTIAN SPIRIT

3. INDEPENDENCE   107
    INVOLVEMENT IN THE DYNASTIC POLITICS OF EUROPE
    STEPS TOWARD FULL INDEPENDENCE FROM ENGLAND
    THE WAR GETS UNDERWAY IN THE NORTH
    WASHINGTON: THE MATTER OF PERSONAL CHARACTER
    THE WAR ITSELF
    THE WAR MOVES SOUTH ... AND FINALLY ENDS

4. THE BIRTH OF THE AMERICAN REPUBLIC   139
    THE MACHINERY OF GOVERNMENT
    THE ORIGINAL INTENTIONS OF THE CONSTITUTION'S DESIGNERS
    THE STRONG CHRISTIAN COMPONENT IN THE DISCUSSIONS
    THE PROCESS OF COMING TO AN AGREEMENT
    A FEDERATION REPLACES THE CONFEDERATION
    A GOVERNMENT THAT DRAWS ITS POWERS FROM THE PEOPLE
    WHAT WERE THE GUARANTEES THAT THIS WOULD WORK?
    THE REPUBLIC IS BIRTHED

5. THE YOUNG REPUBLIC — 174
- GETTING STARTED (1789–1801)
- JEFFERSON BEGINS THE REIGN OF THE REPUBLICANS
- AGRARIAN AMERICA INTRODUCED TO THE INDUSTRIAL REVOLUTION
- AMERICA IS SLOWLY DRAWN INTO THE FRENCH-ENGLISH WARS

6. THE SHAPING OF A NATION — 210
- THE "ERA OF GOOD FEELINGS"
- THE TOUGH QUESTION OF INDIAN vs. ANGLO LAND RIGHTS
- THE JACKSONIAN DEMOCRATIC REVOLUTION
- JACKSONIAN CULTURE
- THE "SECOND GREAT AWAKENING"

7. EXPANSION ... AND DIVISION — 248
- "MANIFEST DESTINY"
- TEXAS INDEPENDENCE
- "TIPPECANOE AND TYLER TOO"
- JAMES POLK AND THE MEXICAN-AMERICAN WAR (1846–1848)
- "WESTWARD HO"
- THE GROWING CONFLICT OVER SLAVERY
- AMERICA AT MID-CENTURY (1850)

8. THE GATHERING CLOUDS OF WAR — 274
- THE STEPS TOWARD WAR
- LINCOLN
- THE NATION FINALLY DIVIDES

9. CIVIL WAR — 292
- 1861: THE LONG-DELAYED WAR FINALLY BREAKS OUT
- 1862: STALEMATE
- 1863: THE NORTH BEGINS TO DOMINATE
- 1864: THE SOUTH UNDER SIEGE
- 1865: THE COLLAPSE OF THE SOUTH ... AND DEATH OF LINCOLN

10. AMERICA RECOVERS: 1865–1880 — 319
- RECONSTRUCTION DURING THE JOHNSON PRESIDENCY
- AMERICA UNDER THE GRANT PRESIDENCY
- THE 1876 ELECTION AND THE HAYES COMPROMISE
- THE BATTLE FOR THE WEST

11. THE "GILDED AGE" OF AMERICAN CAPITALISM — 340
- CAPITALISM IN THE GILDED AGE
- THE RAPID GROWTH OF AMERICAN MATERIAL POWER
- NATIONAL POLITICS DURING THE LATE 1800s
- THE WHEELS OF MATERIAL PROGRESS

12. AMERICAN PROGRESSIVISM — 366
- THE EMERGENCE OF AMERICAN PROGRESSIVISM
- JANE ADDAMS
- WILLIAM JENNINGS BRYAN
- THEODORE (TEDDY) ROOSEVELT
- WILLIAM HOWARD TAFT

13. THE RATIONALIZING OF WESTERN CULTURE　　　387
    UNDERSTANDING THE SPIRIT OF THE TIMES
    THE RISING AGE OF WESTERN RATIONALISM
    ROMANTICISM AND NATIONALISM
    DARWINISM
    KARL MARX
    VLADIMIR ILYICH ULYANOV (LENIN)
    DEMOCRACY AS THE RISING IDEAL OF AMERICAN POLITICS
    WOODROW WILSON, THE DEMOCRATIC IDEALIST
    AMERICAN LIBERALISM
    JOHN DEWEY AS A FOUNDING FATHER OF AMERICAN LIBERALISM
    SUPREME COURT JUSTICE OLIVER WENDELL HOLMES, Jr.
    CHRISTIANITY RESPONDS

14. NATIONALISM, IMPERIALISM, AND THE GREAT WAR　　　436
    EUROPEAN IMPERIALISM
    AMERICAN IMPERIALISM
    THE CLOUDS OF WAR BEGIN TO GATHER
    1914 – WAR FINALLY BREAKS OUT
    1915/1916 – THE EXTREMELY UGLY WAR HAS NO END IN SIGHT
    REVOLUTION IN RUSSIA (1917)
    AMERICA ENTERS THE WAR (1917)
    THE TROUBLED PEACE

15. THE "ROARING TWENTIES"　　　476
    AMERICA DOES INDEED ROAR AFTER THE WAR
    TRADITIONALIST AMERICA ... AND THE NEW CULTURE
    A STRONG SENSE OF CYNICISM IN URBAN AMERICA
    THE AMERICAN QUEST FOR MORAL GROUNDING
    AMERICA CONFRONTS THE WORLD DURING THE 1920s
    THE 1920s COME TO A CRASHING END

16. THE GREAT DEPRESSION (THE 1930s)　　　507
    EARLY ATTEMPTS TO ANSWER THE ECONOMIC CRISIS
    ROOSEVELT'S NEW DEAL
    A SHIFT IN THE AMERICAN SENSE OF ORDER

BIBLIOGRAPHY AND ENDNOTES　　　531

INDEX　　　546

AMERICA – THE COVENANT NATION

Preface to the Two-Volume Series

* * *

THE PARABLE OF THE FOUR GENERATIONS

History teaches us a key lesson: that societies rise – and then fall – sometimes in short order (just a few generations), sometimes slowly over the centuries. But they all do at some point come and then go as strong, viable societies.

For instance, ancient Athens rose to glory and then fell in the span of only a mere century. It did linger on after its fall, but no longer a great society. Rome however managed to hang on for centuries between its gradual rise beginning in the 300s and 200s B.C.* (or earlier if you take into account its very first steps) and its fall, first in the Western half of the Empire du1ring the 400s A.D. (thanks to the Germans) and then in its Eastern territories in the 600s A.D. (thanks to the Arab Muslims) – although it did hang on as a small Eastern power all the way up to the mid–1400s.

In the 20th Century alone, we watched the decline and disappearance of the once-great British, French, Dutch, Belgian, and Portuguese Empires. And we saw both the seventy-year dramatic rise and then dismal collapse of the Soviet Russian Empire. And we got to watch Hitler's "1000-Year Reich" and the great Japanese Empire rise to enormous greatness and then to full collapse – all in a mere dozen years.

And we got to watch America rise from a being secondary power to the status of being the world's sole superpower in the course of the 20th Century.

Thus arises the question: for how long will America hang on to its greatness? Will America be like ancient Athens, holding on to greatness for only about a century (such as what happened also to the great Habsburg Spanish Empire which dominated the entire 1500s)? Or will it manage to carry on over the centuries, like the great Roman Empire?

---

*B.C. – "Before Christ."   A.D. – "Anno Domini" (Latin for "Year of our Lord").

Back in the early 1970s, when I first took up university teaching, that question was put to me by my students, naturally concerned about the direction toward which their American society seemed to be headed. I answered with a story illustrating a society's natural dynamics of growth and decline, a story explaining how strong leadership, inspiring a disciplined social-moral order, could establish and build to great strength an entire society. But the story also illustrated how corrupt or just morally lazy leadership, which seems to come along inevitably with time, would also confuse and severely damage that society and its social-moral order. I called this story the "Parable of the Four Generations." Here is a brief summarization of the parable.

The First Generation. A society typically begins under the mastery or leadership of a very strong-willed individual, not infrequently a young man who climbs out of very tough – even brutal – circumstances. And in overcoming those circumstances he achieves a self-discipline in the face of dangerous challenges, one which so strongly impresses a gathering circle of young warriors that he is able to turn this group into a similarly disciplined band of conquerors. The warrior-leader is very generous to those who would follow his lead bravely, against even the most dangerous of challenges. But he could also be equally unforgiving of those who would fail to live up to his very precise warrior code or his high expectations of a very brave performance in carrying out the warrior duties of those who would dare join him.

But what drives this leader is not just some hunger to force others under his direction for the sheer joy of it. That can come to certain people as a big ego-high. But usually that same urge will blind and ultimately destroy such wannabe leaders. No, what drives this First-Generation leader is vision, a higher vision or sense of call that comes from some source other than the approval of the immediate world around him. It comes typically from a sense, even at a very early age, that Heaven itself has a special commission for this young man to build a society that will serve the greater will of Heaven, God, Providence, Allah, Zeus, Tian – or whatever name is given to this Higher Power. It is the ability of our young warrior to keep his eyes on this higher call that allows him not to fall victim to the flattery of those who would try to use him for their own personal gain. He is immune to such human willfulness. Thus such vision with its call to bold action as well as an unshakable resolve to keep himself and others under the inflexible moral discipline required to see that vision come to reality together make him the powerful leader that he is.

He also occupies a special place in history because his arrival on the social scene is timed with developments well beyond his own political-social designs. In fact, he himself is no such political-social designer. Instead, he is an individual fully capable of taking on fearsome challenges immediately in front of him as they arise to confront him on an almost daily basis. He does not design life, like some lofty intellectual working at a desk and living in a bubble of beautiful ideals and wonderfully rational plans designed to achieve utopia. His world is tough, messy, and unpredictable. But he is fearsomely brave as he pursues this political-social call placed on him by the very power of Heaven. He resolves simply to keep moving forward, even in the face of the most discouraging circumstances.

And thus it is that this man of valor is able to inspire others to join him on this path of overcoming – and ultimately this path of social conquest. He is thus able through sheer doggedness to produce social greatness.*

And in our parable, that conquest would include even the great civilization just over the next mountain range, a civilization that is in deep trouble because it is no longer led by such powerful leaders as our First-Generation founder. This once-great civilization has fallen into deep moral decay, one that inevitably comes along with the rise to power of the Fourth and final Generation. This civilization finds itself caught at this point in time in the throes of social collapse. It is ripe for conquest by some kind of rising power outside itself. And that is where the First-Generation leader finds himself and his men headed in history.

Timing is, of course, also key to success in history.

The Second Generation. The son (the Second Generation) of the original founder-warrior will also have grown up in tough circumstances, though only because of the disciplined social environment established by his father – not because of a threatening political world immediately around him. By the time he is a rising young man, much of that has already been cleared away by his father's early successes. However, the father's grand vision, in which he understood rather clearly the ultimate destiny of his small but growing society, has had the father over the years preparing his son to take up the responsibilities that one day will be passed on to him. The First-Generation father therefore has had his Second-Generation son train and join him in battle, learning the responsibilities of leadership. There is, after all, a world to be conquered by both of them, father and son.

And that conquered world one day will need to be administered by a

---

*Certainly both Washington and Lincoln are perfect examples of this kind of leadership. So also was the largely unacknowledged true Founder of Anglo-American society (at least the New England version), John Winthrop. And this category should also include Hamilton, a fiercely brave soul who took up the unloved responsibility of getting the new Republic started up on very strong financial foundations. These people carried America forward in its development through the most challenging of times.

competent ruler. But it will fall to the son, not the father, to be just that individual. Anticipating this, the father perhaps will have, early along the way, sent his son off to live and study for a number of years within that larger civilization, one that is destined to be ruled by his own rising dynasty. This certainly occurred in the case of Philip II of Macedon, when he sent his son Alexander off to Greece to study under Aristotle. As a result, the son will know and understand the ways of the larger world that one day will be his responsibility to rule.

The son will also know of the Heavenly Commission upon which his society was originally founded by his father, though perhaps only secondarily, through what his father has told him about it. The son will respect that Higher Power and will take its ruling principles into account in his governance. But he will also be shaped by his knowledge of the political codes and moral rules of the society he is about to inherit, its wise counselors, its civilized ways. All of this will come as a blend of the son's own vision and self-discipline. He is more the person of Reason, like the civilized world he has come to know, than of dangerous risk-taking, something required by the social conditions his father grew up in.

Typically, the era of the Second Generation will be understood by historians as constituting the political height of that society or civilization, the one created or restored through the conquering efforts of the First Generation, and the considerable administrative talents of the Second Generation.*

The Third Generation. The grandson/son of the two preceding generations will be personally familiar only with life as lived within the palace that he was raised in. He will know well the stories of the great valor of his grandfather, although such knowledge will have more the nature of folklore than reality to him. He will see and experience directly the blessings of his father's well-administered social-legal order. It certainly will have already benefitted the son greatly. And thus he will be entirely devoted to the idea of completing and securing the full development of that perfect social order. He will spend his time in his royal chambers working on that perfect design, working closely with his highly educated advisors on the specifics of a proposed legal order he wants them to put into place by royal decree.

Along with the proposed legal order, his own vision typically will include the perfecting or beautifying of the visible features of the civilization he has inherited: the beautification of the palace dwellings; the building of

---

*Both Roosevelts, Truman, Eisenhower, and Kennedy would certainly fall somewhere in this category, in the way they worked to maintain and utilize American social power in the face of huge social challenges. Nixon, Reagan, and Bush Sr. probably also belong in this category.

magnificent homes for his huge administrative staff; the upgrading of the public places such as the all-important central market and the houses of worship; the development of public parks and places of leisure (mostly for the privileged urban classes).*

Of course all of this will come at a great cost, especially to those least able to fend off the tax collectors, who fleece the poorer classes to pay for these extravagant projects, projects which will bring little or no benefit to the lower social orders. Restlessness and even occasional revolt will from time to time upset this utopian social order that Generation Three is attempting to put into place. And our ruler will be uncomprehending as to why such turmoil is accompanying his efforts to perfect his people's world. But that is because he lives largely in a social-intellectual-moral bubble of his own making. He is far removed from the hard realities of the larger world around him. Most importantly, he has lost touch with those he is expected to govern. He no longer relates to this people as a moral compass or spiritual guide for them. Trouble brews.

The Fourth Generation. Having grown up in a world of total privilege, surrounded by flattering supporters who were looking to be brought into that world of privilege, our Fourth-Generation leader will have lost touch completely with the hard realities facing his society, the challenges that as society's governing authority he is expected to address and solve. But he lives in a world of massive disinformation (who would dare to contradict the presuppositions of the Great Ruler). He is clueless as to his responsibilities.

Not only is there a total loss of dedicated discipline to his governance, there is not even any particular direction to it. He is a person of no particular vision, except to hang on to all the entitlements coming his way as Great Ruler. He is bored, listless, and dangerous, not only to those immediately around him but also to himself. And most tragically, he is also a great danger to the society he is expected to lead. He indulges in every known diversion possible, being able (he believes) to afford them all: gambling, drugs and alcohol, sex (in various ways), wild spending sprees (for nothing in particular), cruel games (including the torture of individuals he does not particularly care for), and so on.

And as for the general moral order of the society he is supposed to be leading, it now finds itself in a state of collapse. Hungry gangs wander the streets, violating persons and property as they see the urge to do so. It

---

*American examples of this would be Jefferson, Wilson, and Johnson (LBJ), all of whom sought to perfect American society (and even the world in some cases) through highly-planned or rational social redesign. Franklin Roosevelt, Carter and Clinton seemed to have started out this way, but thankfully were forced back into a Second-Generation profile when hard Reality struck!

is dangerous for women and children to go to market for the day's needs, or even to enter the streets at all. Extortionists come around to exact the price of protection on the defenseless people. The social order is simply collapsing. And as for the people's affection for their government, its Great Ruler in particular, there is none. They wish him dead, and would support anyone inclined to cause that to happen.

And that brings us back to the First Generation, for that is where such help is to come from. And thus the cycle begins all over again.

What the parable seems to imply about America today. So, in answering my students' question back in those years of the early 1970s as to where America found itself in this matter of a society's rise and fall, I answered "somewhere in the middle of the Third Generation." We had been trying to perfect the structuring of American society through Johnson's Great Society programming and building a strong South Vietnamese society able to ward off the aggressions of Communism. But instead of achieving wonderful social progress on both fronts, Johnson's programs seemed to have brought to America only shocking social chaos, both at home and abroad. And that chaos merely continued through the 1970s. At times it felt as if we were even heading into the Fourth Generation.

Later, during the 1980s and 1990s, we actually seemed to step back into a profile more characteristic of the Second Generation. But with the beginning of the 21st century we also seemed to skip ahead, down the road heading America toward the Fourth Generation. Indeed, today I would have to say that we stand somewhere in the early stages of the Fourth Generation. We have so thoroughly "Changed" the fundamental moral structure of American society, that America – and Americans – are suffering from a major identity crisis, one characteristic of the Fourth Generation.

Americans seem to find it highly entertaining to tear at each other at home – wielding "Reason" like a club to crush political adversaries. The traditional moral grounding which for generations forced political debate to stay within certain boundaries has disappeared. All combatants today are so convinced of their own righteousness (who needs rules or boundaries when you are certain that you alone are the only one who is Right in these matters!) that Washington politics has become totally uncivil. This is definitely Fourth Generation behavior.

With China on the rise in its effort to become *the* superpower of the 21st century, this is not a good condition for America to find itself in. America seems to be losing serious influence abroad (it was a very strong America, after all, that put in place the shape and direction that moved much of the larger world after World War Two). But the loss of power abroad means also the loss of political freedom at home. A weakened America does not need to be "protected' or "guided" by a newly dominant China.

America needs help, much help, from some source other than its own self-inflicted wisdom or Reason that now pretends to direct it. It is going to need the very power that long ago put the foundations of this great society in place. It is going to need the very power of Heaven, of God himself, to get America back on track as a powerful society. Literally, it needs to restore the Covenant or contractual relationship with God, one that was agreed to four centuries ago (the early 1600s) by the Puritan Founding Fathers. In that Covenant, those leaders agreed to put this country's fate in the hands of God and promised that they would follow God's – not man's – counsel. What they were doing there in New England was totally unprecedented, very risky, and they were going to need God's help in order to succeed in this rather experimental social venture. And succeed they did.

But as with all things in human nature (as our parable points out), success led American society down the road of moral drift – more than once, as it turned out! But God remembered the Puritans' agreement with him and honored the terms of the Covenant. In sending great spiritual revivals or "Awakenings" to America at various points in the county's history, he got America back on course, moving ahead once again. In each of these instances, that Godly relationship – not human social planning – got Americans ready to face some very major social crises that loomed before them. And thanks to God's moral-spiritual renewal of America, America came through these crises stronger than ever.

Now here we are today morally confused and horribly undirected. Worse, we seem to want to fight any efforts to get us up and running again as a truly great society. We need Godly, not more Rationally human, guidance again ... badly.

Thus, recovering that Covenant or contractual relationship with God is a matter of great urgency today.

✳ ✳ ✳

THE PURPOSE AND NATURE OF THIS STUDY

Another central and closely related theme of this study is the fact that, from its founding onward, there have always been "Two Americas." One such America always finds the Americans themselves focused entirely on their own individual or personal success achieved through Rationally-designed self-advancement, calculated to help the individual acquire superior social status, visible clearly to the world in terms of the material display (housing, cars, clothing, etc.) that is supposed to accompany such personal success.

This America finds itself in the category of the Third Generation, which unfortunately slides so easily into a Fourth-Generation situation.*

The other America, however, is characterized by a willingness of Americans to take on huge social challenges as a single people, working closely together – even sacrificially – to bring their beloved society to success. Like the First Generation, they have also well-understood that what truly mattered in life was a very personal relationship with God, one that enabled them to take on unpredictable and thus fearsome challenges in the full confidence that God, not some lofty program of grand Humanist design, would guide and strengthen them through those tough times.

This dual pattern has appeared repeatedly: Americans rather naturally wanting to drift down the self-focused "Rational" Secular-Humanist-Materialist path, and then God through various Awakenings bringing them together back on the course that as a Covenant People they had originally set out on.

This study covers all the typical subjects of an in-depth American political history, but with extensive social-cultural analysis offered by way of a mixture of a strong political Realism and an equally strong Christian cultural and spiritual perspective. The study also includes a close look at a number of individuals, leaders who strongly shaped America's social-moral culture as the country developed. And it always keeps an eye on the changing balance culture-wise between Human Reason (Humanism or Secularism) and Christian morality and spirituality as America moved from one age to the next

This is a study shaped greatly out of a classroom effort to help young Americans come to know personally the narrative of their own society (and eventually also young international students to better understand the same dynamics for their society as well) ... to prepare them to enter a world in which one day they will have to make choices, both personal and social. This narrative was designed to help them gain needed political-moral perspective, to help them rise out of the confusion that has been left for them to deal with by previous generations. They have the huge social responsibility of becoming a wise generation. After all, America is supposed to be a democracy, dependent on the wisdom of all its people and not just on the guidance of a self-proclaimed body of the enlightened few located off in some distant political center. Thus it is that this study is intended for the classroom, at all levels of young adult learning

But actually, this study originated as part of an adult social studies

---

*This is the situation America found itself in during the Roaring Twenties (1920s), materially rich and spiritually impoverished – until the Great Depression of the 1930s brought America out of this moral funk and got the country spiritually ready to take on the huge challenge of World War Two soon facing them.

Preface

program and therefore is also directed toward a fairly adult general audience. It is written at a college level (even grad school level) in terms of vocabulary and social commentary. However, I once asked my high-school students if they had trouble with the vocabulary. They assured me that the meaning of what they were reading was always very clear, even if occasionally above their general vocabulary level!

* * *

THE PERSONAL BACKGROUND TO THIS STUDY*

Ever the political analyst. I am by training and experience not really an historian but instead a political scientist – by very strong instinct. I have long used history as my laboratory in developing an understanding of social and political dynamics. But I am also a dedicated Christian – who had to come to that Christian faith and understanding through a long process of searching for the Truth in life. Actually, it turned out that Truth found me! From that moment on, I have been trying to flesh out the details of that Truth. This study is a part – a big part – of that effort.

Early in my career I was a university professor (international politics) and a consulting political-economic analyst for corporate America. My journey started back in the 1960s at Georgetown University (1963–1968), when I did my master's thesis on South Africa and my doctoral dissertation on Belgium, both concerning the subject of multiculturalism – having become intrigued with the subject because of my junior year (1961–1962) spent at the University of Geneva in multicultural Switzerland. The dynamics by which I came to predict (as it turned out, correctly) that South Africa in the mid-1960s was destined to go down a path different from the one being followed elsewhere in Africa (South African Whites would hold on to their power, at least for another generation) pushed me to dig more deeply into the matter of why societies go this way rather than that. And I arrived in Belgium (1969) just as it was beginning to find relief from the long struggle between the French and Dutch-speaking halves of the country – by instead moving to serve the higher goal of becoming the center of a rising New Europe. I was impressed by how societies that find a higher purpose to their very existence can gain great strength in the process.

As a young political science professor at the University of South

---

*This personal story of mine has been recently published (September 2021) as *The Spiritual Pilgrim – A Journey from Cynical Realism to a "Born Again" Christian Faith*. Its various 250-page print versions can be found online under my name at amazon.com or barnesandnoble.com, as an ebook at kobo.com, or as an audiobook at audible.com.

Alabama (1971–1986), I had the opportunity to broaden this interest considerably, teaching over the next fifteen years not only American diplomacy and international relations, but also regional political dynamics (courses offered annually on Europe, the Middle East and Asia) by which I began to understand how different societies see things differently and thus approach life differently. But I also saw a pattern amidst all these differences and, early on, developed the Four-Generation parable to explain this dynamic. This interest in social dynamics led me ultimately to set up my own consultancy business in political-risk research, working with banks and corporations located across the American South, and ultimately to offer a special contract course on political risk analysis staged at the London School of Economics. Thus it was that I put to work my instinct for *Realpolitik*. This study certainly reflects that same instinct.

The cynical Realist. However, something was missing in all this political Realism. I was quite understanding of the dynamic of the rise and fall of societies, and was not very happy watching American society going through this same dynamic in the 1970s. Sadly, in all this insight, life was showing me no good exit from the cynicism that hard Reality left me with. I was a most unwilling member of a latter-day Lost Generation, having become greatly disillusioned with life.

Encounters with God through contemporary examples of Jesus Christ. Then in 1983-1984 – in the midst of immense spiritual turmoil – God began to reveal himself to me step by step, eventually put clearly before me in the form of a young Catholic priest I worked with in El Salvador (1985–1986), a Christ-like figure loving and encouraging a small community of campesinos being shot up in a savage civil war going on in that country; then soon after that, an Episcopal priest who performed the same act of loving support to throwaway kids living under the boardwalk at Pensacola Beach; and similarly, a local plumber who went fulltime into a deeply caring Christian ministry to the homeless in downtown Mobile. Coming to know and work with these individuals opened up a whole new world for me.

While still teaching fulltime, I found myself undertaking part-time both regional prison ministry and Mobile jail and street ministry, fascinated to see how the Gospel of Jesus Christ brought wonderful light into the human darkness, even when that darkness seemed very dark indeed. As a Realist, I knew quite well that this was a darkness that no human program, no government program, no amount of Human Reason, was going to bring light to. For a natural cynic, the Gospel of Jesus Christ was a huge revelation.

Preface 11

Taking up the call. In fact, this personal Awakening was so huge that it caused me in 1986 to drop my professorship, tenure, status, and all, and head off to seminary in Princeton, simply to devote myself fulltime to deepening my understanding of the Christian social dynamic. Actually, fulltime was even fuller because I almost immediately started up a daily morning street ministry nearby among Trenton's homeless – breakfast, bible study, and just wide-ranging discussion. I would continue my hands-on work there, even for eighteen months after having completed my studies at the seminary – working in construction while awaiting a call!

Something of a side-note on my Princeton days but illustrative of where I come from in life was when in 1989, just a few days prior to the time I was due to graduate, my thesis mentor, a youngish professor at the seminary, finally reported my grade (which I myself had not yet seen) to the Registrar. It was an F! This was his personal assessment of my 260-page senior thesis, which was assembled after I had spent two months in South Africa the previous summer interviewing widely leaders of the various racial groups that made up the South African Society. My thesis concluded that there was going to be no violent revolution that would bring Black power into full play. But instead, an amazing spirit of racial reconciliation was going to achieve the same objective. This fervently Liberal professor, who actually knew very little about South African society and its dynamics, concluded that I had been taken in by South African Fascist deception, and thus I was not worthy of the Princeton stamp of approval. He was so wrapped up in his bubble-world of Liberal Reasoning that Reality found itself beyond his reach. Anyway, as it turned out, I had so many extra academic credits accumulated that much to his surprise I was able to participate in the seminary's graduation ceremonies three days later – thanks to a sympathetic Registrar who immediately refashioned for me my major from Christian Ethics to Biblical Studies. And when I ran into him sometime later, when things were unfolding in South Africa just as I had predicted, he was not interested in following up on the subject!

The discovery of the power of historical narrative. In any case, one of the great wonders that hit me in those seminary years came in acquainting myself with the power of the Judeo-Christian narrative, especially in the original languages of Greek and Hebrew! It was at this point that the idea of social narrative itself took on special meaning, even supreme importance, to me.

This arose from understanding the grandness of what the ancient Jews had achieved when they were dragged off to captivity in Babylon and were no longer permitted to practice their familiar pattern of worship, up until then mostly animal sacrifices performed at the Temple by temple priests. Unable to build a temple for themselves in Babylon, they instead simply reinvented themselves around their own narrative! They were a people anciently covenanted to God to be precisely his people – and as such had a marvelous story to tell about what that had meant to them over many generations. This story, this narrative itself thus became the focus of their devotion to and worship of their God Yahweh and their identity as a distinct people.

Thus it was that these ancient Jews literally created Judaism: rabbis or teachers instead of priests to lead them in their devotional life, rabbis who collected and then issued commentaries (sermons) on the gathered narrative at weekly gatherings at synagogues found scattered among the Jewish population in Babylon. It was thus the narrative itself, not temple sacrifices, that at this point defined the Jewish people and their special relationship with God. This was unique at the time. It was awesome.

And I realized how importantly Christianity was built on this same tradition of the narrative, not only including the Jewish narrative (the Old Testament) but also the story of Jesus's ministry (the Gospels) and the counsel (the Epistles or Letters) of the early saints, in particular the counsel of Paul found in the New Testament. For three centuries, the Bible became brutally-persecuted Christianity's early social-moral foundation ... before the Roman authorities reversed course and adopted Christianity as the Empire's own moral underpinning.

But in reversing this course, Christianity ultimately became "Romanized."

I also understood the struggles of the Christian Reformers of the 1500s and 1600s in their effort to get Christianity back to its original foundations based on the Biblical narrative – and not on just the Romanized ecclesiastical or hierarchical Church-based, legalistic, political-social tradition. I well understood how this also inspired the Puritans who came to America in the early 1600s to put into operation a society that would actually try to live as close to the counsel of that same Biblical narrative as possible. These Puritans were well equipped with highly educated teacher-preachers (like the Jewish rabbis) to keep them aligned with this Biblical counsel – through the weekly holding of Sunday gatherings where sermons inspired by this Biblical narrative were presented on an on-going basis.

While in seminary I had no intentions of becoming a pastor. But pastoring is ultimately the task God called me to in my move into my second career. Over a twelve-year period, three Presbyterian churches were to hear, from the pulpit and through special social-studies courses, sections of that narrative, mixed in with my tendency to move to contemporary social-cultural analysis in the process. I even in the 1990s started up my own website (newgeneva.org, later refashioned as spiritualpilgrim.net).

Preface 13

In my last years of pastoring I put together a team of myself and four other Presbyterian pastors and a Presbyterian businessman and for two years worked on developing a New Geneva study center to retread Presbyterian pastors and elders, naturally around both the Biblical and the Christian West's historical narrative. But with seventeen acres in hand, the project awakened a prestigious Presbyterian Church nearby, which viewed the project as possibly resulting in a sheep raid on their flock and, wielding enormous political pressure in the Presbytery, had us shut down.

Thus it was at this point that God led me to take a position (September 2001) at a new and quite humble but very spiritually and intellectually rigorous Christian school, The King's Academy (TKA). Quite ironically, in my first week at the school I stressed to my students that the days of Fortress America were gone. The two oceans no longer served to protect us from the affairs of the rest of the world. We no longer had an option as to whether we wanted to get involved with events abroad or not. It was our destiny to play a huge role in the world's development, whether we wanted to or not. Also, I stressed that the world now in this day and age would be coming to us – and at us – on its own terms, and we needed to be prepared physically, emotionally and spiritually to face such challenges. In fact, I mentioned in several of my classes how the Islamic jihadists wanted to take down the New York City Twin Towers. Tragically, my point struck home to my students even more deeply, when the very next day the Twin Towers did indeed come down.

I don't know what made me pick that example (I was of course aware of the former attempt in 1993). But that's how doing God's work often goes. That certainly got my students' attention concerning the importance of this learning project we would be working on together. Nonetheless, this was not a happy thing for me. Two of the people who died in the Towers were former parishioners of mine when I served as a pastor in Northern New Jersey. One in fact, the church treasurer, I was rather close to.

Anyway, from this academic base camp at The King's Academy I began to expand considerably my teaching material, which bit by bit made its way to my website ... including Western cultural history, comparative world cultures, biographical sketches, French language development, classic literature, even art history! And this is the material (the American history portion anyway) that would bring me today to produce this narrative that appears before you.

* * *

ABOUT THIS STUDY

As already indicated, this has been a long-researched project that was gradual, changing, and always developing here and there over a twenty to thirty-year period, some of that during a time of pastoral duties, though most of it while teaching my high school students at The King's Academy. It was done with the understanding that this is political science and Christian philosophy as much as historical fact.But in any case, the facts are extensively researched, and abundantly detailed.

Ultimately this particular study is about America and its covenantal relationship with God, offered America by God through the willingness ofAmerica's early leaders to follow Jesus as the Lord and life of this strange venture, this founding of a very new and very unique society. These Founders would be commissioned not only to help all members of this new society to live up to the terms of this Covenant (which the people themselves also agreed to honor) but also to show through the American example the way to such a divine relationship to the rest of the world. In accepting this commission, it was understood by those early Americans that this new society was to dedicate itself to living to great purpose – to be a City on a Hill, a Light to the Nations.

This covenant relationship with God has certainly been one with its ups and downs. But it was always this relationship that clearly moved America forward, eventually to become the superpower of the 20th century. But sadly today, an overly comfortable and smugly self-satisfied America has again drifted away from this relationship, perhaps further than it had in any of its earlier wanderings. We have now raised at least two – and are working on a third – generation that in general knows very little, or even nothing, of this Covenant.

America needs to be awakened to both the blessings and the adversities of life, shown the wisdom of those who went before us, facing most of the same problems – in different packages, but fundamentally the same issues then as now. There is much to be learned in once again hearing the American narrative. There is much that must be learned, or social drift into an ever-darker world will be the foreordained outcome. Even the Puritans – or better, especially the Puritans – who started out this American narrative, were aware of this challenge. And that is why we start with them.

INTRODUCTION

ON BEING A COVENANT PEOPLE

* * *

JOHN WINTHROP AND THE PURITAN COVENANT

In mid-June of the year 1630, John Winthrop, Governor of the new Massachusetts Bay Company, called together aboard his flagship, the *Arbella*, the first group of some twenty thousand Puritans who would be coming to New England over the next dozen years. This initial group of some 1,000 Puritans were about to depart for their new mission in New England.

As Puritans, it had long been their mission to purify the Church of England of its corrupt medieval ways and bring it as close as possible to strict Biblical standards in its operations, exactly as God himself had commanded ancient Israel and the early Christian communities. But finally, Winthrop's group of Puritans had come to the conclusion that hope of reform of the English Church was futile. Thus they needed to take their mission to America. Life under King Charles and Archbishop Laud had become impossible – even highly dangerous – for those who wished to continue the cause of Christian reform in England.

But even this retreat to America was highly dangerous. The general record of English settlements in America was horrifying – hunger, sickness, and ultimately death overtaking more than half of those who attempted the venture. Yet they were willing to face that risk, so great was their determination to succeed in this project of theirs.

It is important to note that this move to America was more than just a gamble of the English to secure for themselves a better life than the one they had in England. Most all of them came from comfortable middle-class homes and had they been less vocal about their concern for reform of the Church of England they could have quietly lived their lives out in relative ease. No, something else was going on here, something that had made them the reformers that they were. They truly believed in their religious cause, so much so that their efforts at reform had brought them enormous problems with the English Church and Crown.

At least now in America they would be free to see these reforms reshape their world, both religious and social. And that, in sum, is why they came – by the thousands.

It is hard today even to begin to imagine the thoughts that motivated these English settlers. Religious idealism is such a secondary matter (if even that) in modern America, where material rewards count so heavily and life is measured in terms of a person's professional success. Yet as hard-driven as Americans are today in pursuit of the American materialistic dream so too the Puritans were hard-driven in pursuit of their religious dream: to live a life in close companionship with God and ultimately, as Christ himself stressed, in close companionship with each other.

Thus just as his shipmates were about to depart on the *Arbella*, Winthrop addressed them with one of the most famous sermons ever preached, a sermon entitled by Winthrop himself, *A Modell of Christian Charity*.[1] Sounding very much like Moses addressing the ancient Israelites just as they were about to enter the Promised Land, Winthrop challenged his fellow Puritans:

> *Thus stands the cause between God and us. We are entered into covenant with Him for this work. We have taken out a commission.*

It was well understood by all that a covenant meant that there were specific terms or obligations that had to be met, something like a legal contract drawn up between themselves and God. They would serve God. And if they were faithful in that service, then God would also faithfully serve them. With God's help they would prosper, in a most miraculous way.

This is what they understood that this whole venture was all about, to prove not only to themselves but also to the wider world the notion that man could live most nobly, most successfully – not in pursuit of personal gain or advantage but instead in pursuit of a closer relationship with the God who presided over all doings in his Creation.

But as with all contracts, there was the down side, relating to failure to keep the Covenant with God. Failure would indeed bring down on them God's wrath. Winthrop warned them:

> *. . . if we shall neglect the observation of these articles, [and] embrace this present world and prosecute our carnal intentions, seeking great things for ourselves and our posterity, the Lord will surely break out in wrath against us, and be revenged of such a people, and make us know the price of the breach of such a*

Introduction: On Being a Covenant People

covenant.

Additionally, the Covenant included a second aspect to it, not just the one linking these Christian souls to Almighty God. The Covenant also required a similar bond uniting them in affection and devotion to each other. Winthrop explains:

> *Now the only way to avoid this shipwreck [of God's wrath], and to provide for our posterity, is to follow the counsel of Micah, to do justly, to love mercy, to walk humbly with our God. For this end, we must be knit together, in this work, as one man. We must entertain each other in brotherly affection. We must be willing to abridge ourselves of our superfluities, for the supply of others' necessities. We must delight in each other; make others conditions our own; rejoice together, mourn together, labor and suffer together, always having before our eyes our commission and community in the work, as members of the same body.*

Then Winthrop went on to remind his fellow Puritans that this venture was something of much greater importance than merely their own success, for God had entered into this Covenant with these Puritan settlers as a demonstration model of how all people should live. Whether this venture succeeded – or failed – would, by God's own intent, come to be a matter of great importance to all the world, a world which would take careful note of exactly how this covenant life in America worked out for everyone. Winthrop stated:

> *We shall find that the God of Israel is among us, when ten of us shall be able to resist a thousand of our enemies; when He shall make us a praise and glory that men shall say of succeeding plantations, may the Lord make it like that of New England. For we must consider that we shall be as a city upon a hill. The eyes of all people are upon us. So that if we shall deal falsely with our God in this work we have undertaken, and so cause Him to withdraw His present help from us, we shall be made a story and a by-word through the world.*

He concludes, citing Moses' admonition to Israel:

> *Beloved, there is now set before us life and death, good and evil, in that we are commanded this day to love the Lord our God, and to love one another, to walk in his ways and to keep*

his Commandments and his ordinance and his laws, and the articles of our Covenant with Him, that we may live and be multiplied, and that the Lord our God may bless us in the land whither we go to possess it.

But if our hearts shall turn away, so that we will not obey, but shall be seduced, and worship other Gods, our pleasure and profits, and serve them; it is propounded unto us this day, we shall surely perish out of the good land whither we pass over this vast sea to possess it.

Therefore let us choose life, that we and our seed may live, by obeying His voice and cleaving to Him, for He is our life and our prosperity.

* * *

AND HOW DO THINGS STAND TODAY WITH THAT SAME COVENANT?

Here we are today four centuries later, indeed a highly successful society – in terms at least of the unprecedented material blessings that we enjoy as Americans. Was this divine Covenant, as Winthrop and the Puritan settlers earnestly believed it would be, the source of this success? Or was it just luck? Or was it simply the cleverness of the American people that brought the country to such success? This a question of huge importance, one that needs some serious investigation. But it is a question hardly heard at all today outside of the tiny ghettos of struggling American churches.

Certainly the Covenant is largely forgotten today, not even mentioned in the public education of America's youth, and only seldom in the public discourse held in the in the halls of the national capital or in the national media. Indeed, according to today's legal interpretation, such religion was never intended to be any part of public America, church and state supposedly having been separated by the First Amendment. But a close reading of the First Amendment* (which few people seem to actually bother with) reveals that the Founding Fathers intended this constitutional principle contained in the First Amendment to protect religion *from* regulation by the state – not for religion's public regulation (and largely exclusion) *by* the state. But this is how generally Americans prefer to understand things today. Authority in the form of the state, not God, is what Americans today believe should be

---

*The First Amendment, protecting the rights of Americans against an overbearing state, reads specifically: "Congress shall make no law respecting an establishment of religion, or prohibiting the free exercise thereof; or abridging the freedom of speech, or of the press; or the right of the people peaceably to assemble, and to petition the Government for a redress of grievances."

Introduction: On Being a Covenant People

the governing voice in American life.

And how is that working out for us today? Were Winthrop's reminders of the negative side of the Covenant (the curses that should fall upon the community should it turn its hearts away from God) simply idle words, spoken out of the superstition of the times? Or indeed was this the deal, then and now?

The best way to answer this question is to take a long, hard look at the record itself, to observe what we can of America's good times and bad, its rises and declines, to see if there is any actual evidence that the Covenant was indeed all that Winthrop had declared it to be.

And thus if indeed it was just contemporary superstition and there is no real evidence in history that it played a significant role in American history, then we can get on with things (materially and professionally) and continue down the path we have been on since the 1960s when we began to let the federal state based in Washington, DC, take the lead in American life. But if on the other hand there is strong evidence that indeed the Covenant was – and therefore still is – fully operative, we should pay close attention to Winthrop's admonitions, and begin to fear ... or better yet, take corrective steps.

And so that is what motivates this work: an investigation into the question of America being a Covenant Nation. And we will begin our investigation at the beginning, not just with Winthrop's New England but also with the royal colony of Virginia. These two simultaneous ventures of the 1600s were themselves very revealing on this matter!

CHAPTER ONE

COLONIAL FOUNDATIONS: THE TWO AMERICAS

* * *

THE TWO DISTINCT CULTURAL MOTIFS SHAPED BY THE LARGER SOCIAL DYNAMICS OF THE TIMES

It is extremely important to note that from its very outset, English America laid out both of the two distinct social traditions mentioned previously. This happened because English America was founded on two very different reasons for the English to want to come to America. Conveniently for our analysis, these two distinct social traditions were based on two different regions along the Atlantic coast of what was to constitute English America.

The first of these is the Southern or *Virginia tradition*, first laid out in 1607 with the founding of the English settlement at Jamestown (Virginia). The second of these is the Northern or *New England tradition* laid out fifteen to twenty years later (1620s and 1630s) in Plymouth and Boston (Massachusetts), Providence (Rhode Island), and Hartford (Connecticut).

Both settlements, Virginia and New England – which were quite different from each other in cultural character and consequently in political design as well – were shaped deeply by the two different European social contexts from which they were drawn. Both settlements came out of a long-standing Christian social cultural tradition. But that Christian tradition itself was highly divided, even by war.

Traditional feudal Virginia. The Southern colony of Virginia was profoundly reflective of the feudal system which, functioning under the direction of the priestly officers of the Christian Church and a variety of kings, princes, and dukes acting as defenders of the Christian faith, had for centuries directed a basically agrarian European society. As a typical feudal society in which the hard working many were commanded by the leisured, aristocratic few, Virginia was founded on the secular quest for wealth and social status measured by the size of someone's landholding and the number of people working that land for the landowner: the more land owned and the more servants working the land, the higher the social status of the landowner.

All of this was considered Christian because the understanding was that such a hierarchical system was something that God himself had ordained, from the aristocratic few at the top of this Christian social order down to the many common laborers, even permanently indentured (ultimately enslaved) workers at the bottom of this same order. The key function of the Christian Church was to morally/spiritually authorize and protect exactly this strict hierarchical social order against all forces attempting to disintegrate it.

Protestant reformist New England. On the other hand, the Northern colonies of New England were deeply reflective of the rising urban-industrial society and culture that had been emerging along Europe's Mediterranean, Atlantic, and Baltic coastlines ... where an ambitious commercial/industrial spirit posed a profound challenge to Europe's older rural feudal system. In full support of the Protestant religious reform challenging all of traditional feudal Europe in the early 1600s, the New England colonists had decided to take their reform efforts to America, seeking to establish there the right to live as God directed – not as man, not even kings or bishops, directed.

The key distinguishing features of this New England social order were 1) the deep sense of equality of all members of society, because ultimately all people were equal in the sight of God; 2) the responsibility of everyone to embrace fully the toil (hard work) in God's vineyard necessary to make this Godly society succeed; 3) the understanding that those who took the responsibility to guide this society (its religious and civil officers) were servants – not owners – of this society, regularly elected to office by its members (and recalled by them if need be), and therefore not constituting some permanently privileged social class or group; 4) the moral and spiritual guidance of each community by means of the careful examination and presentation by highly educated pastors of God's Word to that community, their preaching to serve as the social-moral foundation of this new social order; and 5) the understanding that the English community they purposely set up in the New World was intended to be a social model for all the world, demonstrating how it is that God expects everyone to live.

This dual profile of Virginia and New England not only divided America into two cultural-spiritual camps from the very outset of the colonization effort, it would lead the country in the mid-1800s into the violent conflict we know as our Civil War (1861-1865). And elements of this same cultural-spiritual divide, though no longer geographic, grip America even today.

* * *

THE ORIGINS OF THE WESTERN OR CHRISTIAN SOCIAL LEGACY
OUT OF WHICH COLONIAL AMERICA FIRST EMERGED

Original or Biblical Christianity. Christian civilization marks its origins with what we believe to be (approximately) the year of the birth of Christianity's founder, Jesus of Nazareth, thus the Year One on all Christian or Western calendars. Jesus grew up in a Jewish world (Judea/Galilee) located at the Eastern end of the Mediterranean Sea – at about the same time that the mighty Roman Republic was being transformed by the Caesar dynasty into the Roman Empire.*

In around 30 A.D., Jesus began his active ministry, which according to the records kept by his followers (presented as the Gospels or Good News at the beginning of the New Testament in the Christian Bible) was very brief, lasting possibly only three years. But that ministry, Jesus's tragic death, and his post-death or resurrection appearances before his devoted disciples, had a huge impact on not only his disciples but also on Western society at large – not immediately, but in a strong, growing manner over the next few centuries.

Jesus's teachings, his direct and powerful connect with the world immediately around him, and his way of dignifying and transforming those who followed him with the noble idea of the God of the Universe as their own personal Father, all stood in such contrast to the grasping, scheming, material world of Roman (and also sometimes Jewish) politics and economics that surrounded them. Jesus healed the sick, gave courage to the weak, and hope to the poor at a time when the Roman and Jewish moral-spiritual order seemed to have little to offer the poorer social classes trying to find something in their lives worth living for.

Ultimately, the local authorities, who feared that Jesus's impact would undo their carefully planned and strictly enforced social-legal order, inspired

---

Republic comes from the Roman or Latin words *res publica*, referring to a society that is literally a "thing of the people," meaning a society and its government belonging to no ruling dynasty, no particular social class, no caste, but to the people themselves. *Empire* comes from the Roman or Latin word referring to a society run by the military and its commanders, the *imperators* or emperors, which was what eventually developed with the Roman Republic when it gradually – and tragically – turned its governance over to the strongest military rulers. The emperors supposedly offered Rome greater social and economic stability. But in fact this transition simply stripped from the average Roman citizens control over their government. At this point, Rome belonged to its professional armies and their commanders, who fought bitterly among themselves for control of Rome's political and economic affairs. And thus the Roman *Empire* was born out of the slow death of the Roman *Republic*.

Colonial Foundations: The Two Americas 23

a mob to demand of the local Roman governor that Jesus be executed by crucifixion (slow death on a Roman cross). But by some mystery of God, the grave could not hold Jesus, who, after his death on such a cross, reappeared before many of his followers in a Resurrected body that defied all human logic, but which transformed his followers themselves into powerful ministers of teaching and healing.

Something new had happened, so powerful that it changed multitudes of people in those days – and in the generations that followed – into very different, incredibly courageous people of unequaled faith, faith in the power of life ... and in the life to come. It so inspired Paul, one of Jesus's subsequent followers, that he wrote extensively and organized faith communities widely. Indeed, his impact on the early Christian community was itself so great that his own experiences and counsel concerning the power of his new life in Christ came of themselves to be added to the Christian story or narrative (the New Testament) studied carefully by those who subsequently took up the Way of Jesus Christ.

Ultimately all of this became what the Western world would know as Christianity.

In the generations that followed, the number of followers within the Roman Empire who took up Jesus's Way increased rapidly, many of them becoming by their own rights Christian greats or saints. However, Christians suffered tremendously for not fitting in with the established Roman social order. But their bravery – even in the face of a cruel death imposed on them by Rome's authorities for their unwavering faith in Jesus as the Christ (Anointed One) of God, God's own first Son (as his followers also began to see themselves as sons and daughters of the Father God in Heaven) – stood them out as a most noble people at a time when personal nobility seemed to be largely lacking in the Roman world.

At first it would be the downtrodden, the dispossessed Romans who poured into the Roman cities looking for relief from the crushing poverty that life imposed on them across the Empire, that would flock to the call of Jesus the Christ, thus becoming Christian. But given the moral bankruptcy of Roman society during the 200s A.D., even members of the nobler classes of Romans began to take up this powerful religion. Furthermore, massive persecution by Roman authorities of the Christian movement (reaching fever pitch around 300 A.D.) failed to break its rapid growth. In fact, persecution seemed only to weed out the less stalwart of the faithful, leaving the movement in ever-stronger hands.

Roman or Imperial Christianity. Finally, in the early 300s, when the imperial candidate Constantine took up the Christian cause for himself and his soldiers in his quest for Roman emperorship – and by a divine miracle was able to defeat all other imperial contestants for power – Christianity finally ended its days as a persecuted religion.

Constantine, being Roman and thus coming at his new political responsibilities with a highly organized, legalistic mindset, called together various leaders of the Christian faith (the bishops) to organize this Christian faith into a tightly defined (Roman style) social-religious order. He wanted his new faith to have no religious-spiritual loose ends (as 300 years of underground existence would naturally have produced) but instead be brought to a theologically precise character.

Thus it was that imperial Christianity or Christendom (the official world of social-cultural Christianity) was born.

Indeed, before that same century was finished, subsequent Christian emperors would see that anything that did not fit into a precise or legalistic definition of Christianity would be rejected, and ultimately, Roman style, even be suppressed. So it was indeed that Christianity, under imperial sponsorship, now itself became the persecutor of any religious deviants within the newly Christian Roman Empire.

The irony accompanying Christianity's change in fortunes did not stop there. The traditional paganism of Roman society was placed under intense persecution at a time in which the masses still held close to their hearts certain aspects of traditional pagan Roman religion – as well as a deep reverence for the Earth Mother cults that had been brought in earlier from the East along with Christianity. With the authorities having now outlawed the religious practices in which the little people once looked for assistance to the patron gods of old, pagan deities that once presided over family matters, business matters, travel issues, romance issues, etc., the little people found that by appealing instead to famous Christian saints, reputed to possess the same supportive powers as the former pagan gods, they could satisfy their spiritual-religious hunger. They thus now prayed to the saints rather than to the old pagan deities for their blessings. There was nothing Biblical about any of this (this idea did not originate from Jesus's own teachings, nor those of his original disciples). Yet the Christian authorities let such worship of the saints stand, because it seemed to satisfy everyone and seemed somehow to qualify even as proper Christian practice.

Likewise, Jesus seemed to slip away from the grasp of the little people as he became the friend of emperors, Jesus's primary role now being to certify the rule of imperial candidates by Jesus's own personal endorsement from Heaven. That is, Jesus was now *Christus Rex* (Christ the King), the friend of the emperors, and too lofty to be approached as personal friend and savior by mere commoners. His place in the hearts of the little people now was taken by Jesus's mother, Mary. She was accessible, she was the one that you could go to in order to reach the powers of Heaven. Of course,

Mary-worship quickly and easily replaced Earth-Mother worship, Mary being able to offer a Christian alternative in terms of the same feminine warmth and hope as the older Earth-Mother (Aphrodite, Isis, Demeter, Astarte, etc.) cults had formerly offered the little people. Eventually Mary basically replaced Jesus as the focal point of common Christian worship. Under Roman sponsorship, churches, cathedrals and other centers of Christian worship were dedicated to her honor, rather than Jesus's. Of course, Mary was mentioned in the Christian Bible, but never in this central role, one that Biblically belonged only to Jesus.*

But gradually Biblical writings were fading as the fundamental authority defining the Christian faith. That place was being taken by the church authorities, the bishops and archbishops who presided over the Christian faith, Roman style, whose sacred pronouncements now became the final authority on matters of Christian belief and behavior. An episcopal† bureaucracy whose authority flowed from the religious power-centers of Constantinople, Alexandria (Egypt), Antioch (Syria) and old Rome (Italy) now directed completely the Christian faith, and its leading role in the Roman Christian political, economic and social world.

And thus it was that the Christian faith, which had started out as the source of strength offered the common Roman citizen in an increasingly depersonalized Roman Republic run by military authorities no longer personally accountable to the Roman citizenry, was subsequently stripped of its democratic roots, and itself became part of the highly authoritarian Roman imperial realm.

But its origins as a highly democratic religion would not be completely eradicated, at least not as long as the narrative concerning Christianity's origins were still to be found clearly laid out in the Bible – there to remind some of the faithful of how Christianity originally started out in the days of Jesus and the first century church. But for the time being (for many centuries in fact) Biblical Christianity would be forgotten and be replaced by Episcopalian Christianity, a Christian faith and social order shaped and

---

*It is hardly surprising that the founder of Islam, Mohammed, in his travels (c. 600 A.D.) to the Christian world north of his Arabia, would get the idea that Mary constituted the third member of the Christian Trinity (God the Father, Mary the Mother and Jesus the Son!), he heard so much about the central place of Mary in the Christian faith. Interestingly, although he would reject the notion of the Christian Trinity, he would accept the idea of Mary's very special place in the life of the faithful.

†"Episcopal": a system of bishops (Greek: *episcopos*) controlling and directing the life of the Christian community, from the top down. Thus village priests were under the authority of the regional bishop, who in turn was under the authority of the archbishop, who in turn was under the authority of the Pope (the Bishop of Rome), who then answered to God alone.

enforced by the Church hierarchy of bishops, archbishops and Roman popes on the one hand to define that faith according to the interests of the official Church – and barons, princes, kings and emperors on the other hand to defend or police those Christian interests.

Trinitarian versus Unitarian Christianity. But even with the official Romanization of Christianity in order to rebuild Roman or subsequently Western society on the precise features of the Christian religion, this did not end the debates, some of them quite bitter, as to what exactly such precise Christianity was to look like. In particular, a split developed in such a way that two distinct interpretations of the faith developed within Christendom. *Trinitarian* became the label for those who were able to follow the complexities of deep Greek thinking and interpretation (typical of the Roman authorities now relocated to the Eastern or Greek-speaking part of the Empire) and *Unitarian* the label for those for whom such complex theology was way beyond their comprehension (the German converts, for instance), or for those simply unwilling for one reason or other to go down the Greek philosophical road (the Semitic peoples such as the Jews and Arabs of the Middle East).

The *Unitarian* Christians are the easiest to understand. They believed (and still believe) that the person of God is to be found only in the single form of the God of Heaven. The earthly Jesus, while on earth, was never considered to be God, but merely a human who lived such an exemplary life of piety and personal virtue that upon his death he was seated at God's right hand as God's favored Son, a heavenly Son (and thus at that point able to be considered to be something of a God) to be honored by Christians in following Jesus's life of piety and personal virtue here on earth. Thus, Unitarian Christianity is considered a religion of human "works," whereby a person achieves heaven at death as a reward achieved through his/her own good works modeled on Jesus's own good works. Thus for Unitarians, the cross of Christ is only an identifying symbol, nothing more.

Trinitarian Christians believed (and still believe) in *God in three forms or "Persons"*: 1) the heavenly Father, 2) His Son Jesus, and 3) the Holy Spirit. In Trinitarian Christianity (the theological position of the official Christian Church), Jesus is considered to always have been part of the personhood of God, God come to earth at his own gracious initiative to bring sinful man to full reconciliation between man and God. For Trinitarians, the cross is more than just a religious symbol. It is considered to be a critical part of human salvation, because it was the place where God himself, in the form of Jesus, paid the eternal sacrifice demanded by the law of life, for the sins of all and for all eternity, a moral cleansing offered by God himself, a moral cleansing that that man can never achieve for himself, for his own sins, no matter how hard he tries.

For Trinitarians, the Holy Spirit is critical as the third Person of the Godhead, a part of God sent to aid man because in coming to know and accept personally (by simple faith alone) the saving gift of Jesus – thus becoming "born again" – man would still need God's own assistance, God's own accompanying power, to actually be able to continue to follow Jesus's Lordship through a world of sin everywhere.

This is why Trinitarians claim that salvation happens only by way of Divine *grace* received by people through simple *faith* ... not through their human works. *Faith*, not works, is key to Trinitarian Christianity.

But people like works. It seemingly keeps them in charge of outcomes. Faith requires a person to give up such control, and hand it over to God. That is not something that humans naturally want to do!

The battle between Unitarian and Trinitarian Christianity was – and remains still today – ongoing. Islam basically was modeled by the Arab (Semitic) leader Mohammad on Unitarian Christianity. Also, Roman or official Catholic Christianity itself over the centuries slowly slid into something like Unitarianism (works-righteousness Christianity), which the Protestant Reformation in the 1500s and 1600s attempted to correct.

But much of Protestant Christianity over the years also tended to slip into works-righteousness, by placing its emphasis on acting like Jesus in pursuing human programs of peace and social justice. In taking up such good works, there supposedly would then be no need to seek personal salvation through some kind of a deep spiritual cleansing and conversion. Good works were supposedly able of themselves to lift a person above the world of sin and offer a person a future place in Heaven. No, good works would be just fine. No need for all that born-again stuff.

But God has intervened periodically (waves of Christian Awakenings) to pull Christianity back from its Unitarian tendencies in order to place it once again on the path of a Holy-Spirit empowered (Trinitarian) personal faith, one that moves mountains. That's what being born again means, not just for individuals but even for whole societies as well.

Christianity survives the collapse of the Roman Empire in the Christian West. In any case, the Roman Empire's conversion to Christianity did not ease the problems a struggling Roman Empire was having with its enemies to the East across the Syrian desert and to the Northeast across the Danube River: respectively, the Persians to the East and the Germans to the Northeast. This was a major reason for moving the Roman imperial headquarters out of the city of Rome itself and east to the New Rome of Constantinople, where Roman authorities would find themselves closer to their fields of battle with the Persian and German challengers.

With respect to the Persians, there was little the Romans could do. The powers of both Rome and Persia were so evenly balanced that the wars between these two powers simply played back and forth, brutally. But with respect to the Germans, the solution was simple: move the Germans westward, into Western Europe where Roman authority had recently downgraded the importance of that part of the Empire. Even some of the Germanic tribes (such as the Franks) were invited to relocate themselves within the boundaries of the old Empire, in the hope that they might serve as something of a buffer against other Germanic tribes hungrily eyeing a decaying Roman imperium in the West. On top of that, Germanic troops (mostly Goths) were being recruited for service in the Roman legions, to a point by the late 300s they made up most of the Roman army. How a heavily German-staffed Roman army was expected to enthusiastically fend off fellow German intruders was a problem with no very good solution.

Pressures on the Germanic Goths coming from the Asiatic Huns in the East, plus a violent reaction of the Romans to the growing numbers of Goths in their midst, produced an explosive encounter between the Goths and the Romans ... which did not go well for the Romans. The Goths attacked the Roman Empire, even in 410 sacking and burning extensively the old capital at Rome (which by that time was no longer serving even as the Western Roman capital). That was the signal for other Germanic tribes (principally the Franks, Burgundians, Visigoths, Vandals, and Saxons) to move into Roman territory in the West (today's France, Spain, Northern Africa, and Southwestern England). Tragically, the Romans seemed unable to offer effective resistance. By the mid-400s, the Roman Empire in the West was no more.

The Germanic tribes had not come wanting to destroy Roman society. Instead, they simply wanted to possess it, to make it their own. To align themselves with the Roman way of life, a great number of them had already accepted Christianity as their tribal religion, although it was of the Arian (Unitarian) rather than Trinitarian variety, thanks to the earlier missionary work among them by the Unitarian priest Ulfilas (Wulfila). The Franks (of today's northern France) and the Visigoths (today's Southern France and Spain) finally aligned themselves with Trinitarian or Catholic Christianity, owing to the conversion of their tribal leaders in the 500s and 600s by missionaries sent out by the bishop of Rome (later termed the pope). Christian missionaries also sent out in the 500s and 600s from a recently converted Ireland (resulting from the work in the 400s of Patrick and his disciples) in turn helped bring into Catholic Christianity other Celtic and Germanic tribes, ranging from the Scots and Saxons in Britain to the Burgundians and Alemanni in today's eastern France, western Germany and Switzerland.

Thus it was that although the Roman Empire collapsed in the West, its Christian religious legacy did not. And little by little, the Church, under the talented leadership of a series of Roman bishops or popes, began to bring some degree of Christian cohesion to Western Europe.

Charlemagne, and the shift from tribal to feudal (or dynastic) society. Then in the late 700s, Europe underwent a dramatic transformation as Charles, King of the Franks, better known to us today as Charles the Great or Charlemagne, came into the European political picture. Charlemagne not only inherited the title of King of the Franks from his father, Pepin the Short (himself son of the powerful Frankish leader, Charles Martel), but also succeeded in conquering all the neighboring German tribes in north and central Europe, and even (at the invitation of the Pope in Rome) defeated the powerful tribe of Lombards in Italy. Thus on Christmas day in the year 800, the pope, in recognition of this great military achievement, crowned Charlemagne as emperor, a title not used since the fall of Rome some 350 years earlier.

With this achievement, Charlemagne not only broke the power of the individual German tribes – at least on the European continent* – but had the Church recognize officially his right to rule much of Europe as his personal property or *fief*.

The principle of subinfeudation. However, this fief (Latin: *feudom*) was a vast piece of territory to rule. Unlike the former Roman Empire, Charlemagne had no well-developed bureaucracy of trained government officials placed around his Empire to rule on his behalf. So, Charlemagne instituted the policy of awarding large sections (fiefdoms or feudatories) of his personal empire to various barons (princes and dukes, etc.) to govern on his behalf, that is, in his name. Charlemagne still held the full title to the land since all of this was now considered his (like private property), his to lease out to others as he saw fit. His tenants or *vassals* (the princes and barons) in turn owed Charlemagne loyal service in maintaining the peace of the land and providing him troops in case of war. They did not pay taxes because no one, not even the barons, had much by way of money. The obligation of personal service to Charlemagne as their *lord* was what was required of them.

But even for the barons, the territory they were responsible for was still too big for any one person to govern. So they in turn sub-leased portions of their own lease to lesser land-lords (marquesses and counts,

---

*Saxon tribes in England remained beyond the reach of Charlemagne's political system – until the Saxons were conquered by French Normans some two and a half centuries later.

etc.), under the same type of obligation that they owed the emperor: land tenure (land-holding, not land-owning) for various services in return. Thus, although the barons were vassals to the emperor, they were themselves lords to their own set of vassals lower on the feudal scale.

Finally the system reached down to the masses of peasant farmers and their families (actually about 95 percent of the population!), who were allotted land in return for labor service (working their lord's fields and maintaining his flocks) and the requirement that a portion of their harvest or produce be turned over to the local lord and his court of knights and ladies. The peasants themselves owned almost nothing (except maybe their most humble clothing), usually not even the houses they lived in.

No money was involved, just the right of a certain amount of landholding and the obligation of certain services in return.

This in short was the feudal system.

In theory the emperor was free to extend or take back land rights to whomever he chose, for however long he chose to do so. But over time it became a lot easier for a lord to allow a vassal to pass his land rights on to his sons (or his eldest son only – under the rule of primogeniture that was widely practiced in Europe). After a number of generations, a family would begin to consider this land theirs to have and to hold as they chose. This created difficulties between the lords (such as the European kings) and their vassals (their barons) that were never fully worked out satisfactorily. Some clever dukes were able (through conquest, although most often through marriage) to accumulate sections of land here and there, sometimes at great distances, even under different lords. The Dukes of Normandy, for instance, ended up holding more land of their own than the French kings they were supposedly under (but the Dukes of Normandy were also kings – in England – by their own right).

It could get to be very confusing.

But the principle always remained the same: land, land, land. Social status depended entirely on the amount of land a baron was able to hold. And land tended to stay within the realm of one's family. And thus inheritance (not hard work or industrial cleverness) ruled the status system. A person was born into his or her status, and was carefully married off in accordance with the dictates of that same status system. What possibilities life might bring a person were determined entirely by that person's birth.

And so it was. And so long it was that few ever thought that things could be otherwise.

The deep challenge to the feudal order posed by the rise of the monarchies, supported by a rising urban Europe. That was until things started changing in the 1300s and 1400s with the rise of industry, commerce and banking – centered not in the extensive European feudal countryside but in the fast-growing cities that dotted the Mediterranean, Atlantic and Baltic coastlines.

Contact with the Muslim East (the crusades of the 1100s and 1200s) had birthed a new system of wealth founded not on landholding but on the ability to accumulate mobile wealth (goods, money, bank credit, etc.). Such wealth, like the feudal system, could be acquired and passed on to future generations of the family. But mostly it came as a challenge to each generation to grow its own wealth in industry and trade – something that feudal landholding could not do. Land, of course, could be exchanged with, or seized from, another. But the overall supply of land itself could not be increased any. However, the money economy had no limits placed on its ability to expand.

Feudal lords naturally looked down on the lower-status industrial-financial achievers as mere wannabees, not really worthy of serious social consideration. In short, feudal lords were snobs. But monied wealth had its own way of having an impact, even socially and politically. Kings, who always had troubles with their much-too-independent-minded barons, found that working with these industrial entrepreneurs from the rising urban middle class (neither barons, nor peasants but socially in the "middle") worked to their great advantage.

Kings were willing to license industrial groups (grant them charters as corporations or companies) in return for a tax portion of their monetary earnings or profits, taxes which allowed kings to hire their own soldiers and purchase their own arms, rather than be forced to rely on the not very dependable military services of their barons or lesser lords. Also, with the development of overseas interests on the part of kings and princes, a navy of fighting ships had to be constructed at considerable financial cost, something that only the moneyed classes could fund – but also derive considerable benefit from as much-needed protection in their trading – something also that the landed aristocrats of the countryside had nothing to contribute to or gain from.

For England and France, the Hundred Years' War raging between the mid-1300s to the mid-1400s also served to strengthen the hands of the French and English kings, by simply bleeding off the feudal aristocracy in endless slaughter. In France those wars left the feudal lords so devastated that in 1439 the king was able to put literally the entire military establishment and an entire national tax program into his own hands. In England the chaos continued an additional three decades (until 1485) in an ongoing dynastic struggle (the War of the Roses) between the two royal houses of York (White Rose) and Lancaster (Red Rose) serving to weaken even further the remnants of the old feudal order. In that last year, a distant Lancastrian cousin of the House of Tudor was able to grab power, marry a York princess, and finally, as King Henry VII, bring an exhausted England under his firm grip. At Henry's death in 1509 his son Henry VIII took the throne and continued to strengthen the monarchy, this time at the cost of the medieval Church – whose lands he confiscated in order to award the Church's vast wealth to his own political supporters. Thus in the early-to-mid–1500s, royal absolutism also came to England.

A growing cultural-religious (and consequently political) divide within Christian Europe. The Christian social identity of Europeans had long been the foremost of all the particular identities that a person might hold, back in pre-modern Europe – even more important than English, or French, or Spanish. National identities and national politics, especially on the European continent, were only in their very early stages of development. The people who governed European society married across national or linguistic lines and ruled lands whose inhabitants spoke a variety of languages. Most Latin-speaking European kings and princes viewed themselves not as national defenders but simply as rulers of multi-ethnic lands, personally called to keep the peace and preserve the Christian faith in their assigned lands, wherever those lands might be.

It is important to note that of all their responsibilities, the greatest was still considered their divine call as defenders of the faith. But it was also in this area of defending the faith that considerable tension had been brewing in Europe by the early 1500s. Many Christians felt that the Church had long departed from its original spiritual mission and was more interested in securing wealth and power for itself than in guiding and guarding the souls of its people.* Demands that the Church reform itself had largely fallen on deaf ears among the Church's ruling elite.†

Compounding this theological tension was a deep social-cultural clash between the older feudal order based largely in the extensive rural countryside of Europe and the rising urban, commercial middle class. And it had to do with not only the rise of moneyed wealth and power in competition with landed and titled wealth and power, but it also arose over

---

*The Roman popes at this point were clearly more interested in consolidating their political-military grip over central Italy than in playing the role of spiritual mentor to the huge Christian world of Europe.

†Earlier reformers had not done well in their effort to bring needed reform to the Church. In 1415 The Englishman John Wycliffe was officially condemned as a heretic (forty years after his death in 1384) for having dared to translate the Latin Bible into the English spoken by the common Englishman. 1415 was also the same year that the Czech reformer Jan Hus was burned at the stake as a heretic for his effort to bring the Church back to Biblical standards.

the matter of the high degree of literacy typical of this rising middle class.

Widespread literacy in newly-rising urban Europe. Literacy was rare across the European countryside. Peasants did not know how to read. Aristocratic males were normally fairly well-trained in Latin and therefore literate. But they constituted only a small portion of the cultural world of the European countryside. However, the very rigors of urban commerce and industry necessitated a high degree of literacy in the fast-rising cities, members of this rising urban middle class needing to track financial transactions and engage in correspondence that flowed with their trade.

And accompanying the rapid growth of literacy in Europe's fast rising cities came the ability of members of the middle class personally to open the sacred Scriptures of the Christian faith to their own reading. With the advent of the printing press at about the same time that urban culture was gaining power, the Bible became increasingly available as a book that could easily be afforded by any urban middle-class family, even though Bible-reading by mere commoners had long been condemned by the Church because supposedly the meaning of Scripture could be understood only by those trained as priests.

With a new and closer look in Scripture and how Christian life appeared at its origins in the first century A.D. and how the Christian life fifteen centuries later stood socially, economically and politically, there appeared to be a huge disconnect. In short, what the new class of readers of Holy Scripture discovered in that reading was how far materially, morally and spiritually the contemporary European Church seemed to have wandered from the design or character of the original Christian community or Church as described in the Bible. To the thinking of many of this rising middle class, something therefore needed to be done to bring the Christian world back closer to its roots. Clearly their Christian world needed deep reform.

Luther.[2] But surprisingly, it was not in the cities but rather in the rural hinterland of central Germany that a successful challenge to the authority of the traditional Roman Church first took place. There a very vocal German monk and Biblical scholar, Martin Luther, was so bold in 1517 as to challenge Catholic authorities to justify Church practices on some ninety-five points, earning him the hatred of the Roman Papacy – and the Habsburg Holy Roman Emperor Charles V (who also happened to be king of superpower Spain) whose most sacred job was to defend traditional Christianity from just such religious rebels as Luther.

Luther was upset in seeing how the official Church had moved Christianity slowly over the centuries towards Unitarianism. Under the dominion of the powerful Church, salvation or access to heaven had come to depend less and less on God's grace and the individual's repentance and transformation in being confronted by that grace, which the Bible clearly described as the only path to salvation. Instead, over time the idea of salvation had come to depend on the powers of the hierarchical Roman Church, a community of priests and high priests (bishops) offering ceremonial cleansing by the administration of the holy sacraments, through required confessions which brought priestly forgiveness of human sin (provided that certain cleansing rituals were undertaken as per the instructions of the priest), and finally even payments to the Church in the form of indulgences – which would speed a departed soul through the process of Purgatory (the stage after death in which individuals had to purge or work out the penalties for their sins before they could enter fully into heavenly paradise). In short, the Church was becoming the grace-dispensing institution, not the personal faith of the believer. Salvation had thus become a matter of works (required by the priestly Church) rather than divine grace freely given by God. Luther was loud in how all of this was wrong, very wrong – at least according to Biblical standards.

But such challenges were considered simply as attacks on the Holy Mother Church, and the reaction of the Christian Establishment (the Medici Roman Pope Leo X and the Habsburg Holy Roman Emperor Charles V) was that Luther had to recant ... or disappear (as critics before him had). But ready to defend Luther were some of the princes of Germany, who smarted at the way the Roman Church laid such a greedy hand on the wealth of Germany to finance its various projects, especially the building of the pope's exquisite Vatican Cathedral in Rome. Certainly, as much for political reasons as for religious reasons, they swung their support behind Luther, giving him protection from both the pope and the emperor.

Furthermore, Luther shook the foundations of the Roman Church with his claims that God intended the role of priesthood to be the self-responsibility of all Christian believers, and not just the select few members of the priestly class serving the official Church.

However, when thousands of German peasants, under the leadership of Thomas Müntzer, moved to extend that idea of the sovereignty of the Christian believer to all aspects of Christian life – including their own civil governance – Luther balked. The idea of political self-government was too radical for Luther,* who sided with the German princes, who moved decisively to put down savagely a huge revolt (1524–1525) of the German peasants (supposedly some 100,000 to 300,000 peasants were killed,

---

*In his *Wider die Mordischen und Reubischen Rotten der Bawren* [*Against the Robbing Murderous Hordes of Peasants*] (1525) he advises the German princes to take necessary action against the peasants: "Let everyone who can, smite, slay and stab, secretly and publicly, . . . a poisonous, devilish rebel, like one must kill a rabid dog."

although no one is quite sure of the exact number).

Theologically, Luther was a radical reformer. But when it came to challenging the feudal political order, Luther came out strongly in opposition. Consequently, the feudal order would remain intact in Germany all the way up into the 20th century, despite much of the country's Protestant character.

Calvin's reforms modeled in urban Geneva, Switzerland.[3] A far deeper and more threatening movement for Church reform now shifted to the rising urban society of Europe. And this would be led by the French reformer, John Calvin – who experienced a personal conversion that changed him from a secular-minded jurist (legal scholar) to a true Christian evangelical. This rather quickly got him in trouble in France and in 1534 he fled to Berne, Switzerland, where he began to study and write (first in Latin in 1536 and eventually in French in 1541) a commentary on the Christian faith, *Institutes of the Christian Religion*.[*4] He ultimately ended up in the Swiss city-state of Geneva, invited there by the town fathers to put his ideas of Christian reform into practice in their city. And this he did, turning Geneva into a model Christian city dedicated to honoring God with Christian life and practices conducted in accordance only with Biblical standards, and not the traditional pronouncements of the Roman or Catholic Church.

And in the process, going well beyond Luther's theological reforms, he undertook Christian reform in political or social (or civil) matters as well. In Calvin's eyes, civil and religious life were completely interconnected. One could not be properly spiritually reformed without being socially-politically reformed as well. The witness or outward evidence of an inner salvation – or being one of the elected or covenanted of God – would be clearly demonstrated in the quite obvious way the Christian actually lived in the world: humbly, lovingly, and actively supportive of the greater good of mankind. Calvin noted that a person's works were not themselves required for salvation, yet true salvation nonetheless would inevitably produce good works in witness or testimony of such a Godly salvation. This is what God rightly expected of his Covenant People.

This Genevan or Calvinist project of erecting a purified Christian society, attempting to live by Biblical standards as a Godly witness before the larger world, excited a huge number of this rising class of industrious European urban commoners. They were eager to become part of a society in which individuals presented themselves personally before God on the basis of their personal faith alone, not on the basis of the teachings of an ancient

---

*This work underwent numerous editions, increasing in coverage with each new issue, from a single volume of six chapters in 1536 ultimately by 1559 to four volumes of 80 chapters, indicative of his own development as a scholar-teacher.

religious institution, and certainly not on the basis of the intervention of a class of professional priests. Furthermore, they tended by nature to be a hardworking lot (at a time in which feudal aristocrats looked down on such manual labor) and were pleased to find Christian dignity in their work. Therefore, this rising urban middle class, being an independent, free-thinking and hard-working lot, was quite ready to practice diligently the priesthood of all believers, one that Luther talked about, but one that Calvin actually put into full social practice.

Thus Christians from all around Europe flocked to Geneva to study Calvin's reforms, and to participate in the publication there of the Bible in more of the local European languages. Their personal Bibles provided the common people of Europe the platform on which they could then carry out their part in the priesthood of all believers.

They came to Geneva from France (the Huguenots), from the Netherlands (the founders of the Dutch Reformed Church), from Germany (the German Reformed Church), Scotland (the Presbyterians), England[*] (future Puritans and Separatists), Bohemia, Hungary, Poland, and even Italy and Spain (the political heart of Catholicism.)

The rising Wars of Religion. But with the rise of this spiritual-intellectual awakening, the Christian Church itself became deeply divided between Catholics, who supported the feudal Church and society such as had long existed, and the Protestants, who demanded reform of both the Church and society along more Biblical – even Genevan – lines. And the division became deeper and more contentious with time, Christians fighting Christians over this matter of the Church and its ways, an issue so central to the very identity of all Europeans that the fighting soon became extremely brutal.

For instance, Habsburg Spain under Philip II (ruled 1556–1598) unleashed its armies on the Protestant Dutch lands of the northern reaches of the Habsburg Empire (1560s), arresting and executing the leaders of Calvinist Dutch Flanders (modern Belgium) along with thousands of other Flemish Calvinists – ultimately forcing the region back into the Catholic camp. But the armies of the Spanish Habsburgs found themselves unable to break the resistance further north among the Holland Dutch, who consequently remained in the strongly Protestant (Calvinist) camp.

Also, the autocratic French Queen Catherine de Médicis in 1572 invited the nobility of France to a wedding in Paris on St. Bartholomew's

---

[*]Under the brief rule (1547–1553) of Henry VIII's young but sickly son, Edward, the Protestant cause took great strides forward in England. But when he died, his half-sister Mary took the throne, an ardent Catholic, who was determined to stamp out this new Protestant intrusion into her realm. It was during the violent reign of Mary (1553–1558) that English Protestants fled England, and headed to Protestant Switzerland, coming under Calvin's strong influence.

Colonial Foundations: The Two Americas 37

Day, and had the Calvinist Huguenots among them (about half the nobility at this point) slaughtered. This in turn led further to the killing of tens of thousands of other Huguenots in other French cities as well, all in the name of protecting the True Faith (Catholicism). Thus it was that the spread of the Protestant Reformation was brought to a halt in France.

Feelings separating the Catholics and Protestants thus became very bitter – and the use of power by one group to suppress the other was intense, even murderous. By 1618 the European continent found itself plunged into a savage war (depopulating huge sections of central Europe) which went on for thirty years (thus the "Thirty Years' War"). Finally sheer exhaustion over this matter of religious identity led the wearied dynasties to conclude in 1648 the Treaty of Westphalia. With this treaty the various dynasties agreed to acknowledge that some parts of the continent would probably always be Catholic and others Protestant. There was no point in continuing to fight over this matter. It was time to move on.

The Human Enlightenment – or Age of Reason. And not surprisingly, and quite ironically, all this ferocious religious zeal was to open the way for the rise of the Human Enlightenment or "Age of Reason," as a civilized or "reasonable" alternative to the murderous Christian theological disputes that had destroyed Europe. Scholars and thinkers since the time of René Descartes (early 1600s) had been exploring the idea that all of nature actually operated rather mechanically in accordance with the laws of nature (Natural Law) that were discoverable simply through disciplined study and analysis. The question of God or Catholicism versus Protestantism played no part whatsoever in this new approach to the search for the fundamental Truths of Life. All that was needed was the mature application of Human Reason to the study of the various processes directing every feature in every category of life. The mechanics of life involved in the production of goods, the similar mechanics in the behavior of plants and animals, even in the behavior of men and society, could and should be investigated simply through the process of applying Human Reason – in order to bring life's great Truths to light.

Thus was born the new realm of modern science, although at the time it was called "natural philosophy." Actually, these natural philosophers had begun the process of coming at life with an entirely new worldview, a new religion that needed no reference to the role of God (except maybe as the originator of all of life's natural mechanics) or, for that matter, of any part of the Christian religion. And so it was that towards the end of the 1600s, the Age of the Western Enlightenment – or Age of Reason – was born ... and soon in full growth.

That's what obsessive, eventually murderous, religiosity could bring mankind to. But this also should have naturally raised the question: would this new religion of the exalting of Human Reason not also itself eventually go down this same road, given mankind's love to pursue religious Reason to the point of murderous obsession? It was, after all, obsessive Theological Reasoning – not Jesus or his teachings – that had actually been the cause of Christian theology's murderous disputes.

Only time would reveal the answer to that question.

The impact in England of the Protestant Reformation. In England the split between traditional Roman Catholics and Protestant Reformers was less murderous – though intense nonetheless. English King Henry VIII had split from the Catholic Church during all the commotion of the early years of the Protestant revolt (the first half of the 1500s), but his move was strictly political and not religious. He detested Luther, but had pursued pretty much the same goal as the German princes in wanting to free himself from the grip of the Roman Church and the Habsburg Holy Roman Emperor Charles,* the very conservative "defender of the (Catholic) faith." Nonetheless during Henry's reign, the Protestant cause began to take root in England, notably, of course, within the urban commercial class, especially strong in London.

Henry's daughter, Elizabeth, who came to rule England during the last half of the 1500s, conducted something of a delicate balancing act so as to retain the loyalties of both English Catholics and English Protestants. She had no desire to split her realm into warring factions. Things nonetheless were harder for the Catholics than Protestants in Elizabethan England, principally because her contemporary in Spain, the very Catholic Habsburg King Philip II, was determined to conquer England and force it back into Roman Catholicism. This made English Catholics highly suspect as being possibly pro-Spanish. It also advanced the cause of English nationalism – which was becoming increasingly Protestant in nature.

The Puritans. But Elizabeth's middle-of-the-road policy did not please the Protestant purists (deeply inspired by Calvin's reforms) who felt that if England did not permit worship in the purest, most first-century or Biblical way of early Christianity, then the reform movement in England was merely a sham. Purity of faith was not something about which they were willing to

---

*Charles was the Holy Roman Emperor who tried to stop Luther; Charles ruled both Spain as Charles I and the Holy Roman Empire as Charles V. His was a very long rule (1516–1558) – as was also his son Philip II's reign (until 1598). Philip, however, received only the kingship of Spain, the Holy Roman Emperorship going to Charles's brother, Ferdinand. Thus the House of Habsburg from that point on (mid-1500s) constituted two separate branches, one in Spain and one in Germany/Austria (the Holy Roman Empire).

Colonial Foundations: The Two Americas 39

compromise. And thus this group of Biblical purists collectively came to be known in England as the "Puritans."

In the early 1600s a new ruling line took over England (Elizabeth never married and thus had no heir of her own to whom she could pass on her throne) when her cousin and Scottish King James was brought to the English throne. He was raised as a Protestant and was pleased to authorize the publication of a new English translation of the Bible, the well-known King James Version (although the Puritans were quite content with their English-language Geneva Bible). But he was not willing to go much further in the direction of Protestant reform than that. He, as Henry VIII and Elizabeth before him, was head of the Church of England, personally appointed its archbishops and bishops as well as presided over its theological discussions, and was most unwilling to revise this episcopal or top-down or structure of his English church. He detested the Puritans, but basically tolerated them – as long as they did not get too radical in their demands for reform.

But that degree of flexibility toward the Puritans would not be passed on to his son, Charles, who replaced James at his death in 1625. During Charles's reign (1625–1649) violent religious controversy would explode in England – and result very importantly in how part of English America was to develop.

* * *

THE FIRST YEARS OF EUROPEAN COLONIZATION OF AMERICA

The Spanish first set the agenda. At the time (the 1500s), when these two Catholic and Protestant cultures were first confronting each other, the leading power of Europe was unquestionably fervently-Catholic Spain, under the rule of the Habsburg family. This was due in part to the toughness of the Habsburg kings, Charles and his son Philip, but also in part (in great part actually) to the flow of gold into Spain resulting from the Spanish plundering of American Indian societies, notably in Mexico and Peru.

When, on behalf of the newly combined Spanish monarchy of Ferdinand of Aragon and Isabella of Castile, Columbus had discovered America in 1492, he had introduced Europe (but in particular Spain) to a vast land soon revealed to be of considerable wealth, including very importantly gold. The Spanish were of course the first to benefit from this discovery, and they benefitted royally. The Spanish plunder in gold and silver taken from Mexico and Peru made Habsburg Spain the richest and most powerful society in all of Europe during the 1500s. Spain secured this huge wealth by sending young and aspiring (that is, lesser) noblemen to America to secure the bulk of this wealth for their king – and personal wealth and noble title for themselves in the process. These young men fulfilled their aristocratic ambitions not only by pure plunder, but by taking over the indigenous Indian population and working them in the mines and on the land. This slave-like labor provided an on-going source of wealth for these new Spanish lords.

A feudal-like political system thus settled over Spanish America – much like the system back in Europe where peasants and serfs worked almost endlessly for their aristocratic lords or masters. Thus it was that the opening up of America extended the Spanish feudal system to that continent, a feudal system offering wealth and dignity to aspiring lesser nobility, or to nobility who had simply fallen on hard times economically, or to those simply seeking to escape their positions among the lower social orders of feudal Spain, hoping to rise to the status of noblemen from newly acquired American wealth in land – and servants working that land for them.

Spanish kings however were not very comfortable with the ambitions of these young conquistadores (conquerors), who were merciless exploiters of the labors of the American Indians that had the misfortune of falling into the hands of these adventurers. The Spanish kings considered the Indians their personal subjects, much like the Spanish peasants who worked the aristocrats' lands back in Europe. Also, the Spanish kings felt something of a moral responsibility for extending the reach of the Christian faith to their Indian subjects. So, the kings sent Dominican and Franciscan monks to America to accompany or follow-up the conquistadores, to convert the Indians – and then to protect them from the cruel greed of those Spanish conquistadores. Thus to the mix of a rising Spanish feudal system in America in which Spanish noblemen ruled the surrounding land and its inhabitants from their feudal manors or haciendas, the kings added the political oversight of their colonies through the scattered mission stations of the Spanish Catholic priests. These feudal lords and priests were called on to help keep the American social order under the firm control of the political authorities back in Spain.

Meanwhile other ambitious Europeans looked with envy on the Spanish success in America. But at the time the Spanish navy so completely dominated the water passages from Europe to America that it was very perilous for anyone else to attempt to duplicate what the Spanish were doing in America. The Spanish would simply not allow the intrusion of European outsiders into their American lands. But the rewards were too great for other Europeans not to try to challenge the Spanish monopoly.

The French get involved. Spain had not appeared as interested in North America as it did in Central and South America. Therefore, North America seemed to offer the best possibilities for others to get in on the act. By the beginning of the 1600s it seemed that the time was right –

Colonial Foundations: The Two Americas 41

particularly after the Spanish army and navy had experienced a string of disastrous setbacks trying to keep both their Protestant Dutch subjects from breaking away from Habsburg Catholic Spanish authority and the English privateers (actually merely pirates officially authorized by English Queen Elizabeth) from harassing the Spanish fleets bringing gold from America.

The French thus sent explorers and traders to the Maritime Islands of eastern Canada, and then beyond up the St. Lawrence River – to take advantage of the great wealth in animal furs of the more northerly region of the Americas. But they also sent Jesuit priests to Canada to bring Indian souls to the French (Catholic) Church.[*]

But the chill of the Canadian North proved to be not greatly inviting to French settlers, and the French imperial venture in Canada did not take on great importance in the larger French political scheme of things

The Dutch get in on the act. Since the Spanish quest was for aristocratic status, not success at the game of commerce and trade, very little of this Spanish plunder got devoted to the building up of Spanish industry and commerce. Almost all of it went to the purchase of land, and aristocratic title that went with the land.

However, the Dutch, who were part of the Spanish kingdom[†] (even though way north of the Spanish heartland) and of a strong Protestant-Calvinist disposition, were a different breed. The land of the Dutch was small in land size, highly urbanized along the long coastline, and divided into two distinct regions: Flanders, the region just to the north of France (and directly across the Channel from England) whose coastal cities achieved vast wealth early in the Renaissance period; and, north of Flanders, Holland, much of that region wrested from the North Sea by the Dutch through a laborious process of building dikes to hold back the sea in order to bring up more tillable land, and then draining additional seawater seepage into that land by way of windmills. These Dutch provinces were dotted with cities engaged in manufacture, banking, shipping, and trade. Ultimately, much of the Spanish wealth brought back from America by the Spanish conquistadores tended to end up in the hands of the very industrious and commercially clever Dutch.

Nonetheless, Habsburg Spain, as long as the gold held out, appeared wealthy and powerful, and dominated European life. But when that gold

---

*Eventually both French Jesuits and explorers reached even deeper into the new continent, doing extensive exploration (and some settlement) along the massive Mississippi River, north to south.

†Spanish King Charles I was actually Dutch rather than Spanish by birth – born in Ghent, in Flanders, the Dutch-speaking northern portion of modern Belgium.

ran out (as it was destined to do) aristocratic Spain began to slip rapidly in power. But the Dutch, who had learned how to invest that gold in projects that multiplied their wealth, turned from this small outpost of the Spanish kingdom into a major European power. Little by little (late 1500s) the Dutch began to move toward independence, precipitating a terrible war initiated by Spain in an attempt to force the Dutch back into submission. The Spanish effort succeeded in the Flemish south (ruining the Flemish cities in the process) – but failed to reach that same goal in the Holland north. All this did was to steel the will of the Holland or Netherlander Dutch – and further drain Spain of its wealth (early 1600s).

In the meantime, the Netherlander Dutch had begun their own exploration of the lands to the West in America. They set up a merchant corporation to bring back the wealth of the central shores of North America (a region they called New Netherland), and hopefully to find a passage through America to their valuable commercial holdings in Asia (the Spice Islands of the East Indies which the Dutch had seized from the Portuguese), by way of the Hudson River, along which they established a number of Dutch settlements.

England stirs under the Spanish challenge. At first England's main ambition across the Atlantic seemed to be merely raiding the gold-laden Spanish galleons shipping their Indian plunder back from America to Spain. Under Queen Elizabeth, English privateers were even treated as noblemen: Sir Francis Drake, for instance, excelled at this game of plunder.

Of course the Spanish tired quickly of this English game and in 1588 sent a massive fleet to crush the English navy, and also force the rather Reform-minded or Protestant English back into the true Mother or Roman Catholic Church. But this mighty Spanish Armada ended up itself crushed by foul winds and clever English seamanship. This marked the beginning of the rise of England as a major naval power, and the decline of Spain as the dominant European power.

But it would be a while before the English would themselves get deeply involved in the process of bringing American lands into the English realm.

✳ ✳ ✳

VIRGINIA - AND ITS ENGLISH
ARISTOCRATIC (OR FEUDAL) TRADITION

England finally gets in the game. In the early 1600s it was finally England's turn to play the game. Much like the young Spanish conquistadores coming to America a century earlier, young English aristocratic wannabees,

Colonial Foundations: The Two Americas

or for that matter anyone seeking social betterment, looked to America in the hope of finding American gold with which they could buy land and thus social status. But also English King James needed money to continue England's struggle against Spain and was therefore very willing to charter two new colonization efforts to the New World, to the area at that point known as Virginia.* One such effort was to be located in the northern part of Virginia (roughly what was to become New England) and one in the south (focused on the Chesapeake Bay area of today's Northern Virginia and Southern Maryland). Two companies were set up in England to oversee these colonization efforts, one in Plymouth (the northern colony), one in London (the southern colony).

The first of these ventures (the Plymouth or northern colony) failed. The second one, planted at Jamestown in 1607, was more successful – but barely so. But with its success the first Virginia colony was finally established.

Roanoke – an earlier, but failed, effort at settlement. Actually, Jamestown was not the first English settlement in America. It was only the first English settlement to have survived the rigors of colony planting in the wilds of America. A generation earlier, in the mid–1580s, a couple of efforts were made under the sponsorship of Queen Elizabeth's close friend, Sir Walter Raleigh, to plant a Virginia settlement in a strategic American coastal position from which the English colonists could search for gold – or simply raid passing Spanish galleons. On a second attempt (1587) a group of 90 men, 17 women and 11 children was brought to a spot they named Roanoke, on the Outer Banks of what is today North Carolina. They were left there to establish an English colony, while the ship returned to England for more supplies.

The ship was unable to return right away however, because the English at this point were deeply engaged in this struggle for their very survival against the mighty Spanish Armada. Not until the English survived this danger, three years after originally depositing the settlers in America, was a ship able to send supplies back to the colony. But upon the ship's arrival, the settlers were nowhere to be seen – nor was there any indication of where they might be or what had happened to them.

The news of the Lost Colony put a serious chill on any further thoughts about another such venture – until another generation came along at a time when the lure of gold seemed to be greater than the fear of failure.

---

*The name of the corporate venture, "Virginia," was chosen in honor of the "Virgin Queen" (never married) Elizabeth, who had just given England a long period of stable rule.

The early settlement of Virginia at Jamestown (1607). With the support of King James, financial backers or "adventurers" of the Virginia Company in London were able to amass enough money to outfit three ships (two of them being incredibly small) to bring some 144 (all male) settlers to Virginia. Setting out in December of 1606, the settlers arrived in Virginia a very long five months later in May of 1607. They sailed into the Chesapeake Bay and forty miles up a wide river, which they named the James River. There they found a small island which offered good defense against the Spanish – although a very bad spot for human habitation (swampy, and within a month totally mosquito-infested). They quickly erected a wooden fort, and named their new settlement Jamestown.

Seriously lacking among these men was any sense of how they were to cooperate in order to survive. Beyond the building of the fort, their interests were strictly personal and greedy. The hunt to strike it rich in gold began immediately. They were also unprepared to deal diplomatically with the Powhatan Indians – on whom they would depend greatly for their survival. They had an appointed Council to oversee the venture. But the members of the Council found themselves bitterly at odds with each other from the beginning. Briefly Captain John Smith brought some order to the group – though he was more interested in adventure than in group management. He was soon (1609) forced to return to England after a wound he suffered worsened. He never returned to the colony. Several times supplies – and new settlers – were brought by the Company to add to the colony. But food was never ample and the hungry mouths always seemed to outstrip supplies brought from England.

In general, the colonists themselves refused to provide for their own food stores – for such manual labor would automatically disqualify them from the gentry status they so earnestly sought. A gentleman just did not soil his hands in manual labor!

Thus Jamestown entered a massive starving time during the winter and spring of 1609–1610 in which 420 of the 480 colonists died of hunger or disease. The 60 survivors decided that it was time to abandon the settlement. They were ten miles downstream on the James River headed back toward England when Lord Thomas De La Warr (Delaware) intercepted them coming from England with a boatload of supplies and 150 additional settlers – and orders from the king to do what was necessary to ensure the survival of the colony. The survivors thus turned back. Jamestown was saved.

John Rolfe. Among the newcomers was the London businessman, John Rolfe, who on his way to Virginia had picked up a variety of tobacco seed in Bermuda and who thus began a plantation in tobacco. The first shipment sent back to England in 1614 proved to be highly profitable (although the

Colonial Foundations: The Two Americas

king despised the drug!). Failing to find gold, many of the colonists soon found that tobacco was not a bad substitute financially.

Rolfe himself was a significant part of Virginia's development in more ways than one. His passage to Virginia was itself a most exceptional one. Leaving England in 1609 along with 500 other settlers headed for the new world, his ship *Sea Venture* was hit by a hurricane and wrecked just off the Bermudas. The ship would be slowly salvaged over a ten-month period, in which time his wife would give birth to a child, who would soon die and his wife as well. It was while he was in Bermuda however that he became familiar with tobacco. Ultimately, two smaller ships were made from the wreckage of the *Sea Venture*, one of which brought him finally to Virginia, in the darkest days of its struggle for survival. But his interest in tobacco ultimately helped the colony to survive.

So also did Rolfe's romantic interest in Pocahontas, beloved daughter of local Indian chief Powhatan. She had been captured in 1613 in an attempt to have someone of importance to trade for the release of English being held as prisoners by the Indians. But she stayed on with the English, quickly learned English and became a Christian. And in 1614 the governor gave the enraptured and quite pious Rolfe permission to marry Pocahontas.[5] This actually served finally to put some degree of peace between the English and the Indians. But the bliss of it all was not destined to last. In 1616 Rolfe, Pocahontas, and their son Thomas sailed to England, where they received a royal welcome from the very curious English. Pocahontas wanted to stay on in England, but they were needed diplomatically back in Virginia to help hold the peace between the English and the Indians. But just as they were about to leave, she caught pneumonia and died in England.

A sad Rolfe returned to Virginia, leaving his son in the care of English friends. He subsequently married again, increased his tobacco business substantially, and then died in 1622, presumably in the Indian uprising of that year (although the exact causes are not known).

Some social-political reforms. Despite the economic boom that came to Virginia complements of the tobacco trade, changes were needed to attract more settlers to the colony. In 1617 the Company ended its monopoly on land ownership, allowing private ownership. By 1619 there were ten major plantations in Virginia, mostly along the wide James River. In that year Virginia received a new governor (Lord Delaware had died on a return trip to America) and a new colonial assembly. As part of the plan to encourage settlers to come to Virginia, this legislative assembly was set up to give the settlers their own voice through two elected representatives sent to Jamestown from each of the ten plantations, plus Jamestown itself. Thus in Virginia the idea of representative democracy was first born in America.

Troubles with the Indians. Now the settlers needed land, lots of land – Indian land. In 1622 there was a major uprising of the Indians led by the new chief Opechancanough (younger brother of Chief Powhatan), who had planned a surprise massacre of the inhabitants of the various plantations scattered within what they knew to be their hunting territory. In a single day 300 to 400 colonists were killed – although Jamestown itself was spared such destruction because of a warning issued by an Indian boy to the inhabitants of the town. Yet the uprising failed to kill but a third of the intruding English. The surviving English struck back – and the violence continued for a year until a truce was established. But in fact, the fighting never really ceased completely.

Virginia becomes a Royal Colony. Troubles over the high-handed ways of Delaware's deputy, Samuel Argall, created huge political problems for the colony. Rumors made their way back to England about the colony's difficulties.

Finally in 1624, because of Indian troubles, Argall's behavior, and all the rumors which were hurting the recruitment of settlers, King James suspended the Virginia Company's charter and reappointed Virginia as a royal colony, directly under his own governance (or actually under his appointed crown governor). Virginia was redistricted into counties and towns and the House of Burgesses' power was reduced somewhat. But the major plantations still dominated Virginia's local politics (the prestigious Governor's Council was made up of the heads of the largest plantations).

Growing class distinctions in Virginia. The farming of tobacco would prove to be a highly valuable path to wealth – great wealth – especially for those possessing enough initial capital to purchase the services of large numbers of indentured servants* brought in from Europe (and Africa) to work the land for them. The earliest Virginia planters who purchased the best of the properties along the shores of Virginia's Tidewater region, where wide navigable rivers (the James, York, Rappahannock, and Potomac Rivers) allowed ships from England to pick up their tobacco on docks right at the river's edge, made excellent profits from the tobacco trade – and thus were able to purchase the services of additional indentured workers

---

*Indentured service was something like an apprenticeship in which, by way of a contract (the indenture), a young man agreed to work for a master, who paid for his passage to America and housed and fed him while in his service. In exchange, the servant was to work in the fields and barns for the master. At the end of the term of indenture, usually seven years, the servant was given certain tools and his freedom. And thus with the training he received during his years of service he was ready to start off life elsewhere on his own, now himself as a landowner (usually also as a tobacco farmer) by his own right.

Colonial Foundations: The Two Americas

in order to expand their land holdings and thus overall production. Some of these plantations consequently became vast in size and operation, something like great feudal estates of thousands of acres and hundreds of servants to work those acres. Thus also along the edges of the broad rivers and numerous bays of Eastern Virginia an English aristocracy began to grow up in America, dominated by such families as the Randolphs, the Carters, the Lees, and the Washingtons, whose family patriarchs typically served on the influential Governor's Council. In the context of the times this elite-dominated society appeared quite normal.

But for the other settlers who came later to Virginia – after the flat, fertile, and directly river-accessible Tidewater region of Eastern Virginia was basically settled – opportunities for similar success became quite difficult, if not indeed even impossible. For the newcomers, life was tough because new land was available only by pressing into the unsettled Indian woodlands to the West, involving a dangerous encounter with the Indians. And it took backbreaking labor in the scorching heat of Virginia to clear a rocky woodland for tobacco farming. But even with a small cleared farm ready to produce, a normally servant-less frontier farmer located at some distance from the ships that would pick up his tobacco found it very difficult to compete in the tobacco business. He was barely able to eke out a living in this American land of opportunity.

The governorship of Sir William Berkeley.[6] In 1642, Virginia received a governor who would play a key role in giving this Virginia society something of a more stable footing, at least for a generation or so. Berkeley was the very bright second son of a family of country gentry, who grew up in England educated by both the rigors of agricultural management and a classical education at Oxford. In 1632 he gained admittance into King Charles's literary circle, the Witts, where Berkeley composed several plays performed before the king. Then in 1639 he took a military command under Charles during the rising conflict in England over the reform of the Church of England, gaining for Berkeley a knighthood. His growing esteem in the eyes of King Charles consequently led to Berkeley's appointment in 1641 as crown governor of Virginia.

But Berkeley was the first royal appointee to take more than a nominal interest in his position as Virginia governor.* He purchased for himself a section of land (Green Springs) just to the west of the Jamestown capital and began to grow different crops there as a demonstration model of alternatives to tobacco farming. As governor he worked diligently in

---

*The turnover in Virginia governors was fairly rapid, each governor or acting governor would take his position in Virginia only for a few years at a time, Berkeley being the exception.

encouraging other Virginia planters to also diversify their crops.

He clearly became quite supportive politically of the colony as well, and served to enhance the power of the Virginia General Assembly in order for it to be able to act more independently of the royal government in London.

With respect to religion, he was very loyal to Charles's Church of England and quite hostile to those who questioned the Anglican Church and its authority – notably the Puritans, of course. He kept a very close eye on the doctrines and political ideas being preached in Virginia to make sure that they conformed absolutely to the standards of the Church of England. Likewise, he discouraged public education for fear that it would provoke the growth of unwanted ideas and kept a tight rein on what got published, for much the same reason. In general, his strong views supporting the Church of England during a time of rising controversy about the need to purify the Church met with the approval of the Virginians – especially by the prominent Virginia families, who tended to be very supportive of their social identities as proper Anglican Christians.

A major incident occurred in 1644 during Berkeley's first period of service as Virginia Governor (1641–1652): the very savage conflict with the Indians and their leader, Opechancanough, who struck again at the Virginia settlers, killing about 500 of them. But Opechancanough was captured and killed, leaving the Indian uprising leaderless. The Indian attacks continued into the next year, but had run out of energy after Opechancanough's death. Soon the Indians found their power largely broken in Virginia, at least as far west as the foothills of the Appalachian Mountains – which at that point provided the Indians with a more defensible position against the intruding English. In general, Berkeley's handling of the situation met with the approval of the Virginians.

When King Charles was beheaded during the Protestant uprising led by England's Puritan Parliament at the beginning of 1649, thereby bringing England under Parliament's rule as a new Puritan Commonwealth, Berkeley's days as Governor seemed numbered. Still serving as governor in the early days of the rebellion, he offered sanctuary in Virginia to royalists escaping England – until the arrival of Commonwealth authorities in 1652, who removed him from power, but let him continue to reside in Virginia on his Green Springs Plantation.

For the next eight years Virginia was led by Puritan Commonwealth Governors elected by the Virginia General Assembly.

With the restoration in 1660 of the deposed Stuart monarchy (Charles II now being England's new king), Berkeley was also restored to his former position as Virginia governor. But his horizons soon expanded when in the early 1660s he became one of the co-proprietors of the new Carolina colony to the south of Virginia (his older brother John also receiving land in New Jersey).

Perhaps this served to overextend his responsibilities, because in Virginia he was becoming viewed as being increasingly indifferent to some of the problems there, from the poverty experienced by the lower social orders to the troubles with the Indians experienced by the frontier farmers.

Bacon's Rebellion (1676). In 1674 another Indian War exploded along the Virginia and Maryland frontier. Both sides, English and Indian, raided and slaughtered each other's settlements along this frontier, with efforts at negotiated peace seeming not able to cool down hot tempers on both sides. Berkeley responded by moving to build forts along the frontier, raising taxes in order to cover these expenses. But this angered the poorer of Virginia on whom the taxes fell especially hard and the frontiersmen who considered Berkeley's fortresses to be useless in dealing with their portion of the Indian problem. Political tensions in Virginia began to grow as the frontier question seemed to be finding no good solution.

Problems also began to develop when in 1675 Berkeley brought onto the Governor's Council a young English aristocrat, Nathaniel Bacon,* who came to the Virginia colony to escape a financial scandal back in England. In the midst of the huge Indian crisis, Bacon asked Berkeley for permission to use a 400-500 men militia he had assembled to drive the Indians from the frontier (Bacon actually was aiming at two Indian groups who had not participated in the attacks, but whose land was eagerly sought by the Virginia frontiersmen). Berkeley refused. But Bacon went ahead anyway, bringing the Indians to appeal to Berkeley for help. Berkeley arrested Bacon, whose men then broke him out of prison. Bacon subsequently not only went after the Indians, killing and enslaving many and confiscating their lands, but also issuing a number of manifestos accusing the governor of corruption and incompetence. In essence Bacon was striving to make himself Virginia's effective leader.

When Berkeley assembled his own army to go after Bacon and his militia, a war was on. Meanwhile the King shipped off from England about 1,000 soldiers to help Berkeley put down the rebellion. At first, the course of the conflict clearly favored Bacon, whose militia succeeded in burning Jamestown to the ground in September of 1676. But a month later, Bacon suddenly died of a fever – and the rebellion, lacking a leader, quickly collapsed. Berkeley was thus finally able to restore order just prior to the arrival of the English troops. Berkeley had twenty-three of the rebels hanged, some without even the benefit of a trial.

---

*He may have also had some family ties to Berkeley's wife, Frances.

An investigation into the whole affair back in England brought criticism of both Berkeley and Bacon for their handling of the matter, especially the treatment of the Indians. Consequently, Berkeley was removed from his position as governor. Berkeley immediately sailed to England to protest his dismissal, but died soon after his arrival. Sadly, he was buried in England, far from the Virginia countryside that he had given so much of his life to develop.

From indenture to slavery. The net result of Bacon's rebellion was a deepening of the social gap between the Virginia aristocracy and the Virginia frontiersmen. But also, the aristocrats were so unnerved by the anger of the rebels at this point that the Virginia wealthy lost interest in indenture – and moved to use fully slave labor in its place.

In 1619 some 20 Angolan Africans had been seized from a Portuguese ship (the English privateers were probably hoping to seize Portuguese gold rather than slaves!) and brought to Virginia.[7] That number dwindled ... until 1628 when some 100 more slaves were brought to Virginia. Actually at that time, the slavery of Indians taken in battle was much more prevalent.

The status of such slaves was at first not officially different from that of the Whites brought in as indentured workers. In fact, Africans brought to Virginia were early on classified as indentured workers, subject to certain service obligations, as just as were the White workers brought in from England, Scotland, Ireland and Germany. But clearly, arriving as slaves rather than as contracted workers led to much more rigid terms of service ... some even for a lifetime, although there were no fixed rules about such matters. Not yet anyway. Also to be noted was that White slavery existed, though in only small amounts, as punishment for some kind of crime a person committed.

Actually, by 1645, a number of freed Africans (though by no means a very large percentage of Virginia's total African population) were farming along Virginia's Eastern Shore region.

But as time quickly progressed there was less and less opportunity for freed workers, Whites or Blacks, who had completed their required terms of service to now find good land by which they might prosper. Thus many stayed on with their Virginia masters – becoming as servants a rather permanent part of the plantation system.

This was especially true of the rather compliant Africans, who tended to stay on from generation to generation, each new generation rather permanently indentured. Slowly the Africans were being locked into the indenture system – legally bound for life in service to their masters. Also, since indentured services could legally be bought and sold, soon these African workers and families were looked on not as humans but as property.

Colonial Foundations: The Two Americas 51

Step by step, indenture was transforming itself into slavery.

Slavery as an institution was recognized as a legal matter only in 1654.* But as slavery extended its place in the Virginia economy, the laws regulating and controlling slavery advanced in accompaniment. By 1705 the Virginia Slave Codes defined the institution fairly much as it would be practiced in Virginia for the next 160 years.

The Virginian or Southern social profile. By the very nature of the Virginia plantation system, the lay of the land, the wideness and depth of the Virginia rivers (such as the James or York Rivers) in the Tidewater region – the Southern economy remained essentially rural. Towns were not greatly needed, since the produce of the major plantations could be loaded directly onto ocean-going ships bound for England right at the docks in front of the plantation. There was no need to ship the plantation's produce to some port city or commercial center to be collected there and then forwarded on to England. Each plantation conducted its own business with England right at the plantation. Thus an urban economy did not develop in the South as it would in the American North.

As for the poor dirt farmers scattered throughout upland Virginia, their existence was largely one of mere subsistence farming, their hard work providing barely enough to keep their families alive. This also made the South unattractive to European immigrants to America – as they realized that given this wide gap between the rich aristocrats and the poor dirt farmers in Virginia, they knew exactly in which class they would eventually find themselves, no matter how hard they worked. Virginia was not the land of opportunity for an immigrant. Slave labor and the plantation system that depended on it dictated an economic reality that worked only to the benefit of the early and well-established Virginia aristocracy.

God and Virginia politics. Despite this rather un-Christian social profile of the very rich lording it over the slaves – and also over the upland poor-White dirt farmers – Virginia was not Godless. To be sure, there was a Christian character about the Virginia colony, for that went right along with being English. Much like in the Catholic Spanish colonies, in Virginia the king's official Church of England was expected to be established as part of the (feudal) political order there. However not until well into the

---

*Actually, slavery was practiced widely across the world in the 1600s. The Muslims specialized in it – and were major slave traders. But Europeans engaged in the practice as well, though economically it was not particularly profitable in Europe itself. It really grew big on the islands of the Caribbean where slaves were brought in in huge numbers to work the highly profitable sugar cane plantations. Here Africans virtually replaced the Indian population that had once inhabited the islands.

establishment of the Virginia colony (c. 1620) did some effort take place to bring Virginia under Anglican church structure, with its system of parishes presided over by priests or rectors and the non-clergy vestry. But always there was a shortage of priests willing to come to America. And even with the creation of the College of William and Mary in Williamsburg in 1693[*] (America's second college), there were not many young men willing to take up the challenge of the Anglican priesthood. Ordination could occur only in London, as there never was a bishop appointed to the American colonies during the period prior to American independence in the 1780s. Also, in status-conscious Virginia, there was little status and even less economic reward in being an Anglican priest in Virginia.

Also, attendance at Sunday service was the law, which was seldom enforced – and which thus produced little personal incentive for the Virginians to be very attentive to the colony's need for religious discipline.

Virginia did possess some semblance of democracy. The House of Burgesses continued to give representation to all free Virginians, although over time the vote was limited to only landowners. Nonetheless, the greatest power or authority was based on the Governor's Council, comprised of individuals selected by the Governor to help him with his governing responsibilities. These individuals were nearly always drawn from the class of local Virginia aristocrats, the owners of the major Virginia plantations.

Not surprisingly, Virginians generally were quite accepting of this political arrangement, holding the social or cultural understanding that it was the proper thing to do to defer to one's social betters – just as things worked back in England.

* * *

PURITAN NEW ENGLAND (EARLY 1600s)

Strongly differing motivations for the Virginia and New England colonies. Just as the Virginia colony was basically established for economic reasons, the Puritan colonies of New England were established for religious reasons. The latter is harder to understand today because in our increasingly secular culture, religion seemingly plays such a small role in our lives – or for many, apparently none at all. It is also easy to understand the Virginians' desire to found a colony where they might secure for themselves material wealth and high social status. That is what basically drives modern society. It is not so easy for us to understand the

---

[*]It took 57 years after the Puritans founded Harvard College in New England to train their Congregational pastors for the Virginia Anglicans to do the same in founding the College of William and Mary to train their Episcopal priests.

Puritans' desire to found a colony where they might secure for themselves God's pleasure and his blessings. But indeed that was the case – very much the case.

In short, those two different motivations, wealth/status and religion/purity were basically the source of the major differences between the two colonies. Everything about them followed naturally from these original motivations – one economic, one religious.

A split in England's Protestant ranks: Puritans and Separatists. It is important to point out that even within the ranks of the English Protestant reformers there was a split. The vast majority of the reformers remained loyal to the Church of England – hoping to bring it to Puritan standards. But other reformers took the attitude that reforming the English church was impossible and that the true purists should simply separate from the Church of England and go their own way.

Most of the Puritans disagreed strongly with those they called "Separatists," seeing their giving up on church reform as betrayal in the face of the great task of church reform. Though these two groups of English Protestants never came to blows, certainly the Puritans looked down upon the Separatists as being something like traitors to the Protestant cause.

The Separatist Pilgrims arrive first in New England (1620).[8] With Queen Elizabeth's death in 1603, her cousin and Scottish king James received the crown of England (thus becoming king of both England and Scotland). We have already noted that he fully intended to keep England in the Protestant camp. But loving the privileges of power, he strongly resented mere commoners telling him how to run the Church of England. The Puritans annoyed him greatly – though he tolerated them. But for the Separatists he had no toleration whatsoever and treated them as English traitors. His persecution of the Separatists was intense, even murderous.

Finally, a group of Separatists managed to escape England in 1608–1609 to the city of Leiden in the land of the Dutch Protestants – where a version of Calvinist Protestantism similar to their own was widely practiced. But job opportunities, especially for rural English in a highly urbanized Leiden, were few. Most of the Separatists faced long hours of work at menial tasks. Also, with the Catholic Spanish trying to bring the Protestant Dutch to their knees, it was an exceptionally difficult time for anyone then living in the Netherlands. And with time, these English ex-patriots sensed that they were losing their English identities, especially among their children, who were taking up Dutch ways.

Leiden was not the solution to their problems that they had hoped it would be. Within ten years they knew they had to move on – most likely to the wilderness of America – despite the stories coming from America about the hostile Indians and massive deaths of the colonists in Virginia.

But securing the right to emigrate to America was extremely complicated and proved to be loaded with deceptions that were foisted on the Leiden community. At the same time, English Royalist pressure on the Dutch authorities to squeeze out the Separatists was heightening. Ultimately however the Separatists received permission to settle in the area around today's Hudson River by a newly formed Plymouth Council for New England, itself desperate to find individuals willing to take on the huge risks of settling in their colony.

In September of 1620, 102 of the Leiden Separatists finally were able (after a couple of major mishaps) to put Europe behind them and head toward America. They arrived in America two months later – not at the Hudson River area they were assigned to settle, but well to the north at Cape Cod. November weather and countering winds moving north up the American coast – which they could not sail against – consequently forced them to settle in there at the Cape.

The Mayflower Compact. There were no gentlemen among them who might be expected to take command of the enterprise. They were all simple commoners. There was therefore no typical English political order within their community. They would have to devise such a thing themselves. So they created their own social contract, the Mayflower Compact, by which, still aboard their ship *Mayflower*, they agreed to form their own political community at Cape Cod – complete with their own rules of government, which they all agreed to respect. They were following a format modeled on the church covenants that were used typically in the formation of new congregations by the members themselves (a common practice among Separatists).   William Bradford (one of the colony's frequently elected governors) recorded the Compact as reading:

> *In the name of God, Amen. We whose names are underwritten, the loyal subjects of our dread Sovereign Lord King James, by the Grace of God of Great Britain, France and Ireland, King, Defender of the Faith, etc.*
>
> *Having undertaken, for the Glory of God and advancement of the Christian Faith and Honour of our King and Country, a Voyage to plant the First Colony in the Northern Parts of Virginia, do by these presents solemnly and mutually in the presence of God and one of another, Covenant and Combine ourselves together into a Civil Body Politic, for our better ordering and preservation and furtherance of the ends aforesaid; and by virtue hereof to enact,*

constitute and frame such just and equal Laws, Ordinances, Acts, Constitutions and Offices, from time to time, as shall be thought most meet and convenient for the general good of the Colony, unto which we promise all due submission and obedience. In witness whereof we have hereunder subscribed our names at Cape Cod, the 11th of November, in the year of the reign of our Sovereign Lord King James, of England, France and Ireland the eighteenth, and of Scotland the fifty fourth. Anno Domini 1620.[9]

They thus vowed to form a tightly-knit community rather than just a collection of self-interested individuals. This would be a quite different venture than the one in Virginia.

Settling in at Plymouth (1621). It was a most unfortunate time for arrival, for winter was beginning to set in. They were also positioned at a point along the New England coast where mistreatment of the Indians by earlier English adventurers had left the Indians potentially very hostile. But smallpox had cleared some of the area of its Indian inhabitants.

After three weeks of exploring the area, they found an excellent fresh-water site inside the Cape to lay the foundations for their settlement or plantation, which they called Plymouth. But it was now late December and winter had set in on them. They needed to erect buildings for shelter as quickly as possible to get the people out of the damp conditions aboard the *Mayflower*.

It was a very hard time. Tragically a main building they had just built, one which they hoped could then shelter them, burned down in mid-January. At this point they began to die, losing around half of their members over that winter of 1620–1621. Of the eighteen wives in the group, fourteen died that winter. The children and youth fared better than their parents, but consequently their numbers now included a large group of parentless orphans.[10]

But amazingly as the spring approached, their fortunes changed dramatically. Not one but two Indians able to speak English presented themselves to help them adjust to life in the New World! One in particular, Squanto, would be a Godsend, showing them how to plant and cultivate the corn that would become their life support. And both Indians would introduce them to the Indian chief of the area, Massasoit, whose Wampanoag tribe would become close allies of these English.

The summer yielded a fair crop. Their homes were in place. Yes, they had paid a huge price for their success, having lost half of their members during the terrible winter. Yet though they certainly mourned for lost loved-ones their hearts were glad enough to schedule a harvest feast, to which they invited their Indian friends, in recognizing that God had performed a miracle among them. Their community definitely was well planted and able to survive. They had succeeded against all odds. Now they could expect to live in a world that existed to give God great glory through their human enterprise. Here, as unlike in England, they could live freely to the Christian goals and standards they long had sought.

And unlike Virginia, which went continuously through the hardest of times, these Pilgrims at Plymouth would never again experience the kinds of catastrophes encountered in Virginia. They would face another winter of hardship that very next year when a boatload of more colonists was unloaded at their doorstep. But even then, there would be no dying time – because they all sacrificed together to get everyone through that winter. And their relations with the Indians remained generally friendly (especially their alliance with Massasoit) – unlike Virginia. Then over the next years, the bringing of more settlers (not a large number however) to the area was a regular event. By 1630 there were 300 people living in the Plymouth colony.

Their community had survived and prospered all because (as they saw it) they had been willing to live like true Christians.* Also ironic and sad is that everything that the Pilgrims were ready to sacrifice for is completely ignored by modern secular society, even as it celebrates the remarkable achievement of this early group of English settlers. The Pilgrims motives for this dangerous enterprise are recast by modern Secularists (or Humanists) as simply the quest for freedom. The quest for religious purity is not something that Secularists are either able or willing to acknowledge as the prime reason for the Pilgrims' undertaking of this dangerous enterprise.

It becomes time for even the Puritans to separate (1630). Meanwhile, in 1625 King James had died and his son Charles had taken the throne of England. In theory a Protestant like his father, Charles's devotion to the Protestant cause was easily questionable. His marriage to the Catholic Henrietta of France and his close friendships with the anti-Calvinists Richard Montagu and William Laud were problematic. He was arrogant (raising taxes without Parliament's approval), wed to the idea that the king should have absolute power to rule (the divine right of kings), and lacked a sense of political diplomacy. Tensions began to grow with many of his subjects,

---

*The Pilgrims actually regarded very humbly their own efforts at settlement. They sacrificed most of their earnings to pay off greedy investors back in London – who kept upping the obligations imposed on them. Their children would later drift away to settle in more fertile parts of New England, leaving the legacy at Plymouth somewhat forlorn in comparison to the thriving settlements to the north around Boston. They would have been totally surprised to know that today they are the most celebrated of all people who made the perilous journey to English America – to bring the Christian life to the New World.

Colonial Foundations: The Two Americas 57

especially the Puritans (who dominated the House of Commons).

In the meantime, the English colonization efforts in the area coming to be known as New England were gathering momentum. During the 1620s a number of small companies were formed to settle the area to the north of the Plymouth colony around the Massachusetts Bay. The largest of these, a Puritan settlement at Salem under the leadership of John Endecott, had not fared well: out of the nearly 300 original settlers, over 80 died during the winter of 1628–1629. As a result, only 80 decided to stay on to try to keep the settlement going, and the rest returned to England.

But others were not so easily discouraged. Anyway, life in England was becoming almost impossible. King Charles dismissed Parliament in 1629 and attempted to rule England on his own. The Puritans immediately understood that things were going to get rough for them with the King attempting to rule the country as an absolutist monarch. It was time for the Puritans to leave England.

The Great Migration (ca. 1630–1642). King Charles in 1628 authorized the creation of the Massachusetts Bay Company, assuming that it was another business venture – not understanding that he was authorizing thousands of Puritans to flee to America to get out from under his increasingly oppressive religious control. In 1629 and 1630, under the direction of the Company's governor, John Winthrop – and financed heavily by Winthrop's own personal fortune – eleven ships containing 1,000 Puritan settlers set off for America, to lands in and around the Boston area. Tragically, 200 of that group died the first winter. But like the Plymouth settlement, that first winter would complete the tragic cost of getting the colony up and running. From then on, the colony prospered greatly (despite the ever-present problem of relations with the Indians).

Winthrop's group of Puritans was merely the beginning of a massive departure of settlers from England to America (but also to Ireland, Canada and the Caribbean). During the next dozen years approximately 20,000 English Puritans migrated to the Massachusetts Bay Colony, exchanging economic security in England for the risky opportunity to live in America where they could practice their religion without fear of the civil authorities.

A covenant society.[11] Behind all this was more than simply the desire to escape the tyranny of English kings. In coming to America, they could actually build, from the ground up, a society which would function in the ideal Christian way. And they would be able to succeed in this enterprise because they would be doing it in company with God, by a special Covenant between them, God agreeing to be their God, they agreeing to be his people.

This covenant society would be a grand experiment in showing the world how such a relationship with God could work to great human effect. Indeed, by its very existence, this special covenant society would stand as a city upon a hill, offering the light of hope to a darkened world. It was a huge responsibility that God had laid on their shoulders: to live as God himself commanded them to live ... not as sinful man, with all his selfish instincts, might choose to live.

Laying the foundations of a middle-class Christian society. These were not impoverished or status-hungry refugees. The Puritans in general were well educated and had been a quite prosperous group back in England. Their number included a large group of Cambridge University educated pastors – some of the best English intellectual talent of the day.*

Also they had a very strong entrepreneurial instinct and ability to easily take care of themselves. And they naturally brought with them to America their charter, and all of the rights that it guaranteed them. Consequently, they left behind no group in England that the King could pressure or manipulate into religious and political conformity. The Puritans were on their own in America. And very capably so.

The flow of thousands of Puritans to America continued unabated until 1642, when a confrontation between King Charles and the English Parliament developed into a terrible civil war. This then made it extremely difficult for anyone to find the means to get to America from England. At this point the steady flow of settlers to America diminished greatly.

The Puritan Leader, America's first true Founding Father': John Winthrop.[12] Far above all others, John Winthrop was the one who directed the course of Puritan New England to its success as a grand religious or social experiment. It was Winthrop's sense of vision, his optimism, that kept New England on course as it laid out a Godly society built from the ground up in such a way that it could serve God as a City on a Hill, a beacon light to all the world. It was Winthrop's background and personality that helped steer the course of this development between the dangerous rocks of religious fanaticism on the one hand and heavy-handed legalism on the other.

Winthrop was nobly born to a father who was both a lawyer and substantial landowner as well as a director at Trinity College, Cambridge – which John himself would attend, and there develop close friendships with other Puritan reformers. At age twenty-six his father made John Lord of

---

*Indeed, education was of such importance to these Puritans that once in America they set themselves to the task of founding their own "Cambridge" in America: Harvard College, established in 1636 to train additional clergy that would be needed as the colony expanded.

the Manor at Groton and then later a member of his law firm in London.

John was profoundly religious – his long-developed journal describing the struggles he had in attempting to live worthily as a Christian, and his constant appeals to God's grace to give him the power to live with a spirit of joy, despite the many challenges he faced in both his private and public life. Those challenges included the deaths of his first two wives, and the gradual pressure put on the Puritans by King Charles and his chief advisor, Archbishop Laud.

The latter challenge became particularly troublesome when in 1629 the king dismissed Parliament – fully intending to rule England on his own as absolute sovereign – and dismissed Puritans from public service, including Winthrop, who lost his position at Court. But this freed up Winthrop to spend his time in the autumn of 1629 trying to convince the newly formed Massachusetts Bay Company of the importance of a general emigration of Puritans to New England. At a Company shareholders' meeting in October the decision was made to take Winthrop's advice, and, as he was willing himself to make the journey with the first group of emigrants, he was chosen to serve as the Company's governor.*

Winthrop then organized the effort to arrange for a fleet of ships and supplies necessary to carry out this journey to America. He also was active in recruiting pastors who would be needed to guide the communities that the Company intended to set up upon arrival at their new home in America.

Winthrop could be a tough governor, and he made mistakes, which he freely acknowledged, mistakes which made his heart all the more supple and which drove him to depend ever more completely on the mercies of God rather than on his own sense of right-mindedness to keep things moving forward. He had his detractors, even dedicated enemies, who felt that his hand was too strong – or not strong enough. But his love for his fellow New Englanders was immense – as was their love for him. And it was this love, more than anything else, that gave the New England experiment its strong foundations.

Establishing a viable community in the New World meant having to build on new and untested social principles – where only old English social habits, plus a lot of expectations for a radically new society, had to be carefully reshaped and redirected so as to produce something socially viable in the New World. All of this had to take place in the context of a heated debate raging among Englishmen about proper or Godly social ideals, and more particularly, proper or Godly social authority. By tradition the English were very deferential to the authority of their social "betters,"

---

*Between his election as the Company's governor in 1629 and his death in 1649, Winthrop was for 19 of those years elected annually as either the Company's governor or its deputy governor.

unquestioned social authority typically being bestowed on those favored by upper class birth. Thus in one sense it was expected that those of higher social rank would naturally direct the development of colonial society.

In New England all these social-political ideas and attitudes would come together in tension. Thus Winthrop (and his associates) had to carefully guide this new society through these challenging times in order to develop this new society on firm social and political ground.

Winthrop addressed this matter from the very outset by setting an example personally in undertaking hard physical labor to get housing established for the Puritan settlers in a number of different settlements in what would become the Boston area. He made the message very clear: everyone was expected to labor in God's vineyard. There would be no exceptions, not even for gentry. Hard work was expected of everyone despite whatever social rank they had back in England, work that not only served to get the colony established on solid ground but which also made it clear that there would be no traditional English social ranking in New England. Here all were equal by birth in the eyes of God, and thus they would also be equally born in the eyes of man. The only social rewards to be achieved in New England would be the product of one's own labor. And even these were to be kept within a sense of the fundamental equality, and thus unity, of New England society. That included housing, clothing, and any other visible markings that back in England were designed to announce clearly one's status.

An example of how serious Winthrop took this matter would be the fuss that Winthrop made with his deputy Dudley because Dudley had built his house with excessive decorative woodwork!

The larger legacy of this Puritan venture. Today the Puritan experiment is treated as if it were some kind of terrible period of religious bigotry in American history.* Little is taught and therefore little is remembered about

---

*Very characteristic of how modern America has come to view the entire Puritan enterprise is the way it is summed up in a very popular textbook used recently in America's public schools – to teach a rising generation about its cultural-moral inheritance: Ira Peck and Steven Deyle's *American Adventures: People Making History* (New York: Scholastic Inc., 1991).

After seven chapters (uniformly four pages each) three of which are on the American Indians, one on the Portuguese, one on Columbus, one on the Spanish Conquistadores, and one on the French, the text arrives at a four-page coverage of the Jamestown settlement, and then one on New England, the latter chapter appropriately entitled "They Were Free at Last." All but three concluding paragraphs of this chapter are focused on the Pilgrim settlement at Plymouth, with half of that section on the feast they shared with the Indians.

The only discussion of the Puritans in the entire text of 853 pages is the three small, very negative paragraphs, describing 1) how the Puritans came to America seeking the same religious freedom as the Pilgrims, but were unwilling

those early formative days except a few unflattering episodes selected from the long and complex history of the period, episodes that shed little light on the actual dynamics of the times but instead episodes that point more to the kinds of social priorities that have emerged in post-modern America.

On the one hand, the dissenters of those early years who attacked the moral and political authority of the colony are today held up as the true heroes of early America. On the other hand, forgotten are those that labored hard to keep the society united and moving together against all the forces which threatened to pull that precious social order apart.

The name John Winthrop is barely known today. This is very unfortunate for there are great lessons to be learned from how democracy in America was crafted out of a carefully cultivated spirit of compromise, one which set careful boundaries to political discourse so that tempers and egos of the more energetic type might not wreck the society. Yet it was a system which allowed within those boundaries a wide latitude of freedom of discussion and debate, something that was unheard of in those times. Indeed, such a spirit we would be most unwise not to continue to respect, study, and nurture with the same care by which it was first developed.

For the blessing of so great a social legacy as this home-grown American democracy we may thank God – and certainly also to a very great extent his humble servant John Winthrop, the first of America's great Founding Fathers.

The early development of New England. Those that were able to get to Massachusetts during the years of the Great Migration represented some of the best of England's brains and industrial-commercial talent, benefitting Massachusetts greatly and giving it a very special quality as a true homeland, a highly self-sufficient society. Most of the men were skilled as tradesmen of some kind and were dedicated to the task of finding a respectable place for themselves and their families in the larger social scheme of things. (Virginia at that time was still attracting mostly single men hoping simply to get rich enough to eventually return to England in better economic circumstances than they had left it).

---

to extend that same freedom to others, 2) citing as an example how Roger Williams was banished from the Massachusetts colony because he thought that Puritans had no right to impose their beliefs on everyone and 3) how also Anne Hutchinson was told to leave the colony because Puritan women were required to obey their husbands and clergy, and she actually held religious gatherings in her home.

This kind of shaming of the Puritans tells us more about where our intellectuals find themselves ideologically today, than what history itself might actually teach us about the dynamic that shaped the birth and development of the American nation. In any case this is very typical of how modern teaching wants to depict the very foundational Puritan legacy.

There was nothing attractive about New England for those of any aristocratic nature or ambition, for New England offered no known opportunity for striking it rich. Only those who were content to live merely comfortable – yet free – lives were attracted to the colony. This resulted in a high degree of sense of basic equality within the society. Besides, basic Puritan theology stressed how all people were equal in the eyes of God – and anything otherwise was just sinful vanity.

And thus it was that Middle-Class America was born!

Property rights as the foundation of Puritan economic equality. Property ownership was an important consideration in Puritan society (as it was of course also in feudal society), but only as an assurance that the citizen as property-owner would have a stable or conservative interest in the welfare of the society. And property was fairly abundant in New England (at the great cost, of course, to the Indians).

In fact, there was much attention given to the matter of property by the Massachusetts authorities. Each village or town was understood to have just so much property to offer to newcomers, most of it offered on a fairly equitable basis. When that property was fully distributed, a new town (usually west, towards the expanding frontier) would be opened up for settlement and the property there carefully distributed to a new group of settlers. While this offered no one any opportunity for great wealth, it also offered no urban overcrowding and no poverty such as existed widely back in England.

Early New England government. The matter of the government of Massachusetts went through a difficult process of evolution within those same years. At the outset (1630) the colony was under the authority of the Company – which was directed by the Governor and a Council of eight freemen. But under pressure from some of the settlers, the Council expanded membership on a General Court to include 118 of the men, although the Council still continued to conduct most of the colony's business. When a special tax was levied on the colony in 1632 complaints were quick to arise. In 1634 the settlers discovered that the Company's charter actually had provided for the General Court to be made up of all the freemen. But as the colony had become by this time so enormous, that was not a practical possibility. A compromise was reached in the form of representation to the General Court by two members elected by each town – plus the Governor and the members of the Council. The colony now had its own legislature. The General Court not only voted taxes and other matters of general concern of the colony, it took up the responsibility of electing the Governor. It also promulgated a new code of laws, the Massachusetts

Colonial Foundations: The Two Americas 63

Body of Liberties (1641) which guaranteed a number of personal rights to, but also the duties of, the colony's citizens. Thus it was that a commercial corporation became a representative democracy of its own design.

The New England Confederation. Two years later (1643) the colonies of Massachusetts, Plymouth, Connecticut and New Haven (excluding Williams' Rhode Island, which did not participate) joined together to form the New England Confederation, primarily to unite their defense efforts against the restless Indians – and also against the expansive French and Dutch. But it also coordinated their jurisdictions so that a person could not avoid the effects of law by simply escaping to another of these colonies. And it provided a mechanism for resolving disputes among the colonies – each colony, regardless of size, possessing two votes each on an issue. Thus even though the civil authorities back in England had made no particular provision for the English colonies to work together, the colonies had taken the initiative on their own to meet this need. This inter-colony cooperation would become an important part of the development of English America.

But that was because they were all very aware of the dangers of not working closely together as a new society. The dangers of failure were a clear and present danger to the colonists. The examples of the failure of efforts to settle the New World were numerous and horrible to behold. And thus the need to work closely together was understood by all.

Voices of dissent. Almost all, that is. There were some notable exceptions. Not all of the Puritan settlers were content with the social order in Massachusetts that was quickly taking shape under Winthrop and the other Puritan leaders (mostly pastors of this or that community that dotted the landscape). As is typical of any society, there were critics or dissenters, who for one reason or another found the setup to be not to their liking. As previously noted, today it is these dissenters, not the ones attempting to preserve a viable social order, who have drawn the greatest notice and admiration of modern historians (especially of the revisionist school of history), who find much about the Puritans' demand for unity to be horribly contradictory to their highly cultivated sense of personal freedom.

Roger Williams and the Providence Colony. One of these dissenters was Roger Williams, a supremely intelligent and personable young man, who came to the colony in 1631 and was immediately offered the pulpit of the Boston church. But he was a compulsive perfectionist, unable to locate the perfection he always hungered for, thus finding himself to be a tormented soul under the control of personal instincts that made him an early version of the self-destructive Humanist (in other words, an individual unable to accept the fact that realistically the world will always be full of sinners, no matter how hard you try to rewrite the rules of life). Thus he declined the Boston pulpit – because he felt the church not to be pure enough (it included members who had participated in a Church of England communion service and had failed to repent of this great sin). He accepted the pulpit in Plymouth, but eventually found the church there also not pure enough. He switched to the pulpit in Salem, and from there began a wider quest for purity within the larger Massachusetts colony, particularly over the matter of the very right of the colony to exist at all. His major concern, one that he harped on most loudly, was about the illegitimacy of the charter that authorized the Massachusetts Company to be about its business in America. The charter had come from the English king, not the Indians, the only ones who, according to Williams, had the right to issue such permission.

Also behind his dissent was his strong Puritan belief that no one but God alone truly knew who was saved and who was not. Therefore no one had the right to qualify who had, and who had not, the right to participate (vote) in the political affairs of the community. But since being demonstrably among the saved was key in the Bay Colony's qualification permitting a person full membership in the church and thus also the right to lead (vote) in the affairs of the colony, Williams' theology undercut the entire vision of legitimacy that the Bay colony was trying to build itself on.

His criticisms soon started fraying the nerves of the colony's leaders, who tried to get him to understand how harmful to the spirit of unity of the community his attacks were becoming. Being reprimanded by the Council for his trouble-making, he quieted down for a while. But then he soon started back up again. His attacks on the colony for having received their grant from the king without the assent of the local Indians the Council knew would prove highly offensive to the king should he get wind of Williams' tirades. The whole venture could be compromised by Williams' attacks. He was called a second time (summer of 1635) before the Council for his trouble-making. An impasse developed between the Council and Williams: banishment was finally ordered (October) – but postponed because of the arrival of winter, provided that he stopped his attacks on the colony's authorities ... which he seemed unable to do. Thus about to be expelled, he and a group of followers left the colony (January 1636), taking refuge among the Wampanoag Indians. In the spring, having purchased land from the Narragansett Indians, he founded his Providence Colony (in the future Rhode Island) where he could put his purer social ideas into play.

In accordance with his own fundamental principles, he opened up his colony to full (male) political participation by anyone, regardless of particular religious persuasion. Thus Anabaptists (Baptists) joined his colony. These

Colonial Foundations: The Two Americas

he joined, for a few months anyway – until he found problems with this group of Baptists as well. Then to find refuge in Williams' colony came the hyper-activist Quakers, whose most unusual theological ideas and behavior* were highly contradictory to the fundamental principles of the Bay colony. Williams personally disliked (and debated) Quaker theology. But he nonetheless permitted them to stay. However his colony also became a natural attraction for all the ruffians and malcontents who found the discipline of the Bay Colony not to their liking. Ironically, these newcomers who would soon have the opportunity to quote some of Williams' own earlier sermons, enjoyed denouncing him as a hypocrite when he himself attempted to force some kind of social discipline on his colony!

And oddly enough, several years later he returned to England – to get a charter from Parliament authorizing his new colony of Providence, the very thing that he had been loudest about in his critique of the Bay Colony's legitimacy!

Eventually Williams discovered that grace rather than self-righteousness was the greater Christian virtue. A close friendship he continued to maintain with Winthrop during the difficult startup years of his new colony only deepened with time. And his concern for the Indians proved authentic. And in the end, this spared the Providence colony some of the Indian troubles which would later hit New England.

Anne Hutchinson. Another of these famous free spirits that the moderns love so much to extol was Anne Hutchinson. She and her husband came to New England in 1634 and she immediately gravitated to the Boston pastor John Cotton, whom she had taken a liking to back when he was a pastor in England. She flattered her way into importance in his eyes – and soon the eyes of others in his church. She gathered a group in her home to discuss his sermons,† extolling his great virtues in comparison to other pastors, whom she insisted were less worthy of their calls. Soon she was passing judgment on all the leaders of the community, claiming that only Cotton preached a covenant of grace, the rest a covenant of works. Further, she began to claim that she possessed this power of judgment

---

*The more typical image held of the Quakers today is their quiet manner and spiritual gentleness. But in their early stages of existence (the mid–1600s) they were loud, abrasive, even lewd in their rather violent demonstrations against Puritan piety. The quietist image will not develop until much later.

†Actually holding such discussion in her home was not an uncommon thing among Puritan women, who were actually quite active in forming and leading prayer and discussion groups, ones involving men as well as women. See: Mark A. Noll, *A History of Christianity in The United States and Canada* (Grand Rapids, MI: William B. Eerdmans, 1992), pp. 60–61.

because it was given her by God. She was now posing herself as some kind of prophet, enlightened with spiritual insights permitting her to see into the ministry of others. Eventually she concluded that none of the pastors in the colony (except Cotton) were truly fit to preach the gospel.

Thus she found herself – under divine authority, of course – slandering the community's leaders, gathering a rather large party or group increasingly hostile to those leaders – and in general threatening the harmony of the community. This was more than simply exercising free speech. She was therefore called before the Council (1638).

Much is made by feminists today that she was under indictment simply because she was a woman daring to challenge the male authorities of the Colony. But let the concluding portion of the trial speak for itself:[13]

> **Mr. Winthrop, Governor.** *Let us state the case and then we may know what to do. That which is laid to Mrs. Hutchinson's charge is this, that she hath traduced the magistrates and ministers of this jurisdiction, that she hath said the ministers preached a covenant of works and Mr. Cotton a covenant of grace, and that they were not able ministers of the gospel, and she excuses it that she made it a private conference and with a promise of secrecy, ?c. now this is charged upon her, and they therefore sent for her seeing she made it her table talk, and then she said the fear of man was a snare and therefore she would not be affeared of them. ...*
>
> **Mrs. Hutchinson.** *If you please to give me leave I shall give you the ground of what I know to be true. Being much troubled to see the falseness of the constitution of the church of England, I had like to have turned separatist; whereupon I kept a day of solemn humiliation and pondering of the thing; this scripture was brought unto me – he that denies Jesus Christ to be come in the flesh is antichrist – This I considered of and in considering found that the papists did not deny him to be come in the flesh nor we did not deny him – who then was antichrist? ... The Lord knows that I could not open scripture; he must by his prophetical office open it unto me. ... I bless the Lord, he hath let me see which was the clear ministry and which the wrong. Since that time I confess I have been more choice and he hath let me to distinguish between the voice of my beloved and the voice of Moses, the voice of John Baptist and the voice of antichrist, for all those voices are spoken of in scripture. Now if you do condemn me for speaking what in my conscience I know to be truth I must commit myself unto the Lord.*

Mr. Nowell. *How do you know that that was the spirit?*
Mrs. H. *How did Abraham know that it was God that bid him offer his son, being a breach of the sixth commandment?*
Mr. Dudley, Deputy Governor. *By an immediate voice.*
Mrs. H. *So to me by an immediate revelation.*
Dep. Gov. *How! an immediate revelation.*
Mrs. H. *By the voice of his own spirit to my soul. I will give you another scripture, Jer. 46. 27, 28 out of which the Lord shewed me what he would do for me and the rest of his servants. – But after he was pleased to reveal himself to me . . . Therefore I desire you to look to it, for you see this scripture fulfilled this day and therefore I desire you that as you tender the Lord and the church and commonwealth to consider and look what you do. You have power over my body but the Lord Jesus hath power over my body and soul, and assure yourselves thus much, you do as much as in you lies to put the Lord Jesus Christ from you, and if you go on in this course you begin you will bring a curse upon you and your posterity, and the mouth of the Lord hath spoken it. . . .*
Gov. *The court hath already declared themselves satisfied concerning the things you hear, and concerning the troublesomeness of her spirit and the danger of her course amongst us, which is not to be suffered. Therefore if it be the mind of the court that Mrs. Hutchinson for these things that appear before us is unfit for our society, and if it be the mind of the court that she shall be banished out of our liberties and imprisoned till she be sent away, let them hold up their hands.*
. . .
Gov. *Mrs. Hutchinson, the sentence of the court you hear is that you are banished from out of our jurisdiction as being a woman not fit for our society, and are to be imprisoned till the court shall send you away.*
Mrs. H. *I desire to know wherefore I am banished?*
Gov. *Say no more, the court knows wherefore and is satisfied.*

She took herself and her followers to Williams's Providence Colony. But things did not go well for her in Rhode Island. After her husband died, she moved her family to the Dutch colony of New Netherland (on Long Island) – where in 1643 she and her five children were killed in a local Indian uprising. For someone who was certain that a curse would fall upon the Bay Colony for coming up against her and her prophetic powers to locate the anti-Christ among the authorities of the colony (virtually all the pastors except her beloved Rev. Cotton) it appeared to some at the time that the curse in fact had fallen on her instead.

Thomas Hooker and the Connecticut colony. Hooker was another individual who departed from the colony because of disagreements he had with its authorities over key issues. But his departure was deeply mourned by those authorities, for they considered him one of their very best leaders. Nonetheless they granted him his request to depart, seeing it as God's way of extending the Puritan domain.

Hooker was undoubtedly the most highly respected and beloved Puritan pastor back in England ... and the most detested by the king and bishops. He was forced to flee the country in 1630, make his way to Holland, and then three years later join his fellow Puritans in Massachusetts. He was immediately given the pulpit in Newe Towne (Cambridge) and became a key voice in the life of the Colony.

But he too was bothered by the way religion and politics were bound so closely together in Massachusetts. The colony's officers, both civil and religious (governors, magistrates, pastors, teachers, etc.), were elected only by full members of the Church. Hooker felt strongly however that the elections of civil officers should be open to all citizens, or at least property-holders among them, regardless of their status within the Church. He felt so strongly about this issue – and the Massachusetts officers felt so strongly opposed to his idea – that in 1636 he petitioned the Council and was granted permission to leave the Colony with 100 of his church members to establish a new settlement to the West, at Hartford on the Connecticut River. Here he joined other English settlements at Windsor and Wethersfield, established only a few years earlier along the Connecticut River. In 1637 they combined to fight the Pequot war and in 1639 even formed a joint government, defined in the Fundamental Orders of Connecticut, largely in line with Hooker's philosophy on civil and religious authorities.

His influence remained strong however not just in Connecticut but throughout New England. He continued to be very close to both Winthrop in Massachusetts and Williams in Rhode Island, traveled frequently to Boston and to Providence for consultations, and helped create the notion that despite the doctrinal differences among these leaders, they were still closely united in their vision of creating a New Israel in America.

In addition to these social and theological issues there were a number of economic issues also at work in the development of the Connecticut colony. The land around Boston was stony and ill-suited for farming. And the population was growing rapidly in the Bay Colony, putting tremendous pressure on the land's ability to support community life. But the land along the Connecticut River was fertile and productive. Thus many Puritans

Colonial Foundations: The Two Americas 69

began pouring into the area simply to take advantage of the better soil.

And nearby another colony, New Haven, was set up in 1638 by Puritans who began to feel that Winthrop's Bay Colony was not strict enough in enforcing its Calvinist ideals!

Relations with the Indians. It might be supposed that any troubles that developed with the Indians would have been over questions of land rights. But actually, the first conflict which erupted was over trade, compounded by rivalries among the Indian tribes themselves, and set off by the misadventures of a handful of English and Indians – which step by step escalated into full-scale war in 1636.

The Pequot War (1636). Endecott (not only former governor in the early days of the Puritan settlement at Salem but also former soldier), angry over a local murder by some Indians, led a raiding party against the Pequot – who in turn took revenge. This quickly spiraled into massacres of both English and Indian settlements. The worst was the near total slaughter of the Pequot (600 or 700?) at their village at Mystic by a force of English and their Narragansett and Mohegan allies. This attack and several others like it (though of a smaller nature) broke the power of the Pequot. Some of the surviving Pequot escaped to neighboring lands (the Mohawk, however, turned them over to the English as a show of friendship). But most were given to the Narragansetts and Mohegans as slaves or sold as slaves to Bermuda or the West Indies, or even sold to Puritan families in Massachusetts and Connecticut as household slaves. And Pequot land was confiscated by the English. The Pequot were devastated.

John Eliot and the Praying Indians. John Eliot, as minister/teaching elder, was one of the early leaders of the colony (arrived in 1631). He co-edited the *Bay Psalm Book* (the first book published in the English colonies) in 1640 and set up the Roxbury Latin School in 1645. But his most notable achievement was his missionary work with the Massachusetts Indians. In 1646 the General Court authorized support for a Christian mission to the Indians, and Eliot took the lead in the effort, giving the first sermon that year in the Natick language. His work drew interest back in England and in 1649 the heavily Puritan Long Parliament subscribed 12,000 pounds (silver coinage) toward the mission. He eventually completed a translation of the Bible in the Natick language (1663) and created an Indian grammar book (1666). He also organized the newly converted Indians, called Praying Indians, into communities along the English frontier (fourteen eventually), the foremost at Natick. But these Indian communities served a political purpose as well – for they acted as a buffer between the English and the more hostile Indians.

When however a major English-Indian war finally erupted (1675) the English lost their trust in these Indian allies and confined or resettled them – thus ending the separate status of the Praying Indians.

King Philip's War (1675–1676). In 1675 the very deadliest of all Indian wars in American history erupted – deadliest not because of the sheer numbers involved, but deadliest in terms of the percentages of the inhabitants killed in the fighting. More than half of New England's ninety towns were attacked, almost a thousand English settlers were killed by the Indians, but three times that number of Indians died (mostly of exhaustion and disease) during the Indian uprising. Ultimately the war left the Indian communities in the region totally devastated and the English communities hostile toward or at least suspicious of all Indians.

When Plymouth's long-time Wampanoag ally Massasoit died in 1661, and his older son died suddenly (and mysteriously – even suspiciously) in Plymouth while there on a diplomatic mission, his second son Metacom (or King Philip to the English) took command of the Wampanoag. But Metacom did not hold the same view of the English that his father had. Metacom began meeting with other tribes to organize a massive surprise attack on all the various English settlements in New England.

The Indians were having a hard time with the English. The English had been sending settlements up the rivers and along the coasts, depriving the Indians of some of their best hunting territory. The Indians no longer found in the English presence at least the economic advantage of trade with them for the much-needed tools and weapons the English possessed. The Indians were running out of goods to trade for these English items and were having to resort to the selling of their land instead. Then too the English seemed unable to respect the Indians or their culture, increasingly treating the Indians as pagan children, frustrating and angering the Indians enormously.

The situation was thus already very tense when Metacom began to plot this act of Indian reprisal against the English everywhere. The war erupted in gradually growing stages starting with the murder in 1675 of a Praying Indian who had warned the English of Metacom's plans to attack the English settlements. His Indian murderers were captured, tried and hanged – leading to a countering attack on an English settlement by a group of Indians. The violence now escalated quickly. The Indian attacks against various English settlements gathered momentum during the summer and early fall of 1675. In the early winter the colonist militias struck back furiously at the Narragansetts, who had been sheltering Wampanoags.

The situation however only worsened for the English settlers as a

Colonial Foundations: The Two Americas

gathering coalition of Indian tribes raided town after town, even reaching as far into English territory as the Plymouth Plantation. By March of 1676 it looked as if the Indians were unstoppable. They even burned Providence (Rhode Island) to the ground and a large section of Springfield (Massachusetts). But as the war was becoming a war of mutual attrition, it became a question of which side could resupply itself in food and weapons. The Indians were hoping for help from the French. But the help never arrived. Likewise, the English were hoping for help from the Mother country – which also never materialized. But the English were greater in number in the affected areas and better set up to help each other. Also, some of the Indian tribes, such as the fierce Mohawks, actually joined the conflict on the English side.

Little by little Metacom and his warriors began to lose ground. They had also missed the growing season that they would need to survive the coming winter and they knew that their situation was growing desperate. Warriors began to drift away from Metacom – especially as the English offered amnesty to Indians who would give up the fight (important because continued fighting was resulting in whole Indian units being surrounded and slaughtered, men, women and children). Metacom now had become a man on the run. In August he was finally tracked down and killed by an Indian who was a member of one of the search parties looking for him. Quickly the whole Indian uprising fizzled out.

Many Indians escaped to join other tribes in the neighboring regions. Many others were captured and sold into slavery (mostly in the West Indies). A number of the remaining tribes were virtually eliminated in part by the fighting itself, but even more by the hunger and disease which accompanied the fighting. The English community quickly revived – and found now that it could move westward with less danger coming from hostile Indians.

CHAPTER TWO

THE COLONIES MATURE

* * *

THE VARIETY AND NATURE OF THE AMERICAN COLONIES

Corporate colonies. Thus far we have seen colonies of the types that might be termed a corporate colony, that is, set up and run as a huge corporation – such as the Virginia, Plymouth, and Massachusetts Bay colonies. The corporate colony followed a procedure that is still used today when we incorporate businesses, creating them as legal persons by the consent of the government (English kings back then) according to specific terms listed in their incorporating charter. These legal corporations were/are subject by the governing authority to taxation and to periodic review of their operations to ensure that they continue to serve the purpose to which they were incorporated. If they violate this trust, they might lose their charter rights and be dissolved – as was the Virginia Company in 1624.

In 1500s and 1600s England the idea of corporations was closely tied to the need to gather together large sums of money to underwrite a huge business venture. Such ventures always required more than one person to contribute the investment capital necessary to get a particular industrial operation up and running. So a group of investors (adventurers) would get together and form a corporation. Typically, the adventurers bought shares or percentages of ownership of the corporate company and received accordingly their share of the profits (if there were any) proportionate to the number of shares they owned.

The kings liked these kinds of ventures, because one of the stipulations in creating these corporations was that the king would receive taxes on any profits these ventures made. Being money-short, kings very much liked this kind of business deal.

In the earliest cases of the use of this procedure to finance the startup of an American colony, the adventurers lived back in England and supervised the company from afar (such as the Plymouth Company and the Virginia Company). But the Massachusetts Bay Company had

The Colonies Mature 73

most of its adventurers or owners actually part of the group that settled in America – even taking their corporate charter with them. This gave the Massachusetts Bay Company a tremendous amount of independence of operation – being far removed from the scrutiny of the king! Soon other New England colonies joined Massachusetts in having not just their operations but also their governing councils with them in their colony in America. (The Plymouth Pilgrims did not have that advantage and were exploited terribly by their London adventurers).

Proprietary colonies. There was another type of colony that was also in existence, the proprietary colony. The king, in a feudal-like manner, could grant portions of his kingdom, which included the English territories in America, to personal supporters for whatever reason that moved the king to do so. The king often paid off royal debts this way – or just simply granted the land as a special favor to an individual or group of individuals who had been particularly supportive of his rule.

Those favored by the king (usually always English noblemen) were given proprietorship over the colony by the king, much like a personal fiefdom. They received not only a huge land grant but also royal permission as personal proprietor over this colony to rule it in an absolute fashion – much like a medieval baron. For instance, Maryland (chartered in 1632) was a proprietary colony. The Calverts (Lords Baltimore, father and son) were entitled to govern their colony as they saw fit, develop whatever governmental institutions they found helpful to their rule, and even distribute portions of their land grant to whomever they wished – creating their own lord/vassal feudal relationship. They owed loyalty to the king, of course, with an understood promise to support him whenever the need arose from such personal resources as their properties supposedly offered. But what they did with their colonies was strictly the proprietors' business. Usually this involved granting portions of it to their own friends and putting other portions up for rent, offering land to tenants who in turn would pay the proprietors an annual quitrent.

In general, the nobility who received lordship over these proprietary land grants were not terribly interested in actually living there. And they also had a very difficult time of it collecting the quitrents owed them. Thus these proprietary ventures tended not to turn out to be good money-makers for the proprietors.

Royal or crown colonies. A third type of colony came into being, usually from the failure of one or another of the chartered corporation colonies to perform as the English king had come to expect (such as Virginia in 1624) – or through shifts in the political scene which would cause the English government to seize a proprietary colony (as was the case of Maryland in 1689 – although the colony was returned to the Calvert family in 1715). The king would rescind or terminate the colony's original charter, re-charter it as a crown colony, and send a royal governor to the colony to rule it in the name of the king.

This was generally not a popular move in the colonies. When in 1687 King James II wanted to convert the Connecticut colony from a largely self-running coerporate colony to a royal colony run directly by him, Patriots hid the Connecticut Charter in the cavity of an enormous oak tree to keep it from falling into the king's hands. Of course it ultimately failed to stop the king. But nonetheless it was well-remembered as an early act of defiance of the colonists in protecting their liberties from a king who was determined to hold in his own hands all powers of life and death over his subjects.

* * *

MARYLAND: THE PROPRIETARY CATHOLIC COLONY OF LORD BALTIMORE (OR CALVERT)

Just as New England was settled primarily for religious reasons, so was Maryland – except that it was established not for Puritans escaping persecution, but for Roman Catholics escaping persecution in a heavily Protestant England. George Calvert (Lord Baltimore), a recent English convert to Catholicism, saw a double opportunity in securing land in America – both as a way to enrich his family fortunes, and as a religious refuge for fellow Catholics. In 1629 he petitioned Charles I for a tract of land in which to establish a settlement along the Chesapeake Bay just north of Virginia [he had given up on a similar venture in Newfoundland because it was simply too cold there!] – but died before a land grant was awarded by the king. His son Cecil then took over the project, receiving a royal charter in 1632 – despite the opposition of the Virginians who claimed the same land as part of their colony.

Lord Cecil Calvert needed thousands of settlers to make the colony pay for itself, so he made settlement available also to English Protestants, who would actually outnumber the Catholics, even from the very beginning. Thus Maryland was always officially a religiously tolerant colony open to settlement by anyone, regardless of religious affiliation (Catholic, Anglican, Puritan, and eventually Quaker).

The venture, beginning with only a couple of hundred English settlers in 1634, started off smoothly, with no starving time or trouble with the local Indians. In the area where the Marylanders first laid out a town (St. Mary's) the local Indians befriended them because they themselves were in need of

The Colonies Mature 75

allies against their own Indian enemies. The Indians sold them the land they first settled and also corn to feed the colony. And soon the rich Maryland soil had the Marylanders producing enough food to easily feed the colony.

Lord Calvert was quick (1635) to grant his settlers a voice in colonial affairs with an assembly that operated much like the colonial assemblies of Virginia and New England.

Nonetheless Maryland could not escape the Catholic-Protestant religious tensions that tore at the mother country England, and in 1655 Maryland experienced its own religious civil war, which temporarily brought a Protestant government to power in the colony.

In most respects Maryland differed very little from its neighboring colony next door (Virginia). Tobacco was the main crop, at first worked by indentured laborers – and then over time by slaves. The colony was dominated by an aristocracy, set up early by the Calverts, who gave large land grants to family members and fellow English gentry. This, as in Virginia, created in Maryland a distinct upper class that stood socially far above the common dirt farmers who came to Maryland as indentured workers.

* * *

THE ENGLISH CIVIL WAR, COMMONWEALTH AND RESTORATION (1642–1660)

The practice of granting American lands to royal supporters would fall out of use until the "Restoration" to the English throne in 1660 of Charles I's son Charles II following the end of the English Civil War.

The English Civil War (1642–1649). Just as the bitter conflict between Protestants and Catholics settled down on the European Continent, it exploded in England. The Puritan-dominated Parliament and the English King Charles I, caught up in inflexible religious differences, squared off against each other, complete with armies of their own (1640s). But the Parliamentary Army (mostly Puritan in character), under the highly disciplined command of Oliver Cromwell, proved to be vastly superior to Charles's Royal Army, and Charles fled to Scotland, only to be arrested and sent back to England (1646). But Charles was not finished, and attempted to induce the Scots to change sides and support him (promising to institute Presbyterianism throughout his realm).* The Scots agreed, but proved to

---

*The distinction between Presbyterians and Puritans was actually very small, and only in terms of organization, not theology, as both were fully Calvinist. Puritans believed in the total independence of each local congregation, especially in the matter of choosing their own pastors. Presbyterians believed in a higher

be unable to defeat Cromwell's Puritan army.

Cromwell entered London and authorized a greatly reduced or "Rump" Parliament of Cromwellian supporters to conduct a trial (and conviction) of Charles under the charge of having committed high treason. The Rump Parliament complied, and in January 1649 Charles I was duly convicted and beheaded. Charles's eighteen-year-old son (also Charles) took up the Stuart family cause. But the young Charles II was soon driven into exile in France.

The Puritan Commonwealth (1649–1659). At this point the Rump Parliament declared that England (but also Scotland and Ireland) had come under the governing authority of a Commonwealth (Anglo-Saxon for "Republic" meaning "belonging to the common people") headed up personally by Cromwell. A few years later Cromwell would even be proclaimed Lord Protector for life, satisfying those who still believed that England needed to fall under some kind of royal rule. And indeed, Cromwell's military-run Commonwealth (similar to Caesar's ancient Imperial Rome) finally brought peace to England, Cromwell ruling the country throughout the 1650s with an iron fist. At the same time he continued the brutal effort to crush Catholic rebellions in Ireland – and to a lesser extent Catholic or pro-Stuart rebellions among the Scottish Highlanders.

But the Puritan domination (the era of the Puritan Commonwealth) in England was short-lived. Tragically, this venture in Puritan government in England possessed none of the moral or spiritual qualities that, for instance, Winthrop and others had, a generation earlier, laid out in America with their Puritan Commonwealth. Consequently it failed to win the hearts of the English people.

In any case, Cromwell died in 1658 and his son Richard then took over the Commonwealth. But Richard had no political leverage (such as his father possessed with his army) needed to control the factions that vied for power within the Commonwealth. Consequently, the army began to fall into feuding, and Royalist sympathies quickly began to make a comeback in England.

Richard was soon driven from power by one of the factions, forcing one of Cromwell's generals, George Monck, who had been governing Scotland,

---

union of their congregations at the regional or presbytery level, each of their congregations sending pastors and elders to represent them regionally at Presbytery. The presbytery would have some say in certifying (or rejecting) the pastoral calls to the pulpit of the local congregations within its district. Likewise, the presbyteries would be united even more widely at the synod level, with the presbyteries likewise sending pastors and elders to represent the presbyteries at that higher level. In short the distinction was one of pure democracy versus representative democracy, a distinction that it seems should not have been worth fighting over! Actually the fight was more one of national spirit (Scottish versus English) than it was one of ecclesiastical organization.

The Colonies Mature

to march on London, put in place a new Parliament, and begin negotiations with the exiled Charles II for the restoration of the monarchy in England, something clearly desired at this point by most of the English.

The Restoration (1660). Finally in 1660, terms were agreed on with Charles II for his return from the Netherlands in order to retake the throne of England. With him came numerous Royalists to reclaim their former positions of privilege. The king, in his gratitude to his supporters, even granted them rewards beyond mere restoration of what had been lost. In gratitude for their support during his exile and his return to the throne, Charles presented a number of them with full title as proprietors of new colonies in America – on much the same basiss as those by which his father had some thirty years earlier granted Maryland to the Calverts as a proprietary colony.

* * *

THE CAROLINAS

In 1663, Charles II granted to eight English noblemen a huge grant of land to the south of Virginia, in theory all the way to Spanish Florida. The land was termed Carolina in honor of his father, Charles I. The eight proprietors included Virginia governor Berkeley; George Carteret (also soon to be a New Jersey proprietor); the king's Lord Chancellor, Edward Hyde, (Earl of Clarendon); and his Chancellor of the Exchequer, Anthony Ashley Cooper (eventually the Earl of Shaftesbury) – the last-mentioned who would be the main driving force behind the Carolina colony. They planned to make the colony quite accepting of the widest variety of religious groupings, Catholic and Jewish as well as Protestant, in order to make their investment a success.

Actually, English settlements had already been established just to the South of Virginia along what is today the North Carolina coast. Then Berkeley convinced some of the landless of Virginia to move to his new Carolina colony, although there too they settled only in the area (Albemarle Sound) immediately south of the Virginia colony. But further south saw virtually no settlement – until Shaftesbury convinced the partners to be more active in the enterprise.

Anthony Ashley Cooper, 1st Earl of Shaftesbury.[14] Leading this Carolina venture was an Englishman of exceptional moral integrity – at a time when it could be very dangerous to be a man of such integrity. Cooper was something of a social optimist, yet very much a realist in the way he carefully moved towards his ideals.

Although Cooper was nobly born (both mother and father), he lost both parents by the time he was eight and was raised by various trustees named in his father's will, all of them well connected Members of Parliament. At age fifteen, Cooper entered Oxford (Exeter College), studying under a strong Calvinist master, and then the next year switched his energies to the study of law at Lincoln's Inn, where he was influenced greatly by the Puritan perspective on society.

At this point Cooper confirmed strongly his dedication to what he understood to be the very highest Christian principles. He was never one who was willing to follow particular doctrines and policies just because they were the political trend of the day, whether during the time of the Royalist ascendancy or the time of the Puritan ascendancy. He learned to work with both parties, but always cautiously.

As a youth of only eighteen he was elected Member of Parliament, and at first took a position in support of the king in Charles I's expanding conflict with the growing group of Puritans in Parliament. However when at his own expense he assembled a regiment and participated in a Royalist victory at a battle in 1643, he ended up deeply shocked at how the Royalist commander Prince Maurice ignored the negotiated peace that Cooper had worked out with two Puritan towns, and instead Maurice simply plundered the towns. By 1644, disgusted with the Royalists' behavior – and their increasingly obvious Catholic instincts – Cooper chose to change sides and join with Parliament's anti-Royalist faction. But even then, he showed more the instincts of the (mostly Scottish) Presbyterians than the Puritans in his willingness to find some way to bring peace to the land through compromise with the king. At this point he held back from further political controversy and quietly took up responsibilities as a local sheriff.

Then he turned his interests overseas, purchasing property in Barbados in 1646.

When the monarchy was overthrown in 1649 and the Puritan Commonwealth took command of English society, Cooper was cautiously returned to larger political responsibilities by Cromwell's Rump Parliament and was soon voted membership into that body. Then Cromwell appointed him to serve on the Council of State, helping to create a new legal structure for England. But Cooper seemed more interested in limiting than in authorizing the rising power of the Cromwellian Protectorate, raising suspicions that he was still a Royalist at heart (not true). Somehow however Cooper was able to wade through the accusations and counter-accusations of both friend and foe to continue to keep his seat in the constantly evolving Parliament.

But with Cromwell's death and the inability of Cromwell's son to hold the Commonwealth together, Cooper joined in 1658 with a small group

The Colonies Mature 79

working to bring General Monck and his troops from Scotland to London to restore a degree of order to the crumbling situation. Monck shut down the Rump Parliament, restored the former Long Parliament (itself shut down by the Rump Parliament in 1648), which then subsequently voted for the restoration of the Stuart monarchy under Charles II, before it dissolved itself in 1660. Then Cooper traveled with the delegation sent to The Hague to escort Charles back to England.

This put Cooper in good standing with Charles, who would be looking for supporters in assuming his new responsibilities in London. Indeed, upon arrival in London, Cooper was appointed to the king's new Privy Council. At this point Cooper became a key voice for reconciliation, convincing the king and the Cavalier (Royalist) Parliament to ease off on the severity of the Clarendon Code – rather than take revenge on those English who had been involved in the Commonwealth (excepting those who had been part of the execution of Charles I), a very wise voice in getting England to let go of the past and move on to new things. The king was impressed and in 1661 elevated Cooper to the position of Lordship as Baron Ashley. Ashley (as we will now term Cooper) thus left the House of Commons to take a seat in the House of Lords.

Soon thereafter the king named Ashley as his Chancellor of the Exchequer – the second most important position in the royal cabinet behind that of the Lord Chancellor (or Prime Minister) held by Edward Hyde, the Earl of Clarendon – with whom Ashley would clash constantly during their years of mutual service to the king in the 1660s.

A grand experiment in social planning. Meanwhile Ashley had not forgotten his interest in colonial affairs, and joined a group of eight Lords Proprietors (including Clarendon) in developing this huge tract of land south of the Virginia colony that they had been granted by the king in 1663. Ashley proceeded to work on his Carolina territory with John Locke, who at the time was living under Ashley's patronage as both household physician and personal secretary, to devise a major program of enlightened social structuring for the Carolina colony. Eventually (1670) what resulted was the Grand Model. This comprehensive plan included not only the Fundamental Constitutions of Carolina but also the designs for the actual settlement of the colony.

However, like both Ashley and Locke themselves, the Grand Model was very visionary – too visionary in fact to be of much use as it was drawn up. Locke's design provided for a very orderly division of the land into counties and land parcels assigned to a highly stratified society, from Black slaves and property-less Whites up to the largest landholders, which were the proprietors themselves. Every Carolina inhabitant would receive from none to extensive political rights depending on the amount of property he possessed, Locke (as most of the social philosophers of his time) being convinced that property was the best guarantor of a true sense of social responsibility on the part of a citizen and thus also the amount of social authority that should be entrusted to him.

The Progressivist urge of the rising Age of Enlightenment. However, as things turned out for Ashley and Locke, much of the Grand Model had to be reworked according to the hard realities of life in a largely unmanageable, even highly dangerous, American wilderness.

Nonetheless this noble effort well-represented the kind of social idealism that was coming into vogue in Western culture at that time. Ashley's and Locke's efforts stood at the heart of a rapidly changing attitude among a rising group of Western social philosophers concerning society and its ways. The old social habits that people had long understood as the unquestionable foundation of all social organization seemingly now needed to give way to a new sense of social organization, one born of careful or rational social planning.

In short, the world at that time seemed to need enlightenment, not tradition. Thus political ideals swung slowly toward the understanding that carefully constructed human logic would inevitably produce better ways of organizing life on this planet than had long been the case.* And the New World offered just the perfect opportunity to put these grand ideas into practice – or so the hope was anyway, one that would never die despite the unwillingness of hard reality to give way to such idealism.

Ashley's later years (as the Earl of Shaftesbury). In 1667 Ashley became part of the team or Cabal (**C**lifford, **A**rlington, **B**uckingham, **A**shley and **L**auderdale!) that governed England until 1674. Meanwhile, in 1672 Ashley was elevated to the position of Earl and received a new title, the Earl of Shaftesbury, and soon thereafter briefly served as the king's Lord Chancellor (1672–1673). Anthony Ashley Cooper, Earl of Shaftesbury, had

---

*Tragically, in the abandoning of long-standing tradition, there would be more than just this Ashley-Locke disappointment arising from the effort to find the right utopian formula in the face of life's ever-developing challenges. In fact, failure rather than success – and often very brutal failure at that – would be the normal outcome of such ventures ... over and over again. But there would always be the strong temptation to try again anyway – especially on the part of those who made such armchair social design their main work in life, social philosophers, social critics, journalists, progressive politicians, social studies professors, etc. Despite the miserable historical record of failure of such social ventures, that record would be completely disregarded, so certain were such intellectuals that their newest formula would finally be the one that would bring grand social success (also making them therefore the social genius of their day).

The Colonies Mature

reached the pinnacle of political success in England.

But from there it would be a bumpy ride for Shaftesbury, as his political ideals constantly got him in serious trouble (especially his role in founding the Whig party) – culminating in his arrest (1681) and flight from England (1682) and death (1683) because of his participation in the effort to have Charles's brother and heir to the throne, James Duke of York, excluded from this inheritance because of James's strong Catholic sympathies.*

The Carolina colony moves forward. Meanwhile in 1670, some 300 settlers were enlisted from England to settle in the Carolina colony, although only 100 of them survived the Atlantic crossing to actually settle in the new colony along the Ashley River (named after Ashley of course!). But the colony began to grow. Vital in its growth was a special trading relation with the English Caribbean colony of Barbados, where the slave trade was robust (several of the Carolina proprietors themselves were involved in the slave business). Ten years later (1680) Shaftesbury laid out nearby a new town, Charles-Town (Charleston), located where the Cooper River (also named after him) meets the Ashley River. Charleston was soon to become the hub of an extensive trade between Indians and Europeans in furs and pelts – as well as (after 1700) rice farming, which accompanied the rapid growth in the colony's slave population. By the mid–1700s, with the addition of the trade in indigo, Charleston had succeeded in making itself the most prominent city in the American South.

In the meantime, because the northern and southern parts of the Carolina colony were so far apart, a sense of a North Carolina and a South Carolina began to develop. Adding to this sense of distinction was the fact that the northern part of the colony was inhabited largely by poor Whites (Presbyterian Scots-Irish brought in from an over-crowded Northern Ireland) living on small self-sustaining independent farms, and the southern part of the colony was a highly stratified society, dominated by aristocratic, High-Church Anglicans – much like Virginia society. Fairly quickly the two areas came to understand that they had little in common, culturally, economically and politically. From 1691 to 1708 they were united under a single

---

*Shaftesbury and his fellow Whigs precipitated the Exclusion Crisis when in 1679 they introduced into Parliament the Exclusion Bill, in the attempt to block James's future accession to the English throne. The Whigs were also demanding that royal authority be placed under the discipline of a written constitution, a shocking idea in the days of royal absolutism. Opposing the Whigs were the Tories, supporters of James and defenders of the doctrine of royal absolutism.

These labels "Whigs" and "Tories" were terms of contempt that one party assigned to the other: Tories, the name for Irish Catholic bandits, assigned to those who were opposed to Catholic Exclusion, and Whigs, the name first for Scottish horse thieves and then later for Scottish Presbyterian rebels, eventually assigned to those favoring Exclusion!

governor – but separated again after two years of struggle between the two sections of the colony. In 1729 the proprietors (descendants of the original proprietors) sold most of their rights to the English king, who turned the two Carolinas into two separate Royal colonies: North and South Carolina.

✱ ✱ ✱

NEW YORK

Another piece of American territory to be granted by Charles II as a proprietary colony was New York (formerly New Netherland), seized in 1664 from the Dutch by Charles's navy, under the command of Charles's brother, James, Duke of York (the future King James II). In fact, it was to his brother James that Charles granted this important proprietary colony.

Dutch New Netherland – the early years. Greatly problematic for the English with their Southern colonies in Virginia and Maryland and Northern colonies in New England was the Dutch settlement of New Netherland, wedged into the Mid-Atlantic coast between these English colonies.

In 1609 the Dutch had commissioned the English sea captain Henry Hudson to explore the area in an effort to find a river passage across America (no one at the time knew how broad the North American continent happened to be) as an alternate path leading to their valuable commercial holdings in Asia, the former Portuguese Spice Islands of the East Indies. Hudson's discoveries included the large bay at Manhattan, and the wide North River (eventually named after him) which fed that bay – but also the realization that this river was not the fabled water route to the Far East. However it flowed through very fertile lands which would be quite suitable for Dutch settlement and for a staging ground for trade (in furs, mostly) with the Indians. Indeed Hudson's voyage was soon followed up by further Dutch exploration of the region – and the building of a Dutch fort in 1614 well up the North (Hudson) River at today's Albany.

To further secure their claim to various parts of the New World, in 1621 they set up the Dutch West India Company, which in 1624 planted its first Dutch settlements also at today's Albany and on Governor's Island in today's New York City. Then in 1625 they brought in a small number of additional colonists to establish settlements at what they hoped to be their northern border at Fresh River (today's Connecticut River) and at their southern border at the South River (today's Delaware River). And in 1626 the island of Manhattan at the mouth of the North River was selected as the capital of the entire Dutch province. There they built Nieuw Amsterdam.[15]

But the Dutch colony was not a cohesive venture like the English colonies. Unlike New England, Dutch society did not include any particular group seeking to escape the Dutch homeland, the French-speaking Walloons under the new Spanish Catholic domination (in Southern Belgium) being the exception. In fact, recruiting Dutch for New Netherland proved difficult as individuals were needed for the much more profitable East Indies operation, or just defense at home against the Spanish. Thus they recruited widely across the other European cultures in order to find settlers for their American venture. Also, Dutch *dominies* or pastors sent to the colony were few in number, thus keeping the religious character of the colony very loose. And to make matters even more bizarre, some of the Dutch governors sent by the company to oversee the colony were not of the best caliber, such as Willem Kieft, who needlessly stirred formerly friendly Indians to violent revolt during the 1640s.

Furthermore, it would not be until the 1650s that the Dutch could undertake serious Dutch settlement in their New Netherland colony. The Treaty of Westphalia (1648), which finally ended the very brutal Thirty Years' War, included official Spanish Habsburg recognition of Dutch independence and thus ultimately peace, finally giving the Dutch the chance to move forward in developing their colonial holdings in America.

Nonetheless, the Dutch had much difficulty securing political and cultural dominion in the area. The Company made the awards of huge land grants to *patroons* (essentially land barons) who pledged to settle at least 50 families on their land. This worked (somewhat) along the Hudson River to give it a cultural quality that would last for generations. But otherwise the Dutch colony, in which Dutch was the official or governmental language, remained a wide cultural mix of Dutch, French (Huguenot), German, Swedish, Portuguese – as well as African slaves and allied or dependent Indian tribes – living throughout the colony. It was also more broadly tolerant religious-wise, permitting Calvinists, Baptists, Catholics, Quakers, and even a large number of Jews to practice their religion freely, even though the Dutch Reformed (Calvinist) faith was the official religion of the colony.

The new governor brought to the colony in 1647, Peter Stuyvesant, tried to clamp down on the unbridled ways of the colony, attempting new taxes and a stricter religious conformity to Dutch Calvinism – something that simply was not going to work with the very diverse population of the colony, or with the authorities back in Amsterdam who ordered him to back down and keep the doors open to all newcomers (now including a large number of Jews). But for Lutherans, the matter was quite different, for the Amsterdam authorities authorized Stuyvesant to come down hard in restricting the practice of Lutheranism!

Since the very origins of the Protestant Reformation there had been something of a rivalry between the Lutheran and the Reformed or Calvinist branches, despite efforts of some of the leaders of these two Protestant groups to bring them to greater cooperation. But the theological quibble over the dynamics of the Holy Communion and the question of church organization always seemed to get in the way of such cooperation.

New Sweden – as part of New Netherland. Sweden was also a rising European power in the early 1600s – and joined the European effort to lay claim to American land by settling some of their own people there. In 1637 the New Sweden company (made up principally of Lutheran Swedes, Dutch and Germans) established a settlement named Fort Christina (today's Wilmington) along the upper Delaware Bay. The Dutch had also laid claim to this area, but were not able to enforce that claim until 1655, when Stuyvesant sent a small force to the Swedish settlement and, without firing a shot, forcibly incorporated it into the Dutch New Netherland colony.

James's proprietorship of New York. Back in Europe, the Dutch and English had been locked in a bitter commercial (or just simply nationalistic) rivalry that finally led them to the Anglo-Dutch Wars of the mid-1600s. Their respective colonies in America would certainly be drawn into these wars. King Charles II had wanted to close the coastal gap between his New England and Virginia colonies – and the Dutch province stood in the way. Thus in 1664 Charles dispatched his brother, James, Duke of York, to supervise a naval fleet which would simply take over forcefully the Dutch colony of New Netherland.

The Dutch West Indies Company had made no particular military preparations for such an event. In fact, this had been a major grievance of the Dutch settlers. This lack of military preparation by the Company's governors had made the settlers very vulnerable to Indian attacks. Thus they were greatly disenchanted with the Dutch authorities at the time of the English grab of the colony, even seeing English authority as possibly preferable to the authority (not) offered by the Dutch West Indies Company. With no military and with little popular support, Stuyvesant was forced to strike a deal with the English: the English promised the Dutch no expropriation of personal Dutch property and also the protection of a number of cultural and religious freedoms if the Dutch simply turned authority of the colony over to the English. And so in 1664 this huge Province became English territory – for a few years anyway.

As a reward for his service to his brother, James was granted title of Proprietor over the Dutch Province, which was renamed the Colony of New York, in honor of James as the Duke of York (he was also at this time given territory to the north of New England, which constitutes today's State of

The Colonies Mature

Maine).

The Dutch and English commercial rivalry meanwhile continued unabated and soon had both countries involved in yet another war in 1665-1667 (the Second Anglo-Dutch War). At the war's end in 1667, as part of the peace agreement, the victorious Dutch did not attempt to retake the colony but instead reconfirmed the English claim to it, receiving on their part recognition of ownership of Suriname (on the northern coast of South America), which at that time was considered vastly more valuable as a colony because of its sugar plantations! Then came even another Anglo-Dutch War (the Third) in 1673, and the Dutch retook the New Netherland Province. But the war overall was a disaster for the hard-pressed Dutch (also under attack by the French King Louis XIV) and the Dutch were forced at war's end in 1674 to return the Province of New Netherland to the English. At this point James's colony would remain permanently "New York."

James never visited his colony but ruled it through appointed agents of his own: governors, councils, and personal agents. He at first did not provide for a popularly elected assembly – remembering the English Parliament during the recent past as being no more than a source of constant opposition to royal rule. He had no desire to offer an opportunity for opposition to his rule to arise in his own colony. However, in 1683 the New Yorkers finally got a colonial assembly and a constitution. However, two years later, when James became the king of England, he canceled this by turning his proprietary colony into a royal colony, making him now more completely the ruler of his New York!

NEW JERSEY

Not all of New Netherland had been converted into James's personal proprietorship of New York. James in turn in 1665 awarded part of New Netherland to his own personal supporters as East Jersey and West Jersey. To Sir George Carteret he assigned the more populous section of East Jersey in settlement of personal debts he owed Carteret. To Lord John Berkeley (brother of the Virginia governor William Berkeley) he sold the section termed West Jersey. Carteret and Berkeley worked together to govern and develop the colony as New Jersey, appointing Carteret's cousin as the first governor of their colony. The two proprietors also issued jointly (1665) the Concession and Agreement document granting full religious freedom in their colony – in order to attract as many settlers as possible. But the venture proved to be not terribly profitable, as settlers tended to refuse to pay their quitrent to the proprietors, claiming that they had received title from the governor of New York. Tensions grew between New Jersey and New York.

Ultimately (1674) Berkeley sold his share to a group of Quaker leaders (which included William Penn) – who purchased West Jersey in order to bring in Quaker settlers. In 1688 East Jersey was purchased by another group of Quakers. Although both colonies were in theory Quaker colonies (actually Quakers were by no means numerically dominant in this diverse religious setting), effectively East and West Jersey were now two separate colonies. However in 1702, failing finances forced both colonies to lose their title as proprietorships and become united as a single royal colony (again New Jersey) under the direct authority of Queen Anne of England.

* * *

PENNSYLVANIA AND DELAWARE

George Fox and the Quakers. The story of Pennsylvania begins with the founding of the Quakers (members of the Religious Society of Friends) in England in the mid–1600s. An English shoemaker and shepherd, George Fox, began to spread a new interpretation of Christianity which caught on quickly in England – and which disturbed greatly the more established Anglican and Puritan Christians. Fox did not believe in original sin (thus diminishing the importance of Christ's death on the cross for the atonement of such sin) – and instead put forward a more Humanist idea that everyone could be saved by simply allowing the Inner Light of God within each person to serve as his or her soul's guide along the path to righteousness. This was a private experience – and required no assistance from a professional member of the clergy (who had no role to play in Fox's religious movement). At first persecuted and arrested, he developed a friendship with Cromwell which briefly brought an end to the persecution – until Cromwell's death in 1658. With the Royalist Restoration in 1660, persecution of the Quakers resumed.

The movement initially spread quickly to the New England colonies where it found a grudging permission from Roger Williams to base itself in Rhode Island. Eventually nearly half the settlers there would be Quakers (mostly the other half Baptists).* But Massachusetts and Connecticut

---

*The Baptists were a breakaway group within the Calvinism that was so strong among the English reformers. The critical issue separating the Baptists from the others was the matter of infant baptism, which the Baptists rejected, claiming that only fully believing adults were to be baptized (also by full immersion rather than just the sprinkling of baptismal waters, which was practiced in infant baptism). Calvinists claimed that by making baptism an adult achievement

The Colonies Mature

banned the new movement, convinced that its very character was so far afield of what they understood to be Christian orthodoxy that its mere presence undermined greatly the social order of New England, especially when some of its louder adherents returned to those colonies after having been expelled repeatedly for their efforts to convert their people to Quaker ways. Finally, four of the leaders were even hanged* (1659, 1660 and 1661), before early in his reign, King Charles II decreed an end to such treatment of the Quakers. This was subsequently reinforced in 1689 by the British Parliament's Toleration Act.

William Penn.[16] Ultimately Pennsylvania would become the real center of the Quaker faith in America because of the work of one man, William Penn. William Penn was born to the ranks of English aristocracy, his father being a prominent admiral in Charles II's navy and in fact one of the key agents in the return of England to monarchical rule under Charles. His father had high hopes for William as a leading soldier and politician in royalist England. But William was of a strong philosophical bent (much to the distress of his father), and very sensitive to the suffering that was going on outside of England's palace walls (the 1665 return of the plague and the 1666 Great Fire which destroyed most of London and left the population destitute). William's natural curiosity had him begin to associate himself with the Quakers, which ultimately drew an eight-month prison sentence for William (among several other prison terms he experienced in his lifetime), despite his family's high political connections.

Miraculously, at his father's deathbed father and son were reconciled, in fact his father telling William never to betray what his conscience knew to be true.

With his father's death in 1670 Penn came into a huge fortune, which he began to put it to use to advance the Quaker cause. This is what led him to become part of a group of Quaker investors in the West Jersey colony in 1677. Penn then grew interested in the land that lay to the West of the West Jersey colony and began to press Charles to grant him land rights

---

they were following the detested salvation-by-works policy. But the Baptists protested that adult baptism was simply a matter of the Holy Spirit moving on a fully cognizant adult, a matter of Divine grace and not human works. Neither group was able to find a common theological meeting point. And thus the Baptists became a separate Protestant denomination.

*This included Mary Dyer, Anne Hutchinson's former close companion, who had become a Quaker and who was expelled from the Massachusetts colony four times, the last under the threat of death if she were to return. She did return however, and after some efforts to get her to back down she was finally hung in 1660. But this created an outcry that reached the King in England who finally gave the order to cease all such punishments for mere questions of faith.

there as additional territory for settlement. The area in theory belonged to Charles's brother, James. But a deal was finally worked out in 1681 in which James would give up claim to the western territory as part of his New York which would then come into Penn's hands in 1681 in return for the forgiveness of a huge debt owed by the king to the Penn estate. Thus it was that Pennsylvania (meaning Penn's Woods – a name chosen by the king himself) came into being.

Penn intended to make his colony a model colony of town planning, social reform, and high moral standards. In 1682 he came to his American colony to supervise personally the drafting for Pennsylvania of a Frame of Government which provided for an elected assembly for the colony. He also guaranteed a whole list of personal rights, including total freedom of religion in the colony (these were formally summed up in a Charter of Liberties which he drew up in 1701). And he personally laid out his carefully planned capital city Philadelphia, the City of Brotherly Love, on a square grid pattern between the Delaware and Schuylkill Rivers. He was also careful to give financial compensation to the Indians for the land, and blessed his colony with peace with the Indians as a result.

Soon English Quakers arrived in large numbers, along with also French Huguenots (Calvinists like the Puritans), Mennonites and Amish (German Protestant Pietists), and Catholics and Jews from all over Europe. Pennsylvania was a place where all religious groups were invited to settle in the hope of finding finally a life of peace and prosperity. Actually it never reached the state of perfection that Penn had hoped for, in no small part due to the fact that the Quakers themselves could not agree as to what their new religion actually constituted, or how it was to respond to a number of threats to the colony's very existence. Ultimately, Quaker rivalries proved very disruptive to the Quaker order Penn was trying to achieve.

Furthermore, as with the Jersey colony, the colony did not truly prosper its proprietor. This was in part due to Penn's inability to collect the tenants' quitrent, in part due to his overgenerous nature in extending loans to too many people, and in great part due to too much confidence in his business manager, who cheated Penn out of much of the profitability of the colony. Tragically, he ended up briefly once again in prison as a huge debtor. Although Penn died penniless in 1718 (previously believing himself and his Quaker project to have been a failure) his efforts at building a welcoming model colony ultimately helped to prosper Pennsylvania greatly, both materially and culturally.

Delaware. Three counties extending along the lower western shore of the Delaware River constituted a matter of title dispute between the Penn and the Calvert (Maryland) proprietors. The issue was finally settled by the king

The Colonies Mature 89

in 1682 when the area was recognized as part of Penn's colony. But these three counties, though possessing the same governor (appointed by Penn) as Pennsylvania, were handled differently, eventually (1704) possessing their own assembly to advise the governor. Effectively Delaware was a separate colony under the same proprietorship as Pennsylvania and with much the same freedom as its sister colony.

* * *

THE "GLORIOUS REVOLUTION" (1688-1689) AND ITS IMPACT ON THE COLONIES

Events in England. James II did not long rule England (only three years: 1685-1688). His autocratic and Catholic ways once again stirred the wrath of a very independent-minded Parliament quick to protect its rights and powers against an ambitious king. What finally set off an armed conflict between King and Parliament was when in mid-1688 a son was born to James, thus effectively ending the possibility of the throne upon James's death passing to his Protestant daughter Mary and her Protestant husband, William of Orange, Stadtholder of the Netherlands – who was also her cousin and a grandson of Charles I.

Religious tensions had been running high throughout Europe, principally because in 1685 French King Louis XIV had revoked the Edict of Nantes, a nearly century-old guarantee that Protestants (Calvinist Huguenots) would have the freedom of worship in France. Much of Protestant Europe was up in arms about this revoking of the Edict of Nantes, reactively forming something of a Grand Alliance under William of Orange's leadership.

When in the spring of 1688 English King James concluded a naval agreement with France, suspicions mounted quickly in England that this was the prelude to a formal pro-Catholic English-French military alliance. A group of English leaders agreed with William of Orange that it was time to act. Soon a coalition was formed against James II and Louis XIV, which oddly enough included, at least indirectly, the very Catholic Holy Roman (Austrian) Emperor and the Pope!* The French king took the first action – which then led to full-scale war.

Now it was the turn of William to act. He quickly gathered a huge Dutch naval invasion force – to which James responded rather feebly. With William's landing in England, noblemen began declaring themselves as Whigs for William. James began to lose courage quickly, fearing even the loyalty of his own Tory army. Defeat in small skirmishes and growing anti-

---

*It seems that at that point in this new age of post-Christian Enlightenment, dynastic rivalries now played a much bigger role than old religious loyalties, even for the Catholic Pope!

royalist or Whig rioting in England's cities decided him to flee to France in mid-December. But he was caught before he could complete his escape and was returned to London. However, William did not want the responsibility of taking personal action against his uncle (also his wife's father). Clearly, the best strategy was to allow James to again escape to France. And so at the end of December James slipped off to France to live in exile as a guest of Louis XIV.

Parliament quickly (February 1689) empowered William and his wife Mary to rule as joint sovereigns – under the authority of Parliament. William would rule as English King William III until his death in 1702; Mary would co-rule as Queen Mary II until her death in 1694. Parliament also passed a Bill of Rights (December 1689) clarifying the rights and powers of Englishmen and their government. England still had a monarchy (which it does even to this day) but it was in fact under Parliament's unquestioned sovereignty. Thus to most of those viewing those events, this was indeed a Glorious Revolution.

Events in the American colonies. James had been no less autocratic in his handling of the American colonies. Upon his gaining the throne in 1685, he had abruptly canceled all the charters, constitutions, and compacts of the Northern and Middle American colonies. He intended to unite these colonies into a single Dominion of New England, ruled from Boston by his royal governor, Edmund Andros. Anti-James (or anti-Jacobite) hostility grew quickly in the colonies.

With the outbreak in 1689 of fighting in England between William and James, New York militia captain Jacob Leisler deposed the royal governor and placed himself in control of a newly democratic New York. When in 1691 the recently crowned William sent his own royal governor to New York, Leisler was not willing to step down. A small military showdown had Leisler and his circle arrested. Leisler was tried and hanged as a traitor – and the Leisler Rebellion quickly died down.

In Boston the reaction to the news of the war in England was the same. Rebels took control of the city. Fearing for his life, Governor Andros attempted to flee Boston, but was caught dressed as a woman. He was then sent back to England for trial – but was released upon arrival in England.

Ultimately William renewed all of the charters of the New England colonies and things returned to normal. But the colonists had demonstrated that they could be just as quick to defend their political rights as the English Whigs. Indeed, the term Whig would eventually be assigned to the colonials who in the later 1700s would move America away from the tyranny of royal authority to an independent American republic, and the term Tories to those who chose to stay loyal to the English king.

The Colonies Mature   91

The matter of English or British rule heading into the 1700s. Over the next quarter of a century English royalty changed hands, from the Stuart family to a family of distant cousins in Hanover, Germany.

When King William died childless in 1702, the throne of England passed on to Anne, the sister of William's deceased wife Mary. But the sickly Anne also had borne no heir of her own, and when she also died childless in 1714, something of a crisis descended upon the Kingdom of Great Britain (the name of the union since 1707 of England and Scotland). There was no way that the British Parliament was going to permit any of the very Catholic Stuarts still in exile on the European continent to return to the throne, and the 1701 Act of Settlement outlawed that possibility anyway. Thus at this point the British had to perform a huge genealogical stretch to find a Protestant kinsman to take the British throne.

Finally, the selection came to that of the distant German (Hanoverian) kinsman, George of Brunswick Lüneburg, who as early as 1710 had made it clear that he was the proper successor to the British throne. And so he was. But his accession to the throne was the signal for the Tory-supported Catholic Stuarts to spark a Jacobite rebellion in Scotland, which was quickly put down – but handled mercifully by the new king.

At this point British politics focused primarily on foreign events, especially the dynastic conflicts among the various royal families of continental Europe, conflicts that the American colonies would be caught up in.

George's rule of Britain (1714–1727) was loosely held. He spoke no English and left most domestic governmental matters to his cabinet ministers, thus allowing English government to move more closely to the notion of cabinet rule. At his death in 1717, his place was taken by his son, George II (with whom he had personally maintained only a cold and distant relationship), also not an able English-speaker, who, like his father, continued the policy of leaving domestic politics to his cabinet so that he could participate fully in the game of foreign diplomacy and warfare.

* * *

THE COLONIES' EVER-EVOLVING
INTELLECTUAL-SPIRITUAL CHARACTER

The Halfway Covenant. Meanwhile the Puritan colonies of New England had settled in quite well. Life was very comfortable there now as the 1600s continued. The first New England generations of Separatists and Puritans, who had braved the dangers of founding new colonies in the wilds of North America, were now followed by generations quite familiar with security and prosperity, and thus began to evidence the ancient pattern of the Biblical Israelites. These following generations of Puritans were much less reliant on God for their fortunes, much less spiritual, and much more materialistic in their approach to life. Their lives evidenced little of the spirituality, the mark of true Christian faith, that had been stressed by their elders as essential to being received into full membership in the church – and thus also in the Puritan political ranks.

A bit of a quandary thus emerged, concerning the bringing into the Divine Covenant of infants of the true born-again parents by way of infant baptism. What was to be done about the infants of those later-generation parents who had themselves not yet given to the community a demonstration of their own true conversion? Were their children to be denied the right of the baptismal covenant because of the parents' shortcomings?

In 1662 a compromise was put forth by the community's pastors and elders: the younger generation of Puritans were offered a new, less rigorous qualification for church membership. The younger generation would be accepted into *partial* church membership, a Halfway Covenant, where their children could be baptized, although the unconverted parents would still not be allowed to participate in the celebration of the Lord's Supper or to vote on church business. The hope for these halfway convenanteers however was that they (and subsequently their children) would allow themselves to be guided and instructed by more mature full members, until such time as they could finally demonstrate a readiness by way of the conversion of their souls, one that qualified them for full membership.

But for many, such a time of readiness never came. They either could not convince the more strict, older Puritans of the authenticity of their conversion in the Christian faith – or they simply just delayed and then lost interest in going through the requirements of full church membership. Besides, there was a growing trend (Maryland, Connecticut, and Rhode Island setting the early example; the proprietary colonies of Charles II following up on this idea after 1660) of separating political participation in colonial government from the requirement of church membership. Thus the original ideal of the Puritan societies, uniting both spiritual and political activities as essential to true Christian life, began to lose its hold on the newer generations. They did not at all walk with God the way their elders had.

The Salem Witch Trials. Much attention has been focused on the events of 1692 and early 1693 concerning the accusations, trials and executions of witches in Salem (actually other towns of Massachusetts as well). In not too subtle ways this event is brought out as a general indictment against Puritanism in general – and today's American Christianity (or at least

The Colonies Mature

Protestantism) which is so clearly a direct offspring of the Puritan legacy. It also served recently as a coded story (as per Arthur Miller's 1953 play *The Crucible*) of encouragement to those being subject to the attacks in the early 1950s of U.S. Senator McCarthy, who was orchestrating an hysterical anti-Communist witch-hunt to cleanse America of the terrible Communist political disease that affected the country, even in high places (or especially in high places) – at least as McCarthy saw things.

But what exactly did this event so long ago actually mean? Was it typical of Puritanism in general? Or was it some weird, deviant event in the otherwise honorable history of American Puritanism?

Certainly Puritanism itself had lost much of its original character by the late 1600s. Puritanism was being pulled in several directions at once. A growing Secularist worldview among a new breed of intellectuals was challenging Puritanism's old truth-claims. The religion had also settled into a rather stale, legalistic format, leading many people to seek some kind of spiritual relief by turning to more primitive religious instincts, such as a belief in witches. A sense of spiritual conspiracy or just plain old hysteria also played a huge role in letting things move along toward terrible results.

Certainly the times were right for conspiracy theories and the hysteria which causes and also results from a sense of the loss of order in life. Much cultural, social, economic and political uncertainty was burdening the Massachusetts colony at that time – especially as the colony became increasingly rationalistic in its worldview and thus more expectant of things to follow an orderly pattern (which their Puritan ancestors would not have expected).

On the other hand, for the less-enlightened, it was reasonable in its own way for them to look to the works of the devil and demons as an explanation for the recent Indian uprisings, and the fact that the economy was sagging because the soil was becoming overworked and was overburdened by a growing population it could no longer support.

Also, at this time witchcraft or at least the occult was not uncommon as a practice in Western society, raising the wrath of conservative Christians. France, Sweden, Germany, and other European countries had conducted numerous witchcraft trials over the years since the 1400s, especially during the early 1600s. The height of the Swedish scare in fact was only seventeen years before the Salem events, and in Sweden resulted in numerous executions of those accused of practicing witchcraft, in one instance seventy-one executions in one day alone in 1675.[17] In short, this was not something unique to just Puritanism.

The witch event in America actually started off in February of 1692 as an outbreak of very strange behavior of two girls in Salem, Massachusetts, which then spread to a number of other girls. At first, several older women, social outcasts of one variety or another, were accused of dabbling in the occult (as many did at that time), even of being witches, causing this strange behavior of the girls.

This accusation led to others, finally exploding into a general hysteria in the town of Salem. At trials in March and April, people accused of witchcraft in turn accused others of practicing witchcraft as well.

The witch hysteria meanwhile had been gathering momentum, spreading to other villages in the area. But by the summer, the colony's Puritan leaders were urging caution in the process, for judges to be increasingly rigorous in demanding more exacting proof of reputed behavior. Thus slowly the momentum to accuse others began to slow down. Nonetheless executions of those already found guilty started to take place in the late summer, at the same time that new trials were resulting in people being found innocent of the charges of witchcraft.

Nonetheless, when the momentum finally died in early 1693, by that time, 200 people had been accused of being witches, nineteen people had been found guilty and put to death and five had died in prison.

Within a few years after this event many of those who had been responsible for the wild accusations were backtracking on their earlier claims, even eventually coming to full repentance for their actions. The authorities in fact even had moved to a willingness to give financial restitution to those who had suffered either directly or indirectly (descendants of those put to death) from the trials.

The social-cultural legacy left behind by this event. Nonetheless, this hysteria deeply undermined the integrity of the Puritan experiment, giving rise to thoughts of more enlightened individuals to move to a purely scientific (Secular-Rationalist) approach to life. This move to a more Secular worldview would even sweep up many leading voices in the church. And it certainly would provide Secularists of any age – especially today's Secularists – all the proof they needed to demonstrate that any kind of thought about supernatural forces, including the existence or at least continuing involvement of God, is not only foolish, it is downright dangerous.

And thus it is today that Puritanism has become a slur word, and all of the very best of the Puritan legacy (middle-class democracy) has been ignored and even despised. Secular Rationalism or Humanism has taken the seat of cultural dominance in America today, justifying itself by presenting this brief episode in the Puritan era as the summary statement of all that Puritanism ever stood for, also justifying its call to reject such religiosity at all costs.

The Colonies Mature

The rise of a robust spirit of intellectual Enlightenment. By the early 1700s the European Enlightenment had indeed taken huge steps in putting aside the Puritan religious culture – both in England and America. Logic and a common-sense approach to life was moving rapidly to replace the previous Christian piety of the early Puritans, and for that matter throughout much of Christian America in general. Churches found themselves fairly empty on a Sunday morning – and the pastors complained much about the loss of Christian faith afflicting the colonies.

At the same time, many prominent Americans, taking their cues from the strong intellectual or philosophical trends arising in Europe, were becoming more confident of their own intellectual gifts, their own personal enlightenment, their own powers to fathom the mysteries of the universe through personal study and, of course, through the application of ever-expanding human logic. The old spiritual affections of the early Puritans increasingly appeared to the well-educated American as being nothing more than the result of mere superstition. And the concept of God was slowly turning itself into little more than the idea of the One who long ago set out the self-operating fundamental principles of natural philosophy.

John Locke. Without a doubt the one individual who would have the greatest impact on this Secular-Rational trend in the English-speaking world was the English social and psychological philosopher, John Locke. We have already mentioned Locke's effort in 1670 to draft a constitution for the Carolina colony. Despite the fact that Locke's Grand Model proved to be too utopian to find practical application in the Carolina wilderness, he was hardly slowed up in his efforts to bring a more rational approach to society and its improvement or reform. Indeed, his further studies were received with such acclaim among the community of intellectuals that Locke left a deep and permanent mark on Western philosophy, in America as well as in Europe.

In his *Two Treatises of Government*, written in conjunction with the overthrow of the Stuart monarchy of James II in the Glorious Revolution of 1688–1689, Locke in the *Second Treatise*[18] laid out clearly a very comprehensive worldview that was widely accepted as brilliant and totally compelling, at least to the rising class of enlightened intellectuals.

Locke based this worldview on the belief (a belief held by most everyone in those days) in man's tendency to self-preservation and self-promotion. But he also believed that man was inherently reasonable and would freely submit to society – as he saw personal or selfish advantage in doing so.

Locke contributed further to the growth of the Secular worldview in another field of endeavor: psychology. In his work, *An Essay Concerning*

Human Understanding (1690),[19] Locke treated human life as if it were simply another machine in its operation. His studies of epistemology (why or how man comes to know what he knows) had a tremendous impact on Western thinking about the process of learning and enlightenment. To Locke's way of looking at things, the human mind or brain at birth is simply an empty slate (*tabula rasa*) upon which, as the child begins to encounter life, data ("sensations") from outside the individual are received by the senses and transmitted to the brain. Locke understood that the mind also had, by some kind of instinct, certain abilities through self-reflection to manipulate this incoming data, by associating ideas into working information. In an Aristotelian fashion, he saw man as able to categorize and organize logically this information into the knowledge he would need to thrive in life. It was all very mechanical, this process of thinking and learning.

Locke's philosophy was well greeted by the English Whigs who were looking for justification for bringing James II's government under Parliamentary restraint. James, of course had based his right to expect unquestioned obedience to his rule by his English subjects because he had been appointed to his position as king by God himself. And who would dare to question what God had willed for England? This was of course the classic Divine Rights Theory of kingship proclaimed widely throughout Europe at the time. But Puritans had questioned this theory under James's father, Charles I, stating that God had appointed to all of his faithful believers a degree of personal sovereignty. The Bible itself supported this view, and how could Scripture be questioned, even by kings?

But now Locke had come along and presented a view of life as a natural matter, complete with its own natural laws. And how could an intelligent person question such natural logic? This had nothing to do with God, either good or bad. It was purely natural philosophy (the grandfather of modern science).

With Locke's contribution to Secular thought, the possibility of producing heaven on earth through enlightened human understanding seemed to be beyond the question of any reasonable or enlightened person. God was not a factor in any of this enterprise of social reform. God was no longer needed. History belonged to man, and the decisions he alone made.

According to Locke, this tendency of man to pursue what he understood as self-interest thus could be employed to form a civil society, one able actually to achieve human goodness and development, if properly directed. It simply needed the right mechanical political and economic social instruments (or government) to bring that about, designed and managed by those who were enlightened to these mechanics. In short, government was in reality nothing more than a machine, a mechanism –

The Colonies Mature 97

put together by the consent of those who formed the civil society which this mechanism – by way of its officers – directed or governed.

Deism. Step by step a new worldview was rising rapidly in Europe and America, one which stood halfway between traditional Christianity and the rising world of scientific atheism (which was not as widespread in America as it was in Europe at the time). It was called Deism. Deism believed that God had wonderfully assembled all creation in its present, perfect pattern of operation. God was much like a watchmaker, crafting a perfect self-running instrument. But now wound up, life operated entirely on its own, according to its own natural laws, the iron laws of nature that scientific inquiry was discovering with breathtaking rapidity. Natural philosophers (researchers focused on learning about nature and its ways) were beginning to see the earth (and the heavens) simply as machinery – like the well-crafted watch – every item on earth operating according to strict mechanical laws, laws easily discernable by any logical mind. True, not all laws of nature had yet been discovered. But they were out there, waiting simply for the scientific mind of some natural philosopher to finally uncover them.

It was all very exciting, watching life seeming to come under the total mastery of man – or at least under the mastery of the Enlightened Ones of mankind.

Meanwhile, in such a universe running under its own mechanics or laws of nature, God played no further role in the day-to-day events in life. He was now in some kind of distant retirement. It was up to man now to get along in life according to his own knowledge of how the watch operated.

Enlightened Christianity attempts to reform itself. This piece of logic was so compelling that by the early 1700s even theologians and church officials began to call for a reform of traditional Christian understanding of the Bible – to drop the idea of original sin and to clean up the parts of Scripture that relied on miracles to sell the important moral points that Christianity engendered. Enlightened Christians would in fact perfect their faith by getting rid of such superstitious material and focus purely on natural religion, that is, the moral instruction found in Scripture. Jesus was thus viewed by such Christians – John Tillotson, archbishop of Canterbury, 1691–1694, being such an example – no longer as Savior of sinful men but as moral instructor to those who wanted to perfect their lives. Ah, once again Christianity was sliding into Unitarianism!

Even before the 1600s were out, there had been a call within Christianity itself, notably from bishops in the Anglican church, to reform itself, to make it more enlightened. Miracles such as Jesus walking on water, or his raising the dead, or Joshua stopping the course of the sun across the sky in order to gain sufficient daylight time to fully defeat his enemies, etc., were raising all sorts of arguments. Some sought to justify these miracles on rational grounds, which by definition makes them no miracle at all, such as the Irishman John Toland in his controversial book, *Christianity Not Mysterious* (1696).[20] Others, such as Matthew Tindal in his book, *Christianity as Old as the Creation* (1731),[21] called for Christianity to avoid such questionable or superstitious matters and instead focus itself on the moral-ethical teachings that abounded within Christianity – and for that matter within all the religions of man which have arisen everywhere in the world out of man's natural religious instinct. Thus to such enlightened individuals as Tindal, excellent moral conduct was the supreme virtue of any faith, a virtue and related intellectual discipline that was placing in man's hands the responsibility of seeing heaven brought to earth, as Jesus himself had talked of.

This was all very logical. But to the human spirit, it was deadly. Little wonder that the church of the early 1700s was losing steam.

* * *

COLONIAL SOCIETY IN THE 1700s

Southern culture continues to pursue its aristocratic dream. In the American South the passing of time merely fortified the feudal-like distinction between the firmly established Southern gentry, which increasingly took on the appearance and behavior of English aristocracy, and the poor White dirt farmers living precariously along the foothills of the Appalachian Mountains that rose abruptly to the West of the open, fertile fields of Tidewater Virginia and Maryland. And then there was the matter of the thousands of African slaves, having no freedom to plan a life at all, always treated simply as saleable property. Such oppression of masses of human souls made the Cinderella dream of the Southern aristocracy very fragile. Also, whereas some efforts had been made to introduce some of the Indian neighbors to Christianity, there was virtually no interest in doing the same for the African slaves. Christianity would have to wait a bit longer before it would offer its spiritual counsel to these pitiful slaves.

A classic example of the Southern Gentleman: William Byrd II.[22] The Virginian, William Byrd II, exemplified the aristocratic nature of those who dominated Virginian life during these formative years of the colony. William II was born in 1674 on his father William I's huge Belvedere Estate (later known as the Westover Plantation) near the modern site of Richmond, further up the James River from Jamestown.

The Colonies Mature

As was typical of the Virginia nobility, the young William was sent off to England (age seven) for schooling while living with relatives there. Here for nine years he studied classic and modern European languages and literature. He then apprenticed in London and Rotterdam in the tobacco trade before taking up the study of law at the Middle Temple, London, in 1692. He was admitted to the bar in 1695 and, complements of the support of family friend Sir Robert Southwell, elected to the Royal Society in 1696.

In 1696 he also returned to his native Virginia, which he had not seen in seventeen years. Here, with his aristocratic father's urging and backing, William was elected to the House of Burgesses, representing Henrico county. But finding colonial life lacking the sparkle of English social life, William soon resigned his position and returned to England to practice law. In 1698 he received the appointment as London Agent of the Virginia Governor's Council (the upper chamber of the Virginia House of Burgesses), thus now entitled to the prestigious rank of colonel. However, in this position he became deeply involved in political tensions arising between his father and Virginia Governor Nicholson (the Byrds had been supporters of the ousted former governor, Sir Edmund Andros).

His four years at this position made him a somewhat cynical observer of political behavior. Also this aspiring young colonel found that despite all his close study and discipline in the graces of the English aristocracy, he suffered from the incurable social disease of being a mere colonial, and was never accepted into English society on an equal footing, despite his many social accomplishments.

Thus in hearing of his father's death in 1705, he returned to Virginia to take up the responsibilities of running the huge estate he had just inherited. Those responsibilities included not only supervising the vast production of tobacco by hundreds of slaves, but of representing the Westover Plantation in all its power and social grace to the society of Virginian aristocracy. In this he was well prepared, complements of his years of (unsuccessful) effort in London to achieve entrance into English aristocracy. In 1709 he was appointed to the Governor's Council in the Virginia capital of Williamsburg.

He found a wife from colonial society (daughter of Colonel Daniel Parke II, governor of the Leeward Islands in the Caribbean), Lucy Parke. This high-spirited young lady was a perfect social match for William, though not untypical of high society at that time, William was reputed to be having alliances with a number of other women during their ten-year marriage. In 1715 Lucy died of smallpox. William would remarry eight years later. From this second marriage William III would be born.

This Virginia taskmaster could be tough on his slaves (beatings of slaves for even minor infractions was normal procedure) but also on himself. He rode hard, ventured into the Virginia wilderness to survey the boundary line between Virginia and North Carolina, founded the town of Richmond, and kept himself well-read on all the latest literature, which he added to his classic collection – around 4,000 books in his personal library, which he considered to be nearly sacred ground. He even took up writing book-length studies, most notably his adventures during the Virginia-North Carolina surveying expedition.

When he died in 1744 he left to his son William III family landholdings which at this point totaled almost 180,000 acres.

* * *

GEORGIA – THE LAST OF THE THIRTEEN COLONIES

The last of the American colonies, Georgia, chartered by King George in 1732, was quite different in conception from the others. It was not designed originally as either a place of religious refuge or a money-making venture, though certainly it was hoped that the Georgia colony would be able to cover its expenses. It was primarily a military colony, with the additional idea in mind that it could be a place to resettle England's poor, languishing in England's prisons because of debt.

The main inspiration for the colony came from English General James Oglethorpe, who had been involved in the War of Spanish succession (1701–1713). Although the question of which family should rule Spain had been resolved back in Europe, other questions, including the issue of what exactly were Spain's rights in North America, were still open. Thus trouble from Spanish Florida was expected. Consequently, a fortified colony south of Charleston and north of Florida was seen as a military necessity.

Oglethorpe, as a member of Parliament, had been involved in a study of the conditions in England's debtors' prisons – which he found appalling and little likely to improve the lot of a debtor. So the idea emerged of using this proposed military colony as a place to help debtors get out from under an impossible situation. Oglethorpe and a group of fellow philanthropists thus petitioned King George for just such a colony (1732). The plans were to build forts along the coast of this new colony of Georgia and to locate the colony's capital city (constructed in a very well laid out grid pattern) at the mouth of the Savannah River. Blacks and Catholics were excluded from the colony (during only its very first years) in the hope of ensuring against any danger of religious and racial turmoil.

Actually, very few debtors made their way to the colony. But it soon became a place of refuge for religious minorities from the continent of Europe, and for English tradesmen hoping for a better start in life. Still, the tight supervisory mindset that was supposed to get the colony off in

The Colonies Mature

the right direction seemed to discourage a great number of settlers from heading to Georgia. Most new settlers preferred to head instead to the less restrictive Carolinas. Only after the various laws regulating the character and behavior of the settlers were lifted did the colony begin to receive a large number of settlers. Then (by 1750) the colony began to take on the cultural flavor of nearby South Carolina, and the capital city Savannah some of the character of Charleston.

* * *

THE "GREAT AWAKENING" SUDDENLY AND MYSTERIOUSLY RESTORES THE CHRISTIAN SPIRIT IN THE COLONIES

Then around 1740, just as it appeared that the Christian foundations of early America were about to die out for lack of spiritual interest or even cultural support, something mysterious infected the American heart. The "Great Awakening"* suddenly broke out upon the American scene to restore the warmth of American affection for God and Jesus – and the belief again in God's full sovereignty in America.

This involved an enormous religious revival, drawing thousands of Americans who gathered in open fields to hear evangelists call them back to the old-time religion that their Puritan ancestors had known Christianity to be. This not only rekindled the American sense of being a Covenant people, but in the process revitalized the American sense of the basic equality of all people because according to these revivalist preachers (and the Puritan fathers before them) in the eyes of God all people were indeed equal.

Frelinghuysen and the Tennents. Actually, something of this strong revivalist nature had started some dozen years earlier (1725–1726), just here and there in New England and in the Middle Colonies. Theodore Frelinghuysen had been given the task of pastoring a number of small Dutch Reformed Churches in the Raritan Valley of New Jersey. He understood his central responsibility was to bring the wandering Christian souls back in line with a faith rather than works approach to their Christian life. He issued a strong call to the faithful for repentance, and a return to God as the guiding force in their lives. This call challenged them to take up something much more rigorous than just regular church attendance and proper Christian moral behavior. This was a call for a deep renewal of the people's faith in God personally as director of their lives.

---

*The term "Great Awakening" was first applied to this event with the publication in 1845 of Joseph Tracey's book, *The Great Awakening: A History of the Revival of Religion in the Time of Edwards and Whitefield.*

Something of the same nature was going on at about the same time in nearby Central New Jersey. William Tennent and his sons, particularly Gilbert, found themselves deeply committed to issuing to the Presbyterian congregations of the area a similar evangelical call to spiritual repentance and revival of their Christian faith.

Jonathan Edwards.[23] Likewise, to the north in New England, elements of a similar spiritual revival were undertaken during the mid-1730s by Jonathan Edwards at his quite large Congregationalist church in Northampton, Massachusetts. There was a deep earnestness on Edward's part concerning the sinfulness of the faithful and the need for repentance, which stirred the emotions deeply of his congregation. Some 300 people were brought into fellowship with Edwards' congregation during that period.

But all the emotionalism of such Christian revival began to stir the ire of some of the other pastors of New England and the Middle Colonies. And briefly it appeared that the whole thing would soon die away.

George Whitefield and the Wesleys.[24] Meanwhile across the Atlantic in England something of the same nature was taking place, led principally by the English Calvinist reformer George Whitefield (pronounced Whit-field) and his close friends, the Anglican reformers* John and Charles Wesley. They developed their close relationship (despite some theological differences) during their years at Oxford University where they created and led the Holy Club – before, at different points in time, heading off as pastors for a couple of years to the colony of Georgia to be part of the philanthropic idealism that supposedly had founded this new colony. But Wesley would soon return to England after rather uninspiring efforts in Georgia, something that broke Wesley's heart. But this humbling experience in turn opened him to a truly born-again experience.

Soon a spirit of revival rather dramatically took hold of both Wesley's and Whitefield's ministries. In 1739 this spirit took at first Whitefield and then John Wesley out into open fields to preach the message of salvation to the English working class. Such open-air preaching was a dramatic departure from the type of pulpit preaching expected of pastors. But while this irritated some of the Christian faithful, it succeeded in reaching thousands of people who otherwise would never have found themselves inside a church except for a wedding or a funeral. Something new was happening here!

In 1740 Whitefield returned to Georgia to found an orphanage – and

---

*Or "Methodists" as they had previously been termed contemptuously by their peers in their college days, because of the spiritual disciplines they put themselves under in order to strengthen their faith and to support their work.

The Colonies Mature

then moved on to Pennsylvania to do the same there (in partnership with some Moravians), also preaching every day as he made his way across the colonies. Gradually word began to spread among the colonies about this revivalist preacher Whitefield who was invited (as was customary) to preach in various churches along the way.

Meanwhile, Tennent and Edwards linked up with Whitefield, inviting Whitefield to New Jersey and New England to preach there. With this, full revival began to break out, not just in Northampton and Central New Jersey but at various points throughout the colonies – as Whitefield now preached his way from New England in the north to Georgia in the South. Thus Whitefield found that his mission was no longer orphanages but simply a continuation of his preaching, wherever the Spirit directed his path.

But having found it also easy in England to preach in open-air settings (fields and town squares), he proceeded to do the same in America. For some, this was quite a bit too much and now he found some church doors closing on him. But he continued to preach open-air style anyway.*

The impact of the Great Awakening. Edwards himself became a major figure in this broader revival, with his preaching in 1741 in his church in Massachusetts and then again in Connecticut his famous sermon, "Sinners in the Hands of an Angry God." Although Edwards did not take up the fiery style of Whitefield, his calmly presented sermons had much the same effect on his listeners: repentance and the call to salvation.

The effect of this revivalist preaching was overwhelming. Revival swept like a whirlwind everywhere throughout the colonies, especially in the years 1741–1743. This first truly all-American event went far not only in restoring a deep spirituality in America but also giving the colonists from the North to the South a sense of being a unique people, something akin to a nation. Americans now had national heroes as Americans, revivalists and missionaries well known up and down the colonies as part of the common experience of American life. Whitefield became very well-known from

---

*While Whitefield was busy developing Christian revival in America, his friend John Wesley was busy doing the same in England, thus founding there what was to become the Methodist movement. Eventually (1760 and after) Wesley's Methodist movement would come to America – still considering itself an integral part of the Church of England and under its discipline. But in 1784, with America's break from England following its War of Independence, the Wesleyan or "Methodist" movement in America would reform itself as the Methodist Episcopal Church, coming under its own bishops, Thomas Coke and Francis Asbury. At this point the Methodist Church would truly take off as a massive revival movement, especially as a result of the extensive work of the Methodist circuit riders who carried the spirit of revival to the rapidly expanding American frontier – making it a part of the "Second Great Awakening" that shook the young Republic in its early years (1790s to mid–1800s).

Maine to Georgia, moving up and down the American colonies over the course of the thirty-two-year period (1738–1770) when he visited America numerous times to preach revival.

Also the heroic story of the young Presbyterian missionary (and friend of Edwards), David Brainerd, who wore himself out (tuberculosis) preaching a similar revival to the Indians, was well known across the colonies, making him something of a national hero. And the Presbyterian minister Samuel Davies became a powerful instrument in reaching not only frontiersmen but also African slaves in Virginia with the gospel message. Furthermore, the sermons of the revivalist preachers (especially Edwards' sermons) were read widely throughout the colonies.

The message of this revival was clear and unvarying: God was calling the Americans out of their spiritual slumber to a repentance that would prepare them for a great work ahead of them. As citizens of the New World they had a huge calling on their lives from God to be his people as he, their one and only sovereign, led them. In taking up this call they would show the Old World of Europe, by America's own example, how a people could live to a new and glorious purpose in Christ.

Consequently, such a message repeated over and over again worked strongly to build something of a national spirit – a collective identity among the colonists as "Americans."

Opposition to the new style. Not every American got swept up in this Awakening. There were many hostile critics among the American intellectuals who found this phenomenon most improper.

Unfortunately, the excitement of the new style led some enthusiastic pastors to go overboard in that enthusiasm. For instance, James Davenport went all out not only in viciously attacking people who had not embraced fully the revival, but going through strange emotional highs himself publicly (possibly suffering from bouts of insanity) in the service of his cause, which made it easy to be very critical of the excessive enthusiasm of that cause.

Indeed, for many of the Old Light Christians (led by the Boston pastor Charles Chauncy),* revivalists preaching emotionally charged sermons in open fields before thousands of common farmers and tradesmen and women – rather than to parishioners properly attired in their Sunday finery and seated properly in their pews in church attentive to the theological

---

*But Old Light Chauncy would be just as outspoken in his opposition when talk began to develop (the beginning of the 1770s) in England about placing the colonial churches of America under episcopal authority (rule by bishops and archbishops – and ultimately the king of England himself) of the Church of England. In fact Chauncy's sermons and pamphlets in support of the colonies' War of Independence against England were widely influential in the colonies.

The Colonies Mature

details of a scholarly sermon – was just not proper Christianity. Worse, such proper church-going Christians being called out by the revivalists as sinners needing the forgiveness of God no less than the sinners of the inferior social ranks was considered by those proper Christians as an outrageous idea, even an evil idea inspired by the Deceiver, Satan himself. Then too, many pastors were simply bitterly jealous that while their churches remained empty, hundreds – even thousands – of people found it easy enough to gather in nearby fields to hear the preachers of spiritual revival.* But these critics were a small voice in the scheme of things.†

Ben Franklin's take on the matter.[25] Even the greatest American sage of the time, Ben Franklin, found himself warmed at least intellectually by this massive religious revival. In fact, he personally saw to the publishing of forty or more of Whitefield's sermons on the front page of his newspaper, the *Pennsylvania Gazette*. Indeed, Franklin and Whitefield formed a friendship that lasted the entire span of Whitefield's remaining life (he died in 1770).

God knew that the Americans would need this preparation for the days ahead when troubles would mount between the Americans and the powers of Europe (and also the native Indians). No amount of intellectual Rationalism would give courage to the American colonials, who understood the sacrifices they were called to in taking up the path of rebellion against their king, and the hangman's noose that awaited them as traitors if this rebellion should fail. Americans were going to need a strong faith in God's support in order not to lose courage in the face of these deadly challenges. And so it was that the Great Awakening was well timed to bring exactly such spiritual preparation. God was being faithful to keep his side of the Covenant with America.

---

*A split in 1741 opened up also within the Presbyterian denomination (heavily concentrated at the time in the middle colonies of New Jersey and Pennsylvania) between the New Side and Old Side over the ordination of pastors graduating from Gilbert Tennent's "Log College" (forerunner of Princeton Seminary). New Siders were pro-revivalist pastors, whose numbers increased dramatically – just as the Old Side pastors numbers declined equally dramatically.

†Sadly for Edwards, opposition to his style and message eventually developed within his own church, and in 1750 he was voted out of his pulpit by a quite large majority. He took himself off to preach to the Indians (but still writing at the same time). But he was not forgotten in the larger American world and in 1758 he was called to the presidency of the Presbyterian New Sider's College of New Jersey (the future Princeton University). But he died of smallpox just as he was taking up his new duties.

CHAPTER THREE

INDEPENDENCE

* * *

INVOLVEMENT IN THE DYNASTIC POLITICS OF EUROPE

America begins to sense that it has a political destiny different from the mother country's. Certainly the American colonists knew that they were Englishmen. But they also knew that they were a very different kind of Englishmen than the ones back in the Mother country. It is not that they were first and foremost Americans. They would have seen themselves first as Virginians, or New Yorkers, or Pennsylvanians, etc. But life collectively on the opposite side of the Atlantic from the Mother Country was beginning to have a unique effect on their social self-perceptions.

The new Hanoverian kings of England. With the expiring of the Stuart dynasty in 1714 – and the need of England to go all the way to Germany to fetch a new English king (a distant cousin from the Hanoverian branch of the family), the sense of distance between America and England would begin to grow. We have already noted that George I (1714–1727) and his son George II (1727–1760) were truly German rather than English and tended to isolate themselves in their own familiar world (hunting and sporting), leaving politics to political advisers who understood English ways (and the English language) better than they.

Also they were as interested in European events involving the status of their German holdings in Hanover as they were interested in things English, including the affairs of colonial America. In short, they tended to look much more eastward toward continental Europe (and all the dynastic quarrels going on there) than westward across the Atlantic to what was going on in America. This kind of political neglect by the English kings in the period of 1714–1760 thus strengthened the sense of a going-it-alone in the colonies.

Those years gave American colonials a chance to develop even further a strong sense of independence and political self-sufficiency.

Independence

Europe's dynastic wars. Dynastic wars among European monarchs were constant, involving ruling families in one war after another in unbroken succession. These wars naturally included the dynastic holdings in colonial America (as well as Asia) and thus the American colonies would get involved in one way or another. However, the colonial perspective on these conflicts differed from the European perspective, being fought in America around local interests of the English, French and Spanish, and usually drawing the Indians into the conflicts on one side or the other. A few of these wars stand out because they touched the colonies deeply.

Naturally, where possible, the colonists tried to stay out of the affairs that embroiled European politics. They were, of course, always well aware of the struggles going on back in Europe. But the distance from those events gave the colonists a distinct view or take on them. The colonists were naturally more focused on things closer to home, such as the ongoing troubles with the Indians, and the expansion of the Catholic French into the lands to the West of the Appalachian Mountains, where the Americans were beginning to look for their own expansion. Then there was also the potential threat from the Catholic Spanish to the south of the colonies.

But in the end, the colonies could not avoid getting involved in the ongoing dynastic struggles between the monarchies of England, France, Spain, Portugal, Austria, and Prussia – and the Netherlands (which was not a monarchy but rather something more like a republic, but which was caught up in the conflicts nonetheless). Mostly these wars involved the English against the French (always) and the Spanish (frequently). And these European contests had a way of spilling over into the colonies, forcing the colonies to work together to defend themselves militarily.

But this too would add to the growing sense of the colonists that they were not only Virginians or New Yorkers, but also Americans.

Queen Anne's War* [Europe: the War of Spanish Succession] (1701–1713). This war was fought in Europe over the possibility of a French Bourbon prince, Philip V, becoming the King of Spain (the Habsburg dynasty in Spain finally having expired without an heir). Philip was the grandson of the French Bourbon King Louis XIV and thus also in line to eventually become the King of France. The thought that these two large countries should come under the rule of one person was frightening to much of the rest of Europe, especially the English. A general coalition against the French and Spanish thus gathered and war broke out in 1701. The final result (the Treaty of Utrecht in 1713) was most importantly that Philip renounced his claim to the French throne and thus became only the King of Spain.

---

*Interestingly, these wars were usually known in the colonies by a name which differed from the one used by Europeans!

In the colonies, the English forces made up of Royal troops, colonial militia, and their Indian allies, found themselves fully occupied with fighting along the frontiers both in the North, against the French and their Indian allies – and in the South, against the Spanish and their Indian allies. The fighting was rather constant, ferocious, and inconclusive. English and French forts, towns and farming communities, plus Indian villages were attacked here and there, with first one side then the other gaining a brief advantage – or nobody gaining a victory from the effort. The mighty Iroquois Indian confederation (positioned principally in northern and western New York) insisted on remaining neutral between the French and English, though sometimes the Iroquois gave minor aid to the French or to the English. Mostly the French and English avoided passing through Iroquois territory in order not to upset the neutrality of this strong Indian confederation.

In the end, according to the terms of the Treaty of Utrecht, the French lost to the English their scattered French-Canadian settlements in Newfoundland and the more built-up French-Canadian coastal region of Acadia (Southeastern Quebec). The effect for the Acadian French was the forced Anglicizing of both their Catholic religion and French culture, which would remain a constant sore point for the Acadians, and in the eyes of the English leave the Acadians as questionable citizens within the British Empire.

In the south (in the future Georgia and in Spanish Florida) in addition to the raiding and destruction of coastal settlements of both the English and Spanish (including Spanish Catholic mission stations), the war turned out to be mostly a war of Indian against Indian, tribes being drawn into mutual conflict as allies of either the English or Spanish. The net result was the huge loss of Indian life in the South – in Spanish Florida and in what would become southern Georgia. The Treaty of Utrecht ultimately changed little in the southern political picture. But the Spanish were hit so hard in Florida that they never were really able to recover their position there physically. Ultimately, continuing trouble with Spain in this region was what convinced English King George in 1732 to support Oglethorpe and his associates in their effort to found the English colony of Georgia.

The War of Jenkins' Ear* (1739–1742). This war was fought between England and Spain, largely over the English right to sell slaves and other goods (for the limited period of thirty years) in the Spanish colonies as part

---

*English sea captain Robert Jenkins lost his ear in a struggle when the Spanish boarded his ship in 1731 to block the selling of slaves in the Spanish Americas. The displaying of his severed ear in Parliament eventually stirred the English to go to war against the Spanish. Actually, this smaller conflict helped set the stage for the outbreak in 1744 of the larger War of Austrian Succession.

Independence

of the terms of the earlier 1713 Treaty of Utrecht. By the late 1730s both sides claimed that the other party was not properly respecting the *asiento* (agreement or contract) and war broke out in 1739. The English played the war cautiously, not wanting English success against the Spanish to draw the French into the war on the side of the Spanish.

The war itself proved nothing in America as well as in Europe. Oglethorpe's effort to take Spanish St. Augustine in Florida failed (1740), as did a Spanish attack on Georgia (1742).

King George's War [Europe: the War of Austrian Succession] (1744-1748). This war was fought in Europe ostensibly over the question of the right of a woman, Maria Theresa of Habsburg, to the Imperial throne of the Holy Roman Empire (Austria). Actually, it was part of the on-going dynastic struggle among the Bourbon French, the newly Bourbon Spanish, the Habsburg Austrians, and the Hanoverian English for control of particular borderlands here and there in Europe. But the war introduced a new major player in the dynastic game, Hohenzollern Prussia, under the rule of the very capable Frederick (the Great). France allied with German Prussia in the hopes of further undermining its ancient foe, the Austrian Habsburgs. But Frederick was more interested in the borderlands (Silesia) between Prussia and Austria. In the end – and after much expensive, devastating, and inconclusive battling among nearly all the European monarchs – only Prussia really came out of the war with a true gain (Silesia). France got nothing for its costly efforts except the emptying of the French royal treasury and the deepening of the indebtedness of the French king still trying to cover the costs of his military adventures. Austria got to keep Maria Theresa in place as Austrian empress. But Germany would now and for the next century be the cockpit for an ongoing struggle between Austria and Prussia for ascendancy over the many states that made up the land of Germany – which eventually Prussia would win, becoming the centerpiece (1870) for a new German nation.

As for the English colonists in America, the war brought frustration when the vital French fortress of Louisbourg, located on an island at the mouth of the St. Lawrence River and thus guarding the maritime entrance to French Canada, was returned to the French in 1748 as part of the final peace settlement (the Treaty of Aix la Chapelle). Louisbourg had been captured by American colonial troops at some serious cost to those American troops. But American political interests were of no particular concern to the English monarch, whose sole interest at the time (as with all European dynasties) was how such peace terms played to the political advantage of his own dynasty.

The French and Indian War [in Europe: the Seven Years' War] (1754-1763). This war actually began in the colonies in 1754, a couple of years before it drew the major European powers into full-blown war in 1756. It also actually phased out in the American colonies in 1760, several years before it ended in Europe (and in Asia) in 1763.

The war began in America with a dispute between the French and English over the question of who had the rights to trade with the Indians in the Ohio region – a very complex issue made even more complex by the changing alliances of the Indians themselves – and more specifically over the colonial boundary running along the Allegheny and Monongahela Rivers (where Pittsburgh is located today).

A Virginia officer (major) named George Washington and the colonial troops under his command, sent to establish Virginia's claim to the area, clashed with and defeated a small French force there in May of 1754. Washington then proceeded to build a small fort (Fort Necessity) to defend Virginia's claim to the area. But the fort was soon (that July) lost to the French ... Washington's first of a long string of defeats!

The following year (1755), British General Edward Braddock – joined by Washington – returned to the area to try to seize the French Fort Duquesne, but failed in the attempt. Braddock and his troops were then mauled by Indian allies of the French as his troops retreated. Braddock was killed, the French were tipped off as to British military plans for the entire region, and the British campaign of 1755 turned into a huge disaster.

The only English success that year occurred in the Northeast when the French island fortress of Louisbourg once again fell into English hands. This event was accompanied by the tragedy falling on the Acadian French living in the area, distrusted (for good reasons) in their loyalties by the British authorities, who by the thousands were forcibly removed from the region. Beginning in 1755 and continuing until 1763, over 11,000 French-speaking Acadians were deported and scattered among the English colonies – around 2,000 losing their lives through exhaustion and disease in the process. Some returned to France and others made their way down the Mississippi to French Louisiana where they established a colony west of New Orleans, and thus a particular French-speaking culture there, namely that of the Cajuns (from the French *Acadiens*.)

The next couple of years (1756-1757) did not go well for the English. The worst of the beating that the English took was in August of 1757 at Fort William Henry, along the southern shore of Lake George (New York). A small garrison of English soldiers protecting the Fort and the surrounding English settlement was besieged by the French under Montcalm and a Huron Indian force of over 2,000 (who had gathered from all around the Ohio Territory, even from beyond the Mississippi). The garrison surrendered under the promise of safe conduct extended to the soldiers and civilians departing south to Fort Edward. But as the English soldiers and settlers were making their way through the masses of French and Indians, the Indians set upon the defenseless English, killing and scalping and enslaving hundreds of the English – women and children as well as the men. News of the massacre spread rapidly through the colonies, further embittering settler feelings toward the Indians and making any idea of future friendly relations between the English settlers and the Indians all the more unlikely.

In 1758 things finally began to turn in favor of the English. An English blockade against supplies reaching Quebec, a bad Canadian harvest in 1757, the outbreak of disease (including smallpox) among the French Canadians, and the decision of the French to try to divert the English from Canada by withdrawing troops from Canada in order to further strengthen their forces attempting a direct attack on England itself (which failed miserably), all greatly weakened the French position in North America.

By 1759, the French were losing fortresses everywhere. The worst loss was Quebec, which fell in 1759 and took the lives of both the invading English commander Wolfe and the defending French commander Montcalm. The loss of Quebec then left Montreal vulnerable to English conquest.

By 1760 the French were ready to admit defeat in America. Thus the American portion of the Seven-Years or French and Indian War was essentially over.

For the Indians, who joined in on one side or the other, there was no gain whatsoever by their participation, but only the further weakening of the overall Indian position in the Ohio territory. Promises of security against the further expansion of Anglo settlements into Indian lands were made by the new British King George III (crowned in 1760) to his Indian allies. But these were not promises he was able to keep, and promises that only soured relations between him and his English subjects in America.

Overall, the war was an international struggle among European dynasties which involved the participants in Europe itself, in the West Indies, and in Asia – as well as in North America. Though the war effectively ground to a halt in North America in 1760, it dragged on elsewhere. The final settlement was not concluded until 1763 with the Treaty of Paris. It involved the transfer of power back and forth among the dynasties not only in North America but also in much of the rest of the world, where the Europeans had been active establishing their presence with commercial colonies and trading centers. The results would make England the world's leading colonial power, with a global empire including significant sections of India, the Caribbean, and the African coast, as well as the Eastern half of the North American continent.

The other net effect of the war was that it nearly bankrupted the participating European dynasties. The French, the English, and the Spanish kings found themselves deeply in debt at the end of the war and desperate for new funding (taxes) that could help them restore their respective royal treasuries.

Monumental consequences would arise from the financial predicament in which the war placed the European monarchs.

The Albany Plan: An early attempt at colonial unity. With the onset of the French and Indian War in 1754, the colonies once again felt themselves in danger from the old threat of the French and their Indian allies. Thus in that same year representatives from various Middle and Upper Colonies gathered at Albany, New York, to discuss joint action, including improved relations with their Indian allies. Ben Franklin, who was one of the delegates, proposed a plan to unite the English colonies on a more permanent basis. The Albany Plan provided for an elective Grand Council (two to seven members sent from each of the colonies) that had the power to commit the colonies jointly in a limited number of political areas, most notably the colonies' relations with the Indians. The Grand Council was to be headed by a president, appointed by the king. The delegates approved this plan.

But their colonial assemblies did not, fearing the loss of colonial independence to this colony-wide authority. Such American unity would thus have to wait for a new day.

* * *

STEPS TOWARD FULL INDEPENDENCE FROM ENGLAND

A new and very different Hanoverian king: George III. In 1760, with the death of his grandfather (George II), a young and very ethnically English Prince of Wales (unlike his grandfather and great-grandfather who were quite German) took the throne of England as George III. Almost from the beginning of his reign he ran into trouble with the Whigs, who were used to a quite free hand in their political activity. But George was already in financial trouble, having inherited debts accumulated from the wars of his grandfather, and he pushed for economic policies designed to correct this problem – policies that frequently put him at odds with his Whig ministers. Soon, because of this and other political issues, he was accused of autocratic behavior on the model of the European monarchs who ran their governments as they alone decided to do so. This was not what English politicians (at least Whigs, anyway) expected of their kings. Nonetheless, with considerable encouragement from his mother, George was indeed trying very much to be the king in England

Independence 113

that his Hanoverian predecessors had not troubled themselves to be.

Taxing the colonies to help pay for England's Wars. Problems along these same lines began to develop between the young king and his colonies in America. Since the end of the French and Indian War in 1763, the English had found that although they had gained considerable North American territory from the French because of the war, the English national debt had also nearly doubled in the process. It had been a very costly war. Thus the sentiment arose with both the king and his Tory supporters in Parliament that the American colonists, who had benefited from the increased security of having the French threat removed and the Indian threat (presumably) neutralized, should help repay the debt through the imposition of new taxes on the colonies.

But the colonists were very sensitive to the fact that they themselves had made considerable contributions to the English victory with their own military support – and with the loss of lives and property which occurred during the war. Thus the imposition of taxes by king and parliament, without even any consultation with the colonists themselves (which was the historic right of all Englishmen), seemed totally unfair.

The 1765 Stamp Act. Worst of all was the fact that the first taxes to be collected would be from the revenue acquired by the purchase of official stamps or stamped paper, required to be printed on or attached to all colonial documents – even church documents. Boston Pastor Jonathan Mayhew preached a fiery sermon against this tax, claiming that this was a guise to establish royal control over the voice of the American church. The next day angry Bostonians burned down the home of the lieutenant governor.

But the Virginians were no less outraged, and the burgesses, under the influence of Patrick Henry's oratory, voted a refusal to pay the taxes. British Parliament quickly repealed the Stamp Act (although other taxes would be imposed in place of the stamp tax). But the political damage was done. The Bostonians and Virginians demonstrated that they had no hesitation in rejecting the authority of the King in America if he overstepped the ancient rights of Englishmen.

On this matter they even had supporters in the English parliament back in London, the Whigs, who agreed in principle with the colonists. But the king also had supporters in Parliament, the Tories, who agreed with the king, that he as sovereign had the right to make his subjects pay for the expenses of running the government. Thus beyond the issue of the costs involved in the war, the matter of high political principle dividing Whigs and Tories became a key part of the matter.

The 1770 Boston Massacre. The issue came to violence when an angry group of Bostonians began taunting British Redcoat soldiers stationed in Boston to protect British agents sent to collect the hated taxes. Nervous soldiers fired into the surrounding crowd, killing three and injuring eight (two of whom would subsequently die of their wounds).

Volunteering to defend the soldiers was a dedicated lawyer (and future American president) John Adams. Six of the soldiers were acquitted and just two charged with manslaughter. This was a daring act on Adams's part, considering the temper of the city, but indicative of his moral integrity (or ambition) – which the nation would later recognize and call into service.

Nonetheless, the event itself was an early indication of the mood that was developing in the colonies.

George III's effort to halt the spread West of English settlers into Indian lands. The colonists were also very unhappy that King George III had promised his Indian allies that, in recognition of their assistance in his war against the French (and France's Indian allies), no Anglo settlers would be allowed into the Indian lands west of the Appalachian Mountains. The colonies had long assumed that their boundaries, never fully defined to the West, actually extended westward across the Appalachian Mountains – at least to the Mississippi River (or even beyond).

Colonists had been looking westward in that direction with the expectation that these lands would become available as the lands in the East filled with settlers and their descendants. Indeed, in 1775 Daniel Boone had laid out his Wilderness Road through the Cumberland Gap in the Appalachian Mountains and had founded a settlement in Kentucky (subsequently named after him as Boonesborough).

Thus the proposed restriction by the king on that expansion was a major irritant – if not even a direct threat – to the future well-being of the colonials.

Along the same lines of logic as his promise to his Indian allies, George issued in 1774 a promise to his French subjects in Canada that their Catholic faith and French civil law would be recognized in a greatly expanded province of Quebec, a Quebec which now would include the territories to the West of the thirteen colonies on the other side of the Appalachian mountain range. What?!!! The king was now not only supporting Catholicism in principle but also moving to establish the Catholic church (and its bishops) as the spiritual governors in the colonies' Western territories.

This move to support Catholicism in the Western lands, plus the king's talk of wanting to appoint Anglican bishops to oversee the religious life of the English colonies, appeared simply to be a ploy to bring the English colonials' highly cherished 150-year-old religious freedoms in America to

Independence

an end.

Even before this event, concern had been rising in New England over the missionary efforts of the king's Church of England, not to the unsaved in the colonies, but aimed at good Congregationalists in an effort to bring them under the Mother Church. Already, in the 1750s, the pastor-activist Mayhew had taken up the cause of fending off the efforts of the Church of England to absorb the independent churches of New England, and by 1762, when there was open talk about positioning Anglican bishops over the colonies, Mayhew did his best to stir the stiffest opposition to such an invasion of colonial religious rights.

The Boston Tea Party (December 1773) – and the King's reaction.
What actually caused a full-scale rebellion finally to break forth in the colonies was yet another issue: tea. This rebellion erupted with the move of Parliament to give financial support to the failing East India Company (the English victory in India had not brought the company the profits it was expecting) by way of a number of political maneuvers which not only gave monopoly rights of the company to trade with the colonies (the colonials could actually get tea much more cheaply from the Dutch) but also imposed new taxes on the company's tea. Protests that these taxes were unfair were met by a coldness on the part of the royal government, which had by the early 1770s come to believe that any backing down on this issue would simply encourage further the independent spirit of the king's American subjects.

A major political explosion occurred in late 1773 with the arrival of a huge cargo of the company's tea sent to the colonies. In most cases Americans simply refused to unload the tea (New York, Philadelphia, Charleston). But in Boston the tea was dumped into the harbor in a great public show (directed by Samuel Adams) by Patriots dressed as Indians – stirring the wrath of the royal government. To demonstrate clearly the sovereignty of the king (and his heavily-Tory Parliament) in his colonies, the king's government enacted a number of Coercive or Intolerable Acts (1774) which basically shut down the port of Boston. The goal of the king was essentially to strangle the town's economy in order to bring the colonists back into submission. And to make doubly sure that the colonists got the point, the king sent a huge occupying force of British troops to Boston, and forced the townsmen to house these normally rowdy troops in their private homes – again, to break the independent spirit of his colonial subjects.

However, George's efforts at coercion merely *united* the colonies more closely in a mood of continental solidarity (the other colonies sent considerable financial and material aid to a crippled Boston). Thus in 1774 a Continental Congress of representatives of the thirteen colonies gathered in Philadelphia to coordinate the colonies' efforts to get some relief from King George. But their efforts to change the heart of the king failed entirely. By early 1775 the spirit of rebellion was gathering momentum among the growing number of American Whigs or Patriots. Now it would take only a small spark to set off a full-scale explosion of colonial fury.

The Battles of Lexington and Concord (April 19, 1775). As tensions mounted in the early spring of 1775 the British military in Boston decided that it would be best to disarm their colonial subjects – by seizing and destroying the stores of weapons and powder of the local militias. Thus in April a march of British troops was initiated by night from Boston to nearby Concord to seize military stores located there (however, these supplies had been mostly evacuated by the Americans who were tipped off about British plans). By dawn on the 19th, the troops had reached the town of Lexington, where American militia had quickly assembled to face the large British force.* A shot rang out (no one knows by whom), the British charged the Americans (who were actually in the process of dispersing) and eight were killed (shot or bayoneted) and ten wounded.

Thus the first shot of the War of Independence was fired.

The British troops then moved on to Concord, where they were confronted by a rapidly increasing gathering of Massachusetts militia. Another fight broke out between the two sides at the North Bridge, except this time it was the British who took the blows. British troops did what they could to locate hidden supplies, destroyed what they found (not a significant amount) and then regrouped to head back to Boston, tired and shocked by the day's business. But the worst was yet to come. Militia had gathered along the route back to Boston and began to fire on the exhausted retreating British troops. British reinforcements subsequently arrived from Boston and then both sides began to take large casualties. But eventually the British made it back to Boston. The shooting had now started in full. It would continue for another seven deadly years.

The Battle of Bunker (and Breed's) Hill (June 17, 1775). In response to this event, some 15,000 colonial militiamen soon gathered in the heights surrounding Boston. They were supplied by muskets and cannon seized in May from Fort Ticonderoga by American troops under Ethan Allen and Benedict Arnold. With cannon in the hands of angry colonials dug into the heights surrounding Boston, the British in Boston now found themselves in a dangerous position. Thus in June an assault on the American positions on

---

*The militias are frequently referred to as the minutemen, because they were trained to assemble and move quickly, fully armed, normally to counter a surprise Indian attack.

Breed's Hill and nearby Bunker Hill was ordered – to convince the colonial riffraff not to mess with the British Redcoats. However it took three British assaults on the American position on Breed's Hill to dislodge them, and the American withdrawal took place only after the colonials had run out of ammunition and only after they had inflicted huge casualties on their enemies: over 200 British killed and over 800 wounded, an unusually high percentage of these being British officers. The Americans lost less than half that number, and their retreat was orderly.

The British claimed this as their victory. But it was for them a costly victory – one they could not afford to repeat. Furthermore, the Americans demonstrated that they would not be easily defeated. Subsequently the British attempted no such raid on any of the other American positions surrounding Boston.

The convening of the Second Continental Congress (1775). Following the events at Lexington and Concord, a Second Continental Congress gathered in Philadelphia in May of 1775 to prepare for what was clearly shaping up as a full-scale war between America and England. One of the Second Continental Congress's first acts (June) was to create officially a Continental Army and place George Washington in command of it (he was in New York, heading to Boston to take command, when the Battle of Bunker Hill took place; he arrived in Boston soon thereafter). Also, at Benedict Arnold's urging, the Congress authorized an assault on Canada to try to draw its colonial neighbors to the north into the war on the side of the American rebels.

Thus it was that the Americans found themselves deeply involved in a war – a major war with a major European power. It was going to take a miracle to succeed. But these Americans believed in miracles. They counted on them.

They knew what a deadly mission they had attached themselves to. It was virtually unthinkable for a common people to come up against their king. The king was armed with a mighty, well-experienced army, manned by battle-tested professionals. These colonial patriots would be offering as their own army only local farmers and tradesmen, not professional soldiers used to the discipline of extended military duty.

History had no examples they could think of where a common people ever succeeded in throwing off the power of a major monarch. On the other hand, they had plenty of examples of popular rebellions, all of which ended with the rebels hanging by their necks on the gallows. From this moment forward these colonials would be considered under English law as traitors. And if this venture were to fail, they would all be hunted down and every one of them end up on the traitors' gallows.

But they believed that they had a cause that demanded their lives in full commitment. Their America had been an experiment in government by the people themselves, an experiment ordained by God himself a century and a half earlier. They had answered that call, and God had proven himself faithful in this venture. Thus this was the sole ground on which they stood, with the understanding that this was after all God's war in which they were all merely foot soldiers themselves. God would see them through, for in God they trusted their destinies fully.

* * *

THE WAR GETS UNDERWAY IN THE NORTH

But things do not go well for the American Patriots. Spirits were running high among the Americans as their militias in those first days gave such an excellent account of their fighting abilities. But events would suddenly take the Americans in the opposite direction. It was as if the hand of God was showing them that while they were indeed true soldiers, without his help their efforts would avail them nothing. Disasters struck one after another, disasters which would test profoundly the character and spirit of the American officers and their troops.

Canada (1775-1776). At first the Americans seemed unstoppable in their move on Canada. By the late autumn of 1775 Americans under Richard Montgomery had brought down the forts protecting Montreal. Then they captured Montreal itself. But soon events began to go wrong. Arnold was bringing up troops through New York, intending to link up with Montgomery against the city of Quebec. But hostile Indians, endless swamps and then early winter set in, slowing the movement and greatly weakening the ranks of Arnold's army. By the time the Americans had reached Quebec, the element of surprise was gone – and cold, hunger and disease wreaked havoc on Arnold's army. Arnold was a brave and daring leader. But it seemed as if God himself was dead set against American success in Canada. On the last day of December, a battle with the English at Quebec finally took place. The exhausted Americans were soundly defeated (and Montgomery killed). The survivors retreated a small distance from the city to wait for reinforcements (which never came) and warmer weather. In June of the following year (1776) a second attempt on Quebec was made – with no more success resulting than with the first effort. Another battle in October again brought failure, and Arnold retreated south back to Fort Ticonderoga, his ego greatly deflated. His valiant effort against incredible odds, human and natural, was well acknowledged at the time. But for Arnold it was still

Independence 119

very disappointing. All that effort – and no victory to show for it.

Because of this disappointing outcome, there would be no further effort to bring (or force) Canada into the war on the side of the rebels.

The British vacate Boston (March 1776). While over the winter of 1775–1776 the British and American armies sat facing each other across the watery surrounds of Boston, in a most amazing feat, Henry Knox brought down sixty tons of canons and military supplies from Fort Ticonderoga (November 1775-February 1776) through huge snowstorms – to reinforce Washington's army which was running low on such supplies (but also most everything else). When the British in Boston saw Dorchester Heights newly reinforced by a whole new array of cannon, British commander Howe knew his position was very vulnerable. He decided on a massive assault (March 1776) on the American position, similar to the one at Breed's Hill. But oddly enough (!!!) a huge storm hit as his troops were about to embark, and the attack was called off. Subsequently Howe came to the decision that the British could not continue to hold Boston and finally they and the American Tories or Loyalists who had also gathered there vacated the city. They would not return to Boston during the rest of the war.

The Declaration of Independence (July 1776).[26] American spirits were not dampened. In early 1776, Thomas Paine wrote a pamphlet, *Common Sense*, daring to speak the unspeakable: it was time for Americans to separate from England and establish their own government. In Paine's opinion, a republic was the best type of government for America. The pamphlet was widely read and agreed with by many. It was time to leave the British Empire.

But such action would require the decision of the Continental Congress in Philadelphia. Yet none of the delegates had come to Philadelphia with this idea in mind or with any specific instructions on this matter from the colonial assemblies they were representing. They would have to return to their colonies and secure authorization. Of course this would be hotly contested by many who, though highly irritated at the high-handedness of the authorities in London, were yet quite unwilling to break the link with the Mother country.

The debate in America in the spring of 1776 was intense, although clearly there was a growing momentum in the colonies in support of independence. Starting with North Carolina, one by one some of the colonial assemblies passed resolutions authorizing their delegates to vote for formal independence from England. But action stalled in the middle colonies. When in mid-May Congress took up a Declaration of Independence written by John Adams, four of the middle colonies voted against it. The Maryland delegation even walked out.

But the independence momentum was gathering strength. On the same day that Congress passed the less than unanimous Adams declaration, the Virginia Assembly voted strongly for independence. Thus politically armed, the Virginia delegation arrived in Philadelphia in early June and submitted its own independence resolution for a vote:

> *Resolved, that these United Colonies are, and of right ought to be, free and independent States, that they are absolved from all allegiance to the British Crown, and that all political connection between them and the State of Great Britain is, and ought to be, totally dissolved.*

The debate that followed was intense. But one by one – with the exception of New York, whose colonial assembly was sent scattering by the British occupation before the Assembly had a chance to vote – the colonial assemblies were instructed to vote for independence.

Thus a committee of five was appointed to draft an explanation justifying the move to independence, to be submitted to the Continental Congress along with the resolution. Ultimately the task of drafting such a statement was given to the young, scholarly Virginia aristocrat, Thomas Jefferson. He put together a draft resolution (the language possibly borrowed heavily from Locke's *Two Treatises on Government*) and submitted it to the committee where it underwent changes,* and then it was presented to the full Congress at the end of June. The famous Preamble states the case clearly:

> *We hold these truths to be self evident, that all men are created equal, that they are endowed by their Creator with certain unalienable Rights, that among these are Life, Liberty and the pursuit of Happiness.*
>
> *That to secure these rights, Governments are instituted among Men, deriving their just powers from the consent of the governed, That whenever any Form of Government becomes destructive of these ends, it is the Right of the People to alter or to abolish it, and to institute new Government, laying its*

---

*Words and sentences were revised, and about 1/4th of Jefferson's text was cut out – including an assertion by Jefferson that slavery had been forced on the colonies by Britain – causing Jefferson to be deeply irritated by this editorial slighting of his personal creativity! Also the irony in Jefferson's statement that all men are created equal was the fact that he himself owned a number of slaves, who, though men, were certainly not created equal or endowed with certain unalienable Rights.

foundation on such principles and organizing its powers in such form, as to them shall seem most likely to effect their Safety and Happiness.

When the Congress moved to a preliminary vote on the independence resolution on July 1st there was by no means unanimity in the Congress. Several states voted no. But nine voted yes, so the resolution was approved as ready for a final vote the next day, July 2nd. On that day a formal vote was taken, with Pennsylvania, South Carolina, and Delaware finally lining up in support of independence. New York, still having no instructions from its assembly in exile, again abstained – but got instructions a week later to support independence. The document was put in its final edition on the 4th of July – and then (no one is sure exactly when) the delegates began adding their signatures to the document.

Now the colonies were no longer just that. As they saw things, they were now thirteen free and independent states.

The Articles of Confederation (November 1777). At the same time that the committee was appointed to draft a document explaining America's Declaration of Independence, Congress appointed another committee to draft a constitution for the government that would oversee a union of the thirteen new states in the struggles that lay ahead.

But unlike Jefferson's Declaration of Independence which was drawn up in very short order, work on this new constitution was very slow going. The draft for a confederation of the thirteen states was finally voted on by the Continental Congress in November of 1777 and sent as the Articles of Confederation and Perpetual Union to the states for ratification. But the ratification process was not completed until 1781. Nonetheless the political reality was that the new Confederation was fairly well understood to be operative from the moment that the final draft of the Articles was approved by Congress and sent to the individual states for ratification.

The slowness of the process was not because of the newness of the idea of a written constitution for America. Although the English had a constitution which was largely unwritten but based on time-honored political traditions that all Englishmen understood well, the colonies had been written contractual affairs virtually from their founding. All had been founded in accordance with basic charters that explained in legal detail the purpose and operations of each of the colonies. These had been revised over the years. And in fact, with the declaration of independence of the thirteen colonies, each of them became busied in writing new constitutions outlining their respective structures and functions as independent states.

The problems involved in setting up the Confederation were largely political – most frequently disagreements over border questions. Now that they were independent, each state began to look to its own future, its growth, its expansion. And this frequently brought them into conflict with each other over the question of state title to the western lands.

Nonetheless the states did need to work together. So even if they had not formally signed on to the Articles of Confederation, they operated pretty much as if it were in full effect. Thus the Continental Congress really saw itself early on as the legislative branch of the confederacy, fully ratified or not.

✻ ✻ ✻

WASHINGTON: THE MATTER OF PERSONAL CHARACTER[27]

Washington – the warrior. George Washington's appointment by the Continental Congress as commander of the newly authorized Continental Army proved to be a very Providential (as in Godly) choice. Whereas a number of experienced Patriot officers (having also previously served as officers in the British Army) coveted that position, Washington had not. He accepted the responsibility only because he understood that he was simply answering the call to duty – a call that came not just from men but also from God. He was living out his destiny.

Washington, as sensitive as any of us to the opinion of others, had taught himself at an early age to discipline his feelings and move forward toward his calling regardless of the obstacles (usually human) thrown before him. But he also knew that there was a special hand on his life, a special place in the affairs of Providence (the term for God frequently used at that time) that not only protected him, but opened the way for him to move ahead in life. He thus combined faith and personal discipline in a way that inspired others. He sought honor by seeking first of all to be honorable. He was highly demanding of integrity in himself – to be a man of honor.

As events were soon to demonstrate, he could be rather forgiving of the lack of honor in his associates (such as his colleagues Lee and Gates) who had given him little reason to expect much from them anyway. But he could be quite demanding of integrity of character and action when it came to those on whom he had come to confer his trust (like Arnold). Washington was unbending in his expectation of excellent behavior on the part of the men under his command. But these expectations were always accompanied by his equally strong sense of trust in these same men. This conferral of his trust was a powerful instrument that succeeded in getting the very best from others. The soldiers under his command seemed always to try eagerly and sacrificially to live up to that trust.

Independence

This was leadership, true leadership, and a real blessing to a new nation trying to make its way forward into an unknown future. Washington would not need to bark orders to those around him to get them moving in the right direction. A simple word would be enough to get things moving. People would be moved to right behavior sometimes simply by his mere presence in their midst. This power of his almost wordless presence (which happened daily as he moved among his soldiers in the icy fields of Valley Forge) would prove in fact to be one of his greatest contributions to the American cause, not only in war but also in peace (such as his daily almost wordless contribution as chairman of the Constitutional Convention gathered in Philadelphia the summer of 1787 to write the new American Constitution).

From where then did Washington draw such inner strength of character if it clearly was not the approval of others? In part it was almost something he seemed born with – a burning desire to succeed. But the success he sought was both social as well as personal: he was a man of incredible concern for the welfare of others. And he seemed to have some well-cultivated instinct for doing things right – right not only as social convention demanded, but at an even deeper level, what he understood God or Providence required of him. Washington was faithful in his time spent quietly in private prayer with God and in his attendance in Sunday worship (although not necessarily regular in this latter matter), fully convinced that there was no other way to secure goodness and Truth for his world, personally and socially. His sense of personal responsibility arose greatly from that powerful sense of divine appointment. He lived and served, as he saw things, fully in service to God and country – by God's will.

How that special relationship he had with God in the midst of this crushing responsibility is well illustrated in the *Diary and Remembrances* of a Presbyterian Minister Rev. Nathaniel Randolph Snowden who recorded a conversation he had with Isaac Potts of Valley Forge, Pennsylvania (at whose home Washington was residing that winter):

> *I was riding with him (Mr. Potts) near Valley Forge, where the army lay during the war of the Revolution. Mr. Potts was a Senator in our state and a Whig. I told him I was agreeably surprised to find him a friend to his country as the Quakers were mostly Tories. He said, It was so and I was a rank Tory once, for I never believed that America could proceed against Great Britain whose fleets and armies covered the land and ocean. But something very extraordinary converted me to the good faith.*
>
> *What was that? I inquired. Do you see that woods, and that plain? It was about a quarter of a mile from the place we were*

riding. There, said he, laid the army of Washington. It was a most distressing time of ye war, and all were for giving up the ship but that one good man. In that woods, pointing to a close in view, I heard a plaintive sound, as of a man at prayer. I tied my horse to a sapling and went quietly into the woods and to my astonishment I saw the great George Washington on his knees alone, with his sword on one side and his cocked hat on the other. He was at Prayer to the God of the Armies, beseeching to interpose with his Divine aid, as it was ye Crisis and the cause of the country, of humanity, and of the world.

Such a prayer I never heard from the lips of man. I left him alone praying. I went home and told my wife, I saw a sight and heard today what I never saw or heard before, and just related to her what I had seen and heard and observed. We never thought a man could be a soldier and a Christian, but if there is one in the world, it is Washington. We thought it was the cause of God, and America could prevail.[28]

Washington's understanding of the challenge before him. Indeed the appointment of Washington as the commander of the Continental Army was a Providential choice* also because he understood the way that Americans would have to fight the huge English military machine better than anyone else around him. He understood two things: 1) to engage the huge English army not directly, but indirectly, using the element of surprise (Indian style) and 2) remember that wars are not won in one great battle, but instead through the staying power of one side willing to fight on longer than the enemy.

Battles bring the victor immediate glory. And a great number of the men, especially other generals in the American army, were eager to attain that glory. They were primarily focused on the next battle, eager to get a chance to gain glory. Victory was not only extremely thrilling in its moment of arrival (a kind of military high), it gave the victors greatly enhanced status with others. However, Washington well understood that while victory in battle may bring glory, it does not necessarily win wars. And his sense of duty always made very clear to him that he was called to win a war, not gain impressive victories in battle.

This may seem puzzling to many even today. Aren't the victories in battle what ultimately win wars? Maybe – and maybe not. What actually wins wars is a breaking of the enemy's desire, for whatever reason, to

---

*It was also a wise human choice, because he was a Virginian and his appointment made this more than just a New England rebellion, as it was up to that point.

Independence

continue the conflict. Wars are won when one side or the other is ready to call it quits.

Thus wars are fundamentally about morale, not about military mechanics. Certainly a victory in a particular battle improves the level of morale of one or the other side in a war. But it generally takes more than one, or even several, military victories to reshape morale to the extent that one side or the other is willing to call it quits. Warriors usually have great staying power – and a loser in battle can put this particular defeat behind him with the hope of a possible win in the next round of the conflict. So in the end, a war is won on the staying power of the contenders, not just the military brilliance of one or another army and its commanders.

Washington's strategy. Thus while generals in the various armies under Washington's command seemed out to win battles – and the glory such battles earned them – Washington was doggedly committed to winning the war, regardless of the fortunes of battle. Washington knew that his primary function was to keep his army of rebels (or Whigs or Patriots) intact and still troublesome to the English (even if it was never fully victorious on the battlefield) – until England tired of the game and was ready to call it quits and let the Americans go freely on their way again.

Washington's inability to win the big one year after year drew much criticism from others, especially other generals who coveted the dignity of Washington's top position over the Continental Army. Consequently, they frequently lobbied with the Continental Congress behind Washington's back to have him replaced (by themselves of course). But Washington seemed unruffled by these endeavors of some of his associates. He was given a war to win. And by the grace of God he was determined to fulfill his duty.

Ethical troubles behind Washington's back. So, character and understanding combined in Washington to produce exactly the kind of leadership that the Patriots would need to get through this war successfully. But other generals lacked that same character. And from time to time America paid a big price for these individuals' quest for praise and honor – at the cost of true wisdom and eventually even their own success. In their quest for glory they put themselves at the center of their devotion and lost sight of the bigger agenda, the one which Washington was clearly following. They became like gods in their own eyes, seeking all glory and honor for themselves. Thus they failed to grasp the higher calling on America, the one that God had placed before them, and the one that Washington was attempting to answer. And God was with him. But as for the others, God gave them over to the depravity of their own logic. And they at some point self-destructed, sadly taking a lot of American morale or spirit with them.

...their thinking became futile and their foolish hearts were darkened. Although they claimed to be wise, they became fools and exchanged the glory of the immortal God for images made to look like mortal man ... (Romans 1:21-23 NIV)

General Charles Lee. General Lee was one of those individuals. He had once been an officer in the British army and considered himself more experienced and thus a better candidate than Washington for the top position. As next in command under Washington he had never been particularly supportive of Washington's military efforts. Washington tolerated him and even accorded Lee proper commanding privileges, though he was aware of Lee's maneuvering behind his back. Also Lee was rather skillfully uncooperative as second in command, more than once leaving Washington without his required support, thereby putting Washington at an ever greater disadvantage in facing the enemy.

At one point his purposeful dawdling with his troops ironically gave the British the opportunity to capture Lee and imprison him – until a prisoner exchange could be arranged. Washington was not pleased to have him back. But he said and did nothing to undercut Lee. Eventually it was a near catastrophe in a key battle (Monmouth) caused by Lee's lack of the right kind of military instincts that finally gave Washington the opportunity to rid himself of this nuisance. However Lee fought back before the Continental Congress because of his removal from command by Washington. But this thankfully only worsened Lee's case before the members of the Congress, who were beginning to catch on to Washington's real importance as the glue keeping their army together.

General Horatio Gates. General Gates, the hero of Saratoga, was another one of those individuals. He too had been a British officer and too believed himself to be the better candidate for the top position. Washington's amazing success at Trenton at the end of 1776 ended temporarily Gates's lobbying before Congress for Washington's job. Gates was however eventually sent to take command of the Northern Department. This put him directly in the position of having to face the British at Saratoga in 1777. Saratoga was a success and Gates the hero of the battle, though his fainthearted ways had not been the cause of the victory. That honor truly belonged to others, including Benedict Arnold, whose insubordinate attack on the British had moved the morale considerably from the British to the American side in this drawn-out battle. But in his self-promoting report on the victory at Saratoga, Gates did not bother even to mention Arnold's role.

Gates then soon joined a secret effort of a number of top officers in the Continental Army to have their supporters in Congress remove Washington

Independence 127

from command (the Conway Cabal). This effort fell apart when it was exposed publicly. Gates apologized to Washington and survived politically. When two years later as the Americans were facing terrible losses in the Southern war, the hero of Saratoga was given command of the Southern District. But the job proved greater than his real abilities – and at Camden, South Carolina (1780), Gates' army was crushed by the British. Gates was relieved of command, retired, but then recalled from retirement (1782) to rejoin Washington – where he may have been part of another plot (1783) to have Washington removed. But by then the war was actually over.

General Benedict Arnold. General Arnold was another individual caught up in the maneuvering of Congress in its politically inspired distribution of military commands and military honors. But Arnold's situation was quite different from Lee and Gates in that the maneuvering in Congress seemed, as with Washington, to be aimed against Arnold, a man who was in fact one of the most capable of America's generals. Arnold was constantly passed over in Congress for promotions in favor of others, who often took credit for Arnold's unheralded actions (such as Gates at Saratoga). At one point, Congress even reprimanded Arnold for owing it money – though he had exhausted most of his own personal fortunes on behalf of the American war effort.

However, lacking Washington's moral and spiritual self-discipline, Arnold gradually sunk into a deep bitterness and, encouraged by his young pro-British or Tory Philadelphia bride, Peggy Shippen, he decided to switch his services to the British side of the war. He was planning, as the newly appointed commander (appointed by a trusting Washington) of the key fortress at West Point, to turn the strategic site on the Hudson River over to the British. But his plans were discovered and the plot foiled (1780). However, he was able to make his own escape down the Hudson to British lines. He was soon given command of a British army unit and caused considerable destruction to the American cause with his raids in Virginia and in his home state of Connecticut.

After the war, living in England as an expatriate, he was met by the English with rather mixed emotions. And he himself began to have regrets about his betrayal. Sadly, his last request as he approached death in 1801 was that he be buried not in his British but rather in his American officer's uniform.

The Americans themselves were greatly divided on the rebellion. Dark days lay ahead for the Americans. These dark days would also test the character and spirit of all the colonials, civilians as well as soldiers. By no means were all colonials supportive of this rebellion. A large number of the colonials (estimates vary from 15 percent to 30 percent, with most of those concentrated in the southern colonies) were opposed to the rebellion. As Tories or Loyalists, they stood with their king on the issues. To be sure, an even larger number (estimates from 35 percent to 45 percent) of the colonials were active supporters of the rebellion (strong in New England and the Middle Colonies). As Whigs or Patriots, they filled the ranks of the militia – or as civilians provided (supposedly) support in supplies or finances to the war effort. And the rest, who were quite numerous themselves, were rather neutral, tending to go with whichever side seemed at the moment to have the upper hand.

Sadly some of the Whigs or Patriots supposedly supporting the independence effort proved to be rather unreliable in backing the Patriot soldiers in their attempt to defend that independence. Many were quick to sell agricultural goods to the British army in return for hard currency while their own armies starved.

Also, the states, loud in their support of the idea of independence, were amazingly unwilling to come up with the financial support necessary to pay even the minimum amount needed to feed, arm and clothe the Patriot armies, a matter of huge frustration to Washington, and to the other officers and soldiers sacrificing their fortunes and lives in support of the independence effort.

The clergy and minority groups in the war. The clergy were themselves divided. The priests of the Church of England assigned to parishes in America rather naturally supported the Tory cause and simply retreated to England when the war broke out. However, Congregationalist and Presbyterian pastors typically were strongly supportive of the move to independence, their support at times even active on the battlefield (often commanding militia units themselves), so active that the Tories referred to them as the Black Regiment (clergy wore black robes, though certainly not in battle!).

A favorite story about the involvement of the clergy in the war arose from an event that occurred in 1780, when Presbyterian pastor James Caldwell (whose wife had been killed by Hessian troops when he was away) found the same Hessians soon returning to his village of Springfield, New Jersey. When fighting broke out and the Patriots ran out of paper wadding for their muskets, he ripped out pages of his church's hymnbooks, Watts's *Psalms and Hymns*, and passed them to the soldiers, shouting, "Put Watts into them, boys! Give them Watts!"

On the political front, clergy took major positions of leadership. One of these was John Witherspoon, a Scottish Presbyterian pastor who came to the colonies in 1768 to take the presidency of the College of New Jersey (the future Princeton University). Under his presidency the college became a breeding-ground for young leaders of the movement for independence, he himself then becoming a delegate to the Continental Congress debating such independence. Then as an official of the denomination, he called on fellow Presbyterian ministers to speak out boldly on the matter of American independence. And in 1776 he had the opportunity to sign the Declaration of Independence, the only clergyman (and college president) to do so.*

There were few Catholics in the colonies (mostly concentrated in Maryland and southern Pennsylvania). Their position had always been precarious, and the war at first did not change things. But the alliance with Catholic France helped Catholics serve the Patriot cause. But so did the leadership of the Carroll family, prominent Catholics in Maryland. One of them, Father John Carroll,† in fact a Jesuit priest, early on was asked to represent the Patriot cause to the French Canadians, in the hope of being able to ally with the Canadians in the move to American independence. John's brother, Daniel, was a signer of the Articles of Confederation and later the Constitution of the United States, and a cousin Charles was a signer of the Declaration of Independence and eventually a U.S. senator representing Maryland. The Carrolls, like Jefferson, were understandably strong supporters of the idea of separating religion from the affairs of civil government. For a while, Protestant animosity towards Catholics would subside as a result of the Carrolls' role in securing American independence and subsequently its Republic.

For the German communities, mostly located along the Pennsylvanian and North Carolinian western frontiers, the situation was one that also required much caution. Lutherans were split, some supporting the Patriot cause, others remaining Loyalists, because in coming out of Germany they had found life in English America so much more hospitable and felt that a spirit of gratitude towards English authority for this better life was required of them. Then there were the German Pietists, small groups of pacifists, such as the Protestant Moravians (recently brought there from Germany by Count Nikolaus von Zinzendorf) who found themselves torn as to which way to go in this battle. They were, after all, pacifists.

Zinzendorf and the Moravians. The young Saxon nobleman Zinzendorf in the 1720s had taken in Protestant Bohemian and Moravian refugees escaping Catholic persecution in their homeland (today's Czech Republic), a persecution that reached back to the days of the Czech Reformer Jan Hus

---

*After the war, he would be the one to call together and lead the first national Presbyterian General Assembly.

†Father John Carroll would become the first Catholic bishop in the United States and also found Georgetown College in 1789 along the banks of the Potomac in southern Maryland, now part of Washington, D.C.

(burned at the stake by Church authorities in 1415) when their religious reform movement (*Unitas Fratrum*) got started. Zinzendorf created a retreat center for these Moravians called Herrenhut. But sectarian controversies that developed within Herrenhut and also with the German world around it compelled Zinzendorf to focus his efforts in developing a true spirit of Christian unity, resulting in an amazing Moravian pacifism – and an equally amazing commitment to Christian mission work (the 1730s) under the most difficult of conditions, especially among the African slaves of the Caribbean (but also elsewhere).

It was their missionary work that first brought them to Georgia in 1735, to be part of the philanthropic project that Georgia was announced to be. They did not succeed greatly in that endeavor – except to influence profoundly a young John Wesley, who took up many of the Moravian approaches to ministry in his own subsequent work in England. In 1741, the Moravians moved on to Pennsylvania, finally establishing a successful mission station there at Bethlehem and then soon at nearby Nazareth. From there they sent missions to many other parts of the English colonies, most notably Salem (now Winston-Salem) in North Carolina.

Now in the 1770s their pacifism made things difficult for themselves as their newly adopted country chose sides in this growing conflict between the colonies and their English king. The Moravians attempted to stay neutral, but over time, and quite gradually, found themselves supporting the Patriot cause.

✳ ✳ ✳

THE WAR ITSELF

Meanwhile Washington, who had taken command of the Continental Army at Boston, realized that the British pullout from Boston meant trouble further south along the New England coast. He decided to pull his army out of Boston and reposition it in New York, on Long Island just opposite Manhattan. But the British army arrived by ship in huge numbers and maneuvered Washington's army back into an encirclement along the Brooklyn Heights (August, 1776). Washington and his men were trapped. The only thing Washington could do was to try to slip undetected by night across the East River into Manhattan in order to escape this trap. However, there was virtually no hope of being able to rescue more than a small portion of his army before the British would awaken to the program and shut him down. But he had no alternative. And then came a mysterious fog which covered the East River and hid his escape – lasting miraculously until mid-morning, allowing Washington to get nearly his whole army away to safety. Clearly this

Independence 131

was understood by all Americans as an incredible intervention on God's part.

But of course wars are not won merely by escaping the enemy. But for Washington, this seemed to be his only recourse – again and again. He got his army out of another potential trap in Manhattan – but lost two strategic American forts and over 3,000 troops taken prisoner by the British in the process. New York City would remain in British hands until the end of the war.

Depression. Washington then retreated through New Jersey and crossed into Pennsylvania, the onset of winter and the tradition by which armies rested in the winter rather than fight giving Washington some reprieve from continuing British pressure. Morale was low. People were deserting nearby Philadelphia, fearing a British attack on the city. Washington's Continental Army was down to about 5,000 soldiers, and that number was dwindling fast. Worse, a good number of them had their terms of enlistment running out at the end of December. At the same time, facing the Americans was – or was soon to be – a growing British Army of over 30,000 troops. Things were looking tragically grim for Washington.

> *These are the times that try men's souls*[29]
> Thomas Paine - participant in the retreat of the Continental Army

Trenton (December 25-26, 1776). To break the mood of depression, Washington decided to conduct a surprise attack on the Hessian troops serving the British at Trenton on the night of Christmas, when the Hessians hopefully would be sleeping off heavy Christmas celebrations. It was a daring maneuver: an ice-filled Delaware River to cross and then a nine-mile march south to Trenton in the dead of a dark, freezing, rainy-snowy night. But Washington seemed unshaken by the high risk of it all. His confidence, which came from a serene higher sense of things, inspired a similar confidence in his men. The attack, and a secondary assault ordered by Washington on another British unit posted nearby, succeeded brilliantly, with little loss of American life (two killed) and yet 1,000 Hessians killed or captured (though a number of American soldiers died in the following days from disease and exhaustion caused by the wintery effort).

Princeton (January 3, 1777). His amazing victory (many said miraculous victory) was soon followed up by another – also stunning – victory against a British unit sent to retake Trenton. Washington abandoned Trenton, but defeated this English relieving force at nearby Princeton. At first the battle looked as if it were going to be another disaster for the Americans. But Washington managed to rally his troops and turn a retreat into an attack

– routing instead the British. It was another humiliating defeat for the British.

These two victories of Trenton and Princeton were strategically small militarily, but morale-wise they were huge boosts to the American effort. Few soldiers abandoned Washington at this critical juncture. Indeed, many men now signed up to serve under Washington. The Continental Army remained a viable fighting machine.

Saratoga (September-October 1777). The British had a plan to knock the Northern colonies out of the war by breaking the vital line of communications between New England and the Middle Colonies at New York, along the upper Hudson River. They planned to bring a large part of their army occupying New York City up the Hudson River to meet two other British armies coming South from Canada.

But things immediately began to go wrong for the British. Colonial militia used every trick in the book to slow up the movement of the British groups descending from Canada. And a section of the British army was overrun (1,000 men killed, wounded or captured) at Bennington in August. Another British group returned to Canada when their Indian allies abandoned them upon hearing that Arnold was commanding the colonials opposing them.

Meanwhile the British commander in New York City, William Howe, sent his men not up the Hudson but off on an expedition to capture Philadelphia. Finally in September the remnants of the British army (6,000 soldiers under General John Burgoyne) met the Americans (8,000 soldiers under General Gates) at Saratoga, New York. The results of a hard-fought encounter were at first inconclusive and the situation settled into a stalemate. Burgoyne kept waiting for British reinforcements – which never came. Meanwhile in the American ranks, which were actually growing at this time, friction had grown between Gates and his subordinate commander (but militarily aggressive) Arnold, and a jealous Gates sidelined Arnold, forcing him into a largely inactive role.

When battle resumed in October the British were forced slowly to give ground. Then Arnold disobeyed Gates and led a charge on the weakening British line – firing up the American lines which in turn delivered yet another crippling blow to the British. Surrounded and exhausted, now certain that he would receive no aid from Howe, Burgoyne finally surrendered his entire British army to Gates. Gates thus became the "hero of Saratoga," an irritated Gates endeavoring to make sure that Arnold's role in the victory would go unnoticed by Congress.

The French join the war on the American side (February 1778). With

Independence

this stunning defeat of a large British army by a clearly effective American army, the French King Louis XVI lost all hesitation and openly declared himself an ally of the Americans (the French, along with the Spanish and Dutch, had previously been quietly slipping support to the American rebels). British General Howe had indeed taken the American capital of Philadelphia in September (1777). But that achievement seemed less significant to the French than the American capture of 6,000 British soldiers in October. Thus in February (1778) America and France became wartime allies.

The loss of Philadelphia (1777). For Washington, things had not gone well. He was not part of the glory of Saratoga. Instead he had been trying to follow and anticipate Howe's moves in removing his troops from New York. Howe's intent finally became clear in August when Howe moved by water up the Chesapeake in the direction of Philadelphia. Washington tried to block the advance of the larger army, but was outflanked at Brandywine (September) and thus forced to allow Howe to enter Philadelphia virtually unopposed. Then a stalemate set in as Washington tried unsuccessfully to capture the Germantown garrison just north of Philadelphia (October). And then the British tried, equally unsuccessfully, to take Washington at White Marsh (December).

Wintering at Valley Forge (1777–1778). At this point it was time for the armies to move into winter quarters. It would be another very trying time for Washington's Continental Army. Of the 10,000 troops that went into winter quarters at Valley Forge just outside Philadelphia, 2,500 of them would die there of cold, hunger and disease before the next spring arrived. But it would be a very different army that would finally emerge from the experience. Mere survival that winter, not to mention success in the next year's military campaign, would require discipline. And the troops got just that from the experience. Military training from Prussian Baron von Steuben and spiritual discipline from the pious rigor Washington maintained in his own life and the same discipline he expected of his men (including daily prayers) brought a quite disciplined army back into service in the late spring of 1778.

Monmouth (June 28, 1778). With the French in the war, the British decided to abandon Philadelphia and return their troops to New York, fearing a French naval assault on that city. Howe resigned and General Henry Clinton took over as commander of the British armies in America. All the way from Philadelphia back to New York City, Washington shadowed Clinton's march.

Finally, as the British troops passed the Monmouth Court House,

Washington saw an opportunity and ordered a surprise attack on the rear of Clinton's army. The arrogant and temperamental General Lee originally had refused the honor of commanding a small military unit ordered by Washington to lead the attack – but changed his mind when he saw how glad Washington was that he had said no, and subsequently requested command of the forward attack force. But Lee lost heart in the midst of the battle when British General Charles Cornwallis counterattacked. Without consulting Washington, Lee ordered a retreat – which turned into a rout. Washington came upon the fleeing Americans, took direct command, and quickly reorganized his men for a counterattack. The battle raged back and forth until nightfall, when both sides were forced to break off the fight. That night Clinton slipped his men away to continue their march to New York City.

For Washington this was not the victory he had hoped for, though it finally allowed him to get rid of the troublesome General Lee, who was disgraced by his actions. But it did prove that under proper command his disciplined troops were fully capable of taking on directly an equally manned and equipped British army.

This would also be the last major battle in the American North (although smaller battles would continue in the Middle Colonies).

* * *

THE WAR MOVES SOUTH ... AND FINALLY ENDS

Failing to get any traction in the North, the British decided to move their activities to the South, where it was hoped that a large number of pro-British American Tories might help deliver that part of colonial America over to the British forces. The British were assured that with the show of a few British victories in the South, the Tories would come out in huge numbers in support of the British effort. But making that happen proved to be more difficult than the British at first had hoped.

Early British and Tory (or Loyalist) failures in the South (1776–1778). From the very beginning of the war things went terribly wrong for the British and their Tory Loyalists in the South. The British governors in the South had been trying to form Tory militia since the outbreak of the conflict in early 1775. Plans were also to bring Redcoats to the Carolinas to join up with Southern Tories. But Whig or Patriot militia were also forming rapidly in the South. Hearing of British plans to land a force of Redcoats in the Carolinas, both sides, Whigs and Tories, began to mobilize in anticipation of this event.

Both sides met at Moore's Creek Bridge (North Carolina) in February of 1776 – and the Tories were soundly defeated by the Patriots. Though the conflict was small in scale (less than 1,000 on each side) the result of the conflict was the tremendous quieting of Tory sympathies in the South.

The British now had to depend largely on their own forces. Unable to find a secure landing in North Carolina for the soldiers and supplies necessary to support their effort to crush the Southern rebellion, they turned toward the major southern seaport of Charleston. But they mistakenly landed their soldiers on Sullivan Island, and thus tried to subdue the defending American fort by ship's canon rather than troop assault across deep waters. But the palmetto logs forming the American outer defenses easily took the shelling – and the fort proved impregnable. Thus the British simply called off the attack on Charleston – and pretty much the entire southern effort.

British Florida, protected by the British fort at St. Augustine, remained in British hands – and became a place of refuge for Tories fleeing the reprisals of the Southern Patriots. But the British seemed unable to acquire any advantage from this strategic position (partly due to political squabbles within the British upper political circles). Eventually British Florida would be able to contribute to the war, but not with the impact that it originally would have had on the war if it had been able to get going earlier.

With the failure of the British to gain what should have been a much easier victory in the South, they lost the valuable strategic advantage they had – and probably the war itself. If they had taken the South out of the war in its early days it would have undoubtedly collapsed the entire colonial rebellion. But they let that opportunity slip from their hands. Indeed, for the next two years the Tory or Loyalist position in the South only worsened as British support failed to appear and as Patriots did their best to drive the Loyalists out of the area.

The British now focus their war effort on the South (1778). Then after the Battle of Monmouth, with the growing awareness of the British that they would not be able to make much further progress in the North, British attention turned decidedly to the South. Once again, the hope was to seize a southern seaport in order to offload soldiers and supplies for a major southern offensive. The target this time was Savannah. It was defended only by some 700 Patriots and thus easily taken in December by a British force of 3,500 troops arriving by sea, even before 2,000 British troops coming up from Florida had a chance to assist in the action. The British now had a seaport available to begin bringing in soldiers and supplies to knock the South out of the war. Savannah would continue to serve the British well in that capacity. A French and Patriot effort to retake the city the following year (October 1779) failed miserably, resulting in the loss of about 1,000 French and Patriots killed, wounded or captured.

Things then seemed to go from bad to much worse for the Patriots when British General Clinton directed a joint land and sea offensive of around 14,000 troops and ninety ships against the city of Charleston, defended by a force only about a third that size. British General Charles Cornwallis, who was commanding the land force, was soon able to cut off the land routes in and out of the city and then begin the assault on the city itself. As the weeks went by it became apparent to the American commander Lincoln that the city could not hold out and a decision was made simply to surrender the city and the 5,000 American troops protecting it. It was the worst American military defeat of the war – and sent a shock wave through the colonies.

If things were not bad enough, they got even worse for the Patriots when Gates, the supposed genius of Saratoga, was sent to take over the Southern Department. Believing himself to be something of a brilliant military leader, he decided on the strategy of a direct assault against Cornwallis's well-seasoned army. Gates was commanding a larger army – but poorly organized and mostly inexperienced. In August (1780), at Camden, South Carolina, the two sides met. The results for the Patriots were terrible. Gates's militia troops broke ranks and fled, leaving now only 800 Continentals to face 2,000 British troops. Colonel Banastre Tarleton's cavalry charge quickly scattered even these Patriot troops. The battle was quickly over. The losses for the Americans were enormous (the loss of over 2,000 men), not only numerically but also morale-wise.

The war in the South now turned into a very nasty guerrilla-style action as British troops under Tarleton had earlier moved into the rural interior seeking to break the last of the Patriot resistance with a harsh strategy of burning out Patriot farms and towns as they went. At the battle of Waxhaws (May 1780) the troops of "Bloody Tarleton" had even cut down several hundred Patriot soldiers after they had surrendered. But Patriot partisans (led by such men as Francis Marion, the "Swamp Fox") fought back all the more relentlessly. And Tarleton's tactics ultimately succeeded only in driving many American neutrals into the ranks of vengeful Patriots.

In October (1780) at King's Mountain, North Carolina, a Patriot army of around 900 surrounded and destroyed a Tory or Loyalist army of about 1,400 – also crushing once again Southern Loyalists' enthusiasm for open military support of the British regulars. The war in the South now began to turn in favor of the Patriots.

Then things also turned quite badly for the British regulars. Tarleton had been sent out by Cornwallis to chase down Patriots under the command of Nathanael Greene (who had taken over the Southern Department from Gates). At Cowpens (January 1781), along the flooded Broad River, Tarleton, after a hard forced march of his men in pursuit of retreating

Independence 137

American forces, met an American unit under one of Greene's most able commanders, Daniel Morgan. But Morgan had set up a skillful trap for Tarleton – and the brash Tarleton sent his men straight into it. Tarleton's men were soon surrounded – and annihilated. Tarleton and a handful of his cavalry were able to escape. But the rest of Tarleton's force was destroyed, including some of Cornwallis's best regiments.

Cornwallis was now desperate for a win to undo the catastrophes he had experienced at King's Mountain and Cowpens. He headed north after Greene's army, to try to wipe it out in a decisive blow that might swing the advantage back to the British. Greene and Cornwallis met at Guilford Court House, North Carolina, in May – and Cornwallis army of only 2,000 men indeed succeeded in defeating Greene's army, which was twice the size of his. Greene was forced to retreat and leave the field of battle to Cornwallis. But Greene was also able to give Cornwallis the slip. And though Greene had lost the battle, his army was still quite intact. However, Cornwallis's victory had come at a huge cost in British casualties that he could not afford. Nonetheless Cornwallis persisted in his effort to try to chase down Greene and his Continental Army, only to have Greene constantly give him the slip. The effect on Cornwallis's troops was exhausting.

The siege of Yorktown (September-October 1781) – and the effective end of the war. Then Cornwallis turned his eyes north to Virginia, reasoning that if he did not succeed in breaking Virginia's resistance, he would not be able to solidify his hold over the South. In the meantime, turncoat Benedict Arnold was leading British and Tory troops on destructive raids on the northern Virginia countryside, targeting particularly the plantations and farms of the Patriots (or rebels, depending on how you looked at matters) which Arnold's Tory troops were pleased to burn to the ground.

In May (1781) Arnold and Cornwallis joined forces in central Virginia. Then in June, Cornwallis began to head eastward toward the Virginia coast, to Yorktown, located along the wide and deep York River. His plans were to dig in there with his army while awaiting reinforcements and supplies to be brought in by ship by way of the Chesapeake Bay.

In early August Washington abandoned his plan to attempt to seize New York City with his combined French (led by General Rochambeau) and Patriot forces – and instead decided to head south to Virginia to link up with French General Lafayette (who had been shadowing Arnold and Cornwallis) and even more importantly, to link up also with a huge French naval fleet under Admiral de Grasse heading north from the Caribbean to the Chesapeake Bay. Washington and Rochambeau's move South was miraculously kept hidden from Clinton, who kept his army in New York, believing that this was where Washington was planning to attack.

De Grasse's fleet arrived at the Chesapeake and in early September defeated not only the British fleet stationed there but also another fleet subsequently sent from New York by Clinton to break the French position. British failure left Cornwallis stranded at Yorktown, now surrounded on land by American and French forces and on sea by the French fleet.

The bombardment of Cornwallis' position became relentless and Cornwallis was now running out of food and supplies. Finally, in mid-October, with the Americans* and French able to break through his last line of defense, Cornwallis surrendered himself and his army of 8,000 men. Several days later a relief fleet of 7,000 British troops arrived at the Chesapeake. But hearing of Cornwallis's surrender, and realizing the hopelessness of trying to send an army ashore to a position strongly held by American and French troops, the fleet turned back to New York City.

No more major actions were to take place after Yorktown. As British Prime Minister Frederick Lord North exclaimed upon hearing the news back in England of Cornwallis surrender, "Oh God, it's all over." The war was indeed all over.

The Treaty of Paris (1783). Negotiations formally ending the war got underway in Paris in April of 1782. Representing the victorious former colonies, since 1776 calling themselves the "United States," was a delegation led by Ben Franklin, John Adams and John Jay. The Treaty of Paris, drafted in November of that year, was not formally signed in Paris until September 3, 1783. It was then ratified by the Congress of the Confederation of the United States on January 14, 1784 and by King George III on April 9, 1784 – finally granting formal recognition by the British of the full independence of the thirteen former colonial States. Terms of the treaty included the return of Loyalist property seized during the war (never really honored), British financial compensation to Americans who lost their slaves when the British freed them (also not ever honored), and recognition of the boundaries of the new United States (rather vaguely defined, and later a point of serious contention).

The war was officially over. And a new republic – and the early stages of a new nation – was now about to take its place in history.

---

*The final American assault on the last of the British redoubts (forts) was led by Washington's young staff officer, Alexander Hamilton. Hamilton and Washington had already grown very close as political associates and personal friends.

CHAPTER FOUR

THE BIRTH OF THE AMERICAN REPUBLIC

* * *

THE MACHINERY OF GOVERNMENT

Well, Doctor, what have we got – a Republic or a Monarchy?
A Republic ... if you can keep it.[30]

(Benjamin Franklin's reported response to a question asked of him as the delegates were leaving Independence Hall, having finalized the draft of a new American Constitution in 1787)

It is generally understood today that the term "American government" applies to some kind of self-standing institution, also referred to as the "state,"* assigned the powers to guide or direct Americans toward particular political goals. Supposedly this institution, the government or state, functions according to a set of basic operational rules (the Constitution and its many legal spinoffs) which empower and guide, but also restrict, the state in its operations.

In a typical class on American government it is this institution and its operations that come under study. Quite in line with the Enlightenment's understanding of the dynamics of life, the American government is treated as if it were some kind of great machine (thus the talk of the "machinery of government") that operates rather mechanically in providing guidance for the country. The structure and function of each of the various parts of the governmental machine are brought under careful study: Congress, the presidency, the courts, the bureaucracy, the political parties, the elections that fill the various positions or offices that run this government. The goal is to bring into focus the end products or policies and programs that this governmental machinery produces in order to make a better America:

---

*The English word "state" comes from the French word *état*, which in French means both "estate" and "state." The king's property or estate was the heart of the typical European "state."

road-building programs, assistance to farmers, the regulation of the value of the nation's currency, the policing of criminals, the collection of taxes to run the government, the defense of the nation's borders, etc.

This approach to the study of governmental mechanics is considered to be political science. Universities even offer a special degree to those who take up the advanced study of how such a governmental institution should be managed: the master's degree in public administration (the MPA). It's all very logical, all very mechanical, and ideally all very manageable from the heights of political power.

However, this study takes a very different approach to the idea of government and its mechanics. What this study is founded on is the central idea that government is that which governs (of course!). And what governs a society is largely the inner core of a people's sense of purpose, their sense of right and wrong, their sense of why it is important to work together as a people. A public institution such as the state is helpful to a people in symbolizing or clarifying these rather intangible intellectual, moral and spiritual ideas which govern their thoughts and actions. It is there also to set boundaries on human behavior when such moral discipline finds itself lacking in the hearts of certain individuals, or even whole communities.

But ultimately no mechanical institutions of state that govern the common folk from above can take the place of what the people, by their own training, habit, inclinations or loyalties can do on their own. For truly that which governs best is that which governs the hearts of a people.

* * *

THE ORIGINAL INTENTIONS OF THE DESIGNERS OR FRAMERS OF THE AMERICAN CONSTITUTION

Because of this tendency today of Americans to view their government as a set of mechanically operating public institutions governing the country from Washington, D.C., it is difficult to understand exactly the dynamic which directed the thoughts and actions of the Constitutional Framers back in 1787, as they attempted to put together a new political union. What today is widely understood as government was not at all what they were attempting to put together.

What they were aiming for certainly was designed to be much stronger than the Confederation, the system under which the newly independent thirteen American states had at first been attempting to work together – but not succeeding very well in the effort since the end of their war against England in 1783.

Was this new thing simply a treaty of alliance among thirteen newly independent states? Was it creating a new government? Did it in fact set up a new national state to preside over the affairs of the thirteen newly independent states and their people? What exactly was it?

The Framers termed it a republic. We today think more in terms of the Framers having created a democracy. They saw it as a federal union or alliance of thirteen independent states. We see it today as the foundation for a federal state governing from Washington, D.C. They could not see exactly what it might eventually become. We today have difficulty in seeing what it was and what these wise Framers originally intended it to be.

Certainly the last thing the Framers wanted to do was to create an all-dominant state. They had just gone through a long and brutal revolt against exactly that sort of institution: the monarchy of England. At that time, European kings or monarchs viewed all things within their royal estate – all lands, and all people and building on these lands – as being their property, belonging to their estate, and therefore under their complete dominion. People lived on their land or estate purely at the tolerance of the king, or so the kings claimed anyway. If you did not like this arrangement you could leave, presuming there was anywhere else to go, the dangerous wilderness of America being about the only possibility at the time.

The Framers were very sensitive about the dangers of tyranny coming from a strong central state. This concern was clearly laid out in their Declaration of Independence of 1776, which outlined one after another the many tyrannies that had developed of late under the English royal or monarchical state. Subsequently many young men had died in the effort to preserve the freedom of life in America against such tyranny. And the leaders of this revolt, which included many of those same men gathered in Philadelphia in 1787 to draft a new constitution, had put on their heads the price of treason They all would have been executed by the English authorities if their revolt had failed. They had so recently risked so much to preserve American liberties. Thus they were not in a mood to give those same liberties away to an American version of the English state that they had just succeeded getting the country out from under.

And yet they stood in grave danger of disunion and – if their new United States remained nothing more than a loose collection of very small, rather weak states – becoming easy prey for imperially ambitious European kings. England might return in an attempt to recapture these states. Even France or Spain might attempt something of the same nature if these thirteen newly independent states did not come up with some kind of stronger political union than this very weak confederacy they had been trying to operate under.

A revision or replacement of the inadequate Confederation? Thus they gathered in Philadelphia in the late spring of 1787 under Washington's rather silent leadership (a gathering which would take them into September to complete their work) to come up with a plan that would allow the various states (Virginia, Massachusetts, Pennsylvania, Georgia, etc.) to work together more closely ... and give their new political system more muscle to handle unexpected domestic problems as well.

The original thought was simply to revise the Articles of Confederation by strengthening the Continental Congress in its various legislative or law-making powers. But as they approached the scheduled gathering, a number of the delegates already realized that they needed to create an entirely new institution, one with enough authority to help them work together in some kind of closer harmony, yet with no more authority than absolutely necessary to fulfill that task.

Since the beginning of the revolt in the mid-1770s they had worked together as thirteen former colonies, now thirteen independent states, under some kind of sense of alliance. They had coordinated their revolt in accordance with the Articles of Confederation, which served as their first joint constitution (put together in 1776-1777 and finally fully ratified in 1781). The Articles and the Confederation had served them fairly well (though by no means perfectly) during the heat of battle against the English armies, supporting Washington's army (sometimes barely so!) and keeping them together in one mind and spirit during the dark days of the revolt. Yet now that this danger had passed, they faced a new danger of splitting apart into a number of contending mini-states.

Indeed, the thirteen states had recently begun to actually compete against each other politically and economically. They were putting up trade barriers to prevent the sale in their own states of the products of the other American states, in order to protect the production of their own farmers and manufacturers. They were even beginning to send out their own diplomats to work separate commercial deals with foreign powers (such as France, Spain and even England) in competition with each other.

If they did not cease this competitive selfishness, they would soon find themselves not only deeply divided but also easily conquered. In a condition of weakened disunity, they would most certainly provoke the lusts of power-hungry monarchs to return to America in a power grab designed to absorb these small, vulnerable states into their ever-expanding empires.

Yes, there was a treaty by which the English government had formally recognized the independence of the former American colonies, now fully sovereign states. But also remember that to European monarchs those treaties had no enduring value. They were quickly broken by ambitious kings when any new opportunity to gain additional territory or regain formerly lost territory presented itself. These American Patriots did not

The Birth of the American Republic 143

want their political divisions to offer those monarchs just that opportunity. They needed to come together in a union that would protect the sovereignty of all these new American states. They needed truly to be the United States of America.

Shays' Rebellion (1786–1787) in Western Massachusetts. Also an incident following the end of the War of Independence had put another type of scare on the political leaders of the newly independent states, leaders who came mostly from the ranks of the Southern landed gentry and the New England and Middle States upper middle class of lawyers, bankers, and merchants. This incident was reminiscent of Bacon's rebellion in Virginia a century earlier, and had the same unnerving effect on these gentlemen: they knew that they had to act decisively or face catastrophic domestic political disorder, a danger at home as great as the one posed by the power-hungry European monarchs abroad.

After the war a number of soldiers, who had received little or no pay for their years of service in the Continental Army, returned to their homes in rural Western Massachusetts, only to find that in their absence they had accumulated an unpayable debt on their land for taxes owed the local and state governments as well as unpaid mortgages owed to the merchants of the Eastern seaboard cities (such as Boston). Hard currency was scarce, a deep economic recession had set in upon America at this time, and there simply was no way for these farmer-soldiers to meet these debts. Appeals to the local and state authorities to help them out fell on deaf ears. They requested the opportunity to repay their debts in agricultural goods rather than in the scarce hard currency demanded by their upper-middle-class creditors in the East. But their nervous Eastern Massachusetts creditors insisted on repayment in full, in hard currency. Falling into bankruptcy, the farmers' lands were seized by the local courts for auction to cover the full amount of these obligations.

The farmer-soldiers were outraged at their treatment, and rebellions (one of them led by Daniel Shays, whose name was assigned to the broader event) broke out in a number of places in Central and Western Massachusetts.

It took the violent confrontation by the Massachusetts militia – and the appearance of General Washington on the scene – to break the spirit of the rebellion, just as the delegates were gathering in Philadelphia to consider a revised or even new political union.

This near run-away event was clearly much on the delegates' minds as they arrived to begin their work. They obviously needed some kind of system to bring social order to their new America, or if not attacked from abroad by foreign powers they would be shattered from within by disenchanted social classes of Americans.

Strength and unity without tyranny. Thus those who gathered in Philadelphia in 1787 knew they needed a strong central bond in order to keep themselves fully united, as they had been in the years of the war. But at the same time this bond must not be so powerful as to compromise the powers of the individual states – which they believed were the better preservers of the liberties of the people. Indeed, they needed an idea, a political ideal, that could continue to command the loyalties of all Americans, a governing system with enough power – but not too much power – assigned to a uniting central authority. This required a delicate balancing act which they would have to perform in order to succeed in this enterprise.

Failed historical precedents. But they had no very successful precedents in history that they could model their new system of government after.

They were all well-educated men and quite aware, through their considerable knowledge of both Biblical and classical history, of the lack of long-term success of Ancient Israel, the ancient Athenian Democracy and the ancient Roman Republic, political systems which came closest in form to what they sought to build in America. Sadly, all systems had failed to maintain their original purposes as governments.

Athens as a democracy had been directly run by the citizens of Athens – much as the local communities in the American colonies had been run for the past 150 years. But the Athenian citizens had been easily manipulated by clever politicians (the Sophists or wise men) so as to turn Athens itself into a tyrannical state dominating and exploiting its neighboring city-states, leading to a violent rebellion among those Greek city-states. This produced the ruinous Greek civil war known as the Peloponnesian War – and ultimately the political destruction of Athens itself. Thus the Philadelphia delegates understood clearly that even a democracy, poorly led, could turn itself into a popular tyranny which would inevitably self-destruct.[*]

As for Rome, the delegates remembered that Rome started off quite well as a republic. The idea of Roman government as a republic was that it was intended to be a government of carefully designed and quite fixed and

---

[*]The Greek philosopher Aristotle was cool on the idea of democracy, or any particular form of government, whether by one, a few or the many. To Aristotle it was not the form of government but the morality of the people and their leaders that distinguished good government from bad government. Aristotle's famous teacher Plato was even harder on the idea of democracy, seeing how easily the democratic masses were led to call for the death of Plato's great teacher Socrates. The Framers of the Constitution were well aware of the opinions of both Plato and Aristotle.

permanent fundamental laws, and not just the result of the changing and usually foolish ambitions of particular men, whether a few powerful figures, or the many, as in tribal societies such as existed everywhere in Italy in the formative days of the Roman city-state.

A governing system of laws favored no particular class, ethnic group or even individuals, and allowed the Romans to expand the domain of Rome as neighboring societies were brought under submission – but whose people of these neighboring societies were then invited by the Romans to become part of the Roman Republic itself as its newest citizens under the law. This proved to be a generous and very successful strategy for building and expanding the Republic.

At first, the Republic served Roman popular interests well. Rome was too big to be ruled directly by the people as in the early Athenian democracy. So the people elected representatives to rule on their behalf. The system still belonged to the people but was administered by their elected representatives, much like the American colonies had been governed at the highest level of authority in each of their individual colonies. In fact most of the Framers of the Constitution had a republic in mind as they set out to redesign an American political system.

But sadly, in the long run, the Roman Republic failed to continue to respect Rome's legal ideals, and ultimately therefore failed to represent all the people as well, despite repeated attempts to perfect the system through the implementing of various new constitutions. The Republic eventually became merely the tool of the more wealthy and powerful patrician members of society. Revolts against this tendency of the Roman Republic toward oligarchy (rule by the favored few) were frequent and brutal on the part of the increasingly impoverished and consequently very angry common people (the plebeians).

The military chose to intervene more and more in the name of the plebeians to bring peace to Rome. Finally, the military legions led by the Caesars took permanent control of the Roman government. Thus the Roman Republic gradually transformed itself into an imperium, a military state or empire ruled by the *imperators* (emperors) or commanders of the Roman army, who would govern *for* the people (no longer *by* the people). Tragically, the Republic had failed to maintain itself because of its inability to stay socially self-disciplined by the fundamentals of Roman law, and thus therefore by the traditional political restraints on power politics – even politics conducted supposedly on behalf of the people.

Popular government (government by the people) ... could this turn into a democratic tyranny as in ancient Athens? Or could an American republic preserve itself against the growth of bitterly contending special interests (as in Western Massachusetts farmers versus the Eastern seaboard financiers)

– and the tendency of men to call on the force of arms to decide political outcomes even within a peaceful society as in ancient Rome (also as in Western Massachusetts!)? Nothing was very promising about the historical record left behind by Athens and Rome. They had meant well, had started out satisfactorily enough, but had failed to maintain their original political – or moral – course and eventually turned themselves into tyrannies, and thus declined and died.

* * *

THE STRONG CHRISTIAN COMPONENT IN THE DISCUSSIONS AT THE CONSTITUTIONAL CONVENTION IN PHILADELPHIA

The example also of Ancient Israel. These men were also aware of another example of an ancient people who had tried to be self-ruling, similar to what the Americans were trying to do. These constitutional Framers were quite well read up on the Bible and were very aware of the sad record of the ancient Israelites in their efforts to stay a strong, yet free people. Indeed, as Christians, the Framers were very well aware that human sin (pride, jealousy, lust for power, etc.) stood as a constant threat to any effort to empower a central authority.

For generations, God alone was ancient Israel's sovereign. The Israelites had called on him time and again to protect and preserve them against their enemies – foreign and domestic. But their loyalties to God were most unsteady. Finally at one point, the people called out to their spiritual leader Samuel, "Give us a king." They felt that they could be more successful as a people if they were more like the other nations around them, ruled not by some invisible God but by a very visible, very politically impressive king. But through the counsel of Samuel, Israel was warned by God himself that their effort to have a government like other nations would be their downfall. But they wanted a king to rule over them nonetheless. And so God gave them a king. But as Samuel had predicted, in this move away from God the Israelites soon fell under the political tyranny of their kings. The kings took away the Israelites' liberties and amassed considerable wealth and power of their own at the expense of the people.

The Protestant component. This was exactly what the American colonists had felt had come to pass with the English kings. The English kings had tried to take the place in the life of the nation that belonged only to God. This effort of the kings to play God, claiming Divine Rights to do so, was what had finally prompted their revolt, their War of Independence. All Americans, as Protestant Calvinists (New England Congregationalists,

Reformed Dutch, Middle Colonies Presbyterians, etc.), Baptists, Quakers and even as Church of England vestrymen, well understood that they too had Divine Rights which no king had the right to disregard or trample on.

Indeed, in one form or another nearly all of those who assembled to draft this new venture into republican government were Christians, Protestant Christians. They were politically informed by their own sense of the longer history of the Church. Protestantism was very aware of the fact that prior to the adoption of Christianity by the Roman emperors in the 300s, Christianity had been a free religion, under no central political control, but self-governing by small communities of believers themselves in accordance with their strongly Christian moral consciences and ingrained spiritual beliefs. The Christians of the first three centuries of the Church had survived terrible persecution from the Roman political authorities and yet not only had kept themselves together as a people but had grown rapidly at the same time. Pure Christianity needed no hierarchical authority to organize and direct the faith of the true believer.

But with the conversion of Roman Emperor Constantine to Christianity in the early 300s, Christianity had become Romanized, that is brought under the political organization and protection of the Roman political hierarchy. From the Protestant point of view, this was a horrible step backward for the Christian faith, for this development made the faith henceforth a matter more of the political interests of the politically powerful than that of the personal faith of the individual believer. Protestantism was fiercely sensitive on this subject.

Thus the Framers tended to be strongly anti-hierarchical in both their religion and their politics. The Puritan-Protestant predecessors of the Framers had lived in terror of the forced Catholicization of England which the Catholic powers of Europe (principally their perpetual enemies Spain and France) sought to promote. The sending of the Spanish Armada to England in 1588 was loudly justified by Spanish King Philip II as a result of God's command to him as Defender of the Faith to bring the English back to the True Faith (Catholicism) – by force if necessary.

The humiliating defeat of Philip's mighty naval Armada therefore ranked not only as a victory for English independence but also as victory in the defense of their Protestant faith. This conflict with the Spanish consequently left an even deeper dislike of hierarchical Catholicism among Protestant Englishmen. In part, the Glorious Revolution in England a century later was prompted by the evidence that English King James II was secretly Catholic in loyalties and planning an alliance with Catholic France to crush the power of the highly Protestant English Whigs who controlled Parliament.

Protestantism as political culture. Thus the Protestant faith of the English colonists was a matter of great political, economic and social importance to them. Their personal freedom and their religious faith were to them inseparable items. As Protestants they chose their own pastors, elected their own elders and deacons to manage their local congregations, read and interpreted their Bible readings on their own – without a priest performing that function for them – and came to their own opinions on theological matters themselves as a matter of their basic rights. This was a matter of great personal distinction to them.

Indeed, not only was the idea of having their lands to the West put under Catholic hierarchical authority that reached to Rome – but also the idea (which was being discussed openly by King George III) of putting the English colonies under the authority of the Anglican bishops (which the king himself personally supervised) had been one of the underlying reasons they finally declared their independence from the English king in 1776.

Their Protestant faith registered itself not only in terms of the things they opposed (namely, hierarchically-controlled religion) but the things they aspired to. Their republican instincts were shaped strongly by the way their churches operated. Their church officers were elected by the congregation on a regular basis and, at least on the part of the very strong Presbyterian component among them, they even developed regional representative government in the form of their Synods (Senates) attended by pastoral and lay representatives. Ultimately, community life, both religious and civil – by long established habit – was to their understanding always governed from the ground up, not the top down. They strongly conceived of government as being collegial rather than hierarchical. Generations of them had lived and died for this principle. They would have it no other way.

God as the guarantor of the success of America's new Republic. Indeed, the constitutional Framers who gathered at Philadelphia in 1787 saw themselves and their challenge very much operating within the context of God's will. They were very well aware that God Almighty, which in the fashion of the times they often referred to as "Providence" as in "The One Who Provides," was the one empowerment that had enabled them recently to succeed in their very risky revolt. Apart from the direct – and frequent – assistance from God, it would have been highly unlikely that a handful of mere commoners could have ever succeeded on their own in a revolt against a powerful king and his army.

They knew well, and testified often to the fact, that only God had made the success of the American revolt possible. They all understood that it was not the size of the American army, nor the cleverness of their generals – but it was the hand of God operating among them that had

The Birth of the American Republic

brought them successfully through these trying times.

Ben Franklin's reminder. At one point in late June of 1787, during the heated debates in Philadelphia over what kind of government they had been commissioned to create, Ben Franklin arose to address the assembly, with a proposal that seemed amazingly out of character for this great champion of earthly wisdom – namely, that the group should start each of its daily deliberations in prayer:

> Mr. President
>
> The small progress we have made after 4 or five weeks close attendance & continual reasonings with each other, our different sentiments on almost every question, several of the last producing as many noes and ays, is methinks a melancholy proof of the imperfection of the Human Understanding.
>
> We indeed seem to feel our own want of political wisdom, some we have been running about in search of it. We have gone back to ancient history for models of Government, and examined the different forms of those Republics which having been formed with the seeds of their own dissolution now no longer exist. And we have viewed Modern States all round Europe, but find none of their Constitutions suitable to our circumstances.
>
> In this situation of this Assembly, groping as it were in the dark to find political truth, and scarce able to distinguish it when presented to us, how has it happened, Sir, that we have not hitherto once thought of humbly applying to the Father of lights to illuminate our understandings?
>
> In the beginning of the Contest with G. Britain, when we were sensible of danger we had daily prayer in this room for the divine protection. Our prayers, Sir, were heard, and they were graciously answered. All of us who were engaged in the struggle must have observed frequent instances of a Superintending providence in our favor. To that kind providence we owe this happy opportunity of consulting in peace on the means of establishing our future national felicity. And have we now forgotten that powerful friend?
>
> I have lived, Sir, a long time, and the longer I live, the more convincing proofs I see of this truth that God governs in the affairs of men. And if a sparrow cannot fall to the ground without his notice, is it probable that an empire can rise without his aid?
>
> We have been assured, Sir, in the sacred writings, that except the Lord build the House they labour in vain that build

> it. I firmly believe this; and I also believe that without his concurring aid we shall succeed in this political building no better than the Builders of Babel: We shall be divided by our little partial local interests; our projects will be confounded, and we ourselves shall become a reproach and bye word down to future ages. And what is worse, mankind may hereafter from this unfortunate instance, despair of establishing Governments by Human Wisdom and leave it to chance, war and conquest.
>
> I therefore beg leave to move, that henceforth prayers imploring the assistance of Heaven, and its blessings on our deliberations, be held in this Assembly every morning before we proceed to business, and that one or more of the Clergy of the City be requested to officiate in that service.[31]

And thus Franklin, the widely respected voice of American pragmatic wisdom, summed up the situation that faced the designers of America's new political system.

Madison, who recorded the events of the Convention (including Franklin's speech), noted that the motion was seconded by Roger Sherman, but met by a concern (voiced by Alexander Hamilton) that in taking up this policy at this late date in the process, people would interpret this resolution as merely the result of the embarrassments and dissentions among the delegates (which was indeed the case). Randolph of Virginia then came to the support of the Franklin proposal with a motion of his own specifying how this resolution was to be enacted. But the business of the day ended without any vote on Randolph's motion.

We cannot state that the Constitutional Convention at this point then turned itself into a gathering of some kind of saintly religious synod. But clearly all present understood the significance of what Franklin had just brought to their attention. In the end what would guarantee the wisdom and durability of this constitutional enterprise rested ultimately not on the flawed and contentious wisdom of man, but instead on the mercies of the God that Provides for his people, especially in guiding their thoughts and actions.

Furthermore, the matter at hand was not just one of providing the thirteen states with some kind of political formula for cooperation, but was (as it had always been) that of building a test society, a demonstration model founded specially to give hope to all mankind that a people's government was not only possible, but was also able to stand strong against forces that would like to return the little people, the commoners of the earth, back under the domination of the high and mighty. Thus there could be no failure in this important enterprise.

Franklin.[32] Benjamin Franklin was a very complex individual, witty, even a bit of a showman, a journalist and publisher, a scientist and inventor, a skilled politician and diplomat, and a philosopher possessed of a folk wisdom that cut through folly and conceit in order to bring authentic understanding of life to light. He was a strong Christian, but never dogmatic in his beliefs so that one could therefore identify him with this or that particular religious group. Some identified him as a Deist, who believed merely in some kind of Creator-God that simply observed life from above – and that perhaps (maybe) controlled the gates of Heaven, opening or closing them to a person at death depending on that person's moral performance while on earth. But actually Franklin's Christian faith varied widely over the course of his life, from a very early negative reaction to the strict Puritanism of his parents, to indeed something that looked like regular Deism, to an interest in the power of passionate Christian revival to alter a person's course in life, to an understanding that indeed God is very active in the course of life for both individuals and societies. But in any case, he was a very independent thinker on all subjects near and dear to him (which were vast in scope). Certainly it was easy to believe that he mostly was just a secular scientist focused primarily in studying the mechanics of life (especially this matter of electricity). Yet others could see in him a person seriously concerned about the religious matters that were important to all Christians (or Jews), but in such a way that Christians, ranging from Roman Catholics to Quakers, could easily believe that he was definitely one of their particular faith. The man was brilliant, a Humanist in the very best sense of the word, not really a lofty or isolated Idealist but very much the intensely involved Realist, and a person able to touch the hearts of others in a way that truly stood him out as one of the Greats of the Age.

He was born in Boston in 1706, the last male of seventeen children born to his father and his two subsequent wives, given formal schooling only until age ten, supposing himself headed to the ministry. But at age twelve he took an apprenticeship in a printing business run by an older brother, James. But at seventeen, Benjamin broke from that relationship (an illegal act at the time) and escaped to Philadelphia to work in printing shops there, before heading off to London to do the same. A couple of years later he returned to Philadelphia, where he not only resumed his work in the publishing business but formed a discussion group (English coffeehouse style) of young members that combined their libraries and engaged in far-ranging discussions of social interest. Young Franklin was very interested in public matters, and soon started up a series of newspapers that offered commentary on the world around him, especially on the matter of what brought societies to virtue and thus happiness, a theme that would remain central to Franklin for the rest of his life.

In 1730 he took up a common-law relationship with Deborah Read, whom he was not allowed to marry because she was already married to a man that ran off with her money, never to be heard from again. Franklin brought into that relationship a son, William, born to him earlier by possibly another woman (or perhaps by Deborah herself?) and a surviving daughter, who would accompany and look after her father after her mother died. He and Deborah remained together until her death in 1774.

In 1733 Franklin began to publish his annual *Poor Richard's Almanack*, offering advice on all sorts of daily matters, along with a multitude of witty sayings that became catch-phrases of the day. The work (which ran from 1732 to 1758) was very popular ... whose sales made the Franklin family quite prosperous.

But his curiosity about life and how it worked did not stop there. He loved to experiment with better ways of doing ordinary things, inventing multitudes of new objects along the way, such as the Franklin stove, bifocals, an elaborate glass harmonica, but especially things connected with the new idea of electricity (including eventually the lightning rod, a dangerous venture which killed others who tried to follow his lead). This latter interest soon had him considered to be one of the leading scientists of the day, and he found himself closely involved with the growing scientific community, especially during his many extensive stays abroad in Europe.

He was no less an inventor in the field of education, helping to develop in the 1750s a New-Model college curriculum taught not by tutor generalists but by professional specialists in different academic fields, and then to see this curriculum put into play in the new King's College (ultimately, Columbia University) and the College of Philadelphia (ultimately, part of the University of Pennsylvania) – the latter which Franklin also co-founded.

But it was in the field of politics that Franklin would be best remembered. From the mid–1750s onward, Franklin spent much time in London as a representative of the Pennsylvania Assembly, in part to press the case against the autocracy of the Penn family (Penn's descendants were less generous than their Pennsylvania founder). But eventually his main concern would come to be over the new taxes (especially the expensive government stamps required on all publications) being imposed on the colonies by King George's Tory Parliament. With his opposition to the 1765 Stamp Act, he became well-known back in the colonies as a key advocate for a cause that touched not only Pennsylvania, but all the colonies mutually.

But tragically this would put Franklin in deep opposition to his son William, who by Franklin's own intervention had been awarded the position as Governor of New Jersey. This royal appointment was to make William a very strong Tory leader in the colonies, at the same time that his father was becoming a leading voice in the colonies' rising spirit of rebellion. The

The Birth of the American Republic

two would split over this matter, never to be reconciled.

When Franklin returned finally from London in 1775, the rebellion had already begun, and Franklin was appointed as a Pennsylvania delegate to the Second Continental Congress, where he was also chosen to be a member of the five-man committee commissioned to draft a Declaration of Independence.

But then he was soon sent off to France (1776) to be something of an ambassador to the French court for the new United States. Here he not only worked hard to coordinate the French support of the American rebellion (and its needs for French soldiers and supplies), but he dazzled the French Court with his (purposely stylized) rustic appearance and homespun wit and wisdom (John Adams, who was there with him at the time, found Franklin's folksy theatrics totally distasteful!). Franklin would remain there throughout the War, ultimately helping negotiate the Treaty of Paris (1783) in which the British recognized the independence of the new United States of America. Then Franklin returned to America in 1785, soon after he and Adams were joined in Paris by the young Jefferson. This would bring Franklin back in time to serve (as we have just seen) as a Pennsylvania delegate to the Constitutional Convention being held in Philadelphia over the summer of 1787.

The Framers understood the dangers of building only on human logic. Franklin's appeal registered itself as strongly as it did because all present knew well the Biblical story of the Fall of Adam and Eve from God's Paradise. Adam and Eve had ignored God's warning not to eat from the Tree of the Knowledge of Good and Evil (human logic), but instead had followed the Serpent's advice to do exactly that because it would make them be "like God." The temptation to play God by assuming for themselves the knowledge of Good and Evil was too great for Adam and Eve to resist. But in breaking that command, disaster struck. What they got for their efforts was only a half-truth (the most dangerous of all lies). Apart from the fundamental guidance of God, their logic could not guide them except in merely self-justifying circles. It did not produce true knowledge. Their logic was only technique – not Truth itself.

Truth came from a deeper source of life – from a depth that human logic itself could never reach. Only a close, fully trusting relationship with the Author of Life – and Life's basic Truths as God ordained them – offered true knowledge. But by their disobedience, by their questing for knowledge apart from God, Adam and Eve had ruptured that vital relationship. They were on their own with their own sophistication (as in the sophistication of the Sophists of Ancient Athens). But this sophistication only made them all the more aware of life's shortcomings, especially in others, whom they blamed for their problems. Ultimately this broken relationship with God ended in death – their death. Not a pretty picture!

The Framers understood very well the moral of that story: human logic was not the answer to life's challenges. Relationship, holding together in a spirit of unity, and holding to God as the ultimate judge and ruler of life, was the path they needed to follow. The better way would come if they were willing to submit their particular self-interests, and the moral and tactical logic man used in defense of those self-interests, in support of the greater bond that held them together as Americans – Americans under God.

What they ultimately formulated as their new American government was a rather simple alliance system that encouraged them to work together without according too many powers to the system itself. This new federal system was their response to the challenge.

Even then they knew that this new system would work only if man's hunger for power (as in Adam and Eve's desire to play God) was held in check. A deep respect for – and even fear of – God among the people was the only way they felt that things might stay on course as they faced the many challenges ahead of them. This was a component missing in the logical systems of the philosophers, ancient and modern. It was not missing in the thinking of the Framers of the Constitution. In fact it held a central or foundational place in their understanding of things.

> *For my own part, I sincerely esteem it [the Constitution] a system which without the finger of God, never could have been suggested and agreed upon by such a diversity of interests.* Alexander Hamilton – 1787[33]

> *Of all the dispositions and habits which lead to political prosperity, Religion and Morality are indispensable supports. . . . And let us with caution indulge the supposition that morality can be maintained without religion. . . . Reason and experience both forbid us to expect that national morality can prevail in exclusion of religious principle.* George Washington – Farewell Address, 1796.

> *We have no government armed with power capable of contending with human passions unbridled by morality and religion. Avarice, ambition, revenge, or gallantry, would break the strongest cords of our Constitution as a whale goes through a net. Our Constitution was made only for a moral and religious*

people. It is wholly inadequate to the government of any other.
John Adams – to the Massachusetts Militia, 11 October 1798.

The belief in a God All Powerful wise and good, is so essential to the moral order of the world and to the happiness of man, that arguments which enforce it cannot be drawn from too many sources nor adapted with too much solicitude to the different characters and capacities to be impressed with it. James Madison – Letter to Frederick Beasley, November 20, 1825

Comparing the Christian American and Secular French efforts at republic-building in the late 1700s. Contrast the American approach to self-government in 1787 with the French Revolution which broke out two years later in 1789 – just as the American Constitution went into effect. The French were led simply by their belief in the power of human reason or logic – especially their own logic (that is, the logic of their political leaders) – which they supposed would produce a Platonically perfect French Republic.

God played no part in the plans of the French reformers. Indeed, their mood was generally hostile to the idea of God (whom they frequently mocked), for they understood liberty as freedom from religion. They viewed religion, the Christian faith in particular, as a key component of the very Old Order that they were bent on overthrowing. They were determined to be ruled not by God but by man – by man's basic ability to do the right thing, the logical thing.

But when finally, with the eruption of the French Revolution in 1789, given the chance to put their philosophy to practice, the French revolutionaries could not agree among themselves as to what exactly constituted the right thing, the reasonable, or logical thing. One man's logic was not another man's logic. Soon they fell from their Idealism into mutually hostile intellectual camps – and then proceeded to bring each other to slaughter under the French guillotine (the Reign of Terror: 1792–1794).

Ultimately, their attempt to found their new system on the belief in the great powers of human Reason – that such Reason provided the assurance that the system would work harmoniously – resulted only in disaster. So their experiment in republican democracy proved ultimately no more successful in producing utopia than the ancient Athenian democracy when it came under the ideological domination of the Sophists.

Finally the dictatorship of Napoleon (1799–1815) brought the French under some kind of political order. It took a new form of tyranny to rescue them from the tyranny of unrestrained human self-interest – and the reason or logic used to justify such self-interest.

So much for human Reason and the Idealistic belief that man's Reason opened the way to some kind of absolute Truth and Goodness! Yet it would be a sophisticated belief that would never seem to die, despite the ugly historical record of man's continuing attempts to build utopias on the basis of human Reason alone.

The Framers of the Constitution for the most part* were very aware of such potential dangers. Thus the American "Revolution" they presided over, suspicious of unrestrained human behavior and thus cautiously minimalist in its utopian efforts, succeeded awesomely in creating a viable republic – whereas the French Revolution failed miserably.

* * *

THE PROCESS OF COMING TO AN AGREEMENT

A note of caution here. It is extremely important to note that the delegates who gathered in Philadelphia to devise a new political formula for the purpose of a closer political union among the thirteen states, were not (like the French) inexperienced in republican self-government. Not only had Americans been operating for years under the Confederation government, but the states these delegates represented had already put into effect their own constitutions as independent states. Thus each of them had a pretty good idea of what American government was to look like, at least in principle.

Indeed, Americans had been practicing some form or other of constitutional self-government since their ancestors put England behind them in coming to America, some century and a half earlier.†

Thus it is important to note that these Founding Fathers of the late 1700s were not inventing self-government. They already understood quite well the principles involved in effective self-government. Rather, they were

---

*Except probably Jefferson, who anyway was away during the drafting of the new Constitution, serving as America's Minister (Ambassador) to France (1785–1789). In Paris, he was wholly enraptured by the reformist spirit of the French *philosophes* (intellectuals or philosophers), a spirit which was clearly driving France toward revolution. Jefferson, being himself a utopian idealist, long remained a devout defender of the French Revolution, which finally broke out in 1789 (just before he returned to America). Indeed, he was one of the last to finally admit that the murderous Reign of Terror into which France soon fell had tragically betrayed the original high ideals of the French utopian philosophers he once so greatly admired.

†The royal charters of the 1600s that birthed each of the American colonies were themselves "constitutions" of sorts, describing precisely the purposes and practices that the colonies were to live by.

The Birth of the American Republic 157

trying to figure out a formula for collective self-government that would allow them to continue to work together as a union at a level higher than each newly independent state.

They were not naive (like the French, and like many Americans today), believing that some utopian formula discovered by some political genius among them was what they needed. Rather, they knew that each delegate that gathered there had a somewhat different political agenda he would be pursuing – and they were going to have to work together in full respect of those different agendas or interests if together they were going to find the necessary common ground on which to build a new union government.

With the benefit of considerable political experience, and with God's counsel opening their hearts to each other, they would succeed.

In short, American government itself was not birthed in 1787 – as we so often tend to imply when we talk about the birth of the Republic that year. Actually, long-standing traditions in American government were simply adjusted to meet the ever-clearer needs for a more effective union among the thirteen newly independent states.

Divergent interests. By no means did the fifty-five delegates who gathered in Philadelphia at the end of May in 1787 have the same idea, some widely agreed upon logic, as to what was supposed to result from their work. They represented not only a wide array of states, big and small, but also different life-styles (major plantation owners, prosperous urban tradesmen, lawyers, etc.). The states they represented also found themselves in deep contention about how exactly their particular borders extended to the West beyond the Appalachian Mountains. And most important, they held very different ideas about what kind of government reforms they wanted to see take place.

Federalists and Anti-Federalists. Some like Washington, John Adams, Alexander Hamilton, and James Madison were strong nationalists or Federalists who were hoping to see a much stronger political hand holding the thirteen states together. But others who came to Philadelphia were of the opposite opinion, thus strongly Anti-Federalist, fearing that just such a political union would usurp the very freedoms they had so recently fought to secure against the ambitions of the English King George III. In fact, major figures in the recent War of Independence, such as Samuel Adams and Patrick Henry had refused to participate in the Convention, fearing that it would saddle them with just such a government. Likewise, the tiny state of Rhode Island did not even bother to send participants to the meeting, fearing the loss of their independence to the interests of the larger states such as Massachusetts, New York, Pennsylvania and Virginia.

The Virginia Plan. Almost immediately upon arrival to Philadelphia the delegates set aside the idea of merely amending the Articles of Confederation. Indeed, James Madison had busied himself in drafting up a proposal before the Convention had even convened. His proposal set out some basic principles which pointed to a national government with a number of strong powers, which his own Virginia delegation and the Pennsylvania delegation were quick to agree on, thus giving it considerable weight. Indeed his Virginia Plan was put forward at the Convention as the opening document, calling up countering documents, or at least offering itself as a document to which amendments and details could then be added.

His Virginia Plan provided for a bicameral legislature of two separate bodies, an upper and a lower house, on the order of the English Parliament with its House of Lords and House of Commons, a principle followed as well in the design of the governments of most of the individual states. In this it departed from the Confederation's single or unicameral assembly (the Continental Congress), which had demonstrated how a unicameral legislature tended to be easily susceptible to the swings of political mood which accompanied popular politics (politics of the people). The hope was that a second legislative body could counterbalance the passions of a popular assembly because, like the English House of Lords, the second body would be expected to be made up of a smaller group of more distinguished statesmen. However, how that group might be chosen was left open as a key question.

Also Madison's Virginia Plan provided for a stronger, more independent executive, not quite like a king but stronger than the executives of the Confederation – and many of the states – who were largely dependent on the legislative bodies for their powers, and thus lacking in any significant power to direct and lead the nation. Anyway, most of the delegates were expecting Washington to head up the new government, and it was important to assign him sufficient powers and independence of action to bring his talents to full service to the country. But the question remained: was he to be the sole executive (and thus more like a king) or was he to share his function with one or two others (as was done anciently)? What would be his term of service: serving for life (and thus indeed like a king), or elected, and probably re-elected, annually or for periods of greater length?

And there was the matter of the judiciary or body of judges, who by English tradition were extensions of the king's authority. Efforts of the states to make their judges instead dependent on the appointive powers of the legislatures had produced less than distinguished judges, and elements of well-known political corruption. How such judges should be selected was thus a major problem that brought on much debate.

The Birth of the American Republic

The debate begins. The first issue to come under heated debate was the selection of the representatives to the new Congress. The Virginia Plan assumed that the size of the representation in Congress (both upper and lower houses) would be on the basis of the number of voters in each state, which would clearly give the bigger states a dominant voice in the new government. But Virginia seemed willing to listen to some kind of compromise that would bring the states together in their thinking.

The smaller states were hoping for equal representation by the states, irrespective of size. Representing the interests of the smaller states, the New Jersey delegates thus offered a counter-proposal to the Virginia Plan which called for the continuing existence of the Continental Congress as a single unicameral body, with each member state holding equal representation, despite the size, large or small, of each state.* But it would be given new powers such as in the collecting of taxes and the power to override the state laws. This gave the smaller states a rallying point to put forward their political interests. But overall it was an idea that the larger states clearly were unwilling to accept.

The Connecticut Compromise. Then Roger Sherman of Connecticut offered an idea supporting the Virginia Plan's call for a bicameral Congress, but with one chamber (the House of Representatives) giving the states representation on the basis of the relative size of their population, but the second chamber (the Senate) giving each of the states equal representation (desired by the smaller states). At first Sherman's idea was rejected, as the states large and small were holding out in protection of their respective political interests.† Also there were other issues that undermined the spirit of compromise necessary to break the political impasse.

One of the issues that would long stir turmoil in the new Republic was this matter of slavery. Almost half of the delegates to the Convention (and all of the Virginia and South Carolina delegates) were slave owners. But in general Northerners tended to be adamantly opposed to the idea and practice of slavery; indeed many of the Northern states had included a total prohibition of slavery in their new state constitutions. But Southerners could not bring themselves to imagine seriously a Southern economy able to function without slavery. Some made it clear that they would not join the new Union if slavery were somehow disallowed.

---

*The Continental Congress which had guided the 13 states during the War of Independence had given each state simply a single vote, regardless of the number of individuals – usually two to six or seven – a state had representing it in Congress.

†It was at this point that Franklin asked the Convention to bring God into its deliberations as a means of transcending their deep differences.

Moreover, the Southern states were adamant on the matter of including their slaves in the calculation of the representation in the House of Representatives. But Northerners were quick to point out that slaves weren't citizens. Thus should they be counted at all? Some Northerners even quipped that since slaves had merely the status of property rather than of free citizen, Northern cattle should be added to the count for the Northern representation in the House of Representatives!*

Ultimately another compromise was eventually reached when it was decided that slaves should count as three-fifths of a person!

Anyway, most of the Southern Framers were of the opinion that slavery would soon die a natural death, though they had no idea of how that might happen. And so they basically dodged the issue – and would continue to do so until it blew up in their faces in the early 1860s.

* * *

A FEDERATION REPLACES THE CONFEDERATION

What the Framers ultimately came up with as they concluded their work in mid-September was a central or federal political authority with just enough power to keep the states working together in a sense of American unity, but with enough limits to its powers to insure that it would not fall into the human sin of unchecked power hunger that led inevitably to tyranny.

Congress or the legislative branch of the federal government. In a sense what they had finally agreed on was a new treaty of political alliance among the thirteen independent states,† a treaty stronger than the one that had empowered the Confederation. This new treaty instead provided for a federation, meaning a political union with strong powers (though only in certain carefully prescribed areas of governance) assigned to a central authority by the still quite strong individual state governments that made up the Union.

The heart of this federation was to be a newly empowered Congress (one with wider powers than the older Continental Congress), which would meet periodically to enact certain categories of legislation for the Union. This Congress, as per the Connecticut Compromise, was to be made up of two separate assemblies. The lower house, the House of Representatives, would represent the American people directly, elected by them and thus

---

*Indians were never part of the count!

†Although Rhode Island did not send a delegation to participate in the drafting of the new Constitution, Rhode Island did finally join the Union in 1790

giving the new federal Union something of a democratic quality. But the upper house, the Senate, would represent instead the states, each of the participating states being permitted to select and send two of its most respected statesmen to Congress to give direct voice to the interests of their respective states. Also, the Senate was supposed to be something of a more aristocratic assembly, a council of political dignitaries who were to keep cooler political heads than what might be expected of the representatives of the people in the House of Representatives.* But in any case, Congress would be able to function only as both the House and the Senate worked together.

The president or the executive branch. Congress was intended to be the political center of the whole system: a place where representatives of the states and the American people themselves might gather to do the business of the Union. But the Constitution provided also for an executive officer, a president, whose primary job was to oversee the ongoing unity of these United States. He was to be no king but only a political supervisor elected for a term of four years (presumably renewable however), elected not by the people, but by the states whose union he presided over. Actually it was the duty of an electoral college to choose the president (called into existence every four years solely for that single purpose), each state accorded a number of electors equal to the number of representatives they were entitled to have in the House of Representatives, plus an additional two electors (as thus also each state had two senators). Each state was given the right or responsibility to decide who those electors were to be, with the important restriction being that they could not be chosen from among the ranks of a state's congressional representatives or senators.

The president was given a key leadership duty in being the one to call Congress into legislative session (even call special sessions of Congress if need be) and to report to Congress on his observations as to the "State of the Union." He was also expected to be the enforcer, that is, the one assigned the task of seeing that the laws passed by Congress were indeed faithfully executed or followed throughout the Union. In short, he was seen primarily as an executor of Congress's legislation, although possessing limited veto or blocking power if he deemed such legislation inappropriate to the health of the Union. But even then, if Congress could on a second attempt at passage gather, instead of just the usual simple majority for passage, a full two-thirds vote approving the proposed bill (a much more difficult political feat to carry off), Congress could override the president's veto, and the bill would become in fact actual law.

---

*However the Senate was "democratized" in 1913 with the passing of the Seventeenth Amendment, having the voters of each state, rather than the state assemblies, select their two senators.

The president did have additional functions that fell to him alone, such as sending and receiving diplomats, symbolizing the majesty of the United States, and along those same lines was given the responsibility of overseeing the country's relations with other countries. He also was given the responsibility of serving as the commander in chief of the U.S. military, a vital role in the follow-up to his foreign policy responsibilities (however he could not actually employ this military except when specifically authorized to do so by the Congress). And also, as Congress met only periodically, he (and his cabinet staff) was given the task of the ongoing or day-to-day administration of the federal system at the all-union or national* level.

The Supreme Court or the judicial branch. The Constitution also described a Supreme Court of federal judges or justices, largely expected to act in accordance with British legal tradition in seeing to the fair application of the laws of the legislature (Congress) in disputes that might arise with the actual application of the law to particular circumstances. The judges were to see that such disputes were indeed settled in accordance to their well-informed understanding of the meaning of the law (they were themselves lawyers of course).

The judges would be appointed by the president, but be able to take office only after a confirming vote by the Senate. At the time it was anticipated that the federal judges would be involved mostly in issues arising largely around this tricky matter of the relationship among the different states of the Union.

The Framers obviously did not foresee that the judges or justices serving on the Supreme Court (but also the district courts as well) would step by step go well beyond the scope of the originally designed Constitution to begin to reshape the law according to the judges' own "more enlightened" personal interpretations as to how the law ought actually to read in its application to national life. By this is meant the justices' ability to shape, revise, or even set aside the law of the land in accordance with merely the personal ideological, moral or "rational" inclinations of the nine supreme court justices themselves – or often only upon the decision of a simple majority five of the nine justices, against the objections of the other four. In short, over time, step by step, these individuals, possessing unchecked and thus unlimited legal powers, would succeed in making the Supreme Court – not Congress – the supreme legislative or law-making body found within the American federal system. But we will have more (much more) to say about this matter in later chapters.

---

*Actually, it would be wrong to characterize the United States as a nation at this point. Certainly citizens had some kind of collective or national identity as Americans. But that sentiment would develop in depth only later. At the moment they still saw themselves primarily as New Yorkers, Virginians, Georgians, etc.

The limited powers of the central government. Indeed, there was only a very limited internal or domestic governmental role anticipated for the newly created Congress and President (and Supreme Court) by the Framers of the new Constitution. It was understood that the principal concern of Congress, the unifying voice of the different states and the American people, would be limited to those matters primarily concerning the new Union's foreign civil and military relations with the outside world.

There were some domestic responsibilities assigned to Congress. It had a number of financial powers, such as creating its own tax sources; establishing, regulating and protecting a national coinage or currency; borrowing on credit; standardizing the rules of bankruptcy throughout the United States. Congress could establish a Union-wide postal service and post roads. It was to encourage the development of science and the arts through standardizing weights and measures, creating uniform copyright or trademark protections. It was to create uniform rules by which people could attain citizenship ("naturalization").

The most interventionist of the clauses of the Constitution in the domestic affairs of the Union was the power assigned to Congress to regulate commerce among the states (the inter-state commerce clause). But inter-state commerce was seen simply as the issue of the states raising trade protections against each other – a practice the Constitution was designed to bring to an end. It was not intended as an open door for Congress (or the president or the Supreme Court) to become involved in the internal affairs of America (as would in time indeed become the case).

The residual powers of the states in the federal system. So, with the exception of the specifically named powers of Congress to act on domestic issues, the states – and the states alone – were the only part of the federal system authorized to provide the people domestic government, that is, government inside the Union itself, as the American people themselves chose to do so through their representatives elected and commissioned to serve on their state assemblies and governing councils.

A republic rather than a democracy. It is important to note that the word "democracy" never appeared in the Constitution. The Constitution did define the political nature of this new political order as being republican – very specifically stating that any new states eventually joining the Union (Kentucky stood at the door expecting to become part of the Union very soon at that point) must be republican in character. The republican character of the Union was a matter that Congress itself was importantly to look after.

The rule of law rather than personal or even popular will. To the

Framers, democracy, as much as monarchy or aristocracy, implied the rule of the human will, whether the will of the many, of only one or of a special few. The framers understood that any form of government directed by the will of human agents, however many or however few, was easily susceptible to tyranny.

Rather, the Framers were looking to establish the rule of law – concrete principles that could be etched into stone or inscribed in bronze (as they anciently had been in the Roman Forum), principles that would stand for all times for the community. Humans and their personal desires would come and go. But laws carefully enacted through the constitutional directives they were putting into effect would not be easily swayed by changing human desires and fancies. No, the new government would be a government not of men but of laws.

The Romans had constructed such a political system. They too had believed (in accordance with the ancient Roman's typical love of order over impulse) that a government should be a system of laws, not personal wills. The Framers agreed strongly with this same principle. Their hope was that, unlike the Romans who failed to hold to this fundamental principle, Americans would remain vigilant in maintaining the idea of government as a regime of laws rather than human wills.

This was the central idea directing the deliberations of the Framers of the Constitution that summer of 1787. They would create a Republic built solidly on constitutional law. But the question still remained: would the American people be able to maintain this Republic any better than had the Romans?

*** * * ***

A GOVERNMENT THAT DRAWS ITS POWERS FROM THE PEOPLE – NOT VICE VERSA

Further securing the rights of the people against governmental tyranny – through the addition of 10 Amendments. Not surprisingly, the final draft of the Constitution the Framers put together still left unresolved considerable concern among some Americans about the dangers of potential tyranny in this new system. Consequently, in order to win over the reluctance of such Anti-Federalist or states'-rights people as Jefferson and other prominent Virginians, a promise was made by the Framers that the Constitution would be immediately amended upon taking effect to include a number of additional constitutional Articles further guaranteeing American freedoms against this new government, something Americans know today as their Bill of Rights.

Prominent among these guarantees is the very First of these Amendments:

> Congress shall make no law respecting an establishment of religion, or prohibiting the free exercise thereof; or abridging the freedom of speech, or of the press; or the right of the people peaceably to assemble, and to petition the Government for a redress of grievances.

This Amendment concerning the people's right to worship, speak, read, gather peacefully and petition their government was placed in the prominent position as the First Amendment to the Constitution, emphasizing the guarantee that the new federal authority would not infringe on the personal rights of Americans, rights that Americans had built their lives on and therefore rights that they demanded full respect for by any governing body taking social authority in their world.*

The Second and Third Amendments concerned respectively the right of the people to keep and bear arms, and the forbidding of the stationing of troops in people's homes without their consent.

The Fourth, Fifth, Sixth, Seventh, and Eighth Amendments concerned the rights of the people in the official process of an arrest, trial and sentencing.

And the Ninth and Tenth Amendments made it clear that the states and the people retained full rights on all matters not specifically assigned by the Constitution to the central authorities within the federal system:

> 9. The enumeration in the Constitution, of certain rights, shall not be construed to deny or disparage others retained by the people.

> 10. The powers not delegated to the United States by the Constitution, nor prohibited by it to the States, are reserved to the States respectively, or to the people.

---

*Note that the First Amendment makes no mention of the "separation of church and state" which has come (via Thomas Jefferson) to be understood today as meaning that traditional religion (Christianity, for the most part) may not be practiced or involved in the ever-widening realm of the nation's public domain (most notably, public schools and public grounds of any kind). Actually, the Amendment clearly meant that the state had no business whatsoever regulating the practice of religion – which it does extensively today via the federal courts – in *establishing* Secularism (Humanism) as the only religion allowed to be practiced in the public domain. Precisely, the Supreme Court has taken the authority to describe in detail exactly when and where religion could be practiced legally, and where it is to be *prohibited* from being freely exercised – in clear and total violation of the First Amendment.

These last two Amendments were extremely critical – in promising that other than the powers specifically described in the constitutional document as accorded to the central or national branches of the federation, all other powers of government would remain reserved entirely as the privilege and responsibility of the states, or the people of those states.

The question nonetheless remained: would such constitutional guarantees be sufficient to hold back the tendency of social authorities, especially those who see themselves as exceptionally enlightened, to want to expand their powers of control over the people? This was very much part of the great political question that had bothered philosophers since ancient times: *quis custodiet ipsos custodes* / who (or what) will govern those who govern? Will the people control their government – or will their government control them? Who will be sovereign: the people themselves, or some special government authority towering over them?

This matter of sovereignty. The issue of sovereignty, whether the states' or the people's, had weighed heavily over the proceedings of the Constitutional Convention. The word sovereignty means rule over. According to long established European political custom, the sovereign was the king. The king ruled over his subjects. The people literally lived and functioned at his tolerance and under his direction. French King Louis XIV (1643–1715) had perfected this idea in France: the king rightly should enjoy total or despotic powers over the people because he would be expected to be the most enlightened member of the community and therefore in the best position to know what was right for the community he ruled over. This idea was then quickly picked up by other European kings, including, a century later, the English king George III.

This piece of royalist logic did not sit well with the American subjects of the English king. For a century and a half, since they had left England and crossed a great ocean to start life anew in America, they had needed no king to do their thinking for them. For that century and a half they had been left alone to rule themselves. Families and local communities managed their own affairs on a daily basis, and on special occasions when there was a need to do some colony-wide business, they would elect representatives to be their voice in the management of the larger affairs of the colony. They had done just fine as self-sovereigns and resented it immensely, finally to the point of rebellion, when George III and his Tory supporters in Parliament attempted to bring these free peoples under tight royal control.

The people's divine rights. Lingering behind this debate was the question of political legitimacy. European kings founded or justified their despotic

The Birth of the American Republic 167

powers not just on the basis of enlightenment (for even commoners could bring themselves to enlightenment) but also on the basis of Divine will. For centuries European kings had been claiming that they enjoyed their sovereign position because of the desire of God himself that they should so rule. God caused them to be born to this position. So how could anyone question what God had decreed. After all, *Deus vult,* "God wills it."* European kings (as they saw things) thus ruled by divine right.

But Americans not only had learned the art of self-rule through a century and a half of effective self-government, they too felt that they had done so as a legitimate matter – also of divine rights. They were Protestants, heavily shaped in their thinking by the Protestant Reformer Calvin,† who had raised the idea that all people, kings and commoners, enjoyed equally important responsibilities before God even though the roles they played in society were different. As the Apostle Paul pointed out in his letter to the Corinthians, although people are gifted in their service to the community differently, they are all equally important in the eyes of God and in the functioning of the community. Each person has a distinct calling (vocation) from God to play a key role in the life of the community. Each receives empowerment from God in the performance of his or her vocation; each is equally responsible before God for the proper carrying out of that vocation. There is no room for laziness, no room for cheating, and no room for lording it over others, for God's justice is not to be mocked. Their ultimate accountability therefore is not to some human authority, but to God himself.

Thus when English King George III invoked divine rights in his attempt to bring the American colonies under his complete control they answered with their own Divine Rights Theory.

Again, this is well stated in the opening paragraphs of the Declaration of Independence:

> *We hold these truths to be self evident, that all men are created equal, that they are endowed by their Creator with certain unalienable Rights, that among these are Life, Liberty and the pursuit of Happiness. That to secure these rights, Governments are instituted among Men, deriving their just Powers from the*

---

*An expression that went all the way back to 1096 when Christian Crusaders headed off to the Middle East to liberate the Holy Lands. But eventually it became the proclamation of English kings as they authorized new royal rules.

†Especially the Puritans or Congregationalists, the Scottish Presbyterians, and the Dutch Reformed, the German Reformed and French Huguenot communities in America. The Baptists (offshoots of Calvinism) and Quakers also had this same understanding of society and its politics.

consent of the governed ...

Thomas Jefferson elaborated on this a few years later in his *Notes on the State of Virginia* (1781), although note that he was talking about slavery in the harshest of terms (odd, he himself being a slaveowner):

> God who gave us life gave us liberty. And can the liberties of a nation be thought secure when we have removed their only firm basis, a conviction in the minds of the people that these liberties are a gift from God? That they are not to be violated but with His wrath? Indeed I tremble for my country when I reflect that God is just, and that His justice cannot sleep forever.[34]

Regardless of the source of the problem (King George's tyranny or the evil of slavery), it was quite obvious that there was a strong understanding in America at the time that the rights of the people did not come from some human authority, nor from some human institution. Those rights (and accompanying responsibilities) came from God, and God alone.

So for those who gathered in Philadelphia in 1787 to work out the Constitution of a new American government the question of political sovereignty was clear: it belonged (by the will of God) to the people – or to them through the states, which, through their elected representatives, the sovereign people controlled with their right to vote. The rights of the American people did not, and would never, derive from the institution of some governing state, whether kingly, or aristocratic or even bureaucratic (professionals working full-time for the state). It belonged naturally, by the will of their Creator, with the people themselves. The new federal government with its carefully defined and limited authority would function only as the sovereign American people should empower it, either directly through the House of Representatives or indirectly through the Senate (representing the states, whose own political officials were generally elected in whole or in part by the people).

Protecting and preserving the sovereignty of the people. The people's rights, of course, are hard to hang on to, as the Framers of the Constitution were well aware, having just fought a bitter battle against the English king and his armies to preserve their rights as Americans. What could possibly serve as some kind of guarantee that these rights would not be lost again, that some kind of tyranny of those who lust after political power (and find ingenious ways of justifying this lust morally) would not eventually arise in America? They were quite familiar with the failures of Athens, Rome and Israel in this regard. What could guarantee that this would not also

The Birth of the American Republic 169

happen to them? This is why Franklin answered the query as to what the Constitution architects had created: "A Republic ... if you can keep it."

✳ ✳ ✳

WHAT WERE THE GUARANTEES THAT THIS WOULD WORK?

But all of them knew the answer to that question: their sovereign rights, their personal freedoms, could be guaranteed by no living being, no matter how kindly disposed he might originally be. According to their Puritan understanding, man was by nature invariably a sinner. Given enough opportunity, power would corrupt any human heart.

A mechanical system of checks and balances. Certainly they had been careful to build into the government a system of checks and balances which would actually use human selfishness or political greed to good effect. The system was set up so that cooperation among a number of various branches of government would be required to make the system work. And cooperation meant compromise, the necessity of having to give up the desire for total power, in order to employ any power at all. If one of the branches of government would start to assume more power for itself (a rather certain possibility) this would stir the indignation of the other branches, which out of a self-serving sense of the relative loss of their own power, would gang up on the usurper of their joint power! A very ingenious system!

In God We Trust. But by no means did they rely entirely – or even mostly – on this ingenious mechanical system. They were well aware, just as Franklin had stated, that this whole enterprise would ultimately succeed or fail on one issue, and that alone: the will of God. They needed to stay closely in line with the will of God, who after all had given them the victory against royal tyranny in the first place. They needed to look to God in full trust for such protection, look to God as "In God We Trust." Otherwise nothing, not even clever mechanics, would protect them from human evil. George Washington stated the case very clearly in the speech he addressed to the nation as he took office in 1789 as America's first president:

> *It would be peculiarly improper to omit, in this first official act, my fervent supplication to that Almighty Being, who rules over the universe, who presides in the councils of nations, and whose providential aids can supply every human defect, that His benediction may consecrate to the liberties and happiness*

> of the people of the United States, No people can be bound to acknowledge and adore the invisible hand which conducts the affairs of men more than the people of the United States. Every step by which they have advanced to the character of an independent nation seems to have been distinguished by some token of providential agency, We ought to be no less persuaded that the propitious smiles of Heaven can never be expected on a nation that disregards the eternal rules of order and right, which Heaven itself has ordained.

This was not mere political posturing, this reference to the all-important role that God had played in winning for America its national independence, Washington's appeal to Americans to continue to look to that same God for divine support as the nation now moved forward. This appeal to God's favor was very serious business for it rested on a Truth that recent experience had made very, very clear. This was not just religious platitude, designed by Washington to comfort the people with an assurance that he was a proper church-going Christian (which he frequently was not). This was testimony to the reality of politics that all of these quite astute practitioners of politics had come to understand – at a very deep level. The American venture would not fail, as had Athens' and Rome's and Israel's attempts at self-government, as long as it retained a very deep sense of connectedness to God and his hand in the affairs of man.

Christian Realism – and the Christian Covenant. In the end what we will term as the philosophy which guided these framers of the American Constitution is "Christian Realism." This philosophy was founded on the understanding that man can be both an angel and a devil, prone to do good and prone to do evil. Man must be allowed enough opportunity to put into effect his ability to do the good, while at the same time be put under enough legal restraint to check him against his equal ability to do evil. Ultimately only God could be counted on to do the truly good. But man and God could work together, with man operating under God's judgments, inspired by an awe of God and desire to please God – yet at the same time fearful of what might happen if he did not remember to obey God. Thus this Constitution would work for American society, as long as Americans understood the rules and as long as Americans freely chose to keep this Constitution as a Covenant with God. Anything else would fail.

As Christians, the Framers of the Constitution were well aware of the words of advice – and warning – that Moses gave Israel as it entered the Promised Land (the very same verses that Founding Father John Winthrop referenced in his 1630 sermon, just as the Puritans were about to embark to begin their great Puritan experiment):

> *Observe the commands of the LORD your God, walking in his ways and revering him. For the LORD your God is bringing you into a good land – a land with streams and pools of water, with springs flowing in the valleys and hills; a land with wheat and barley, vines and fig trees, pomegranates, olive oil and honey; a land where bread will not be scarce and you will lack nothing; a land where the rocks are iron and you can dig copper out of the hills.*
>
> *When you have eaten and are satisfied, praise the LORD your God for the good land he has given you. Be careful that you do not forget the LORD your God, failing to observe his commands, his laws and his decrees that I am giving you this day. Otherwise, when you eat and are satisfied, when you build fine houses and settle down, and when your herds and flocks grow large and your silver and gold increase and all you have is multiplied, then your heart will become proud and you will forget the LORD your God, who brought you out of Egypt, out of the land of slavery. ...*
>
> *You may say to yourself, My power and the strength of my hands have produced this wealth for me. But remember the LORD your God, for it is he who gives you the ability to produce wealth, and so confirms his covenant, which he swore to your forefathers, as it is today.*
>
> *If you ever forget the LORD your God and follow other gods and worship and bow down to them, I testify against you today that you will surely be destroyed. Like the nations the LORD destroyed before you, so you will be destroyed for not obeying the LORD your God.* (Deuteronomy 8:6-20 NIV)

* * *

THE REPUBLIC IS BIRTHED

The process of ratification. Whereas some of the states were quick to approve (ratify) the new Constitution, not everyone was completely sold on the new Constitution. As a result, it was not until June of the following year (1788) when New Hampshire, the ninth of the thirteen states voting to ratify, finally put the Constitution into full effect.*

---

*Delaware, Pennsylvania and New Jersey had quickly ratified in December of 1787 and Georgia and Connecticut followed soon after in early January of

During the debate over ratification, Anti-Federalists, such as Samuel Adams and Patrick Henry, had voiced their fears through various newspaper articles that the individual states were simply surrendering too much of the people's sovereign rights to this new central authority. What were the guarantees that this new government would not come to assume the powers of the royal government they had so recently fought to free themselves from?

Federalists were quick to take up the challenge, James Madison, Alexander Hamilton and John Jay writing replies to these questions under the pen name Publius. Some eighty-five articles were published by these three men, each article carefully explaining the workings and benefits of this new Constitution, a collection of articles which have come down to us today as the famous *Federalist Papers*. Madison turned some of the criticism of the Anti-Federalists on their head, pointing out that factions would form within the government, simply because of the size of the new country, but these factions would serve the useful purpose of checking each other's ambitions for power, forcing debate and clarity of thought in government, and encouraging the people to follow political developments closely rather than just letting government officials go about their business quietly out of the public sight, where tyranny might then truly develop. Hamilton, for his part, stressed how a stronger central authority would more likely attract society's natural leaders, involving them more closely in the building of a financially sound economic system, the best guarantee of a society's stability (and consequently its ability to protect personal freedom and prosperity).

And thus it was that the Federalists were able to bring the country to approving this new experiment in republican government.

The last days of the Confederation. The new federal Constitution was not submitted to the Congress of the old Confederation, where it probably would have faced such resistance that it would not have passed, but was sent directly to the states for their approval. Each state was invited to set up its own process of ratification, usually through a special session gathered for specifically that purpose: to approve (or reject) the new Constitution. Thus the Congress of the Confederation was left entirely out of the process that would bring its own existence to an end.

However, the Confederation did perform for the new nation one final

---

1788. Massachusetts (narrowly) ratified in February, Maryland in April, and South Carolina in May, before New Hampshire signed on in June. However, Virginia followed later in that same month, and New York in July, thus assuring the Constitution that it would have the full support of the heavyweight states. North Carolina did not ratify until December of that year. Rhode Island, after first voting against ratification, finally in May of 1790 approved the Constitution.

The Birth of the American Republic   173

and very important service when in 1787 it set out clearly with the passing of the Northwest Ordinance the basis for designing and admitting new states into the Union. Having been accorded the right by the Treaty of Paris to develop the land west to the Mississippi as American land, the Congress had a two-fold job: 1) get the states to stop arguing over the ownership of that land and 2) instead set up in this territory, at least in the Northwest, a number of candidate-states, open to settlement and to eventual admission to the Union as full members states – as they gained a certain size of population and established their own state Constitutions.

Thus it was that the Northwest Territory (today's Ohio, Indiana, Illinois, Michigan, Wisconsin, and what would become the eastern portion of Minnesota) was divided originally into a number of territories or future states (ten originally, but ultimately the five-plus described above). Also plans were drawn up for the creation within these territories of towns and townships – according to a precise grid pattern where each township was defined as a square of six miles on each side, further divided into thirty-six sections of 640 acres each (one square mile). Also a section within each township was ordered by the Northwest Ordinance to be set aside for sale for the support of public education; and a public university was also to be established within each of these major states.

CHAPTER FIVE

THE YOUNG REPUBLIC

✱ ✱ ✱

GETTING STARTED (1789–1801)

Although the young American republic had a new Constitution, it was a very slender affair outlining very little of what we have come to understand today as government. That was just as well. Its brevity sufficed to bring renewed unity to the competitive-minded states, and its vagueness in detail left exactly just those details to be developed by the individuals who would take their place as officers of the new republic.

George Washington. It was understood and expected by all (except perhaps by Washington himself who, after the war, was looking forward to ending his public duties and heading back to his farm at Mount Vernon to enjoy a less frustrating set of labors!) that the person to lead the republic as its new president was to be George Washington. After some soul-searching he once again yielded to the call of duty when it was apparent that no one else but he was expected to be the country's new leader. Thus on April 30th, 1789, he stood on the balcony of Federal Hall in New York City to take the oath of office as the republic's first president.

How would he handle the office? There were a multitude of problems facing the new Republic, none of them particularly military (at least for the moment) and so his sole experience as a military officer would not give much indication as to how he would handle the challenges of civil office.

The Constitution mentions only that a president is chosen for a four-year term, but elected officials in the colonies could be, and frequently were, repeatedly returned to office with a new election. Would he leave after serving only four years? Would he want to stay on repeatedly, like a monarch, ruling until he drew his last breath? Some bitter Anti-Federalists even claimed that Washington would try to make himself king – although those who knew him well were quite aware that this would have been the *last* thing Washington would have wanted for himself.

The Young Republic 175

In any case, how would he get things started as president? What kind of legacy would he leave for others to live up to and develop?

The answer came quickly as he gathered together a small group of advisors to whom he could assign particular functions, a group or council similar to the British royal cabinet. Although the Constitution mentions no such institution, Washington, and all presidents after him, chose to make very important use of a cabinet of officials, some serving as personal advisors and some serving as heads or secretaries of government institutions that American presidents have long used to administer the office of president.

Alexander Hamilton.[35] Once again, Washington called on the one person he trusted most for hard work and natural brilliance of mind (and bravery), the one person he had relied on, time and time again, in the years of the War: Alexander Hamilton. With the financial status of the new republic being the new Union's biggest challenge, Washington was quick to assign Hamilton as the United States' first secretary of the treasury.

Hamilton was actually born (year uncertain) not in one of the American colonies but in the Caribbean, under peculiar family circumstances (that would be the object of much commentary by his later political enemies) and was forced to look after his own survival at a very early age.* But he was a very avid reader, bi-lingual (English-French), and a self-educated apprentice clerking for a local merchant (possibly his actual father), and at seventeen wrote an essay published in the local newspaper. The essay was sufficiently impressive that it led local community leaders to gather a fund to send Hamilton off to New Jersey in 1772 for formal education (prep school). In 1773 he began his studies at King's College (Columbia University) in New York, where he quickly distinguished himself as an excellent orator supporting the colonies' growing spirit of rebellion against British royal authority. Hamilton also wrote at the same time a number of outstanding articles and essays in support of the same cause.

Yet he was also of a cautious or fair mind (perhaps because of his own sufferings as a youth) and in May of 1775 came to the defense of the college president, allowing the man to escape an angry mob, while Hamilton challenged the mob not to attack Loyalists or their cause in this manner.

However, Hamilton was himself quick to take up arms and join with friends in the New York militia, undertaking at the same time (again,

---

*His mother was married but separated from another man when she met and married (thus illegally) James Hamilton, Alexander's presumed father. When her legal status was brought to light, James left her and young Alexander. Then when Alexander was only thirteen his mother died, leaving Alexander an orphan.

on his own initiative) the study of military history and military tactics – and soon put that knowledge to use in leading a raid on a supply of British cannons in the Battery! He then went on to organize his own artillery company, elevating himself thereby to the rank of captain. His company soon joined with Washington's troops in the various battles that raged across New York City, and then across to New Jersey, where his artillery kept the Hessians under fire at the Battle of Trenton.

His talents were quickly recognized, and he was asked by various generals to join their staff. Yet he understood that glory was to be found on the field of battle, not on the general staff of a commanding general ... that was until Washington made the same request. That was an offer that Hamilton was willing to accept. And this changed his life, and America's, forever.

As chief of staff he was assigned the task of maintaining written communications with the Continental Congress, the governors of the new states, and with other generals. Over the course of four years, as Washington's confidence in Hamilton became virtually total, Hamilton himself issued detailed military instructions to officers under Washington's command, and supervised both diplomatic and intelligence operations coming from Washington's command. Thus it was that he met French General, the Marquis de Lafayette, and became close friends with him in the process.

Finally at Yorktown, Hamilton's long desire to actually serve directly under fire, came into play – with Washington's very hesitant permission! It was Hamilton himself who led the American attack on one of the two vital redoubts still holding the British line in the latter's desperate defense at Yorktown. It was a brave, but probably very foolish, move on Hamilton's part. But he obviously survived, adding even more to his enormous stature in the eyes of Washington.

After the war he formed a law partnership with a friend and found himself, among other things, defending Tories who were suffering from the post-war anti-British backlash, typical of his sense of fairness. But he was nonetheless very interested in seeing his new Republic move forward into its own distinct future, and thus in 1784 founded the Bank of New York, the beginning of his entry into the world of large-scale financing.

He was as interested in the political future of the country as its financial future and two years later attended the Annapolis Convention, drafting the resolution which called for the Constitutional Convention that eventually produced the U.S. Constitution. The next year he became an assemblyman in the New York State Legislature, which sent him as one of its three representatives to the Convention in Philadelphia. And of course it was he who wrote many of the articles that formed the famous *Federalist*

Papers, advocating the adoption of the new Constitution.

Washington had not forgotten Hamilton and the military service he had performed for him. He knew Hamilton to be intensely loyal personally, intensely brave, intensely intelligent, intensely competent, and intensely dedicated to serving his newly independent country. And so it was that Washington turned to Hamilton to see what Hamilton could do to help him put the new country on a strong financial footing. Thus he asked Hamilton to become his secretary of the treasury.

Hamilton's debt assumption program. As it had always been during the war, one of the biggest problems facing Washington and the struggling young Republic he was expected to lead was money. Always money! By war's end, the Continental Congress had run up a $54 million debt, and the states an additional $25 million. Also, the promissory notes or bonds issued during the war by the Continental Congress, by the various states, and by the army had been bought up by speculators after the war at fifteen cents on the dollar. Most people believed that they were not worth even that much. In other words, the creditworthiness of the Republic was almost nil.

Hamilton however had some well-developed ideas as to how he wanted to meet that challenge. He proposed to Congress (January of 1790) a method of clearing the debt by what he called assumption: the federal government would assume all of the debts and begin the process of repaying them – at full value! America would pay its debts. The world could take confidence in that. It was indeed financial confidence that Hamilton was trying to restore. To meet this obligation, the Republic would itself borrow (issuing its own promissory notes or bonds) to cover the debt through bonds issued by a newly created national bank: the Bank of the United States (BUS). Besides financing the repayment of the national debt, principally through heavy taxes on imports, the BUS would also fund public economic infrastructure projects and private industrial investment for national development.

Hamilton's program was designed to found the nation not on the democratic whims of the masses but the hard-nosed realism of the moneyed class that commanded the American economy. Understanding the mind-set of America's moneyed class, Hamilton planned to involve this class in the new government by inviting wealthy financiers to exchange the old Continental Congress's bonds with the Republic's new bonds. This would give these individuals a very strong financial interest in seeing the new government succeed. And, most importantly, it would place the new government's finances on very strong foundations.

Money is power. And the new nation needed power in order to survive in a very competitive world. Strong financial foundations were absolutely essential for a Republic trying to establish itself as a serious, viable institution in a very challenging world.

But the reaction to his proposals was swift. The heart of the reaction was this matter of great principle found in the personal debts hanging over the Patriot foot soldiers during their wartime service (loans or mortgages for their homes and land they owed various banks), when they were in no position to meet or pay down on those debts. After the war they had returned to civilian life only to find that those debts had grown even larger while they had been away in the army. Worse, they had been paid for their wartime services with the almost worthless notes issued by the Continental Congress. They retrieved what value they could by selling these notes to speculators for whatever they could get, never enough however to meet the heavy financial obligations hanging over them. And now, here was Hamilton paying those speculators full value for these notes bought on the cheap from penniless citizens. This all seemed very unfair, sort of a double slap in the face of America's small heroes.

And there was also the irritation of the states such as Virginia, which had paid off its own debts in full. Why should they be part of a program assuming the debt of the states that had not done what they had done?

There was lot of anger that arose over Hamilton's program. Jefferson's friend Madison was most vocal in his indignation at Hamilton's idea of debt assumption because it seemed to be developing at the heart of the federal system a power center on the order of the royal tyranny America had just freed itself from. Madison's strong stand eventually pushed Jefferson into an ever-stronger States-Rights (or Anti-Federalist) position. And it cost Hamilton his friendship with Madison, who as former Federalist, now turned into an equally dedicated organizer of an Anti-Federalist group headed up by his fellow Virginian, Jefferson.

As it turned out, Washington threw his support behind his treasury secretary and Congress moved ahead to approve Hamilton's program. And indeed, it did put the new Republic on fairly firm financial footing. But it had opened a wide political wound between the Federalists and Anti-Federalists that would not be healed. As Madison himself had forecast (and in the Federalist Papers had justified as necessary to the proper functioning of a representative government) America took its first steps toward a two-party political system: Hamilton's Federalists in competition with Jefferson's Anti-Federalists, who under Madison's tutelage would organize themselves as the Republicans (not related to the modern Republican Party).

The Whiskey Rebellion of 1791–1794. But paying off that debt was proving to be highly difficult. When Hamilton had raised import duties as high as he felt he could go before it would start crippling American business, in 1791 Hamilton placed an excise tax on the production of whiskey, a basic essential in the diet of the American farmers – and also a means of currency in the farmers' businesses. Understandably, the new tax met with the same resistance that had George III's 1773 tea tax imposed on his American subjects to pay for his wars. Westerners from upstate New York, through Western Pennsylvania, into Ohio and Kentucky, Western Maryland and the Western Carolinas all got increasingly involved in the refusal to submit to Hamilton's tax.

Complicating matters was the fact that Eastern distillers could be much more efficient in the massive production and local distribution of their product and thus proportionately much less burdened by the excise taxes than the frontier farmers. Consequently, Eastern distillers offered no objection to the new tax. However, this differing situation facing the Eastern producers and the Western farmers merely added to the enormous frustration of the latter group.

Washington, however, agreed with Hamilton that the toleration of the insubordination in the West would collapse the authority of the Republic. It was a hard thing to do to come up against these strong souls, many of whom had fought alongside Washington in the War of Independence, a war that had had similar roots in its resistance against George III's new taxes. But ultimately the question was not about taxes (for a government cannot operate without an income stream of some kind) but about the legality of those taxes. The Republic needed everyone involved in the support of their new government, not just the business and financial classes of the Eastern cities, in order for the Republic to succeed and not fail.

And finally, just as in the need to maintain discipline in a war-time army, the Republic would fail in peace-time unless it too could get compliance to its laws, laws properly or legally instituted and properly enforced. Lack of political discipline would certainly destroy the Republic.

Events going on in Paris (the French Reign of Terror, 1792-1794) at that very same time were making this matter quite clear. Street mobs had taken control of the effort to birth the new French Republic and it was looking increasingly likely that the French Republic was thus going to fail in its efforts to get itself established. Now the very same threat seemed to hang over the young American Republic at this point.

Thus in August of 1794 Washington led a 13,000-man army into Western Pennsylvania to confront protesters (who quickly melted away at the appearance of Washington and the army). The show of force broke the rebellion. The authority of the Republic's government was thus confirmed. But ultimately, the event only deepened the distrust by the rural Westerners (and Southerners) of the moneyed class of up-East Federalists.

The Kentucky Question. This event and the growing regional distrust would register itself clearly in the form of a dispute when Kentucky applied for statehood. The up-East Federalists dragged their feet, fearing they would be overwhelmed in Congress by a growing Southern/Western coalition lined up against them. Finally a compromise was reached in 1791 when New England's Vermont was admitted to the Union, opening the way in 1792 for Kentucky to be admitted as a new state as a counterbalancing principle in the politics of statehood, a principle that would be applied again and again as the country struggled over deep cultural differences that separated the various regions of the country.

Thomas Jefferson.[36] Washington had appointed Jefferson to his cabinet as his secretary of state, charged with overseeing America's diplomatic missions abroad and (supposedly) advising Washington on foreign policy matters as the need arose. Jefferson would not be easy to work with.

Jefferson was born to a Virginia planter family, with important family ties – especially on the side of his mother, Jane Randolph, a cousin of Peyton Randolph, who was a leading political figure of Virginia during the 1760s and early 1770s.* At an early age Jefferson was tutored along with the Randolph children, and as a youth, in classic aristocratic fashion, he was taught Latin, Greek and French, along with history, science and the classics. At age sixteen he entered the College of William and Mary, where he continued his study of these same disciplines. He graduated two years later to begin his study of law under the prominent George Wythe. And at age twenty-one he inherited 5,000 acres and fifty-two slaves from his deceased father's estate, including the land where he would begin the building of Monticello, the place of perfect habitation developed from his own ideal design.

He was admitted to the Virginia bar in 1767 and as a practicing lawyer represented his county as a delegate to the House of Burgesses (1769–1775). In 1772 he married a third-cousin, Martha, and settled into a period that was perhaps the happiest of his life. In the ten years of their marriage she bore him six children, only two of which survived to adulthood.† They also inherited from her father another 11,000 acres and 135 slaves to work the land, but also a heavy debt that accompanied the title.

---

*Randolph was speaker of the Virginia House of Burgesses (1766–1769), was the president of the First Continental Congress (1774) and president of the Virginia Convention debating independence from Britain (1775, just before his death that year).

†Already sick from diabetes and her frequent childbirths, she died in 1782 at age thirty-three in delivering their sixth child.

The Young Republic 181

When he was sent to represent Virginia at the Second Continental Congress in 1775, he befriended John Adams. And thus he was invited to join the committee assigned the task (supposedly Adams's responsibility) of drafting a Declaration of Independence, the startup version which was ultimately assigned to Jefferson. Some changes were subsequently made to Jefferson's draft by the committee, then by the full Congress (as we have already noted, about a fourth of the whole was cut out, including a section connecting King George and the slave trade!).

At the time, the Declaration seemed to be a much less significant matter than all of the new state constitutions being drafted by the thirteen newly independent states!

Shortly after this (September of 1776), he was elected to the new Virginia House of Delegates. Here he served on the committee working on the new Virginia Constitution, and sponsored the Bill for Establishing Religious Freedom, forbidding state support of religious institutions or doctrines – which however failed to pass. Two years later he was given the responsibility of reviewing and editing Virginia's system of laws. And the year after that (1779) he was elected as the state's governor, undertaking at that point to institute new laws in pursuit of his personal worldview concerning religion, education, property rights, etc.

When in 1781 Benedict Arnold, at that point serving the British, attacked the new Virginia capital at Richmond, Jefferson and members of the Assembly were able to escape to Monticello (Richmond was burned to the ground). Then when Cornwallis approached Monticello, they escaped from there to another of his plantations to the West.*

After the war (1783) he became a delegate to the Confederation Congress where he chaired the committee that drafted the 1784 Land Ordinance, removing the Northwest Territories from the on-going land title conflicts among the states by making them territories eventually eligible to become states of their own. Also, slavery was to be outlawed in these territories.†

In 1784 he was sent to join Franklin and Adams in Europe in the effort to negotiate trade agreements with England, France and Spain (Franklin returned to America the next year). Jefferson quickly (1785) made himself at home among the French, befriending the Marquis de Lafayette in his effort to develop improved trade relations between the U.S. and France.

---

*It was later that year decided by the Assembly that Jefferson had acted appropriately. But he had lost such stature that he was not reelected governor.

†His anti-slavery provision was not approved at the time, though reintroduced and subsequently approved when the ten territories were consolidated into five territories, the future states of Ohio, Indiana, Illinois, Michigan and Wisconsin.

He also fell in love with the French lifestyle (including its wine and books). Then soon after the French Revolution broke out in July of 1789, he returned to Virginia, intending however to return soon to Paris. But the request by Washington to serve as his new secretary of state (charged with the responsibility of supervising the country's diplomatic mission) caused him to remain in America.

But this would bring him into direct contact with Hamilton, a man whose views Jefferson by instinct opposed on virtually every front. Hamilton was very supportive of a strong central government, able to unify the functioning of the thirteen states, politically as well as economically. This Jefferson opposed strongly, fearing that such a strong central authority would compromise greatly the states' rights to conduct their own affairs as they chose. He was thus highly opposed to the concept of a national authority (until he himself later became president of that very nation!).

Furthermore, unlike the almost spiritual rapport that existed between Washington and Hamilton, Jefferson and Washington lived in very different universes when it came to foreign policy and diplomacy. Even though Jefferson was supposed to be in charge of the conduct of foreign policy, it was usually to Hamilton that Washington turned rather than to Jefferson when faced with a foreign policy issue needing to be resolved. Jefferson grew increasingly resentful over this.

A big part of the problem was that Jefferson was by nature an intellectual who lived in a world of perfect plans and grand schemes. He was also personally smitten by French culture and had become deeply involved in the Enlightenment dreams of the French intelligentsia that eventually took over the French Revolution – and drove it to the human butchery of the 1793–1794 French Reign of Terror. And Jefferson, even though saddened by the gruesome excesses of French Republicanism, refused to admit that there was any injustice in how these cruel events were unfolding in France. A greatly self-blinded Jefferson was quite certain that 99 percent of the Americans supported strongly, even gladly, the events going on in France. Thus despite the carnage, he convinced himself that it was France that needed America's total support in the ongoing English-French conflict.*

Hamilton and Washington, on the other hand, despite the recent war

---

*When William Short, a Jeffersonian supporter, wrote Jefferson from Paris that mobs had taken over the French Revolution and had executed some of their French friends, Jefferson in early January of 1793 wrote back a sharp rebuke: "The liberty of the whole earth was depending on the issue of the contest, and was ever such a prize won with as little innocent blood? My own affections have been deeply wounded by some of the martyrs to this cause, but rather than it should have failed I would have seen half the earth desolated; were there but an Adam & Eve left in every country, & left free, it would be better than as it now is."

The Young Republic 183

with their English cousins, still considered England as America's best partner when it came to the contests involving European politics and economics, which seemed always unavoidable, especially to such a trading people as the New England Yankees.

There really was no way to side-step the ongoing French-English conflict, and neither France nor England would let America get away with being merely neutral in the struggle. One way or the other, America would constantly have to choose sides, not usually happily, whatever the choice. And in choosing sides it usually ended up pitting Hamilton and Washington against Jefferson (and Madison).

Jefferson grew increasingly furious about how Washington was lining up behind Hamilton and the pro-British Federalists and in December of 1793 resigned his position on Washington's cabinet. From then on, he and his Republicans would be active opponents of Washington and his Federalist cabinet.

Citizen Genet. This Federalist-Republican conflict came clearly into public view in 1793-1794 when the new French Republic sent Citizen Edmund Charles Genet to America as its diplomatic representative. Jefferson was enthusiastic in receiving this polished Frenchmen. Then the problems began. Genet treated America as if it were a poor step-child. When Washington declared America neutral in the French-English war, Genet began to go around the authority of the president, maneuvering in different ways to involve America in the war on the French side. Genet disregarded all diplomatic protocol by setting up Americans to attack English and Spanish positions in Florida, Louisiana, and Canada, even hiring privateers to attack American shipping heading toward England! Washington was furious. And at this point even Jefferson and Madison were ready to back away from him.

In any case when in 1794, during the French Reign of Terror, the extremely radical Jacobin Party began executing not only "enemies of the Revolution" but also the rival revolutionary (though less radical) Girondist Party, of which Genet was himself a member, Genet himself realized that he was now a man on the run. Washington was gracious enough to grant him asylum, and Genet spent the rest of his days quietly in America!

Jay's Treaty (1794). Despite the formal signing of the 1783 Treaty of Paris marking the end of the American War of Independence, the British had been disregarding the specific terms of the agreement as if they had never existed. The British had failed to pay the promised compensation to slave owners whose slaves the British had freed during the War. But America had also failed to keep its promise to compensate American Tories who lost their property when they fled to Canada during the War. In any case, the British continued to occupy their forts in the Western territories, and even allied with Indian tribes to block the spread of the American settlers into those territories.

But what was most disturbing was the high-handed way the British impressed sailors by boarding American ships and seizing sailors they claimed were simply their sailors who had deserted to the easier life under sail in America. In fact, many of these sailors pressed into British naval service were simply the hardiest looking American sailors, and not British at all. To try to get the British to ease up on impressment and to honor the terms of the Treaty of Paris, Chief Justice John Jay was sent in 1795 to London to negotiate a better working relationship with the British.

But America was in a distinct position of having to negotiate from weakness, at a time when the British were more focused on winning the on-going struggle with the French than on making Americans happy. As a consequence, Jay returned from England with a new treaty ("Jay's Treaty" as it was scornfully termed) that seemingly offered America very little. The idea of Britain compensating the American slave owners for their property loss was dropped (infuriating the Southerners) and America agreed to accept limited trade rights as neutrals in exchange for the British to finally vacate themselves from the American West. Although Jay could not have extracted anything more from the British than what they had agreed to in this new treaty, Americans of all political shades were outraged. Even Washington came under abusive attack in the press for his acceptance of the treaty.

After a bitter debate in Congress, the treaty was approved (barely) by the necessary two-thirds vote in the Senate. But Jefferson's Republicans, holding a strong voting position in the House of Representatives, were determined to block the appropriations (spending) necessary to bring the treaty to full force. Discussions in the House dragged on for months, with both England and France lobbying representatives to vote up (the British) or down (the French) the necessary legislation. In the end (by a majority of only three votes) the House approved the appropriations bill backing the treaty.

But the emotional price paid for passage had been very, very high. Jefferson's Republicans had lost no opportunity to slander the Federalists as pro-monarchist because of their pro-British sentiments. The Republicans awarded themselves the title of true Republicans because of their support of the French Republic, Americans not yet having realized, or at least not having been willing to acknowledge, the brutality of events in Republican France. The American Republicans were totally supportive of the French Republic's devotion to spreading, quite violently, anti-monarchical – and

The Young Republic 185

often even anti-church – Republicanism to the rest of the civilized world. Thus Hamilton was greatly slandered by the Republican press for his pro-monarchist loyalties (but he was actually not at all a pro-monarchist, as his actions in the recent war had clearly demonstrated), because he was not willing to join with the Republicans in their enthusiasm for what was going on in France. That was a cheap political shot aimed at Hamilton by the Jeffersonian faction. But Washington was slandered no less for the same reason!

But the press campaign was very effective. It marked the beginning of the decline of the Federalist Party.

Washington refuses to take on a third term as president. Washington had originally agreed to serve only one term as president (1789–1793), but had been prevailed upon to run for a second term in the approach to the 1792 elections. He grudgingly accepted the request. But now in 1796, as he approached the time for the elections for a third term in office, he made it very clear that under no circumstances would he continue to serve as president once his second term in office ended in early 1797. He was tired of the bickering between the Federalists and the Republicans and wanted simply to go home to his farm at Mount Vernon. Washington was thus more than willing to oversee a smooth handover in power to his successor, which in this case was his vice president, John Adams.

And so it was that Washington set the constitutional tradition that two terms in office was something of a limit to presidential service. America would not be saddled with a president-for-life, as so frequently happens in new republics.*

John Adams.[37] Although Adams was a staunch Federalist, he was very sensitive to his own place in the scheme of things politically and socially, and found himself frequently at odds with not only Jefferson and his Republicans, but also Hamilton, who after Washington, was the strongest figure among the Federalists. A man of high moral principle, Adams unfortunately was lacking in the tact necessary to put those principles to use without raising a lot of powerful opposition. Sadly, he went largely unappreciated in his own days and by his own people for the way he helped follow up Washington's lead in bringing the country to even greater stability and security – at a time when huge dangers still swirled around the young Republic.

Adams had grown up in a small Massachusetts town to a family that

---

*President Roosevelt, however, would run for a third and even fourth term in the 1930s and 1940s using the emergency of the World War (Two) as justification for doing so. But Washington's "two-terms-only" presidential tradition was ultimately confirmed as a Constitutional Amendment (the Twenty-Second) in 1951.

held strongly to the original Puritan beliefs and ethics, stressing basic human equality in God's (and thus man's) eyes, the importance of working to achieve rather than merely inheriting one's place in life, and the critical nature of personal integrity, no matter the possible social cost for living true and honestly. Also in typical Puritan fashion, there was an early emphasis in his family on the importance of formal education which Adams began at age six, then continuing into Latin School, and at age sixteen entering Harvard College.

But he disappointed his father when he dismissed any ideas of becoming a minister and graduated from Harvard instead as a teacher, pondering the question (that he faced most of the rest of his life) of how to become great. This of course put him in conflict with his sense of Puritan morality, a conflict that he would never successfully resolve.

Law nonetheless seemed to offer the best path to the greatness that he so eagerly sought. Thus he clerked for a prominent local lawyer and in 1758 received his master's degree from Harvard and was soon admitted to the bar. Eventually his legal work would draw him into the cause against growing royal authority in the colonies, for which he began to write (anonymously) in the Boston newspapers.

In 1764 he married a third-cousin and preacher's daughter, Abigail, and proceeded to have six children in fairly rapid succession (the last however did not survive birth), the second born (and first son) being the future president, John Quincy Adams.

Adams came to public attention when in 1765 he published a letter sent to the Massachusetts legislature concerning the highly controversial Stamp Act, restating in very clear and compelling terms the rights of Englishmen concerning both taxation and judicial treatment by the authorities. This helped to bring about his election to public office as a representative on the town council.

In 1768 he moved his family and law practice to Boston. But his law practice did not come into prominence until he defended the British Redcoats accused of murdering members of the Boston crowd who had been taunting the soldiers. He claimed that he feared that this might damage his reputation. But instead it helped him to gain a Boston seat on the Massachusetts legislature three months later and a considerable increase in his law business.* Seemingly Adams had finally found his path to greatness. But this came amidst growing chaos in Boston, and in 1774 Adams moved his family back to the family farm in Braintree – permanently.

---

*Analysts determined that he had skillfully selected just the right jury members (many of whom later became pro-British Loyalists), and that from that moment the outcome of the trial was a foregone conclusion (six soldiers were acquitted and two convicted of the lesser crime of manslaughter).

The Young Republic

However, he continued his work in Boston in the thick of a darkening war cloud. He delivered a hallmark speech in the legislature challenging the British governor with the claim that Massachusetts had always been self-governing; that its charter was only with the King, not Parliament; and that the colonies would have no other recourse if Massachusetts' rights were not respected by British authorities than to take the road of full independence from Britain. These ideas were then extensively developed in a publication that clearly outlined the legal arguments behind them. At this point Adams had secured a very prominent position in the growing debate.*

Quite naturally Adams was sent by his state as one of its representatives to the First and Second Continental Congresses (1774 / 1775–1777). At first he was looking for ways to bring Britain and the colonies back into a better relationship. But seeing no flexibility coming from London, he soon found himself working hard to convince his colleagues that full independence was the only path at that point open to the colonies. And in mid-1775 he was the one who put forward the name of Washington as the one to lead the colonial army gathering around Boston (a careful move to secure Virginia to the cause). In 1776 he got confirmation from Virginia with that colony's Resolution joining the cause, and was subsequently appointed to head the committee assigned the task of drafting a Declaration of Independence. Jefferson wrote most of the draft, but it was Adams who guided its passage through the Continental Congress.

Soon after this, Adams was sent with Franklin to hear the terms that General Howe was willing to offer after a series of defeats of Washington's army in New York. But the discussions led nowhere when the American representatives showed no sign of compromising on their decision for full independence. Adams was now a hunted man (on the list of treasonous colonials who would have been shown no mercy if the rebellion had finally been put down by the Redcoats).

During the next couple of years Adams worked tirelessly on a number of committees backing the war effort, learning important administrative procedures through his extensive service to the cause. Then in 1778 he was appointed (along with Franklin and another American) to represent the new United States in negotiating a treaty of alliance with France, then returning home – only to be sent back the following year to begin discussions in Paris with British representatives to work out some kind of peace terms (Adams in the meantime developing some fluency in the French language!).

Adams was a contentious person (as he himself well knew) and did not find it easy working with Franklin, whose well-staged homespun

---

*His more flamboyant cousin Samuel Adams being at the time even more prominent – having led the Boston Tea Party dumping tea in the Boston harbor in 1773!

manners that so attracted the French Adams himself detested with equal vigor. Nonetheless, the British (especially after the humiliation at Yorktown in 1781) were gradually willing to back down and acknowledge American independence, and work out the compromise (land rights to the West and compensation for civilian property losses on both sides of the conflict) that eventually led to the Treaty of Paris in 1783.

In the meantime, Adams had been appointed ambassador to the Dutch Republic (1780), securing that country's recognition of American independence in 1782 and also securing from Dutch banks valuable loans needed to help the American states get on their feet after the war. With peace at hand, Adams was appointed in 1785 as America's first ambassador to the English Court of St. James, where he sincerely sought to restore friendship between the English-speaking peoples on both sides of the Atlantic. Here in London he put together another written work, defending the new U.S. Constitution just after its adoption in Philadelphia in 1787. Though not as famous as the *Federalist Papers*, it was itself a very clear definition of how in a republic a system of checks and balances among different branches of the people's government was essential to keeping power operating safely within the bounds that the designers of the Constitution intended.

When elections for the presidency of the new Republic were held in 1789, Adams came in second behind Washington in the count, thus by the understanding of the times becoming the nation's first vice president. But with this, Adams disappeared from public view, as was typical of those called to that office. Washington never drew on Adams' services, never consulted Adams on any issue. This left Adams resentful against Hamilton whom the president frequently consulted and even against the president himself whom he visibly supported but for whom he developed a personal dislike. But at least the office put him in something of a position to be the heir-apparent to the presidency when Washington indicated in 1796 that he definitely was retiring from public service.

But Adams was going to have to face Jefferson and his alliance of mostly Southern Republicans, plus the question as to whether or not Hamilton would put his Federalist support behind Adams (he did, because Hamilton despised Jefferson more than he disliked Adams!). In the end Adams narrowly defeated Jefferson with his seventy-one electoral votes to Jefferson's sixty-eight votes, the voting being almost entirely a northern versus southern state electoral division. Thus Adams became the nation's new president, and Jefferson (being in second place) became the nation's vice president.

The XYZ Affair. Troubles with Europe continued to rock American politics as Adams assumed his presidential office. But it was now France's turn to

The Young Republic

play the role of seizing American vessels, hundreds of them. Jefferson and his pro-French Republicans were embarrassed into silence over this French arrogance. As for Hamilton and his pro-British wing of the Federalists, they jumped at this opportunity to demand a declaration of war against the French.

Adams sent a delegation to Paris in 1797 to try to find a remedy to the problem. But the delegation was met by French agents X, Y and Z, who demanded bribes and a loan before the Americans would be allowed to meet with French foreign minister Talleyrand. The Americans refused and returned to the U.S., with the news of the "XYZ Affair" stirring even greater war fever among the indignant Federalists under the slogan, "millions for defense, but not one cent for tribute!"

The Alien and Sedition Acts (1798). But this then raised among nervous Federalists the specter of pro-French treason at home (not too subtly aimed at their Republican rivals). In 1798 the Federalist majority in Congress rushed through to passage four Alien and Sedition Acts (which Adams unfortunately signed into law) empowering the president to deport pro-French traitors and to penalize any pro-French seditious language that might come from (Republican) newspapers and public speakers. In the end all this succeeded in doing was drive the Republicans even deeper in their resolve to oppose the Federalists at all costs.

The doctrine of nullification. The strongly Republican Southern and Western states of Virginia and Kentucky, in bitter reaction to these Acts, passed their own Resolutions (authored by Jefferson and his ally Madison) affirming that Congress had no constitutional right to intervene in the internal affairs of the states and their people. As the Constitution was the product of the action of the states (or so the Republicans claimed anyway), it was the states, not Congress that had the last say in what was constitutional and what was not. The states were the ultimate sovereign authority within the Union, not Congress. The states thus reserved for themselves the power to nullify acts of Congress which they regarded as being unconstitutional.

This constitutional issue, of course, would be a matter that would continue to be hotly debated until it finally led to full civil war in the mid–1800s.

The Quasi-War with France. The conflict with France finally boiled over in early 1799 when America's new navy found itself fighting a "Quasi-War" with France on the high seas. Fired up by a major sweep of the 1798 elections (thanks to the XYZ Affair), the Federalists now pressed harder for a declaration of war against France.

Finally Adams took matters in hand to solve this issue tearing the country apart, and sent an envoy to Paris to negotiate an improvement in

U.S.-French relations. In the resultant treaty, the French agreed to leave American shipping alone, thus bringing the Quasi-War to an end.

The treaty did not at all please the Hamiltonian Federalists, nor did it suffice to restore for Adams friendly relations with the Jeffersonian Republicans. But he signed the treaty anyway, suspecting that by doing so it would end his political career. Indeed, one month later, during the 1800 presidential elections, Adams was voted out of office, having served only one four-year term. And thus it was that Adams had given up the presidency in order to bring the country back from the brink of war.

The "midnight" judicial appointments. Interestingly, the very last act of his presidency would be the one thing of his presidency that would come to have lasting constitutional value: the creation by Congress and appointment by Adams of individuals to some six dozen judicial posts, including the fateful appointment of the Virginian John Marshall as chief justice of the Supreme Court.

These mostly new positions resulted from Congress's recent Judiciary Act of 1801, which expanded the number of judicial posts (which indeed were too few to handle the large case load before them), an act that was rushed through a lame duck* Congress of a majority of Federalists, many of whom had just lost the federal elections to a new Jeffersonian Republican majority, but had a few weeks of time remaining in office before the newly elected Congress could take its place in the new capital city of Washington, D.C. (actually at this point a forlorn collection of shacks, muddy lanes, and farm animals!). In fact the job was so rushed that Adams spent his last night in office completing the task of making these judicial appointments, thus earning them the reputation from the Republicans as the "midnight judges."

With this last act of public service completed, Adams quietly slipped away from the capital to his home in Massachusetts, a rather tired and bitter old man. He hadn't even bothered to stay long enough to see the new president of the United States, his once close colleague but now strong political rival Jefferson, sworn into office.

But once again, the simplicity of this procedure would demonstrate that in American political culture, defeat in an election meant not a prolonged challenge to the results by a resentful loser, but a peaceful transfer of power to the winner. It had been that way since the founding of the Anglo-American society in the early 1600s, and would continue as an important

---

*The term "lame duck" refers to office-holders who have been voted out of office in an election that went against them, but who still hold the office for a brief period until the newly elected officials can take their place. A lot of frantic legislation is often passed by a lame duck assembly, realizing that it is about to lose power to its opponents.

The Young Republic

political tradition into this new era of Republican government.*

* * *

JEFFERSON BEGINS THE REIGN OF THE REPUBLICANS

With Jefferson's election to the presidency in late 1800, there would be a dramatic shift in the character of the new Republic. The Federalists were out; the Republicans were in. The Federalist emphasis under Washington (inspired by his close advisor Hamilton) had been to serve primarily the urban, commercial interests of the coastal East. The Republican emphasis under Jefferson (and the fellow Virginians who followed him to the presidency) would be the rural South and West.

Reshaping the Republic's finances. Hamilton had used a growing (but responsible) national debt as a means of locking the financial leaders of the new country into full support of the new Republic. However, inspired by the American farmer's instinctive dislike of the banking world, Jefferson moved immediately to undercut Hamilton's strategy by reducing the size of the debt. He had his new treasury secretary, Albert Gallatin, abolish domestic taxation (such as the hated excise tax on the farmers' whiskey) and instead raise revenue through enhanced customs duties ... and the sale of land in the Western territories. The former measure would put most of the new tax burden on the commercial Northeast. The latter measure, through actually rather inexpensive land sales, would bring about greater American settlement in the Western territories, putting further burden on the Indian tribes living there. Jefferson's intention was clearly to strengthen the political voice in the new Republic of the rural South and West at the cost of the heavily urban Federalist Northeast.

Also in line with his Republican dislike of a strong central authority (preferring "states'-rights" instead) and as part of his strategy to reduce the Republic's debts, Jefferson moved to reduce the government budget by half, and thus also to reduce the federal bureaucracy by nearly the

---

*That important principle however seems to have been abandoned in the 2016 election, which brought the Republican Trump to the White House. Democrats not only went to the streets in loud protest over the results, but Democrat congressmen/women supported by a very Liberal press corps began immediately to look for grounds to impeach Trump for having committed "high crimes and misdemeanors" – and would stay completely focused on that effort for years thereafter. And four years later, Trump supporters would return the favor in their physical attack on Capitol Hill when Trump lost the 2020 presidential election to Biden. This is Third World politics, typical of what happens in elections (should they even have them) in Asia, Africa and Latin America. For America this has constituted a grand departure from America's great constitutional tradition.

same amount. A particular target was the collectors of the excise (mostly whiskey) tax. Also, as the bureaucracy had been previously staffed almost entirely through Federalist appointments, Jefferson's Republicans were placed immediately in half of the remaining positions.

The war with the Barbary pirates. Jefferson was also adamantly opposed to maintaining at the public expense a huge standing army. Using the logic that the Indian tribes to the West had been pacified, Jefferson was eventually able to cut the size of the army in half.* He also had a similar goal with respect to the navy, wanting to replace the navy's six new fighting ships (frigates) with smaller coastal vessels, used primarily to catch Northeastern shippers trying to avoid Jefferson's new customs duties.

However, before he got going on his naval reduction program, he found himself facing a huge problem that had long infuriated the Americans: the Barbary pirates of the North African Mediterranean coast. Operating as privateers out of the Muslim states of Tripoli, Tunisia, Algiers and Morocco, these pirates had long raided Christian shipping, seizing not just the ships and their cargo but also the sailors who manned them, holding them for ransom or even selling them into slavery. America paid a huge ransom each year to bring release for its captured sailors: approximately one million dollars annually, roughly ten percent of the government's total budget.

Jefferson had long protested the decision of Washington and Adams to pay this ransom, and now, as president, was determined that this policy was going to come to an end. When the Bashaw of Tripoli declared war on the United States in 1801, Jefferson responded by sending Commodore Preble, who linked up with the King of Naples (Italy) to attack Tripoli's pirates. Then Preble set up a blockade against the Barbary states with an increase in the American naval presence in the Mediterranean. But in late 1803 one of his frigates (the *Philadelphia*) ran aground in the Tripoli harbor. However rather than let the ship fall into the hands of the pirates, in early 1804 Americans boldly slipped into the harbor and set the ship ablaze. Then in 1805 the American consul in Tunis gathered a band of mercenaries and crossed the Libyan desert to seize the coastal town of Derna, just as also the American fleet arrived to bombard the town from the sea. The Barbary pirates were ready to sue for peace. And thus the Americans proved themselves quite ably on the high seas.

But growing problems with England and France as the Napoleonic Wars heated back up again would pull the Navy from the region in 1807. It would not be until after those wars were brought to an end in 1815 that a

---

*However, he did perform one great service to the military by establishing a military academy at West Point, the goal being to bring young Republicans into military command.

The Young Republic

final victory over the Barbary states would be accomplished.

The Louisiana Purchase (1803). At the same time that he was reducing the influence in the Republic of the urban (and Federalist) Northeast, Jefferson busied himself looking to the territory across to the West of the Appalachian Mountains. The new American Northwest beckoned thousands of agrarian (and thus Republican) settlers. As nature would have things however, to bring their produce to market these settlers would have to look to the rivers which flowed west and south away from the mountains and toward the mighty Mississippi River, which however flowed through French territory as it approached, via the town of New Orleans, the Gulf of Mexico and thus the high seas.

So it was that Jefferson asked his ambassador to France, Robert Livingston (who was later joined by future president James Monroe) to negotiate with Napoleon the purchase of this French town, for $10 million. But America was in for a surprise when Napoleon offered not just New Orleans, but the entire French territory (Louisiana) to the west of the Mississippi River to America – for a mere $15 million dollars.

The Louisiana Territory (which reached westward all the way to the Rocky Mountains) had been originally French but was turned over to the Spanish in 1763 as the price of France's losing the French and Indian War (Europe's Seven Years' War). But in 1800 the French Emperor Napoleon forced Spain to give it back to France in anticipation of renewing the French Empire in America. But failure in 1802 to suppress a Creole (African) independence uprising in the sugar-rich Caribbean island of Saint-Dominique (Haiti) and a renewal of hostilities with England had left Napoleon desperately in need of cash. This is what moved Napoleon therefore to sell off the whole Louisiana Territory to the new United States. In any case, Napoleon saw no immediate economic advantage in possessing this vast continental wilderness, and fifteen million dollars seemed much more useful to his European ambitions. And thanks to Hamilton's having put the young American Republic on strong financial footing, America was well able to afford the Europe-recognized rights to this very valuable Western territory.*

In effect this nearly doubled the size of the new American nation. And it ended (for a while anyway) French ambitions in America, and put America on a new international footing. As Robert Livingston himself put things at the time of the signing:

We have lived long but this is the noblest work of our whole

---

*The Indians, of course, would offer no such recognition. But that legal matter counted for little in the American thinking at the time.

lives. The United States take rank this day among the first powers of the world.*

The Lewis and Clark Expedition (1804–1806). Jefferson was quick to send army Captain Meriwether Lewis (accompanied by William Clark) and a team of fifty men to explore this new territory. Leaving St. Louis in May of 1804, they headed west up the Missouri River, hoping to find finally a water route to connect with the Pacific Ocean, reaching today's North Dakota as winter set in. Here they hired a French fur trapper and his Indian wife (Sacajawea) to guide them further west. The next summer they reached the headwaters of the Missouri River in the high Rocky Mountains, disappointed in not finding the water route they had hoped for. Then they pushed westward beyond the Rockies (and thus the boundaries of the Louisiana Territory) until, after an incredibly difficult time, they reached the Pacific Ocean in November. There they wintered, turned back eastward in early 1806, and arrived in St. Louis in September – welcomed with great enthusiasm as heroes.†

Federal land development. In looking West, Jefferson saw the need to connect that part of America with the home base east of the Appalachian Mountains. Western land sales were booming and the U.S. Treasury thus was well endowed to finance public roads and canals. A Republican Congress in 1806 authorized Jefferson to construct a national road reaching into the Ohio territory. But this was just the beginning. Treasury Secretary Albert Gallatin began work on a proposal for massive development of America's agricultural hinterland, to help the farmer get his goods to market by road or by canal. In 1808 he proposed a multi-million-dollar (sixteen to twenty million) plan to build a canal to connect the Atlantic (via the Hudson River) with the Great Lakes and to construct additional national roads, some of the plan financed directly by the national government, some of it through private contractors financed by loans from the government.‡

Thus it was that the small-government mentality of the Republicans was easily reversed when it came to the role of the government in supporting

---

*Notice that the "United States" is used in the plural! The Union is still seen at this times basically as an alliance of numerous independent states rather than as a single political entity.

†Jefferson would also send out other teams to explore the new territory, including that of Gen. Zebulon Pike who in 1806 ventured as far west as the territory that would become Colorado (who also was captured by the Spanish in the process, but released in 1807!).

‡In the end, most of this project was financed by private interests or the States rather than by the federal government.

The Young Republic

the American farmer!

Hamilton v. Burr (1804). Aaron Burr was an ambitious American "who would be king." He headed up the New York wing of Jefferson's Republican Party, and was selected to run with Jefferson in 1800 to balance the ticket (Virginia South and New York North). But at the time, the vote was not set up in a way that could distinguish a presidential vote from a vice-presidential vote and Burr had the same number of votes as Jefferson.*

Hamilton took this opportunity to harass his old political opponent Jefferson by urging the Federalists to tie up the vote when it went to the House of Representatives (to break the tie between the two candidates). Yet in the end Hamilton disliked even more intensely Burr and finally threw his support to Jefferson, not gaining any appreciation from Jefferson however, but gaining a deep hatred from the extremely ambitious Burr.

The rivalry finally reached crisis proportions four years later in the heat of a New York governorship election in which Burr was a candidate (he had been dropped by Jefferson as his running mate in Jefferson's reelection bid that year). Deeply derogatory anti-Burr letters that Hamilton had written, intended for private usage only, ended up being submitted for publication (no one is quite certain by whom), producing the sense of deep insult that back then demanded remedy in the usual way: a pistol duel. This was quite illegal, but widely practiced at the time. Most of these duels ended up with both parties purposely shooting wild, not hurting anyone, but satisfying the code of honor. Hamilton had participated in ten of these prior to his meeting with Burr on July 11, 1804, though his son Philip had been killed a few years earlier in a duel when the shot-less strategy went awry.

Anyway, Hamilton shot first, a bit wide of the mark (accidently or purposely?). Burr returned the shot, mortally wounding Hamilton, who died the next day from the wound.

Burr was subsequently indicted for murder, although the charges were soon dropped. But sensing that he had just killed not only his enemy Hamilton but also his own political career, Burr retreated to South Carolina. Then he returned to Washington, D.C. to finish out his last months as Vice President, before heading West to the recently acquired Louisiana Territory to start a new life (of political intrigue?). He had plans of a strange sort which were later reported by (an even bigger schemer) Wilkinson as involving the creation of an empire with Burr as its head (never really proved – nor disproved). Burr then moved to Europe, finally returning in 1812 to his law practice in New York, spending the rest of his life quietly

---

*This error would be corrected by the 12th Amendment to the Constitution, fully ratified by the States in 1804.

out of politics!

The development of the powers of the U.S. Supreme Court. One part of the Federalist heritage that the Republicans could not undo was the Supreme Court and its various Federalist appointees by Adams, most notably the U.S. Supreme Court Chief Justice John Marshall. Marshall was a strong Federalist, unlike most of the rest of his fellow Virginians, who tended to be Jeffersonian Republicans. He had declined Washington's offers of being a part of his Administration (turning down the offer first to be the nation's attorney general and then ambassador to France) and even Adams' first attempt to nominate him to the Supreme Court. But considered one of the most brilliant lawyers of his days, he was again nominated to the Supreme Court as its chief justice in Adam's frantic effort to put Federalists in office before the Republicans took control of both houses of Congress and the White House in early 1801. This time Marshall accepted the offer.

Jefferson and the Republicans were furious about the Federalist judiciary, especially by the way the Federalist-dominated courts had treated Republicans under the ill-fated Alien and Sedition Acts, and were determined to clean the courts of the midnight judges. Jefferson's secretary of state, Madison, refused to sign the commission of the Federalist William Marbury, a commission appointing Marbury as justice of the peace in Washington D.C. Marbury sued Madison, bringing before Marshall's Supreme Court the famous case of *Marbury v. Madison* (1803).

But ultimately Marbury lost the case, due to Marshall's questioning about who exactly had the right to bring this case before the Supreme Court. In theory Marbury had a right to his appointment. But it was done under a law, the Judiciary Act of 1789, that supposedly gave Marbury that right to bring the case directly to the Supreme Court. But Marshall argued that the Constitution itself permits original jurisdiction for the Supreme Court only to foreign policy issues or state issues. Marbury's case involved neither factor, despite what the 1789 law seemed to authorize. In fact, the 1789 law of Congress was invalid, because it was "unconstitutional." Thus Marbury had no right under the Constitution to proceed as he had.

In one short stroke, Marshall had just accorded to the Supreme Court the power to decide what laws of Congress were and were not constitutional. Though the Constitution itself mentioned no such power belonging to the Supreme Court, Marshall's decision was not contested. At the time, it seemed like a win to the Republicans. But the Republicans did not see that the principle underlying Marshall's decision laid the groundwork for the Supreme Court to continue to move down this road of making itself the ultimate decider in the land as to what was law and what was not, or worse, how the law might be better interpreted by progressive judges.

The Young Republic

For the next three decades Marshall and the Supreme Court rendered various decisions which further strengthened not only the voice of the Supreme Court, but also the supremacy of the Washington, D.C., government over the various state governments. For instance, in the *Fletcher v. Peck* (1810)[38] decision, Marshall's Supreme Court affirmed that federal authority took precedence over the laws of the individual states. In *McCulloch v. Maryland* (1819),[39] his court denied the rights of the states to tax federal agencies (in this case the Bank of the U.S.). In *Cohens v. Virginia* (1821)[40] Marshall declared that the Supreme Court had review powers over the decisions of the state courts.

* * *

AN AGRARIAN AMERICA IS INTRODUCED TO THE INDUSTRIAL REVOLUTION

Beyond mere self-support, the American economy since its founding as a group of English colonies was designed from the point of view of the English mother country largely with one purpose in mind: to supply England with raw materials needed to feed its growing industrial society. New England, however, tended to pursue an economic agenda arising from a strong instinct for full economic self-support (food, housing, personal items), with its Puritan ideal of Christian self-sufficiency. However, the American South from its founding had been deeply supportive of the mother country's hunger for raw materials: tobacco, dyes, and – at first – small amounts of cotton.* But by the end of the 1700s all of that was about to change.

The beginnings of America's Industrial Revolution. Samuel Slater was an Englishman who had apprenticed as a youth to Richard Arkwright, the inventor of the water-driven machinery which spun raw cotton into the thread needed for England's growing textile industry. Slater slipped off to America in 1789 with the knowledge of this process in his head (such technology was considered such a strategic secret that what Slater was doing was highly illegal in England), to set up a spinning mill of his own in Rhode Island in 1790. So successful was his mill that Slater soon expanded his operations to Massachusetts, Connecticut, and New Hampshire.

Slater's contribution to the American economy coincided with the contribution that Eli Whitney made, when as a youth he moved from

---

*In comparison to the Caribbean Islands, which supplied to England the commodities of sugar and rum – highly sought after at that time – the English colonies of continental America were considered to be interesting, but of much lesser value as economic assets.

Massachusetts to Georgia to study law. Observing the painfully slow process by which slaves extracted seeds from cotton balls in order to ready the cotton as raw material for yarn production, in 1793 Whitney came up with a machine that could perform that same process mechanically, greatly speeding up the process – and the profitability of Southern cotton production destined for the English textile mills (and soon the rapidly growing number of Yankee textile mills in New England).

Indeed, this simple invention revolutionized the South, confirming the South as an agrarian society focused on the growing and exporting of raw cotton, but also confirming slavery as a Southern institution, as thousands of slaves would be needed to plant and pick the cotton now so vital to the Southern economy (and to the small Southern aristocracy whose wealth soon became founded almost entirely on this single industry).

Growing sectionalism. What was taking place was the widening of the gap that separated the Northern or Yankee culture from the Southern slave-based aristocratic culture. Yankee culture extolled hard work and inventiveness, and produced not only an ever-widening variety of industrial products but also a rapid growth in inventions that would quickly bring America into the industrial revolution that had been shaking Europe. In fact, very soon, Yankee America would surpass Europe itself in the vastness of its industrial creativity and energy.

It was heady stuff, stimulating a culture that became increasingly fascinated with its own human ability or powers to shape the world according to its own design. It did not at first see itself as leaving behind the deeply devout Christian culture that had originally formed New England. It was simply moving ahead or progressing (supposedly to the pleasure of the Creator-God) in bringing the wonders of a perfect heaven to an ever-perfecting earth.

The South, on the other hand, seemed to be moving in the direction of Jefferson's idealized agrarian utopia, where a leisured gentry would preside over a highly structured, even rigidly stratified, agricultural society. Supposedly this presented a picture of agrarian bliss, with the slaves singing in the fields as they produced the harvests that brought the valuable revenues to the entire community, and the aristocracy conducting their rounds of intellectual discourse and genteel socializing as the confirming symbol of the success of it all. Of course few people lived lives that measured up to this bliss. But it was a beautiful social picture, so compelling that it led even poor White farmers to believe that someday they would share this same bliss with their cousins enjoying the refinements of plantation life.

In many ways this was the cause of the bitterness that separated Jefferson and his Republicans from Hamilton and the Federalists. Hamilton

The Young Republic

came of questionable social circumstances and had worked his way forward in society through simply a lot of hard work and sheer determination. To Jefferson, born to social privilege, Hamilton's type of social climbing seemed vulgar (as it did also to all English gentry) and inappropriate as a social model for the emerging American culture.

Indeed, these two life-styles, these two cultures, not only had little in common except the name American, they were in so many ways mutually antagonistic that there was no way that some kind of cultural, social or even political battle was not inevitable.

And Hamilton's death at the hands of the aristocratic Burr (who, though a New York northerner, shared Jefferson's view on how America should take shape) was perhaps symbolic of the bitter struggle to come. Southern honor, after all, simply could not be allowed to suffer the indignities of upstart Yankee presumptuousness.

* * *

AMERICA IS SLOWLY DRAWN INTO THE FRENCH-ENGLISH WARS

Jefferson's last years in the White House (he served two terms or eight years) were tough on him, as tough as they had been for Washington in his last years as U.S. president. The primary cause was the bitter English-French feud stirred by Napoleon with his efforts to spread to the rest of Europe, by military force if need be, French Enlightenment ideals (that is, anti-monarchy ideals, and to a lesser extent anti-church ideals). Although Napoleon clearly was a French dictator, there was something about French culture that appealed to the Jeffersonian Republicans. They also still harbored very strong anti-British sentiments. On the other hand, the Federalists (who were quickly dropping in political importance) looked to England rather than France as their natural allies. But in any case, whatever the sentiments, there was no way America, whose economy was built heavily on trade, could stay out of the French-English conflict, even as neutrals.

During these troubled times, the British had never ceased their impressment of American sailors. But in 1807 a British warship attacked an American warship just off the American coast when it refused to allow the British to board them for a sailor hunt. Americans were outraged and it was all Jefferson could do to keep his Republican Congress from pressuring him to issue a declaration of war against Britain.

What Jefferson did however was almost as ruinous as war would have been at that time: he decided that somehow placing a block or embargo on American trade with England would bring the British to their senses (he had the idea that this would stir up worker unrest in England!). His rather naive analysis blinded him to the fact that this would actually put America in alliance with France, which was trying to bring the English economy to collapse by a similar embargo against English goods traded on the European continent, a continent that Napoleon now dominated. The economic stakes were so high in the British mind that this American embargo would only inflame them further against the Americans, not bring them to their knees! He also failed to realize that this policy would force American traders into bankruptcy, or into smuggling. Hoping to placate the opposition which exploded when he announced his embargo, he announced that the same policy would hold true also with respect to trade with France. But this pleased no one either.

To make bad matters even worse, Jefferson chose to meet the European challenge by not building more warships (frigates), the likes of which had proven themselves so capably in the war with the Barbary states. He figured that not having a fighting navy would help keep Americans from making the mistake of wanting to go to war with either France or Britain.*

Instead he chose to build a number of much smaller gunboats. These would not be terribly effective in defending American shipping overseas, but certainly could be used to help prevent the American smuggling that his embargo encouraged.

Such dangerous folly did not escape the notice of the American press, even bringing fellow Republicans to loud complaint. But Jefferson stood firm, and thus finished his second term in the midst of a national uproar. However in early 1809, he finally saw the logic in repealing the much-hated embargo, just prior to his junior colleague, Madison, taking office as the country's next president.

James Madison.[41] Madison had started out as an ardent Federalist, one of the co-authors (with Hamilton and Jay) of the *Federalist Papers* advocating brilliantly the acceptance of the federal Constitution. But with time he found himself swinging his loyalties behind Jefferson, who looked upon the national government with deep suspicion as a potential confiscator of the

---

*Liberal Humanists such as Jefferson have always supposed that it is weapons that cause wars – and thus disarming the people will automatically cut back on the dangers of the people falling into a war with someone else. But in fact self-disarmament – that is, disarmament if not mutual on the part of all contending societies – will merely undercut the ability of a society to protect itself against another society that has come to hold such power that it no longer fears the consequences of its efforts to bully others into submission. Weapons are not the problem. The political-moral intentions of societies are what are critical in matters such as this.

The Young Republic

rights of the states and their people. Then when the strongly pro-Federalist Hamilton purposely built up the powers of the central government through a policy of attaching it to the interests and thus support of the moneyed banking and industrial class – and when Washington and Hamilton began to swing their support behind the English in their war with the French at a time when Madison's mentor, Jefferson, had brought Madison strongly into his pro-French camp – Madison found himself jumping fully into Jefferson's Anti-Federalist faction, which he then helped organize as a proper political party: the Republicans.

Madison was an individual of varying opinions, highly supportive of the idea of intellectual or ideological variety itself being a very healthy approach to life, not just for himself but for society in general. He came to this viewpoint through his own personal development. He was raised conventionally enough as a Virginia Episcopalian of a highly respectable blood line, but instead of attending the Episcopalian College of William and Mary he headed off to Presbyterian Princeton, where he came under the direction of its president, Witherspoon. Presumably he studied theology under Witherspoon, but stayed on after graduation to continue the studies in Enlightenment philosophy. He returned to his family home at Montpelier and became involved in local politics, supporting not only a distancing of Virginia from increasingly aggressive royal authority, but also the disestablishing of the Church of England, in favor of religious freedom.

Of rather poor health, he would serve during the war which soon broke out as a political voice rather than a military officer on behalf of Virginia, participating in the discussions and the drafting of the numerous documents that clarified Virginia's political goals in the war. He was brought on the governor's council of state and also the Second Continental Congress, developing a close relationship with Jefferson in the process. Madison became a very strong nationalist, working hard to reform the Articles of Confederation. But when that did not work, he continued the cause as a delegate to the 1787 Constitutional Convention in Philadelphia. He helped prepare the Virginia Plan brought to the Convention, which started the debates, then personally kept notes on the entire proceedings (thus we have Franklin's prayer proposal!). And after the Convention he worked closely with Hamilton in writing numerous articles (the *Federalist Papers*) defending the new Constitution, as it faced the challenge of ratification.

When the new Constitution went into effect, Madison was elected to the House of Representatives – after overcoming considerable opposition from his Anti-Federalist rival Patrick Henry and Henry's ally James Monroe by promising to push for the passage of a number of amendments to the Constitution securing the civil rights of the Americans. And this he did, helping greatly in authoring the First Ten Amendments or Bill of Rights.

During Jefferson's eight-year presidency Madison had served loyally as Jefferson's secretary of state and right-hand man, and was the obvious choice of the Republicans to take over the presidency when Jefferson was ready to leave office. For Madison it was an easy glide into office (Madison secured almost three times the electoral votes as his Federalist opponent). But nothing after that remained so easy.

Madison tried hard to pacify the British, but the British were not interested in changing their policies toward America. Then the Republicans in Congress weakened America's diplomatic hand further by cutting deeply the funding for the army and navy!*

Tecumseh. But this unwise reduction of the U.S. army also weakened the defense of the American settlers along the frontiers with the Indians, at a time when the Indians were deeply involved in military alliances with the British. Thus it was that while American relations were worsening with the British over their treatment of the U.S. navy and its sailors, the Shawnee chief Tecumseh and his brother, the Prophet, organized for war. Tecumseh gathered a huge Indian confederation dedicated to driving White settlers from the Indian lands of the Great Northwest. Although Tecumseh received a stinging setback by Harrison's troops at the Battle of Tippecanoe† in 1811, his confederation continued to give serious trouble to the White settlers in the Great Northwest. And when the War of 1812 broke out the next year, he was quick to join the British as an ally against the Americans.

The rise of the young Republican War Hawks.[42] The Republican Party was beginning to register the first of a generational change from the older Jeffersonian Republicans to a younger breed of Republican activists. They soon came to be known as the War Hawks – Henry Clay of Kentucky and John C. Calhoun of South Carolina prominent among them.‡ They demanded

---

*Jefferson and his Republicans also had the strong notion that state militias, not a standing federal army, provided the country its best defense. They identified a standing army with the tyranny of European kings and emperors and the militias with democracy.

†Thus gaining fame for Indiana Governor and commanding officer Gen. William Henry Harrison, who with his men bravely stood their ground when, instead of meeting to discuss peace, the Prophet attacked the White army come to meet with him. The Harrison victory was such that it undercut the Prophet's standing among the Indians, and later (1840) had Harrison elected as U.S. President.

‡In fact many young Federalists had joined the growing Republican Party, helping to reduce further the size and impact of the Federalist Party, but also helping to promote this new nationalist look among the Republicans. This group of new Republicans included even John Quincy Adams, son of the ardent Federalist and former U.S. President John Adams.

The Young Republic

action: action against the Indians who attacked American communities on the frontier and action against the British who armed the Indians and who insulted America on the high seas with their policy of impressment of U.S. sailors.

National fervor was definitely on the rise. In this, the younger Republicans seemed to be departing from the original principles of the Republican Party set out originally by Jefferson (the priority of the states over the nation). In many ways they were acting more like the Federalists of an earlier generation. Even Madison found himself swinging back to his earlier, more Federalist, attitude as the nation came under greater threat.

War is declared. A particular action this new breed of Republicans called for was the conquest of Canada: to rid the North American continent of the British presence (and support of the Indians) forever. Thus in June of 1812, Congress declared war against England – but with considerable opposition in both houses (not a good sign when going to war).* Tragically, Congress went to war without considering how it was that Americans were supposed to fight, much less win, this war after having previously cut back the army and the navy to a pitiful status.

The first round in the War of 1812. Immediately things went badly for the Americans. The Americans expected an easy time in conquering sparsely populated Canada. But the British were quick to respond, seizing Fort Mackinac in July before the Americans at the fort were even aware of Congress's declaration of war. This bold move so encouraged the Indians that they eagerly joined the British in the attempt to break the power of the Americans in the Northwest Territories. The British, who were in the midst of this huge war with Napoleon's France and thus unable to supply a large English military force in North America, were more than willing to accommodate the Indians in their desire to crush the Americans.

An American army under General William Hull immediately invaded Canada, only to find that the Canadians were of no mind to surrender. The British responded to Hull's move into Canada by moving around him toward Detroit, which Hull realized he could not protect. Fearing a Shawnee massacre, in mid-August he ordered the Detroit garrison simply to surrender.

Likewise, fearing that the Americans would not be able to hold on

---

*A large number of Federalists were strongly opposed to the war and did not support it militarily or financially. When America finally emerged from the war not only with its honor intact, but buoyed up by an even stronger sense of American nationalism, Americans turned strongly against the Federalist Party, causing it nearly to cease to exist.

against the British and Indians at Fort Dearborn (Chicago), Hull at the same time ordered the soldiers and militia stationed there to abandon their position and retreat east toward safer territory. The retreating Americans were promised safe conduct through Potawatomi territory by the local Indian chief. But younger warriors attacked the retreating party and slaughtered not only half of the soldiers and militiamen but also women and most of the children, carrying off the rest for ransom or slavery.

Americans were outraged at the news. This Indian victory would in the long run cost the Indians dearly. It would also cost Hull his command. He was replaced as commanding general by America's Tippecanoe hero, William Henry Harrison.

On the high seas Americans performed much better, though against a navy as immense as the British navy (175 warships and 600 ships overall!), that hardly made any strategic difference in bringing the war to an American victory. But psychologically, events such as the defeat of the English frigate *Guerrière* by the American frigate *Constitution* in August were a shock to the British and an enormous boost to American morale. Other naval engagements that year also played to the American advantage.

1813. Things were again off to a bad start for the Americans as 1813 rolled around. In January a large detachment of militia from a number of American states (including Kentucky) was defeated in a failed attempt to retake Detroit (nearly 400 killed and over 500 taken away to Canada as prisoners). Wounded Americans were left behind, only to be slaughtered by Indians that the British could not control.

Thus American bitterness against the Indians only deepened. And the Kentuckians became more resolved than ever to bring the British – but especially their Indian allies – to defeat.

But the Americans would make a huge mistake in Canada when in April of that year they attacked the capital of Upper Canada at York (modern Toronto). The American victory was costly (including the death of the American commander Zebulon Pike). But the worst part of the mistake was when the American officers lost control of their men, who proceeded to plunder and burn the town, stirring among the British and Canadians a determination for revenge. They would soon have that opportunity at Washington, D.C.

Then the Indians struck again in late August, this time in the deep South at Fort Mims, Alabama. A branch of the Creek Indians called the Red Sticks harbored a deep hatred of the Whites – and also of their fellow Creek tribesmen who had been more accommodating to the Whites. The Red Sticks overran the Alabama fort containing around 500 men, women and children: White, Black (slaves) and mixed-breed Creeks. A large

The Young Republic

number of the White militia were killed in the action, as well as women and children (burned to death when they took refuge in an inner stockade that the Indians torched). About 100 of the Blacks were spared their lives, but taken off to slavery nonetheless. Only a small group (fifty of the original 500) escaped the massacre or enslavement.

In the meantime, finally realizing the foolishness of the previous naval cutback, Congress voted to construct six more frigates, thus giving the American navy a total of twelve warships! However, though small in number, they gave good account of themselves when facing the British. But just as important, American privateers were very active capturing British merchant ships. Yet overall, the British presence on the high seas was so vast that this hardly slowed up the British. They replaced lost British shipping faster than the Americans could bring down British ships.

On the Great Lakes that stood between New England and Canada both sides raced to build up their fleets of fighting ships. Battles on the water and in the coastal towns raged back and forth inconclusively, though with much loss of life and destruction of property. Americans made an attempt to capture Montreal, but failed miserably in the process.

But two American victories would more than compensate for the failure to take Montreal. In September on Lake Erie, an American fleet under the command of Oliver Hazard Perry soundly defeated a British fleet sent out to destroy the Americans, and thus gave America control of the all-important Lake Erie. Now the way was finally opened to recapture Detroit. Then in early October the Americans met up in Ontario with a retreating British army and with Tecumseh and his Indian confederation. In the Battle of the Thames, Tecumseh was killed and the British army soundly defeated. With the news of Tecumseh's death, the Indian resistance collapsed. Indeed, his death would mark the collapse of his huge Indian confederation. All in all, it was a major American victory.

1814. The Americans took their revenge on the Red Stick Creeks the following March in nearby Mississippi when General Andrew Jackson led his Tennessee militia, allied with Cherokee and friendly Creeks, against the Red Sticks at Horseshoe Bend. The slaughter of the Creeks was extensive (800 of the 1,000 Creek warriors killed; Jackson's side lost only 49 killed), breaking the power of the Red Stick Creeks – and establishing General Jackson as a military hero.

When Napoleon finally was brought to defeat in Europe in May of 1814, the British were then able to turn their attention more closely to the war going on between America and Canada.* They devised a grand

---

*Napoleon was exiled at the end of May in 1814 to the island of Elba off the Italian coast.

strategy to hit the United States from three directions: from Canada in the North, up the Chesapeake Bay toward Washington and Baltimore in the East, and at New Orleans in the South.

However, both sides, American and British, were tiring of the war. A British blockade of American ports had reduced American shipping and trade to a point of near economic collapse. But the British were becoming war weary, taxes were running very high, and trade with Canada and the British Caribbean was suffering. Thus both sides agreed to meet in August in Ghent (Belgium) to explore the possibility of peace. But the English, feeling that they had the military upper hand in the negotiations, demanded full British naval control of the Great Lakes, unrestricted access to the Mississippi River, and the creation of an Indian buffer state between Canada and the United States. The Americans were incensed at these demands. But British voices (including England's military genius and hero Arthur Wellington) also objected to these demands as being highly unreasonable and not likely to bring the troubles to an end (in this they were quite correct!).

However, the defeat of Napoleon had also taken care of some of the issues that had brought America to war in the first place. Britain was no longer on a war footing and therefore the British no longer felt the need to pursue the impressment of sailors. With the war with Napoleon seemingly over,* there was no longer any need to block American shipping to France or the French colonies in the Caribbean.

Nonetheless the war with America continued.

The British burn Washington, D.C. Americans were stunned by the arrival of the British fleet in the Chesapeake Bay in August. The American effort to fend off a large British army put ashore near Washington, D.C., failed miserably. The Americans were unorganized, poorly led, and poorly equipped to face this experienced British army. The British proceeded to humiliate the American militia gathered at Bladensburg on August 24th as they advanced on the American capital. The commanding American general lost his nerve, and he and his men fled (as did Madison and his presidential cabinet), leaving the capital open for the British to enter that evening. Then the British proceeded to burn to the ground: the White House, the Capitol building, the Library of Congress, and anything else of

---

*Or so it seemed at the time. However, in March of 1815 Napoleon would escape from the island of Elba to the mainland of France, gather a new French army and begin again his attacks on Europe's monarchs. But his Hundred Days was brought to a close in July when a grand coalition of Austria, Prussia and Britain met and defeated him at Waterloo. He was then banished to an island in the middle of the South Atlantic, where he lived out has days as a comfortable prisoner.

The Young Republic

value. In part this was done as repayment for the American action in York (Toronto) the previous year.

The Battle of Fort McHenry. From there the British headed confidently up the Chesapeake Bay toward Baltimore in September, but with a very different outcome this time. American militia stopped the British at North Point. And Fort McHenry, guarding Baltimore, held out boldly against the heavy bombardment from the British ships on September 13th.* Thus, unable to get past this unyielding resistance, the British finally withdrew, all the way back to Jamaica.

American victory on Lake Champlain. Meanwhile a major American victory took place on September 11th on Lake Champlain in New York, when a British fleet attempting to extend English control into the heart of the American nation was soundly defeated, losing three British ships to the Americans in the process. This fairly well ended the part of the grand plan to squeeze the Americans from the north. At this point the British turned their attention to the part of their grand plan which included the assault on New Orleans, scheduled for the beginning of 1815.

However, in the South, along the Gulf coast, Americans were holding fast against British efforts to gain a foothold there. The British gathered at Pensacola (Florida), but were easily overrun by General Jackson's troops. Jackson then moved to New Orleans, suspecting (correctly) that this would be the next British target.

The Treaty of Ghent (Christmas Eve, 1814). Meanwhile, by the end of October, both the British and Americans seemed to agree that the best thing to do was simply return things to the way they were before the war (*status quo ante bellum*), and began to fine-tune a treaty, which the diplomats of both sides signed on December 24th. British Parliament approved the treaty three days later, and it went by sea to America, arriving in mid-February of 1815. The Americans were also quick to approve.

The Battle of New Orleans (January 8, 1815). On the Gulf coast, neither the British nor the Americans were aware that the Treaty had been signed in Ghent, and on January 8th, they proceeded to battle. Jackson's men were unwavering against multiple British assaults on well-held positions outside the town. Jackson's troops were well-protected by a wall of cotton bales

---

*A witness to this British failure at Fort McHenry was Francis Scott Key, who wrote a poem about the flag remaining aloft through the night of heavy bombardment. The poem was eventually put to music and became the American national anthem, *The Star-Spangled Banner*.

they had erected against the advancing British, whose guns were totally ineffective in breaking down the American defenses. The net result was a disaster for the British: 291 British dead against 13 American dead, 1,262 British wounded against 39 Americans wounded and 484 British captured or missing. Although the battle took place after the war was officially over, it had its own very serious consequences: America had indeed established itself as a strong nation not to be taken for granted.

The greater results of the War of 1812. Wars have huge psychological/spiritual (as well as political) consequences – for both the winners and the losers. For the American Indians, their power had been rather permanently broken by the war. From then on, the Indians would be forced on a continuing retreat, fighting as they went, but retreating nonetheless, with little likelihood that they would ever be able to stem the flow of Anglo Whites into their lands.

As for the Americans, they now experienced a new sense of being American nationals, as well as (and maybe even more importantly than) Virginians, or New Yorkers, etc. And the war had put a new name on their lips: General Andrew Jackson, a person with an obviously major destiny ahead of him as a national leader.

The war would also mark the death of the Federalist Party. Federalists had resisted the war effort every way legal, and often illegal (trafficking with the British enemy). Interestingly, they now took the states'-rights position of the older Jefferson Republicans, just as the Republicans were turning increasingly nationalistic. The Federalists were bitter about the complete Republican domination in Washington, accusing Republicans of everything imaginable, including even being nothing more than Jacobins (the butchers of the French Revolution).

So alienated were the Federalists by political developments that they even met secretly in Hartford, Connecticut (mid-December 1814 to early January 1815) to consider New England's secession from the Union, even as the Treaty of Ghent ending the war was being finalized. The timing could not have been worse for the Federalists. Jackson's victory at New Orleans had the American national spirit running so high that the Federalists now appeared to be even treasonous. The Federalists backed down from their call for secession. But it was too late anyway. As a party, they were finished.

Madison's last days as president (1815–1817). The last two years of Madison's eight-years as president were largely without major controversy or issue. The nation was ready to get back to the business of growing, economically and territorially. Madison sponsored tariffs to protect a growing American industrial sector and busied himself in securing federal grants for

The Young Republic

the states for the building of roads and canals to link the interior with the East coast. He even backed down from some of his earlier Jeffersonian tendencies, bringing back into existence in 1816 a second Bank of the United States (BUS)*, and supporting the establishment of a professional military. At this point he was again definitely following in the footsteps of his once friend Hamilton – not his former mentor, Jefferson.

But a huge controversy arose in the very last days of his presidency over the Bonus Bill of 1817. It called for profits and dividends from the new national bank to be used to fund more roads and canals. Though Madison was a supporter of exactly just such internal development, he felt that the Constitution did not allow for the federal government itself to become involved directly in this action. He thus vetoed the bill just prior to leaving office. In this he was drawing from his former Jeffersonian dislike of empowerment of the national government (over the states). But he was also treading on the ground of an issue that would come increasingly to trouble all national politics: the growing sectionalism that seemed to arise over every issue. For one thing, development of the West, at the expense of Eastern financial interests, drew off workers necessary for development of the eastern industries. But for another, it constantly raised the question: is a rising Western territory to develop as a slave or free state?

---

*Madison and the Republican Congress had earlier refused to renew Hamilton's Bank of the United States (BUS) when its charter expired in 1811.

CHAPTER SIX

THE SHAPING OF A NATION

* * *

THE "ERA OF GOOD FEELINGS"

James Monroe (the fourth Virginian president: 1817–1825). In December of 1816 the electoral college gave a complete thrashing to the dying Federalist Party when it elected the Jeffersonian Republican James Monroe to the presidency by 183 votes in his favor, against only 34 votes for the Federalist Rufus King of New York.

Monroe was not an exciting politician. But he more than made up for his lack of charisma with his personal dedication to the young American nation that he had served so well. He served in Washington's army and took part in many of the famous battles of the War of Independence, rising to the rank of colonel before he resigned his commission to study law under Jefferson. He would follow in the footsteps of Jefferson, becoming America's minister to France, then governor of Virginia. He then became President Madison's secretary of state, and thus a natural choice of the Republicans for the presidency when Madison indicated his intention to step down from the presidency after two terms.

America relaxed greatly in finally finding peace with England and France in 1815, producing a lively sense of optimism which in turn in 1817 prompted a Boston newspaper, the *Columbian Centinel,* to entitle the new post-war period the "Era of Good Feelings." Yet there were a number of problems still facing the country.

The Economic Panic of 1819–1821. The biggest problem the nation faced at this point was the state of the nation's economy. The war had thrown the government treasury into deep debt, a debt financed largely by the government's borrowing from a number of private banks. This borrowing in turn flooded the economy with new bank notes, producing a currency inflation that threatened the financial stability of the country.

Furthermore the private sector was in just as much trouble. With

The Shaping of a Nation

the end of the Napoleonic wars in 1815, the demand in Europe for American agricultural goods, which had produced much of the prosperity of the Era of Good Feelings, dropped away rapidly (European soldiers had returned to their farms, thus ending the demand for American farm goods). The price of farm products faded away in America, leaving farmers unable to pay the debts they had acquired in buying more land to meet the former high European demand. Land prices also fell as farmers scrambled to sell off some of the land they had purchased.

Banks that held farmer's mortgages soon also found themselves in trouble as well, the banks demanding from the farmers cash payments, cash which the farmers simply did not have. The bankrupt farmers being forced to turn their land titles over to the banks was no help to the banks, as the land was now valued at much less than the original loans the banks had extended to the farmers. Also, people now began to make a run on potentially troubled banks, demanding specie (gold or silver) for the bank notes issued previously by the banks. As the banks had issued paper notes ten times the value of the metallic specie they held in their vaults, they were simply forced to shut down. By 1819 and 1820, banks, farms, and other businesses were closing down everywhere

Understanding the economic dynamic. This was the first major panic, like those that would hit the country at regular intervals, such as in 1837, 1857, 1873, 1893, and 1907. The pattern of the 1817 panic was also very similar to the one that developed within rural America just after World War One (1919–1920) when American farmers and their banks found themselves in exactly the same situation. And there were similar elements in the situation during the 1930s Great Depression when American manufacturers found that the market for their new consumer goods was saturated, most Americans now possessing the radios, cars, sewing machines, washing machines, etc., that had the industrial market running so hot in the 1920s.

It is the very nature of venture capitalism to get caught up in these wild swings of fortune, especially because of the aggressive – and risk-taking – nature of capitalism itself. A capitalist economic system is shaped very heavily by the personal economic decisions that the individual members of society themselves make. At the same time, the system is subject to unpredictable forces, simply because there are so many forces at play in a free or open national economy. But history has demonstrated over and over again that it is better to let those mysterious factors play out than to try to bring them under the mastery of some small group of enlightened economists or social planners. Such Socialism, in trying to bring these mysterious social and economic forces under human control, simply ends up snuffing them out. Invariably Socialism brings into being the most oppressive and impoverished of all economic systems.

Of course, some moderate amount of governmental refereeing of the economic game played in a market open to all private producers and consumers is wise. But the governing referee must never start trying to play the game itself or the game will simply stall. This would be, after all, just another version of Socialism.

Actually, in 1816, just prior to the outbreak of the Panic, Congress had voted into existence the second Bank of the United States in order to bring the economy under some kind of stricter management. Eventually the financial discipline that the BUS imposed on the nation (tightening the country's money supply) brought down the inflation, and helped stabilize the value of the nation's currency. At first this intervention merely deepened the crisis, leaving many businesses, large and small, facing collapse when they could not repay the cheap money they had borrowed earlier with the money now due on their loans, money (especially silver and gold coinage) that was now much more scarce and thus more expensive for them. Then when in early 1819 American cotton prices crashed as a result of the British purchase of cotton from India, panic set in. But the BUS did not let up on its tight money strategy, despite the country's economic reversal from inflation to deflation.

Finally the economy settled down and began to revive, though less from any activity of the BUS than from the availability of new Mexican silver to back an expansion of America's money supply in metallic specie.

But not surprisingly, as with the first BUS, the second BUS would come under the intense dislike of America's vast legion of farmers – who, as always, loved cheap money and inflation since it allowed them to repay their mortgages and other operational loans much more easily with cheaper or inflated dollars. Besides, to their way of looking at things, the banking world was simply the tool of wealthy exploiters operating out of the industrial East.

Thus sadly, the stumbling economy, and the government's efforts to revive it, had undermined the spirit of national unity produced by the war, and revived the old sectional rivalries that divided the country.

These events would also split the Republican Party into the New Republicans (in many ways similar in their economic and political philosophy to the former Federalists) and the Democratic-Republicans (closer to the original Jeffersonians).

These events would also bring the short-lived Era of Good Feelings to an abrupt end.

Florida. The Napoleonic Wars of 1800–1815, during which Spain had been torn between French efforts at political control of their country and

The Shaping of a Nation

desperate Spanish efforts to throw off the French grip, had left Spain greatly exhausted. As a result, Spain proved to be powerless in its efforts to head off independence movements among its Spanish colonies in America (for example, Mexico, Colombia, and Argentina) which erupted during this period. And where Spain continued after the war to hold on to some kind of position in America, that hold was very weak. This certainly was the case in Florida.

Seminole Indian raids from Spanish Florida into Georgia and Alabama ultimately decided the fate of Florida. Because of these raids, American Secretary of War John C. Calhoun in late 1817 ordered the hero of New Orleans (and Horseshoe Bend) General Andrew Jackson to take action with respect to the Seminoles. Jackson interpreted this as being more than a call for the defense of the American borders. With the coming of the next spring (April and May of 1818) he invaded Florida, not only decisively defeating the Seminoles but seizing all of Spanish Florida, declaring it to be thus a territory of the United States. President Monroe and his secretary of state, John Quincy Adams, were embarrassed. But the American nation was thrilled by Jackson's heroics.

Spain at this point decided that wisdom called simply for the sale of Florida to the United States (for the price of $5 million) confirmed in the Adams Onis Treaty of 1819. With the American payment in 1821 of that sum, the United States in fact came into undisputed possession of Florida.

The Missouri Compromise (1820). In 1819, Missouri applied for statehood, opening up a bitter controversy arising from the question about whether Missouri would enter the Union as a slave or free state. At this point there was a balance of eleven free and eleven slave states making up the Union. But the balance was precarious, stirring fears of the Southern slave states that adding more states would swamp them in an anti-slave mood arising from the North. Slavery had been forbidden in the states of the Northwest Territory. And Louisiana had been admitted in 1812 as a slave state, and thus there was some kind of expectation that future Southern states would join the ranks of the slave states. But Missouri was a border state, with slavery practiced in parts of the state, but not in others. Was Missouri thus to be considered slave or free?

The Constitution itself made no mention of the issue, although one of the last acts of the Continental Congress in 1789 was to set up the Northwest Territory as a free zone forbidding slavery, indicating that the federal Congress might have such authority as well concerning the admission of territories as new states. The Southern states claimed that the issue was entirely a state issue, not a federal issue; each state could of its own decide whether it was to be a slave state or not.

Nonetheless, slavery was not really a legal issue as much as a deep moral issue, with slavery clearly coming under ever deeper moral questioning.* This made the Southern states all the more uneasy, because the lifestyle, the Southern fantasy of living the life of plantation aristocracy, as well as the tobacco/cotton economy itself was completely dependent on the institution of slavery. There was no longer any talk in the South about the institution simply withering away by itself. Indeed, any talk of limiting the institution was taken as an insult or threat to Southern culture.

But the North was deeply involved in a spiritual movement of Christian revival, in which slavery certainly appeared to be one of the sins of the nation that needed cleansing. The abolition of slavery was indeed soon to become a major topic of conversation in the North, a conversation that made the South very nervous.

On top of this, the population of the North was expanding much more rapidly than that of the South because the freer culture made for greater personal opportunity. It thus drew adventuresome Americans – and even Europeans – to the North rather than the South for settlement.

All this tension came to a head with the question of admitting Missouri as the twenty-third state. But then Maine requested entry into the Union as a new state, and the possibility of compromise seemed to present itself.

Henry Clay – the Great Compromiser. Henry Clay of Kentucky stepped forward to offer specifics as to how this compromise might be achieved. As a package deal, Clay proposed admitting both states – one slave, one free – thus preserving the balance, coupling this with the stipulations that a line would be drawn across the country at the 36°30' parallel running west from the Mississippi River, distinguishing future slave and free states. This would run along the southern border of Missouri, but exempt Missouri, allowing it to be admitted as a slave state. He added also the provision that the property interests of Southern slave-owners would be fully protected, including the return of runaways and the ability of Southerners to travel north with their slaves without the fear of the legal loss of their slaves once in the North. And he cleverly bundled this as a single proposal so that it could not be amended by those wanting to pick its provisions apart.

At the time this compromise seemed to be a brilliant solution to the problem, which many hoped would now go away as an issue. But Clay's

---

*Prior to the War of Independence – even during the Great Awakening of the mid–1700s – most Americans avoided the issue concerning the evils of slavery, even as an additional 150,000 slaves were imported to America from the 1720s to the 1760s. But the Quaker John Woolman took up the cause in the 1740s, and in 1758 was instrumental in getting the Yearly Meeting to set up a committee to look into this issue. But this was merely a very slow start of what eventually would become Abolitionism.

The Shaping of a Nation

compromise did not solve the problem. Instead it brought out into ever-stronger light the deep moral-cultural division separating the North from the South, a division that clearly was not going to go away on its own and indeed would only grow larger with the recurring matter of the country's taking in new states to the West.

The Monroe Doctrine. Meanwhile, with Spain caught up in a struggle at home in Europe between Republicanists and Monarchists, Spanish power overseas in the Americas was clearly slipping. After ten years of struggle, New Spain or "Mexico" finally (1821) secured its independence from an exhausted Spain – with Central America following right behind.

When in 1822 France, backed by other monarchs of continental Europe, moved to oust a constitutional republic in Spain and restore the country to monarchy, concern developed in America that Spain, or even (and more likely) France, might want to impose imperial rule in the Americas again. But Britain was just as alarmed as America about this. Britain had its own reasons for not wanting to see this happen. Britain was always suspicious of any rising European power that might upset the balance of power on the continent and overseas, for such a development would usually end up isolating Britain from the rest of Europe (and from the lucrative overseas trade that Britain's economy depended on), always a dangerous position for Britain to find itself in. Britain had been developing growing commercial relations with the newly independent republics of the former Spanish (and Portuguese) Empires in America, which they did not want to lose through a renewal of Spanish (or French) imperial or mercantilist designs* on the Americas.

Thus it was that British Foreign Secretary Canning inquired of Monroe's secretary of state, John Quincy Adams, the son of the former president, John Adams, about America's interest in a policy of blocking the restoration of European imperialism in the Americas. It was understood that the British navy would be ultimately the enforcing agency of such a policy, but without any formal connection (which might also stir up accusations about Adams being pro-British).

The answer was in the affirmative, and took the form of a message to Congress by Monroe in 1823 (actually written by Adams), in which Monroe made it clear that the Americas had a destiny separate from Europe's, and America would defend that separation by whatever means necessary. European monarchs scoffed at Monroe's presumptuousness, but in fact were well aware of the reality of British interests behind this pronouncement and did not actually challenge it.

---

*Mercantilism was commonly practiced in European imperialism, in which only the European mother country was allowed to trade with its overseas colonies.

Monroe's final years as president (1823–1825). And thus it was that Monroe finished out his presidency in 1825 with the country once again in excellent shape. The economy was booming with the expansion of American industry and trade, the American population was expanding to lay full claim to its western territories, and America found itself in no major crisis with one or another of the major European powers. The Era of Good Feelings had been restored!

The election of 1824. With the collapse of the Federalist Party, the American two-party system had thus also collapsed, complicating greatly the selection of candidates for the presidential election. The Republican Party itself was consequently split into a number of contending factions, built mostly around prominent personalities, the various geographic regions that supported them, and the spoils system of political rewards that generated widespread personal support for the leaders in Washington (with the notable exception of John Quincy Adams who found such political wheeling and dealing to be personally distasteful).

Four different candidates presented themselves for the presidency, John Quincy Adams, William Crawford, Henry Clay and Andrew Jackson. As a consequence, none of them received a majority vote (at least 50 percent of the total vote) and the election of the president (according to the Twelfth Amendment) was given to the House of Representatives to decide. But only three candidates were eligible for consideration under the provisions of the Twelfth Amendment. Jackson had received by far the most popular votes of the four (though only a small plurality in the electoral college) and was expecting the House to elect him. Clay, who was the fourth in the electoral count and thus not eligible for House consideration, nonetheless commanded considerable power in the House of Representatives as its Speaker. Clay personally disliked Jackson and was closer to Adams in political thinking. He convinced his supporters in the House to vote for Adams, giving Adams a full majority on the first ballot, and thus the presidency.

John Quincy Adams (President 1825–1829).[43] Then when Adams named Clay to be his secretary of state (so far, the one position that seemed a natural stepping stone to the presidency), Jackson exploded in fury. He claimed that the deal was simply a corrupt bargain,* and hammered away

---

*This was quite an unfair accusation, as Clay was an outstanding statesman, very well suited for the job. Jackson's team in fact had also courted Clay in the hopes that he would swing his votes in the House towards Jackson. Part of Jackson's fury was a result of Clay's earlier strong stand in Congress against Jackson's invasion and grab of Florida.

The Shaping of a Nation 217

on that claim for the next four years.

John Quincy Adams was much like his father, John Adams, lacking personal charm or charisma, but possessing a brilliant mind and a strong moral character. He did not particularly like politics, or even the office of presidency, and did very little to build up a corps of political support beneath him. He preferred to focus instead on programming various physical and intellectual improvements for the nation, from roads and canals, to the encouragement of industry, to the advancement of education, to the support of the sciences. He worked hard to reduce greatly the national debt. But he faced tremendous opposition from Jackson and his supporters in Congress on every one of his programs.

He did not have an extensive foreign policy program to deal with because as the former secretary of state he had overseen tremendous improvements in the country's international position. He also believed that it was America's duty to not act the part of an ambitious imperialist nation, but instead to focus on the development of the Republic at home.

He tried to be fair in the handling of the nation's relations with the Indians – especially concerning the land rights of the large Cherokee nation in the American Southeast.* But on this issue Jackson's opposition was extremely strong, as this was a matter of great interest to Jackson's natural constituency of Southern and Western Whites, who were demanding that the Indians be removed to a location somewhere West of the Mississippi River.

Overall, John Quincy Adams, though an excellent administrator as U.S. president, was sadly out of touch with a dynamic America, which others, such as Jackson, understood instinctively. Thus Adams would serve only one term as president.

* * *

THE TOUGH QUESTION OF INDIAN vs. ANGLO LAND RIGHTS

The English/American understanding of land ownership. Land – Indian land – had long been a big part of America's sense of personal salvation. Americans understood that God saved the soul. But they also understood that land saved the body! From the very moment that Americans landed on the Atlantic or Eastern shores of North America they

---

*The Cherokee had gone to great lengths to accommodate themselves to Anglo culture, most of them becoming Christians and giving up their hunting economy to become settled farmers like the Whites. Although they presented no danger to the Whites, Southern Whites could not get past their general hatred of all Indians – or anyway the general hunger to confiscate Indian lands.

had developed a very strong interest in the land, the low mountains and dark forests that lay just to the West of them. The Indians who lived on that land were not numerous and thus the lands seemed virtually empty, just waiting for the English colonists to come and settle there.

At first the English settlers and Indian hunters attempted to stay on friendly terms with each other. But their concepts of land ownership were so different that conflict – deadly conflict – was inevitable. To the English, land ownership was demonstrated in a person's working of that land. Whoever cleared the land, cut back the forest and planted crops in these new clearings could claim unchallenged title to the land. Idle land, land that was not farmed or grazed, was not owned by anyone. Indeed, unfarmed land was simply uninhabited land. Thus the Indians as hunters requiring the woodlands for the survival of the game they hunted just did not factor into the English understanding of things.

To the English way of thinking, Indian land was simply there waiting for the taking by some industrious individual. But according to the Indian way of thinking, the land was there for hunting, not farming – and the English were no more than thieves, stealing their land.

In this contest for the land the Indians were technologically, numerically, and socially greatly outmatched. Not only did the English settlers possess superior weapons, they also had more highly disciplined or unified social power. The Indians were not only small in number on the land, they were highly divided among themselves – ancient enemies, one small tribe against another. The Indians thus were tremendously handicapped in their efforts to hold back English expansion into their ancestral territories. Consequently, by the early 1800s, the expansion into the Indian lands of the West and South by land-hungry Anglo-Americans was rapid.

There had been efforts from time to time, even from the beginning of the earliest English settlements, to legalize or regularize this question of land ownership. For the English this was done through written legal assignments of the land in the form of deeds. Such legal assignments not only awarded ownership to an individual but also to that individual the rights of transfer of that land to another – as a grant (often in marriage, often as the terms of peace after a war) or as a sale. Treaties as a follow-up to a war very often included the idea of the transfer of land from one individual (a king, for instance) to another.

The weight or worth of treaties. Indians were aware of such arrangements – entering into arrangements among themselves similar to the European concept of treaty. And thus on many occasions the English and tribal chiefs transacted land deals – that is, entered into treaties with one another. The Dutch thus purchased the island of Manhattan for their

The Shaping of a Nation

New Amsterdam and Roger Williams so also purchased from the local tribes the land at the head of the Narragansett Bay for his Providence Colony. But in general, even this nicety was ignored by the English who pushed into Indian lands to make way for their own settlements, unaware of or ignoring the Indians' land rights.

There often were treaties signed between the English and the Indians – usually following another bitter conflict or local land war. These treaties usually simply acknowledged another loss of land by the Indians, though they were frequently accompanied by some comforting section which recognized the rights of the same Indians to other, uncontested territory. But treaties back in Europe among kings had very little longevity – quickly broken by their kings at the earliest opportunity. And so it was with the treaties the English signed with the Indians. These agreements were treated with the same lack of sense of anything permanent about them. This the Indians did not understand, for their idea of a treaty was that it formed a perpetual or permanent right to land use, one that would be handed down as a matter of honor by generation after generation. Sadly, the Indians were to learn that things just did not work this way with the English.

Besides, frontiersmen paid little attention to the land arrangements entered into with the Indians by their colonial governments. Such governments were far away and the local frontiersmen lived in a world far removed from the halls of the colonial governments. Frontiersmen conducted their own affairs pretty much as they saw fit, regardless of what the colonial authorities had agreed to.

The Christian understanding of all this. Why didn't Christianity soften this kind of hard-handed land seizure? Christians after all were instructed by Jesus to love their neighbor as themselves. But their Bible also told them of the command of God to the Israelites to enter the land of the Canaanites and clear it of both the people and even the herds and flocks of the Canaanites. This was a necessary precondition for God to be able to settle the Promised Land with his Chosen People.

Of the two viewpoints, Christlike love or Israelite aggression, when it came to dealing with the Indians, the tendency of Christian America was to take the Old Testament approach. Christian Americans generally saw themselves under the same instructions by God to clear the land to make way for the People of God.

The huge demographic or population pressures behind the expansion. Anyway, whatever the legal or moral points involved in this takeover of the land, there was little likelihood that the Indians were going to be able to hold back the flood of Europeans into their tribal territories.

Since the late 1300s the European population had exploded and land hunger in Europe was very intense. This was the case not just in England but in the Netherlands and in German-speaking central Europe. The English first attempted in the 1500s to put excess population in Ireland, this being justified in the English mind by the primitiveness of Irish society (in the same way English land settlement would soon be justified in America). But some of this Irish land soon filled up with settlers from Scotland – the Scots-Irish – who in turn (by the early 1700s) would push on to America and become major settlers along the American-Indian borderlands or frontiers.

Even by the time of American independence, numerous European settlers in America had left the coastal lowlands along the Atlantic coast and were settling in various places in the Appalachian Mountains to the West. Some had even crossed those mountains and had begun to settle in the rolling hills of Kentucky and Tennessee to the West of the Mountains.

As we have seen, one of the last tasks of the Continental Congress in 1787 was to design an orderly system of settlement of the land in the Northwest Territory awarded the Americans in their peace settlement that ended the War of Independence with the English. Swift action was required to get settlers into these territories – before the English found some new excuse to break the peace treaty with the Americans and seize these lands again.

Of course, the Indians were not consulted in this matter. They, as "savages," counted not at all in the plans to map out a program of systematic land development in the West.

And now that the legal reach of Anglo-America extended, through the Louisiana Purchase, even to the Rockies (and possibly beyond), life was going to become very tough for the American Indian.

* * *

THE JACKSONIAN DEMOCRATIC REVOLUTION[44]

The new Jacksonian Democrats. One of the unintended and unwanted achievements of the one-term Adams presidency was the creation of a new and very strong political force, the Democratic Party, whose sole purpose – besides supporting Jackson in every way possible – was to block Adams in every way possible.

Instrumental in getting this new political force organized was Martin Van Buren, a New Yorker who personally had an intense dislike of the remnants of the upper-class Whig elite of the American Northeast who held to the older notion that politics (and economics) should be directed by society's better elements: lawyers, bankers, manufacturers, shippers, etc. Jackson's (and

Van Buren's) Democrats represented the other side of the social scene: the common man, the day laborer, the Western woodsman, the trapper, the river boatman, but especially the farmer, the backbone of American society.

Where the Southern aristocrat fell in this newly rising social order was complex. The Jeffersonian aristocrats were themselves moved aside by this new political arrangement. The older Jeffersonian Republicans nonetheless would identify with the new Democratic Party, because of its Southern/Western orientation. But the days when the Southern aristocrats would preside over the Southern/Western political caucus were over. Mostly they continued to exercise whatever influence they could from behind the scenes. Out front, leading the political caucus were the brash, unrefined, champions of the people.

The 1828 election. This election was vulgar in tone, with candidates – or their supporters, anyway – hurling coarse insults against each other.* But the results regardless were a major landslide victory for the Westerner, Andrew Jackson (Tennessee) and his running mate, the Southerner John C. Calhoun (South Carolina).

So, Adams was out. Like his father, Adams quietly slipped away from Washington without attending the inauguration of the new president.

Andrew Jackson (supported by Van Buren) was projected as a man of the people, in contrast to Adams who was portrayed as a New England elitist, a social snob. On both counts this was a major exaggeration. Adams was colorless in personality, but in his own way was as interested in the welfare of the American people as Jackson.

Jackson played to the crowds. Indeed, on inauguration day, throngs of very ordinary people attempted to gather to see and hear their hero being sworn in as president, and then join him at the White House for a major reception. Even in through the windows the crowds came, muddy boots and all, stepping on the furniture, knocking over tables, smashing china. Jackson slipped away from the adoring crowd and quietly had dinner with close associates. Jacksonian democracy was all a grand show, but one for which Jackson himself had no personal interest. He would let Van Buren take care of the political image-making. As for Jackson, he had other things he would rather be doing!

So, the age of elite-led politics was over. The noblemen (Washington, Adams Sr., Jefferson, Madison, Monroe, and Adams, Jr.) who formerly had

---

*In the case of Jackson, it was slander about the legality of his marriage to his wife Rachel, so vicious that it may have been the reason Rachel died of a heart attack in December 1828, shortly after Jackson's presidential victory, but before he was sworn into office. Jackson, understandably, remained forever bitter about this incident.

quietly assumed the presidency in order to serve the nation, would now be replaced by the politically ambitious, who knew how to work the political imagery necessary for getting elected to public office. In this Van Buren, on behalf of Jackson, was a genius. He understood what it took to appeal to the common voter. He understood the press and its ability to create reality. He knew how to line up voters and get them to the polls, especially in the newly emerging democratic age of the general electorate.

With the advent of full democracy (at least with respect to the House of Representatives), there was a much lower voter turn-out percentage-wise than in the days when voting rights were tied closely to property ownership. Voting then was viewed as a responsibility, and the turn-out proportionately vastly greater, even though the total numbers were also vastly lower. Now it would take all kinds of political cleverness to get sufficient voter turnout to get a candidate elected in a very competitive election.

Paying for rounds of whiskey or beer for those who came out to vote for a candidate was probably the most obvious technique employed.

The spoils system.* This term derives from the manner in which Andrew Jackson treated his electoral success in 1828. For a successful political candidate, the greatest form of spoils was the numerous offices to which he could appoint his supporters. Thus with a candidate's electoral success came long lines of job-seekers, each hoping to get an appointment to a public job. In those days there was no professional civil service, selected through special qualifying exams for various government jobs. Instead jobs were filled on the basis of personal support of a candidate, regardless of whether a person was qualified or not. Such a payoff for electoral support was simply what everyone under the new democracy expected from the political system. That's how democracy was expected to work.

Financing democracy. A great warrior and political charismatic Jackson was indeed. But a presidential administrator obligated to help keep the vast American economy healthy, Jackson was not. As a result, the young nation would face a series of crises that would challenge the heart of its economy – and its politics.

A part of the problem had already taken root in the last year (1828) of the Adams presidency over the question of tariffs. Tariffs on imported goods were understood to serve a dual purpose: to protect the American producers from cheaper goods coming from India (cotton) and machinery

---

*From the statement coined by New York Senator Marcy, "To the victor belong the spoils," following Andrew Jackson's election to the U.S. presidency in 1828.

The Shaping of a Nation 223

(England), and to pay for all the infrastructure projects reaching into the expanding American West, such as roads and canals. The tariffs themselves were disruptive of American political interests, as protection of one industry, such as the higher price of Southern cotton, came at a great cost to another industry, such as the New England textile mills that needed cheap cotton to compete with cheaper English textiles. Thus when a bill was introduced in Congress in 1824 to raise a whole range of duties on imports, it was met with mixed emotions, and took four years to finally pass. When it did, it plunged America into a new crisis, political as well as economic.

A grand strategy of Calhoun, who introduced the bill, was to call for an increase in the tariff so high that (he presumed) his own bill would naturally be killed. He and the fellow Jacksonians were actually opponents of the increase, seeing no great benefits to themselves in this legislation. But the New Englanders, including even Van Buren, were not shocked into opposition as Calhoun had hoped, so the bill advanced slowly, almost imperceptibly, until in 1828 the Tariff of Abominations was passed (over finally Calhoun's own strong opposition!).

With Jackson and Calhoun swept into power in the 1828 elections, the two running mates would find themselves slowly splitting in their political philosophies, in no small part due to the new tariff. Jackson turned out to be a major supporter of the tariff, for it afforded him the monies needed to pay for roads and canals of special interest to his political supporters in one state or another. True, most roads were private or state funded. But the truly big projects, such as the national road west into Ohio could be funded only by a larger single source, namely the national government. And Jackson enjoyed being in the position to oversee just such development, especially when he could use his power to exclude similar projects in the states of his political opponents!

Calhoun, however, saw the expanding powers of the national government increasing the potential of granting it greatly increased authority to take action in other areas, such as in the question of slavery. As a politically sensitive Southerner, Calhoun was well aware of the growing swell of anti-slavery sentiment growing in the North and was fearful that the rapidly increasing Northern population would eventually give Congress sufficient votes to ban the practice of slavery altogether. As a result, Calhoun, once a strong nationalist, now became an increasingly strong voice in support of states' rights, meaning that the states, not the national government, should have sole right to determine their position on the slavery issue. This would throw President Jackson, a strong nationalist, into increasing opposition to his vice president, Calhoun. Thus with the new round of presidential elections coming up in 1832, Jackson replaced Calhoun with his loyal supporter Van Buren as his new running mate.

Western land sales. The other chief means of raising federal revenue besides tariffs was the sale of Western land. New Englanders wanted the land sales to slow down because it drained off workers needed in the New England factories. Southerners however were big supporters of the opening of Western land for sale, in part because, with slavery, the South was not really the land of opportunity for its slowly rising White population and because cotton production tended to deplete the energy of the soil. Therefore new lands were needed to be opened up for cotton production. Thus whereas the North proposed increasing the price of Western land (presumably to increase federal income), the South proposed the opposite: to lower the price of land, and if no buyers could be found, to simply give the land away. Thus along with tariffs, the issue of land sales deepened the North versus South (and West) split.

The Webster-Hayne debate (1830). And here too in the land sale debate, the issue of slavery would insert itself. The opening of Western lands would always bring forward the question of whether this new territory was to allow slavery or not. Thus the great debate between the Northerner Daniel Webster and the Southerner Robert Hayne about Western land sales quickly turned itself into a question about the future of slavery. But it also even got down to the question of the future of the country as a united people.

Hayne raised the specter of a South being forced to change its lifestyle by an imperialist North and countered with the old Jefferson-Madison nullification doctrine, that the Union was simply an agreement among sovereign states and that the states themselves had the final say on what went on politically within the Union. The implication was that if the states did not agree with political developments, they had even the right to secede, to end that relationship and go off on their own (as the New Englanders themselves had considered doing during the days of the War of 1812).

Webster countered that the very freedom enjoyed by the nation, a nation created by the people themselves and not just the states, was a result of the tremendous strength of the Union, and that to lose that unity was to lose the freedom that Americans enjoyed.

It was now easy to see that the new nation was headed for major trouble over this very strong cultural split which ran through its very heart, multifaceted in character, combining the issues of federal revenues, Western expansion, economic lifestyles (feudal vs. industrial), and ultimately slavery, forging itself into a sharp sword which was cutting the country in half. Slavery especially stood at the heart of the division, for the idea of a White man holding a Black man in subjugation as property was understood

The Shaping of a Nation

to be vital to the very life of the South – and at the same time understood by the North as a gross sin likely bringing the wrath of God down on a people allowing such an abomination to occur within its society.

The 1836 Gag Rule. There seemed to be no way to bridge this widening cultural gap. Eventually, however, Congress came up with the supposedly ingenious idea (proposed by Representative Henry Pinckney of South Carolina) that the way to avoid the slavery issue from causing an irreparable split in the country was to get congressmen to agree simply to avoid the subject, not ever to bring it up in discussion. The explanation was that it was a state issue anyway and Congress had no constitutional right to interfere in the matter.

Whereas this may have helped smooth the problem over in the short term (but most politicians trend only think in the short-term anyway, or at least only as far forward as their next election) avoiding the subject ultimately meant that it would become even harder to resolve in the future.

Jackson and the 2nd Bank of the United States (BUS). Jackson was coming up for reelection in 1832, opposed in the electoral campaign by his old adversary Clay. In the midst of the campaign the BUS got dragged front and center into the Jackson-Clay battle. The question was not most importantly one of economics, such as the issue of coin versus paper money (which was a favorite subject of dispute among American politicians), as much as it was one of political patronage. The BUS was coming up for a renewal of its charter in 1838, though its supporters proposed an early renewal just to get things squared away sooner. But the fact that it was Clay and his supporters who made the proposal automatically infected the idea in the eyes of Jackson.

Jackson was not opposed to the BUS in principle, but wanted to reshape national banking in such a way that gave him the right to preside over the personnel and policies of such a bank. A national bank was a huge source of patronage, and Jackson disliked the idea that the BUS seemed to be the instrument of the up-East business class. He especially disliked it when Clay threw his support to the renewal of the BUS charter because it meant securing Clay's BUS patronage rights if the charter were renewed, and the loss of Jackson's patronage rights if his own idea of a national bank were thus set aside. Consequently, Jackson decided to fight the BUS with all of his typical Jacksonian ferocity.

The election of 1832. Thus the BUS became a major issue in the election of 1832. Jackson used all of his folksy language to depict the BUS as the tool of the up-East elite, succeeding in connecting his opponent Clay in the minds of the common folks with greedy elite trying to take the country away from the people. The strategy worked, and Jackson was reelected by a large popular majority and an even larger majority in the electoral college. Thus Jackson would be president for another four years, with Van Buren as his new vice president.

And Jackson would withdraw all government deposits and suspend all future business with the BUS in 1833, depositing government funds instead in a number of state and local banks, termed by his opponents as Jackson's "pet banks." He would block the renewal of the BUS's charter in 1836, and ultimately leave it struggling as something of a private bank (which finally closed in 1841), leaving the U.S. government without a strong financial instrument to combat economic crises, a major one which exploded in 1837 and lasted until revival finally began to occur in 1842/1843.

The Indian Removal (1830s).[45] Although Jackson had great respect for the American Indians as warriors, he nonetheless had no particular compassion for them as they faced the pressures of an ever-expanding Anglo population. And Jackson, ever-sensitive to his image as champion of the common (White) man, knew what his supporters' sentiments were with respect to the Indian: they wanted them removed as far away as possible from their own world. And in general, that meant moving the Indians beyond the Mississippi River.

This process had been urged since early in the Republic, had been going on slowly under various presidents, but had stalled during John Quincy Adam's presidency. Jackson's supporters in the Deep South (Georgia, Alabama and Mississippi) wanted the process resumed. If the federal government was not going to take action, then the states would – as part of the principle of states' rights

Particularly interested in such removal was the government of the state of Georgia, which eyed the Cherokee lands with envy. The fact that the Cherokee were Christians, literate, settled as farmers and peaceful, came as no defense in their effort to hold on to their ancestral lands. Also, the discovery of gold on Cherokee land made the situation for the Cherokee even much worse. The government of Georgia wanted the Indians gone, and signed a treaty with some compliant Cherokee chiefs authorizing the purchase of Cherokee land, coupled with the promise of land in the Oklahoma Indian territory as additional compensation. But thousands of Cherokees refused to accept the treaty.

Meanwhile Jackson got into the act, in part to bring the federal government rather than the states as the ruling voice in this issue. He pushed through Congress the Indian Removal Act of 1830 requiring the Indian tribes of the South to move west of the Mississippi River, principally

The Shaping of a Nation

to the designated Indian territories of present-day Oklahoma. The bill had originally implied that the removal would be voluntary. But by the time the bill was finalized the voluntary part had been lost along the way.

Cherokee attempts to fight the legality of Indian removal finally reached John Marshall's Supreme Court, which on the one hand had determined in 1831 (*The Cherokee Nation v. Georgia*)[46] that the Cherokee had no right to be treated as a sovereign nation, but on the other hand in 1832 (*Worchester v. Georgia*)[47] that the state of Georgia had no right to engage in a treaty (forced or voluntary) with the Cherokee because that right existed only for Congress to exercise. Thus the official Georgia deal to remove the Cherokee was unconstitutional. Presumably the removal was now blocked. Or was it?

Jackson supposedly replied to Marshal's decision: "John Marshall has made his decision; now let him enforce it." Certainly Jackson had no intentions of getting in the way of the removal and he knew therefore that the removal was inevitably going to go forward, the Supreme Court notwithstanding.

The Indians resisted as best they could. In Illinois the Sauk and Fox Indians, led by Chief Black Hawk, revolted against the order and had to be put down violently by the Illinois militia (including in its ranks Captain Abraham Lincoln).*

But one by one the Choctaw (1831), Seminole (1832),† Creek (1834), and Chickasaw (1837) were forced to move. Finally the Cherokee were also forced to join the exodus when in 1838 General Winfield Scott and an American army confronted the Cherokee with the fact that it was now time to move.

Thus in a process of removing one Indian tribe after another in the period 1831 to 1838, 46,000 Indians were relocated in order to open the way for Anglo-American settlement in their traditional lands. All Indian tribes in the Southeast were forced to make the long trek to the Oklahoma Indian Territory without adequate support in food or shelter along the way. The worst suffering occurred among some 13,000 Cherokee, who in 1838 were first herded into camps in Tennessee and then force-marched westward through a freezing, snowy winter by General Scott's soldiers. Cold, disease, and starvation took a huge toll in their numbers. Thus many

---

*The Sauk and Fox had previously moved West across the Mississippi, but found themselves under attack by the Sioux Indians, and had moved back to Illinois, trying to avoid extinction.

†But the Seminole were the most resistant of the Indian tribes to the removal, engaging in savage war against the Whites from 1835 to 1842, during which many took to hiding in the Florida swamps. Ultimately three thousand were killed and the rest finally forced to move.

died along this Trail of Tears, possibly as many as a third of all Indians involved.

The Van Buren presidency (1837–1841). As Jackson's chief political supporter, as secretary of state and as vice president it was inevitable that the Jacksonian Democrats would look to Van Buren to take the lead as Jackson completed his second and final term as president in early 1837. Van Buren won the 1836 election easily over his Whig* opponents, who had mistakenly hoped that by dividing their candidacies they would throw the election into the House of Representatives where they commanded a strong majority. But little else about his presidency would be so easy.

The 1837 Economic Panic, and Depression (into the early 1840s). Van Buren would be saddled with a huge economic crisis that was not really his fault (the roots of it reached back into Jackson's presidency), which nonetheless he would be personally blamed for, and which guaranteed that his presidency would be short-lived (only one term).

The wild speculation in Western land, the decentralization of the banking system with Jackson's shutdown of the BUS, the extensive printing of paper money (as opposed to specie in the form of silver or gold coinage), and an overly optimistic consumer society (an economic bubble) all contributed to the crisis. But the brewing crisis itself was set off by events far away in England when the Bank of England, detecting an economic downturn in Great Britain (poor wheat harvests and the need to spend specie to purchase food from abroad), undertook policies to tighten up the money supply, sending shock waves throughout the rest of the world dependent on British finance as the international standard. This included importantly a number of American banks in the East, who were forced to follow the British lead in tightening their lending policies, sending out ripples, then waves, of financial fear into the previously overly optimistic economy.

Also the land speculation bubble was quick to burst when in 1836 Jackson issued an executive order demanding that Western land payments be made in gold and silver specie rather than paper money, coinage which most people did not have. Prior to this, land speculators had been buying up huge amounts of land employing only a rather seemingly inexhaustible supply of paper money issued by the numerous state and local banks on

---

*The Whig Party was formed in 1834 out of the regional and social interests of what had once been the heart of the Federalist Party: Up-East banking and manufacturing interests. Whigs also tended to oppose Westward expansion, in part out of the dislike of seeing slavery extend itself Westward, and in part out of a desire to slow down the movement of needed industrial laborers from the East to the Western frontier.

which the value of the dollar depended now that the BUS had been shut down.

Hard money advocates urged Jackson to take action, to bring real wealth into all this land speculation. And thus the 1836 Specie Circular was issued as one of Jackson's last acts as president, adding to the panic which broke out early in the next year (February-March of 1837) as Van Buren took office. Now speculators were holding land that could not be financed except by specie, at a time when those holding gold and silver specie were afraid to let go of it, hoarding it and taking it out of circulation – which merely depressed the economy further.

But it was not only land speculators that got hurt but the American banks themselves that got crushed in the panic. During the bubble, banks had been issuing those same paper dollars for mortgages and personal loans, careless in connecting those dollars to the real value of gold and silver coinage held in their vaults as reserve. As panic set in, people conducted runs on their banks, demanding the exchange of their paper money for gold or silver specie, which the banks simply did not have. At this point banks had only one of two options: to call in for full payment loans and mortgages extended to their customers (but who had the money to suddenly pay off their loans in full?) or to simply close their doors. Within a short time nearly half of America's banks, especially the small ones, indeed closed their doors.

Thus people held onto their money for fear that spending it might leave them penniless. But this only worsened the contraction. Prices on commodities fell as producers attempted to lure forth nervous consumers. All of this ultimately acted together to sink the American economy in a spiral downward of economic contractions affecting virtually every sector of the U.S. economy.

The first and worst to get hit was the cotton export business of the American South, which had to lower cotton prices by as much as 25 percent in order to hold on to industrial customers both at home and abroad. This immediately threw the cotton-dependent South into deep recession. But wheat prices were close behind in the collapse, hurting the Western farmer almost as badly.

In the industrial East, workers were let go as businesses floundered, to a point where in many cities almost a third of the workers found themselves unemployed.

State governments also hung on the edge of bankruptcy, having relied on the Jacksonian banks to hold their reserves, supply them with loans, and provide a tax base (on bank profits) which allowed the states not to have to tax their voters. It had all worked very nicely in the days of the bubble. But when the bubble burst, states across the country found themselves in deep trouble, not able to finance even the slenderest of their operations.

To top it off, Van Buren gave orders that the federal government would no longer distribute funds to the states (which had been part of Jackson's policy of building state support at the cost of the national government). His goal was at least to keep the national government solvent. But this only made the economic contraction all the worse.

It was thus unsurprising when in 1840 Van Buren faced a disillusioned electorate and went down in dismal defeat in his bid for reelection, 234 electoral votes for his Whig opponent Harrison and only 60 votes for Van Buren.

✳ ✳ ✳

JACKSONIAN CULTURE

Tocqueville's *Democracy in America*.[48] In 1831 the Frenchman Alexis de Tocqueville arrived in America, ostensibly to study the American prison system. But he and his associate Gustave de Beaumont were truly more interested in studying the American society in general, a subject of great interest to the French. Tocqueville published in two volumes the results of his study as *Democracy in America*, appearing in 1835 and 1840 at the height of the Jacksonian era. It provides an incredibly insightful view of the American culture by one standing outside that culture.

He noted the hugely individualistic spirit of the typical American and the restlessness of the American heart, which was already looking for the next challenge before it had completed the work on a previous challenge. He also noted the spirit which defended the basic equality of all (Whites), ever-ready to challenge presumptions of superiority on the part of others. He correctly attributed the origins of this egalitarian spirit to the Puritans of New England as well as the principle of the sovereignty of the people founded in the early Puritan covenants and state constitutions.

But he also noted the contradictions to all this posed by the agonizing question of slavery. Also, from a Frenchman's view with its more liberal attitudes toward marriage and the sexes, he was distressed at how rigid were the sexual roles assigned to men and women, both in and out of marriage (but this also was a Puritan legacy, unknown in France). He was also concerned about the dangers of democracy turning into a tyranny of the ignorant majority, unrestrained by the more enlightened understanding of social dynamics by society's more polished and better educated social elite. And he correctly predicted the tragedy of war that would eventually occur over the wrenching issue of slavery. In short, he described clearly the good and the not-so-good of Jacksonian America, at least as the French

The Shaping of a Nation

understood the social ideas of good and bad.

The Industrial Revolution continues forward in the East. The restlessness of the American heart that Tocqueville noticed was clearly obvious in the incredible amount of industrial activity – and innovation – pushing the American economy ever-forward. The development of the steam engine permitted extensive mechanical operations to take place where no water power was readily available to turn the wheels of industry's many new mills appearing across the North (by 1840 there were some 1,200 cotton mills in operation, mostly in the American Northeast).

Foodstuffs, raw materials, and even finished goods were constantly on the move in America – along the turnpikes and the many canals being laid out across the East. By 1818 the National Road had been completed linking the American East at Baltimore and Philadelphia with the Ohio River valley at Pittsburgh and thus providing access to the American interior all the way to the Mississippi. With the development of steam power,* paddlewheel boats able to go both ways on the great rivers of the American interior were soon moving vast amounts of produce from the West back to the East – and people and their goods headed to new lives in the West.

The Erie Canal. Not to be outdone by Baltimore and Philadelphia, New York, under the direction of its industrious Governor DeWitt Clinton, decided in 1817 to dig a canal from the Hudson River at Albany all the way to Lake Erie at Buffalo, thus gaining access to the American interior by way of the Great Lakes. The 363-mile project was open for business by 1825 (which turned out to be a highly profitable venture!).

The first railroads. In 1827 the town fathers of Baltimore, seeing water traffic outbid their wagon road, decided to investigate the possibilities of laying a railroad, similar to one under development in England. In 1828 they laid the first rails and by 1830 they had completed the first portion of the Baltimore and Ohio Railroad.

Then, not to be outdone by New York with its Erie Canal and Baltimore with its railroad, Massachusetts in 1830 and 1831 decided to undertake the building of a railroad across the low mountains to the West, to link Boston with Albany on the Eire Canal, completing the program by 1842.

Eight years later (1850) almost 3,000 miles of rail line then connected New England towns with even the Great Lakes. And by 1852 the Baltimore

---

*In August of 1807 Robert Fulton's steam-driven dual paddlewheel *North River Steamboat* made the amazing 150-mile boat trip up the Hudson River from New York City to Albany in 32 hours of actual travel (not counting stops along the way).

and Ohio Railroad was the first Eastern railroad to reach the Ohio River. This was such a boon to business, that the following year (1853) the mighty New York Central Railroad was formed by consolidating ten smaller railroad companies.

Meanwhile in the South, in 1828 the town fathers of Charleston decided to open up their city by rail all the way south to the Savannah River (to gain some of the trade which was prospering rival city Savannah tremendously). When it was completed in 1833 it was at that point the world's longest railroad. Eventually the South extended the reach of its rail system, by 1851 reaching Chattanooga on the Tennessee River and from there ultimately Memphis on the Mississippi River.

The mechanical reaper revolutionizes agriculture. In 1831 Cyrus McCormick held a demonstration of his new reaper, which with one mule and one driver could harvest wheat at six times the rate of a single farm worker.* Needless to say, the reaper now became not only highly sought after, it soon became standard equipment on the large farms of the American Midwest, which themselves were industrial enterprises rather than just mom-and-pop operations designed merely to support a single family.

Individualism and isolation of life in the opening West. The American world was changing fast, and change itself produced its own problems, psychological as well as physical.

On top of all this change, it was obvious by 1830 that the land was playing out in the East. The stony soil of New England had never been that great and – stressed by a rapidly expanding population – the region was unable to sustain a stable agricultural existence. So the 1830s and 1840s saw streams of New Englanders heading West across the Appalachian Mountains and down the Ohio River to find new homes in Ohio, Kentucky, Indiana, Illinois, and across the Mississippi into Missouri. Likewise, the cotton farms of Virginia, the Carolinas and Georgia were playing out, sending settlers West into Alabama, Mississippi, Louisiana, and even into the northern Mexico territory of Texas.

Unlike the planned movements and settlements of the Puritans two centuries earlier, there was no organization or coordination to this movement. Individuals just simply up and moved in the hope of starting a new life in the West. But life in the West proved to be isolating, and

---

*McCormick's claim to have invented the reaper was challenged by another inventor, Obed Hussey, whose 1833 invention was in fact a better machine. The two improved their models and competed until Hussey was finally driven out of business.

The Shaping of a Nation 233

dangerous under the constant threat of Indian attack.* Yet such a life produced highly independent and self-sufficient Americans, hunters and riflemen, well able to secure meat from nature, and prepared to fend off the dangerous Indian.

Unitarianism and Deism flourish in the East. At the same time, for others, especially those living along East-coast America, a comfortable small-town life (dependent on an economy other than just agriculture) seemed to have a natural peace and prosperity to it. Not surprisingly, life took on a more rational character, thus stepping back from its previous fervency in its Christian spirituality. Americans, especially among the more leisured professional classes, found themselves less interested in what God might do in their lives and more interested in what they might achieve for themselves under this more rational social realm emerging around them.

They did not abandon Christianity, because being Christian was understood to be the same as being civilized. But the faith component (trust in God as the essential higher power in their lives) was disappearing. Its place was being taken by a rational morality, a key part of Enlightenment Humanism that was sweeping intellectual circles at the time, in America as well as Europe. Such Humanism usually claimed the moral teachings of Scripture, especially the teachings of Jesus, as its Christian foundation. But in the end, no such connection was absolutely necessary, for these were self-evident truths that any rational person would understand as the foundation of any life well lived (French revolutionaries had gone so far as to disdain even this slender Christian connection with their utopian Idealism).

Once again (as in the enlightened days of the late 1600s and early 1700s) enlightened Americans of the early 1800s were convinced that Human Reason was vastly superior to the pre-scientific superstitions about life held by simpler Americans – Americans who were intellectually unable to shake off the irrational beliefs about people walking on water and raising the dead back to life. The enlightened ones were easily disdainful of those who clung emotionally to a religion drawn from a darker past. Of course, they failed to notice that their new Rational Humanism was no newer than the story of Adam and Eve's fall in the Garden of Eden or the long Biblical narrative about the repeated wandering of ancient Israel away from the counsel and discipline of God – and its tragic results.

Christian Unitarians. In the early 1800s a huge split occurred within the Congregationalist churches of New England, a split that ultimately came

---
*The results were always murderous for men, women and children, or worse, torturous, because Indians loved to gather to watch their captives writhe in carefully administered pain until they finally expired.

to center on the professorship of theology at Harvard College, a position which remained empty from 1803 to 1805. When the position was finally awarded to the Liberal Henry Ware, the conservative Calvinists left Harvard and founded the Andover Seminary. There they would be joined by the more evangelical members of the New Divinity* group. Meanwhile, Harvard College moved off more strongly in the Unitarian direction.

Inspired by a sermon preached in Baltimore in 1819 by Boston pastor William Ellery Channing, entitled "Unitarian Christianity," a sermon that found itself well-received among numerous New Englanders, the Unitarian movement began to grow rapidly, particularly among a large number of (mostly Congregationalist) pastors. This soon (1825) led over a hundred Unitarian pastors, again, mostly from New England, to come together to form the American Unitarian Association, in part to undo the Calvinism that had earlier formed the foundations of the New England Congregationalist churches. Their goal was to bring Christianity more in line with the recent discoveries of science, and with simple Humanist logic that found much of the traditional Biblical claims of Christianity to be completely unbelievable, most notably about man's inherent sinfulness, and need of repentance and renewal by the Holy Spirit. They proposed a simpler formula of good works undertaken by a kindly heart as the goal that a single God (the one and only God) set out for all mankind. In taking this position, they were certain that they were strengthening the foundations of a more progressive Christian religion, one that promised to underlay a newly-arising and fast-developing post-Trinitarian American society and culture.

Another individual to figure big in this rising Humanism around this same time (but now in his later life) was Thomas Jefferson. In 1822 Jefferson wrote his friend Dr. Benjamin Waterhouse attacking the foundations of traditional Christianity, pointing out in particular the ancient apologist Athanasius and the more recent Calvin as false shepherds and usurpers of the Christian name

> teaching a counter-religion made up of the deliria of crazy imaginations, as foreign from Christianity as is that of Mahomet. Their blasphemies have driven thinking men into infidelity.[49]

In that same letter Jefferson (who had published an updated Bible

---

*A major leader in the New Divinity movement was the religiously conservative Yale College president Timothy Dwight, who worked very hard to head off the Deism and Unitarianism spreading among the New England clergy. Dwight was also the head of the Federalist Party in Connecticut and an early supporter of the inter-faith American Board of Commissioners for Foreign Missions (ABDFM) created in 1810.

eliminating all the miracle stories and focusing only on the moral teachings of Scripture) professed that the simple doctrines of Jesus (to love the only God with all one's heart and one's neighbor as oneself) had been perverted by adding Platonizing doctrine (Jefferson did not like Plato very much either) most evident in Calvinist dogma.

But he was confident that such dark days were becoming a thing only of the past. Thus he states:

> *I rejoice that in this blessed country of free inquiry and belief, which has surrendered its creed and conscience to neither kings nor priests, the genuine doctrine of one only God is reviving, and I trust that there is not a young man now living in the United States who will not die a Unitarian.*

For those living in the comfort of a secure existence and untroubled by enemies or economic hard times, the promise of the Enlightenment seemed to be beyond all serious question.

Robert Owen and his communitarian or socialist experiments in America. Right in line with this rising Humanist Idealism were many experimental communities set out in America to show how a perfectly designed social order could produce unprecedented prosperity and happiness. One of the most active of such idealists was the Scottish social philosopher, Robert Owen. He actually set up a number of such utopian societies in America. But the most famous of these, the one he put his heart and soul into, was his New Harmony community, set out in the frontier land of Indiana. Owen bought the land in 1825 from a community that had also, under the leadership of the Lutheran Pietist George Rapp, attempted a similar experiment in perfect Christian Socialist living, a Harmony project that failed because of the inability of the German immigrants to live up to Rapp's great hope for them.

But anyway, what textile manufacturer Owen was proposing to do in his New Harmony had nothing to do with Christianity. A huge effort was made to make his New Harmony the perfect setting of purely Secular economic and social perfection. While Owen went around to promote support elsewhere for his New Harmony project, he left its supervision to his sons. They in turn ran into all sorts of difficulties when well-intended and not so well-intended individuals flocked to the project, a project that was designed to become self-supporting through the industrial enterprises Owen attempted to start up there. Some were willing to accept the responsibilities required of this communal (Socialist) venture. Many were not. Chaos quickly set in. Ultimately no moral structure (other than a breezy Humanism) underlay the project. Owen himself was strongly anti-Christian, and strongly pro-Humanist, but like all Humanists, could never figure out how to get a free people to accept social responsibilities on the basis of their own instincts. Other prominent Humanists visited and offered counsel to the community. But they got no further in getting a true social order up and running. Two years later (1827) the Owens had to abandon their project – without having learned anything in the process.

Emerson and the Transcendentalists. Another version of this development was found among the Transcendentalists, who reached well beyond the purely rational world of the Unitarians and other Humanists with their mystical quest for the Divine as a higher order of disciplined thought. They sought, through different forms of spiritual discipline, to embrace Divinity both in a oneness with nature and a sense of reaching beyond even the natural. They sought to be as fully human as possible so as to find the Oneness of Divinity as fully as possible. They too tended toward lofty communalism in the hope of reaching beyond the coarse nature of selfishness and sin, to find a more perfect human harmony.

Ralph Waldo Emerson, Henry David Thoreau, and Amos Bronson Alcott (father of novelist Louisa May Alcott) were neighbors in Concord, Massachusetts, who set the pace of Transcendentalism. Thoreau attempted to find serenity in two years (1845–1847) of relative isolation in the woods at Walden Pond,[50] Alcott in his experimental school in Concord, and Emerson in his philosophical lectures and writings.

Emerson,[51] born in 1803, grew up as the second of five sons (two daughters and another son died in infancy) of a Unitarian minister William and his wife Rebecca. His father died when he was almost eight and he was raised by a circle of women, including an aunt with whom he would become very close. At age fourteen he entered Harvard College and graduated at age eighteen (surprisingly, only in the middle ranking of his class). He went to work with a brother, William, teaching young women at his mother's home. When William went off to Germany to study divinity, Emerson then established his own school. Several years later he himself entered Harvard Divinity School for study. In early 1829 he was ordained to the ministry at Boston's Second Church as its junior pastor.

Then tragedy began to hit Emerson. In 1831 his young wife Ellen died of tuberculosis. Then a younger and very brilliant brother, Edward, who also had long been struggling with his health, both emotional and physical, died of the same disease in 1834. Finally another younger brother, Charles, died in 1836, also of tuberculosis. Emerson was devastated.

Following his wife's death, he began to distance himself emotionally from traditional Christianity. The following year (1832) he resigned his position at the church to begin the search elsewhere for the answer to life's questions. At the end of that year he departed for a grand tour of Europe, where he would meet a number of such intellectual luminaries as the English philosopher John Stuart Mill and the Scottish lecturer and social commentator Thomas Carlyle. In Paris he would become intrigued by the botanical gardens of the Jardin des Plantes, where he hit upon the thought of how all things in life seemed mystically interconnected.

Returning to America in October of 1833 he contemplated Carlyle's career as a lecturer, and the next month undertook the first of the 1,500 lectures he would offer over the next near-half century. These lectures would be his stock-in-trade, the source of a number of books he would publish.

In 1835 he remarried (Lydia or Lidian) and they moved to Concord, where two sons and two daughters were born. Here, in company with three other scholars, the Transcendental Club was founded (1836) – with the hope of birthing a community similar to the salons of Europe where intellectuals would gather to discuss weighty matters of life. Among those who would join them was Thoreau, for whom Emerson took on something of a role as a father-figure.

Emerson's split with Christianity became evident when in 1838 he delivered a lecture at Harvard Divinity School, affirming that Biblical miracles and the claim of Jesus' divinity were merely the inventions of the classic mind that assigned God-like qualities to their heroes. Emerson instead advocated something of a Humanism that freed the soul from the shackles of traditional religion so that it could soar in search of the higher meaning of life. Harvard Divinity School was scandalized by his bold Humanism (he would not be invited again to lecture there, until thirty years later when even Harvard Divinity School had begun to come around to holding many of Emerson's Humanist ideas).

Efforts were made by Emerson's neighbor Alcott to put their organic philosophy into full operation as an experiment in communal living, when the entirely vegetarian farm Fruitlands was established. It was not a grand success. After it failed, Emerson purchased another farm for Alcott for a second attempt. He even purchased two sections of land for himself (though he himself did not work the land). As it turned out, the Transcendentalists were better at thinking, discussing, lecturing and publishing than at securing material success, although Emerson's lectures were beginning to pay well and his books were being widely read.

Emerson now branched into esoteric or Universalistic study, taking up the study of Hindu Vedanta, reading the *Bhagavad Gita* and commentaries on the Vedas by Henry Thomas Colebrooke. His philosophy of the Oneness of Life had the larger religious confirmation of the Hindu religion. This fit his temperament better than traditional Christianity.

The earthier intelligentsia. Meanwhile, for those less comfortable, where life's dangers were not guaranteed to be manageable, where life could suddenly take a violent turn (hunger, disease, Indian massacre) such Humanist Rationality seemed as absurd as their personal trust in a God of miracles seemed absurd to the Humanists.

Indeed, even Nathaniel Hawthorne, who once was a neighbor of the Concord Transcendentalists, eventually became something of an anti-Transcendentalist, tending to delve more into the darkness of the religious ethical issues of his era in his novels *The Scarlet Letter* (1850) and *The House of the Seven Gables* (1851). Likewise, Edgar Allan Poe could be just as abrasive in his dislike of the romantic optimism of Transcendentalism.

There were also a number of other American writers and artists who represented well the life of the common man, the serene primitiveness of the American landscape and the exotic culture of the Indians, giving excellent characterization of the democratic realities of life in America. James Fenimore Cooper wrote elegantly of the complexities of life in America in such novels as *The Pioneers* (1823) and *The Last of the Mohicans* (1826). And in the field of graphic art, the works of Thomas Cole and others of the Hudson River School were on a parallel with the best of European landscape artists of the same era, as were the works of George Bingham who, in addition to his beautiful landscapes, portrayed insightfully democratic life in the Mississippi and Missouri River valleys.

* * *

THE "SECOND GREAT AWAKENING"[52]

As far back as the 1790s, the first decade of the new Republic, it appeared as if Christianity might be resolving itself simply into a civic religion serving to provide a moral foundation and discipline for the emerging United States as a distinct society. Certainly that was how the intellectuals, especially the Deists among them (most all intellectuals at that point), understood things. But such civic religion did not fill churches, for it resided solely in the independent thinking and behavior of citizens as they went about their daily routines. It did not need pulpits to show the people how to go about doing such things. Human logic itself seemed pretty good at constructing such moral-intellectual systems.

Part of this developing religious dynamic of Christianity as principally a civic religion was the result of the way that the war and the consequent independence of American society had a tremendous impact on the

The Shaping of a Nation

religious character of America. The Church of England, well beloved by the Tories particularly numerous in the American South, was devastated by the war. Eventually it was able to service Anglican loyalists in America by establishing its own Episcopal authority, and thus be able to carry on as before, but independent of England itself in doing so.*

As for the Calvinist Congregationalists in New England and Presbyterians in the Middle Colonies that had been active in leading the independence movement, post-war America had been expanding in population at a far greater rate than the slow process of producing seminary-trained pastors could meet the demand for new churches and individuals to pastor them. Also the very logical character of Congregationalist and Presbyterian theology, especially among the more highly educated of the membership (including, importantly, pastors), caused many to be quite comfortable in the Deist camp, leading some of them even to switch their loyalties to the growing (for the time being anyway) Unitarian movement.

Baptists and Methodists however did not have this same problem, being open to the recruiting of lay pastors (not seminary trained but simply called out of general society to Christian ministry). These individuals had been led to take up their calls not by academic logic, but by a highly personal, and most frequently highly emotional, sense of personal judgment, moral cleansing and new purpose to their lives, a purpose calling them into full service to the very process that had personally saved them out of a world of sin. They were on fire to bring others to this same spiritual renewal or revival that they themselves had gone through personally. And they were willing to face all sorts of obstacles, both by nature and by man, in order to bring (especially to the frontier where churches were virtually non-existent) the gospel of salvation in Jesus Christ to hungry hearts there. This was not mere civic religion. This was religion of a very personal spiritual nature.

Millennialism† and perfectionism. Behind all this religious activity was

---

*In the years between the 1st Great Awakening and America's war for independence, the Church of England's Society for the Propagation of the Gospel not only sought to bring the unchurched of America to Christ, but more importantly, it set out to bring non-Anglican Christians to leave their Congregational, Presbyterian, Quaker churches and join the Church of England, being far more active in setting up Anglican churches in coastal New England and the Middle Colonies than along the American frontier. As we have already noted, this assault on highly independent American Protestantism was another one of the ways that England had infuriated the colonies and driven them to want full independence from the mother country!

†A belief that the coming of Christ will usher in a 1,000-year Golden Age, a long period of time prior to the Day of Judgment, and the establishment of a New Heaven and a New Earth.

something very much part of the spirit of the Jacksonian times. As Tocqueville had noticed, Americans had a strong sense of personal destiny, an urgency to accomplish some greater work, to move forward, to fulfill some nobler purpose in life. Life was viewed as a challenge, one faced with many obstacles, many of them deficiencies in the people themselves, personal deficiencies or sins that needed cleansing, ones that required some act of purification which would clear the way for them to gain some personal victory. Christian revivals offered exactly just such an opportunity for getting things right with God.

Empowering this activity was an abiding sense that history was about to find completion in the form of the second coming of Christ and his final judgment of all people, saints and sinners, a widespread sentiment of the times due in part to the horrible 1837–1841 Depression which undercut severely the American belief that life moved forward along largely logical lines. Surely this grand catastrophe pointed to the ultimate and thus final judgement of God in the form of the long-awaited coming of Christ as the ultimate judge of life on earth.

Consequently, many Americans came easily to the conclusion that they were approaching the millennium described in Scripture (Revelation) in which all must be made perfect in preparation for that final coming of Christ. Sinful behavior needed to be corrected, both for society as well as the individual. Perfectionism or social reform was thus urgent. The institution of slavery in particular needed to be abolished – immediately. Alcoholism, which was rampant on the Frontier and in the workshops back East, also needed to be curbed. Caring for the poor became a priority. Injustices of whatever variety needed to be addressed, the treatment of women being one of the issues taken up by a new generation of feminists. Social experiments accompanied this mood, in which varieties of utopian programs were put in place to answer the challenge of the times. Most of these failed miserably, but failure did not seem to discourage others from trying.

Sadly, the quest for perfection usually set one group against another, even splitting groups time and again as perfectionists understood faults in the others, even small faults, to be the work of the devil in his attempt to stop the arrival of the millennium. It got confusing, and at times it became very bizarre in the routes such perfectionism took this rather primitive religious instinct so endearing to the American frontiersmen. But it made those simple souls, those who had moved to the frontier because their lives back East amounted to so little, now understand how special they were, even how royal they were, their purity of conscience bringing them into a very special relationship with God. On this sentiment they were very ready to build a new world.

The Shaping of a Nation

Francis Asbury.[53] Highly empowered by this national mood was the rising body of Methodists. Earlier, Methodism's actual founder, John Wesley, had originally been very opposed to the American rebellion against English royal authority. Consequently almost all of the preachers Wesley had sent to the colonies returned to England when the war first broke out. But Francis Asbury stayed behind, to organize Methodist lay preachers to help nurture American hearts during the dark days of the war. After the war, Wesley agreed to ordain American Methodist pastors – including Asbury, whom he named as one of his two Methodist superintendents in America, authorized to supervise those pastors – in order to bring the Methodists into some kind of proper or apostolic communion with the English Methodists. Thus it was Asbury and his lay preachers in America who would push Methodism forward, preachers who fit more closely the democratic mood of the times, able to relate better to life on the frontier. Estimates are that Asbury himself, in order to preach on virtually a daily basis, traveled thousands of unimaginably horrible miles each year in hunger, cold, wet or heat, frequent loneliness and extreme exhaustion, for a possible total as much as 275,000 miles in order to deliver a total of 16,000 sermons! During his time of leadership (1784–1816) the Methodists grew in number from 1,200 to 214,000 members, with 700 ordained preachers to pastor the flock.

The Methodist circuit riders.[54] Also playing a key role in this development were the Methodist circuit riders, formed from that same adventurous spirit of the frontier culture, who had answered a call from God to head out alone on horseback into the Western wilderness. Here they faced storms, hunger and hostile Indians – to bring the comfort of the Christian religion to scattered settlements and cabins that dotted the wilderness. Their offerings were not just the assurance that God was with these settlers but that they were also somehow still connected with the rest of society, which was also with them. The way the circuit riders helped settlers to keep body and soul together was thus enormously appreciated on the Western frontier, where the Methodist church – or at least the Methodist movement – grew rapidly, soon to become the largest of the Christian denominations in America. By 1840 some 3,500 circuit riders and some nearly 6,000 pastors were supporting the faith of 750,000 Methodists!

The African Methodist Episcopal (AME) and AME Zion churches. The Methodists were officially opposed to slavery from the beginning of the denomination's entry onto the America scene in the 1760s. Asbury was hotly opposed to the practice, but learned that to reach Black audiences held in bondage as well as Whites, he would have to tone down his rhetoric on the subject. Otherwise he would send slaveholders off into fellowship with Baptists and Presbyterians, which at the time took no such position on the subject. But the Methodist position did not go unnoticed by free Blacks, and Methodism would have a tremendous impact in getting their Christian world organized and up and running.

Richard Allen was a Black slave who was able to work to pay for his freedom from his Philadelphia master. In earlier years he had been very attentive to the Methodist circuit riders who had come to his plantation, and even before securing his freedom he had become active in encouraging fellow slaves with the gospel message. Once free he continued this activity, forming one small society and then another, until in 1816, in association with another free Black pastor, Daniel Coker, five newly developed congregations in Philadelphia were able to hold their first Methodist General Conference. Taking up the spiritual disciplines of Wesley's Methodists, they took the identity as the African Methodist Episcopal (AME) Church, the beginning of what would eventually turn into another of one of America's larger denominations.

Meanwhile in New York City in 1800 another group came together to form the Zion Church which grew significantly, until in 1821 they were able to constitute themselves as the African Methodist Episcopal Zion Church under Bishop or Superintendent James Varick. The AME Zion Church too spread across the country among free Blacks. Both Methodist churches would compete in eventually playing a leading role in shaping the religious lives of newly freed slaves after the Civil War.

Camp meetings.[55] Meanwhile, off on the American frontier, the highly individualistic but also highly isolated life on the part of those Americans that lived well away from the comforts of the East produced among Westerners a hunger for personal meaning within the context of community, membership in larger society being a rare but well-appreciated commodity. Most frequently this took the form of huge gatherings whenever a local Christian revivalist appeared in the region. Thousands would turn out to spend a week at an improvised encampment listening to an array of preachers, singing and dancing, shouting and fainting, and having a thoroughly good time.

Finney.[56] Taking a more structured (and thus "logical") approach to revivalism was the lawyer-turned-Presbyterian-minister Charles Grandison Finney. Though a Presbyterian, a denomination which traditionally viewed salvation as solely a matter of God's graceful election (and thus not really a personal work or achievement of man himself), Finney fit better the spirit of the Baptist and Methodist revivalists. He was required to appear before a Presbyterian board to examine his views on faith versus works, an issue

The Shaping of a Nation

which has caused considerable controversy since almost the founding of Christianity. In the end he satisfied the board that he preached a doctrine of grace rather than works, although his revivals' goal of cultivating immediate repentance and renewal had something of the quality of works before grace.* His careful structuring of his revivals, taking place in the period 1825 to 1835 in both the rural setting of up-state New York and the urban setting of New York City, became a model that other revivalists would follow. It helped not only tone down (somewhat) the emotional level of these revivals, it also put them on steadier religious foundations.

Millerites and Seventh-Day Adventists. Another New York revivalist who played big on these instincts was the farmer and Baptist lay-preacher William Miller, who in 1833 predicted (on the basis of calculations he drew up from the Book of Daniel) that the long-awaited event of Jesus Christ's return to earth was going to take place sometime in the period 1843–1844, the accompanying rapture also ending life on this planet. His views began to gain wider acceptance as the 1840s loomed into view, his prophecy even taken up by followers in England, Norway and Chile. Ultimately in 1844 he and his followers gathered on hilltops and rooftops in March, again in April and finally in October in anticipation of the rapture. But instead a Great Disappointment occurred when Jesus failed to show up on schedule, causing his following to break up.

Surprisingly, however, this was not the end of his massive religious movement. Others picked up Miller's vision (particularly its millennialist perspective), importantly the female prophet Ellen G. White, who cultivated a huge group of followers that would eventually take the name Seventh-Day Adventists. They took up perfectionist ways in the avoidance of alcohol, meat, and other foods, advocating instead vegetarianism. From this group would eventually come such famous breakfast food producers as Kellogg and Post.†

The Burned-over district.‡ One of the places that seemed to be particularly active in this new religious dynamic was the "burned-over district" of Western New York. Here wave after wave of millennialist revivals

---

*But this is a subject that no Christian has ever satisfactorily resolved by mere logic or precise theological argument!

†Vegetarianism was a common trend among the millennialists, who believed that meat-eating made man a brutal beast.

‡The term burned-over district was assigned by Finney to this region because it had held so many revivals that Finney was certain that there could be no one there left to convert.

occurred, producing some of the most notable elements of the Second Great Awakening. The Millerites were very numerous in this region. Shakers were also numerous in this part of the state.* The utopian Oneida Society was also established there to practice the idea of social communalism.

The Mormons. Certainly the most amazing phenomenon to come out of all this millennialism, and in this case even this same burned-over district of Western New York, were the Latter-day Saints or Mormons, a group that followed the prophecies and teachings of Joseph Smith, Jr.

As a teenager, Smith claimed that he had a number of visions, the most important being a visit by the Angel Moroni in 1827, who directed him to a place where he uncovered a book of golden plates on which were written in some form of reformed Egyptian the story of the ancient Jews and of Christ and his visit to America. Using a special technique, he translated what he saw written there by ancient authors (Mormon being chief among them), which in 1830 Smith published in English translation as the *Book of Mormon*.† That same year he formed his first congregation as the Church of Christ, teaching his followers the new doctrines, and then sending them west to spread the new revelation as Latter-day Saints.

His ultimate goal was to establish a new Zion, a community of the Latter-day Saints, to prepare the way for the coming of Christ. At first he thought it would be in Ohio, where in 1831 a large group of his followers assembled. But then some of his followers moved on to Missouri, planning to establish his New Jerusalem or Zion there. But they ran into trouble when the local citizens reacted to the Mormons pouring into their area. Smith ran into the resistance of the local Missouri militia when he arrived in Missouri to try to secure the land for his followers, and thus he decided to build his temple in Ohio. But a major bank failure (resulting from the panic of 1837) undermined the harmony of his followers and Smith migrated with those who still remained with him back to Missouri. Once again he faced stiff resistance there, except this time organized by the governor of

---

*The Shakers, as the Quakers before them, were noted for the shaking of their bodies when they entered into a rapturous union with the Spirit of God. They were notable also in that they believed that sex was bestial behavior and thus they did not have offspring of their own, forcing them to keep the community going through converts. Their religion required all property to be held jointly; the equality of the sexes; children (brought in from the outside world) belonging to the whole community; the profits of workmanship shared communally, etc.

†The book states that tribes of Israel (the Ten Lost Tribes?) had managed to get themselves to the New World – as well as Jesus himself, who appeared to the Indians soon after his Resurrection, producing several centuries of exceptional peace among the Indians. Indeed, the book claims that the Indians were in fact descendants of these migrating Israelites.

Missouri, who in 1838 was determined to drive the Mormons from his state. Thus some eight thousand Mormons followed Smith to Nauvoo, on the Illinois side of the Mississippi River.

For the next few years he was able to proceed in the building of his temple, until the citizens of Illinois – seeing the land being overrun by these Mormons and shocked at the practice of polygamy taken up by Smith in 1843, a practice that seemed now so central to Mormon social organization – thus also began to take up arms against the Mormons. Then in June of 1844 Smith and his brother Hyrum were killed by an angry mob, throwing the Mormon community into confusion as to who was then to lead them.

At this point a number of Smith's colleagues stepped forward to claim succession. Brigham Young took the lead, although other individuals also claimed the title and led their followers off to form their own separate Mormon communities. But after two years of trying to make things work out for them in Illinois, Young decided in 1846 to take his thirty-five wives and hundreds of followers West, all the way to the Utah territory in 1847 where they hoped to be able to build their community in peace. There indeed they found just such security – at least for a decade – and from there began to send out missionaries to the larger world around them, to build the new faith in anticipation of the coming millennium.

New School versus Old School Christians. All of this highly emotional spiritual adventure impacting the young Republic was having the effect of splitting the old Calvinist religions (Congregationalists, Presbyterians, Dutch Reformed) between two camps: the New School group, supporting the revivalist trend, and the Old School group opposing it. Once again, similar to the earlier Great Awakening of the 1740s, the highly emotional character of these revivals seemed to Old School conservatives to be a most undignified way to bring people to Christ and also very shallow in how it might develop Christian life over the long-term in comparison to well-thought-through traditional Christian understanding. Worse, New School revivalism seemed to support the Arminian (or Methodist) idea that man was somehow able on his own to rise above his state of moral or self-focused depravity and elect or choose entirely on his own his personal salvation. Also, of course, the very idea that a person was not properly aligned with God without having one of these highly emotional moments of conversion seemed highly offensive to those raised since their youth to follow the lines of the faith as best as they could, understanding that they were indeed sinners, but always throughout their lives as faithful Christians sensitive to the need to keep themselves open to the judgments of God. For this latter group of Old School or Christian conservatives the suggestion that the path they were on was not sufficient because it had never arrived at an emotional crisis point of decision was outrageously ridiculous.

Christian mission societies. However, the Second Great Awakening did not in fact somehow leave the Old School churches out of the religious developments of the early 1800s. On the contrary, there were some very significant developments that took place among these older denominations. Although they did not take on the colorful features of New School revivalism, they went a long way in developing the religious character of the young Republic.

What is being described here is the birth in the 1810s and 1820s of a large number of interdenominational Christian societies that sought to set Christianity to the task of taking on a number of social problems, blemishes that embarrassed good Christians. These Old School Christians also believed strongly that America had a vital role to play as a model of Christian virtue to the larger world. These new societies were thus set up to provide Christian demonstrations as to how such issues as poverty, illiteracy, and just plain ignorance of the Christian gospel were to be taken on by the faithful.

Working across denominational lines (Baptist, Methodist, Congregationalist, Presbyterian, Dutch Reformed, etc.), Americans were very active in forming such groups as The American Bible Society (to help every American family find itself in possession of a Bible), the American Sunday School Union (to develop Biblical literacy among the children of all social classes), the American Tract Society (to put in the hands of everyone the simplest explanation of and call to Christianity), the American Anti-Slavery Society, and the American Temperance League (both fighting particular social evils). Then there was the inter-faith (Congregational, Presbyterian, Dutch Reformed) American Board of Commissioners for Foreign Missions (ABDFM) created in 1810, which sent missionaries to the Cherokee (and other American Indians) and ultimately overseas to Hawaii, China, India, the Middle East and finally Africa. These volunteer organizations became a vital part of the American social-cultural dynamic that developed in accompaniment with America's spread across the North American continent, and soon across the world.

Christian colleges. As we have already noted, from the time of the Puritans' early settlement in America, higher education was a matter of vital necessity, not only in training the pastors who would be expected to lead the Christian communities the Puritans were establishing but in training in other areas such as the law, business, finance, and teacher training – all so vital to the life of their communities. Thus Christian America founded

The Shaping of a Nation

Harvard, Yale, William and Mary, King's (Columbia), Georgetown, the College of New Jersey (Princeton), New Brunswick and Andover Theological Seminaries, as well as colleges such as Mount Holyoke, designed to give women the same opportunity at a higher education. In fact, in the period between the founding of the colonies and the mid-1800s, over 500 colleges were founded by America's various denominations. This too was a key part of Christian America's larger mission to be a Light to the Nations.

Horace Bushnell.[57]   And then there was the compelling voice of a Connecticut pastor calling for interdenominational compromise, a spirit of Christian unity ... and in doing so would greatly impact his times (and continue to do so even through the rest of the 1800s): the persuasive voice of Horace Bushnell. He took a unique position that aligned him exactly with none of the contending Christian groups, yet found value in all of them. With respect to the Old School Christians, he was quite respectful of the way traditional Calvinist Christianity was able to shape from a person's very early life, even childhood, key Christian understandings that helped direct a person (elected purely by the grace of God to the privilege of being born into full Christian fellowship of Christian family and church) toward a long-term and deeply faithful Christian life. This understanding was clearly laid out in his very popular book, *Christian Nurture* (1847).[58] At the same time, he was highly supportive of the Unitarian (and Arminian or Wesleyan or Methodist) viewpoint that man did have the responsibility (and thus the choice in the matter) of disciplining or ordering his own thoughts and actions as part of the mature Christian life. And for a period of time he was quite supportive of the Transcendentalists' mystical approach to God, seeing such a higher reach of the soul as vital to a strong personal relationship with God. However, in early 1848 he found himself decisively back in the support of the idea of God, not in the form of the Transcendentalists' Universalist Deity, but rather in the traditional Trinitarian view of God as Father, Son and Holy Spirit. But even in this retreat, he continued to believe that although emotional revivalism was not necessary for everyone to reach God, it certainly served very well those who had become quite lost in their journey in life and was an authentic way of bringing such lost but spiritually hungry souls to Christ – provided that such revival always was followed up by on-going fellowship with a worshiping community, in order to make the salvation-event a lasting transformation.[59]

Although he would draw criticism from all the communities for his less than full embrace of their respective positions, his ability to see Christianity above these divisions would come to be of great value to American Christianity in the days ahead.

CHAPTER SEVEN
EXPANSION ... AND DIVISION

✳ ✳ ✳

"MANIFEST DESTINY"[60]

In 1845 the publisher, lawyer, and strong Jacksonian Democrat, John L. O'Sullivan, popularized the term "Manifest Destiny" when he wrote articles in his own periodical, the *Democratic Review*, concerning both the American acceptance of the request by the Republic of Texas to join the Union and the need to get fully behind the American claim in the boundary dispute with Britain over the Oregon territory. O'Sullivan explained that it was America's manifest destiny to overspread the continent given it by Providence for the free development of its yearly multiplying millions and for the development of the great experiment of liberty and federated self-government. In general, this represented well the view of the Jacksonian Democrats.

But the Whigs were fervently opposed not so much to the high democratic ideals expressed by O'Sullivan as to the implications this had for the westward spread of slavery and for unwanted foreign (and Indian) conflicts it seemed to invite. Some Whigs were even so bold as to accuse the doctrine of being simply an excuse for imperialism.

But the reality was that the American population instinctively believed in such ideals without the prompting of journalists or congressmen. It was a central part of American culture, both spiritually and materially. It was part of American culture materially because Americans believed that it was their natural right to seek new opportunities in the West as those opportunities faded in the East (a rapidly expanding population, exhaustion of the soil, but most importantly, little new land for cheap purchase for a new generation trying to start out life). The land to the West was simply there for the taking by any young (or old) family willing to face the risks involved.

It was also a central part of American culture because it was a key part of the Second Great Awakening, in that Americans had a fervent sense that as the New Israel, they were commanded by God to fill the land

Expansion ... and Division

with His People. Their westward expansion was actually a divine duty. Protestant Christian Americans were expected to fill the empty spaces sparsely inhabited by only pagan Indians or Catholic Hispanics.

California and the rich Pacific coast was one of the points of destination. But the place that would receive the greatest attention and be the cause of the express formulation of the Manifest Destiny doctrine was Texas. Texas would be the test case for Manifest Destiny.

* * *

TEXAS INDEPENDENCE[61]

Anglos to Texas. Texas (Tejas) was originally a sparsely settled northern portion of New Spain. In 1821 there was a general revolt of the Hispanic population (The Mexican War of Independence) against the authorities back in Spain, which resulted eventually in the creation of the Republic of Mexico two years later. The huge northern region was so sparsely settled that two huge regions were formed into the single state of Coahuila y Tejas.

The Comanche Indians were a constant problem for the Hispanic settlers and the decision was made in 1824 to encourage European and Americans to settle in the area. This had already been happening on a small scale – as in the case of the *empresario*, Stephen Austin, bringing some 300 Americans to settle along the Brazos River in 1822. Then with this decision a large number of others, mostly Americans, were settled in Texas under a number of similar empresarios. Finally the influx of Americans was so overwhelming in numbers* that in 1830 Mexican President Anastasio Bustamante closed the borders to further immigration.

But the American immigrants, sensing the Mexican effort to isolate them, fought back – at the same time that a revolt against the Mexican president was taking place in the Mexican capital. Taking advantage of the political chaos and supporting the party of Mexican Federalists fighting the Mexican Centralists, Texans gathered at the Convention of 1832 to discuss the option of independent statehood. The spirit of independence was thus birthed in Texas.

The Battle of Gonzales and the Consultation (1835). When in 1835 a small Mexican military contingent was sent north to crush this spirit, a similarly small group of Texans fought the Mexicans to a standoff at

---

*At the beginning of the migration in 1825 there were only about 3,500 settlers in Texas, mostly Hispanic. Less than ten years later that figure was over ten times that size, about 80 percent of them Americans, with a substantial number of slaves among them.

the Battle of Gonzales, merely strengthening the desire of the Texans to achieve independence. They gathered that same year (The Consultation), declaring their reasons for seeking independence and setting up a provisional government and General Council. They also established a Texas army under Sam Houston.

But political controversy immediately plagued the new government, which collapsed in early 1836. However, another gathering that spring produced quickly a formal Declaration of Independence (March 2nd, 1836) and the announcement of the creation of the Republic of Texas.

The massacres at the Alamo and Goliad (March 1836). At the same time, the new Mexican president (and military *caudillo* or strongman), Antonio Lopez de Santa Anna, had already headed north with the intention of crushing this Texas rebellion. Santa Anna's army[*] surrounded the Alamo Mission near San Antonio and finally, after a siege of almost two weeks, overwhelmed the approximately 185 defenders (March 6), killing all of them to the last man. But in fact it was quite an expensive victory, costing Santa Anna the loss of 400 to 600[†] of his army in dead and wounded.

At about the same time another large Mexican Army began to move north from Matamoros, overwhelming small Texas units as they went. In mid-March a larger Texas unit confronted the Mexicans in three days of fighting. But the Texans ran out of ammunition and were surrounded and forced to surrender as they attempted a retreat. The Texans were marched back to Fort Defiance in Goliad. Then, under the orders of Santa Anna, the Mexican troops proceeded to massacre over 300 of these prisoners (March 27). But rather than breaking the spirit of the Texans, the event merely steeled their determination to secure Texas independence at all costs.

Texas victory at San Jacinto (April 1836). The next month Sam Houston and his Texas army joined battle with Santa Anna at San Jacinto. A Texan surprise attack on a wearied Mexican army and a twenty-minute battle turned out to be a disaster for the Mexicans. They tried to flee but were simply hunted down and killed on the spot, to the cries of "Remember the Alamo" and "Remember Goliad!" (some 600+ Mexican soldiers were killed this way). And Santa Anna was captured, disguised as a servant in an attempt to escape. Amazingly, only eleven Texans died in the battle.

---

*The exact size of the Mexican army and the portion actually involved in the final assault on the Alamo are not known, though figures vary from 1,800 all the way up to 6,000.

†Some estimates are much higher ... but are hard to confirm because of the political implications of those numbers at the time.

Expansion ... and Division   251

At this point (and after three weeks of captivity) in order to secure his own release Santa Anna had to agree to recognize Texas's independence. But Santa Anna would immediately repudiate the agreement once he was safely out of Texas.

The debate over Texas joining the Union (1837–1845). Almost immediately (1837) a split occurred within the leadership of the new Texas Republic between those wishing to retain and expand Texas as an independent republic (possibly extending its borders all the way to the Pacific Ocean) and those who wanted to see Texas annexed as a new state joining the U.S. The debate was finally decided in favor of the annexation group when Mexico sent troops back up into Texas and had to be fought off with much difficulty. This seemed to establish in Texan minds the importance of being closely connected to the greater power of the U.S.

But Texas allowed slavery, stirring debate within the United States itself as to whether or not Texas ought to be admitted as a new (slave) state. President Van Buren did not want the slave issue to work its political damage at a time when he was struggling with the economic Panic of 1837 and so he tried to hold off the issue of Texas admission throughout his entire four-year tenure as president. Also he did not want to find the country at war with Mexico – which had never accepted the idea of the independence of Texas. But he faced a lot of adversity from Southerners, especially from Calhoun who was making it an issue of the South's willingness to stay in the Union if Texas were not admitted. But opposing Calhoun was John Quincy Adams, who had returned to Washington after his presidency to become a very powerful voice in the House of Representatives, and who spoke for three weeks in opposition to the admission of Texas.

* * *

"TIPPECANOE AND TYLER TOO"

Even though by 1840 there were signs that the economy was beginning to recover (though the psychology of recovery takes longer to register among the people than the material fact of economic recovery itself), Van Buren faced a major uphill battle for reelection. His efforts to hold at arm's length the question of slavery had only alienated much of his following in the Democratic Party. Besides, he was facing the war hero of Tippecanoe, William Henry Harrison, who though he once was a states'-rights Democrat was now running as a moderate Whig. However what his precise views on politics happened to be was largely a mystery to most everyone. His running mate, the Virginian John Tyler, he too being a Whig moderate, was also hard to pin down as to where he actually stood on a number of issues. Thus the campaign slogan "Tippecanoe and Tyler Too" gave the American voter little idea of what a vote for this team actually would mean if they were successful.

The importance of Tyler however would arise soon, for the aged Harrison caught a cold delivering his overly long inaugural address and died of pneumonia only one month into office. Tyler quickly cleared up the uncertainties of the Constitution about exactly what was to be the actual capacity of a vice president occupying a vacated presidency by assuming the title and the full powers of the presidency.

Tyler's presidency however would be marked by controversy, much of it involving a personal rivalry which developed between Clay and himself. And it would first arise over the old question of the Bank of the United States (BUS), seemingly a source of constant controversy within American politics. Clay championed the bill for a new BUS – which Tyler vetoed, not liking some of the provisions concerning BUS lending to local bank branches (he actually was not opposed to the BUS in general). Clay pushed through another attempt, this time mostly as a personal challenge to Tyler, who vetoed it a second time. At this point Clay began to maneuver within the Whig party to undercut the party's own Whig president! Under the urging of Clay, the cabinet Tyler inherited from Harrison soon abandoned him. Within a short time he found himself being something of a political loner in the White House.

High tariffs had been put in place in earlier years to protect the budding American industry from cheaper British industrial goods. But a schedule for the gradual reduction of those tariffs had been put in place at the same time, the presumption being that the industries would not continue to need such protection as they matured. But it had come to the point that these tariffs were a major source of income for the federal government. Consequently, a mood grew within Congress (under Whig domination) to delay putting into effect those tariff reductions. Thus the Whigs proposed new laws to postpone these scheduled reductions – which Tyler vetoed.

Finally with a third attempt by Congress, Tyler agreed to some delay in the reductions, but under the conditions that federal monies would not be used to fund the operations of state governments. But this undercut the deal that Whigs had with the Democrats to keep them cooperating with the Whigs in Congress. The Democrats, seeing the potential loss of financial rewards for their state supporters, abandoned the Whigs in the 1842 election. The unhappy Democrats ran quite successfully by pointing out this loss to their voters. This in turn caused the Whigs to lose their place of leadership in the House, which the Democrats now took over. Tyler,

Expansion ... and Division

of course, was blamed for it all.

The Webster-Ashburton Treaty (1842). In the field of foreign relations Tyler was more successful, backing his secretary of state, Daniel Webster, in negotiating with the British diplomat, Lord Ashburton, a Canadian-American border treaty. This treaty finally put to an end a number of crises that had occurred over defining exactly where the border was located between the U.S. and Canada (from Maine in the East to the Rocky Mountains in the West).*

* * *

JAMES POLK AND THE MEXICAN-AMERICAN WAR (1846–1848)[62]

The 1844 elections: Clay vs. Polk, vs. Birney. In the 1844 elections, the Whig nominee Clay found himself up against the Democrat (Tennessean) James Polk. President Van Buren had alienated so many within his own Democratic Party that the party's presidential nomination ultimately had gone to Polk, something of a dark horse that had not been one of the early frontrunners in the party. Polk subsequently ran his campaign on the promise that if elected he would admit both Texas and Free-Soil (no slavery allowed) Oregon as new states, thus offsetting some of the northern opposition to the admission of Texas as a slave state.

Clay, his third time as a presidential candidate, ran on the typical Whig platform of Clay's own American System: protective tariffs to promote American industry, a strong central bank, and the building of the commercial infrastructure of canals and roads. These all tended to favor the conservative interests of the up-East financial-industrial class, and undercut his support among Westerners and Southerners.

But a "third-party-spoiler," the Liberal Party's James Birney, was also running, drawing support away from those who otherwise would have voted for Clay. This would prove ruinous for Clay. So it was that Polk handily won the electoral vote, including even a large number of northern states.

The admission of Texas to the Union. But as a lame-duck president, Tyler, sensing that the election had served as a referendum strongly supportive of the admission of Texas as a new state, moved ahead in his last days in office as president and proposed to Congress a resolution opening Texas to membership in the Union. This was the final blow in undercutting

---

*But the treaty left undefined the Canadian-American border west of the Rockies – that is, the Oregon Territory – which would remain in dispute until resolved by the Packenham-Buchanan Treaty of 1846.

his Whig political base, causing the president to be expelled from his own Whig party!

The Whigs fought the annexation with all the strength they could muster. John Quincy Adams, who as a strong anti-slavery voice in the House of Representatives had fought bitterly the admission of Texas as a new slave state, voiced this move as being a devastating calamity for the Union. But like the Federalists before them, the Whigs were up against a growing Manifest Destiny fever which seized the country. Remembering the fate of the Federalists, they voiced their opposition carefully.

But Whig opposition would not be enough to stop the entrance into the Union of another, quite large, slave state. Ultimately Tyler succeeded in getting Congress to authorize the annexation of Texas, not by a treaty requiring a 2/3rds vote for Senate approval (which would not have been possible due to the strong Whig opposition) but instead by a mere joint resolution of both houses of Congress, which required only a simple majority in both houses! Finally the resolution providing for the annexation of Texas was signed into law by Tyler on his last day in office.

And his presidential successor, James Polk, would see the annexation completed when the huge slave state Texas formally accepted the invitation to join the United States in December of 1845 as its 28th state.

Steps toward the Mexican-American War. Mexico had made it clear that it would never accept the loss of its Texas province, particularly if it were then absorbed into the United States. Then when the discussions between the Republic of Texas and the United States started referencing as Texas's southern border with Mexico not the Nueces River but the Rio Grande – much further south and thus deeper into Mexico – the Mexicans were outraged.

In many ways the new president, James Polk, was something of another Andrew Jackson: a strong personality who was unafraid of stepping on toes in order to get done exactly what he wanted. He also knew that Mexico was furious enough over the admission of Texas to the Union that war could easily develop between the two nations. He was prepared for that possibility as well.

But also Polk was by every instinct the lawyer who believed that it was better to work out a deal with litigants than go to court. By those same instincts he was hoping he could work out a deal with Mexico, perhaps purchase his way to a settlement. He was prepared to offer Mexico millions in assistance and even in purchase of Western territory itself.

He knew of course that the Mexicans themselves were fired up for war and wanted satisfaction for their bruised sense of honor. Money would not restore that sense of honor. Americans themselves were also getting

Expansion ... and Division

fired up for war. Thus war was likely. But Polk wanted to make sure that if and when it occurred, it would take place on America's terms, not Mexico's.

The situation was complicated further by the fact that relations between the Americans and the British were quite unresolved in the far West. The British claimed Canadian territory along the Pacific Coast deep into the Oregon region. There were rumors circulating that the British were interested even in extending their imperial hold all the way into California and were thinking about purchasing sparsely inhabited California from Mexico. The Mexicans were possibly considering this as preferable to having as northern neighbors more Americans, who also were eying that land. Thus some kind of Mexican-English relationship was possibly building which would have weakened the American hand considerably in any war with Mexico..

Furthermore, though humiliated in the Texas war of Independence, the Mexican military was considered to be no joke of an army. European military experts in fact expected that in any direct military confrontation with America, the Mexican army, huge and well disciplined, would make quick work of the motley crew of American militia and the rather small national army. Indeed, many were certain that the superior Mexican army would quickly roll back the Americans all the way to Washington, D.C.

Seeing the war clouds darken, in mid-1845 Polk ordered General Zachary Taylor to move American troops into Texas and position them on the Nueces River, waiting to see what might develop. He also sent a small military group (sixty men) of explorers under General John Frémont to Oregon through California (still part of Mexico), whose larger purpose was a mystery to the Mexicans. Highly suspicious of Frémont, the Mexicans ordered him out of California.

Then in early 1846 Polk sent an offer to Mexico to purchase California and New Mexico. He also in April ordered an American warship to move into the San Francisco Bay to protect Americans living in California.

Meanwhile Mexico itself was undergoing tremendous political turmoil (4 different individuals succeeded each other in the Mexican presidency in 1846, 6 in the war ministry and 16 in the finance ministry). A big part of the problem was that the Mexican leaders themselves could not agree on what to do in the face of the growing possibility of war with America. Centralists demanded war; Federalists requested negotiations. Back and forth the controversy swayed, until the military party of Centralists seemed to have grabbed firm control.

War is declared (May 11, 1846). Polk then ordered Taylor to move his troops all the way to the Rio Grande, where Taylor constructed a fort. For the Mexicans this was the final insult, as they still claimed the land south of the Nueces River and north of the Rio Grande as theirs. In late April of 1846 they issued a declaration of intent to fight a defensive war and sent a detachment of 2,000 Mexican soldiers to expel the Americans from what they considered Mexican territory.

In the process, the Mexicans overwhelmed a small patrol of seventy American soldiers in the disputed territory, killing sixteen of the Americans. On May 11th, claiming that Mexico had killed American soldiers on American soil (for that was the American view on the matter of the territorial boundary), Polk asked Congress for a declaration of war. The Democrat-dominated Congress obliged him – though the Whigs, seeing this as playing to the advantage of the Southern slave states, were highly opposed to this decision.

Action in Texas actually had taken place even before the American declaration of War. Mexican and American armies had met at the Rio Grande earlier in May, and the results were disastrous for the Mexicans. From then on, the southern front in the war would be fought in Mexico, not Texas.

California was next to become the scene of battle. In June of 1846 Frémont returned to California to openly invite a revolt (the Bear Flag Revolt) of Americans in Sonoma (northern California). This all looked quite similar in character to the Texas rebellion ten years earlier, except that the Californians moved immediately to replace the California Bear Flag with the American flag. Frémont's army moved south to capture Los Angeles, and was joined by the army of American General Stephen Kearny, moving in from the East across the vast southwest desert, who easily took San Diego. By January of the following year (1847) the Mexicans were forced to surrender their claim to California. England, meanwhile, had elected to stay out of the conflict.

In the meantime, Taylor began to advance his troops into Mexico from the northeast. His troops were a wild collection of volunteers, undisciplined, and at times functioning more like a drunken mob than an army (raping and pillaging as they went). It took considerable effort for Taylor to finally be able to shape his *gringos** into a disciplined army.

Taylor's first major encounter with the Mexicans was at the city of Monterey (September 1846) where his army, unused to urban warfare, ran into stiff resistance from Monterey's troops and citizens. Ultimately to achieve a win, Taylor had to resort to an armistice allowing the Mexican soldiers to leave the city peacefully. Technically this marked an American victory. But Polk was furious about such a weak showing by Taylor.

---

*There is some dispute about the origins of the term *gringo*. Some claim that it originated from the song that the Americans sang, "Green Grow the Lilacs," as they marched through Mexico!

Expansion ... and Division

Meanwhile Santa Anna had again seized control of the Mexican government and had come out to fight the Americans. In February of 1847 Taylor's and Santa Anna's armies met at Buena Vista – with the Mexican army over three times the size of the American army. Santa Anna was able to surround Taylor's troops and inflict huge casualties on them, though the Americans held their position. Both sides were exhausted. But Santa Anna got news of political troubles back in Mexico City and had to abandon the conflict, leaving Taylor in control.*

During all of this confusion the Comanche and Apache Indians had been conducting raids on the Mexicans. Thus as American soldiers advanced from the northwest toward Mexico City, they found the countryside deserted and the towns unwilling to resist the advancing Americans.

At the same time, Americans under naval Commodore Matthew Perry were fighting the Mexicans along the Mexican shores and tributary rivers of the Gulf of Mexico, inflicting humiliating defeats on the Mexicans as they went.

Polk now turned to General Winfield Scott (working closely with Perry) to lead an assault in March of 1847 on the Gulf of Mexico coastal town of Vera Cruz, to reduce the walls protecting the city in preparation for a massive amphibious landing of American troops whose ultimate destination would be Mexico City. Seriously outnumbered by this attacking American force, the Mexicans were only able to hold out a dozen days before having to surrender Vera Cruz to their American attackers.

The Americans then headed west to Mexico City and, after overcoming stiff resistance to the north of the city at Chapultepec (including the brave fighting of the Mexican students at the military academy located there), were able to enter the city in mid-September. Santa Anna was overthrown and fled the country. The Americans were now in total control of the Mexican political heartland.†

The question then arose: what to do with Mexico? Some political voices speculated that the Mexicans themselves might greet annexation to the United States gladly. The Whigs were however strongly opposed to the annexation of Mexican territory, fearing it would only expand the political weight of the pro-slavery portion of the nation. But in fact, neither the Mexicans nor most Americans had any interest themselves in such a union.

---

*Taylor would make much of this victory in his successful bid for the U.S. presidency in 1848.

†Marines were put on guard duty at the Mexican National Palace, the "Halls of Montezuma," completing the opening line of the Marine's hymn: "From the Halls of Montezuma to the shores of Tripoli..." [from Mexico City to the shores of the Barbary Pirates].

The moral impact of the Mexican-American War. Many of the Whigs of the American North had viewed the Mexican-American War as little more than an effort of the South to strengthen its political position in Congress by adding newly conquered territories, and thus subsequently future states, to the pro-slavery roster. Most notable in their opposition to the Mexican-American War in this regard had been Henry Clay and John Quincy Adams. They employed every argument possible concerning the moral degeneracy of the imperialism America had inflicted on its Mexican neighbors. However most Whigs certainly encouraged the idea of American expansion westward – as long as any newly acquired territories remained in the Free-Soil category.

Then in August of 1846, during the debate approving the $2 million in appropriations underwriting potential negotiations with Mexico (which it was hoped at the time might end the war) the gauntlet was thrown down in Congress by Representative David Wilmot. He wanted attached to the appropriations bill the proviso that would ban slavery in any of the lands that the Mexicans might turn over to the Americans (the Mexican Cession) as a result of a much hoped-for negotiated peace settlement. The bill passed in the House, but failed in the Senate when Congress dismissed without considering the resolution. When Polk later that year made another request for funds to negotiate a peace settlement with Mexico the Wilmot Proviso was reintroduced and hotly debated. However as debate developed, an additional demand was added the following year that the prohibition of slavery be extended to any new territory acquired by the United States. Tempers were now hot.

Then Alabama Representatives proposed a counter-resolution which would leave the slavery issue to the individual territories to decide (building on the philosophy of the sovereignty of the states, or states' rights). The measure failed to pass, but united the Southern representatives into a strong regional bond, one that would build and become the main political identifier among the members of Congress.

America's major political division now followed not the more traditional Whig/Democratic Party lines, but ominously North/South regional lines. The parties themselves were splitting into North-South factions, especially as the Wilmot Proviso kept getting introduced time and again in the North's hope of finally forcing the end of slavery on the South.

Finally, with the American military victory in Mexico City, negotiations got underway in January of 1848 at the town of Guadalupe Hidalgo, and within a month the two sides agreed on terms: Mexico would receive $15 million in payment from America for the acquisition of California, Texas to the Rio Grande, and the territory in between (which would eventually become New Mexico, Arizona and Utah.)

Expansion ... and Division

John Quincy Adam's death, and the finalizing of the Guadalupe Hidalgo Treaty. When the Guadalupe Hidalgo Treaty was submitted to the Senate for ratification in February, the Whigs were bitterly opposed to any affirmation of the Mexican-American War and its outcome because of the blatant imperialism involved. Even with the revealing of the generous terms offered to and accepted by Mexico in the negotiations of 1848, a storm erupted. Certainly the generosity undercut some of the imperialist argument, though others were appalled at just that generosity. But mostly the eruption occurred over the idea of a number of potentially new states in the Southwest being lined up for statehood and how this would tip the balance in the growing North-South split over slavery. Leading the attack on the treaty was the distinguished Whig senator from Massachusetts, Daniel Webster, the Great Orator.

Then in the middle of discussions going on in the House, John Quincy Adams was felled by a heart attack, bringing the proceedings to a halt over the next days as the nation stood watch over the last man with personal connections with the Republic's Founding Fathers, and who himself had come to grow greatly in the esteem of his Congressional colleagues because of his cool wit and sharp insights. When he died on the 23rd (of February) the nation mourned.

The effect was to sober the proceedings in the Senate, which in early March finally moved to approve the Guadalupe Hidalgo Treaty, 38–14.

The size of the financial award offered to Mexico for the loss of its territory still caused some to question exactly who it was that had won, and who had exactly lost the war! But it was a wise move, giving a degree of fairness to the war's outcome, because Mexico might otherwise have continued to harbor a deep resentment over a total loss – such that Mexico would have been tempted to renew the war at a time when America was less able to fight, as would have been the case when America fell into its savage Civil War thirteen years later.

* * *

"WESTWARD HO"*

The Oregon Question. The Oregon Territory had been left out of the 1842 Canadian-American border treaty because both sides, British and American, were unwilling to flex on the issue. The British claimed the area south to the Columbia River (today forming most of the border between the

---

*Originally the call of London boatmen serving as taxis on the Thames River, taken as the name of an English play in 1607, later carried to America and popularized in an 1832 novel of that name by James Kirke Paulding.

states of Oregon and Washington) whereas the Americans claimed the area north to the Russian border at Fort Simpson on the Fraser River or roughly to the 54°40' parallel.

Polk had promised in his presidential campaign that along with the Texas issue he would bring the Oregon border conflict with the British to some kind of resolution. Polk thus proposed a compromise of extending the 49th parallel east of the Rockies now all the way to the Pacific, though swinging that line a bit just below Fort Victoria on Vancouver Island facing the strategic Puget Sound.

At first the British rejected this proposal. But the Americans made their original claim to the 54°40' parallel something of a war cry ("Fifty-Four Forty or Fight") and the British decided that the pressing of their own claim was not wise. They thus instructed British negotiator Packenham to come to terms with American Secretary of State James Buchanan on the basis of Polk's original compromise. Terms were quickly agreed on. Thus in mid-June of 1846, just as the Americans were moving against Mexico, the Senate approved the Oregon Treaty.

The Oregon Trail. Even before the treaty was signed, both Christian missionaries seeking to bring the Indians to Christ and land-hungry Americans had begun pouring into Montana, Idaho, and the Pacific Northwest. Starting their trek from Independence Missouri, they followed the Missouri and Platte Rivers west to the Rockies, crossed rivers, mountains, snow, and ice before descending down into the lush Oregon territory along the Columbia River. By the time of the 1846 treaty more than 6,000 Americans had made their way to the Oregon Territory, to begin a new life there.

Gold in the American West. But soon many using the Oregon Trail were merely passing through Oregon on their way to California, where gold was discovered in 1848 at Sutter's Mill, fifty miles upriver from Sacramento in northern California. Almost immediately the Oregon Trail had become a flood of migrants – the "Forty-Niners" (1849) – mostly male, heading to the gold fields of California in the hope of striking it rich (only about one in a hundred would find success however).

By 1855 some 300,000 Americans had made their way to California, some by the Oregon Trail, some by the long sea route around South America, in either case a long, arduous journey. What they found when they arrived, besides a vastly beautiful landscape, was a wild, unruly collection of hard-working, hard-drinking prospectors, mixed in with thieves and con-artists, prostitutes, and a handful of lawmen trying to build some kind of social order out of the chaos. This was natural man. But it was hardly the kind idealized by the 18th century Frenchman Rousseau (and nearly all comfortable intellectual-utopianists since then), supposing what man in his natural (that is, pre-civilized) state was like. The reality of the West was that it was a dangerous place where survival itself was not guaranteed. It made for very rough personalities and very rough behavior, men and women alike. But it also produced a tough breed of Westerners.

The pattern was very similar elsewhere in the West, especially when gold was discovered in Colorado and Arizona, the latter necessitating the creation of the Santa Fe Trail to the American Southwest. These gold rushes produced virtually overnight towns founded on this wild social order, towns which would just as quickly turn to ghost towns when the gold ran out and the gold-hungry citizens moved on to new fields.

But some places, such as San Francisco (the transportation and financial center for the fast-rising economy of Northern California) would indeed turn themselves into more conventional-looking American cities as middle-class life began to replace the unruly culture of gold prospecting. By 1850, Manifest Destiny had a full plate in just trying to bring the West into the older American social mainstream.

* * *

THE GROWING CONFLICT OVER SLAVERY[63]

In the meantime, American culture was splitting ever more deeply over this persistent question about Americans holding slaves. There was no way that the problem was going to simply go away on its own or just be avoided, as many Americans had earlier held the hope that this might be possible. But high-sounding principle was easier to achieve than actual plans of action.*

Unfortunately, such a large part of American culture (especially in the South and parts of the West) was built on ideals requiring the labor services, voluntary or involuntary, of other people. To undo such a social system was to destroy the cultural ideals of economic and social success themselves.

Christian Abolitionists. But there also was no way that the spirit of Puritan Protestantism widespread in the North could ever come to tolerate intellectually and emotionally this behavior in the land of freedom. Slavery violated every Christian sensibility of the Northerners, to a point that some in the North grew increasingly impatient at the willingness of even their

---

*Jefferson, for instance, though admitting the wrong of slavery, could not bring himself to free his slaves. Instead in his will he required the sale of his slaves to other slaveholders to pay for the debts he had run up by constantly redesigning his Monticello home in his effort to perfect it as a miniature utopia.

own Northern politicians to tolerate or ignore this stain, this sin corrupting the soul of the great American nation. Americans were understood to be a Covenant people called to display to the world the glories of living as Christ's people, to be a light spreading hope into the darkness of the surrounding world. Surely slavery made a mockery of this Covenant. Some felt very strongly that God would curse the nation for breaking this Covenant that their forefathers had agreed to two centuries earlier. And the Republic that had been put into place only a few generations back, a Republic dedicated to the high calling of being a light to the nations, would fail ... fail miserably. Thus the institution of slavery had to be abolished immediately. And so it was that those who advocated such action came to be called Abolitionists.

Abolitionism and the Second Great Awakening. In fact, many Abolitionists saw in slavery the seeds of certain destruction of the American people and society, by the hand of God no less. Indeed, the religious fervor of the Second Great Awakening, which continued to burn forward through the 1830s, 1840s and 1850s, had made slavery its main hot-button issue. Preachers, newspapermen, self-appointed social reformers and even a small handful of congressmen saw this issue intimately tied up with how God was looking in judgment at his Covenant people. America could not afford to lose its soul over this issue.

In general however, aggressive Abolitionists were not widely popular, not even in the North at first. They were viewed as being dangerously disruptive of the good order of the Republic. Those who viewed themselves as being of a wiser nature tended to presume that the good moral sense of Americans would eventually work this problem out. Thus it was in 1836 that Congress had placed its gag rule on any further discussion of the slavery issue. Nonetheless, the issue was a big part of what would go on to divide the New School and Old School Presbyterians in the late 1830s, the division tending to follow North-South lines. Likewise, in 1845, the Baptists also split quite permanently along North-South lines over the matter.

Europe's example. Then also there was the fact that the English had already set the noble example in 1807 by abolishing slavery within England and then in 1833 by extending abolition to the entire British Empire. France had outlawed slavery as far back as 1794 during the French Republican Revolution (though Napoleon had reintroduced the practice somewhat after 1804) and in 1848 France made the move to abolish slavery throughout all of its colonies. Thus also to the American Humanists, America's failure to follow the moral example of England and France brought unbearable shame to America as the supposed model of Enlightened Republicanism.

Most American supporters of freedom for the slaves advocated a

Expansion ... and Division 263

gradual process of emancipation. They considered this to be the more responsible solution to the problem. Others supported the idea of sending Blacks, both free or slave, back to Africa where it was supposed there would be a more natural fit for them. Thus Liberia had been established in 1820 by President Monroe (and thus Liberia's capital Monrovia) as a resettlement colony on the West coast of Africa.

Abolitionist voices. However, the Abolitionist William Lloyd Garrison, founder of the American Anti-Slavery Society and publisher of the newspaper, *The Liberator*, wanted abolition to occur immediately and fully. He even went so far as to accuse the U.S. Constitution of being a pact with slavery. This ranked him among the most radical of the Abolitionists.

A number of other newspapermen, such as Horace Greeley, editor the *New York Tribune*, were also constant in their verbal assault on the vile practice of slavery. But this could be a very dangerous issue for newspapermen to pursue. In 1837 an angry pro-slavery mob attacked the newspaper office of the Alton (Illinois) *Observer* run by the Abolitionist and Presbyterian preacher Elijah Parish Lovejoy, the fourth such attack on him and his press. But this time they murdered him, making him a martyr to the Abolitionist cause and pushing his brother Owen into the leadership of the Illinois Abolitionists.

The Abolitionist cause was also moving front and center in the midst of a growing feminist movement in America. Alongside the temperance movement to slow down or prohibit entirely the consumption of alcohol (Amelia Bloomer and Harriet Beecher Stowe), the public-school movement to extend public schooling into the poorer neighborhoods of America's fast-growing cities, and the movement to reform prisons and insane asylums (Dorthea Dix), the call for the abolition of slavery stirred women to tremendous public action (making even some male social reformers nervous!). The Grimké sisters, Angelina and Sarah, were Southerners who moved to the North to get away from the horror of slavery. And from their new home in the North they dedicated themselves to opposing the practice by any means possible, particularly through the distribution of pamphlets and lecturing around the country. As a Quaker, Lucretia Mott put her views to work in lectures enjoining women to see it their duty to push for the immediate end to slavery. Also joining the Abolitionist movement would be future suffragists (demanding the right of all women to vote) Susan B. Anthony and Lucy Stone.

Free Blacks also joined the Abolitionist chorus, speaking from the horror of personal experience. Thus Sojourner Truth and Harriet Tubman worked actively in support of immediate freedom for the slaves, Tubman becoming active in aiding escaped slaves to head North through the

Underground Railroad and Sojourner Truth joining the speaking circuit to publicize the need for immediate action on the issue. But undoubtedly the most important voice coming from the Black community itself was that of Frederick Douglass, whose obvious intelligence put to lie the idea of inherent Black inferiority on which the South built their moral case. Douglass was one of the greatest orators and writers on the subject, his books *Narrative of the Life of Frederick Douglass, an America Slave* (1845) and *My Bondage and My Freedom* (1855) both becoming best-selling works.

And working from within the political system was once the ever-vigilant John Quincy Adams. He had taken the bold course of presenting himself for election to the House of Representatives in 1830, after having lost to Andrew Jackson his bid for reelection as president in 1828. Then as a Massachusetts representative in the House, he proved to be far more politically effective than he had been as president. And on the basis of his strong opposition to slavery he built an ever-growing reputation, both in focused support and in focused opposition. He had simply ignored the 1836 gag rule and pushed the issue ever before Congress, frequently by stirring his pro-slavery opponents to wrath and thus actionable rebuttal. He had made dedicated enemies, of course. But he also had begun to have his impact in Congress, as he rose higher as a clear moral voice that constantly forced Congress to face the issue of this vile institution. He even became close friends with his former arch-rival within his Whig Party, Henry Clay.

The slave-holders' moral response. Southerners, such as the fiery-tongued Calhoun of South Carolina, were quick to react to the moral condescension coming from the Abolitionists and soon formulated a moral reply of their own. As the slave-holders themselves now in essence put things: slavery existed as a divine ordinance of God himself because Blacks were unable to function outside the system of mastery by the Whites. Thus slavery was more than merely a legal matter. It was a racial and even religious matter as well. Whites and Blacks were two different breeds of people, obviously (to any reasonable observer) unequal in their nature or character. Blacks were clearly destined by God himself to serve (as the sons of Ham) the superior White race.* Messing with God's ordinance, as

---

*Because Ham saw the nakedness of his father Noah, this Biblical pronouncement fell upon him and his descendants: "Cursed be Canaan [son of Ham]; a servant of servants shall he be unto his brethren. And he said, blessed be the LORD God of Shem; and Canaan shall be his servant." (Genesis, 9:25-26 KJV), "Hamite" was a term applied to one of many African groups, and Southerners concluded that it was through this Biblical reference to Ham and his descendants that the curse of servanthood fell eternally upon the Hamites, i.e., those of African descent. Clever, but horribly flawed, logic – not to mention terrible Biblical exegesis [analysis]! But it seemed to many Southerners to suffice as a compelling moral argument.

Expansion ... and Division

certainly the Abolitionists were doing, was itself going to bring on America the wrath of God.

The moral chasm deepens. So there it was. Two opposing viewpoints, both enshrined with a keen sense of divine legitimacy, both employing precise human logic to develop and deepen their two contradicting moral positions. There was no way that the issue therefore was going to simply go away on its own. The challenge of answering the moral question of slavery had spun America into two moral camps with only a small and rapidly declining moral realm still uniting them.

Once again, Human Reason was not going to provide America with any clarity or Truth that could bring it out of this growing hostility. Human Reason merely fortified the two bitterly opposing social viewpoints, even at this point religious worldviews. Conflict – vicious conflict – was increasingly the only way this critical issue was going to be resolved.

Zachary Taylor elected U.S. president (1848). Clay now supposed that he had the Whig nomination all sewed up as he approached the nominating convention in Philadelphia. But the Mexican-American war had put General Taylor front and center in the hearts of the American people, especially among a younger generation that had less reverence for the Great Compromiser Clay. Similarly, the long-standing political star Daniel Webster suffered from the same loss of relevance to the younger generation. Webster finally threw his support behind Taylor, who in turn offered him the position as his vice presidential running mate, which Webster declined (though when Taylor died sixteen months into his presidency, Webster would regret not having taken up the offer). So Taylor turned to the strongly anti-slavery New Yorker Millard Fillmore as his running mate.

Taylor's political views were largely unknown. He was a Kentuckian and a slaveholder (a rather unusual social profile for one who confessed himself to be a Whig), though he seemed to have no strongly-held views on the issue of slavery. He was a soldier first and foremost, a strong American nationalist, and a national hero. And that is what the American people found so appealing about him.

Running against the Whigs was a new face in the competition, a new third party, the strongly Abolitionist Free Soil Party, which ran Van Buren as its presidential candidate (actually drawing about ten percent of the national vote). And, as usual, opposing the Whigs – but also now the Free-Soilers as well – was the pro-states'-rights Democratic Party, with its strong Southern support, which ran Lewis Cass as its presidential candidate.

In the election itself, in which the voter turnout was quite light, Taylor won a slight (five percent) majority of the popular vote, although he ultimately received 163 electoral votes to Cass's 137 votes in securing for himself the U.S. presidency. All in all, the election was a clear indication that the nation was ready for a break from the tensions of the Mexican-American war and the slavery issue. But sadly, the latter was not destined to be.

* * *

AMERICA AT MID-CENTURY (1850)

The widening social-cultural-moral gap between the North and the South. Behind the moral-legal battle in Congress, in the press, and in the pulpit stood a stark social reality that was forcing both North and South into ever more inflexible positions as the two sections of the country faced each other. A big part of the problem was of course the slavery issue. But there were other issues that were pushing the two sections of the country further and further apart – also in part related to the slavery issue but more importantly related to the way that the social-cultural dynamics of the two regions (with the young West beginning to form a third part of the social-cultural distinction) were rapidly unfolding. Both key sections of the country were heading down very different socio-economic paths. This would only add to the inability of the two main sections of the country to understand or even just work with each other.

The North. The North was prospering in a way that the South, despite all its romantic ideas of the elegance of Southern plantation life, could not match in terms of economic achievement. An observer of life in the North would have been quick to note all the infrastructure recently completed or under construction in the North: roads, canals and railroads. True, these were also developing in the South, but at a much slower rate than in the North. For each mile of track laid out for railroads in the South, three miles were being constructed in the North. And even at that, the Northern lines tended to run East and West linking the industrial East closely with the expanding Western frontier. Comparatively few of the roads ran north and south to link more closely the Northern half of the country with the South.

The coastal cities of the North (Boston, New York, Philadelphia and even Baltimore) were bustling with new life, much of it from European immigrants – who knew of the lack of economic opportunity in the American South and thus headed from Europe to America's Northern coastal cities.

Much of this new life coming to the North was chaotic, fueled by a mass of Irish coming in from Ireland to escape the horrible 1840s potato famine which was devastating their country. The Irish came to all of the major cities of the North (but also the rather Catholic New Orleans in the South), disrupting the calm composure of White Anglo-Saxon Protestant (WASP) America with their Irish Catholicism and defiant Irish attitudes (they disliked the Anglo world intensely for the highhanded ways the English had dealt with the Irish crisis). Under the impetus of this Irish invasion, New York City, for instance, became a very vibrant but also a rough place in which to live and do business, with its tough neighborhoods, its Irish gangs, and its corrupt political wheeling and dealing.

To the Irish, as would also be the case for the Southern Italians and Sicilians who would flock to the country early in the next century, social justice or law had little to do with abstract Constitutional principles and political offices developed in the long English tradition of both England and America. Instead, they saw justice as vested in local urban bosses whose job in government was to use the public treasury to take care of their own people. This Irish paternalism was something the WASPs called corruption, but something the Irish instead looked upon as being simply what any person had the right to expect from government.

Further West into the heartland of the American North were a large number of prosperous towns and cities – large and small – and a multitude of small and well-kept farms dotting the Northern landscape, from upstate New York and Pennsylvania in the East to the fields of Wisconsin, Minnesota, Iowa and Kansas in the West. All of this seemed to evidence solid success, even if only on a small scale. There was a sense of inventiveness, of activity, of progress, of confidence, of accomplishment, energizing the average Northerner, who looked with pride on his or her work in the home, in the field, in the shop.

Here too immigrants added to this picture of vitality, notably the Germans and Scandinavians, who however blended into the American Midwestern landscape more readily than did the Irish in the American urban East. These northern Europeans were a more communal group, especially the Mennonites and the Amish among them, with a communal work ethic in many ways even more rigorous than the highly individualistic Yankee work ethic of the Anglo North. Very obvious material success followed their efforts, adding considerably to the picture of rural prosperity in the North.

With the opening of the West all the way to California, the Northern pattern tended to be the one that reached into the new western territories. There were slaves that accompanied some of the White newcomers to the West, though they constituted only a small part of the population that crowded West to lay claim to the new land. Slavery was not very useful in terms of the types of challenges these newcomers faced in the new West. Indeed, frontiersmen were very much the same individualists as the American Northerners, depending on their own talents to survive and prosper in a highly competitive world.

The South. The South could easily sense that the social dynamics of a rapidly growing America were not going its way. A mood of defensiveness was settling in on the South, still proud of its own distinct cultural traditions – and the peculiar institution of slavery that Southerners understood as constituting the foundation of it all. The more the North pressed them on this matter of slavery the more defensive they became in asserting the correctness of Southern social values.

But sadly, despite all the romantic swooning about the aristocratic plantation life in the rural South, the material reality was not quite so elegant. To be sure there were endless rounds of social visits (in the style of the British aristocracy that Southerners attempted to duplicate), fancy balls, fox hunts, etc. to occupy the privileged members of the plantation class. But behind this pleasant façade stood a troubled reality. All of this style stood on very shaky economic ground.

Cotton was king in the South, so much so that for a long time there had been little interest in the production of anything else. The amount of cotton that was produced was truly vast, which meant that the price per bale produced would remain competitively low. And it would reach an even lower low when cotton production from India began to hit the world market. The plantations, despite all the flow of cotton from their vast fields, were stretched greatly to make an adequate profit able to sustain this luxurious life style.

Urban life of course existed in the South, but not generally of the bustling industrial variety found in the North. Urban life was largely an extension of the all-prevailing cotton economy. Towns such as Richmond, Columbus and Atlanta existed mostly to collect and market the cotton of the rural areas immediately around them (plus buy and sell slaves as an accompanying activity). On the Atlantic and Gulf coasts cities such as Baltimore, Charleston, Savannah, Mobile and New Orleans* served as points of departure in the shipment of cotton to both British and New England textile mills.

Beyond cotton, the South was slow in its uptake of the new industrial revolution. Steel was manufactured in the South as well as the new tools and equipment to aid the economy of the Cotton South, but not at the rate that it was being produced in the North. Nonetheless, despite the smaller scale of the industrial revolution in the South, rather substantial profits were to be had by those who ventured into the competitive world

---

*New Orleans was actually the third largest city in America at the time. Being the primary port of the huge Mississippi River watershed region, its economy was much broader, of course, than just the cotton trade.

Expansion ... and Division

of industry. Yet, the status and prestige that Southerners sought was not assigned by Southern culture to the world of capitalism. It belonged largely to the romanticized world of the rural plantation. This was what truly slowed the South in its economic development, at least in comparison to the rapid industrial growth of the North.

Worse, no industrial invention had provided an alternative to the hard reality that cotton was still picked by hand. Cotton picking or chopping was a painful finger-bleeding and exhausting back-breaking labor as well as often a spirit-breaking activity, especially when accompanied by the whip of a White overseer who had the responsibility of making sure that the Black slaves under his charge met high-reaching production quotas.

Cotton farming did not make for much happiness, not just for the slave but also for the White farmer who could not afford slaves – as indeed the vast majority could not. The Southern dirt farmer was by economic reality reduced to a material standard of living hardly better than that of the slave, often occupying shacks no more comfortable than the ones the slaves occupied on the plantations. Of course the White farmer was free and the Black slave was not. And on that difference the poor-White farmer staked his entire self-image, to ensure that at least that small achievement would not be taken from him by freeing the slaves and thus putting him on a par with them. To protect that slim social distinction, he would be willing to fight fiercely. Beyond that he dreamed the Cinderella dream that he someday might find himself elevated to the social level of the plantation elite whom he admired greatly (when he was not resenting them). The dream sustained him somehow, even though there was virtually no likelihood of it ever coming true.

As for the slaves, the tragedy of the lives of the masses of these captive workers was almost beyond endurance. It was not just that they were worked to exhaustion daily but that they had no sense of the future ever holding anything positive for them. In fact the future held the agonizing possibility of their much-loved spouses or children being taken from them by a cash-strapped owner who needed to sell them to pay off mounting debts. They were treated like commodities, similar to cattle, and even bred like cattle in order to build up their numbers as an economic asset, averaging in value at that time around $1000 apiece if they were young, strong and of a fertile age. And of course there were the young masters who could not keep their hands off of attractive female slaves, humiliating both slaves and White family at home with their sexual adventures, which no one dared talk about even though it was widely practiced.

And connecting the slave and the slave owner besides the whip was the regime of fear produced by the whip. Although to ease its conscience White society attempted to dehumanize the African slave, there was no way that the Whites could get past the understanding of exactly how the slaves must truly feel about their White masters. That link of fear was based heavily on the constant concern about the possibility of a slave rebellion (such as the successful slave rebellion in Haiti or the failed one of Nat Turner in Virginia in 1831). The White South did not know what to do. To keep the slaves in submission they would have to be unflinching in their harsh discipline, which they knew darkened ever deeper the slave heart. Yet to try to win slave hearts was to have to release that grip, which could then explode the very social foundations of the South.*

The Compromise of 1850. The American acquisition of the Western territories resulting from the Mexican-American War had sadly and even tragically merely presented another round in the North-South contention over slavery and its extension westward. Promoted strongly by former General and now President Zachary Taylor was the idea that California, New Mexico and Utah should be brought directly into union with the U.S., and not go through the stage of first being territories prior to statehood. Furthermore all three future states had expressed the intention of being brought into the Union as Free-Soil states. This was not going to please the South.

At the same time, Southerners were already talking about disunion. In late 1849 Mississippi called for Southern representatives to meet the following year in Nashville. The purpose of this meeting though unstated was obvious. They were going to be gathering to discuss this very possibility. Needless to say, all this created quite a stir in Washington.

When the candidacy of California was put forward for statehood at the very end of 1849 tempers in Congress flared. California was going to be admitted as a free state, ending the tradition of maintaining a balance in the number of slave and free states. The speeches for and against grew hotter as they took on very biting moral accusations and moral justifications concerning the central issue of slavery. One vote followed another as the two sides deadlocked over the issue.

Once again the Great Compromiser Henry Clay (but now also a very weak old man) stepped forward in the Senate† at the end of January (1850)

---

*White Southerners were keenly aware of what had occurred in the French colony of Haiti in which in 1791 the African slaves successfully rose up against their French masters, defeated an effort in 1803 by Napoleon's military to bring the slaves back into submission and ultimately in 1804 butchered thousands of French, forcing the French to finally acknowledge the obvious: Haiti was free of White oppression.

†Of course both houses of Congress were debating the same issue, but the nation's eyes tended to be turned more to the Senate where debate was viewed as having more of a strategic nature, especially when it involved an address to

Expansion ... and Division

to offer a set of proposals that he hoped would smooth feelings on both sides, and ease the way for California to achieve full statehood. The bill authorized the admission of California to the Union as a Free-Soil state; it set the Western boundaries of Texas, thus ending the contention Texas had with New Mexico; it designated both Utah and New Mexico as territories, with each possessing the right to determine how they would eventually enter the Union, as free or slave states; it called for the end of slave sales within the Washington, D.C. capital (though not the end of slavery itself in the nation's capital); it required Congress to drop any claim of authority to regulate the interstate trade in slaves; and it required the North to return escaped slaves to their owners in the South, a measure that was designed to calm the fears of the South about Northern Abolitionist ambitions.

As compromises typically fare, it pleased the moderates of both the North and the South but also succeeding in angering the extreme wings of the Abolitionist Northerners and increasingly independence-minded Southerners. Particularly upset were the Northern Abolitionists to whom the idea of the forced return of slaves that had escaped to the North was an abominable idea. They would have none of it, even if it meant defying the nation's laws.

But not everyone in the South was appeased by this compromise either. At the beginning of March, Calhoun, too weak to deliver his speech himself to the Senate, had someone read for him the biting accusations about the rising tyranny of the North, and his call for an amendment to the Constitution that would give the nation a dual presidency and the right of each state to veto any act of Congress. Also, Southerners should be able to go anywhere in the Union without the fear of having their property confiscated. Slavery must be protected throughout the Union. Anything less than that would be answered with the secession of the Southern states.

The speech shocked everyone, yet had the effect of emphasizing even more the importance of compromise in order to save the Union from dissolution.*

Several days later it was the turn of the third elderly member of the Great Triumvirate, Daniel Webster, to address the issue in the Senate. In his three-hour speech, he recalled the history of the slavery issue as it had taken on ever greater importance to the nation, the efforts to bring the issue to compromise, and the overriding importance of maintaining the Union. He also projected that any move to disunion would throw America

---

the Senate of one or another of the Great Triumvirate of Senators Henry Clay, Daniel Webster and John C. Calhoun

*John C. Calhoun died some four weeks later. With Calhoun dead, the Nashville conference got put aside, and the secessionist mood in the South subsided, for a while anyway.

into chaos, and ultimately murderous conflict. With this he was stating what was becoming increasingly obvious to all, that if America continued to behave as it had been recently, there would be no escaping some horribly violent outcome. The nation had to come together.

Then four days after Webster's speech, it was the turn of a rising star within the Senate, William Seward of New York, an Abolitionist Whig, to be heard. He put forward the claim that there was a higher law than even the Constitution that he answered to, the Law of God. That higher law would never permit him to return an escaped slave back into the arms of immoral, illegal servitude. Southerners were furious. Even Northerners were stunned. But Seward had laid the seeds of an argument that would gather force among the Northerners.

A Congressional committee was set up to consider Clay's proposals and finally in May these proposals were brought before Congress in the form of an omnibus* bill: all measures to be voted up or down jointly in a single vote.

Meanwhile tensions were growing between (slavery) Texas and (free) New Mexico, as Texas claimed that the eastern half of what was being designated as New Mexico territory was in fact an integral part of Texas. Texas was willing to enforce that claim by military action if necessary.

But President Taylor weighed in against Texas and demanded immediate accession of New Mexico as a new state, and as an old soldier was willing also to enforce his viewpoint by military action if necessary. Southerners then were quick to join Texas in their outrage over this move by the president because the accession of New Mexico would mean one more free state being added to the Union. War clouds began to gather in the West.

Then in the midst of the furor, President Taylor got sick attending a long, hot 4th of July ceremony in the capital, worsened (by the help of doctors who bled him extensively and pumped him with narcotics), and died five days later. The nation was stunned.†

But this automatically elevated Vice President Millard Fillmore to the presidency. And he was willing to take a more centrist position, consulting both Clay and Webster, both well known as willing to compromise on this matter.

But at this point it was time for yet another key figure to take center-

---

*This was a term that Taylor came up with, unhappy at how all these measures had been thrown together, like being put in an omnibus, a large city carriage that anyone could ride for a fee. The term stuck and is now used regularly in Congressional legislation.

†Rumors persist to this day that Taylor may have been poisoned. In 1991 tests were made that said no, but even the tests have been contested.

Expansion ... and Division

stage: Illinois Democrat Senator Stephen A. Douglas. Though Douglas was a major slave owner (thanks to his wife's inheritance of a 2500-acre plantation in Mississippi, which he rarely visited but which was for him a constant source of revenue) he was a Democratic Party moderate on the slavery issue. He proposed that the various portions of the omnibus bill be broken out into their different parts and be considered separately. This lowered the tension about the all-or-nothing character of the legislation. Also with the radical pro-slavery Calhoun gone from the scene and with the death of the strongly Free-Soil Taylor also no longer in the picture, tensions eased. Talk of war subsided. Now a new mood opened the opportunity for compromise.

An exhausted Clay called on Stephen Douglas to run his measure through the Senate again. This time the Compromise made its way successfully through Congress in September in the form of a number of pieces of legislation. Texas was willing to give up its claim on New Mexico (and adjust its territorial boundaries elsewhere as well) with the assumption of $10 million in Texas debt by the federal government. And the part that the Abolitionists hated so fiercely, the promise of the North to return all escaped slaves to the South (coupled with massive fines slapped on anyone aiding and abetting any escape of a slave), was finally passed as the Fugitive Slave Act.

Now the thought arose that the slavery issue had been resolved once and for all. The Union was saved. But Southerners remained skeptical. To them, whether the Union held or not depended on how faithfully the North enforced the Fugitive Slave Act. They were soon to find out.

CHAPTER EIGHT
THE GATHERING CLOUDS OF WAR

***

THE STEPS TOWARD WAR

Harriet Beecher Stowe's *Uncle Tom's Cabin* (1851–1852). The answer to the question of how well the North was going to stand by its promise to enforce the Fugitive Slave Act came quickly in the form a broad reaction of Northerners to a piece of literature that took the North by storm: Harriet Beecher Stowe's *Uncle Tom's Cabin*. This story, first published as a periodical series in 1851 then as a novel in 1852, depicted the suffering and bravery of Southern slaves (most notably the slave Tom), the tragedy of the South caught in the trap of its own slavery system, and the power of Christian love to overcome evil. It was an immediate best-seller in the North,* and moved the North vastly closer to the Abolitionist position. It also put the South again on the moral defensive,† which in turn hardened Southern attitudes against the Union.

As far as the Fugitive Slave Act of 1850 was concerned, the popularity of the novel fairly well undercut any idea of a serious enforcement of the Act in the North. In fact it merely encouraged yet another feature that had been developing on the American stage: the Underground Railroad.

The Underground Railroad. The Underground Railroad was the term used in reference to a system of aiding the escape of slaves from bondage to freedom in either the Northern states or Canada. The system was neither underground nor involving primarily a railroad, but was a complex arrangement of safe houses where escaped slaves could hide and of guides who would escort these escapees from one safe house to the next.

This process had actually been going on for quite some time. But

---

*It sold 300,000 copies in the first year of its publication alone.

†It was of course also read in the South, though interestingly with some degree of sympathy – at least initially – until its strong political implications became increasingly clear.

The Gathering Clouds of War

during the period 1850 to 1860 its activity increased dramatically, though it is hard to know exactly how many slaves were moved North by this escape system, precisely because of its secret nature. Certainly, thousands made their way North.

Both North and South were aware of its existence. Both sides claimed that it was extensive in nature, though the North would have cited huge numbers as a matter of pride in its accomplishments; and the South would have made a similar huge claim, though only to emphasize how great was the Northern violation of the agreed upon Fugitive Slave Act.

The sight of Southern lawmen – but especially Southern bounty hunters – coming to Northern cities to look for just such escapees and under the authorization of the Fugitive Slave Act dragging them back into Southern slavery was more than Northern sensitivities could bear. Indeed, there was evidence that even free Blacks – and more horrifying, defenseless children – were simply kidnaped off the streets by Southerners seeking bounty money. This was pushing the North into the arms of the Abolitionists, Abolitionists who even recently had been declared by moderate Northerners as being dangerously radical. Now rather quickly, the Abolitionists were seeming less and less radical and more and more correct in their fierce opposition to slavery.

The South, on the other hand, was outraged at the violent reaction of the Northerners to the Southern lawmen (and bounty hunters) who, under the full authority of the law, were simply in the North to recover the South's lost property. The South seethed in anger at how the North could so willingly violate the law of the land.

So indeed, the Compromise of 1850 was turning out not to have achieved anything in the effort to settle the hostilities growing between the North and the South. If anything, it had succeeded merely in heightening and sharpening those hostilities.

The passing of the last of the Great Triumvirate. We have already noted that John Calhoun died in the very midst of the debate that ultimately produced the Compromise of 1850. But the other two members of the Great Triumvirate were soon to follow. The passing of these three greats marked the end of another era of American politics and the beginning of yet a new one as the country marched toward a violent split.

At the end of June 1852, the Great Compromiser Henry Clay passed from the American scene. He had served the country since first entering the U.S. Senate in 1806, then serving in House of Representatives from 1811, eventually becoming its speaker in three different sessions. He then became the secretary of state under John Quincy Adams and afterwards returned to the position of senator until his death. He had campaigned for the U.S. presidency in 1824 and again as candidate for the Whig Party (of which he remained leader for the rest of his life) in 1832 and 1844, though he lost all three elections.

In late October of that same year the third member of the Triumvirate, Daniel Webster, followed Clay into eternity. Another Whig, Webster was famous for his eloquent defenses of American nationalism and for his support of the American business class which he felt strongly held the greatest responsibility for the success of the new nation. Webster served in the House of Representatives for ten years, in the Senate for another nineteen years and served as U.S. secretary of state under presidents Harrison, Tyler, and Fillmore, occupying this position as of his death in 1852.

Both men worked hard to hold back the forces that wanted to divide the country over slavery. They both suffered sharp opposition from the most aggressive members of the extreme wings of the Southern Secessionists and the Northern Abolitionists. But they held strong at the middle. But the middle was already losing power by the time of their deaths. With their deaths there now was little to hold the two conflicting sides together.

Franklin Pierce, the Young-America Expansionist, elected. The Whig Party was in major disarray. The Compromise of 1850 produced a deep sense of alienation by many Northern Whigs, who felt betrayed by some of their leadership, most notably the newly installed President Fillmore, whose support of the Compromise won him no affection from the anti-slavery branch of the Whig Party. On the other hand, the Democratic Party counted the Compromise as being a major success, especially by Southern Democrats because the Fugitive Slave Act clearly supported the Southern view of slaves as property rather than as humans. Also political moderates, both North and South, though not greatly fond of all the details of the Compromise, felt that nonetheless its passage had thankfully finally put the slavery issue to rest. The nation could now relax.

In the Congressional mid-term elections of 1850 that November, the Democrats swept the Whigs aside, securing two-thirds of the seats in the House. Sensing that they were headed for victory in the up-coming presidential election in 1852, the Democrats began immediately to prepare for it. Meanwhile the Whigs found themselves stunned by the huge 1850 setback. They were not sure which way to turn. Certainly there was no way they were going to support Fillmore in his bid for reelection. But who would they support?

At the Democratic National Convention in 1852 the Democrats once again nominated (on the 49th ballot!) a Northerner of Southern principles: Franklin Pierce of Vermont – a lawyer with an acceptable military record as

The Gathering Clouds of War

brigadier general in the Mexican-American War (but wounded and thus not able to perform dazzlingly). The Whigs responded with their own military hero as nominee, General Winfield Scott – whose Abolitionist principles at that point however were too strong for the taste of most Americans. Consequently, Scott and the Whigs were trounced in the 1852 elections, Pierce receiving a 50.8 percent of the popular vote (to Scott's 43.9 percent) and 254 electoral votes for Pierce versus Scott's forty-two. The Free-Soilers (4.9 percent of the popular vote) and other fringe parties (such as the Liberty Party and the American Party) made up the balance in the popular vote.

Overall, this election began the decline and ultimate death of the Whig Party. It would dissolve before the next presidential election in 1856, with most Whigs joining the newly constituted Republican Party (no connection with Jefferson's former Republicans, however).

The Gadsden Purchase (1853). By 1850 America had laid more railroad track than any other nation and over the next ten years the amount of track laid would more than triple. Most of this occurred in the North. But even the South by 1860 would have more track laid than any European country.

It was during Pierce's presidency that his secretary of war, Jefferson Davis (soon to be president of the Southern Confederacy), began to push for a Southern railroad to reach all the way to the Pacific. This would have put the South ahead of the North in its reach West, possibly giving slavery a boost in the Western territories for which slavery was to be a local option chosen by the people of the territory themselves. Thus Davis convinced Pierce to send rail magnate James Gadsden to negotiate with Mexican President (again!) Santa Anna for the purchase of a section of Arizona border territory that would have helped the South more quickly reach its goal of a southern transcontinental railroad. The purchase price of this section of land (popularly termed the Gadsden Purchase) was for $10 million, badly needed by Santa Anna whose government was once again on the verge of bankruptcy. With this purchase, the territorial reach of the U.S. was complete (until a century later in the 1950s when Alaska and Hawaii were added as distant states).

Cuba and the Ostend Manifesto (1854). The island of Cuba, not far from the southern shores of Florida, was still held by a greatly weakened Spain, which however posed no particular threat to America and its Monroe Doctrine. Consequently, over the years it had attracted little American attention.

However, following the admission of California to the Union and the unlikelihood of the New Mexico and Utah territories joining the Union as anything other than as Free-Soil states, the South turned its eyes to Cuba as a possible slavery territory and future state offsetting the North's gains. At the urging of Pierce's secretary of state, William Marcy, a meeting of American diplomats posted to Europe met secretly in Ostend, Belgium, to discuss a strategy for either purchasing Cuba from the Spanish, or just simply taking it by force. But news of the secret meeting got out, causing a huge outrage in both Europe and in the American North, and a major embarrassment to the Pierce government. The timing for this was terrible, because it coincided with another issue that was tearing the country apart.

The Kansas-Nebraska Act of 1854. A combination of land hunger from American farmers being pushed West in search of new lands to open up, plus the commercial interests of railroad magnates seeking the riches that came with the land-for-rails exchange,* put the huge Nebraska Territory just to the west of Missouri up for development. This of course brought forward the persistent question with reference to the Nebraska Territory: slave or free?

According to the Missouri Compromise of 1820, the Nebraska territory, being entirely above the 36°30' line separating in the Western territories' Free-Soil land above that line and slavery territory below it, should automatically have been classed as a free state. But as some (notably Democrat Party leader, Illinois Senator Douglas) pointed out, California and New Mexico were well below that line and had entered as Free-Soil states under the principle of popular sovereignty (letting the state's citizens themselves decide the matter of slave or free). Indeed, Douglas made it a personal mission of his own to get Congress to accept this same principle of popular sovereignty for the new Nebraska Territory. Southerners joined with Douglas, and went even further in attempting to amend the bill by adding the provision making the Missouri Compromise now null and void.

President Pierce, his cabinet and Southern Democrats were all highly favorable to this proposal. Even Southern Whigs supported the idea. But Northern Whigs were furious, and Northern Democrats were none too pleased. In all, the issue would finally finish off the Whig Party through an irreparable split in its ranks. But the Democratic Party would also find that its huge majority would mean little in Congress when it too was deeply split over this issue.

Pierce attempted to hold the Democratic Party together by making

---

*Railroad companies were given huge land grants in return for laying track in the Western territories. The land then was sold to new settlers, to compensate the railroad companies for their building expenses. It was to the great advantage of the railroad companies to bring in as many settlers as possible, pushing the rapid development of these territories.

The Gathering Clouds of War 279

support of the Nebraska Bill the measure of party loyalty and the distribution of party favors. He even proposed to pass responsibility over to the Supreme Court by getting it to declare the Missouri Compromise as unconstitutional.

In January of 1854 the bill was reintroduced in the Senate, calling for the repeal of the Missouri Compromise and dividing the Nebraska Territory into two parts, Kansas to the south and Nebraska to the north. The new northern section of Nebraska was clearly going to be free territory, by the obvious choice of the settlers themselves. But the southern section of Kansas was understood as being capable of going either way in a popular vote.

With Democrats possessing a large majority in both houses of Congress and Douglas using all his energies to gain passage of the bill, it finally passed both houses after four months of bitter fighting, 37 to 14 in the Senate (early March) and 113 to 100 in the House (May 22), with Pierce signing it into law on May 30th.

Despite Congress's resolution of the Kansas-Nebraska matter, the country as a whole was taking a position very different from that of Congress. The North, containing the vast majority of the nation's population, was distressed by the political slick that had just occurred in Washington, and was more determined than ever in its stand against the extension of slavery. The South, on the other hand, was not moved to a greater affection for the Union because of the new Act, becoming instead even more skeptical that union with the anti-slavery North was going to last much longer.

The Congressional elections of 1854. In the elections of 1854, the Democratic Party experienced a huge setback delivered by its Northern constituents. Of the 91 Free-Soil or Free-State Democrats in the House at the time of the election, 66 of them were not reelected by their voters (mostly in New York, Ohio, Pennsylvania and Indiana), leaving only 25 Northern or Free-State Democrats to return to the House in 1855.[*] They would fail to recover any of those lost seats in the upcoming elections. As a result, the Democratic Party turned itself into a heavily Southern Party.

In all, six parties now competed in the House. A coalition of the American Party or Know-Nothings[†] (52 seats) and the Opposition Party formed the new majority in the House. The American Party supported curbs on immigration, which voters felt were overwhelming the Anglo-Protestant

---

[*] As senators were still chosen by their state legislatures, the Senate profile changed very little in 1854.

[†] The American Party was built mainly on a number of fraternal lodges whose members operated under a pledge of secrecy (as was common in men's organizations at that time). When quizzed about their doings they responded with "I know nothing," thus acquiring their nickname as the "Know-Nothings."

character of America. For a while it looked as if the American Party might replace the Whigs as the main adversary of the Democrats. On the other hand, the Opposition Party was simply a loose coalition of the remaining members of the Whig Party (now holding only 15 seats), the Anti-Nebraska Party (22 seats), the People's Party (9 seats) and the new Republican Party (13 seats).

This latter party, that of the new Republicans, would however soon absorb the last of the Whigs (and their political and economic philosophy) and the Anti-Nebraska Party. Also a large number of the American Party or Know-Nothings would accompany their leader, House Speaker and soon to be Massachusetts Governor Nathaniel Banks, in moving into the Republican Party. Thus the Republican Party, rather than the American Party, would move ahead to face the Democrats as the Democrats' major opponent.

This would then form the Republican-Democratic Party dualism that exists to this day.

Bleeding Kansas.[64] With the Kansas-Nebraska Act's call for popular sovereignty in determining the future of Kansas, there was a push on by both Northerners and Southerners to increase the supporters among the Kansans of one side or the other. From Missouri came pro-slavery settlers (termed "Border Ruffians" by angry Free-Staters) to augment the ranks of those ready to vote for slavery for Kansas. But the Free-State side had their "Jayhawkers" who entered Kansas to build up the ranks of the free vote. Thus Douglas's popular sovereignty turned out to be not the solution Kansas needed to avoid conflict, but the very cause of its growing intensity.

Conflict thus began to mount between the two groups, so much so that the strongly pro-slavery territorial capital at Lecompton became a very dangerous place for Free-Staters. This caused the Free-Staters in 1855 to establish their own legislature at Topeka and to elect their own governor and senators.

Kansas newspapers chose sides and hyped the intensity of the bitterness mounting between the two parties. This in turn invited vigilante action in which one or another of these newspapers were ransacked and their presses destroyed.

The Brooks caning of Sumner (May 1856). While Kansas bled away, an incident occurred in the U.S. Senate that would add fuel to the growing fire. The strongly Abolitionist Massachusetts Senator Charles Sumner, who had a knack for delivering sharp insults, in his "Crime against Kansas" speech unloaded a stream of insults on the Kansas-Nebraska Act's coauthors, Douglas and South Carolina Senator Andrew Butler. Butler's cousin, South Carolina Congressman Preston Brooks, decided to avenge Butler's honor by entering the Senate and pounding Sumner nearly to death with a cane (requiring Sumner two years to recover), making Brooks a hero to the South and Sumner a martyr to Northern Abolitionists.

John Brown. At about the same time, the appearance of the wild (and possibly slightly insane) self-proclaimed Abolitionist leader John Brown and his sons, plus a handful of other followers, only heightened the violence in Kansas. In May of 1856 they executed five pro-slavery farmers in the Pottawatomie Massacre in revenge for the sacking of Lawrence by pro-slavery forces. In retaliation, in August several hundred Border Ruffians, equipped even with cannons loaded with grapeshot, attacked the town of Osawatomie, where Brown's family was living. With only 40 defenders as his support, Brown was forced to withdraw after having lost two of his sons and several other Free-Staters killed. Then the Border Ruffians proceeded to loot and burn the town. But John Brown would survive to become a central figure in the growing bitterness between the North and the South.

From then on, the Kansas violence would only escalate into full scale guerrilla-style warfare, complete with the killing, looting, and burning of settlements and the destruction of crops across Kansas. Not only was Kansas bleeding, but in Kansas the Civil War had already begun. And Kansas would continue to bleed until the last shot of the Civil War was fired in 1865.

James Buchanan elected (1856). By 1856 the Republican Party was registering rapid growth, and ready to field its first candidate for the U.S. Presidency. Leading the organization were Ohio Senator (and soon-to-be Governor) Salmon P. Chase and New York Senator (and former Governor) William H. Seward. Although the Republicans took up the former Whig Party agenda of national banking, protection of industry, and infrastructure improvements (roads, canals, and railroads), the main issue they pursued was the issue of slavery. Though not radical (and thus demanding an immediate end of slavery), they were very much behind the idea that it was time to begin to put an end to slavery through financial compensation to slave owners and recolonization to Africa if necessary.

But the Republicans passed over Seward as their presidential candidate, choosing instead California war hero John Frémont. However, in the national elections in November the Northern vote was split by the Know-Nothings who fielded former President Millard Fillmore as their own candidate. This split caused neither Frémont nor Fillmore to be elected. Instead the Democratic Party candidate, former Pennsylvania senator, U.S. secretary of state and ambassador to England, James Buchanan, won the election (45.3 percent of the popular vote for Buchanan, 33.1 percent for

Frémont and 21.5 percent for Fillmore, though with 174 electoral votes for Buchanan, 114 for Frémont and only 8 for Fillmore).*

Buchanan had been in England during the Kansas-Nebraska crisis and thus was not identified strongly with either side in the issue. He intended to keep it that way, claiming that he alone at this point could bring healing to a disunited country. He would be above politics. Anyway, he was counting on the Supreme Court to settle the question of slavery in the territories.

The Dred Scott Case (1857).[65]   And the decision of the Court came only two days after Buchanan's inauguration (early March 1857). The case concerned a Black man (Dred Scott) and his wife and their daughter, as to whether nor not under the law they had – because of their long residence in the anti-slavery North (before being brought back to pro-slavery Missouri) – attained the status of free citizens. It was in being shifted from owner to new owner as slaves that Scott decided to bring his situation to trial. He filed in the Missouri courts for recognition of his free status – whose jury initially agreed with him. But he lost that favorable decision on appeal by his owner Sanford. Scott filed the case again, *Scott v. Sandford*,† this time in federal court, and his case made its way through appeals all the way finally to the U.S. Supreme Court.

On March 6, 1857, Chief Justice Roger B. Taney issued the Court's 7-2 decision, finding against Scott and in favor of Sanford. Taney's findings were supposed to put the issue of the legality of slavery in the new territories to a final resolution. But in fact they did quite the opposite, deepening further the hostilities separating the free North and the slave South. Firstly, Taney said that since Scott was a slave and not a citizen, he had no right to bring suit against Sanford in a federal court. That should have been then the end of the legal issue for the Court. But Taney went on to touch further on the legal implications of the case. He claimed that Scott had no right to citizenship because no slave had the right to citizenship, because none of the slaves had origins as free citizens, even the ones who had received manumission (being freed) by their owners. He stated also that no states had the right to pass laws that offered manumission to slaves living within their jurisdiction. Further, Congress had no Constitutional right to make

---

*At their National Convention, the Democrats had passed over their own White House incumbent President Franklin Pierce to give Buchanan a plurality, though not a majority, on the first ballot. Party leader Stephen Douglas started out a distant third, then began to pick up additional votes with each round of new party elections, at the cost of Pierce. Finally Douglas threw his support to Buchanan, giving him the party's nomination on the 17th ballot.

†The federal courts had misspelled the defendant's name, causing confusion in how to spell the name of the case all the way down to today.

The Gathering Clouds of War

any determination of the slave or free status for any state or territory, as no such authority was given Congress by the Constitution. In fact the only relevant Constitutional provision in the matter was the Fifth Amendment which protects a citizen's property rights in all parts of the Union. Taney went so far as to affirm that no state had the right even to grant citizenship to Blacks, slave or free, because the Constitution was written only for the superior race of Whites. Blacks were unfit to associate with the White race and had no natural rights that Whites were bound to respect.

Northerners were furious with the Court's ruling.* Southerners were now no longer the only section of the country sensing that their values would have to be defended by force. The idea that Congress had no right to exclude the enslavement of men anywhere in the Union was too galling an idea to ever be accepted in the North. And at the rate of pro-slavery progress moving across the American political landscape, the states of the North could wake up to find themselves suddenly declared slave states by the Supreme Court.

The moderate Senator Douglas did not challenge the Court directly, but stated that regardless of a territory's inability to exclude slavery, it could refuse to offer police enforcement or protection to the practice of slavery. But this piece of logic proved compelling to no one, Northerner or Southerner.

Southerners now went so far as to claim that the Dred Scott decision had fully vindicated the practice of slavery, in any part of the Union. Some even claimed that it was time to go on the offensive and push to have slavery allowed in all the Union, therefore preserving the Union's integrity and unity in having no longer two but now one fundamental social vision (that of the slave culture of course). There was of course no way that Northerners were going to yield even an inch to that kind of argument.

Thus overall, the Supreme Court's intervention in the sectional dispute only made things worse, pointing the nation ever more in the direction of armed conflict similar to the Kansas variety, except a violent conflict located in the very heart of the Union.

The Economic Panic of 1857. On top of that, the Supreme Court decision put a huge chill on investment fever that had been pushing the fast-growing railroad industry westward at a frantic pace, dreaming of catching huge profits in the process. Suddenly the bubble burst as investors realized that the Dred Scott decision threw the future of Western development into question. Everyone was aware of the trauma of Kansas attempting to sort through the issue of slavery. Now it was clear that the Supreme Court had

---

*Nonetheless, a previous owner of Scott paid for the freedom of Scott and his family even as the Supreme Court's findings were being announced!

laid the same conditions for the rest of the Western territories. The decision as to whether a territory was going to be slave or free was no longer set by law, but by Senator Douglas' popular sovereignty, which meant by pitched battles between well-armed advocates of both sides. This was not a situation designed to invite economic development.

Investors began to back out of the railroad enterprise (at least the railroads running West from the East, for North-South lines were not affected).   Now the railroad companies could not pay off loans to Eastern banks, setting off a round of fears about the strength of the Eastern banks. Virtually overnight a huge financial panic set in in the North.

The South experienced virtually none of this panic, presuming that it was because an agricultural economy based on the certainty of cotton sales was vastly superior to the highly speculative realm of the North's industrial capitalism. This only confirmed in the Southerners' minds the correctness of their (slave-based) agricultural society, which they were ready to defend to the death. And indeed, they would soon be called upon to do just that.

John Brown's raid on Harpers Ferry (October 18, 1859). Meanwhile, John Brown had moved his abolitionist campaign East, and began plans to gather a small fighting force of his own to spark an uprising that he expected would be joined by hundreds of slaves throughout the South. The beginning of the uprising would be signaled by his attack on the U.S. military arsenal at Harpers Ferry, just up the Potomac River from Washington, D.C. But when the event occurred, only twenty men joined him, and a marine detachment under Colonel Robert E. Lee was immediately sent to the arsenal to put an end to Brown's rebellion. Ten of the raiders were killed on the spot, and Brown was wounded, captured, tried, and soon executed along with four other raiders. A few escaped and others were freed.

The nation found itself deeply divided over this event. To the growing ranks of Northern Abolitionists, Brown was a great martyr whose efforts exemplified the noble qualities that had made the nation what it truly was, since the days of its own rebellion against English tyranny. But to Southerners he was viewed as an extremely dangerous villain, typical of all Abolitionists thirsting to destroy the South by inciting a massive and brutal slave rebellion.

Thus because of events such as Brown's raid on Harpers Ferry, the lines of a coming war between the North and the South were clearly beginning to be set in place.

Statehood for Bleeding Kansas. To gain statehood, two different Kansas Constitutions were sent to Washington for approval, the Lecompton and the Topeka Constitutions, along with claims and counter claims involving

The Gathering Clouds of War

massive fraud in the Kansas elections ratifying one or the other of these constitutions. Buchanan supported the pro-slavery Lecompton Constitution, whereas Douglas supported the Free-Soil Topeka Constitution. Eventually the Lecompton Constitution was defeated both by another referendum in Kansas (1858), and by a vote in Congress to admit Kansas as a free state, with yet another constitution, the Wyandotte Constitution of 1859. The latter vote in Congress in January of 1861 to admit Kansas as a new state occurred just as the nation was breaking apart, with the withdrawal of the Southern states from the Union.

* * *

LINCOLN[66]

It was an act of God that brought forth out of relative insignificance the one person mentally, morally and spiritually equipped to save the Union. Abraham Lincoln had been born to extreme poverty in Kentucky, lost his mother at an early age, and as a youth followed a hard-handed father into Indiana and then Illinois in search of a better life. He loved to read, no matter what his other activity at the time (reading while plowing?), and had an enormous capacity to remember vast details. Exposed at an early age to extensive tragedy and hardship, he had a susceptibility to depression, which he learned to relieve by studied patience and humor. He was a master story teller, making him easily popular with common folk. But he himself was no common person.

He trained himself in the law and set up practice in the Illinois state capital at Springfield where he developed legal expertise in virtually every branch of the law. He was interested in politics and was elected as a Whig first to the Illinois House of Representatives (1834–1846) and then to the U.S. House of Representatives. But in the latter, as he had promised, he served only a single term (1847–1849), and returned to his law practice supposing that his political career was over.

In 1842 he married a Kentucky socialite (from a slave-holding family), Mary Todd, who would be both a source of unyielding resolve and frequent irritation for Lincoln. They had four sons, the second of whom Eddie would die in 1850 at age four. A third son, Willie, was born in the same year as Edward's death, but would himself die in 1862 while the Lincolns were living in the White House. Both parents remained forever distraught over these deaths, deepening Lincoln's sense of melancholy and frequently driving Mary to hysteria. Thus Lincoln developed a huge capacity to carry on in the midst of deep tragedy.

As it turned out, his political career was not over (Mary was not about to let that happen!). In 1854 he put himself forward in the contest in the Illinois Assembly for the position of U.S. senator representing his state. He failed (narrowly) to get the appointment, but left a deep impression concerning his dedication to the ending of slavery. He thought of himself as a moderate Whig, focused less on the moral issue of race and slavery than on the obvious contradiction of allowing slavery in a Republic founded on the legal equality of all its people. His most immediate concern was not the total abolition of slavery, but instead the prevention of the spread of slavery into the rest of the nation, a dangerous threat to the Republic as clearly demonstrated by the strife going on in Kansas.

With the death of the Whig Party after 1854, Lincoln joined the new Republican Party. At the 1856 Republican National Convention his name was put forward as candidate for Republican vice president, in which he subsequently placed second in the vote. At this point people were beginning to take notice of him as a national political figure.

The Lincoln-Douglas debates (August-October 1858). In 1858 the Republicans nominated Lincoln as their candidate for U.S. senator from Illinois, running against the Democratic Party's candidate (and Democratic Party leader in Congress), Stephen Douglas. The two men agreed to meet each other in various parts of the state of Illinois for a series of seven debates. The nation watched closely as the famous Douglas met this new challenger, a seeming country boy with little to commend himself as he took on the "Little Giant" Douglas. But it soon became apparent that this Lincoln was no pushover. Douglas accused Lincoln of being simply another Abolitionist (not yet very popular, even in the North) and Lincoln accused Douglas of surrendering the original moral principles of the Republic in his failure to take any kind of stand against slavery.

Thousands gathered, plus the national press, to hear Lincoln and Douglas go at each other. In the end, the Illinois representation was skewed by the way the state was districted and although the Republicans gathered more votes than the Democrats, the Democrats received more seats, and thus the Illinois Assembly re-elected Douglas to represent the state in the U.S. Senate.

The Cooper Union speech (February 1860). But the Republicans did not forget the brilliant way Lincoln put his arguments together, and in 1860 asked him to address a group of Republican leaders at Cooper Union in New York City. There he recalled the vision of the Republic's Founding Fathers and how they struggled over the issue of slavery. He then answered point by point the arguments of Southerners and of Northern Democrats as they either defended or permitted slavery. And he addressed the threat

The Gathering Clouds of War

issued by the South that if a Republican were elected president, they would secede. The Republican leaders were impressed.

Nomination as the Republican presidential candidate (May 1860). In May the Illinois Republicans decided to get behind Lincoln in a bid for nomination as the Republican Party's presidential candidate. This would be for Lincoln an uphill battle because William Seward and Salmon Chase were widely understood to be the front runners for the nomination. But with a bit of help from his Illinois friends, and much to the surprise of many, Lincoln was nominated for the spot on the Republican National Convention's third ballot. His well-reasoned moderation on the slavery issue and his strong support for the old Whiggish agenda of protective tariffs and internal infrastructure development had won him the day.

Meanwhile the Northern Democrats had nominated Douglas as their presidential candidate – although the Southern Democrats withdrew from the Democratic National Convention and nominated their own candidate, John Breckinridge. Lincoln did not campaign directly, as did his opponents. But the Republican Party did the campaigning for him, running on his image as a simple American farm boy who, in the best spirit of the Republic, made his way to success through hard work and study. The tactic worked well.

On to the U.S. presidency. In November, with a huge turnout of voters, Lincoln won a plurality of the popular vote, 1.87 million votes for Lincoln, 1.38 million for Douglas, 850 thousand for Breckinridge and 589 thousand for a fourth candidate, John Bell – but an absolute majority of the electoral vote, 180 votes to his opponents combined total of 123 votes. Lincoln was thus elected to be the nation's sixteenth president.

A "Team of Rivals."[*] Lincoln then took the somewhat unprecedented step of appointing to his cabinet a number of his major political rivals, William Seward, Salmon Chase, and Edward Bates, among others. At first these political dignitaries tended to be contemptuous of him[†] and his country boy ways. But gradually they all (except Chase) came to see Lincoln's true political genius and came to full support of him as their president. Chase was retained in Lincoln's cabinet despite his behind-the-scenes maneuvering

---

[*]*Team of Rivals* is the title of a Simon & Schuster 2005 Pulitzer Prize-winning book by Doris Kearns Goodwin, in which she demonstrated the political genius of Lincoln in appointing to his cabinet a number of his recent political opponents.

[†]Seward even at first proposed to Lincoln to have him turn all real powers of the presidency over to himself, and then proposed a bizarre foreign policy to isolate the South, all of which Lincoln politely ignored as he moved steadily ahead with his own policies for dealing with the rising crisis.

to have himself replace Lincoln as Republican candidate in the elections coming up in 1864, because Lincoln respected Chase's financial skills. Lincoln eventually (1864) appointed him as chief justice of the Supreme Court, removing a constant irritant on his cabinet, but giving the country a chief justice guaranteed to stand in support of the rise to citizenship of America's freed slaves. As for Seward, he soon became a totally-devoted supporter of Lincoln's, very important to the president during the dark days ahead.

The war president. Lincoln had only very limited war experience and no formal military training, in contrast to his chief adversary, Jefferson Davis, Confederate president and graduate of West Point and a commanding officer (colonel) in the Mexican-American War.* But Lincoln had a keen mind for strategy, a deep insight into the character of others, and an awareness that he needed wise war counsel – which he got from the elderly Winfield Scott† and eventually from his war cabinet. Being a lawyer, he tended to think through objectives better than the military men under him, who tended to think mostly in terms of battle strategies designed to win *battles*. Lincoln however thought in terms of war strategies (economics, diplomacy, ideology, morale, as well as military engagements) designed to win a *war*.

Lincoln the Christian. There seems to have been nothing particularly remarkable about Lincoln's religious or spiritual nature going into the White House in 1861. As president he would attend frequently the New York Avenue Presbyterian Church in Washington. But he was definitely not what you would call a churchy individual. However, the four years of the presidency would have a tremendous impact on how he made his way forward through life's many challenges. He was a sensitive man, which made him all the more vulnerable to the criticism and personal attacks that others would aim at him. He was called on to lead a war, which meant the deaths of countless young men, both Southern as well as Northern Americans, all of which burdened his heart deeply. There would always be political voices claiming that he was going too slow – or too fast – in his conduct of the war. There would be subordinates who would disappoint him deeply with their failures to live up to their responsibilities, others who because of their own political ambitions would undercut him in order to bring him down. Even within his cabinet – even within his own home (his

---

*Davis presumed himself to be militarily wise and thus failed to seek good counsel. In fact he involved himself too deeply in the running of the war at the field level, making things even more difficult for his generals.

†Lincoln's Anaconda strategy, to surround and strangle the South into submission, was the brain-child of Scott.

The Gathering Clouds of War

wife could be brutal in her sarcasm and withering criticism) – he often had to face dispiriting opposition.

What held Lincoln together was not man, not man's opinions, not man's advice. What kept Lincoln going during these extremely stressful years was his growing sense of the hand of God in placing him in the presidency, and the grace of God in providing the only counsel he could depend on.

He had an ever-deepening sense that all of this tragedy was a way that God was cleansing the nation of its sins, in order to restore it to its longstanding status as a model society, a true Christian nation and thus a greatly needed democratic light to the world. As he put the matter at Gettysburg in November of 1863 in honoring those who had died for this just cause: Americans must "resolve ... that this nation, under God, shall have a new birth of freedom – and that government of the people, by the people, for the people, shall not perish from the earth."

This attitude was brought into even higher relief in his second inaugural address in March of 1865 (just weeks before his assassination) when the entire second half of the speech focused on how the nation must answer to the righteous judgments of God, and how it is imperative at this point "with malice toward none, with charity for all, with firmness in the right as God gives us to see the right, to finish the work, to bind up the nation's wounds, to achieve a just and lasting peace among ourselves and with all nations."

Here was truly a man of God.

* * *

THE NATION FINALLY DIVIDES

The Role of the Second Great Awakening in the Civil War. Sadly, it is hard for us today with our highly Secularized culture to understand the importance of Christianity in the way the Civil War played out for nearly all Americans in the 1860s. Morally it was very hard for Americans to want to kill other Americans. Southerners of course would quite naturally want to fight to fend off Northern aggression. But for Northerners, who personally knew of slavery mostly through stories and reports of others, the issue of slavery was largely a moral abstraction. It is easier to find cause to go to war for the defense of one's home and land when they come under attack. The South certainly felt that this was the case for them. It is more difficult to find the will to go to war for moral abstractions.

However the Second Great Awakening provided exactly the required sense of moral commitment to those Northerners who took up arms. To Christian Americans, the nation had always been a divine experiment, a model of how it was possible for a people to live freely in a post-feudal society in which a perfect God – not a sinful and blemished man – stood over them as director and enforcer of life. To such Christians it was imperative therefore not to lose that relationship with God lest the Republic under God should fail and bring down man's great hope for democracy with it, possibly discouraging any further attempts at democracy, ever.

Appropriately enough, while Southern soldiers sang romantically about the land of Dixie that they were defending, Northern armies went into battle singing *The Battle Hymn of the Republic*,* a call to join with God in his mighty hand of judgment on the nation. Through the horror of the war that challenged America, God's Truth, God's Will, would prevail.

> *Mine eyes have seen the glory of the coming of the Lord;*
> *He is trampling out the vintage where the grapes of wrath are*
>   *stored;*
> *He hath loosed the fateful lightning of His terrible swift sword:*
> *His truth is marching on.*
>
> *Glory, glory, hallelujah!*
> *Glory, glory, hallelujah!*
> *Glory, glory, hallelujah!*
> *His truth is marching on.*
>
> *I have seen Him in the watch fires of a hundred circling camps,*
> *They have builded Him an altar in the evening dews and damps;*
> *I can read His righteous sentence by the dim and flaring lamps:*
> *His day is marching on. ...*
>
> *He has sounded forth the trumpet that shall never call retreat;*
> *He is sifting out the hearts of men before His judgment seat:*
> *Oh, be swift, my soul, to answer Him! be jubilant, my feet!*
> *Our God is marching on.*

The formation of the Confederate States of America. The election of Lincoln was the signal for the Southern states to begin to announce their secession from the Union. On December 24th (1860) South Carolina was the first Southern state to announce its withdrawal. Six others (Mississippi, Florida, Alabama, Georgia, Louisiana, and Texas) soon joined South Carolina and on February 4, 1861 they announced at a meeting in

---

*The words were written by Julia Ward Howe (using the melody from an old Methodist hymn "Say Brothers" – or more popularly at the time, "John Brown's Body") and published in the February 1862 edition of *The Atlantic Monthly*.

The Gathering Clouds of War

Montgomery, Alabama, the creation of the Confederate States of America. There a provisional government was established, with Jefferson Davis as the provisional Confederate president.

Initially the moral claim of the new Confederacy was that it was simply confirming the basic rights of the states, rights that reached back to Madison and Jefferson, rights that they claimed former Federalists and contemporary Unionists had been stealing from them. And indeed, the Confederacy was built loosely so that the states did indeed seem to be nearly fully sovereign and the Confederacy simply a coalition of rather independent states.

Yet there were strong forces holding the Confederacy together. Actually, the very looseness of the Confederacy required as a matter of extreme necessity a strong, commanding hand to hold it together. And that hand appeared in the form of Jefferson Davis, the Confederacy president. In many ways, the struggle of the South to secure its independence militarily required him and his administration to take on almost unlimited powers.

But holding the Confederacy together was the even more powerful ingredient: fear White Southerners had of their Black population – both free and slave. The Black population was growing at such a rate that Whites were terrified by the thought of being outnumbered in their Southern homeland by Blacks. The preventing of the spread of slavery into the new Western territories – as Lincoln and most of the North had committed themselves to doing – would imprison the South in a confined world over which they feared they could soon lose control.

Paranoia and thoughts of anti-White conspiracy coming from multiple directions gripped at the Southern imagination, forging Southerners into a tight bond. But that bond would soon deprive them of the real sense of freedom that they claimed they were achieving in breaking from the Union. The South became an oppressive land, whose laws and cultural vigilance tightened down on society. Free Blacks living in the South soon found themselves under the threat of being forced into slavery. And war fever in the South demanded that any Northern Blacks captured in battle (those not just killed outright), or simply captured as farm workers in the process of the Southern armies advancing across the land, would be carried off into Southern slavery.

As both Jeff Davis and his vice president, Alexander Stephens, put it, Blacks by their very inferior nature were intended by God to thrive only within the context of eternal servitude to the superior race of Whites. Enslavement of any and all Blacks was actually a necessary part of the advance of civilization. This credo was thus the real glue holding the Confederacy together.

CHAPTER NINE

CIVIL WAR[67]

* * *

1861: THE LONG-DELAYED WAR FINALLY BREAKS OUT

Fort Sumter. With the formation of the Confederacy, vast numbers of Southern officers in the U.S. Army withdrew to the South and began to take command of the 100,000-man army called for by Davis. Canons designated for the federal or Union garrisons were seized by Confederate officials and gold and coin of the federal mints in the South were confiscated.

South Carolina then demanded that federal troops vacate their various emplacements in the Charleston Harbor region. Union commander Robert Anderson refused and pulled his troops back to the most defensible position at Fort Sumter. President Buchanan (who still had a couple of months to serve before Lincoln took over) attempted to reinforce the fort, but called off the effort when on January 9th a Union supply ship was fired on by shore batteries in Charleston. President Buchanan ultimately chose to do nothing in response, realizing that Lincoln was going to have to deal with the situation after his inauguration on March 4th.

Thus the relief of Fort Sumter became the first order of the day for the new president. But Lincoln could do little to help the heavily besieged fort. On April 12th, Charleston shore batteries opened a withering fire on Fort Sumter. After thirty-four hours of bombardment and with little food, water, or ammunition left, Anderson surrendered the fort to the Confederate forces. The South was thrilled and the North was exasperated.

Lincoln's call to arms, and the South's response. The war had begun. On April 15th, Lincoln called on the states for 75,000 volunteers to build up the Union army in preparation for the conflict ahead. The Tennessee governor flatly refused, indicating his readiness to join the Confederacy – which Tennessee did on May 7th. Arkansas announced its decision to secede on May 6th. Virginia voted in convention on April 17th to secede, confirmed in a popular referendum on May 23rd. And on May 20th North

Civil War

Carolina also joined the group of secessionists. The Confederacy now had eleven members. Kentucky also refused to send troops to Lincoln, though Kentucky was not going to be joining the Confederacy but instead was going to remain neutral. However, in a number of important ways, this proved to be strategically more beneficial to the Union than to the Confederacy.

Slave-holding Maryland and Delaware did not secede, in part because they were divided in opinion on the matter and in part because they were under the federal gun not to secede. Lincoln was intent in not having the Union capital at Washington lose its link with the North by being surrounded by a rebellious South. Lincoln moved swiftly to stop any idea of Maryland seceding, declaring martial law,[*] sending troops in to secure strategic positions in the state, arresting large numbers of Maryland officials, and suspending the writ of *habeas corpus*,[†] despite the protest of Supreme Court Chief Justice Taney (himself a Marylander).

Missouri, like other border states, was divided in its loyalties. But in the end a Missouri convention called to decide the matter chose almost unanimously to remain loyal to the Union. Missouri Governor Jackson took the opposite position and called out the state militia to enforce his pro-slavery stance. But he was attacked by federal forces, chased with his supporters out of the Missouri state capital, and pushed down into the southern part of the state. The members of the convention choosing for the Union then took over the running of the state. But Missouri would itself remain a center of the North-South struggle for the rest of the War.

In Virginia citizens of the western counties were opposed to Virginia's decision to secede from the Union and instead chose to secede from Virginia and the Confederacy, forming the new (pro-Union) state of West Virginia.

Gearing up for war. In the meantime, thousands of soldiers rushed to join the state militias both North and South, excited to get involved in this opportunity for personal glory. But as with all such early rushes to war, the excitement would quickly subside once the cruel reality of war began to register.

In material terms, this was bound to be an unequal fight. The North had three times the number of men eligible for military service as the South – Southern Blacks of course excluded. And while the huge number

---

[*]Martial law is a much stricter form of law than civil law, enforced by military authority operating under the emergency conditions of war.

[†]A written summons issued by a court of law allowed to any person being held in detention without a formal charge or trial first having taken place, requiring that the authority holding that person show a specific cause under the law for the detention, or else requiring the immediate release of that person for failure to show just cause.

of Southern Blacks provided work units supporting the Confederate army, they needed considerable supervising to ensure their cooperation, taking a good number of Whites out of military service. Also, the emphasis of "Cotton as King" now would haunt the South because it had caused the region to ignore emerging industrial development. Thus the South fell way behind the North in the production of everything from ammunition and uniforms to canons and railroad engines.

On the other hand, Southerners had made up a disproportionately large percentage of America's experienced (Mexican-American War) army officer corps prior to the war. Most of these would quit the U.S. army to take assignments in the Confederate army. The superior quality of the Confederate officers would show in the way the South tended to embarrass the Northern armies whenever they met in battle, at least during the first years of the war. The fact that even with all this material superiority it took the North four years to bring the South to defeat stood in part as testimony to the superior military leadership found within the Confederate forces.

The strategies of war. The purpose of war is to get an adversary to stop doing – or even being – what it is that a society pursuing war finds detestable in the thoughts and behavior of that adversary. To get the adversary to yield in this matter requires an enormous amount of pressure put on the adversary. That pressure can take all kinds of forms, military, economic, psychological. But whatever it takes, the object is always the same: to get the adversary to stop whatever it is that they have been doing – to just quit.

For the South, the strategy was simply to get the North to let the slave-holding states withdraw from the Union so that the South could continue to pursue its cultural dream of an elegant semi-feudal social order consisting of a genteel plantation society engaged in endless rounds of fancy social gatherings, the whole social program supported by the labors of multitudes of Black slaves.

For the North the goal of war – and thus the strategy involved – was much less uniform in inspiration, Northern groups often working at odds with each other. For some, the goal was to eradicate the institution of slavery from the entire North American continent. For others it was to simply force the South to continue to honor its commitment to the unity of the United States of America, even if that meant backing off on the slavery issue. Yet for others it was a similar hope of enforcing that unity, and ending slavery in America as well. This lack of unity of purpose would make things very difficult for anyone given presidential responsibility, as previous holders of the office of U.S. president had already discovered. Thus the newly installed president Lincoln knew that he had been called to undertake a task of unimaginable difficulty.

He had therefore a dual set of responsibilities, as he understood the challenge personally. He was determined fully, almost regardless of the costs involved, to maintain the unity of the federal Union. That meant full war against any states undertaking rebellion against the Union. But he also had to provide the North with a rallying point that would unite all these conflicting Northern viewpoints. Failure in holding such unity of purpose in the North would be to deliver the South the victory it sought.

As far as the slavery issue went, Lincoln was very cautious about waving the flag of Abolitionism, because not only would it complicate the task of keeping the North united, it would merely steel the resolve of the South to continue its struggle, regardless of the costs involved. After all, the purpose of war is to weaken the resolve of the adversary, not strengthen it.

Nonetheless, Lincoln well understood that the slavery issue was at the heart of the crisis that had split the Union. One way or another the slavery issue could no longer be allowed to infect America's national health. Slavery was going to have to disappear. But just how that would happen, Lincoln seemed to have no particular strategy in mind. He seemed resolved to leave that question up to the fortunes of war – and to God, on whom he relied ever-heavier as the war between the Northern and Southern states dragged on.

What Lincoln was clear on was his military-economic strategy by which he intended to force the Southern states to give up their rebellion and once again take their place as full members of the Union. Basically, his strategy (aided tremendously in its conception by his military advisor, the old warrior General Winfield Scott) was to surround and isolate the South militarily – north, south, east and west – and thus shut down their cotton-export economy on which the Southern dream depended so completely.

This was going to hurt the textile mills of the North, which depended heavily on the ability to acquire Southern cotton. But that would be one of the sad prices of war. But Lincoln was aware that this war was going to be costly – very costly – on a number of fronts. But the Union had to be preserved at all costs, or there would be no very good future for any of the states, North or South.

And thus it was that in pursuit of this strategy of strangulation (the Anaconda Strategy as it was termed), the Civil War was conducted simultaneously on a number of key fronts. The most important front was the one that developed in Northern Virginia, the spiritual heartland of the South. Another was the maritime front that extended from the Chesapeake in Virginia, south along the Carolina and Georgia coasts, around Florida, and into the Gulf of Mexico just south of Alabama, Mississippi, Louisiana, and Texas. Another was along the Mississippi River, which separated the

Confederate states of the Deep South (Georgia, Alabama, Mississippi, and Louisiana) from the Confederate states of the Southwest (Texas and Arkansas). A fourth front was at the very center of the North-South border, basically within the states of Kentucky and Tennessee (and the northwestern section of Georgia). Four different fronts, and four different armies (or navies), all trying to tighten the noose around the rebellious South.

Not only would the political task of maintaining unity at home against the partisan political interests of ambitious Northern politicians be a constant challenge for Lincoln, but perhaps even weightier would be the task of finding military leaders able to understand Lincoln's strategy of war. Again, soldiers are notorious for wanting to win battles (and thus battlefield fame) without seeming to understand how that connects with the larger challenge of winning the war that has called forth these battles. General Washington understood this. So did General Winfield Scott. But Washington was long dead, and the very elderly Scott was not far behind him. Lincoln needed a wise, not just an ambitious, general to supervise the military portion of his general strategy. Lincoln would soon discover how difficult it would be to find just such a general.

Robert E. Lee.[68] At first Lincoln turned to the veteran general, Robert E. Lee, asking him to take command of the Union troops. But when Virginia declared itself to be withdrawing from the Union as a member of the new Confederacy, Lee understood that his loyalties to Virginia stood well before his loyalties to the Union and turned down the offer. In due course, the Confederacy would come to see in Lee what Lincoln had observed and make Lee the commanding general of the South's military (although former general and now Confederate president Jefferson Davis actually seemed to want – and often undertook – that responsibility himself).

The First Battle of Manassas or Bull Run* (July 21) gets the war underway. The capital at Washington was surrounded by a number of forts held firmly by the Union. Thus Virginia had to accept the loss to the Union of the northern part of the state, including Confederate General Robert E. Lee's plantation home in Arlington just across the Potomac River from Washington.

But Virginia was not going to let that go unchallenged, and the Army of Virginia gathered forces to head north towards Washington. Lincoln sent out the Army of the Potomac, with its 36,000 men under an inexperienced General Irvin McDowell, to stop them. The two armies soon met at the Bull

---

*The Union tended to identify battles by a nearby body of water or creek; Conferates did so by the name of the closest town. Such was the case, for instance, also at Antietam Creek or the town of Sharpsburg (September 1862).

Run creek near Manassas. Then just as McDowell moved against the smaller Confederate force of around 20,000 men under General P.G.T. Beauregard, another Confederate force of around 12,000 men under General Joseph Johnston arrived unexpectedly on the scene, stealing from McDowell what he was hoping would be an easy victory.

Meanwhile, spectators came out from Washington in their carriages and with their lunches to watch the spectacle. But the spectacle turned out to be much more than they had bargained for. Both armies executed rather clumsy maneuvers with their inexperienced troops. In the end, the Confederates were able to hold their ground, with General Thomas Jackson standing like a stone wall with his troops. Thus he became known to his men as "Stonewall Jackson"!

The Union lines began to break, and then a retreat turned into a humiliating rout of the Union troops. The spectators themselves then took flight, racing all the way back to Washington with the troops when they realized what was happening.

Fear that the Confederate troops might now even turn and continue to march on the capital seized the crowds. But it was not to be. Both armies had suffered casualties far beyond what they had expected, approximately 850 men killed in the brief action, with several thousand wounded or captured or missing. It proved to be a very sobering experience for both sides. It now dawned on many that this civil war may indeed not be "over by Christmas."

The Civil War uniforms. At the beginning of the War, the American regular army was quite small. There were however, numerous state militias. These were the mainstay of the army in its first days – both North and South.

At the Battle of Manassas or Bull Run in July, considerable confusion existed once the armies met in close combat – because of the diversity of the uniforms worn by the various state militias. The Union Army, of course, wore its official navy-blue uniforms. But the state militia uniforms were mixtures of navy blue, light blue, grey, green, red – on both sides, North and South. Confederate militias however tended to favor the popular grey worn in the military academies by the cadets. But the New York militia was also decked out in the same grey. The confusion proved deadly.

As a result of this confusion, the South put the Dress Regulations into effect in September whereby all Confederate troops were to wear the grey uniforms: jackets, trousers, caps and greatcoats. Soon thereafter, the New York militia felt compelled to re-uniform itself with the navy-blue colors of the North's regular army.

In time, light blue trousers began to replace the navy-blue trousers of the Union army, fairly widely so, although the superior officers tended to stay with the all-navy uniform. At the same time these same light blue trousers made their way into the Confederate armies as the Confederate soldier's trousers wore out and the only available replacements were those seized in a raid on Union supplies or even, when things got truly desperate, those stripped off dead Union troops.

Indeed, the problem of resupplying new or replacement clothing became critical to the South. The blockade had deprived it of imported cloth – a major problem for a society that produced enormous amount of cotton, but principally for export to clothing mills found in the North or in England. Homespun uniforms, dyed with rust or acorn juices to an earth-colored tan or butternut, thus rather rapidly replaced the imported grey cloth worn by the Confederate soldier in the early years of the war. Indeed, by the end of the war, any clothing that was still fit to wear became the uniform of the Confederate soldier.

The battle further west. Over in the West, Missouri Governor Jackson's pro-slavery militia confronted in August a Union force that was less than half its size just southwest of Springfield at Wilson's Creek. In the battle the Union army lost its commander, yet managed to hold off three assaults by the Confederates before running out of ammunition and having to retreat into Springfield. The Confederates were themselves too exhausted to pursue, both sides having lost over 250 killed, over a thousand each wounded, making it the Bull Run of the West. In theory it was a Confederate victory, but again, all the killing advanced the cause of neither side. The basic profile of the Civil War was beginning to reveal itself.

During that first year of the War there were a multitude of smaller North-South skirmishes and minor battles scattered all over the countryside, though the greatest number took place in Virginia, Kentucky and Missouri. Again, none of them proved conclusive, but all of them involved more killing and wounding (wounds themselves often proving fatal in the long run) on both sides.

Ulysses S. Grant.[69] One of the battles occurred (November 7) at Belmont on the Missouri side of the Mississippi just opposite Columbus (Kentucky). A portion of the Union Army of Tennessee had been advancing toward Columbus under a somewhat unknown Brigadier General Ulysses S. Grant. He had just scored a victory against the Confederates at nearby Paducah (Kentucky). Now at Belmont, he attacked a similar-sized army of Confederates. The battle proved inconclusive, with both sides each losing over 600 killed or wounded. However, it attracted the attention of Lincoln because of the reports of Grant's impressive leadership. Lincoln would see more of that in the months to come.

Civil War

The Mason-Slidell or *Trent* Affair. On November 8th, an American ship intercepted the British ship *HMS Trent* with two Confederate officials aboard who were heading for England in the hopes of securing British recognition of the new Confederacy. Official recognition would have given the South considerable international leverage (even financial and military support) in the battle with the North.

The Confederate officials, James Mason and John Slidell, were taken from the ship, causing a major uproar in both the South and in England. The British demanded the release of the prisoners and an apology, underscoring their annoyance by strengthening their military presence in Canada.

Several weeks later Lincoln officially distanced himself from the actions of the American ship's captain and had the two Confederates released, who then continued on to England. But there they failed to receive the diplomatic recognition sought so dearly by the South. Soon thereafter the diplomatic crisis facing the North blew over.

✶ ✶ ✶

1862: STALEMATE

Hampton Roads, or the Battle of the Ironclads (March 3). With the Union naval blockade in place and the South now unable to get to or from the high seas, the South's vital export business was crippled.

But Confederate naval designers came up with an ingenious plan. They would restore the sunken Union steam-driven frigate, the *Merrimac*, and cover her topsides with steel plating which would make her invulnerable to Union cannons. This would turn her into a terror against the blockading Union fleet.

On March 2nd, renamed the *Virginia*, this ten-cannon monster (operating under steam power and thus needing no masts, and showing only slanting ironclad sides above water) steamed into the Union fleet blockading the mouth of the Chesapeake Bay, creating havoc. She rammed and sank the *Cumberland*, sank the *Congress*, and ran the *Minnesota* aground before night set in and she returned to port.

On the following morning she headed out toward the Union fleet with the intention of finishing off the *Minnesota* and then turning on the three other Union ships still blockading the harbor. But she was met by an equally strange ironclad sailing vessel, the *Monitor*, that the North had hastily put together when it first got wind of the South's intention of building an ironclad ship. The *Monitor* was just a round turret with two canons inside sitting atop a flat barge whose deck barely rose above the water. These two monster machines met and for four hours blasted away at each other. The match finally ended when the *Virginia* withdrew. Overall however, there was no victor and no vanquished in this battle.

The two ships never met again. Then that May, the Union army captured Norfolk, the operational base of the *Virginia*. Thus with nowhere to operate from, and with the South not wishing to surrender the *Virginia* to the North, her crew blew her up.

The battle in the West. Over in the West, in Central Tennessee along the Tennessee and Cumberland Rivers at Forts Henry and Donelson, a series of fierce battles in February raged back and forth between Union and Confederate troops, with Grant inflicting a huge loss on the Confederates (15,000 of their troops captured), essentially knocking Kentucky and much of Tennessee out of the war.

But a Confederate comeback at Shiloh in April caught Grant by surprise (he was resting his troops on his approach to Memphis), causing 10,000 Union casualties over the two-day battle. However, it was a costly victory for the Confederates, losing almost an equal number of their own men, plus on the first day of the battle their capable commanding officer Albert Johnston.

Also in April, Union forces under Naval Captain David Farragut captured the strategically key city of New Orleans at the base of the Mississippi River. This opened up this vital waterway to a massive Union advance that would cut off Texas and Arkansas from the rest of the Confederacy.

Meanwhile, Grant quickly recovered from the blow at Shiloh and moved from the north down the Mississippi River until he approached the well-fortified town of Vicksburg located atop high cliffs overlooking a sharp bend or loop in the river. Vicksburg needed to be taken to complete the Union control of this vital waterway, a task that would prove to be daunting.

At first Grant attempted in December a direct assault on Vicksburg from the river, securing nothing in the two-month-long process. Then he attempted the laborious process of building levees in order to divert the river through the swamps, again making no real headway in the process. But Grant was not one to quit. But the year would be out before he was able to attempt yet a different move on Vicksburg.

McClellan's Peninsula Campaign and the Seven Days Battles. Action now began to pick up in the East over in Virginia. Lincoln had transferred command from McDowell to General George McClellan, the latter being an expert strategist and excellent organizer and builder of an efficient fighting force (Lincoln learned a lot of military strategy from him). But he had two major flaws: he had a very high esteem of himself (having U.S. presidential plans in mind) and a low esteem of both Lincoln and Lincoln's main military strategist, General Winfield Scott; and worse, he had a very hard time committing to action the troops he had trained and equipped. He loved his men, and they loved him. But they were after all trained for battle, deadly battle, and that is the part that McClellan found hard to stomach. Consequently, he was overly cautious about committing his troops to battle and selected actions only when there were strong odds in his favor for victory ... and glory for himself.

Lincoln wanted him to make a quick move south to attack directly the new Confederate capital at Richmond. But instead McClellan chose to bring his men by boat around to the peninsula southeast of Richmond and to march on the capital from that direction. General Johnston moved his Confederate army quickly to confront the overly cautious McClellan and they met in battle at the Siege of Yorktown (April 5–May 4) and again along the Chickahominy River, where Johnston was badly wounded. The Confederates then regrouped under their new commanding general, Robert E. Lee. Now the war would be more than a battle of armies. It would be a contest between generals. And McClellan was not the type to do well against the elderly, but very aggressive Lee.

Immediately Lee, joined with Stonewall Jackson, took to the offensive against McClellan's forces in a number of pitched battles (the Seven Days Battles, June 25–July 1) during which the Union lost 16,000 of its 105,000 troops. But Lee lost even more, almost 20,000 out of his 90,000 troops. After the last of the Seven Days Battles (at Malvern Hill), McClellan pulled his troops out of action, disappointing Lincoln because of the missed opportunity to end the war quickly.

The Second Battle of Manassas or Bull Run (August 29–30). With McClellan halting his troops in the Virginia southeast, Lincoln was forced to set up yet another army under General John Pope to help protect Washington and to press Lee from the north while Lee stood facing McClellan to the south. Lincoln in fact hoped at that point that Pope and McClellan might engage Lee from both the north and the south in a pincer movement that might finally bring Lee to defeat.

But Lee, rightly unconcerned about McClellan, instead attacked the advancing Pope, also sending Jackson to the north around Pope's army, now putting Pope in the same trap that Lincoln had hoped to put Lee in. The two armies met again at Manassas, with Pope's army losing 14,000 of his troops. It all appeared to be something of a Confederate victory. But the results were almost as devastating to the South, having themselves lost 8,000 men in the process.

McClellan does his own thing. Subsequently in August McClellan, who had avoided any involvement in the action, instead returned his army by ship to Washington, and himself back to his adoring supporters, to lobby with the politicians there for more troops and equipment. His goal, he claimed, was to smash Lee Napoleon-style with a single massive pitched battle. Indeed, this latter-day Napoleon did not approve of the less dramatic process of winning the war with General Scott's Anaconda strategy of gradually strangling the South. In fact he threatened to resign his commission if Scott were not dismissed as commanding general and he himself appointed in his place (to which Lincoln finally yielded). Such a Napoleonic self-image did McClellan hold of himself that it even caused some in Washington to suspect McClellan of planning a Napoleon-style military takeover of the Union!

Antietam or Sharpsburg (September 17). In early September Lee decided to take his army across the Potomac into Maryland with the intent of invading the North and taking the pressure off his home state of Virginia. He divided his army into three groups, with the same idea he had used at Manassas of surrounding from three directions and entrapping a Union army he was expecting to come after him. But the plan was discovered by a couple of Union soldiers and relayed to McClellan. McClellan now had the opportunity to attack in full force one of the three Confederate groups before they had a chance to converge. But he refused to go after any of the Confederate groups. Thus Jackson, leading one of those three groups, moved on Harpers Ferry, capturing 12,000 Union troops before joining Lee for the main battle which broke out at the Antietam Creek near Sharpsburg.

The fight at Antietam lasted all day and produced the highest one-day casualty rate of the entire war, in fact in any war America has ever been involved in. For instance, in one Union charge against the Confederate lines, 2,300 Union soldiers fell in just 20 minutes. Overall, the North lost over 12,000 men, the South lost over 10,000. But Lee was stopped and his plan (at least at this time) to take the war to the North was completely undone by the battle.

The next day Lee retreated back across the Potomac into Virginia, stunned by the losses. But McClellan did not pursue him (of course!) – much to the intense displeasure of Lincoln. Ultimately Lincoln decided to relieve McClellan as commander of the Army of the Potomac (November 7th) – and to turn that responsibility over to General Ambrose Burnside, a rather unwilling recipient of this responsibility.

The Emancipation Proclamation (September 22). The issue of slavery as a cause of war remained quite controversial. Abolitionists had been pushing from the outset of the war for Lincoln to take a strong stand against slavery, making it the primary cause of the war. Lincoln, though highly opposed to slavery, was more moved by the needs of preserving the unity of the American nation against the divisiveness of Southern instincts. He was also afraid that a strong stand against slavery might alienate the border states of Maryland, Kentucky and Missouri.

But he knew it must be done, for there was talk of the English and French possibly recognizing the independence of the Confederacy. But if Lincoln were to make the war seem more like a contention over slavery, both the British and French would want to avoid appearing to be in any way supportive of a slave-holding South. Lincoln therefore had to take some kind of public position that clearly cast this war as a battle over slavery.

Thus on September 22nd, having the victory of Antietam to show that he was not making this move out of desperation, Lincoln announced that effective January 1st of the following year, the slaves of any rebellious state would be considered by the United States government as free persons. Further they could be enlisted in the Union's military service.

This had the effect of further weakening the South's social structure as more slaves poured North to escape slavery, many of the men even taking up arms as Union troops against their former masters.

It also made the war more clearly a civil rights campaign – which had the effect in Europe of undermining any thoughts of ever extending official diplomatic recognition to the Confederacy by a European government, thus further isolating the South politically and commercially.

Fredericksburg (December 11–15). The newly appointed commanding General Burnside knew why Lincoln had dismissed McClellan: Lincoln wanted unrelenting action against the Confederate army on the part of the Union army – not intermittent and inconclusive skirmishes. Lincoln wanted Richmond, the capital of the confederacy, taken. But marching on Richmond meant having first to take the town of Fredericksburg which lay across the path of the northern approach to Richmond.

But Fredericksburg lay on the southern or opposite side of the wide Rappahannock River and furthermore was backed up by towering cliffs which stood over the city, from which the Confederates could put up a stiff defense of the city and its bridges. Nonetheless, Burnside decided that Fredericksburg had to be taken.

The only possibility of success lay in a surprise attack on the city, before the Confederates could get an army in place in the heights above Fredericksburg. But for Burnside, such a surprise would not be forthcoming. It took two weeks for his engineers to get pontoon bridges in place across the river, and by that time the Confederates were well-situated above the city. When finally Burnside moved his troops across the river and into the abandoned town, butchery resulted. Almost 13,000 Union troops fell the next few days trying to take the heights (though amazingly so did over 5,000 Confederates defending the heights). Defeated in this venture, Burnside withdrew his army, leaving Lee still in command of Fredericksburg.

* * *

1863: THE NORTH BEGINS TO DOMINATE

Fredericksburg (again!). Burnside knew he had to rescue his badly tarnished reputation by another assault on Fredericksburg. On January 20th he began moving his army back toward Fredericksburg, only to be greeted by rain, and more rain. The roads turned to a sea of mud and his army bogged down, exhausted from four days of futile effort to move forward. The endeavor was another disaster – though only to the army's morale and Burnside's personal reputation. Three days later Lincoln replaced Burnside with "Fighting Joe" Hooker as commander of the Army of the Potomac.

Mounting Opposition to the War. From a point very early in the war the enthusiasm of the young men called to do the fighting subsided. By the beginning of the second year of the war both North and South changed from a situation of having too many volunteers to train and equip, to not having enough to make up for the heavy losses suffered in the numerous battles occurring everywhere.

The South, despite all the bravado about the Southern military ethic, was the first to have to resort to conscription. In April of 1862 the Confederacy passed a draft law calling into service all men (with a number of exempted categories by profession) between the ages of eighteen and thirty-five. In July the North followed, asking the states to institute the draft when they could not meet their quotas.

German and Irish immigrants contributed greatly to the Union Armies, as did free Blacks and liberated slaves when the Emancipation Proclamation was announced, opening up military service to the Blacks as of the beginning of 1863. The South, of course, could not or would not increase their number in arms in a like manner.

But by 1863, with the war seeming to drag on endlessly with no end in sight, resistance to military service, and especially the draft, began to rise. In March, Congress allowed for draftees to pay a fee for exemption – or to find a substitute to take the place of a draftee, a sort of bounty system. But this merely raised questions of integrity and commitment to the cause at a time when enthusiasm for that cause was dwindling rapidly (in both the North and the South).

The New York City draft riots. In New York City, Irish who had been signed up for American citizenship (to build up the city's Democratic Party regime of boss William M. Tweed and his corrupt Tammany Hall cohorts) found out that in doing so they had also signed up for the draft.

In mid-July this discovery led to a major riot of working-class Irish against the system in which wealthier Americans could buy their way out of the draft. They vented their anger particularly against Blacks (but also the homes of Abolitionists, Protestant churches and a number of businesses), turning the event into largely a race riot. Troops had to be called in to help the New York police and state militia finally crush the rebellion and restore peace to the city. But it left the city shaken badly, especially among the Blacks who moved out of the city to either Brooklyn (not part of the city at that time) or New Jersey. And the South was quick to point up the event as an example of the true nature of Northern race relations.

Vallandigham and the Copperheads. Meanwhile considerable trouble was being stirred up by another group of opponents to the war, largely from among the anti-War Democrats in the North (especially Ohio) – who eventually drew the label "Copperheads." Under the leadership of Clement Vallandigham, they opposed the draft, opposed "King Lincoln," opposed the Emancipation Proclamation and called for an immediate peace with the Confederates (which would have left the issue of Southern slavery untouched). Republicans accused the Copperheads of treason, and in May of 1863 Vallandigham was arrested by a military tribunal for encouraging Americans to take up arms against the Union.

Much controversy followed his arrest, so Lincoln decided that rather than try him for treason, Vallandigham was to be banished to the Confederacy. Vallandigham eventually made his way to Canada, and proceeded from there to be nominated as a Democratic Party candidate for Ohio governor. He subsequently lost the election, but deepened the division among the people of Ohio over the questions of the war and of slavery.*

However, with the continuing advance of the Union armies against the Confederacy, support for the Copperheads would eventually fade away. But they would be a serious problem for Lincoln until things finally began to improve.

---

*While still in Canada Vallandigham attempted to set up a Northwest Confederacy of Ohio, Kentucky, Indiana, and Illinois as an ally of the Southern Confederacy. But nothing came of the plans. He slipped back into the U.S. in order to be able to attend the 1864 Democratic National Convention (Lincoln decided simply to ignore him) hoping to be the party's presidential nominee. But that honor was to go to the ambitious General McClellan instead.

Chancellorsville (May 1–6). Meanwhile back East in Virginia, Union General Hooker had spent the winter months of early 1863 rebuilding the demoralized Northern Army of the Potomac. In the spring, he set out in the direction of Fredericksburg, but swung to the west of the town to draw Lee's army away from it. At a crossroads clearing known as Chancellorsville, elements of the two armies met.

But despite having more than twice the number of troops as Lee, at this point Hooker strangely took a defensive position, though he sent part of his men to try to sweep in behind Lee. Lee then attacked Hooker and for two days both armies fought fiercely, until Hooker disengaged and retreated back across the Rappahannock River, humiliated in his inability to defeat an army less than half the size of his. Lincoln would soon replace him with yet another general, George Meade.

But the loss was great on both sides. The Union lost 17,000 soldiers, and the Confederates nearly 13,000 soldiers. But the Confederates also lost Jackson when a Confederate guard mistakenly shot Jackson while the latter was out late at night studying the land in preparation for the next day's action. Jackson died on the 10th of May, a huge loss to the South.

Gettysburg (July 1–4). After Chancellorsville, Lee understood that his best strategy would be once again to take the war into the North and conduct a bold strike against the Northern army, which in turn would likely force Lincoln to have to give in to the rising voices in the North demanding immediate peace with the South.

When Meade got his new orders to take command of the Union Army of the Potomac, Lee already had a number of his troops in southern Pennsylvania, with the Confederate cavalry leader Jeb Stuart raiding the countryside. It looked as if Lee intended to grab the Pennsylvania capital, Harrisburg, so Meade gathered his forces and headed northwest from Maryland to intercept him. On June 30th, at the small Lutheran seminary town of Gettysburg, forward elements of the two armies met.

For the next three days the two armies fought each other, the Union armies holding defensively the upper grounds and the Confederate armies attempting to dislodge or even surround the well-entrenched Union position. This time the immense boldness of Lee did not suffice to carry the day, despite the enormous effort Lee applied to the task of overrunning the Union position. Even a massive frontal assault across one mile of open field produced merely huge Confederate losses. Finally, on July 4th, Lee ordered the retreat of his army – back toward Virginia.

Tragically, Meade did nothing to pursue the retreating enemy. He and his troops were exhausted. But so were Lee's. Once again, like the generals before him, Meade could not think past the issue of the battle at hand and understand that he had a war, not just a battle, to win. By letting Lee escape back to Virginia, he had let slip by the opportunity to end the war then and there. Lincoln was pleased with Meade's victory, but was upset that Meade had missed what to Lincoln was an obvious opportunity to crush Lee's army and end the war.

Yet it was still a grand disaster for the South – and Lee recognized immediately that he had gambled the lives of his men foolishly. He lost 28,000 of his 70,000 troops. But it had been costly for the North as well. Meade had lost 23,000 of his army of 90,000. Nonetheless, it was Lee, not Meade, who had been broken by this action. Lee would never be able or willing again to try an assault on the North. Henceforth, the war would involve the South trying to protect itself from invading Northern armies. Gettysburg (and Vicksburg) then marked the turning point of the War, although at the time this was not widely understood in the North.

Grant's victory at Vicksburg (also on the 4th of July!). Meanwhile off in the West, things were finally beginning to improve for the Union Army. Grant had finally succeeded in getting his Army of Tennessee swung south around Vicksburg and inland toward the Mississippi state capital at Jackson. He was able to bring that vital Confederate city to surrender (May 14), opening the way for him to swing west and attack Vicksburg from its less well-defended eastern approach by land. Vicksburg was now surrounded on all sides by Union troops, and the slow process of strangling the city now began. For a month and a half, the citizens of Vicksburg withstood constant bombardment and loss of supplies to feed the town. Finally, on July 4th, with the citizens of the town nearly starved to death, Vicksburg capitulated.

Thus Grant was able to present Lincoln with the wonderful news of the full control of the Mississippi River, another Independence Day gift (along with Gettysburg) given to the much beleaguered president! The Union could now move supplies up and down the river unimpeded. At the same time, the Western Confederacy, most notably Texas and Arkansas, was now cut off and isolated from the rest of the Confederacy.

Southeastern Tennessee. The action now moved to the center of the North-South line of battle, along the Tennessee River in Southeastern Tennessee. Union General William S. Rosecrans's Army of the Cumberland had been pushing General Braxton Bragg's Confederate troops south through Tennessee, and having reached Chattanooga in August they were ready to now push into Georgia. In the meantime, Rosecrans had sent Burnside to Knoxville (where there was considerable pro-Union sentiment) to secure that city for the North. It had all been fairly easy. But that was about to change.

Chickamauga (September 19-20). In his push south into Georgia, Rosecrans did not get very far before running into a deep forest along the Chickamauga Creek where (unknown to Rosecrans) Bragg's forces had been reinforced by Confederate General James Longstreet's troops. Although operating blindly in the dense forest, the Confederates found a gap in the Union lines, split the Union forces in two, and then turned hard on one of the two Union groups. It was a Union disaster. But the other half, under General George Thomas (a Virginian who had stayed loyal to the Union), held off the Confederates long enough to let what was left of the Union Army retreat back to Chattanooga.*

It had been a devastating battle for the Union ... but also for the Confederates. The Confederates suffered 21,000 casualties compared to 16,000 Union casualties. Thus the Confederate "victory" at Chickamauga had come at a huge price that the South could ill-afford.

Chattanooga (November 24-25). The situation in Chattanooga for the Union army grew desperate, as it was now surrounded by well-positioned Confederate troops who had cut off the Union army's line of supplies (including food). In October, Lincoln had put the entire central and western command under Grant, who in turn replaced Rosecrans with Thomas as the new commander of the Army of the Cumberland. And Grant pushed strongly forward to make sure that supplies and troops (Hooker's troops from the East and the troops of General William Tecumseh Sherman from the West) would make it past the Confederate blockade. By late November the Union army was finally resupplied and ready to fight.

The biggest challenge was the huge Lookout Mountain from which the Confederates could still threaten Chattanooga and hamper the movement of goods and troops in and out of the town. That had to be taken – although it was well defended by Confederate troops atop a 500-foot-high cliff. In fact, it was so well defended that Bragg decided to send Longstreet and his troops off to retake Knoxville, considerably reducing the size of the Confederate army in position at Chattanooga.

Grant's plan was to send Hooker's troops around one side of the mountain and Sherman's troops around the other side, with Thomas's troops to hit the mountain straight on, mostly as a diversionary action until Hooker's and Sherman's troops could get into position. But Thomas's troops, once they got going, refused to halt at the foot of the mountain, and began to climb wildly straight up its heights, terrorizing the Confederates, who could hardly believe what they were seeing. In the end, the Confederates scrambled back up the mountain and then over the other side, and did not

---

*Thomas would be called the "Rock of Chickamauga" for his role in saving Rosecrans's army.

Civil War

stop running until they were well out of range. The Union army had thus broken Bragg's position, and now a humiliated Bragg was forced to retreat south.

In the meantime, Union General Burnside had been able to hold off Longstreet's Confederates at Knoxville, and with Sherman now able to come to Burnside's assistance, Longstreet was forced to break off his efforts to retake Knoxville.

At this point the Union army settled in at Chattanooga for the winter – in preparation for the next spring's offensive against central Georgia, the very heart of the Confederacy.

* * *

1864: THE SOUTH UNDER SIEGE

Grant takes over the effort to bring Virginia to defeat. In early 1864, Lincoln promoted Grant to Lieutenant General, giving him command of all the Union armies. Grant turned his armies (the armies of the Tennessee and Cumberland now combined) over to General Sherman and headed to Washington to take command of the entire war effort. His plan was to have Sherman march south into Georgia from his position at Chattanooga, in order to take the vital Confederate heartland at Atlanta. At the same time Meade's Army of the Potomac would attack Lee's Army of Northern Virginia (with Grant in camp with Meade) from the north and General Benjamin Butler would attack Richmond coming up from the south along the James River (similar to McClellan's Peninsula Campaign two years earlier.)

It would be total war, designed to crush the South's economic and emotional as well as military capacity to wage war. Under Grant's command the war would be fought very differently, smaller battles, but one immediately after another, with no letup in the hits the Union troops were to make on the Confederate troops.

Lee now understood that he was in trouble, with the Union troops unwilling to break off after a battle but instead hanging onto his troops like bulldogs, wearing the Confederates down little by little. And thus it went, at the Battle of the Wilderness (May 5-7), Spotsylvania Court House (May 8-21), Cold Harbor (May 31-June 12), with Grant attempting to swing around Lee's forces, and Lee being forced to give ground little by little in order not to be flanked or surrounded by Grant's forces.

At the Spotsylvania Court House and Cold Harbor Grant learned a lesson that he would not repeat: do not break off from your adversary long enough to give him a chance to dig in. Grant's attack on Lee's Bloody Angle at Spotsylvania had proven to be very costly to Grant, and at Cold Harbor a dug-in Lee proved impossible to dislodge by direct assault. From this, Grant learned to never again attempt a direct assault on a well-defended position, as modern arms give the defenders a tremendous advantage.*

Once again Grant swung his forces east and south, determined not to give up despite the terrible thrashing his men had received at both Spotsylvania Court House and Cold Harbor. He had lost over 52,000 men in the period since he started his Overland Campaign in early May. But Lee had lost 33,000 men, a much larger loss proportionately to his total troop size, and thus was much less able to afford such a high loss.

Petersburg (July 1864–March 1865). At this point Grant decided to move his troops south past Richmond and seize the town of Petersburg, a vital rail link to Richmond. But Beauregard was able to hold off Grant long enough for Lee to get his forces in place to protect Petersburg, and a long Union siege set in. At one point the Union troops dug a long tunnel under the Confederate lines, then exploded it with the intention of rushing troops in through the gap in order to seize the city. But the Union troops were slow to move forward and found that the crater they had created was so deep that they could not easily move across it, but instead down in it they became easy targets for the gathering Confederates. With this failure, the siege of Petersburg settled down to a long stalemate.

Sherman's March on Atlanta (May–September). Meanwhile, further to the West, by the month of May Sherman was ready to begin his assault on the northwestern region of Georgia. Sherman too preferred flanking movements around the enemy rather than frontal assaults and thus time and again Sherman would swing (usually to his right) around the Confederates, forcing them to fall back to avoid being surrounded.† And bit by bit this ballet continued, slowly advancing Sherman down through northern Georgia.

---

*During World War One (1914–1918) European military strategists failed to learn this same lesson and for four murderous years would throw their troops into the enemy's grinder of breech-loading rifles, machine guns and cannister artillery, killing hundreds of thousands of troops without gaining any particular advantage in doing so. They just could not break themselves free from the habit of designing battles with grand frontal assaults, as in the day of troops possessing only slow-loading muskets, in which direct and quick frontal assault was the best tactic in gaining battlefield victory. In the days of modern weapons this was now a pointless and murderous tactic to put soldiers through. But the European generals were slow to figure this out. Grant, however, was not so dimwitted!

†A notable exception was at Kennesaw Mountain where Sherman attacked Johnston directly, losing 7,000 troops in the process – whereas the Confederates lost only 700. The frontal assault thus was a maneuver that Sherman (like Grant) learned to avoid.

By July Sherman's army was on the northern outskirts of Atlanta. At this point the Confederates in Georgia (now under the Command of John Bell Hood) were resolved to give no more ground to Sherman. But six weeks of attacks on Sherman's forces bled the Confederates greatly. Furthermore, Sherman had sent troops around to the south of Atlanta, cutting off Confederate supplies to the city. Realizing that they were about to be trapped, on the night of September 1st Hood managed to pull most of his troops out of Atlanta, burning what supplies he had left to avoid having them fall in the hands of Sherman. Atlanta now belonged to Sherman.

Atlanta burns (early November). Hood left a section of Atlanta burned out because of some of the measures he took to destroy supplies. But this would be small in comparison to the widespread torching – indiscriminately undertaken by Union foot soldiers who understood that there would be no punishment to come their way for acts of arson. In early November, fires thus swept through Atlanta. Sherman ultimately did nothing.

Atlanta's destruction demoralized greatly the Southern spirit. But that too ultimately served Sherman's purposes quite well. For after all, this was what war was all about: to fight until such time as your enemy has lost all desire to continue.

The Battle of Mobile Bay (August 5-23). Meanwhile the North learned of another major victory against the South. Mobile, at the Southern tip of Alabama on the Gulf coast was the last major Confederate port east of the Mississippi still open to the Confederates. Rear Admiral David Farragut was commanded to seize it.*

Mobile was protected by three forts at the mouth of its huge bay and a number of Confederate ships in the bay itself, plus an array of floating mines (called torpedoes at the time) and the ironclad ram *CSS Tennessee*. Farragut commanded 18 ships, including four new ironclads. Additionally, 1,500 troops were put ashore west of the bay to take the western-most fort (Fort Gaines) guarding the bay.

On the day of the direct assault on Mobile Bay, Farragut pushed his men to ignore the mines and get past the forts as quickly as possible. Then the four Union ironclads took on the *Tennessee*, which received such a pounding that it finally brought the ruined ironclad to surrender. With that, the Confederate fleet was virtually defenseless against the Union fleet, which now controlled Mobile Bay.

Now Union attention was turned to the forts, two of which were fairly quickly brought to surrender. The third, Fort Morgan, would hold out for

---

*Despite Union efforts to blockade the bay, blockade running was still taking place out of Mobile.

two more weeks before it too surrendered. This now left the city of Mobile itself isolated, though still well protected by Confederate forces.

The Shenandoah Valley Campaign (August to October). Lee hoped to draw off Grant by sending (mid-June) Confederate cavalry under Gen. Jubal Early to relieve the Confederate troops located in Western Virginia, in the Shenandoah Valley – a region of highly productive farms suffering greatly from Union attacks there. Early was able to drive back these Union forces, and then continue north up the valley until he crossed into Pennsylvania. Then he turned (mid-July) southeast towards Washington, attacking one of the city's defending forts in the northwest.

At this point Grant dispatched his own cavalry commander Philip Sheridan to the upper Shenandoah region to draw Early into battle.   As Sheridan marched to meet Early, he destroyed as he went, attempting to collapse the economy of this region, which provided much of the food needed by the Confederacy. In mid-September the two armies met in two battles, with Early taking a beating from Sheridan in both. Then at Cedar Creek (October 19) Early nearly delivered a crushing blow to Sheridan ... though Sheridan was able to rally his troops later in the day and completely reverse the situation. In fact, the result of this encounter left Early with such a badly crippled army that Sheridan was now able to move his army east and rejoin Grant at Petersburg. The Shenandoah Valley would no longer concern the North, having been fully neutralized by Sheridan's actions.

The Election of 1864. Things had looked quite negative for Lincoln in the early months of 1864, as both the Republicans and Democrats made preparations to choose candidates for the presidency. No president had been reelected since Jackson's reelection in 1832. Nonetheless, Lincoln was able to receive the nomination of his Republican Party, with Andrew Johnson, a Southerner loyal to the Union (and military governor of Tennessee), named as his running mate. On two key points the Party's platform was quite clear: unconditional surrender of the Confederacy and a constitutional amendment abolishing slavery everywhere within the U.S.

The opposing Democratic Party was split between War Democrats and Peace Democrats, the former continuing to support the war as it stood, the latter demanding a negotiated peace. The Party finally created a compromise, by nominating the popular General McClellan as a War Democrat for president, and anti-war Congressman George Pendleton as their candidate for vice president. But the balanced ticket only confused Americans as to what exactly the Democratic Party's intentions were if the McClellan-Pendleton combination were elected to office.

In any case, by November's elections, things had turned very favorably for the North. Lee was clearly on the defensive deep in Virginia, Mobile Bay had been taken from the Confederates, Sherman had conquered Atlanta and the Shenandoah Valley had been neutralized. The North seemed clearly to be winning the war and thus Northern voters were now swinging strongly behind their president.

Thus in the elections, Lincoln won the popular poll by over 400,000 votes and the electoral college tallied 212 votes for Lincoln and only 21 for McClellan.* Americans clearly wanted Lincoln returned to office for four more years.

Hood attempts to cut off Sherman's line of supplies. Confederate General John Bell Hood swung from Alabama north into Tennessee in an attempt to draw Sherman back away from Atlanta. But Sherman had other plans, and instead sent Thomas north with some of Sherman's troops to take a stand against Hood at Nashville.

Hood's attempt to cut off Thomas's movement failed. He suffered severe casualties at Spring Hill and Franklin, Tennessee, in late November and was completely humiliated two weeks later at Nashville when a massive attack by Thomas drove him and what was left of his army back to Mississippi. No further attempts against the Union armies would be coming from that direction.

Sherman's March to the Sea (November 15–December 21). The next move was designed by both Grant and Sherman with a dual purpose: to cut a wide swath of morale-crushing destruction through the heartland of Georgia, one that reached from Atlanta all the way to the Atlantic port of Savannah, and then turn north in order to put such pressure on Lee in Virginia that this would allow Grant to finally break the stalemate at Petersburg.

The plan was to break free from the need to maintain a supply line to the Northern troops and simply (and brazenly) to disappear with his army into the midst of enemy territory, living off the land by foraging widely (at times about sixty miles in width) from the local economy as they went. And they were to destroy local infrastructure (bridges, rail lines, telegraph lines, mills, barns) in areas where they ran into resistance.

Unfortunately for the South, Hood's decision to abandon Atlanta and retreat into Tennessee in the hope of drawing Sherman off in that direction had greatly reduced the South's ability to hold off Sherman's invading army as it headed toward Savannah. Sherman, in the meanwhile, had succeeded

---

*Of course the eleven Southern or Confederate states still in rebellion did not participate in the election.

in keeping the South confused as to his ultimate destination.

Savannah (Christmas). With little Confederate resistance, Sherman's army reached the outskirts of Savannah within a few weeks of its departure from Atlanta. There Sherman's army linked up with Union Admiral Dahlgren's fleet, and the two Union forces began to attack Savannah from both land and sea. Sensing the trap, the Confederate forces defending the city escaped by the one route still open. Thus on December 20th Sherman marched into the city to receive its surrender, under the promise – which was honored by Sherman's troops – not to destroy the city. Sherman was pleased to present Savannah to Lincoln as a Christmas present!

1865: THE COLLAPSE OF THE SOUTH ... AND DEATH OF LINCOLN

Sherman continues his march north through the Carolinas. After a month's rest in Savannah, Sherman turned his army northward toward Virginia, with the same intention as had been the object of his march through Georgia: to cut a wide swath of destruction through the South in order to cripple Southern morale – and help bring the war to an end. Again, with little Confederate resistance, by mid-February he had reached the South Carolina capital city of Columbia, whose central city – like Atlanta – proceeded to burn to the ground (to this day no one is sure whether by Union troops or by retreating Confederate forces). A week later Wilmington, North Carolina, surrendered, the Confederacy thus losing its final seaport (although it had been largely shut down earlier by the Union blockade). As he headed his troops through North Carolina, he encountered torrential rains and snake-infested swamps along the way. But North Carolina had never been very enthusiastic anyway about the Confederate cause and Sherman's troops made their way through the state without their usual devastation along the way. In the only serious engagement with enemy troops in North Carolina, Sherman's forces overran Confederate General Johnston's Confederates at Bentonville on March 19–21. At this point Confederate resistance was collapsing rapidly.

Lincoln's Second Inaugural Address (March 4).   In the meantime, Lincoln was sworn in to the office of the Presidency for a second term. Lincoln sensed that the war was finally drawing to a close, although exactly when the killing might end was still an uncertain matter. But in his Second Inaugural Address, Lincoln was already looking to what lay ahead as the Union moved to reunite and mend the wounds of the war. He reviewed

Civil War

the course of the war, spoke lengthily of the hand of God in using the war to transact justice in a morally challenged (slavery) America, and looked forward to a postwar healing of the entire nation, North and South. In the first part of this address he went over the origins of the war. He then continued:

> ... Neither party expected for the war, the magnitude, or the duration, which it has already attained. Neither anticipated that the cause of the conflict might cease with, or even before, the conflict itself should cease. Each looked for an easier triumph, and a result less fundamental and astounding. Both read the same Bible, and pray to the same God; and each invokes His aid against the other. It may seem strange that any men should dare to ask a just God's assistance in wringing their bread from the sweat of other men's faces; but let us judge not that we be not judged. The prayers of both could not be answered; that of neither has been answered fully. The Almighty has His own purposes.

He then explained that slavery was one of those offenses against God that God would allow – but only until such time as he was ready to exact his judgement, through the terrible war they had been experiencing.

> If we shall suppose that American Slavery is one of those offences which, in the providence of God, must needs come, but which, having continued through His appointed time, He now wills to remove, and that He gives to both North and South, this terrible war, as the woe due to those by whom the offence came, shall we discern therein any departure from those divine attributes which the believers in a Living God always ascribe to Him? Fondly do we hope – fervently do we pray – that this mighty scourge of war may speedily pass away. Yet, if God wills that it continue, until all the wealth piled by the bond man's two hundred and fifty years of unrequited toil shall be sunk, and until every drop of blood drawn with the lash, shall be paid by another drawn with the sword, as was said three thousand years ago, so still it must be said the judgments of the Lord, are true and righteous altogether.

He concluded:

> With malice toward none; with charity for all; with a firmness

> *in the right, as God gives us to see the right, let us strive on to finish the work we are in; to bind up the nation's wounds; to care for him who shall have borne the battle, and for his widow, and his orphan – to do all which may achieve and cherish a just, and a lasting peace, among ourselves, and with all nations.*

These were the words of a great leader, made ever wiser by the very impossibility of meeting the challenges he had facing him solely through his own intellectual abilities. Lincoln had learned to persevere in the face of massive uncertainty and huge risk, simply by trusting that he was merely a servant of the will of God himself and that it was up to God – not Lincoln – to bring the true and the good to bear in this Covenant nation that God himself had, centuries earlier, called into being. Indeed, this was the kind of wisdom that few American leaders after Lincoln were able to match even on a partial basis.

The crushing of the Deep South. After his victory at Nashville, Thomas sent General James Wilson to head south through Alabama all the way to the Gulf coast. Following a policy similar to Sherman's, Wilson destroyed the last of the South's industrial capacity as he went, notably at Birmingham and Selma (where he also crushed Nathan Forest's Confederate cavalry), and even burned down the University of Alabama at Tuscaloosa in the process. At the same time a Union army under Edward Canby overwhelmed the Confederate defenses at Spanish Fort, which in turn finally brought the town of Mobile to surrender (April 9).

The Fall of Petersburg and Richmond (April 1–3). Upon Sheridan's return to Petersburg from the Shenandoah Valley, he was given orders by Grant to undertake a flanking attack to the West of Petersburg, to cut off the final supply line supporting Petersburg. Confederate General Pickett was sent by Lee to counter Sheridan's move, a move initially successful, but then set back with a major defeat at Five Forks delivered by Sheridan on April 1st.

The next day Grant's forces attacked a greatly weakened and thinly stretched line of Confederate troops south and southwest of Petersburg, and swept away the Confederate defense. Lee pulled his forces from both Petersburg and Richmond and headed them west with the intention of then turning south to join up in North Carolina with what was left of General Johnston's Confederate army. Both cities were quickly occupied by Union troops on April 3rd, though most of the Union troops were sent in pursuit of the fleeing Confederates. But the Confederate army was finding itself cut off from supplies and was being forced in huge numbers into surrender.

Lee's surrender at Appomattox Court House (April 9). Lee's hope to join his forces with Confederate troops still operating in North Carolina was anticipated by Union cavalry, who positioned themselves in front of his path of retreat. When in attacking these cavalry units at dawn on the 9th, Lee came immediately to realize that they had been joined by two corps of Union infantry, and that effectively he was surrounded by a Union army far larger than his. He also was running very short on food and supplies. At this point Lee knew that it was time to surrender. At 8:00 in the morning he rode to the McLean House to meet Grant to sign the terms of surrender.

Lee's surrender effectively brought the Confederate will to continue to a nearly complete halt. Skirmishes here and there between the two sides would continue for a while longer. But for all practical purposes, the war was over.

Lincoln is assassinated (April 14). Lincoln was already at work seeking ways to bring the nation back together ... minus slavery. The Thirteenth Amendment to the U.S. Constitution, ending slavery anywhere within the United States, had been ratified by the Senate in April of 1864 and in the House of Representatives finally (following a bitter contest there) at the end of January (1865), just a few months previously. It was yet to be submitted to the states – Northern only at that point – for their ratification. But the amendment was expected to be easily approved by the states.

As Lincoln had stated in his second inaugural address, he was indeed looking for ways "to bind up the nation's wounds; . . . to do all which may achieve and cherish a just, and a lasting peace." That would not be an easy task, given the level of hatred still smoldering in many Northern hearts, and given the bitterness Southerners felt about their humiliating loss to the Unionists. However, achieving a just and lasting peace was where he was now directing all his efforts.

But success in that endeavor was not to be. On the night of April 14th the actor John Wilkes Booth was able to complete part of his plot to kill Lincoln and Grant while attending together the play *Our American Cousin* at Ford's Theater in Washington (but Grant had instead left to visit his children in New Jersey), as well as Vice President Johnson and Secretary of State Seward (the legal successors to a vacated presidency). Lincoln was shot in the back of the head – and then Booth escaped by leaping from the balcony to the stage and then fleeing the city. Lincoln died early the next morning. Meanwhile Seward was attacked and nearly killed the same night by another of the plotters, who after repeated attempts to stab Seward to death finally fled into the night when confronted by other members of Seward's family. Seward survived. Booth was found with a co-conspirator in Virginia twelve days later, surrounded and shot. Arrests of other members of the plot soon followed. On July 7, four of the conspirators were hanged.

Taking stock of it all.* And so the war was over. The South found itself desolate and the North simultaneoulsy found itself in a condition of profound mourning. The whole thing had been a sad tragedy, pushed to monumental proportions by the inability or unwillingness of American leaders before Lincoln to confront the slavery issue directly. It finally took not political reason, but war and devastation of monumental proportions to bring this burning issue to a resolution. But so often is this the case. Passion, not Reason, plus the mysteries of circumstances seemingly beyond human control, quite frequently bring human crises to a resolution ... not pretty, but well resolved.

Most tragically of all, a Southern bullet had taken the life of the one person who could have healed the nation's wounds and brought the South back to life more quickly than turned out to be the actual case. As it was, the bullet left many in the North without pity for the South and its vast suffering, and left the South itself to begin a process of recovery that would take generations to complete. Such is often the cruel irony of history.

---

*Of the approximately 2.6 million who had enlisted in the Union army and the 1 million in the Confederate army, 360 thousand Union and 258 thousand Confederate soldiers had died either from battlefield deaths or eventually from wounds, disease, etc. The total casualty count is around 1.5 million of those 3.6 million men serving (civilwarhome.com/casualties.htm). In addition to the 620 thousand deaths, there were 476 thousand counted as wounded and another 400 thousand as captured and dying in prison, or missing. One in four of the Civil War soldiers never returned home after the war. The number of Americans killed in the Civil War exceeded the total of the American losses in all of its other wars from the War of Independence through the Korean War (battlefields.org/learn/articles/civil-war-casualties).

CHAPTER TEN

AMERICA RECOVERS: 1865-1880[70]

* * *

RECONSTRUCTION DURING THE JOHNSON PRESIDENCY

Johnson versus the Radical Republicans.[71] With Lincoln's assassination, Vice President Andrew Johnson was automatically elevated to the presidency. But he had neither the personal skills nor the political support necessary to carry the nation forward through a post-war healing process. Johnson was a Southerner (from Tennessee) with something of Northern attitudes, and as a Democrat (not a Republican, as was Lincoln) put on the presidential ticket with Lincoln in 1864 to flesh out the National Union ticket that both Lincoln and Johnson ran under. This left Johnson in the peculiar position of being on the political spectrum too moderate for many Republicans and too radical for many of his fellow Democrats.

He generally believed that he understood and supported the policies that Lincoln had previously laid out as his intentions for the South, but would find it virtually impossible to carry out those policies. He had no personal political leverage that would enable him to do so.

Thus despite the Constitutional powers of the presidential office, Johnson himself had no real personal political power to mobilize in his effort to follow up the Lincoln policy, a reminder that the man makes the office rather than the office makes the man.*

Johnson was opposed to slavery, but as with many in the North, was not convinced that freed Blacks or "freedmen" were yet capable of conducting the responsibilities of citizenship (voting and holding office).

---

*This would be a matter that Americans in general would have a very hard time understanding, especially those who get caught up in the glory of nation-building, devoted to designing for others (and imposing, if possible) a perfect social-political system of various offices and powers drawn up on paper – as was the case of American involvement in Vietnam, Afghanistan, and Iraq. There were even strong elements of this same mentality in Wilson's taking America into World War One with the idea of freeing and redesigning many of the world's societies around Wilson's own highly idealized principles of democracy.

Thus he was in no hurry to see the right to vote extended to the freedman. Rather, he turned his attentions to the issue of reintegrating the Southerners back into the Union. Like Lincoln, he generally opposed the widespread retribution against Confederates called for by Northern Radicals. Thus to the Radicals, in particular Thaddeus Stevens and Charles Sumner (the latter who had finally recovered from his nearly fatal beating in 1856 by Southern Democrat Preston Brooks), Johnson seemed treasonously pro-South.

The Congressional election of 1866 returned a large number of Republican Radicals, who then began to design their own Reconstruction policy (whose bills Johnson vetoed – only to have each veto overturned by a two-thirds vote in Congress). And thus it was that Johnson found himself slowly alienated from the powers that ruled Washington. Earlier that year, the split between Johnson and Congress was birthed by the 1866 Civil Rights Act affirming the legal equality of American Blacks, which was passed despite his veto (Johnson claimed that as per the Tenth Amendment, only the states had the right to determine the legal status of its citizens). And seeing a challenge to the new law coming from the South, Congress then authored the Fourteenth Amendment reaffirming the intent of the Civil Rights Act (full equality for all Americans, although exempting Indians and Confederate army veterans!). Johnson's opposition to the Fourteenth Amendment thus merely served to build the strength of the Radicals in the 1866 elections, and point to his own political demise.

Eventually, in early 1868, Johnson would be formally impeached by the House of Representatives (March 2) and placed on trial by the Senate for his unconstitutional behavior,* nearly being found guilty and thus removed from office (May 16). Only the lack of a single vote to produce the Senate's two-thirds majority necessary to convict spared him this enormous humiliation. But in any case after that, during the remaining two years in office, Johnson proved totally powerless in trying to shape events developing in the country, both North and South.

Reconstruction in the South.[72] Southern Reconstruction had actually already begun before war's end, as Lincoln had placed pro-Union administrations in each of the Southern states as they came under Union control: specifically Tennessee, Arkansas and Louisiana. Slaves had technically been freed as of Lincoln's Emancipation Proclamation coming

---

*Of the eleven charges brought against him, the primary charge concerned his removal of the Radical Republican Edwin Stanton as secretary of war and replacement by the more moderate Ulysses S. Grant. This was in violation of the Tenure of Office Act passed in 1867, itself a highly questionable constitutional act that Congress enacted specifically to end Johnson's power to remove cabinet appointments (such as in the specific case of Stanton, where considerable friction had been developing between Stanton and the president).

America Recovers: 1865-1880

into effect on January 1, 1863, but the economic reality of what newly freed slaves might do to feed and take care of themselves had created a huge amount of confusion. Many joined the ranks of the Union army, thus fitting them into some kind of a place within the social scheme of things. That helped. But with war's end, the future of the freedman was still in doubt. Radicals talked of giving each freedman some forty acres and a mule to start out life with.* But that idea had never been put into some kind of specific political formula before Lincoln's assassination.

Anyway for most Blacks who received no title to any land, the only alternative they had was to sign on with a White plantation owner either as a tenant farmer, or as a sharecropper, where the plantation owners provided the land and the sharecroppers the labor (actually the majority of Southern sharecroppers were poor Whites). Lacking property, the Blacks soon were to discover what poor Southern Whites had long known, that they were unlikely to achieve the American dream (although in fact a small number of Blacks were ultimately able to acquire land and a settled place in the Southern scheme of things).

Indeed, the situation for the Whites was often not much better than that facing the Black freedmen after the war, haggard soldiers and starving women and children scrounging through burned-out towns and farms looking for food or anything else of value.

And there was the question of what to do with those who had served in the Southern rebellion as Confederate soldiers. Radicals were ready to have every Confederate officer imprisoned and many even executed. A number of Confederate families, expecting the worst – or just monumentally angry over the war's outcome – left the country, Mexico and Brazil being favored destinations. For his part, Lincoln had wanted the South reintegrated as quickly as possible, and stood adamantly opposed to the vengeance sought by the Radicals. But the South tragically had lost Lincoln's critical advocacy. Then when Johnson tried to follow Lincoln's program, but lacking Lincoln's political base, he ended up merely making his personal political standing in Washington all the worse.

What Johnson decreed as the requirement for a Southern state's readmission to the Union was a minimum of ten percent of that state's population to pledge allegiance to the United States. The Radicals were hotly opposed to these easy terms. Even more, they were outraged that readmission to full status in the Union legally exempted the Southerners from having their land seized, something the Radicals eagerly sought as a means of redistributing Southern land to the benefit of property-less Blacks.

---

*This idea had actually been put into action by Sherman as he swept through the South, settling some forty-thousand freedmen on South Carolina's Sea Islands.

Further, this meant that Southerners could elect their own state officials and send Congressional representatives to Washington, many of whom were simply former political leaders and military officers of the Confederacy. The Radicals were furious, and refused to seat these Southern representatives in the House and Senate.

Nonetheless, little by little and in subtle ways, traditional Southern culture began to reassert itself. And whatever plans the Radicals had for reforming the South were to come to nothing. Black codes were passed throughout the South, forcing Blacks to contract their labor to Whites, requiring Blacks to obtain official permission to travel or move outside their counties, and imposing harsh vagrancy penalties of stiff fines or even imprisonment on any unemployed Blacks. Also, the professions and skilled trades tended to be closed to Blacks. And Blacks were forbidden to bear arms (in clear violation of the Second Amendment).

Then there was the creation (1866) of the Ku Klux Klan, headed up by Confederate cavalry General Nathan Bedford Forrest, which terrorized the Blacks in order to keep them in their place. But the KKK could be just as hard on Southern Whites whom they interpreted as being too sympathetic to the Blacks, burning crosses being left prominently at strategic spots by the KKK to remind the terrorized individuals as to who and what was in charge of Southern society.

Black Reconstruction. Facing this recalcitrant Southern attitude were large numbers of Northern Whites who descended on the South, many sent by the new Freedmen's Bureau, to help the Blacks make the transition away from slavery. These "carpetbaggers"* were disliked intensely by Southern Whites (especially the poorer Whites), but they did help bring some education to thousands of Black children (although absenteeism among Black students was very high and a serious problem in trying to bring the Black population into mainstream American culture).

These reformers were backed by an 1867 Military Reconstruction Act which stripped the South of its governments set up under Johnson's liberal reconstruction policies. The new law dismissed these state governments and divided the South into five military districts commanded by Union generals and enforced by a 60,000-strong Union Army positioned throughout the South. And the terms for readmission to the Union now required not ten percent but a full majority of a state's citizens, which now included Black voters.

In fact, the tendency of White voters to boycott the new elections advantaged considerably the Black vote. As a result, the South saw its

---

*Named for the type of luggage they arrived with: a large bag made of heavy cloth or carpeting.

first Black politicians (almost universally members of Lincoln's Republican Party) take their place in the states' assemblies, and even in the nation's Congress.

None of this however served to bridge the ever-widening emotional gap between Southern Whites and Blacks. But for the time being – as long as this military administration was kept in place in the South – there was little that Southern Whites could do about a situation that they detested (including their anger directed at the North for its "imperialistic" behavior).

* * *
AMERICA UNDER THE GRANT PRESIDENCY[73]

Grant elected president (1868). The Republicans were quick to nominate Civil War hero Grant as their party's candidate for president in the 1868 elections. The Democrats dumped Johnson and nominated New Yorker Governor Horatio Seymour (whose White racist views made him appear to be opposed to the North's tough Reconstruction policies). Thus a half million Black votes helped Grant win (53 percent) in this election with an untypically high voter turnout. But the electoral college, as usual, skewed the vote even further in favor of the winning candidate, Grant with 214 electoral votes to Seymour's 80.

The election was so close that Republicans realized that if Confederates disqualified by the Fourteenth Amendment had been able to vote (plus the three unreconstructed Southern states not yet allowed to vote), the election would have gone badly for the Republicans. Sensing that any potential Democrat victory would undo the Republican Party's Reconstruction program, Congress was quick to put into play in 1870 the Fifteenth Amendment, making it illegal for a state to deprive a citizen of the right to vote because of race, color or previous condition of servitude. As a condition for readmission to the Union, the last three hold-out Southern states – Texas, Mississippi and Virginia – had to approve both the Fourteenth and Fifteenth Amendments.

But Grant as a president was going to be much less aggressive than he had been as a general. Tragically, he tended to trust too much those he had placed in positions of authority and tended to be slow to check out rumors of corruption rampant in his administration, or at least within the higher realm of politics within the America he was supposed to be inspiring and directing. Grant himself was not involved in the corruption and often did act – usually belatedly – when a national scandal broke out.

The Fisk–Gould gold scandal. A scandal that erupted early during the

Grant Administration was the effort in 1869 by Wall Street tycoons Jim Fisk and Jay Gould to corner the American gold market. Buying up all the gold they could at $135 an ounce, thus diminishing the nation's gold supply and driving up the price of gold to $160 an ounce, they anticipated gaining a huge windfall profit when they finally unloaded their gold. But Grant learned of their scheme and stepped in to release some of the federal government's gold supply, thus bringing down the price of gold. Fisk and Gould thus came away with a much smaller profit than they had anticipated. Sadly, although Grant's action was quite correct, he could not escape the tendency of people to blame the president for allowing this to happen in the first place.

The Crédit Mobilier scandal. An even bigger scandal broke out when the public got wind in 1872 of the widespread corruption involved in the huge project of laying railroad track designed to connect the nation East and West. As early as 1862, during the Civil War, the federal government had authorized $100 million in capital to build a 1750-mile railroad westward from Council Bluffs, Iowa (on the strategic Missouri River) by the Union Pacific Railroad Company and eastward from the Pacific Ocean at San Francisco by the Central Pacific Railroad Company – through desert, mountains and unfriendly Indian territory. It was undertaken as a matter of national interest rather than as a money-making capitalist enterprise because it was not expected that the venture could ever recover its costs simply through the revenues it would acquire when it was actually up and running. It simply had to be built, by public funding if necessary.

The public funding actually took the form of federal land grants to these railroad companies of approximately twenty million acres, valued at somewhere around $50–$100 million, and cash loans of around $60 million, the loans to be eventually paid off by the sale of the land granted to the railroad companies. To handle these financial transactions Union Pacific director Thomas Durant set up the banking firm, Crédit Mobilier of America (which had no connection whatsoever with the famous French banking company of the same name).

Of a very highly questionable nature* was that the directors of both the Union Pacific and the Crédit Mobilier happened to be the one and the same individuals. Worse, Union Pacific stocks were sold to its directors and also to a number of United States congressmen whose vital votes supported this expensive venture (some thirty representatives from both parties were involved). Stocks were sold to these insiders at par value,

---

*There was considerable opposition within the general public and in Washington to the venture by those who did not see the strategic need for such an expensive venture.

well under their market value, thus securing enormous profits for these privileged investors (some estimates put their profits at around $20 million total) when they turned around to sell their shares on the open market.

Further, the railroads were granted $16,000 for each mile of track laid on flat land, $32,000 for hilly terrain, and $48,000 for mountainous terrain, tempting the companies to wander across as much terrain as possible and also to exaggerate their claims of miles of track laid, a monumental piece of corruption which finally in 1872 the New York City newspaper *Sun* uncovered and ran a damaging exposé about, just in time for the 1872 national elections.

Once the revelation of the scandal broke in 1872, Union Pacific stock dropped in such value that it left other stockholders nearly bankrupt. And once again Grant was blamed by an outraged media for not having intervened to block this whole corrupt venture.

But it was a sign of the times. Such scandals, especially related to the hugely lucrative business of railroad construction (which was expanding rapidly everywhere in the country), would unfortunately be very typical of the way America found itself developing economically in the last quarter of the 19th century.

Boss Tweed of Tammany Hall. Another scandal of the times, not connected to the Grant Administration however, was the New York City Democratic Party's political machine, Tammany Hall, operating under the direction of William "Boss" Tweed. Tammany Hall was originally set up as an organization designed to help immigrants (notably the Irish) get established in America. Such assistance, of course, came with the expectation that immigrants would then support the organization when it came time for local elections, ensuring Democratic Party control of the city and all its patronage jobs. Boss Tweed, who took over the organization in 1863, served on a number of city and state committees and boards and even on the New York State Senate (1868–1873). He eventually ended up controlling much of the New York state legislature, New York courts, the city treasury, and the huge cash flow that accompanied his various positions

He was reported to have helped Jay Gould and Jim Fisk take control (1866–1868) of the Erie Railroad from the equally adventuresome Cornelius Vanderbilt with fake stock (which Boss Tweed was able to get the New York state legislature to authorize), receiving a considerable share of that stock himself plus a position on the company's Board of Directors.

The amount of graft that Boss Tweed acquired is still uncertain, it was so extensive. He was accused and tried in a series of court cases starting in 1873 for stealing from the New York taxpayers an amount ranging from $25 to $45 million (more recent estimates put that figure at closer to 100 million in 1877 dollars). He was in and out of prison (at one point he even escaped to Spain) until 1878, when he died in prison at age fifty-five. But Tammany Hall itself quietly survived Boss Tweed's demise, to conduct business as usual well into the 20th century.

The 1872 national election. All this corruption, well-covered by press exposés, naturally called forth the need for extensive political reform in the North itself. Consequently, a new political grouping came into being in advance of the national elections: the Liberals. Taking a broader view of the South than the vengeful Radicals, the Liberals found themselves joined with the Democrats (ironic for such a reformist grouping, since the Democrats were identified closely with Tammany Hall) in calling for a lifting of the heavy-handed Reconstruction program imposed on the South by the North. In anticipation of the 1872 presidential election they nominated newspaper editor and ardent reformer (also Socialist) Horace Greeley, to run against the Republican Party's candidate, President Grant.

In the election itself Grant won handily the vote of the electoral college (300 to 60), though Greeley won 44 percent of the popular vote. Thus Grant was going to have four more years in the White House. But Grant's second term in office would be as troubled as his first term.

The 1873 Financial Panic. The failure of a major brokerage firm, brought down by its heavy involvement in Northern Pacific railroad bonds, set off a financial panic on Wall Street which soon led to the collapse of a number of banks and other investments houses. The situation became so bad that Wall Street shut down business for ten days to cool down the panic.

Worse, this crisis was timed with the decision by Grant to remove readily available silver as a standard for the dollar, leaving the dollar reliant only on gold as its metallic standard. While this may have strengthened the dollar, it restricted dramatically the ability of investors and entrepreneurs to gain easy credit for opening up or expanding their business base. This hit particularly hard the massive farming industry which always relied on bank loans to carry farmers from planting time in the spring until harvest time in the fall, when finally the farmers would see income.

Grant did not understand the severity of the financial crisis that hit the country in 1873, thinking the downturn in the nation's economic activity to be merely a normal fluctuation in the economy – which certainly happens from time to time. But this was no mere fluctuation, the economy going into a stall which lasted five long years (termed at the time the Long Depression) and which saw almost ninety railroad companies go bankrupt. Grant refused to back down from his tight monetarist strategy, believing that the strong dollar was more important to the nation's economy than the easy-credit strategy that the nation had been pursuing, a strategy leading to the vast corruption that had sullied the reputations of the railroad and banking companies.

But this was a bad time to put additional brakes on the nation's economy, because it would have severe political as well as economic consequences. As a result of the 1873 Panic, there occurred a major sweep in 1874 of the Republicans out of office everywhere, including the U.S. House of Representatives, where the Democratic Party took control. This did not bode well for a continuation of the North's Reconstruction program for the South.

"The South will rise again." In the meantime political tensions had been building in the South, where the Democratic Party was regaining political ground under the leadership of former Confederate officials, termed Bourbon or Redeemer Democrats. They had been gathering Southern White political support by stoking the Whites' fears of the rising political power that the Blacks had acquired through Congress's Reconstruction policies. Also the KKK was gathering strength – and vindictiveness.

This in turn brought Congress to pass another round of legislation (1871–1872) designed to protect Black voting rights in the South and curb the behavior of the KKK and other Southern organizations like it. But this only inspired even greater bullying behavior on the part of those White racist organizations, making life even more difficult for the Southern Black.

One by one these Redeemer Democrats were able to take over the state legislatures of the South and begin the passing of a round of segregationist "Jim Crow" laws. But in addition to playing the race card as their ticket to power, they employed other populist tactics such as calling for the end of the huge indebtedness of their state governments – by simply repudiating those debts – and by calling for the end of government subsidies for businesses (such as the railroads). It made for great popularity among frustrated White voters, but foolishly undercut the possibility of the South working its way out of its poverty (repudiating debts was a sure way of cutting off any future investments in the Southern economy). And prolonged economic hard times would only harden the attitudes of a racist South.

Grant finishes out his presidential term amidst more rumors of massive scandal. Grant's tendency to grant unreserved trust to those he had appointed to office would shake his administration to the core. Worse, he would tend to side with those accused of corruption, seeing them simply as victims of political opportunists. Indeed, he seemed totally blind to the corruption going on around him, which was rampant. Payoffs for appointments by officials below him, such as Grant's personal secretary, Orville E. Babcock, were normal procedure during the Grant years. Within his Treasury Department a tax collector had set up a scheme to overlook owed taxes, until a sufficient amount had accumulated that he could then go in and collect, plus a sizeable fine which went into the tax collector's pocket.

Meanwhile a huge Whiskey Ring owing enormous amounts of taxes ($3 million) on their whiskey had been allowed to develop, until finally Grant appointed an honest treasury secretary who went in and cleaned house. But when Babcock was also implicated in the deal, Grant threw his protection around his personal secretary, and even pardoned a number of leaders of the Whiskey Ring who had been found guilty and imprisoned.

Corruption touched everything from the War Department to the Department of the Interior as Grant appointees used their power to extract bribes and other payoffs for their services, becoming simply part of business as usual when dealing with the federal government.

Grant did appoint reformers empowered to clean out such corruption. But the corruption was so extensive that his efforts brought little relief from his growing reputation as running a very corrupt Administration. As a consequence, in 1876 the Republican Party distanced itself from him at the convention called to select a new Republican candidate for the presidency.

✳ ✳ ✳

THE 1876 ELECTION AND THE HAYES COMPROMISE

Hayes vs. Tilden. The 1876 national election pitted the Civil War hero, then post-war Ohio governor, and strong Reconstructionist Republican Rutherford B. Hayes, against the Democratic Party candidate, New York Governor Samuel J. Tilden, well-known because of his crushing of the Tweed machine. Both men were excellent choices for the presidency.

The election was close, so close in fact that the results went into prolonged contest. Votes were recounted and challenges were made by both sides of the nearly equal results in a number of states contests. Eventually the matter went before a congressionally appointed commission. But in the meantime Hayes had struck a deal with a number of Southern politicians, promising for their support the withdrawal of federal troops from the South, the support of a Louisiana governor's election in exchange for the promise of the protection of Black rights in that state, and the acceptance of a number of Southern politicians on his cabinet. This ultimately (March of 1877) swung the final decision of Congress in his favor, and finally in the summer of 1877 the new Hayes administration was ready to get down to business. But it would be an administration hampered greatly by the

America Recovers: 1865-1880 329

widely publicized compromises it was forced to accept in order to gain the White House.

Labor troubles. In 1877 violence shook the Baltimore and Ohio Railroad Company, which was having a hard time maintaining profits and thus had announced a reduction in workers' wages. Strikes broke out across parts of Maryland, Pennsylvania, Ohio, and New York, and became violent when replacements (or "scabs" as the workers called them) were brought in to take over the jobs of the striking workers. Times were tough and replacements, particularly Chinese laborers,* were abundant.

President Hayes refused to get involved, although he did bring in troops to protect the property of the railroad companies. Eventually the strike simply limped to an end on its own. However Hayes did succeed in enraging the railroad workers when he then vetoed a bill passed by Congress restricting the use of Chinese laborers. Hayes's veto in turn helped to promote a Democratic Party victory in both houses of Congress in the 1878 elections.

The end of Reconstruction. Despite Hayes's strong support of the rights of the Southern freedmen, the reality was that he was in no position to help them in the face of the rising White reaction building in the South. Also, mounting Indian problems on the American frontier were forcing Hayes to have to move his troops rather immediately from the South (which he had promised anyway) to the West to protect American frontiersmen. And with the removal from the South in 1877 of the military authorities charged with enforcing the Reconstruction laws, Reconstruction itself finally came to a dismal end. Blacks were now on their own in dealing with White power in the South.

* * *

THE BATTLE FOR THE WEST[74]

The American Indian Wars during the Civil War. Wars between the American settlers and the American Indians had been going on, of course, virtually since the arrival of Englishmen to the shores of North America in the early 1600s. Certainly they continued even while America was caught up deeply in its Civil War – and particularly during those times – because

---

*The use of Chinese labor in labor-intensive industry was not uncommon in those days. The tracks of the Central Pacific Railroad had been laid across the high mountains of California and over the Nevada desert by huge numbers of marginally-paid laborers brought in from a war-torn and opium-ravaged China.

federal troops protecting settlers had been pulled from Western service to fight the Confederacy. Thus the Civil War days saw some intense fighting between the settlers and the Indians. There were hundreds of Indian attacks in an Indian effort to drive the White settlers off their lands. There was no sparing of women, children and the elderly as these were battles of whole communities over the matter of land ownership, vital to the survival of both Indians and Whites. In the span of the four years of the Civil War over a thousand settlers' lives were lost to these Indian attacks.

The most intense action occurred in Minnesota in 1862 when Dakota tribes attacked German settlements at New Ulm and Hutchinson, killing several hundred (300-400) settlers. Local militiamen did what they could to hold back the Sioux, and Lincoln quickly sent federal troops to help them. Battles thus broke out between the federal and Indian troops over a six-week period, resulting finally in breaking the Sioux offensive. Over 400 Sioux were subsequently arrested, 300 of which were convicted of murder and sentenced to be hanged. Lincoln however pardoned most of them (much to the great irritation of local White authorities) and only thirty-eight of them were subsequently hanged, the largest such event nonetheless in American history.

Ultimately such Indian attacks brought a bitter White response, in the form of countering attacks of White militia and federal troops on the Indians. There was an attempt to be fair in the size of the response. But the anger raging between both sides made this a matter very difficult to manage. A huge and unwarranted loss of Indian life during this period occurred at Sand Creek in eastern Colorado in late November of 1864, when some 700 federal troops attacked a peaceful community of Cheyenne and Arapaho Indians, most of whose men were away hunting buffalo. 130 were killed or wounded, mostly women and children but also a number of the members of the Cheyenne Council, tragically those most supportive of the idea of peace with White society. This action thus strengthened the hand of the pro-war Indian Dog Soldiers. It also brought into action a federal court of inquiry and condemnation of the federal officers involved. But no other punishment resulted.

Kit Carson. Meanwhile in the American southwest, action led by Union General Carleton – but carried out largely by the living legend Kit Carson* – was undertaken in early 1863 to round up the Navajo and Apache tribes and move them to a reservation along the bleak Pecos River, where they could be more easily prevented from making raids on the White settlers

---

*Penny novels were already being written about his exploits as a mountain man and Indian hunter.

America Recovers: 1865-1880

in the New Mexico Territory. The roundup proved difficult because the Indians knew how to hide themselves in the mountains, driving Carson to take harsher measures to break the will of the Navajo (the ones who had not already joined the Apache in a flight to the West to form an anti-White army.) By early 1864 Navajo resistance had been broken and thousands of them were rounded up and sent off to the reservation, where many died of cold and hunger. Eventually they were allowed to return to their former homes, though as a submissive people.

By late 1864 Carson had turned his attention to the Kiowas and Comanches who had been conducting raids on White settlements in the Texas Panhandle region. In November Carson and his men met a grand Indian coalition of several thousand warriors at the Battle of Adobe Walls. Carson's men were vastly outnumbered and quickly out of ammunition and thus forced to retreat, but managed to inflict massive casualties on the Indians in the process. This battle proved to be a turning point in the Indian wars in the region, greatly undermining the power of both tribes and ultimately bringing the Kiowas and Comanches to sue for peace in 1865.

Geronimo and his Apache raiders. But alongside Kit Carson, the Indians could provide heroics of their own, such as the Apache raider Geronimo. He was part of a military tradition that reached back to the wars earlier in the 1800s between the Apaches and the Mexicans. These wars were constant and without definitive results. Then when the American frontiersmen came on the scene, Geronimo included their settlements in his raids. He actually never commanded a band larger than forty or fifty warriors. Yet his skills brought his name to some kind of fame among the Apache – and the White settlers as well! He eventually was forced into retirement on the Apache reservation by the U.S. military (with also Mexican cooperation), breaking out three times between 1876 and 1886 when he grew restless under the restrictions of reservation life. Eventually he and his Chiricahua tribe were moved to Florida and then to Oklahoma. But his name was so well known that several times he was featured at several major expositions back East and even rode horseback (in native attire, of course) in Teddy Roosevelt's inaugural parade in 1905!

The grand Western migration. On they came – White men, women and children – by steamer or river barge (as far as the rivers would take them westward), then by wagon train, following trails set out by trail-blazing frontiersmen, and eventually by train as the American railroads pushed West and Southwest deep into Indian lands. They laid claim to railroad land and set up their own farms, as well as towns to service the fast-growing farming world of the West.

The Mormons. Some such as the Mormons came looking for religious utopias, much in the manner that had brought the Puritans to America in the early 1600s. Indeed, Brigham Young's Mormons were particularly successful in this matter, developing communities centered on their City of Zion of Salt Lake City (founded by Young in 1847), but reaching far and wide from Utah into Idaho, Arizona, Nevada, California, Colorado, and even northern Mexico.

In 1857 a war began to brew between the Mormons and the U.S. government, the latter in 1850, after having secured the area from Mexico in the Mexican-American War, declaring the region to be off limits to the practice of polygamy (a common practice among the Mormons). U.S. troops were sent to Utah to enforce the ruling against the rebellious Mormons, although the Mormons fought back mostly by simply refusing to supply the troops with needed food and material. Then in the summer of 1858, just as the Mormons were making a move to leave Utah, pressure from Congress brought U.S. President Buchanan to declare an end to the Mormon suppression. The war was now officially over and the Mormons returned to their homes in Utah.

One unfortunate result of the war however was the massacre* by Mormons (disguised as Indians) in 1857 at Mountain Meadows in southern Utah of a party of 120 to 140 adult Arkansas "Gentiles" (non-Mormon Whites) passing through Mormon territory with a huge herd of cattle on their way West to California. All were killed, except children under six who were spared however and taken in by Mormon families. Blame for the massacre was never fully ascertained (Young claimed to have had no involvement in the decision to execute the group of Gentiles), and only in 1877 was one of the supposed perpetrators finally successfully tried and executed.

Miners. The rumors of gold (but also silver and copper) also brought Americans west, though not usually entire families but instead merely single male fortune hunters. States such as California, Nevada (with its fabulous Comstock Lode), Montana, Idaho, and Washington were states particularly sought out by these fortune hunters. Towns would quickly appear wherever mineral sites were discovered, bringing not only the fortune-hunting miners, but also barkeeps and prostitutes to entertain the miners, but also bankers, clergy, and general store operators to bring some degree of American civilization to the towns as well. Then when the mines yielded up all their bounty, everyone moved on to opportunities elsewhere

---

*The decision to massacre the entire group was made when the Mormons feared that some of the Gentiles had discovered that their attackers were Whites (Mormons) and not really Indians.

– and then yet another bustling mining town would turn into a deserted ghost town.

The West's Cattle Kingdoms (1860s-1880s). With the advent of the railroads into the West, new opportunities opened up for the lucrative trade in beef cattle. Thousands of cattle would be herded north from the grasslands of Texas, through the Indian territory of Oklahoma, to the various railheads of the Kansas Pacific Railroad. For instance, in 1867, when the new Chisholm Trail was first laid out, 35,000 head of cattle were brought up from Texas to the railhead at Abilene in that first year alone. From Kansas the cattle were then herded onto boxcars and shipped up to Chicago (or west to Denver for shipment to the Pacific coast). In Chicago the slaughterhouses would be kept busy preparing meat to be shipped up the Great Lakes waterway to the populous Eastern cities.

From the end of the Civil War to the mid-1880s the cattle business boomed, making a lot of cattle barons very rich – and creating a fabled American proto-type, the American cowboy. The battalions of cowboys conducting these drives were hard-working, hard drinking, young men on whom endless popular stories of American fortitude would be based. They were a restless lot, not destined to set down family roots while they remained in the business of cattle herding. Greatly exaggerated however were the multitude of stories of gun battles conducted by them in the Kansas bars, where, being finally paid for their work, they were supposedly emboldened by booze and prostitutes to the point of murderous manliness (but still, these stories made for great reading!). Nonetheless, the cowboy exemplified a spirit that seemed to simply roll out of the manliness demanded of the American male during the Civil War. The cowboy was, indeed, an inspiring symbol of a young, aggressive, expansive America, a nation with a growing sense of destiny.

Cattleman versus farmer. But three things would bring this era to a close: the steel-bladed plow, the barbed-wire fence, and the over-grazing of the cow trails. The grassy plains through which the cattle trails led were covered by a thick undergrowth of tough grass with deep roots, which made the land prohibitively difficult to plow – that was until the steel plow began to come under wide usage (sometime in the 1870s and 1880s). With this invention, homesteaders could now begin to settle the plains, with their plowed fields and domestic animals able to support the lives of their families. To protect their investment, they began to secure their landholdings by the relatively cheap means of the new barbed wire fencing (developed in the mid-1870s).

Now the cattle herds found their paths along their cow trails blocked here and there by these fenced-in homesteads, and trouble began to brew between these two categories of Westerners, the farmer and the cattleman. For years the cattlemen had been allowed freely to graze their herds on the vast federal lands of the Great Plains (reaching from Texas to the Dakotas). But now homesteaders were rapidly filling these open lands. Little by little the cattle herding business was pushed ever more westward, increasing the difficulty and costs of the herding itself.

Furthermore, the herds had expanded to such a size that the price of beef began to drop – at a time in which the cattle lands and trails were beginning to be overgrazed by this vast number of cattle. When a very bad winter hit in 1886–1887, hundreds of thousands of cattle died from exposure and the lack of sufficient grass or even grain for feed. A number of cattle barons never truly from recovered from this bitter blow.

The rise of the American farmer. Anyway, the business of farming was slowly taking over from the business of cattle herding. And truly a business it was. The families who came West and acquired their 160-acre tract of land found that 160 acres in the West did not provide the financial security that 160-acres in the East once had. At best these small homesteads could feed their large families. But beyond that, there was little additional income from their fields that could allow them to purchase the extras needed for the good life. For instance, the Great Plains was devoid of woodlands and thus wood had to be purchased rather than simply cut from the surrounding woods as was the case back East. Sadly for many homesteaders, their sole building material was the sod they cut from the ground and turned into something like bricks to frame their houses and barns. The sod houses that dotted the landscape of the Great Plains were hardly a lasting solution to the challenge of settling the West. In short order, numerous homesteaders (perhaps as many as three-quarters of them) had to simply abandon the effort and move on to try their luck elsewhere.

But this opened the opportunity for the more entrepreneurial-minded homesteader to pick up abandoned neighboring land, adding to his holdings until he possessed many hundreds of – even a thousand – acres of farmland.

This was nicely timed with the invention of farming machinery that made the plowing, cultivation and harvesting of vast fields an attainable goal for an industrial farmer. And indeed, America began to see such industrial farms grow in number during the latter part of the 1800s. In America, farming had finally become very big business, the Western farms fully able to feed the Eastern cities which were also growing rapidly in size.

Towns located along the growing number of rail lines crisscrossing the American Great Plains or Midwest began quickly to develop as economic and social centers for the agricultural industry of entire counties. Thus

America Recovers: 1865-1880 335

as the farming business boomed, churches, schools, banks, and general stores began to appear in these towns, bringing American civilization to the Midwest. In many ways this too, along with the cowboy, was fast becoming a major cultural symbol representing the young and fast-growing America.

Meanwhile, the American South. Sadly the South had slipped out of the picture, caught up locally in trying to heal the economic and cultural wounds left by the Civil War. It would take many generations before the South was finally able indeed to rise again.

The Indians' Last Stand. At the end of the Civil War whatever Indian communities still remained East of the Mississippi were quite small and isolated, hardly registering at all in the social-political scheme of things. However, in the American Southwest, widely scattered communities of Navajo and Hopi maintained something of an undisturbed, though marginal, agricultural existence (their land was arid, even much of it desert.) Neighboring Apache meanwhile led a nomadic lifestyle hunting game from horseback. In the American Northwest a number of tribes led fairly comfortable and quiet agricultural lives, along the lines that the Eastern Indians had once led, prior to the arrival of the European.

The most active, and violent, Indian-European dynamic was on the Great Plains, where Indians constantly struggled against White Americans for control of the land. The Plains Indians had once been farmers. But with the rapid growth of the herds of Spanish horses that had escaped to the wild – horses that the Indians learned how to tame – the Indians had developed great skill as horsemen and left the farming world for the world of the hunter, becoming dedicated hunters of the vast bison herds which covered the Great Plains. They had so completely adapted to the lifestyle of bison-hunter that without these herds to hunt they would not know how to survive. And therein lay one of the biggest problems for them.

The other problem of course was like the one also faced by the American cowboy: the American homesteaders who were moving onto the Great Plains to establish fenced-in farmlands for themselves and their families. By the last quarter of the 1800s it was increasingly apparent to the Plains Indians that the two societies could not coexist. For the Indians, survival meant simply chasing the American homesteader off the land. Thus Indian-American war loomed.

The decline of the buffalo herds. Concerning the bison or buffalo herds and their rapid decline, there is still much controversy as to the cause. But certainly the effect was clear enough: deprived of their buffalo, the Plains Indians could not survive as a society. Explorers to the West prior to the

Civil War were astounded by the size of the buffalo herds, hundreds of thousands of them in a single herd. But already by the time of the Civil War the herds were beginning to thin out. The Plains Indians themselves were well-known for their extravagance in the killing of the herds, given their own marksmanship with the hunting rifle and skill on horseback. The herds also lacked protective instincts and so they were easily slaughtered in vast numbers.

The Whites of course also participated in the slaughter, hunting them for their hides, sometimes just hunting them (for instance from passing trains) for sport – or ultimately to deprive the Plains Indians of their sustenance. By the 1880s the total number of buffalo had dropped to only mere hundreds, to the point of near specie-extinction.

The debate over what to do about "the Indian Problem." While events on the frontier itself seemed to take their own course as frontiersmen saw the necessity, back East a huge debate raged over what the proper policy toward the Indian should be.

Humanism was a response natural to those back East who were comfortably removed from the terror of frontier life. In a Rousseauian fashion,* Humanists took the rather romantic view of the Indian as the pre-civilized natural man, possessing all the pure or sinless qualities of man that he possessed before Adam and Eve's Fall into sin (or before the corruptions of civilization had produced their disastrous effect). Humanists thus believed that the Indians should be simply left alone, that White intrusion into the West should be slowed up or even halted completely. But that romantic dream was also simply not going to happen. Thus the Humanist program was largely irrelevant to the solution of the Indian Problem.

Others, notably evangelical Christians, felt strongly that God wanted Christian Americans to help the Indians come out of their primitive (and pagan) ways, to personally bring them the good news of the higher life to which God called all his American children (including the American Indians). Thus missionaries took themselves to the tribal lands of the Indians to bring them to Christian ways and to the life-style of Anglo-Americans – setting up

---

*Jean-Jacques Rousseau was a French-speaking Swiss philosopher of the mid-1700s who in his widely-read book, *Social Contract*, idealized the "natural man" – even citing the American Indian as a perfect example – claiming that sin and corruption was not itself natural to man, but came upon the social scene only with the rise of civilization. Of course he had the very obvious corruptions of the European royal courts in mind as he wrote, and from a commoner's point of view such highly "civilized" courts (as kings and their attendants saw themselves) were indeed very corrupt, with their perfumed wigs, expensive entertainment, and general uselessness as overseers of the lives of the multitudes of Europeans not part of the privileged class.

America Recovers: 1865-1880

schools and churches to show the Indians the way to proper or civilized life.

But as the Cherokee and other Southeastern Indians themselves had discovered earlier in the 1800s, converting to the settled, agricultural, Christian life-style of the White frontiersman did not guarantee any kind of larger protection when these White frontiersmen sought their land. Thus ultimately this was not a terribly good solution to the Indian Problem, at least not from the Indian point of view.

Ultimately the decision came in the form of the policy of rounding up the nomadic Plains Indians tribes and placing them all on Indian reservations, promising that within those reservations they could live as they chose – but that they were not ever to leave those reservations or they would face the wrath of the U.S. military sent to enforce the reservation policy of Washington's Bureau of Indian Affairs.

As Commander of the U.S. military enforcing that policy, Civil War veteran cavalry leader General Philip Sheridan proved to be a strict enforcer. The only problem here was that the Indians themselves knew from previous treaties undertaken with the U.S. government that these reservations were generally only temporary promises of respect for Indian rights, before such reserved territory was once again taken away from them by land-hungry Whites.

Ultimately, the Indians understood that they were going to have to have their own say in shaping policy, which meant only one thing: they were going to have to fight – and fight savagely – to protect themselves from extinction as a unique society or people.

Custer's Last Stand. Meanwhile wars between the Indians on the one hand and White settlers and U.S. Army units on the other had been fairly constant on the American Plains since the days of the Civil War, with the Indians typically receiving the worse end of these encounters. But by the mid-1870s the Indians were putting aside their ancient tribal differences and beginning to work in concert with each other.

Thus in 1875, Sioux (or Lakota) Chief Sitting Bull and his tactician Crazy Horse decided it was time to leave the Dakota Reservation to take to the offensive against settlers invading the Dakota Black Hills, sacred Sioux land. By the summer of the next year (1876) Sitting Bull had linked up with a large number of Northern Cheyenne and Arapaho warriors in Southern Montana. Sent to deal with this huge gathering of thousands of Indians was Sheridan's cavalry. Sheridan divided his cavalry into separate units, to converge on the huge Indian gathering from three different directions and force these Indians back onto their reservations.

Things did not go well for Sheridan, as the Indians took on one of these detachments and forced them into humiliating retreat. Trying again,

Sheridan sent out 700 troops under the colorful Civil War celebrity, George Custer, Custer dividing his force into a number of units, he himself leading a large detachment of those men. On June 25-26 at the Little Bighorn River he and his soldiers were also to discover the fighting prowess of the Indians, when his entire detachment, including Custer himself, was either killed (268 men) or severely wounded (55 men, 6 later dying from their wounds) in an encounter with Crazy Horse and his warriors.

But this massacre did not break the will of the U.S. military. Ironically it had the opposite effect, turning Custer into some kind of iconic martyred hero, and merely deepening the determination of the military to crush definitively all Indian power. Realizing that his actions had simply awakened an angry and massive White nation, Sitting Bull reappraised the situation and decided simply to take himself and his people back to their Dakota reservation. And this would be the last of the great Indian efforts to hold off by force the advancing White Americans.

Indians assigned to Reservations under the Dawes Severalty Act (1887). Finally in 1887, Washington came to some kind of conclusion about the Indian Problem when it passed the Dawes Severalty Act. It attempted to turn the Indian reservations into homesteading territories, each Indian family assigned the proverbial 160 acres, all Indians to receive English instruction, and eventually all becoming U.S. citizens. That these proud nomads however were not naturally farmers was clearly demonstrated in the crushing of the Indian social morale, and the widespread alcoholism that quickly descended upon the reservations. But at least from White America's point of view, the Indian Problem had been solved.

In keeping with the moral climate of the times, it was not long until the Bureau of Indian Affairs fell right alongside the railroad business into deep corruption. Government money, unaccountable to market forces but distributed solely through political considerations, invited all sorts of patronage appointments, at a cost (kickbacks) of course. But it was not long before a vigilant news media caught wind of the corruption, and scandals erupted into the public view, dirtying the reputations of a number of American politicians.

The Ghost Dance, Sitting Bull, and Wounded Knee (1890). But White Americans were not the only ones to take note of the corruption, which merely added to the Indians' sense of demoralization. Nothing that they could do seemed to improve the Indians' sense of social significance. They were an entirely defeated people. Thus it was that in 1890 the Sioux got caught up in the Ghost Dance craze, believing that the performance of this ritual would finally clear the land of the White man, even with the wearing of special shirts to make the Indians invulnerable to White man's bullets if it should come to armed conflict. And it soon came to such conflict – in which Sitting Bull was killed along with a dozen of his warriors. Then the 7th Cavalry was sent in to impose order and at Wounded Knee even greater fighting broke out, in which 200 Sioux men, women and children were killed – along with 25 U.S. soldiers killed and 39 wounded. It would be the last sad (and probably accidental) such episode in the long-standing feud between the American Indian and the American White.

Indeed, the Indian Problem had now been solved definitively.

CHAPTER ELEVEN

THE "GILDED AGE" OF AMERICAN CAPITALISM

✻ ✻ ✻

CAPITALISM IN THE GILDED AGE[75]

During the time of post-Civil-War recovery, a new social dynamic had been rising within the fast-growing American cities: the adoration of modern technology and those who provided it, the promise of wealth flowing out of this dynamic, and the seeming control over life provided by the scientific mentality that undergirded this whole social-cultural revolution. This was due in no small part to the Civil War and its lasting effect on the American economy. The war's demand for steel, and the iron ore and coal to make it, and the railroads and boats to ship it, and the financial institutions to fund its initial outlay, and the laborers to work the whole system – all this had made a deep impact on what was formerly almost purely an agrarian society.

Apart from the early railroad ventures during and immediately after the war, the government played in the post-war period only a minimal role in the on-going development of this new industrial society, especially as the war and its needs receded from view and the system seemed to run simply under its own dynamics rather than on the basis of popular social-political demands.

Nor was God invited to play a role in the development of this new society. America's Grand Destiny now seemed to be driven forward largely by the huge material rewards that fell to the particularly ambitious and fearless. Fortunes could be made rather quickly by very enterprising individuals (and they could be lost almost as quickly). And these fortunes were awesome, often exceeding (sometimes vastly) the levels of wealth of the European nobility. Indeed, it was a Gilded Age (Age of Gold) for successful American industrialists.

This was a perfect setting for the spirit of Darwinism to soar. Certainly the basic theme of this rising social order was quite Darwinian: progress through survival of the fittest. To the strong belonged the spoils of their conquests. But for those who fell to the wayside in this struggle for survival there would be no tears wept. But the risk of this competitive struggle seemed worth it, at least to those who anticipated striking it rich in this new game of potentially limitless opportunity (if you were willing to play it hard and fast).

For others, however, this game offered virtually no opportunity – only drudgery and painful hardship on this path of survival. With the closing of the Western frontier and loss of the ability to secure cheap Indian land, farm boys were forced to find work in these industrial enterprises, not with the hope of striking it rich, for there was almost no entry point for them into a game that required substantial startup money or *capital* to get up and running in this new capitalist system. These farm boys came penniless, offering only their labor. But for their labor they received very little in return. In the eyes of the Darwinists these new industrial workers were not seen as people, as fellow Americans to whom they owed some sense of mutual responsibility. Instead they were viewed by the rising class of wealthy capitalists only as economic costs, costs which they had to keep low in order to gain the profits that would win them victory in this Darwinian game.

What was happening to America? Had it gone from African slavery only to replace it with a shockingly similar wage-slavery? Was this the social outcome that so many young men had given their lives for in the recent Civil War?

The Captains of Industry (or "Robber Barons" as others termed them). The rapidly widening gap between hard-working American laborers and the Captains of Industry was vast ... and shocking. According to a survey done in 1896,* of a total of 12½ million American families in 1890, 125,000 very wealthy families, or 1 percent of the total number of families in America, earned over 50 percent of America's total family wealth. The well-to-do, comprising about 11 percent of the total number of families, earned about 35 percent of the nation's family wealth, the middle classes, comprising about 44 percent of the total, earned about 12½ of the total wealth, and the poorer classes, comprising another 44 percent of the families, earned only about 1 percent of the total wealth.

And among this very wealthy 1 percent of the population, an even smaller number of families stood out way above the rest. A few are mentioned here just to point out how capitalism was working in the latter

---

*Charles B. Spahr, *An Essay on the Present Distribution of Wealth in the United States*, New York: T.Y. Crowell & Co.,1896, p. 69.

part of the 1800s.

Cornelius Commodore Vanderbilt. Vanderbilt was nicknamed "Commodore" because he got his climb out of poverty as a boat operator back in the 1810s, ferrying New York passengers between Staten Island and Manhattan. It was a very competitive business, but Cornelius Vanderbilt knew how to compete. He fought against the well-defended steamboat monopolies that had secured privileged routes around New York, buying out companies, although at times he even had some of his own operations bought out by others.

But by the end of the 1830s, Vanderbilt had secured a number of his own steamboat monopolies, and in the early 1840s he began to manage small railroads that connected with his steamboat lines. In 1847 he took over a major railroad running from New York to Boston, and bought out a number of competitors, putting his railroad line in a dominant position on that vital route. Then with the beginning of the California gold rush in 1849 he switched to shipping on the high seas, even at one time attempting to put together a group to build a canal across Nicaragua between the Atlantic and Pacific. He failed at this attempt, but did set up a land and water connection between the two oceans, and then developed a Pacific steam line to California.

In the 1850s he bought a large company that manufactured the steam engines for the steamboat industry, and also jumped into the trans-Atlantic steamship business. Even at one point he found himself deeply involved in Central America against a major competitor – and various authorities supporting that competitor ... including some military action. So Vanderbilt moved his operations further south to Panama and then acquired a monopoly on a steamship line running from there to California.

During the Civil War he donated and staffed at his own expense his flagship, the *Vanderbilt*, which was used to hunt Confederate raiders (such as Confederate Admiral Semmes and his warship, *Alabama*).

After the war he was joined by his son Billy in acquiring a number of New York railroads, and brought them together as the future New York Central Line, one of the first corporate giants in America. He also constructed a large railroad terminal in Manhattan on 42nd Street, also the forerunner of the New York's Grand Central Terminal, the world's largest train station.

The only time Vanderbilt found his move blocked was in his attempt to buy up the Erie Railroad, which Jay Gould and his associate James Fisk fought off by watering down stock (quite in violation of the law, which Fisk avoided by bribing New York legislators!), to weaken Vanderbilt's position after Vanderbilt had bought up, at some considerable expense, what he thought would be a controlling share of the business. This massive issue of new stocks by Gould and Fisk devalued Vanderbilt's stocks so badly that his losses were enormous. This created a deep and lasting enmity between Vanderbilt and these two equally ambitious and notoriously clever financial wizards. But Vanderbilt would not again be on the losing side of this rivalry, a rivalry that lasted all the way up to his death in 1877.

At his death he was worth the monumental sum of $100 million,* most of which went to his son Billy (although he was very generous to his other many sons and daughters). He also donated the $1 million that founded the university in Nashville, Tennessee, that still carries his name, which at the time was the largest charity contribution ever offered by a single donor. He also gave rather generously to churches, including the 8½ acres which he gave to the Moravian Church on Staten Island for a cemetery, where he himself is buried.

Andrew Carnegie.[76] Carnegie came with his very poor parents from Scotland to Pittsburgh in 1848 at age thirteen, to live with relatives, and soon found a menial job to help support the family. But he quickly taught himself to read Morse Code messages without having to first translate them, impressing officials at the Pennsylvania Railroad who hired him for just such work. Obvious to his supervisor, Carnegie was an eager and fast learner, and as he studied the larger world of business he proved to be a great strategic thinker – one who thought about how different industrial operations could be combined to produce a complete in-house operation, from securing a company's own raw materials, to building its own machinery, and shipping on its own carriers to its own distribution centers. Taking up this process of industrial combination himself, Carnegie detected the central importance of the iron industry and set up his own company to build the iron bridges that would be needed by the railroad industry. He then branched into the world of iron production, supplying his bridge company with its own iron. He then advanced to the bigger business of steel production, assembling a huge team of steel engineers, and soon was helping America to outpace Britain and Germany (Prussia) in steel production. He then complemented this business by going into the coal/coke business to supply his ever-improving furnaces with their own fuel. His operations were so efficient that he was able to slash steel prices, increasing immensely the demand for his steel production. By the end of the 1800s Carnegie was producing steel at the rate of 6,000 tons per day.

---

*This would make him the second richest man American in history, ranking only behind Rockefeller. The $100 million would be approximately equivalent to $150 billion in todays dollars. Interestingly, he lived modestly. All the lavish Vanderbilt estates that were built across the American East were actually commissioned later by his descendants.

But his aggressive industrial empire-building put him at odds with his skilled laborers (as opposed to the larger unskilled work-force he employed), who were driven less by a desire for personal success than by a desire to see high wage rates applied collectively to their craft union. As Carnegie viewed matters, this was designed merely to produce among the skilled workers a sense of wage and labor security rather than individual opportunity for advancement. And worse, the union seemed to be running his Homestead Plant ever since their victory in the 1889 strike. Thus when in 1892 Carnegie's aggressive corporate supervisor Henry Clay Frick decided to break the growing power of the craft union by declaring a huge reduction in skilled workers' wages, a massive strike was again called by the union at the huge Homestead plant. (This strike Frick would have to deal with himself because Carnegie was back in Europe at the time). The strike was finally broken by the heavy-handed measures of the Pinkerton agents (resulting in deaths on both sides of the conflict). And Frick was shot twice by a frenzied anarchist, but survived the ordeal, the shooting helping to stir a general antipathy against the striking workers.

Soon after this, Carnegie was ready to get out of the business world (the Carnegie Steel Company had by that time achieved the awesome goal of producing more steel than all of Britain's mills combined!) and in 1901 sold his entire operation to the financial titan J.P. Morgan for $480 million (the largest such corporate transaction ever, amounting to over $13 billion in today's dollars), thus helping to create the United States Steel Corporation. This also made Morgan the uncontested giant of the American financial world and Carnegie a very rich man, though over the next years Carnegie would give most of that wealth away to various charities and social endeavors and spend the rest of his life traveling.

John Pierpont (J.P.) Morgan.[77] Morgan was born in 1837 at the opposite end of the social scale from Carnegie, Morgan being the son of a very successful Connecticut businessman and banker, schooled in his youth at fashionable schools in Boston, Switzerland and Germany. Finishing his schooling, he joined his father's banking office in London for a year before returning to the States to work for his father's company in New York City. He was a clever financier, for instance during the Civil War purchasing 5,000 rifles from a Union depot at $3.50 and then reselling them to the U.S. Army for $22 each!

Over the years he demonstrated his skill at buying up struggling companies at bargain rates and then reorganizing them into profitable operations. He even at one point came to the aid of the U.S. Treasury in the midst of the Panic of 1893, when by 1895 the Federal Treasury was nearly out of gold and facing financial default. Morgan joined with the Rothschild bankers of Paris to offer to sell the government 3.5 million ounces of gold in exchange for thirty-year bonds. At first U.S. President Cleveland turned down the offer, but then realizing how close the government was to default, finally accepted Morgan's offer. It indeed saved the status of the U.S. Treasury, but undercut Cleveland's standing with the agrarian wing of his Democratic Party

Again in 1907 Morgan stepped in to rescue the American economy, this time caused by a massive sell-off on Wall Street after the failure of a large copper venture threatened to pull down a number of banks that had invested heavily in the venture (actually Knickerbocker, New York's third largest trust company, did fail). This crisis was so big that Morgan did not attempt to answer the challenge alone, but gathered a number of other New York banks to join him in putting money back into Wall Street and restoring investors' confidence, thus averting a stock market collapse.

Another crisis soon followed, this time caused by the collapse of a major industrial conglomerate invested in coal, iron, and railroads. With President Teddy Roosevelt's permission, Morgan stepped in to take over the fallen conglomerate, aware that this would invite charges of monopolistic behavior. But it had to be done to avert yet another panic in the world of American investment.

But as a result of these interventions, the U.S. government finally (1913) made the move to set up a government agency, the Federal Reserve, to intervene when such economic crises began to show signs of developing. In a sense, Morgan himself had shown the U.S. government the proper procedure by which to intervene when necessary, contributing greatly to the stability of the U.S. economy, which throughout the 1800s had experienced one speculative crisis after another.

John D. Rockefeller.[78] Rockefeller was raised in tough circumstances in upstate New York and then in Ohio, his father being a wandering con-man who only infrequently visited the home, his mother however being a very strong, positive influence on his life. As a youth he proved himself to be very bright, quick with numbers, hard-working, and loving learning, putting himself through a large amount of schooling. He was also a person of deep Christian faith. Together these elements made him an eager challenger of the larger world.

During the Civil War he and his brother raised the capital to found a business providing produce to the Union armies, and then the two of them in 1863 joined a team of investors to build in Cleveland's fast-growing industrial area an oil refinery designed to produce kerosene, helping to move the country away from expensive whale oil as the source of its lighting. In 1865 he bought out the leading partners of the business and through considerable borrowing put himself (and the remaining investors, including his brother) in a well-placed position within an economy turning more and more to the use of kerosene.

By 1870 he moved to establish the Standard Oil Company, which quickly became Ohio's largest oil company. Then moving into the shipping business, he was able to acquire for his oil business special railroad rates that allowed him vast advantage in his competition with smaller oil companies, which he was quick to buy out when they stumbled. Then in 1874 he signed a secret deal with his largest New York competitors, Pratt and Rogers, to buy out their oil company and bring the two on his company as partners. And thus Rockefeller proceeded to move through the infant oil industry, buying out company after company until, by the end of the 1870s, Standard Oil owned 90 percent of America's oil business. He even at one point took on the huge Pennsylvania Railroad Company, starting a price war in shipping rates, which finally forced the railroad to sell its own oil interests to Standard Oil (actually Rockefeller was moving away from shipping by rail to shipping by pipeline). But this in turn brought charges of monopolistic practices (not the first time, however, nor the last) in the courts of Pennsylvania and other states. These court cases Rockefeller found himself battling constantly, gaining for Rockefeller a very negative national reputation.

Adding to this negative image was when in 1882 Rockefeller set up the Standard Oil Trust, a move to bring the many separate state corporations under a single domain (at that time companies were licensed to operate within only the state granting the corporate license). Not only did the creation of this new trust produce a huge outcry of monopoly in the nation's press, other corporations, seeing the benefits of this move, were quick to set up similar organizations, birthing the age of the massive American trust companies. He also birthed the practice (taken up by New York's National Petroleum Exchange) of selling oil futures on the open market as shares or certificates based on oil held in storage, thus making the pricing of oil a public matter.

Eventually Rockefeller ventured into the growing world of international oil production, then moved from kerosene production into the business of natural gas, and even the refinement of gasoline (previously considered just a wasteful byproduct of kerosene production), just as the world of automobiles, with their new internal combustion engines, was opening up.

But the 1890 Sherman Antitrust Act, originally designed to break up labor organizations, would soon be turned against Rockefeller, especially as he moved to acquire oil fields in other American states, his vast oil fields in Pennsylvania beginning to play out. He also entered the business of iron ore production and shipment with Carnegie, causing a huge public uproar.

The "Gilded Age" of American Capitalism

With the arrival of the 20th century, Rockefeller found himself under constant attack, by U.S. President Teddy Roosevelt, wielding the Sherman Antitrust Act wherever he could; by Ida Tarbell, publishing a lengthy exposé on Standard Oil's underhanded business practices; and finally in 1911 by the U.S. Supreme Court, which handed down the decision that as a monopoly violating the Sherman Act, Standard Oil had to be broken up into thirty-four separate companies (eventually becoming Conoco, Amoco, Chevron, Exxon, Mobil, Sohio, Pennzoil, etc.). Yet Rockefeller remained a significant stockholder in these various companies, and the oil business continued to be personally very profitable for Rockefeller. This eventually made Rockefeller the richest man in the world at the time (and by comparison, even still today!).

But like Carnegie, Rockefeller's business sense was based on a larger view of his responsibilities to the world around him. He never saw the making of money as evil, seeing how though some people would fall by the wayside in the competitive world of business and finance, the overall effect was clearly one of economic advancement for the society as a whole.

True, some benefitted vastly more than others in this trend, but even here Rockefeller felt a sense of responsibility to his world, setting up charity organizations designed to help the young and ambitious climb to greater social heights. Indeed, this was part of his understanding of his Christian responsibilities, which began with his church tithing even as a teenager, and which interestingly included teaching Bible at the Baptist church he attended as an adult. But his charity helped turn by 1900 a small Baptist college into the University of Chicago, his grants to church mission produced the Central Philippine University in 1905, and ultimately his sense of charity led to the creation of an outstanding medical research center in New York City. In 1913 he established the Rockefeller Foundation, granting it $250 million to aid in medical research and training, and in 1918, granted $550 million for another foundation (later absorbed into the Rockefeller Foundation) for social research.

* * *

THE RAPID GROWTH OF AMERICAN MATERIAL POWER

America as a brash, young, industrial giant. As powerful as the financial-industrial giants Vanderbilt, Carnegie, Morgan, and Rockefeller were, they were not the only thing powering America. There was a sense of dynamic infecting the entire country, born of the very obvious changes in the material foundations of American society. America was quite obviously joining the ranks of the great powers of the world. You did not even need to be told this. The feeling was just there.

But there was indeed a factual basis for this feeling. By the time just prior to the outbreak of the Great War (World War One) in 1914, America alone was responsible for one-third of the world's total industrial production, more than Britain, France and Germany combined! That figure alone spoke volumes about what America was becoming. After all, there was evidence everywhere you looked.

Yet, as the 1800s came to a close, it was generally considered by those outside America to be the Age of Europe, with European empires stretching around the world, bringing British and Dutch business practices to Asia, French culture to virtually all parts of the world, the division of the African continent into spheres of English, French, Portuguese, German and even Belgian political-cultural control. Islamic culture was in a mood to copy European ways, as was the Japanese culture as well. Europe understood itself to be the world's arbiter in the matter of what was good, what was worthy, and what was not.

It is not that America went unnoticed. But it was viewed by upper class Europeans as a primitive land of cowboys and Indians, and by working class Europeans as a place to escape to in order to find work, any kind of work. None of this presented a picture of sophistication or anything worthy of social attention.

Yet the fact was that America had just reached the status of being an industrial giant, the largest in the world, at about the time that Europe had reached the peak of its glory. And what Europe did not understand was that the next century (the 20th) would be a time of decline for itself. And it would also be a time when America would finally register itself – internationally – as the world's greatest power.

The railroad industry. Railroads were encouraged to reach West across empty plains, deserts and high mountains by governmental financial incentives. But overall and even more importantly, as more railroads spread elsewhere and everywhere across the nation, it was the huge private (non-governmental) financial trusts that were able to amass the capital necessary to finance this massive construction of rail-lines.

These vital rail-lines spanned the nation from ocean to ocean, from Canada to Mexico, carrying a massive amount of goods needed to fuel the huge national economy (food and raw materials headed East, finished goods headed West) built on farming, mining, manufacture. And they carried a restless population always looking for new horizons and new opportunities in this vast nation.

The telegraph and the telephone. Keeping the country linked together

The "Gilded Age" of American Capitalism

was also the telegraph*, which followed the railroad lines so that a flow of vital information kept up with the huge flow of goods and people across the nation. Never before had such a huge territory possessed such instant linkage, so that these massive distances from ocean to ocean found themselves melted down to the level of human horizon that only a couple of generations previously would have reached out only ten or so miles (the distance from the farm to the local town nearby). Distance seemed virtually to have been annihilated!

In 1876 Alexander Graham Bell patented the phone and formed the company of his name, taking phone service in 1877 from three thousand users to 260 thousand by 1893, when his patent ended his exclusive right to operate a phone service. Then thousands of independent companies jumped into the market and soon even poorer Americans could afford the luxury of a phone. By 1920 thirteen million phones were providing service to over a third of the American households, rural as well as urban.

The American iron and steel industry. Of course the railroad steam engines and the vast use of iron rails called forth a massive iron industry, and from that eventually the more expensive but more sophisticated steel industry. Soon steel would be a key part of America's industrial success. From 1870 to just before World War One, America's annual growth rate in steel production averaged 7 percent (thanks in great part to Carnegie), whereas Britain's was a mere 1 percent (Germany's was 6 percent; the rate for France, Belgium and Russia, the other major steel producers, was a little over 4 percent). Overall, American annual steel production climbed from 380 thousand tons in 1875 to sixty million tons in 1920.

The oil industry. We have already seen that the oil industry got off to a huge start when it was discovered how to replace expensive whale oil with kerosene refined from the crude oil seemingly abundant in Pennsylvania. The age of the machine also required oil as a lubricant. Then with the development of the internal combustion engine fired by gasoline or diesel fuel, the demand would grow even stronger for oil's distillate, gasoline.

Gas and electric lighting. Gas lighting (distilled from coal) was already in wide use in England in the early 1800s, lighting streets (making them safer at night), factories (24-hour work was now possible), theaters (much brighter than candles), and even homes (of the wealthy, of course). America quickly caught on to the possibilities, and Baltimore (1817) was

---

*In 1844 Samuel Morse and Alfred Vail built a transmitter that was able to send by wire from Washington to Baltimore a message written in Morse's own code.

quick to adopt the use of gas for lighting. By the mid-1800s gas lighting (and the lamp-lighter who moved from lamp to lamp to light them at night) was a regular feature of America's major cities.

But gas had one major disadvantage. It was dangerous. Theaters burned down when something went wrong with the gas distribution or lamp system. Homes could also suffer the same catastrophe. This then led by the 1870s to electric lighting in theaters, but also in city streets and businesses, using the electric arc system that produced a very bright light (used also in coastal searchlights). Helping to develop this technology into a huge business venture was the amazingly versatile inventor, Thomas Edison (he held over 1,000 patents).

Thomas Alva Edison. Edison grew up in Michigan selling newspapers and candy on trains, but also conducting chemical experiments aboard, which eventually got him in trouble. He turned to printing his own paper, the beginning of his very successful business career. He became a telegraph operator and then news wire operator for the Associated Press. Meanwhile he engaged himself on the side in experimenting with electricity, batteries, and transmission lines. Moving as an impoverished young man to a friend's house in New Jersey, he there developed the stock ticker and then patented (his first) at age twenty-two the electronic vote counter.

Although being hard of hearing, he went on to develop the first phonograph (1877, age thirty) on tin foil wrapped around a cylinder, being invited to Washington to demonstrate his invention before U.S. President Hayes and the Congress. He was now a celebrity inventor!

He moved on to develop his own research lab (which eventually expanded to two city blocks), financed initially from a sophisticated telegraph bought from him by Western Union. Here, with the help of hired assistants, he went about the business methodically of conducting experiments involving a wide array of instruments and machines, and ultimately the incandescent light bulb. He began experimentation on such a light in 1878, the next year ran a successful test on a low voltage (thus inexpensive) carbon-filament light that lasted for over thirteen hours. With some more improvements, he was able to patent the year after that (1880) a very durable light using a bamboo filament that could burn for over 1,200 hours.

He was tireless in his pursuit of invention, commenting at one point: "I have not failed, I've just found 10,000 ways that won't work"!

He had an excellent eye for the business aspect of his inventions. While still conducting his lighting experiments, in order to manufacture and market his lights he set up the Edison Electric Light Company in New York City in 1878, including J.P. Morgan and some of the Vanderbilts as

The "Gilded Age" of American Capitalism 351

investors. From this venture he then went on (1880) to form the electricity utility, Edison Illuminating Company, to distribute electricity to New York City using a 110-volt generating system – establishing that as the American standard (a 220-volt system is used in Europe).

Then he ran into trouble with his direct current (DC) system when George Westinghouse began to compete with an alternating current (AC) system that distributed electric power much more widely and cheaply than Edison's DC system. A corporate battle thus erupted between the two men, one that Edison was not destined to win. By 1890 he was forced out of his own company by J.P. Morgan, and the company merged with an AC company, to become General Electric (a huge AC company which then controlled almost three quarters of the electrical business, Westinghouse being the largest holder of the other quarter of the business).

Edison went on to develop motion pictures, his first invention in 1891 being a kinetoscope, or peep-hole viewer. Then in 1896 he invented a movie projector able to cast a film image on a screen in front of a full audience. He even invented a recording machine able to synchronize the sound with the film. His movie projector proved to be a grand success, his film studio making almost 1200 short films, and prospering Edison greatly.

He was active in other fields as well, the rubber industry, mining, x-ray (which he learned the hard way was very dangerous because of its radiation). And besides his activity in New Jersey he had a house built in Fort Meyers, Florida, next door to a man who had once worked for his lighting company – and whom he took a liking to and encouraged his own development: Henry Ford. The two would remain close friends all the way until Edison's death in 1931.

✳ ✳ ✳

NATIONAL POLITICS DURING THE LATE 1800s[79]

Presidential and congressional politics were fairly tame during the late 1800s. With the issue of Reconstruction simply fading away and with the government-financed railroad to the Pacific completed, the federal government seemed to be called on to play only a secondary role in the further development of American society. America seemed to run mostly on the basis of its own industrial-economic dynamics, rather than on the deep involvement of the Washington government in the life of the nation, such as was the case during the Civil War and Reconstruction.

Social reform would be a big issue during this time. But the initiative for action came not from the halls of Congress or the White House but from the public itself. Through the publicity of America's newspapers, from books written by social reformers, from Christian pulpits, much energy would be given to the idea of perfecting American society. And it would eventually involve the national government, in the form of legislation designed to firm up a reform that the public was demanding. But in this, the government played not the initiating role but merely the confirming role.

One issue however did occupy much governmental attention: the vast corruption going on within its own ranks. President Hayes had tried to clean up some of the corruption left behind by the Grant administration. But Hayes's effort to do so only weakened his position in the face of the considerable political forces benefitting from the spoils system of awarding political appointments as reward for the political support needed to bring politicians to power. The spoils system was understood simply as how politics was expected to work. To try to change things would merely upset the entire political system.

But such spoils became easy targets for journalists looking for a spectacular story to uncover and report. Consequently, there was considerable pressure coming from such molders of public opinion to do something about the problem.

Hayes tried to answer this call for reform when he took action to remove Chester A. Arthur from the lucrative (in terms of spoils) job of director of the New York customs-house. This brought the wrath of New York Boss Conkling, and the anti-reformist Stalwarts in the U.S. Senate who, with the Democrats, held up confirmation of Hayes's subsequent government appointments. Then the Democrats reversed the publicity spotlight, turning it on the Republican Hayes, bringing up the corrupt nature of the deal Hayes had worked with the Louisiana governor to get himself elected to the presidency. But this merely unified Republican Party support for Hayes, though it hardly appeased the press.

The election of 1880, and Garfield's brief presidency. But when election-time came around again, Hayes could not muster enough support from his Republican Party to get himself re-nominated. There were a large number of contenders, including Grant, who was supported by the Stalwarts for a third term. Finally, after 36 ballots, the Republicans turned to a relatively unknown James A. Garfield, and, to Hayes's great shock, Chester A. Arthur as his vice-presidential running-mate.

Garfield was actually an excellent choice, hard-working, intelligent (once a college president), brave (rose to the rank of brigadier general during the Civil War), and politically experienced (having served in both houses of Congress). Running against him as the Democratic Party nominee was the well-known (but politically inexperienced) former Union General Winfield Scott Hancock. The election was close, except again in the

The "Gilded Age" of American Capitalism

electoral college where Garfield gained 214 votes to Hancock's 155.

Chester Arthur's vice-presidential nomination had been the price paid to get Conkling's New York support. But once in office, Garfield had other ideas about how much he owed Conkling in patronage and worked hard to get truly qualified individuals posted to government jobs. In the end, Conkling overplayed his hand, and New Yorkers turned against Conkling.

But also in the end, it was this patronage question that made Garfield's presidency short-lived. He was in office only a few months when he was shot by an unhappy and mentally unstable office seeker – and Garfield died 2½ months later of the wound doctors were unable to heal (they could not find the bullet).

Chester A. Arthur. Actually, the man who had been dismissed from his job at the New York customs house proved, in inheriting the office of U.S. president, to be one of the country's leading anti-corruption reformers. He personally vetoed bills coming out of Congress (most importantly the Rivers and Harbors Act) that were merely opportunities for more political patronage and financial corruption. He also signed into law the 1883 Pendleton Act which turned an increasing number of civil service appointments over to a Civil Service Commission charged with the responsibility of filling government positions on the basis of proven merit rather than political connections.

Finally gaining the deep respect that few at the outset of his presidency ever would have expected, he nonetheless chose to retire from politics after one term in office rather than run for re-election (he was suffering from poor health).

The 1884 election. The 1884 election was fought largely over the issue of personal integrity, the Republican candidate, James Blaine, suffering from a well-known history of deep involvement in the railroad industry spoils system and the Democrat candidate, Grover Cleveland, on the other hand well-recognized for his incredible integrity – except for the claim raised by Democrats that the unmarried Cleveland (but he would soon marry in the White House) had once fathered a child out of wedlock.

The election was so very close that it came down to the electoral vote of New York, in which the final tally gave Cleveland a little over a thousand more votes than Blaine out of a total of over a million votes cast in New York. Part of what ended this long Republican control of the presidency was when a number of reformist Republicans, the Mugwumps,* cast their votes

---

*From an old Algonquin term meaning "a person of importance," implying that those who bolted from the party were being ridiculously sanctimonious or morally condescending in refusing to support their party's candidate, Blaine.

for the Democrat Cleveland because they viewed Blaine as being simply too corrupt.

Grover Cleveland.[80] During his first term in office (1885-1889) Cleveland faced the usual problem of filling government jobs with personal appointments, a deep change in personnel usually accompanying the election of a new president, especially if from a different party than the previous president. But Cleveland announced that he would not remove office holders because of their political affiliation, though he did intend to reduce the size of a greatly inflated federal bureaucracy (because of the spoils system). But eventually he bent to pressure from fellow Democrats to replace some of the Republican officeholders with Democrats, though he was even then restrained in doing so by comparison to previous presidential administrations.

He also tackled the job of improving the navy, by getting rid of inferior ships built by corrupt contractors. He also had much of the railroad land in the West claimed by the railroads, but undeveloped by them, returned to federal government control. And being a limited-government supporter, he cut back on the government's financial support of veterans and farmers that he felt appeared more like spoils than compassion, and which he was certain would merely set up a form of dependency on continuing government bail-outs.

Gold and silver. Another troubling (and persistent) issue he faced was over this matter of the value of the national currency, the U.S. dollar. The country was caught in deep controversy over the matter of inflation, easy credit, and a cheap dollar – versus a tight money policy. Logically speaking, it would seem that this was a matter for the government's financial experts to handle. But after the Civil War this issue had become a matter of almost religious dimensions, so much had been printed and proclaimed on the subject. It had become a matter of simple faith, especially among America's large farming and industrial working-class sectors, that the road to happiness would be easy credit and inflation: to gain higher wages at the workplace or to be able to pay back a loan later in currency that was cheaper in value than when the loan was first assumed. The best way to do that was simply to have the government print dollars, lots of them. Industrial owners and financiers however were very concerned about rising labor costs and the relative loss of the value of their investments through just such inflation and therefore they wanted dollars to remain relatively scarce and thus of ever-greater value.

For most ordinary Americans, the monetary theories involved in this matter were far too complex to follow, so they used the symbols of silver

The "Gilded Age" of American Capitalism

and gold to represent their respective positions. Gold was scarce, and the tight money people insisted that each dollar printed be backed up in the nation's treasury by an equivalent value of gold, and gold alone. Silver, on the other hand, was considered to be abundant and ever-increasing through the relatively easy possibility of more silver mining, and the easy-money people demanded that instead of gold (or at least in addition to gold) silver be the metallic basis for the nation's dollar supply.

So, silver versus gold became the hot national issue, symbolizing the deeper antagonisms between the industrial workers on the one hand and the business owners on the other, between the much humbler American classes in rural America and the growing numbers of up-East financiers – especially problematic if they happened to be Jewish.

In short, gold and silver became the rallying points in a growing class or social-cultural struggle tearing at the nation. Of course these tensions had complex causes, but how easy it was to sum it all up in the question of gold versus silver! And it all made for great conspiracy theories so appealing to the people who struggled to make sense of the difficult times they faced.

Like Grant before him, Cleveland was a gold man. Cleveland responded by attempting to cut back on the silver coinage which the government was required to mint under the Bland-Allison Act of 1878. This cutback merely put Southerners and Westerners and their representatives in Congress in a deeply angry mood, inspiring Bland, author of the 1878 bill, to try to pass a new bill in 1886 calling for the unlimited minting of silver currency. The bill did not pass, but left a bitter issue unresolved.

The tariff question. Another issue Cleveland was forced to tackle was the U.S. tariff. Cleveland strongly opposed the high tariffs imposed on foreign goods in order to protect the pricing of goods produced in America. The tariff revenues collected on imports by the government were so high (about 47 percent of the value of the product itself) that the government was actually registering an embarrassing surplus in its operating budget. But in trying to reduce those tariffs, Cleveland encountered stiff opposition from congressmen fearing that American industry might be damaged badly if those tariff protections were lowered. Thus he got nowhere on this issue.

Benjamin Harrison wins the election of 1888. Although Cleveland won the popular vote in the election, he lost the electoral vote and thus his bid for a second term. A big part of his defeat occurred because of his position on the tariff issue (he lost most of the northern industrial states). Also the team of his Republican opponent, Benjamin Harrison, had conducted a very aggressive (and somewhat questionable) campaign. Cleveland even lost (narrowly) his home state of New York, because of the opposition organized against him by Tammany Hall. If a mere 600 New York votes had gone to Cleveland instead of Harrison it would have given Cleveland the New York electoral vote (and the presidency), the voting being so close.

Harrison was the grandson of the Harrison who served only briefly as U.S. president before dying from a cold caught during his long inaugural address; grandson Benjamin's speech was half the length, also conducted in the rain, under an umbrella held by outgoing President Cleveland!

Harrison reversed Cleveland's course with respect to the tariff and veteran pensions, but tried to emulate Cleveland in appointing government personnel on the basis of proven merit rather than mere political connections. But his idea of merit tended to favor those of his home state of Indiana and his Presbyterian church affiliation, to the anger of politicians from other parts and religious convictions of the nation. And his generous pension payments to Civil War veterans (regardless of the merit) merely opened the opportunity for graft within the Pension Bureau, and a much-criticized reduction in the federal surplus. And with the passage of the McKinley Tariff, Congress went even further than Harrison wanted to go, increasing the tariff even more, purposefully making some products impossible to import.

In answer to the clamor of farmers and miners, Harrison stood behind an Act sponsored by Senator John Sherman, thus the Sherman Silver Purchase Act of 1890. Government purchase of silver had long been a goal of the farming world, and to this was added the voice of the mining world which was panicking because of the oversupply of silver produced by the metal's easy availability. The price of silver dropped away (making it even more attractive to debtors as currency) putting the silver mining industry in a panic. Silverites wanted full acceptance of silver as currency backing, at a fixed rate (well above the actual market value of the metal). Sherman did not meet the full expectations of the Silverites, but did commit the government to a fixed amount of silver purchase, helping to keep the silver market from collapsing and confirming the government's commitment to silver as currency backing. This was not a good long-term solution to any problem – and would ultimately serve as a major contributor to the Panic of 1893.

On the more positive side of the political ledger during Harrison's presidency was the antitrust legislation sponsored by the same Senator John Sherman (the Sherman Antitrust Act as it has been known subsequently) which Harrison signed into law in 1890. Actually, the motivation behind the law was originally aimed as much at organized labor (labor unions) as it was at the huge financial trusts that controlled a great deal of the American rail, steel and financial industry.

The "Gilded Age" of American Capitalism

Harrison also attempted to extend through the Justice Department protection of the civil rights of Black Americans by prosecuting those violating protective legislation already in place. But this effort was stymied by the unwillingness of White juries to convict these violators. Harrison's civil rights push for Blacks in other areas also failed in the face of opposition which arose in both Congress and the Supreme Court.

But towards the end of his presidential term the economic picture of the nation was worsening (just ahead of the Panic of 1893). Things were not looking good for his re-election. Republicans had already lost seats in the 1890 elections and Harrison was experiencing the loss of support by members of his own party (many still upset over the lack of government appointments by Harrison). Also American producers were awakening to the fact that the McKinley Tariff was hurting themselves badly as consumers. As a consequence, though re-nominated by the Republican Party, Harrison faced the national election without the party support nor the popular enthusiasm needed to retain the presidency.

Harrison found himself facing his old opponent, the Democrat and former President Grover Cleveland, replaying the same issues as four years earlier. But unlike previous elections this one would be clean, and quiet. In the end, the 1892 election would prove to be a sad event for Harrison, not only in losing the election rather decisively but also his wife to tuberculosis just two weeks prior to the election itself.

Cleveland returns to office just in time for the Panic of 1893! A combination of bad economic news that hit at about the same time (early 1893) caused a run on Americas scarce gold supply, leaving the federal treasury nearly out of gold and facing financial default. The Philadelphia and Reading Railroad had become too ambitious and instead found itself in deep debt, so much so that just before Cleveland was sworn into office in March of 1893 the railroad company declared bankruptcy. This was combined with a huge drop in wheat prices, a major international income earner for the nation. Nervous investors, both at home and abroad, holding national and corporate bonds began to demand banks, including the U.S. Treasury, to exchange their bonds for gold. Seeing this trend, others jumped in quickly, including the holders of silver coinage – which was greatly overvalued because of the nation's huge silver production stimulated by the Sherman Silver Purchase Act.

Seeing the Sherman Silver Purchase Act as part of the problem, Cleveland convinced Congress to repeal the Act, ending the requirement of the government to purchase a fixed amount of silver. This in turn caused the price of silver to drop drastically, hurting people who held cash reserves in silver (which included a lot of people!).

But Cleveland's action did not bring the Panic to an end. Businesses and then banks began to fail, one after another as investors backed out of the world of investment, or simply just failed as stock values crashed.* Soon unemployment went from 3 percent in 1892 to nearly 12 percent in 1893, to over 18 percent the following year, and then it hung at around the 14 percent figure for the next three years after that.

Labor unrest rocked the nation. In 1894 Ohio businessman Jacob Coxey led a march of unemployed workers on Washington. Many dropped out along the way and the final demonstration was fairly tame, though it certainly alerted the nation to the growing discontent of the U.S. workforce. More violent was the Pullman Company strike by workers (organized by the Socialist leader Eugene Debs) demanding an end to the policy of low wages and the twelve-hour work day. The strike quickly spread to other railway workers until by mid-1894, 125 thousand of them were on strike, virtually shutting down the U.S. rail network. Since the trains carried the mail, Cleveland went after the strikers for violating federal law, resorting finally to sending troops to various points across the nation to make his point.

Meanwhile, Cleveland's assault on the silver market led the Populists (widely popular among American wheat and cotton farmers) to claim that undercutting silver and trying to rebuild the nation's gold holdings was simply an international conspiracy – predominantly Jewish – designed to destroy the American economy. However, at this point America was bleeding its gold reserves badly, not rebuilding them.

Then the formidable J.P. Morgan proposed to Cleveland that he would join with the Rothschild bankers of Paris to sell the government 3.5 million ounces of gold (about $65 million in value at the time) in exchange for thirty-year bonds. As previously mentioned, at first U.S. President Cleveland turned down the offer but finally in 1895 accepted Morgan's offer. Thus the U.S. Treasury was spared default.

The 1896 elections.[81] Cleveland's efforts to resolve the complexities of the Panic seemed merely to undercut his standing with the agrarian and labor wings of his Democratic Party, which suffered a huge setback in the 1894 Congressional elections. Then when in the summer of 1896 the Democratic Party gathered to nominate a presidential candidate, Cleveland was faced by William Jennings Bryan, of the strongly populist and Silverite wing of the party – a fiery orator who roused the convention with his challenge, "you shall not crucify mankind upon a cross of gold." Bryan was subsequently nominated by the Democratic Party, and Cleveland went into political retirement at Princeton, New Jersey (becoming a trustee of the

---

*Estimates are that 500 banks and 15 thousand businesses failed during the 1893-1898 years of the Panic.

university).

William McKinley brings the 19th century to a close.[82] The victor in that election, the Republican candidate William McKinley, represented the transition from the late 19th century governmental minimalism and the governmental activism initiating the 20th century. He was the last president to have served in the Civil War (starting as a private but advancing to brevet major) and as president was an unapologetic supporter of American imperialism, viewed at that time as a natural part of the international responsibilities thrust on America as a rising power. He had been an Ohio lawyer elected in 1876 as a Republican representative to Congress where he sponsored the McKinley Tariff protecting American industries from overseas competition. He lost his seat in 1890 with the huge Democratic victory of that year, but the next year he was elected Ohio governor and again two years after that (1893). As governor he gained a reputation as a skillful mediator between business and labor, and his very skillful political campaigning for the Republican Party in 1892 and in 1894 brought much party attention to him as a possible future presidential candidate. His close friend Mark Hanna skillfully worked those expectations into a reality at the 1896 convention where he was chosen as the Republican Party candidate to come up against the Democratic Party candidate Bryan. The Democratic Party was deeply divided over the gold-silver issue (as was also the Republican Party – although to a lesser extent) which undercut severely national support for the dynamic speaker Bryan, despite his strong standing among midwestern farmers. Indeed, McKinley barely left his front porch during the campaign and yet was able to gain a substantial victory in the hotly contested November elections that year, largely because Hanna had been as busy as the Democrats in issuing endless publications, focused heavily on the gold-silver issue. Also with McKinley's high tariff and pro-gold stance, he easily drew strong support from the industrial East.

Protective tariffs and the gold standard. As president, McKinley made good on his campaign promises, signing into law in 1897 the Dingley Tariff, offering strong protection of American industry, and in 1900 the Gold Standard Act, establishing gold as the sole standard in the redemption of the dollar, making the dollar very strong, and expensive (the gold standard was dropped in 1933 as one of the first acts of Roosevelt's New Deal).

American imperialism. But it was in the area of foreign affairs that the most notable feature of the McKinley presidency stands out. America had long been taking a protective interest in the events occurring to the South of the country in Latin America. But a rebellion in Cuba by those seeking independence from Spain became a major political issue in America when the uprising turned particularly brutal. In 1898 McKinley led the nation to war against Spain, eventually securing not only Cuban independence (under American protection) but also full American possession of the former Spanish colonies of Puerto Rico, Guam and the Philippines. And on top of that it was during McKinley's presidency that America seized the Republic of Hawaii as a new U.S. territory.

The election of 1900. When the reelection campaign rolled around again in 1900, McKinley again found himself facing Bryan as his opponent. McKinley's vice-presidential running mate ended up being New York's governor, Theodore (Teddy) Roosevelt, put forward by New York's Republican Party boss Thomas Platt, who promoted Roosevelt in order to remove him from New York politics! The vice-presidential position was intended by Platt to shift Roosevelt to a place of little significance.

Although the campaign might have appeared as a replay of the 1896 election, America had changed greatly during the four years of McKinley's first term. The nation was experiencing a "Full Dinner Pail" as the Republicans termed the prosperity that the nation was experiencing. Also American victory in the war with Spain had American pride (and support for their president) running strong. And Bryan's running on the silver platform now had none of the impact that it did in 1896. Also his criticism of American imperialism under McKinley lost him a lot of national support. Otherwise the campaign style did not change much, Bryan on the road delivering endless speeches and McKinley greeting visitors from his porch in Ohio.

And the results were again the same, although McKinley registered a slightly larger majority of the votes than in the previous election. Thus McKinley took office for a second four-year term.

But McKinley was only six months into his second term when he was shot in the stomach twice by a deranged anarchist at a presidential reception at the Pan-American Exposition in Buffalo, New York. A week and a half later he died of his wounds. The insignificant Vice President Roosevelt was thus thrust into the office as the nation's new president.

This would move the pace of political change started under McKinley even further, much further.

✳ ✳ ✳

THE WHEELS OF MATERIAL PROGRESS CONTINUE TO ROLL ON INTO THE EARLY 20TH CENTURY

The automobile industry. In the field of transportation, new ideas were

The "Gilded Age" of American Capitalism

quickly being put to use to revolutionize private or personal transportation, in the form of the "horseless carriage." Steam engines mounted on carriages were attempted as the first automobiles, as in the 1878 200-mile (33-hour) race in Wisconsin between two such vehicles. This steam technology used in automobiles (as in the popular Stanley Steamer*) would continue to develop even into the 1920s. But by that time gasoline-powered internal combustion engines (ICEs) were beginning to rule the road.

No single person was responsible for the invention of the internal combustion engine, but it was a technology developed in a vast number of ways, including even the idea of using of gunpowder to fire the device. Inventors in Europe and America built on the discoveries of each other, finding new improvements to patent.

In the mid-1880s, the German Karl Friedrich Benz and the Englishman Edward Butler almost simultaneously developed something like modern gas engines to power their automobiles,† and the race was on by inventors to build varieties of this new engine.

The competition included a number of American builders. By 1904 the Olds Motor Vehicle Company (founded in 1897 in Lansing and then later moved to Detroit, Michigan) was the leading mass-producer of the American automobile.‡

Then when in 1913 Henry Ford introduced his mass-assembled Model T Ford (you could order it in any color, as long as it was black!) the automobile industry in America grew explosively. And eventually offered at just under $500 per car (approximately $7,000 today), the Model T put ownership of an automobile within the reach of millions of ordinary

---

*The Stanley twins (Francis and Freelan) were early entrants into the automotive industry, with their production of over 200 steam-powered cars, making them the largest producers in the 1898-1899 period. In 1902 they founded the Stanley Motor Carriage Company and produced the famous Stanley Steamer, an amazing vehicle which in 1906 was able to reach 127 miles per hour over a one-mile course at Daytona Beach, Florida. By 1917 their rate of production peaked at 500 cars. But Ford's gasoline-powered internal combustion engine Model T cut drastically into their market and they closed their business in 1924.

†Butler's petroleum four-stroke engine was simpler but earlier. Foolishly, British authorities passed a law restricting the speed of his vehicle (requiring a flag-bearing person to walk in front of the vehicle in order to give a safety warning to others!), and soon other requirements that stalled British development of the automobile. Benz's petroleum-fueled two-stroke engine came with a battery to fire the spark plugs, a carburetor to regulate the oxygen intake, the clutch and gear shift to engage the engine at different road speeds, and a water radiator to cool the engine, the basics of a modern automobile engine.

‡No, Henry Ford did not invent the assembly line. That honor really belonged to the Olds Company. But Ford did perfect it by making it a moving line of assembly.

Americans.

Henry Ford. Ford grew up on a farm in Michigan, but disliked farm life and instead in 1879 at age sixteen took up the work as a machinist apprentice in Detroit. But three years later he returned to his father's farm and there familiarized himself with the Westinghouse portable steam engine, leading him to be hired by Westinghouse to service their machinery. On his off-time he studied bookkeeping at a business college, giving him knowledge of the world of business and finance. In 1891 he went to work for the Edison Illuminating Company, becoming a chief engineer in 1893. At the same time, he began his experimental work on gasoline engines, which in turn led him to produce in 1896 a motor-driven four-wheeled cycle. Encouraged by Edison to develop his work further, he finished a second vehicle in 1898, and with some outside financial backing the next year he left the Edison company and founded the Detroit Automobile Company, which however did not succeed and which he had to shut down in 1901.

Not one to be discouraged easily, he built yet another model soon after and which he raced successfully, leading his financial backers to support him in forming in 1901 yet another manufacturing company, the Henry Ford Company. But he left the company the next year (which became the Cadillac Automobile Company) to build a new eighty horsepower automobile, which Barney Oldfield raced famously to victory that same year. He now partnered up with a Detroit-area coal dealer, and he proceeded to work on developing an inexpensive model which would market well within the rapidly growing world of automobile ownership. But although financing was still tight, he secured some additional backers, and in 1903 formed the Ford Motor Company. He then had Oldfield drive his car around the country, attracting wide interest in the Ford model.

Then in 1908 he introduced the Model T Ford, inexpensive and easy to drive and repair. It was $825 in its 1908 offering, with Ford being able to drop the price every year after that as he streamlined production and established an efficient system of dealerships. The efficiency jumped even more in 1913 when he introduced the moving assembly line in his factory. Also his introduction in 1914 of the unheard-of $5 per day wage rate for his workers had the effect of stabilizing and motivating his work force to double their productivity. That same year he sold over 250,000 of his cars to the public. And by 1918, half the cars on the road were Model Ts.

In 1918 he made a move to buy up the stocks held by other investors, ultimately succeeding in making the Ford family the sole owners of his company.

Also during these years he established manufacturing plants abroad in Europe and by 1929 he had plants operating on all six continents. He believed firmly that bringing the benefits of modern technology to the world would promote peace in the best way possible. Indeed, Ford was an economic idealist, something becoming more prevalent in those days. After the unprecedented disaster of the Great War, the hunger for international peace was immense, and business leaders found it easy to believe that prosperity extended to the people of the world would make the world a happier place. Certainly this was the case for Ford.

During the mid-1920s the Model T found itself falling behind in technology as other manufacturers added new features to their models, and Ford was forced (pressured in part by his son Edsel) to think past the Model T. And thus the Model A was born in 1927, reaching 4 million in sales over the next four years. From that time on, Ford made it a policy to introduce new models annually (a policy which General Motors had just previously put into practice).

Much of the credit of his grand success as a businessman goes to the fact that he was as mindful of his social responsibility as he was of his engineering, financing and production. Not only did he offer high wages to his workers (who themselves could now afford to buy their own Fords), he also introduced profit-sharing to his (qualified) workers and in 1926 the five-day work week. But at first he insisted that his workers live responsibly and offered his profit-sharing to only those who could demonstrate a respectable life-style (he had inspectors constantly looking into his workers activities). Eventually he backed away from his paternalism and simply made his policies a general practice to all his workers, regardless of their private lives.

He was at first adamantly opposed to labor unions and did what he could to keep the United Auto Workers (UAW) union out of his operations. He believed that the union bosses were too easily intoxicated by their own power and merely a disruptive influence on business. He hoped that his fair treatment of his workers would suffice to keep the unions away. For a while he was successful, though not without incidents of violence as the UAW sought eagerly to unionize the Ford Motor Company. Finally facing the possibilities of a sit-down strike in 1941, he yielded and signed his first union contract. Perhaps surprised to discover that this did not bring down his business, he in fact subsequently became one of the most generous with respect to workers' contracts.

He had also in the meantime ventured into the new field of commercial flight, putting into production in 1926 his own commercial plane able to fly (uncomfortably) 12 passengers. Almost 200 of the planes were sold, before he closed the business in 1933 due to the Great Depression. Then with America's entrance into World War Two in 1941 he turned to the business of producing the B-24 bomber at his Willow Run plant, at the height of production turning out a B-24 every 58 minutes, for a total of 9,000 planes or half the total built in America during the war.

But by the time the war was over he was losing his mental powers, his son Edsel had died in 1943 and the company was facing bankruptcy, when his grandson, Henry Ford II, took over the business and brought it back to life.

In 1947 Ford died at age 83.

The development of the airplane. One might easily suppose that the airplane would have come along much later than the automobile as a technological development since getting things off the ground would seem to be a much more difficult task than simply getting them to roll along the ground. But that was not the case. Airplane development seemed to parallel closely the development of the automobile.

Balloons offered the first possibilities of human flight (back even in the late 1700s), and by the late 1800s airships or dirigibles with cabins slung below them and with electric-powered rotary blades to drive them looked as if they would be the route that air-flight would take. But they were soon challenged by heavier-than-air flying machines, the modern airplane.

Of course there were a number of inventors across the Western world busily engaged in trying to create just such a flying machine, but the Wright brothers were clearly the real pioneers in the field.* The brothers had carefully studied the dynamics of glider flight (over 200 models tested in a wind-tunnel that they created) and were able to conduct a number of very successful glider flights in 1902. They also built a small engine to power their plane. Finally on December 17, 1903 they were ready to test their new airplane. The first flight lasted only 12 seconds and flew a distance of only 120 feet (captured in the famous picture of this very first event). Later that day they reached a flight of 59 seconds covering 852 feet. Their success (only they, however, could have handled that very unstable first plane!) led them to develop further their design and in 1904 and 1905 they introduced newer and stronger models (the 1905 model flying 24 miles in just over 39 minutes).

By 1906 inventors in other countries were taking an interest in the idea of airplane flight and a huge number of different models began to appear, especially in France where the interest seemed strongest (their flights at first paralleled only the Wrights' 1903 achievement rather than the Wrights' much more sophisticated 1906 success). In 1908 the Wright brothers traveled to France to demonstrate (to the amazement

---

*There is still controversy about the claim of the German-turned-American Whitehead (Weiskopf) of having in 1901 successfully conducted manned flight in Connecticut, 2½ years before the Wright brothers.

of the spectators) the possibilities of the airplane, and to encourage its development in Europe. In this they succeeded grandly, leading a British newspaper to offer a £1,000 reward, taken up by a French flyer who in 1909 was the first to fly across the English Channel.

The military use of the airplane became immediately obvious and was used by the Italians in 1911 to bomb Muslim troops in Italy's seizure of Libya from the Turkish Ottoman Sultan, in order to make it part of the new Italian Empire. Likewise, the Bulgarians used the airplane to survey and bomb Ottoman positions in the First Balkan War of 1912-1913. And of course it was used extensively in the Great War (World War One) that broke out the next year (1914) in Northern Europe.

CHAPTER TWELVE

AMERICAN PROGRESSIVISM

* * *

THE EMERGENCE OF AMERICAN PROGRESSIVISM[83]

The social challenges prompting the Progressivist Movement. It was certainly very easy to be excited about the times. The changes in life-style had been so amazing, so extensive, and in such a short stretch of time. In only a couple of generations Americans had gone from horseback to automobiles, and even to flight. Electricity lit up not only cities but also homes, news of the larger world arrived almost instantly to an increasingly attentive population, personal phones put people in direct communication with each other across even the miles, and wealth reached down into even the middle classes, who knew that they were living better than kings and queens had lived only a few centuries earlier. All this change was very heady stuff.

But there clearly was a downside to all this change. The American population was climbing rapidly. In the forty-year period between 1870 to 1910 the population went from 38.5 million to 92.3 million, growing by about 25 percent each decade (28 percent by 1880, another 27.6 percent by 1890, and another 21 percent for each of 1900 and 1910). This time period also marked a huge shift in the nation's demography, 10 to 11 million (figures are not exact) Americans moving from farms to Americas fast-rising cities, where they were joined by another 25 million immigrants streaming in from Europe.

Not everyone headed to the cities was going to find the streets paved with gold. On the contrary, urban slums – with all the accompanying problems of filth, disease, violence and just simply human degradation – greeted the vast majority of these urban pilgrims.

Also with over fifty percent of the nation's total wealth owned by one percent of the population and nearly a half of the population owning only one percent of the nation's total wealth, it was a certainty that there was going to be a huge outcry about this outrageously huge social disparity in the land where supposedly "all men are created equal." This in itself gave sufficient cause to those with a crusading heart to take up the cause of social justice. Thus developed a rather spontaneous and very diverse social and political movement which historians have termed Progressivism.

Progressivism was not the program of any particular social group or even political party. The state itself played a rather minimal role in its many initiatives, although the state did tend to follow up on social initiatives in many cases with legislation solidifying the gains of the Progressivists. The church also played a minimal role, although much of what moved Progressivism was the Christian conscience.

By and large Progressivism was the instinct of crusading individuals – and groups which these individuals were able to gather around their particular social cause. These individuals were often writers and journalists, they were often educated and socially comfortable individuals with a crusading zeal for social reform, and occasionally they were political leaders.

The basic features of the Progressivist Movement. The Progressivist Movement actually took on many dimensions, sometimes some of them seemingly a bit contradictory. A good example of the contradiction rested in the desire to give the state wider powers to regulate the economy to make it more fair or just to all, yet at the same time the desire to place the state under greater democratic control because of the widespread corruption that seemed to accompany the widening powers of government at that time, especially at the local and state level (though by no means was the national government itself exempt from such corruption).

It was no secret how party bosses ran huge political machines that controlled local politics, especially in the growing industrial cities. Thus Progressivism sought to make local government more democratic and more efficient (also often contradictory concepts!) by introducing the ideas of popular recall of corrupt public officials, the party primary which allowed the voter rather than the city machine to choose the local candidates for public office, even the idea of hiring a professional city manager who would supposedly be neutral in the realm of party politics.

Progressivism was also very focused on finding remedies to the corruption that also infected urban and industrial society in general. Progressivism attempted to place restrictions on child and women's labor in the factories and mines. Indeed, Progressivism demanded better working conditions for all laborers. Progressivism was dedicated to the goal of improved public education, especially for the poor living in urban slums. It fought for quality control of foods, especially meats, sold to the public. It pursued a fight for greater protection of the natural environment against the wholesale plunder of the nation's natural resources. And it included the ideas of turning prisons into reformatories that would reform rather than just merely punish offenders of the law.

Christian Progressivism. Many of these Progressivists were profoundly inspired by long-standing Christian ideals. To them this sad social development pointed to a huge loss of the original Puritan vision that had set the country out on a mission to be a city on a hill, to be a light to the nations, showing the world how the sovereignty of the people was supposed to work.

For many Christians, especially some of the Evangelicals within the Christian community, Christ called them to go out into the broken world, teaching, preaching and healing – in order to bring up the quality of the people's lives, in preparation for Christ's second coming – the Millennium – which they believed was imminent.* To such Evangelicals, Christian action was needed now, to avoid the wrath of a God who had every right to expect his people to better the world they had been given. With Christ's second coming, judgment of all people was going to be swift and sure.

Secular or Humanist Progressivism. Others reacting to the social problems around them were more inspired by the rising Humanism that had captured numerous American hearts. These Humanists were generally intellectuals – writers, journalists and educators for instance – who cared somewhat abstractly for the category of those less fortunate than themselves. Their caring generally took on the form of calling for social justice through governmental action or legal reform.

Such Humanism was very Rousseauian, in that the Humanists had little doubt about the basic goodness of man – if given the right opportunity to demonstrate that goodness. All that stood in the way of bringing this human virtue to light was a corrupt society built on corrupt laws and consequently corrupt social practices. According to the Humanists, society needed only to reform the social laws that enabled and encouraged these corrupt practices, and the utopian bliss which they were positive awaited mankind would dramatically appear. God's justice played no role in this matter. It was all simply a case of employing human logic – or social

---

*Actually, there was something of a big divide within this community of Christian Evangelicals or Millennialists. Progressive Christians tended to be Postmillennialist in believing that the thousand-year reign of Christ (the Millennium) would come only after a fully successful conversion of the world had taken place, a matter requiring ever-greater effort of Christians to bring Christianity and its civilizing qualities to the world. The Premillennialists on the other hand believed that only a time of great tribulation (not human progress) would announce the arrival of the Millennium – requiring of the faithful spiritual vigilance, rather than the progressive works of the Postmillennialists.

science, as this logic came to be termed.

Economic justice for the American worker. The first and foremost problem that Progressivism felt needed to be tackled was that of relieving the suffering of those whose lives had been thrown into turmoil by all the industrial change.

This group of industrial victims included the small farmers who found themselves unable to compete with the larger industrial farms arising in their midst, industrial farms that were able to secure special rates from the grain elevator companies that stored and prepared the farmers' grain for shipment, and special shipping rates from the single (thus monopoly) railroad company that connected their region to the customers back East. To the smaller American farmers, who were having a hard time earning a living from their small plots of land, this special treatment extended to the wealthy industrial farms was outrageously unfair. Something needed to be done to curb the power of the high and mighty, and restore power to the small American farmer, the mainstay of American Middle-Class society.

This category included also the industrial workers who worked long hours in the newly-rising enterprises which hired their services or labor. Skilled workers were accustomed to being respected for their special industrial talents, and were unhappy that their services were so poorly compensated in comparison to enormous earnings of the financial managers or owners of the enterprises that contracted their services. In another way, they were incensed when they were gradually reduced in status simply to that of laborer, hardly different from the masses of unskilled labor who poured into the industrial cities looking for work of any kind.

This latter group of unskilled laborers was actually itself divided into a number of different groups. One was that of the Anglo-White laborers, usually former farmers or their sons unable to secure or hold their lands in the increasingly competitive world of American farming, Whites that were driven to the cities to find any work that they could. Another was that of the Southern Blacks who came North looking for work, no different from the White farmers turned laborers – except for the sadly major distinction of skin color. And then there were the European immigrants (and on the West Coast the numerous Chinese) who came to the country with virtually nothing except the hope that they would finally find success in the America whose streets (they were told) were paved with gold.

This labor mix was characterized by powerlessness in the face of the wealth (and consequent political power) of the industrial elite, or "robber barons" as both the laborers and their spokesmen among the Progressivists termed them. It was also characterized by confusion and disunity within the ranks of the workers because of these many social divisions that set one labor group off against the others. United, they could have constituted a major political force. And indeed many Progressivist reformers attempted to do just that, unite the American labor force into a single labor movement. But in the highly diverse America, that would prove to be an almost impossible task.

The Knights of Labor. An example of the difficulty organized labor faced was the Knights of Labor, founded in 1869. Because of its strong advocacy of the eight-hour working day, it had reached a membership total of almost 30,000 members by 1880. Four years after that its membership figure reached 100,000 and then two years after that (1886) nearly 800,000 members, making it by far the largest labor organization in America at that point.

But the organization itself was weak. And although the Knights of Labor was politically republican in character, it became identified in the press and by its capitalist adversaries as a dangerously militant organization in the manner of the anarchists, who were very influential among many of the immigrant German and East European workers. Indeed, this unfair comparison crippled the organization after the disastrous Haymarket Square Riot of 1886*, with most of its members soon abandoning the organization. By the time of the economic Panic of 1893 it had become only a very small operation.

The American Federation of Labor (AFL). The organizing of American labor was subsequently taken up by the American Federation of Labor (AFL) founded in the pivotal year of 1886 by Samuel Gompers as a result of a dispute with the Knights of Labor over competing labor contracts. It united a number of guilds or unions of skilled workers and craftsmen (as opposed to common day laborers) – beginning with the cigar makers' unions. Then as the Knights of Labor faded away during the later 1880s, the AFL held steady, even picking up new members.

Overall, it supported the idea of capitalism, simply attempting to put skilled workers in a better position to take advantage of the huge profits being accumulated in the industrial revolution sweeping America.

---

*At a gathering of workers at Haymarket Square in Chicago who were demanding the eight-hour working day, an unknown person threw a bomb at police who were in the process of dispersing the crowd, killing seven officers and a number of civilians. On the basis of scanty or non-existent evidence seven (mostly German) anarchists were sentenced to death by hanging (a number of them had not even been present at the gathering) for their contribution to the tragedy. Only four were actually hanged, as one committed suicide in jail and the two others had their death sentences commuted to life imprisonment, but were pardoned by the Illinois governor in 1893 who (as did many) considered the trial a total travesty of justice.

American Progressivism

Its political caution – and especially its patriotism (most notably during World War One) and its willingness to oppose more radical (mostly immigrant) labor organizations such as the "Wobblies" (the Industrial Workers of the World) and the more radical Socialist Party – helped bring the U.S. government alongside the AFL in support of its labor program. By 1920, the AFL had grown to nearly four million members.

The American women's or feminist movement. American Progressivism also included a very strong women's – even feminist – movement. For a number of American women, the prohibition of the sale of alcohol easily brought them to political action. Far too many husbands were returning home from work on payday completely empty-handed, having stopped at the local bar along the way to find some liquid joy in their hardscrabble lives. All too often this visit to the bar was as far as their paycheck got them, leaving their wives to wonder how they were to pay for the food and the other requirements of their meager lives. Something needed to be done to solve this problem, to halt the scourge of rampant alcoholism.

In this, women particularly put the moral muscle of Christianity behind their efforts – eventually generating the idea that any alcohol-drinking at all was un-Christian (a rather recent Christian virtue – although drunkenness had always come under strong Christian condemnation). And thus the Women's Christian Temperance Union (WCTU) was born.

Right along with this anti-alcohol movement went the issue of women's suffrage (voting rights). In most states, women were not given the right to vote. Voting was considered an expression of the will of the entire family – men, women and children – which men, as head of the family, were supposed to represent in voting. But the women claimed that men were not handling that responsibility well and therefore the vote should be opened up to women, who as mothers and wives would bring a more moral tone to politics.

The more radical among the feminists of those days however pushed for voting rights simply as a matter of social justice, a right that should flow from the basic natural equality of men and women, regardless of whether or not it better-served American family life.

JANE ADDAMS[84]

There were a huge number of very capable individuals who dedicated themselves to one or another area of the Progressivist cause in America. But a few stood out spectacularly, particularly Jane Addams. At one time or another she was involved with almost every aspect of the Progressivist Movement.

Her mother died when she was only two, and she grew up deeply influenced by her father, who was a successful Illinois businessman, co-founder of the Illinois Republican Party, and friend of Lincoln. She wanted to be a doctor helping the poor, but her father paid for her to attend a women's seminary instead. When he died leaving her $50 thousand (roughly equivalent to $1.23 million in today's dollars) she and her family moved to Philadelphia where she and her siblings could all attend medical school. But she was forced back to Illinois because of severe back problems she was experiencing. An operation later and a two-year tour of Europe to recover (emotionally as well as physically) taught her that she did not need to be a doctor to help the poor. While in London she became inspired by Toynbee Hall where British from various social classes lived together in some degree of harmony. This would become the model for her when she used her money in 1889 to purchase a run-down mansion, the Hull House, in Chicago.

Other women of wealth joined her in the enterprise of bringing together women of different social and national backgrounds in an effort to demonstrate the possibilities of a life that reached closer to utopian proportions. Then with additional funding she added the feature of both an art gallery (with art classes offered) and a library to the Hull House, to bring working-class children into contact with the higher cultural realm. Little by little the Hull House expanded itself in the Chicago multi-ethnic neighborhood, until it included thirteen separate buildings and a playground.

The Hull House thus became a showcase for experiments in social improvement, so vital to the Progressivist Movement. And she herself entered the world of Progressivist politics in helping to start up the Progressive Party that sponsored Theodore Roosevelt in his third-party run for the U.S. presidency in 1912. From her work with neighborhood families she expanded into the world of public health, public morals (fighting rampant prostitution), and the increasing involvement of women as moral crusaders cleaning up Chicago society and politics, especially when that touched on women and children.

Her intimate relationships were all with women, something that today would possibly qualify her as a lesbian, though the practice then among unmarried women was so common that no label was applied at the time to her lifestyle. In fact she saw herself as a strong Christian (a Presbyterian) who also attended a Unitarian Church and had an excellent working relationship with the local Jewish community.

She also was an anti-imperialist and a pacifist, and when World War One broke out in 1914 her activities led to her being elected chairman of the Women's Peace Party. She subsequently joined the leadership of the International Congress of Women which gathered at The Hague (in neutral Netherlands) in April of 1915 to search for a way to end the war. Her pacifism in turn brought her much harsh criticism when in 1917 the U.S. joined the war effort – and the spirit of militant nationalism swept the nation.

After the war she was elected chairman of several international women's groups focused on securing world peace (by this time with the approval and support of U.S. President Coolidge). In 1931 she was voted the Nobel Peace Prize by the awards committee virtually unanimously, capping a long career which exemplified in so many ways the very heart of Progressivism. Four years later she died, deeply mourned by the American nation which saw in her only goodness and inspiring hope (much needed at a time when America was going through the Great Depression).

✶ ✶ ✶

WILLIAM JENNINGS BRYAN[85]

Another key Progressive was a man who ran as Democratic Party nominee for the U.S. Presidency three times, though he was not successful in any of those three attempts. William Jennings Bryan was something of a common man who identified himself with rural and small-town America, in opposition to the wealthier and more sophisticated segments of society whose arrogance and greed he claimed were destroying the democratic foundations of America. To the latter group, however, Bryan was simply a living-breathing symbol of the grievous ignorance of an American society that needed deep reforming. His unflinching Christian faith and his confidence in the long political-social Christian legacy (which he often romanticized) that touched the heart of the common man, were exactly the things that stirred rather fully the wrath of the intellectual Progressivists of the newly rising Secular Humanist variety. Yet Bryan, in his own way, was very much a Progressivist, just operating from a different vantage point than many of the other segments of the Progressivist Movement.

Bryan was born in rural southern Illinois in 1860 to a Baptist mother and a Methodist father, and went his own way religiously because of a Christian revival when he was fourteen that led him to be baptized as a Presbyterian – the most important day in his life he would say. His father was an avid Jackson Democrat and an Illinois circuit judge and the family lived comfortably and respectably. In order to prepare him for college he was sent in 1874 to attend Whipple Academy in Jacksonville, connected to the Presbyterian Illinois College, which he also attended after completing high school at the Academy. Following graduation in 1881 (he was the class valedictorian) he attended Union Law College in Chicago (the future Northwestern University School of Law). After graduating, he taught high school and married Mary Elizabeth Baird (1884). The two then settled in Jacksonville, where both William and his wife Mary practiced law.

Greater opportunity beckoned from fast-growing Lincoln, Nebraska, and the Bryans moved there in 1887, where he soon became involved in local politics. He ran for U.S. Congress in 1890 and was carried into office with the landslide victory of the Democratic Party that year. He was reelected two years later but then in 1894 he lost a bid to become one of Nebraska's two U.S. senators when the Republicans took control of the state legislature (at that time senators were still selected by the state legislatures).

But he had a crusader's heart, had limitless energy, and a commanding voice that put him on the lecture circuit, where he could spread his message of social reform. A number of issues found their way to the heart of his lectures, particularly the gold-silver crisis (the Panic of 1893) that had the nation deeply divided at that time. As noted previously, when President Cleveland repealed the Sherman Silver Purchase Act in 1893, it caused the value of silver to drop away drastically. While this saved the day for America's major industrialists and financiers, it left the American farmers and miners in a terrible situation. Banks wanted payment in stable currency (gold), something that the farmers did not have, especially at a time of greatly reduced food prices caused by the massive production of farm products. Also at the same time, Western miners found themselves simply out of work.

The 1896 presidential election. It was Bryan who took up the cause of the farmer and miner, delivering powerful speeches on the lecture circuit attacking the great gain of the rich with their gold strategy.* Then in 1896 he mesmerized the Democratic National Convention when he delivered his "cross of gold" speech. The speech changed the entire course of the convention, and the young Bryan (just thirty-six years old) was chosen by the Democratic Party (Cleveland was out) to be its presidential nominee for the 1896 national election, running against the Republican McKinley.

Bryan then took to the road, to deliver more of his speeches (500), fully expecting this to turn the election in his favor. Of course this election was not just about gold, but also about the huge industrial and financial trusts that controlled the nation's economy, the railroads that practiced monopolistic pricing that crushed the farmer, and the politicians in the

---

*Bryan had actually started doing so on the floor of Congress in 1893 when he was a Representative, opposed to the repeal of the Sherman Act.

American Progressivism 375

pockets of the big-money boys.

But the economy was settling down at this point and Bryan did not have the impact that he was hoping for. As we have already seen, he lost to McKinley, gaining 46.7 percent of the popular vote to McKinley's 51 percent, carrying twenty-two of the less populous southern and western states compared to McKinley's victory in twenty-three of the vastly more populous states of the Northeast and Midwest and the Pacific coast, and thus taking a beating in the electoral college (271 to only 176). Still, it was a respectable result, so much so that he would become the party's candidate again in 1900.

The question of imperialism and the Spanish-American War. In the meantime, Bryan (like the rest of the nation) got caught up in the growing problems with Spain over its cruel actions taken to suppress rebellion in the remaining Spanish colonies in the Caribbean. Bryan was an ardent anti-imperialist. He considered imperialism to be nothing more than crude bullying, justified by Darwinist rhetoric (which he also detested) about the necessity of the strong dominating the weak.

Yet he was himself caught up in the rising democratic Idealism that made democracy the answer to the world's problems. Thus he put aside his anti-imperialism and took up the American nationalist cause of intervening in the Cuban and Puerto Rican rebellion to help those two lands acquire their own democracies – drawing criticism from his anti-imperialist supporters who saw such American involvement as merely another form of imperialism. It also brought sneers from his detractors for his being so confused about exactly where he stood on matters.

But then when a piece of follow-up legislation to the Treaty of Paris calling for independence for the Philippines failed to pass in Congress, Bryan began once again to take up his anti-imperialism stance.

The 1900 presidential election. Indeed, anti-imperialism was his main theme at the 1900 Democratic National Convention, where Bryan was again chosen to be the party's presidential candidate. Then once again he became a whirlwind of activity, delivering an endless round of speeches denouncing American imperialism – and pressing still for a return to silver currency. Yet at this point the nation had largely moved on past both issues. America was enjoying the Full Dinner Pail, which McKinley reminded Americans that they had come to experience under the last four years of his presidency. Consequently, Bryan's results in his re-match in 1900 with McKinley were an even greater disappointment to Bryan and his supporters than they had been in 1896.

At this point Bryan devoted himself to the lecture circuit, especially at the rural Chautauquas that economically-comfortable people attended, particularly in the summers to escape the stifling heat of the American cities. Here whole families encountered a full program of entertainment, sports and cultural exposure. Clearly, Bryan was the most popular of the speakers with his coverage of subjects running from social reform to the Christian faith, especially the latter. One of his favorite subjects was Darwinism and the threat it posed to American morality. He was less interested in the debate raised by Darwinists over of the Bible as scientific Truth (the inerrancy issue) than he was in the way the growing Darwinist mindset of modern culture was undermining Christian morality.

He even went abroad with his lectures (and just touring) from 1904 to 1906, in a sense taking a vacation from American political issues.

The 1908 presidential election. But when the 1908 election rolled around (and Roosevelt was stepping down from the Presidency in favor of his friend Taft) the Democratic Party again looked to Bryan to run for the presidency. Bryan had a comprehensive Progressivist program to run on, including a constitutional amendment calling for federal government income and inheritance taxes, full disclosure of corporate contributions to political campaigns, the program of the initiative and referendum (citizens having the right to initiate legislation of their own), and more trust-busting. But Bryan just could not excite the electorate with his program, aimed at an opponent (Taft) who himself was a recognized trust-buster, as well as inheritor of the Roosevelt mantle. This, Bryan's third and last attempt at gaining the presidency, brought him even more disappointing results than the two times earlier. It would be his last run for the presidency.

Bryan's appointment as secretary of state in 1913. Once again Bryan returned to the lecture circuit. But when the 1912 election came around, he chose to merely support a Democratic Party candidate rather than be that candidate himself. The Convention itself was split among a number of contenders, and finally Bryan threw his weight to New Jersey Governor (and former Princeton University professor and president) Woodrow Wilson, who, with Bryan's support, finally on the 46th ballot was chosen as the party's candidate.

Wilson, subsequently elected to the presidency on a mere plurality of votes – because of a split among the Republicans between followers of Taft and followers of Roosevelt – in turn appointed Bryan to the position of secretary of state. Although this was considered the most important of the cabinet positions, actually under Wilson, Bryan would be relegated to a very secondary role in the conduct of the secretary's usual business in foreign affairs – because the idealistic Wilson wanted to conduct American foreign policy himself. But the rest of Bryan's story will be found here in the chapters that follow.

✳ ✳ ✳

THEODORE (TEDDY) ROOSEVELT[86]

Another major figure in the Progressivist Movement was none other than President Teddy Roosevelt. He too was an individual involved in almost every aspect of Progressivism, including its more militant varieties. Personally, he was himself a militant when it came to a cause, any cause. Like the robber barons – with whom he often battled (when not befriending them) – he was the picture of Darwinian fortitude, pressing, pressing, pressing forward whatever agenda he happened to be involved with.

From asthmatic to sportsman. From his birth in 1858, he grew up in an environment of social privilege, a New York City Roosevelt of a long line of successful Roosevelt businessmen. But young Teddy suffered badly from asthma, which, though nearly killing him, did not keep him from being a most energetic and inquisitive youth. He had a keen interest in biology, plus history, French, German and geography (he was home-schooled but also highly self-taught), resulting greatly from the trips he took abroad with his family to Europe and the Middle East. Also, climbing the Alps with his father, he learned the importance of exercise in fighting the asthma and in rebuilding his body. He eventually even took up boxing.

Studies, and his first steps into politics. He went on to study the standard curricula at Harvard, excelling in science and philosophy with his nearly photographic memory. The study of military history also focused much of his attention, as did also boxing and rowing. He was inducted into the prestigious Porcellian Club, was editor of the *Harvard Advocate*, and graduated Phi Beta Kappa and magna cum laude in 1880. He then went off to Columbia Law school, but found his heart to lie not in law books but in the practical field of politics, becoming active in the local Republican organization. At about the same time (1882) he published research he had undertaken at Harvard on the War of 1812, still even today one of the best studies of that war in print. In the same year he became a member of the New York State Assembly.

Tragedy. But tragedy as well as stunning accomplishments followed his life. His father had died in 1878 during his second year at Harvard, leaving him deeply stunned. He married four years later in 1882 at age twenty-two, but his wife died two years later in delivering their first child, Alice. Furthermore, his mother had just died in the same house ... only eleven hours earlier.

Anti-corruption Progressivist. In deep shock, Roosevelt buried himself in his work, investigating governmental corruption in New York City and taking aim at individuals such as the scheming financier Jay Gould and at corruption both in the Albany capital itself and on the judicial bench. And as chairman of the Committee on Affairs of Cities he was a prolific drafter of reformist legislation. He also in 1882 joined the New York National Guard as a second lieutenant, moving up the ranks to captain, gaining military experience that he would put to use later when the Spanish-American War broke out in 1898.

In 1884 he reached higher in Republican politics, gaining chairmanship of the New York Republican Party delegates sent to the national convention that year, over the opposition of Blaine and Arthur. But in the end, he reluctantly agreed to support the Party's ultimate nominee, Blaine. And in the process, he was called upon to deliver a speech before ten thousand delegates, bringing him into the national political spotlight. Blaine went on to lose the election to Cleveland, and Roosevelt retired to his ranch out West in the Dakotas along the Little Missouri River. Shortly after that (1886), as the "Dakota Cowboy," he ran an unsuccessful race for New York City mayor. But that December he finally found success in marrying in London his second wife, Edith, who would deliver five strong children!

In 1888 he returned to public life campaigning for Benjamin Harrison, who in becoming president appointed him to the Civil Service Commission, on which Roosevelt served for the next seven years in Washington, D.C. The purpose of the Commission was to counter the spoils system, and Roosevelt proved himself to be a strong enforcer of that policy. This again brought him much favorable public attention.

New York City police commissioner. In 1894 he declined the offer of New York Republicans to run again for the office of mayor, and then soon regretted the decision. He retreated to the Dakotas again to think things through, and then quickly accepted the offer to become a member of New York City's Board of Police Commissioners. Here his strong will to clean up urban political corruption virtually remade the New York City police, Roosevelt even going out on his own to inspect officers on the beat, but also noting along the way the deplorable state of the city's poor. Eventually his rigor drew the wrath of New York's Tammany Hall and its Boss Platt, Platt finally taking action to have the Board of Police Commissioners eliminated.

American Progressivism

Assistant secretary of the navy. Then in 1897, Roosevelt's friend Henry Cabot Lodge promoted the appointment of Roosevelt to McKinley's cabinet as assistant secretary of the navy. It was a very logical appointment, given Roosevelt's proven knowledge and interest in all matters concerning the Navy.* With a sickly secretary of the navy as his boss, Roosevelt soon found himself conducting most of the affairs of the navy secretary, including advising McKinley on naval matters, particularly as war with Spain loomed into view. He even took over the preparations for naval war after the blowing up of the battleship *Maine* in the harbor of Havana, Cuba.

The Spanish-American War and Roosevelt's "Rough Riders." War against Spain was declared on April 25th (1898) and Roosevelt then resigned his cabinet position soon thereafter to take himself to Texas to form, finance, and train his own cavalry regiment, popularly known as the "Rough Riders." A month later this strange array of adventure-seeking young men (ranging from Ivy Leaguers and Eastern gentlemen, to miners, hunters, cowboys and even Indians) shipped off to Cuba. After some minor experience in battle, in June they were directed to act in support of a massive but dangerous charge of American troops uphill across open ground defended by Spanish regulars armed with the latest weaponry, including machine guns and repeating rifles. However, the American machine guns (Gatling guns) poured such fire onto the Spanish during the charge that the Spanish failed to offer effective resistance. Of course the attack involved thousands of other American troops besides the Rough Riders (the Rough Riders actually charged nearby Kettle Hill while the rest of the Americans charged San Juan Hill). This attacking party included numerous Buffalo Soldiers (American Blacks). The latter did much of the heavy fighting, but (of course) received little if any recognition for their effort.† Actually, the action had cost the Americans dearly: 200 killed and 1,000 wounded, about five Americans for every Spanish soldier suffering the same fate. But the Spanish were put on the run and Santiago was captured two weeks later, virtually ending the war.

Colonel Roosevelt was careful to narrate to an adoring press the adventures of his Rough Riders in a way that complemented the other troops, but clearly left the focus on his own troops. As a result, he came out of the action a national hero. He would also remember this event as

---

*Roosevelt, along with many others, including European heads of state, had been strongly influenced by the 1890 publication by Alfred Thayer Mahan, *The Influence of Sea Power upon History, 1660-1783*.

†Lieutenant Ord, who lost his life in the attack, and his Buffalo Soldiers, who actually reached the heights of San Juan Hill first, were largely overlooked when honors were being passed around.

the very best moment in his life.

New York Governor. So well-known was his name at this point that he was asked to run for the position of New York Governor in 1898, which he won in a very tight race. As New York Governor he was immersed in the kinds of larger political issues that would prepare him well for higher office (such as U.S. president). He had corruption to clean out, monopolies and trusts to hem in, labor problems to resolve, and, close to his heart, the conservation of New York's extensive woodlands and rivers to embrace. And he leaned on wealthy businesses to give financial support (taxes) to the New York community that so prospered these businesses. His program he summed up as the "Square Deal" (sounding a lot like his nephew Franklin Roosevelt's term "New Deal" of some 30 years later). In all this he skillfully led Boss Platt to become an actual supporter of his policies, thus helping Roosevelt get his ideas actually put into play. That was political diplomacy at its finest.

The 1900 election. It was this political skill (plus again some intervention by his friend Henry Cabot Lodge) that brought him to the attention of many political figures, both positively and negatively. Both his friends and his enemies saw his selection as vice president as an opportunity ... to march him toward the White House (his friends) and get him out of New York (his enemies). With no one else being put forward for the thankless job of vice president, Roosevelt was nominated as McKinley's new running mate in the 1900 election. It would be a fateful choice.

Vice president. Roosevelt campaigned hard for the Republican Party (he loved the challenge dearly), the Party once again running against the equally tireless Democratic Party candidate, Bryan. That November the Republicans delivered an even bigger blow to the Democrat Bryan than before. And Roosevelt stepped into the quite powerless job of vice president. Roosevelt would discover during this time how much he disliked being out of the real action.

President. With McKinley's assassination six months into his second term in office (September), Roosevelt stepped up to the office of U.S. president. In some ways he continued McKinley's political program (pro-gold, high tariffs and imperialism) and in other ways he went well beyond McKinley in the way he went after the big trusts that dominated American business, and the way he supported American labor. He faced a huge strike of American coal miners, threatening to send federal troops to break the strike, yet being willing to set up a commission to arbitrate the dispute – which ended

American Progressivism

in a compromise acceptable to both sides. A Square Deal had been struck.

He also backed federal regulation of railroad rates (the 1906 Hepburn Act) to neutralize the monopolistic effect of the industry (only one railroad running through town charging whatever prices it wanted, there being no alternative). The Pure Food and Drug Act was passed also in 1906 (along with other legislation supervising the health of the food and pharmaceutical industries). And being the lover of the woods, fields, steams and mountains of America – and the animals living there – he was particularly active in using federal power to protect undeveloped lands, transforming them into national parks, national forests and game preserves.

The Election of 1904. Roosevelt easily won re-election to a second term in 1904, but made the fateful declaration at that time that this would be his last term in office (but serving only two terms was something of a long-standing presidential tradition anyway). It would be a declaration that later he would regret, which he would go back on, producing disastrous unintended consequences, at least for his Republican Party (and, depending on how a person feels about Woodrow Wilson as president, perhaps for the nation).

Roosevelt's second term in office. Roosevelt pushed his assault on the wealthy, calling for a national income tax, although the Supreme Court had already ruled that the Constitution allowed for no such tax, which would be permissible only through the passing of a constitutional amendment (which eventually occurred, but not until 1913). He also attempted to reach federal authority into other walks of American life, finding the way blocked again by the fact that there was little or no constitutional warrant for doing so, no matter how noble the cause. He did, however, see through to success the 1907 Tillman Act outlawing corporate contributions to federal political campaigns, a significant step forward (not always respected however) restricting big money manipulation of national elections.*

The Panic of 1907. Once again panic hit Wall Street when a greedy scheme to buy out the stock of huge United Copper Company instead collapsed the value of the company's stock, causing people to withdraw deposits with banks invested in the company. This in turn spread quickly into a general banking and Wall Street scare, forcing bankruptcy on numerous state and local banks, including New York banks holding the reserves of these regional

---

*Those restrictions would even be strengthened by follow-up legislation, until 2010 and then also in 2014, when in two separate decisions, the Supreme Court ruled that any restriction in the right to contribute to political campaigns is unconstitutional.

banks. It also dropped overall stock values on Wall Street to half of what they were the previous year. Finally, when the huge Knickerbocker Trust Company collapsed, J.P. Morgan – under an agreement with Roosevelt – stepped in to help buy out failing companies and restore investor confidence in Wall Street. Morgan's U.S. Steel Company also bought out the Tennessee Coal, Iron and Railroad Company (TCIR) just as it too was about to collapse (also under agreement with Roosevelt). Thus it was that during his last years in office the strongly anti-monopolist Roosevelt had to turn to one of his targeted monopolies for help!

* * *

WILLIAM HOWARD TAFT[87]

We bring up another Progressivist for close study at this point because he took up exactly at the point when Roosevelt had to make good on his promise and step down from the presidency at the end of his second term. William Howard Taft was Roosevelt's friend, and a logical successor to Roosevelt in the White House in 1908. Once again, the Democrats put Bryan in the running as their presidential candidate, and for the third time in a row he went down to defeat, this time by the Republican candidate Taft.

Taft was born into an Ohio political family, his father having been both U.S. attorney general and secretary of war under President Grant. Young Taft grew up under strong parental discipline which made him a hard worker, and eventually a successful student at Yale (graduating 2nd out of 121 students and a member of the prestigious Skull and Bones society). He took up study of the law and was in 1887 appointed a judge by the Ohio governor, while only twenty-nine! In 1886 he married Helen Herron – who continued the push he had received from his parents growing up, helping him reach ever higher in the world of law and politics.

Although he hungered for an appointment to the U.S. Supreme Court, President Harrison in 1890 appointed him as U.S. solicitor general (at age thirty-two), where he at least was allowed to argue cases (winning 15 of his 18 cases) before the Supreme Court. Then in 1892 Harrison appointed him to the Sixth Circuit, a natural stepping stone to a Supreme Court appointment. He held this position for the next eight years, becoming a law professor in Cincinnati at the same time.

Philippine governor. In 1900 he was appointed by President McKinley to head up a commission charged with organizing a new government in the recently acquired Philippines (a trophy from the Spanish-American War), under the agreement with McKinley that Taft would receive McKinley's next

American Progressivism

Supreme Court appointment if he agreed to serve in the Philippines. But McKinley did not live long enough to make good on that promise. With McKinley's death in 1901 Roosevelt now served as U.S. president.

Taft and Roosevelt begin working together. Taft and Roosevelt had become friends back in 1890 when both were posted to Washington by President Harrison, Taft as solicitor general and Roosevelt as a member of the Civil Service Commission. Taft put his support behind Roosevelt's appointment as assistant secretary of the navy when McKinley was first assembling his new cabinet (1897). Several years later, with Roosevelt now as U.S. president, Taft was called to Washington to explain developments in the Philippines, and Roosevelt sent him to Rome to try to get support from the Pope in getting cooperation from the Catholic Church in selling to the Filipino farmers the vast amount of land held by the Church in the Philippines. Then when a Supreme Court vacancy opened up, Roosevelt wanted to appoint Taft, except that the latter declined the offer – because he felt this his work as Philippine governor was not yet complete. And it was important work, Taft being well-recognized in the press for his labors in the Philippines. Then Roosevelt took another tack, asking Taft to serve as his secretary of war (like Taft's father), with the understanding that as such he would still be in charge of the Philippines, since the War Department was at that time still responsible for governing the Philippines. Taft accepted the offer (December 1903).

Roosevelt's personal assistant. Actually since Roosevelt himself wanted to direct America's military affairs, Taft found himself serving more as a personal assistant to the president, even giving campaign speeches for Roosevelt in the 1904 national elections, in 1904 traveling to Panama to meet on Roosevelt's behalf with officials there concerning the building of the Panama Canal, in 1905 traveling to Japan for talks prior to the peace conference between Russia and Japan held in New Hampshire a month later, and in 1906 traveling to Cuba to try to resolve deteriorating political conditions there. The relationship between Roosevelt and Taft was so close that when offered Supreme Court appointments both in 1905 and 1906 Taft again declined the offers.

The 1908 election. As Roosevelt was completing his second (and supposedly final) term as president, it was widely understood that Taft was likely to be the Republican Party's new nominee for U.S. president, and thus next U.S. president, given the dominant position the Republican Party seemingly held in the matter of presidential politics. Roosevelt made sure that his friend would receive the nomination without serious opposition, through some maneuvering of his own to get full party backing. Taft himself was not eager for the job. Roosevelt, of course, was, and there was considerable talk of him running again. But Roosevelt had made a promise which he intended to keep. He refused to run. And thus Taft was nominated on the very first balloting.

Once again, the Democratic Party candidate was Bryan, who claimed that he was closer to Roosevelt in his effort to reform American politics than was Taft. But Taft made it clear that he intended to continue Roosevelt's reform programs, though less through Roosevelt's style of presidential action than through the lawmaking efforts of Congress. Indeed, this became a matter of criticism, that with Roosevelt behind Taft's presidential efforts, Roosevelt himself was planning still to run the country. And maybe he was, because Roosevelt hated being out of the seat of American power. In any case Taft won the presidency, although with only 51.6 percent of the vote, though naturally with a bigger electoral college victory, with 321 votes against Bryan's 162 electoral votes.

Trust-busting. However, Taft was quite determined as president to be his own man, keeping only one carryover from Roosevelt's cabinet.* He pursued trust-busting under the 1890 Sherman Antitrust Act even more rigorously than Roosevelt, undertaking seventy cases in his four years in office (Roosevelt had undertaken forty such cases in his eight years in office.).

But all this vigor brought tensions between Roosevelt and Taft, when Congress undertook an investigation into J.P. Morgan's U.S. Steel buyout of the failing TCIR during the Panic of 1907. Taft had supported Roosevelt's approval of the move, but now as president, his Justice Department decided to go after U.S. Steel for that action, implying also that Roosevelt had supported monopolistic practices. Taft claimed he did not know that his Justice Department was up to this, a disclaimer that Roosevelt rejected. Tensions worsened between the two when the next year, a presidential election year (1912), Taft supporters went after Roosevelt, who after a four-year absence was clearly up and running again for the Republican Party presidential nomination, for his earlier failure to act against the huge International Harvester Corporation (farm machinery). Roosevelt pointed out that Taft had at the time agreed with Roosevelt to take no action against the company. Roosevelt was furious that now, several years later, this issue should come up in order to cast a shadow over Roosevelt's integrity.

---

*After Taft's inauguration, Roosevelt supported his friend's independence by taking a 15-month trip abroad, most of the time spent hunting in Africa. They rarely communicated with each other during this time period.

American Progressivism

The Roosevelt-Taft split. Other things were separating the two former friends. Roosevelt was very vocal about his opposition to the growing involvement of the Supreme Court in the nation's politics, something that Taft disagreed with strongly. Also, Taft's leadership of the Republican Party seemed to slip when as a result of the 1910 elections the Democrats took control of the House and lost numerous seats in the Senate, which led Roosevelt to be loudly contemptuous of Taft's role as leader of the Republican Party. In that same election future U.S. president, Republican Warren G. Harding, strongly supported by Taft, failed in his bid for the Ohio governorship. At the same time, Democrat Woodrow Wilson won the governorship of New Jersey, a humiliating defeat for the Republicans.

Further, as Roosevelt's intentions to run again for the presidency in 1912 became increasingly clear, it also became increasingly clear that Taft was not intending simply to step aside for his former mentor. He intended to run again – but on his own merits this time. Thus as the 1912 election approached, the break between the two was now complete.

The 1912 Republican National Convention. Going into the convention Roosevelt had a substantial majority of the delegates chosen through the new primary system (Republican voters themselves choosing their delegates). But Taft held the support of the delegates appointed under the old system of local party caucuses, outnumbering Roosevelt's delegates, with Southern delegates also inclining toward Taft. Roosevelt was loud in his denunciation of the old system of back-room delegate selection. But it did not sway the political weight of the convention, which on the first ballot went to Taft (though most of Roosevelts delegates had not voted once it became clear that they were outnumbered, though only slightly).

Disgruntled Roosevelt delegates now bolted from the Republican Party and set up their own third party, the Progressive Party (more popularly known as the "Bull Moose Party" in reference to the character of the party's leader, Roosevelt). Meanwhile the Democrats nominated the New Jersey reformer, Governor Woodrow Wilson.

The 1912 election. With a three-way race it was likely that none of the three candidates would be able to secure a full popular majority in the November 1912 election. In effect a divided Republican Party faced a more unified Democratic Party, giving Wilson the opportunity to win a race that otherwise, had there been only one Republican candidate, he would have lost. But that's what happens with third party runs. They do not win races, but merely take away votes from one of the two major parties. The final tally was Wilson with 42 percent of the national vote, defeating both Roosevelt with 27.5 percent and Taft with 23 percent of the national vote.

The electoral college vote was even more harsh to Taft, who received only 8 votes, to Roosevelt's 88 votes, and Wilson's 435 votes.

After stepping down from the presidency, Taft moved on to Yale Law School to lecture and teach classes. He also stayed active as president of the commission directing the building of the Lincoln Memorial. Taft and Roosevelt did not reconcile, helping Wilson to win reelection as president in 1916. Taft, unlike most of the rest of his party, supported Wilson's League of Nations proposal. But he also supported a number of reservations to the treaty, concerned about protecting American sovereignty in the conduct of its foreign relations – which embittered Wilson greatly. But when in 1920 the Republicans won back the White House and Taft's old friend Harding became U.S. president, Taft was finally appointed to a seat on the U.S. Supreme Court, as the Court's chief justice. This would be a position he would hold until just prior to his death in 1930.

CHAPTER THIRTEEN

THE RATIONALIZING OF WESTERN CULTURE[88]

* * *

UNDERSTANDING THE SPIRIT OF THE TIMES

Thus far we have been looking at the Progressivist Era largely in terms of its material quality, presented in terms of the vast material wealth that a number of Americans enjoyed, or the lack of that same wealth suffered by others, and the politics involved in trying to make such materialism work to the greater advantage of individuals, groups of individuals, and even the nation as a whole. We have looked at individuals whose energy made much of this possible, the captains of industry and finance (or "robber barons" if you were distressed at how poorly this rising wealth was distributed more broadly among the American population) and the inventors and technical innovators whose ideas kept the Progressivist Era moving ever forward to new and truly amazing material inventions and developments.

The Age of Progress and the "Revolution of Rising Expectations." But at this point we want to look more closely at the spirit of the times, the intellectual, moral and spiritual character of American culture, and the forces that shaped it. It is important to note that the very idea of wealth, or of poverty, is not itself an objective matter, like an automobile, a large or small house, the clothes someone wears, the humble or exotic nature of what is found on the dinner table, etc. Indeed, the very poor were actually better off materially than the middle classes of just a couple of centuries earlier, when the planet was less able to support a large human population. People of course still suffered from fatigue, hunger, disease, and just plain aging. But the profile of Westerners at the turn of the century demonstrated actually a vitality among vast numbers that would have been unthinkable just generations earlier. Yet poverty was there, bitter poverty for some, especially for those (mostly in America's fast-rising cities and industrial towns) whose lives contrasted so sharply with the lives of the very, very wealthy, who benefitted awesomely from the labors of these poor souls.

Yet the poor souls were actually doing much better materially than their medieval counterparts. But expectations were there nonetheless that justice was not being well served by the way America's vast wealth was being distributed. Certainly that idea formed much of the drive behind the Progressivist Movement. If the gap between rich and poor (as it has always been through the ages) had remained largely unchanged, little would have been said about the matter. It would have been accepted as the normal scheme of things (as it was for centuries). But things were changing rapidly, and with them the expectations of the benefits, the fruits of change. And those expectations, emotional and intellectual, were the reality that people actually responded to. And they were rising as fast or faster than the actual material growth of the American economy and technology.

With time the simplest of Americans would be drawn into the world of the new gadgets and lifestyle possibilities, because such fast-developing wealth needed the American people themselves (what ultimately we would identify as the consumer) to absorb the end products of the economic system. Henry Ford understood this principle very well, and got very rich from it.

But America's reality at the turn of the century was not really in just interesting material statistics, but in the fact that America was going through a "Revolution of Rising Expectations." And those expectations were the reality that Americans responded to.

So at this point we turn to the all-important question: what exactly were those expectations? What was it exactly that Americans were thinking concerning their situations, their lives?

The mechanics of social thinking. People themselves are actually not very innovative thinkers, but borrow thought from larger society. Individuals have personalities of their own, of course. But even more importantly they develop social personalities, a sense of personhood drawn from the cultural themes around them, themes that others generate for them individually (opinion leaders) and collectively, out of a commonly-perceived social experience they find themselves in. In other words, people mostly follow the crowd of one kind or another. And what they do, how they act, how they react, is shaped not so much by their own personal reasoning as much as by the reasoning of the social group they identify themselves with – or actually groups, some cooperating to give even more cohesion and strength to a person's social identity, or on the other hand clashing, causing much personal confusion and frustration.

So again, what were Americans thinking at this time? How were they redesigning their personal universe? Something big was going on – because all this material change was stirring new cultural ideas that challenged Americans to rethink their world.

Europe's lead in the emerging "Post Christian" culture. One more point. America itself was not doing this in isolation, but was itself participating (mostly willingly) in a larger rethink of all of Western Civilization. This civilization used to be called "Christian Civilization." But although people still used that language in describing a desirable Christian world, a larger Christian moral code, a set of Christian social goals, the reality was that Christianity was not any single social-political idea – as the violent Protestant-Catholic Wars of Religion of the early-mid 1600s clearly demonstrated. In any case, new ideas were on the rise within this Christian West that had no connection with the idea of the sovereign rule of God or the saving power of Jesus's lordship over the world. Something else in the West was fast replacing Christian culture, a new culture identified by various labels: Materialism, Empiricism, Darwinism, Secularism, Humanism, Socialism, etc., all of which developed from this rising sense of man's own powers to conquer and reshape the world by his own designs, his own logic, his own powers, his own ability to see his human programs put into place to make this world a much, much better place. All of this mental energy was thus serving in different ways to give Western Civilization a new and very aggressive character.

It was all very heady stuff. Just in looking around at all the material bounty that came with this new-think, it is not surprising how very compelling this new culture was. Christianity, with its call for humility in approaching life and its emphasis in trusting God alone to get things right, just did not appear to be the sure and certain formula for acquiring the offerings of this new world of material bounty. And thus people's minds and hearts were fast shifting to this exciting new world of what could be summed up basically as Secular Humanism.

In this development, Europe was way ahead of America. But America was learning quickly. America had its own new ideas about life. But by and large Americans found themselves greatly attracted to the high level of social thought coming from Europe. In fact it was considered to be the height of sophistication to go off to Europe to study (the reverse was hardly the case yet!). Indeed, in the realm of higher thought, America mostly found itself simply responding to European developments that were well underway across the Atlantic.

And that would even take America right into the Great War (World War One, 1914-1918) which America long debated before making the fateful decision to jump into the event.

And thus, for much of this section, we want to look at Europe, and the thought processes going on there, and how that shaped global events, ones that formerly isolationist America avoided during its fragile early development. Now America found itself unable to resist the European dynamic but instead joined in – unfortunately in full measure.

* * *

THE RISING AGE OF WESTERN RATIONALISM

The very ancient roots of the central problem arising with the adulation (even worship) of Human Reason. The use of human reason rather than reliance on divine guidance is not a new issue on this planet. It certainly did not arrive for the first time with Europe's step into the Modern Age, considered by historians to have started somewhere around the mid-1600s, with the end of the Wars of Religion.

The very ancient Judeo-Christian Bible begins its narration with this very issue – immediately after the story of divine creation. The narration centers on man's first temptation: to go his own way rather than to go with God. That is the essence of the story of the Garden of Eden when God had forbidden Adam and Eve to eat of the Tree of the Knowledge of Good and Evil. He did not explain why, because they were still obedient to God rather than deciding themselves what was good and what was evil. However, the Tempter in the form of a serpent soon intervened in the story to put the thought in the minds of this primal couple, that knowing on their own what was good and what was evil would make them like God. That was (and still is) quite a temptation, one they could not or anyway would not resist. And so, they ate of the forbidden fruit, and troubles began immediately.

Western Civilization continues to wrestle with this same issue. It's a great story, absolutely ageless in its wisdom, as Europe was already discovering. And if they had not learned about the Truth of the narrative in observing the events of the Wars of Religion (also known as the Thirty Years' War of 1618-1648) or the French Revolution at the end of the 1700s, they were about to have the issue put squarely in front of them again in the form of the Great War (World War One, 1914-1918), which, unknown to them, was about to break out in seemingly unprecedented fury. But that part of the story belongs to our next chapter.

But in any case, let's at this point take our story of Western Civilization's effort to make sense of this newly emerging world, all the way back to Europe during the times of the European Enlightenment, beginning in the later 1600s, truly blossoming in the 1700s, and challenging in so

The Rationalizing of Western Culture

many different ways the 1800s. Looking at the birth and development of these modern trends of social thought and action should help us not only to understand how we got this way, but also the difficulties we will have if we do not learn from the past.

We have already discussed Locke and Rousseau in some detail. But they were children of the European Enlightenment, not its founders.

The Puritans were actually major contributors to this emerging "Enlightenment." This "Age of Enlightenment" had its origins in the early 1600s, with the rise of "natural philosophy" – something we today term as "science." Very active in this matter of the "philosophy of nature" were the English Puritans, led by such intellectuals as Francis Bacon, who at the turn of the 1600s celebrated the new discoveries of the workings of the natural world ... seeing the hand of an incredibly awesome God in the newly discovered grand designs of nature. Bacon's "science" was treated as almost an act of worship ... as it would be for so many of the other Puritans – who, for the same reason (seeing their natural philosophy as a witness to the glory of God), took the lead in England's scientific revolution that broke forth in the 1600s. And much the same was the case for the Puritans' Calvinist cousins over in the Netherlands!

Descartes[89] (early 1600s) challenges Christian Truth with a new reliance on Pure Reason. But at approximately the same time, the Frenchman René Descartes wrestled with the epistemological problem of understanding how we can be certain that what we claim to be true is indeed true – because there is such a huge gap that separates our mind from what we believe we see out there. How do we actually know what is true and what is not?

This was not just some philosopher's idle question. Descartes was living at a time in which the wars between Catholics and Protestants and between rising monarchs in different parts of Europe were constant and having a deadly effect on European society. Each of the contenders justified his brutal violence on the basis of one or another truth-claim. So Descartes took up the challenge of trying to lay out a basis by which the contenders could pursue these truth-claims logically, rather than violently (presuming that these contenders were indeed all that interested in Truth rather than just domination).

Descartes observed that the world around us operated purely mechanically (or mathematically), and that if we disciplined our minds to work in the same way (rationally or mathematically) we could actually close that gap between our minds and the surrounding world. There was no need for inspiration, no need to rely on tradition or the conventional teachings of society. Man was fully capable of arriving at all truths – even able to prove the existence of God – simply through the exercise of precise human reason. With that Cartesian challenge, the Age of Reason was off and running.

Newton[90] – Leibniz[91] – Locke.[92] Three individuals stand out in particular in the follow-up (the later 1600s) to Descartes' birth of the Age of Reason: the two Englishmen Isaac Newton and John Locke and the German Gottfried Wilhelm Leibniz.

Leibniz and Newton were both brilliant mathematicians. Both seemed to have discovered calculus at about the same time (around 1670). Leibniz tended to follow more closely the lead of Descartes and other Rationalists on the European continent in believing that pure reason, built simply on logical principles arrived at through clear thought, could design a perfect world – and was optimistic that such was soon possible.

Newton tended more to the empirical side (typical of the British), believing that nothing could be considered true until it had been observed to actually work in the real world. But he was also something of a Christian mystic, which in general the continental school of Rationalism rejected completely.

We have already met Locke (a friend of Newton's) who too believed in the power of human reason to solve life's various problems, whatever they might be. Locke, like Newton, was also a highly empirical philosopher who stressed the importance of putting our ideas to the test of observing their success (or failure) in the actual world of people and things.

We also know that Locke was very much a social philosopher. But he was also a student of human psychology, able to put the two worlds of the individual and society together in a rational order. His understanding was that human thought is importantly a collective matter, shaped by the thinking of the larger social world and the particular experiences that this social world was facing and how a society interpreted those experiences. But again, his belief was that this social world could be – must be – improved through the careful thinking through of life's processes, in order to bring life closer to perfection.

Locke and his writings would go on to influence deeply the philosophy of most of the social philosophers of the 1700s (including importantly Thomas Jefferson).

Rousseau[93] and early Romanticism. Of a very special or distinct philosophical contribution to the discussions of 1700s France was Jean Jacques Rousseau. He was to have a huge impact on the thinking of the European continent's Age of Enlightenment (the 1700s).

He was French-cultured Swiss whose writings, especially The *Social Contract* (1762), were very popular in France. He raised the question of political sovereignty, where it was lodged and how it functioned to best serve the people.

Rousseau claimed that originally man lived in some kind of simple natural state of harmony, without laws or government. But life had evolved over time into a more complex form – civilization – requiring as it developed greater mutual dependence among men for the orderly working of society, and thus also a more complex system of moral instruction or law to guide this more complex society. Man accordingly had to give up his total personal sovereignty to come under the protection and nurture of more complex society. But he was giving it up not to some ruling individual but to the larger idea of the society as a whole, the general will – in particular its laws, which were the clearest expression of a people's general will.

The laws, not any particular individuals, were the locus of sovereignty in the truly good society. Unfortunately, ignorance of this good had clouded people's political understanding, causing them to slip into all forms of political tyranny (absolute rule over society by particular individuals such as kings and dukes, which was the general pattern of his day).

Rousseau's hope was to open men's eyes to the understanding of what was truly right and good about society, that such knowledge would free men to usher in a good or utopian society that was truly the right of everyone to enjoy, not just the privileged few. All the superfluous fluff of decadent civilization (in particular French civilization as it was viewed in his own time) would be simply swept away by the opening of the eyes of the people to the Truth.

With the *Ancien Régime* (the Old Order comprised of the officers of the king and church that dominated all European society in the 1700s) thus swept away, society would be free to create or contract a social system as simple and basic as possible, a social system directed by a set of basic laws that restored to man his fundamental liberties, allowing him to live as close to the original state of nature as possible.

The French were strongly impacted by Rousseau's theories – as have been many revolutionary-minded secular philosophers since Rousseau (as well as modern 'hippies' trying to go back to nature in simple communal living). Rousseau's vision of primitive society even found its way into the polite social gatherings or salons of Europe's ruling classes and their intellectual tutors. Thus it was that the future queen Marie Antoinette used to love to play in the Versailles palace gardens (with fellow maidens at the French court) at being a peasant girl herding her sheep. It was all so quaint, so romantic.

The French monarchy was sick, very sick. Reform was needed. But by Rousseau's logic, that reform was going to have to be extensive for the good society to result. The Old Order was going to have to be set aside in its entirety in order to make way for the new. Thus with Rousseau's encouragement, the French political mood was becoming increasingly revolutionary as the political debate in the late 1700s intensified in France.

The further reaction to Europe's Rationalism. In the American colonies in the mid-1700s the Western Enlightenment was answered by the mysteries of the Great Awakening – led by such figures as Edwards and Whitefield, and by the broad popular response of the common people to that dynamic. While continental Europe in general was by-passed in that event (the British, however, certainly had their own version of the Great Awakening), nonetheless as the 1700s moved along, something of a strong reaction to Rationalism also set in among some of the Continental European as well as British philosophers and scholars, something however that had very little to do with going back to Christian basics. That non-Christian reaction to Rationalism would take very different forms – tending to Empiricism in Britain and Romanticism in Continental Europe (though varieties of Empiricism and Romanticism could be found in both locations).

British Empiricism. To begin with, the British were of a more practical mindset in their love of hands-on experimentation than their continental cousins, who loved to sit at their desks or gather at polite salons to indulge themselves in the world of pure thought. During the Enlightenment the British were too busy inventing new material technologies – and developing the industries to put those technologies to practical use – to be wasting time speculating about hypothetical realities. They were all, by nature, Empiricists.

David Hume[94] promotes Empiricism. In the mid-1700s the Scottish philosopher David Hume had his own answer to the Rationalism that infected so much of European society. As a philosophical empiricist, the widely read and respected Hume found sufficient Truth for life in simply observing actual behavior, and the results it produced. Results were to Hume real Truth. Long-abiding custom (in other words, social rules that actually worked over the long run) were for Hume the foundations on which to build human life.

Likewise, Hume was most unimpressed by the great intellectual "spins" that philosophers wove around hypothetical behavior in building their great systems of thought. For Hume reality was in the doing, not in the hypothesizing about life.

Widely studied, Hume became well-known in his time for his skepticism about speculations about God, or great systems of religious Truth, or the validity of "objective" ethical systems, even the claims of science to have established an explanation of all life in terms of cause and effect. All this was to Hume mere intellectual humbuggery.

Hume's impact lived long after him. In fact it was Hume that awakened the great German philosopher Kant from his "intellectual slumber" (as Kant himself put it) and caused Kant to undertake the task of responding to the challenge that Hume had issued to those who would claim to understand human nature, even life itself.

Adam Smith[95] explains capitalism. In the meantime, the British were very busy inventing new material technologies, and developing the industries to put those technologies to practical use.

Building on this attitude was the fellow Scot, Adam Smith, who in his *Wealth of Nations* (1776) wrote a compelling explanation of how simply letting the competitive marketplace bring forward the material blessings of life – and the pricing involved for such wealth – would also naturally bring forth human progress. He was much opposed to the idea of forcing on society the designs of utopian social planners, who would soon enough make a mess of things with their well-reasoned schemes.

In fact, Smith was strongly opposed to any kind of "intervention" into this market mechanism by the government or any other outside societal institution. To Smith (and all capitalist philosophers since then) this independence of commercial action was the key doctrine of Capitalist philosophy.

But at the same time, Smith was highly opposed to market insiders getting together to conspire to set prices through a withholding of goods or services to create an artificial scarcity. He was thus opposed to cartels, monopolies, and unions, of any variety. He also considered the danger of rapid population growth distorting the labor market and driving prices down to subsistence levels. But he felt that economic growth of the whole industrial sector would constantly increase the demand for labor and thus prevent such cruelties from occurring.

Kant[96] attempts a compromise between British Empiricism and French Rationalism. Immanuel Kant was something of a father to German philosophy, setting out, just prior to the French Revolution, to locate some kind of intellectual bridge between the powerful philosophies of French Rationalism and British Empiricism.

Kant agreed with Hume's empiricism, namely that essential to human knowledge is our sense experience – the experience of the seeing, feeling, hearing, etc. of real material objects around us. But he also agreed with the continental Rationalists (most notably Leibniz, whose writings also were a major influence on Kant) that knowledge is also a matter of the exercise of human reason, in particular the use of innate human ideas ("categories") which we are born with and which help us to organize this empirical information. Thus Kant saw himself as closing the intellectual gap between the British Empiricists and the Continental Rationalists.

Kant also saw himself as answering Hume's skepticism about ever knowing with any degree of certainty the Truth of transcendent ideas, such as moral laws or ethical principles (not to mention the idea of Heaven itself). In Kant's *Metaphysics of Morals* (1785) and *Critique of Practical Reason* (1788), he proposed a new moral/ethical "categorical imperative," one that did not require the existence of God for its validity. It involved an ingenious piece of moral logic: we ought to act in such a way that our act could become accepted as a universal principle of behavior. If it were not able to attain such a universal validity (because, for instance, of an internal contradiction in logic) then that action, by "practical reason," was obviously not to be pursued.

Taking this logic of "practical reason" a step further, he turned to the issue of the existence of God. He agreed with Hume that no rational argument could be given for God's existence – that is, "pure reason" could not build a case for God's existence. But "practical reason" could. Pursuing a traditional line of reason that went back at least as far as Ockham in the early 1300s, Kant claimed that human reason cannot establish the "fact" of God. But in observing the moral instincts of people we can see (through the eyes of faith) that there is some kind of source beyond the mere human will itself that directs life. That higher moral grounding is by definition God. Thus God exists. (This kind of theological reasoning did not impress the Prussian government, which censured his work).

Finally, so impressed was Kant that we humans could live in accordance with such higher moral imperatives that in his *Perpetual Peace* (1795) he laid out a vision for a new world order. Here (despite the Reign of Terror going on in France) begins the utopian idealism that will absorb the thoughts and aspirations of intellectuals for generations to come.

The French Revolution plunges ahead, seeking a rational utopia. Of course Rationalism was by no means dethroned by Rousseau's Romantic reaction or the challenge of British Empiricism, because it was pure Rationalism that drove French intellectuals (and Paris mobs) to their violent behavior during the French Revolution, a revolution that soon produced horrors on the scale of the Religious Wars of the 1600s that had first inspired Rationalism. During the violent revolution that broke out in 1789, absolute Reason brought forward powerful people who became also absolute in their authority, and thus highly susceptible to very sophisticated self-deception as they murdered people by the thousands in the name of Reason.

What these Rationalists failed to see was how easily reason, in the face of the serious challenge of ruling a very diverse people, could be so easily twisted to serve merely their own narrower self-interests*, rather than the dreamy goal of serving all the people according to some kind of higher interest they claimed they were pursuing. What these utopian Rationalists had naively come up against was the complex issue called reality, something of which in their lofty world of aristocratic salons they knew virtually nothing.

Reactions to the French Revolution. With the exception of Jefferson, who while living in France just prior to the 1789 Revolution fell entirely in love with French Rationalism, Americans in general took the same attitude as the (Irish) Edmund Burke, who expressed eloquently the horror that all of Britain felt about the very barbaric results of the noble effort of the French people trying to be entirely rational. Burke pointed out (like Hume) that long-established tradition served the people well and should only be reformed carefully as necessary, not overthrown.

Like the French, the Americans at the time were birthing a new Republic. But unlike the French, the American Republic was built cautiously on a very limited or restricted basis on political traditions and practices already well-established in the colonies over the previous century and a half. Americans were not setting up a new government built on untested new principles dreamed up by social planners, like the French were attempting. And (as we have already seen) the results consequently were quite different from America to France.

The Napoleonic challenge. Eventually (1799) France was rescued by the military dictator Napoleon from the murderous folly of the French Revolution's "Reign of Terror" (1792-1795) and the political chaos that followed it.

Napoleon retained technical features of the Revolution and even improved on them, for instance, supporting the metric system and rationalizing regional government through a new bureaucratic system which replaced the chaotic array of multitudes of local feudal domains each with their own laws, standards and social interests.

---

*But isn't this what we pay lawyers to do for us: use powerful "Reason" on our own behalf? Isn't this what both sides are doing in a civil or criminal case, with its opposing lawyers each skillfully presenting rational arguments on behalf of their particular clients before a judge or jury? Even mobsters have well-paid lawyers to defend rationally or "justify" their behavior in court.

Pierre Simon de Laplace gives Rationalism a new lease on life. Newton had earlier outlined the gravitational theories designed to demonstrate that the planets moved about the sun in accordance with immutable mathematical principles. There were however still unexplained small variations in Newton's computations: he had not taken into account the gravitational attraction also working among the planets themselves. These small variations had the ability to destabilize Newton's mechanistic model of the solar system. But Newton was enough of a mystic to look to God to regulate the small variations so as to keep the whole system in order.

This idea of a small residual divine intervention was not a satisfying concept to the French Rationalist Laplace. He understood the universe to be totally operative under the impersonal, mechanical laws of nature. So in 1773 he set out to give full mathematical explanation to the motions of the heavens – in such a way that there would be no more need to call in God as the residual part of the equation. This he successfully completed years later an unprecedentedly in-depth mathematical calculation of the eccentricities in the planetary orbits, taking into account their gravitation attraction to each other as well as to the sun as they moved through their respective orbits. This work was eventually compiled into the five-volume study: *Celestial Mechanics* (1799-1825.) And it earned him a place in the prestigious French Academy of Sciences.

It also removed the idea of God further (if not completely) from the mechanistic cosmology that had been unfolding over the previous century. Not even Deism could stand up to this assault.

Indeed, the story goes that when Laplace presented a copy of his work to Napoleon, the latter uttered a concern that Laplace had made no mention in his work of the divine "Originator" of this marvelous system. To this, Laplace replied quite simply: "I had no need for that hypothesis!"

✳ ✳ ✳

ROMANTICISM AND NATIONALISM

French nationalism. Ultimately Napoleon had achieved stability and unity in Revolutionary France only by focusing the country outward towards its neighbors – in an imperialist quest to establish, through his conquering armies, control over all of Europe (and supposedly also a quest to bring to Europe French Enlightenment and political-social reform in the process). Bringing the peasant class into the highly respected role of soldering made Napoleon extremely popular with that class. In essence he moved out into the world with a new national army, far more powerful (highly motivated,

The Rationalizing of Western Culture　　　　　　　　　　　　　　　　　　　　399

like a tribe) than the professional or paid troops of the European dynasties that Napoleon set out to topple.

But his popularity and dominating role in French politics and French imperialism came at the price of making enemies of everyone else in Europe that was not French or was not completely engulfed in French culture (which at the time was the unifying culture of Europe's ruling classes).

Ultimately what Napoleon did in developing the idea of the French nation set loose the desire of other Europeans to find their own paths to acquiring a similar nationhood, whether Russian, Italian, German, Polish, etc. Other countries, England, Spain, Dutch Netherlands, who already had laid out something of national foundations of their own, also found those respective nationalist sentiments strengthened further by the same Napoleonic challenge.

American nationalism. America of course also had laid out something of a national identity during its War of Independence from Britain. But with the lifting of the British challenge (not completed until the conclusion of the War of 1812), internal cultural differences rather quickly began to trouble America's own national journey. This led to the horrible Civil War, a vicious battle over the matter of whether the United States would indeed stay united or instead would split into a number of smaller political units, not just North versus South but also East versus West. Under Lincoln's leadership (and with Divine counsel to Lincoln) this issue in America was finally resolved – brutally – at the same time that Germany and Italy were struggling, also brutally, to find unity as new European nations.

The role of Romanticism in growing the sense of nationhood. The French Revolution had initially challenged Europeans to investigate further this idea of building human progress on the basis of the ability of man (any man / all men, potentially) to reason clearly ... if properly brought up to do so. But when given the chance to put this utopian dream into practice, the French ultimately had failed miserably – very, very miserably.

A reaction against such worship of Human Reason naturally set in, not just among the skeptical British Empiricists but among a number of continental scholars, especially the German Romanticists. This latter reaction developed on the European continent especially when it became obvious that under Napoleon what stood behind French power was not Reason, but some kind of special Spirit that rose naturally out of the soul of an energized people themselves (French peasants becoming national warriors).

This quest for such Spirit (German *Geist*) would mark much of European philosophy during the 1800s, especially that coming out of

Germany, whose philosophers seemed to dominate the field of intellectual inquiry on the European continent that century, the way the French had done so the century before.

The German Romanticists Herder and Goethe. Two young Germans, Johann Gottfried Herder and Johann Wolfgang von Goethe helped found together the *Sturm und Drang* (Storm and Drive) Movement of the 1770s, celebrating the spirit of struggle as the necessary element in achieving what the Rationalists had felt would be achieved simply through pure reason.

The clergyman Herder studied under Kant at Königsberg, but moved away from Kantian rationalism into a mystical world presided over by God. As a young pastor he met Goethe, inspiring the latter with his insights into Biblical literature. He recognized that the Hebrew literature of the Old Testament was more of the nature of poetry and folk narrative than technical science (which was how Rationalistic Western society was coming to think and operate at that point), and that it was necessary to understand the Hebrew writings as such – not as mechanistic science but as deeply inspired narrative or parable – in order to comprehend their great truths.

The two men became good friends whose speculations together about human knowledge birthed the Sturm und Drang Movement of the 1770s, elevating human emotions above human intellect. Eventually their thinking would settle down a bit and evolve towards Classicism, or love of the styles of classical or ancient Greco-Roman antiquity in an attempt to balance human emotion and human intellect.

Herder was a strong German nationalist, at a time when Germans were attempting to construct the idea of a German nation (Germany at the time was divided into hundreds of independent states, large and small). Yet he was cautious about letting the highly emotional tribal spirit of nationalism get too far away from practical reason.

Then with the outbreak of the French Revolution in 1789 Herder would support the Revolution, producing a split between himself and many of his friends, including Goethe. Finally, his dedication to refuting Kant's theories would place him pretty much in isolation within the German academic community.

Goethe was an individual of wide tastes and talents, being a poet, dramatist and scientist all in one. He was early influenced by Herder, who inspired in him a deep appreciation of German folk culture and consequently a spirit of German nationalism.

But Goethe was also a profound individualist, intrigued by the power and depth of personal experience and emotion. In his first play, *Götz von Berlichingen* (1773), Goethe explored the depths of individual human sentiments – helping to lay the foundation for the Sturm und Drang

Movement, which, among other things, advocated personal freedom in the face of oppressive, medieval attitudes in Germany concerning the role of the individual in society. This Sturm und Drang Movement would later blossom into German Romanticism.

In the 1780s Goethe went to Rome to study classic art, architecture, and literature and for a while came under the more formalistic style of the neo-classicist movement. But on his return to Germany he found little appreciation for his new views. He then turned to science for a while. But his longer-standing romantic inclinations reasserted themselves, and his independent individualist style returned to the fore. This culminated in his all-time great work, *Faust* (actually written and rewritten in two parts over a long period of time reaching perhaps from 1772 to 1829), which was an epic tale of the search of the individual for that which is of a lasting or transcending value in the face of freedom's great opportunities – and uncertainties.

His *Faust* would become the best-read work of German literature (roughly equivalent to the place Shakespeare has long enjoyed in English literature), inspiring young Germans for generations to quest for the German ideal, the romantic spirit or soul that made Germany unique among the nations.

Herder's and Goethe's ideas would leave their mark on German nationalist thinking by putting into place a powerful intellectual legacy for others to pursue, with the idea of exploring the spirit of man as well as his intellect. However both of them eventually moved on to the philosophy of Classicism, which idealized the cultural and political achievements of the ancient Greeks and Romans, who became for them models that Europeans should attempt to emulate (as it was also for Americans at the time, who took up the Roman idea of the Republic as the political structure they were trying to set up in 1787).

Georg Wilhelm Friedrich Hegel:[97] historical progress through struggle. Just as Goethe was to become Germany's grand poet of the century in Germany, Georg Wilhelm Friedrich Hegel would become Germany's grand philosopher of the century. Hegel built on the Sturm und Drang idea of the blessings of struggle, seeing in the tension between opposing forces (usually in the form of newer, radical ideas and practices challenging older, established ideas and practices) the possibilities of birthing a new standard, one operating at a higher social level than previously. This idea eventually became his famous dialectic, the struggle of two opposing things eventually birthing a third, superior thing – a dialectical dynamic supposedly found in all aspects of material as well as biological and social or cultural development on this planet.

But he added to this purely mechanical formula the idea that the process itself was not random, but instead guided by a superior *Weltgeist* / World Spirit or World Mind (or just simply God) that was directly involved in the entire process as part of a quest for the completion of history, with the full union, in a state of perfect love, of all things together. Even God (especially in the form of the living Jesus) was part of this process, seeking his own completion in union with man – or man in union with him, when all would be one in a perfect state of love and peace.

From this point on, virtually all the 1800s sense of progress (not just in Germany but in much of the whole of Western Civilization) was shaped by the idea not just of philosophers sitting in their salons directing others rationally toward a utopian world, but by the direct involvement of those who would bring history forward, through noble struggle, struggle directed by some great Spirit. Without such struggle, violent though it might be, progress was impossible.

Hegelianism also touched on group pride, as nations or classes came to see themselves as being under the special anointing of the World Spirit to take the lead to direct history into the next era. This fed powerfully into German nationalism, with its sense of special German historical destiny.

But this also fed powerfully into the working-class movement also arising at that time, a movement which came to view the industrial workers of the world as the true moral underpinning of the world to come.

* * *

DARWINISM

When in 1859 Darwin published his book, *On the Origin of Species* – the culmination of years of research and earlier publications – he shook the moral foundations of Western civilization. This occurred not because Darwin invented a new worldview out of thin air. The ideas of progress through struggle were by this time rather widely accepted. The British Whig party, in fact, was built on this idea: that Britain should be run by those proven strongest in life's competition and that no tears should be wept for the poor swept aside by life's struggles, because that would only hinder human progress.

No, it was not the newness of Darwin's ideas that made his works so spectacular, but it was because he gave such precise explanation – and justification – to these Whiggish ideas. His great contribution to this debate of worldviews was that he built his Darwinist theory of life on a vast field of scientific evidence, something that had by that time become the absolute requirement for any claim to Truth.

Also, he was building his ideas on a well-established base of earlier works on this matter of evolution.

Robert Malthus[98] ... and early versions of "survival of the fittest." Since the publication in 1798 of the book *An Essay on the Principle of Population* by the English clergyman Robert Malthus, there was considerable discussion in England about the problems created by a rapidly expanding human population on the earth, the issues of hunger, disease and war that this would produce. Consequently, by the time of Darwin's 1859 publication, a number of leading political and intellectual figures in England had already taken the social position that the best thing to do about the rising number of English poor was – by a process of natural de-selection – simply to let them maintain a natural balance with their world by the thinning of their ranks through hunger and disease. It was thus wise not to encourage their expansion through unnecessary charity.

Jean-Baptiste Lamarck ... and genetic progress. Going at the issue of evolution from a different perspective, the Frenchman Jean Baptiste Lamarck had concluded in his 1809 *Zoological Philosophy* that through chemical influences acting on organisms to create new traits and by the environmental forces shaping these traits through necessary adaptation, organisms had progressed over time. This included humans, in which human learning did not start out with a blank sheet (as per Locke's theory) but was built in part not only on the development of natural biological adaptation but also on the received aspects of learning derived by a person's ancestry. Thus learning could be understood as potentially progressive, evolving from one generation to the next, if carefully engineered with that understanding.

An earlier Darwin. It is important to note that Lamarck was himself influenced by Darwin's grandfather, Erasmus Darwin, who in 1796 described in his publication *Zoonomia* how species had developed slowly over the generations by their abilities to pass on from generation to generation not only their basic traits, but also useful alterations in those traits. Thus Erasmus's grandson Charles Darwin came from a family already securely located in the evolutionist camp!

Darwin himself.[99] What Charles Darwin had achieved his 1859 book *On the Origin of Species* was to show through actual scientific analysis how living creatures on this planet could have evolved slowly over an enormous expanse of time from a small number of simpler forms into a vast array of much more complex species. All of this could have been achieved entirely through a natural or mechanical process by which the very competitive nature of life rewarded the stronger offspring of any species the better chance for survival, and the privilege of birthing a new generation that retained that superiority. Eventually this struggle for life – and its continuation from generation to generation – would, over time, bring into existence a distinctly new, more complex specie, one better adapted to the complexities of life.

Thus every living creature we saw around us was naturally evolved from a less complex ancestor by a process termed "natural selection." In short, morally speaking, life was at its core simply a matter of the survival of the fittest.

Herbert Spencer.[100] Darwinism was further buttressed by the writings of other social philosophers of the day. Besides Darwin's pupil Huxley, who actually coined the term "survival of the fittest," there was Huxley's friend Herbert Spencer, who had been moving in the direction of Darwin's thinking even before Darwin published his first work in 1859. Spencer had been working on both social theory (his 1851 *Social Statistics*) and personal development theory (his 1855 *Principles of Psychology*), his work heavily influenced not only by Malthus but also by the theories of Lamarck. Then when Darwin's work was published in 1859 Spencer came out full force in his support of evolution as the basic doctrine of life, in every aspect of life on earth.

Soon Spencer would even outdistance Darwin as the most recognized philosopher of the late 1800s. But the very names Darwin and Darwinism would still serve as the most powerful symbols able to raise strong debate, pro and con, not only well into the 20th century but still even today.

Nietzsche.[101] The German philosopher and writer Friedrich Nietzsche was not exactly a Darwinist, but certainly was – or would soon become – a voice of his times (the late 1800s), a period deeply steeped in the Darwinist mindset. In his multi-volume series *Also Sprach Zarathustra* (*Thus Spoke Zarathustra*), he gave the German culture the ideal of the *Übermensch* – except that he was referring to the highly achieved individual – not some racial group, such as the Nazis would eventually use the term in reference to the German people as a whole, seeing themselves as a superior breed. Nietzsche was referring to the highly self-cultivated individual who (reflective of Nietzsche's own personal struggles) had come to put aside all other values (wealth, sex, even happiness) in order to focus completely in meeting fully the high calling that fate had placed on that person. Such a person strove to rise above the mere animal call to life – to rise above (*über*) mere common existence as a person (*Mensch*).

In fact, with respect to the ideal of the racial *Übermensch*, he was actually much opposed, getting himself in trouble with the German authorities for his strong anti-nationalism. He even at one point renounced his Prussian citizenship. No, Nietzsche was extolling the powerful individual that he claimed should be directing human life on this planet, not the group-think of the rising nationalist spirit that he saw developing around him – one which would eventually lead Europe into the disastrous national or tribal conflict known in its time as the Great War and to us today as World War One (as well as its continuation as World War Two a generation later).

He also was distinctly an atheist – informing the world that "God is dead." He (like Marx) saw the Judeo-Christian religion as offering humanity only enslavement to earthly commonness by teaching people to aim not for greatness in this life – but instead to aim for some supposed afterlife that Judeo-Christianity claimed awaited the humble and faithful at death. Nietzsche was very emphatic in stating that there was no evidence whatsoever that such a Heavenly life actually existed.

The assault on Christian morality. As an Anglican clergyman, Malthus himself had, back in the late 1700s, wrestled with the problem of why God would allow suffering to occur within his creation. Malthus finally concluded that God wanted man to rise to the challenge of life, to succeed in the face of life's difficulties through the discipline of hard work. Those who fell short of the challenge were simply some kind of disappointment to the great Creator.* Those who failed merely reaped that which they had sown. This in essence was the British version of Sturm und Drang!

Malthus's explanation of course was a terrible reading of what the founder of the Christian faith himself had taught the world. Jesus put the challenge not in terms of natural selection, but quite the opposite. According to Jesus, the challenge of life was to find ways to help the poor in the face of the huge challenge of survival in a competitive world of economics and politics. This ability to do charity, when the opposite would be so much more tempting, was for Jesus the measure of greatness of anyone in God's kingdom.

At some point people were going to have to choose between the two, Jesus or the Darwinists. The original Puritans had chosen Jesus, and built an experimental society of mutual service among social equals based precisely on the spiritual ethics of Jesus Christ. The Virginians, not exactly Darwinists but of the same mindset, chose instead personal success at the cost of others (the slaves). Thus by the mid-1800s this was not a new issue. It is simply that Darwinism finally gave aggressive selfishness the

---

*It is truly amazing the extent to which man can go in rationalizing about God and God's intentions.

moral justification that an increasingly aggressively selfish society seemed to require.

But Darwin himself, very sensitive to the importance of human charity and mutual concern in human society, was quite aware of this ethical matter, and actually troubled by how many were choosing to read cruel ethical justification into his theories.

KARL MARX[102]

At the same time that German (and other) social philosophers were seeing in the fast-changing dynamic of their days the fulfillment of history through the rise through struggle of the tribal nation (France, Germany, Italy, etc.), German expatriate philosopher (in exile in London) Karl Marx headed down an entirely different road in his explanation as to where history was headed. He saw history fulfilled not in the struggle among nations but instead in the struggle among economic classes, principally between the owners of wealth and the subject classes (proletariat) that produced that wealth for the owners through their labors. Marx was so insistent on this matter that he actually despised nationalism and all the discussion going on about nationalist struggles, seeing that as a distraction leading people away from the real struggle that lay before them, the industrial class struggle that was about to unfold – and lead the world into its final stage in history.

The Hegelian dialectic applied to Marx's economic theory. In 1848 Marx published his famous 30-page *Communist Manifesto* in the hope of capitalizing on the spirit of political rebellion that was rocking continental Europe at that time.

His *Manifesto* outlined history as a series of quite Hegelian dialectical struggles over time between those who legally owned the land, tools, machinery (what Marx summed up as social property or the "means of production") that produced the wealth that the people of society lived off of, and those (the proletariat*) who, though they owned none of those means of production, labored physically in using those means of production to bring forward the wealth that society lived off of. Typically in history, in the distribution of the wealth that a society jointly created for its survival and prosperity, most all of that wealth went to the class of property owners, with very little making its way to the hands of the proletarian workers. This would bring tremendous tension to society, which eventually

---

*A term drawn from Roman times in reference to the members of the Roman working class who held little or no property and thus few or no political rights.

The Rationalizing of Western Culture

would turn into physical conflict because of this social injustice. Again, in Hegelian (and eventually Darwinian) dialectical fashion, such conflict or class struggle would then move history forward to a new, and better social system, shaped by the way the opposing classes synthesized their social positions into a new social structure.

In his analysis, he carefully described the situation around him in Europe where the feudal system, once dominated by landed aristocrats, had been challenged by a new social class of industrial and financial capitalists, thus creating the age of capitalism. But he also saw how capitalism in turn had created its own opposing social force in the form of the industrial workers (the industrial proletariat) whose labors supported the capitalist system. And he predicted that conditions were quickly rising that would cause the industrial proletariat in its turn to rise up against the capitalist class, and through the necessary historical conflict or revolution open the way to a new social system.

Time was on the side of the worker, because capitalism by its very nature is highly competitive even among the capitalists themselves – each capitalist trying to eliminate his competitors in order to gain greater control over the market. This way they could increase their profits, even establish total or monopolistic control over the whole process. But of course as they drove each other out of business, they were inadvertently thinning out their capitalist social ranks, making their numbers smaller at the same time that the ranks of the proletariat were growing. Thus simply the calculus of the few against the many meant that the days of capitalism were numbered. At that point (which supposedly was now upon them) all the proletariat had to do was rise up and seize control of the means of production, thus destroying the power of the capitalist class, and the public government that had been protecting the capitalists. Thus in rising up against their capitalist oppressors, they had "nothing to lose but their chains."

A property-less, state-less, utopia. But, according to Marx, the resultant social system would be different, it would be utopia itself. There would be no further class of dominators or exploiters of the proletariat, because the new society would be made up solely of industrial workers. There would be no other class of people in the new society but this one single industrial class. Everyone would now live as social equals – as comrades, rather than as a two-class system of gentlemen lording it over a servant class. Being equals, all would live communally, as in all land, tools and machines being owned jointly by all – and by nobody in particular.

Consequently, there would be no need for the political enforcing agency of the state or government. It would simply wither away, because the sole purpose of the state was to protect the interests of the privileged class of property owners, whether feudal, capitalist or whatever. In the communist society there would be no personal property, thus no state. Something like a Rousseauian bliss would then hold this happy world together.

Communism as the last stage of history. Also, the new society would end the long historical dialectic of a ruling class and a proletariat class finding themselves once again in conflict. With no division under communism between a propertied class and a proletarian class, there would be no cause for social conflict, no tension, no stress, only blissful peace. Thus this last historical revolution would bring history to a completion, the kind of millennialist completion that everyone was expecting because of the unprecedented progress they had been observing coming forth at mind-boggling speed. All history was supposedly about to fulfill itself, and Marx was showing how that was to be accomplished.

All very scientific. This was all pretty powerful stuff. And it appealed to the interests not only of European industrial workers, but also to intellectual Progressivists – not only in Europe but also in America. Marx's theories seemed to be irrefutable because they were built on hard fact. Unlike the philosophical speculations of social philosophers before him, but quite like Darwin, Marx had thrown a lot of data into his analysis, supposedly hard economic data, thus qualifying his theory as "scientific socialism," making him – and those who followed his lead – "scientific socialists."

Marx's militant atheism. As all materialists or mechanists, Marx had no need of the concept of God, or some divine hand driving forward the economic process he had outlined. It all worked – similar to Darwin's theories – entirely mechanically. Marx personally was an atheist. In fact he was quite opposed to the Christian religion, or any religion that saw history shaped and judged by a Supreme Being. As for Christianity, he saw the religion simply as a cruel psychological tool used by Europe's ruling classes (most lately the capitalists) that savagely exploited their own servants or workers, by excusing their horrible treatment of the workers under the promise that if the oppressed workers all cooperated with the system and behaved themselves (not rebel against their oppressors) they would be rewarded in the next life with heaven. To Marx, such religious theory was only a form of spiritual opium given to the masses to keep them docile.

Marxism in America. Even though America was going through the same process of social industrialization as Europe, America really never connected with Marxism the way Europe did. Marxism had virtually no place in the semi-feudal South, and even in the industrial North it gained only a marginal position among the American industrial workers. Intellectuals took an interest in it, largely because of its utopian features. But in general Americans developed their own versions of intellectual utopianism, quite apart from Marxism. There would be some similarities, which would get these intellectuals in trouble, especially during the Red Scares that hit America from time to time.

American anti-Socialism. But by and large, America did its own thing. From their very founding, the New England and mid-Atlantic colonies had been opened up, settled, and defended not by resident kings and feudal lords but by a huge class of commoner individuals and their families – giving American culture its individualistic character. With America's expansion west across the Appalachian Mountains, the rural Midwest and the frontier West were settled by the same type of very individualistic Americans. To these proud Americans the very idea of giving up their independence to some kind of hovering governmental institution was itself anathema. Socialism – or government by a politically entitled set of enlightened supervisors – would not gain ground in America ... until the second half of the 20th century. But we will have more – much more – to say about that in the next volume of this historical study.

The spread of Marxism among Europe's intellectuals. Meanwhile, as Europe headed into the Twentieth Century, clearly a growing number of social and political philosophers were convinced that, through some kind of Darwinian process, Western civilization (and, via the West, also world civilization as well) was moving into a bright future in which utopian existence for all – even (and especially) the unwashed masses – seemed to loom into view. Society just needed some adjustments here and there – led of course by these political philosophers or social scientists – in order to bring this process to completion. "Historical progress" and "democracy" – however conceived specifically (and the variation was indeed huge) were the bywords, the slogans, the shibboleths, of those who supposed that they possessed special intellectual insights into where the world was headed.

Within that group of Western social reformers was a large group of Marxist ideologues and political activists – forming the Social Democratic Party in a number of European countries – whose expectations were that Marx's Communist revolution would soon break out across Europe. This supposedly would occur naturally first in a society experiencing the most advanced state of capitalism, probably Great Britain or Germany. After all, Marx's scientific socialism would not work except under the historical circumstances he had so carefully described. Every stage of historical development had to be completed before history would be ready to move on to the next step or phase in its development. The dialectical method demanded that kind of historical precision.

* * *

VLADIMIR ILYICH ULYANOV (LENIN)[103]

Yet oddly enough Marxism was very popular among a number of intellectuals in Russia, where industrial capitalism had barely got itself underway as it slowly emerged from under the Russian feudalism that still largely dominated the Russian social scene. Surely by Marxist logic, Russia was hardly ripe for revolution.

Skipping the capitalist phase, in order to move directly to Communism. However, a Russian intellectual, Vladimir Ilyich Ulyanov, known more popularly as Lenin, found himself not bothered by the inconsistencies between Marx's scientific socialism and the kinds of conditions that Russians like himself were working under in order to bring to Russia their own proletarian revolution, one leading to a workers' democracy. Lenin was a strong advocate of the idea that Russia could skip the capitalist phase of history and move directly from feudalism to full communism.

This of course caused a number of Marxist purists in Russia to oppose Lenin, who was a fast rising voice within the Russian Communist cause. This in turn lead to a split in 1904 in the Russian Social Democratic Party, with Lenin taking complete leadership of one of the two groups, the Bolsheviks (meaning majority even though they were at first the smaller of the two contending Communist groups).

Revolutionary change led by the "vanguard" of the industrial proletariat. Lenin explained in his popular writings that proletarian democracy was of course the goal of everything he believed in. But he was certain that Russia did not need to wait to go through the whole, long capitalist phase of history, but instead could move here and now, even in semi-feudal Russia, directly to a workers' (and peasants') democracy.

Clearly Marx had supposed that a glorious workers democracy would come about naturally through a spontaneous uprising of the oppressed industrial working class when their growing numbers, as opposed to the declining numbers of the capitalist (or bourgeois or middle) class, finally weighted the impulse of history in the workers' favor. To Marx this would require a natural rise and then self-inflicted decline of the capitalist bourgeois class before history would be ready for the move of the industrial working class to seize history.

Marx was thus discussing a workers' revolution whose dynamic would spontaneously unfold from the ground up in a truly democratic fashion.

Lenin disagreed with Marx's insistence that this was the inevitable path by which such revolution would unfold. According to Lenin's thinking, in his native Russia, where industry was only slightly developed and a Russian capitalist class therefore was still rather insignificant politically, a socialist/communist revolution could be undertaken to bring forth a fully modern, industrial Russia – an industrial democracy controlled by the industrial workers themselves – without having to go through a necessary capitalist phase of history.

How was this sidestepping of Marxist logic possible? Lenin argued that such a marvelous industrial democracy could be brought directly into existence, here and now, even in semi-feudal Russia, if it were directed by an intellectual elite well studied in Marxist scientific socialism. Such an elite would be aware of history's ultimate intention (full communism) and with this idea leading them forward would be able to bring society to such a utopia directly through scientific (Marxist) management, without having to struggle through a capitalist phase of industrial history. These Marxist specialists or social scientists were best positioned to do the thinking for the masses of humanity because they were fully studied in Marxist logic, in the Marxist dialectic, in the main tenants of scientific socialism. This small elite group, the "vanguard" of the proletariat could guide and control the people's revolution – get it going and ultimately secured on firm grounds.

So there it was, another "democratic" revolution, led not by the people themselves but instead by their social "betters," intellectuals like Lenin and his Bolsheviks, who would do the thinking and thus the directing of the "democratic revolution from above," from their positions of social "enlightenment."

In any case, by doing it Lenin's way Russia could supposedly skip all the historical necessities and move directly from feudalism to full socialism, and even to the pure state of communism.

The termination of property rights. The key to this Leninist jump away from pure Marxism was found in this matter of land or property rights. According to Marx, it was, is and always will be, the ownership of land and commercial industrial infrastructure (a society's property) which determines the shape, structure and operation of each historical phase of human society. For instance, in the case of feudalism – which Russia still was largely identified with – land was mostly owned by the Emperor, plus a small number of aristocratic families as well as officials of the Russian Orthodox Church. On the feudal estates owned by this small ruling class millions of peasants worked – receiving whatever benefits this ruling class extended to them (usually very minimal).

Under capitalism, which by the 1800s seemed to be in the process of overthrowing or replacing these feudal landowners everywhere (except maybe in Russia), key property rights (land, buildings, roads, etc.) were now coming into the possession of the rising moneyed middle class: the capitalists. Under Capitalism, society's property could be bought and sold by those possessing moneyed wealth.

As Marx was outlining his understanding of social history during the mid-1800s, this system too seemed clearly to benefit only a small percentage of the population. Under industrial capitalism (at least in Europe, though hardly was this the case in America), the vast majority of the members of European society still owned no land and very little other property, but merely worked as rightless (or proletarian) miners and factory workers, to the great financial benefit of this rising class of propertied capitalists.

But according to Marx, the beauty of communism (destined historically soon to replace capitalism) was that in the final phase of history – when capitalism would be overthrown by the huge class of property-less industrial workers – no one would hold title to the land and its industrial infrastructure. With the rise to power of the unpropertied working class, all property or "means of production" would be considered to be communal property – belonging to the society as a whole and to no one in particular (thus Communism).

Lenin's contribution to Marxist logic. However, if the property of the few Russian lords or landowners was simply taken here and now from this small privileged feudal group, the same historical results would take place: a property-less society enjoyed mutually by all. Everyone could then move directly to the bliss of shared or mutual cooperation of full Communism. Each person would give to society according to his or her means or ability to contribute socially, and receive back from society according to his or her specific needs.

And since (according to Marx) governments exist only to protect the exclusive rights of the property-owning classes, under Communism there would be no need for the government or State. It would simply wither away to nothingness.

In short, Lenin proposed the idea that if Russia were to move directly through the guidance of the insightful Communist intellectuals, the Vanguard of the Industrial Proletariat, to an unpropertied society, Russia would not have to go through a capitalist phase in history, but could move quickly toward the state of Communism.

The "Socialist phase" of the transition to Communism. But this move of Russian society from feudalism to communism would nonetheless require a transitional time (the socialist phase), necessary to reform the people's antiquated cultural thinking. The Bolshevik Vanguard would have to continue to control the social revolution until such time as the masses were culturally retrained sufficiently to be ready to assume full responsibility for democratic self-rule. Then, and only then, would we see a withering away of an unneeded State. Then, and only then, would the people be ready to step into a totally free, totally State-less, truly Communistic, stage of social development.

Once again, here in Lenin was an Idealist, positive that the intellectuals with the right Ideas were the ones best entrusted with the responsibility of bringing society to a wonderful utopian future that only they could truly understand and know how to manage.

Needless to say, such self-serving Idealism found wide acceptance in one form or another in the intellectual circles of Western (and even American) society.

Elitist intellectuals versus middle-class commoners. However members of the West's property-owning middle class – and certainly that included the vast number of middle-class Americans – loved their private property and not only had no interest in the idea of intellectuals taking command of society in order to bring their world to some kind of utopian property-less democracy but were positively horrified at the idea.

Indeed, in Puritan America (colonial New England) it had been well-understood that property ownership was crucial to the development of a sense of social responsibility, which is why new Puritan settlements were designed with small but equal property allotments given to each new family joining the community. Thus it was that – to what eventually became Middle-Class America – the ownership of a home and adjoining property was an absolutely foundational principle never to be violated. Any talk about removing property rights of the people was absolute anathema to such Americans, and a key part of the fear or Red Scare that would occasionally sweep America when intellectuals were heard talking of social property rather than private property.

In any case, Marxist-Leninist ideas were rampant in Western intellectual circles, especially with Lenin's successful overthrow of Russia's very brief middle-class democracy and, as a result of the very brutal Russian Revolution and Civil War of 1917-1921, the installing in its place of a Communist working-class democracy ... a "democracy" directed and controlled by Lenin's Communist Party elite, of course.

Indeed Lenin – and his chief partner and heir-apparent, Leon Trotsky

– intended their Russian Revolution to be merely the first phase of a larger, world-wide revolution designed to sweep away bourgeois, middle-class culture and society and replace it everywhere with a Communist working-class society – directed by the vanguard of the proletarian revolution, the Communist Party elite.

And it looked for a while as if they might actually succeed in spreading their revolution, at least to the defeated powers of the Great War, Germany and Austria-Hungary, when Communist uprisings occurred in the capitals Berlin and Budapest.

Thus while Marxist-Leninist thoughts delighted a good number of Western intellectuals, who found it easy to identify with such high ideals (and such marvelous political opportunity for themselves as society's managers), it set off a Red Scare among the comfortable middle classes of Western societies everywhere.

And thus also a serious social cultural breach between intellectuals and Middle-Class or bourgeois commoners began to grow within Western society, especially in America. A battle between "high-brow" intellectuals and "low-brow" commoners* was beginning to form. The battle would become intense and bitter – and rather persistent through the rest of the 20th century (and even still today).

Anarchism. We need to include another political philosophy that developed along these same lines towards the latter part of the 1800s, Anarchism. Anarchism was not a movement or an ideology. Instead it simply was a mood that infected European politics as the familiar feudal world began to fall apart and as the emerging post-feudal Europe was not yet moving towards any set social form or structure. Anarchism might be considered Rousseauian. It might be considered Marxist. Both philosophies stressed how a better world would be one in which the little people led their lives without having to live under powerful overlords who wanted to control their lives. But anarchists were not the type to wait for revolution to develop. They simply took matters in their own hands, and assaulted those leaders themselves. In short, they were simply assassins assuming the heroic responsibility of removing evil overlords from society, or else they were just socially maladjusted individuals, bitter because things were not working out for them socially and taking their sense of vengeance out on the leaders who symbolized an uncaring society.

In any case there would be a rash of anarchist events in Europe in the late 1800s and early 1900s, and even in America (President McKinley was shot and killed by one). In fact it was a small group of anarchists (believing

---

*Or "deplorables," as Democratic Party presidential candidate Hillary Clinton labelled them in a September 2016 campaign speech.

themselves also to be loyal Serbian nationalists) who, in assassinating the Austrian Grand Duke and his wife in 1914, would set off a huge war that brutalized and ultimately crippled European civilization itself.

✳ ✳ ✳

DEMOCRACY AS THE RISING IDEAL OF AMERICAN POLITICS

Meanwhile, across the Atlantic, as we have just seen, America was developing its own new thoughts on the matter of society, and how progress could be brought into play to make for a much better world. Interestingly, much of the American individualistic mindset found itself easily forming around this term that about this time was gaining great currency: "Democracy."

Democracy in the American context was not Marxist, Socialist or even particularly Darwinist – as was the case generally in Europe. But it did have strong elements of Rousseauian utopianism in it. And it seemed also to be a natural fit to the spirit, the mood, of America as it entered the 20th century. American Democracy was built on the instinctive idea of the full sovereignty of the millions of individuals that made up American society. They alone as individuals were responsible for their futures. They alone governed their lives. They were truly members of a great Democracy.

Democracy or Republic? Thus it was that with the arrival of the 20th century, Americans began more frequently to refer to their society as a democracy rather than as a republic. Probably Americans thought that the two were the same thing.

They were not and never have been the same thing. America is indeed a republic, just as the framers of our Constitution intended. America is not a democracy. Nor has it ever been a true democracy – though it certainly possesses a great spirit of full and equal sovereignty among its people.

Why the confusion? A big part of the confusion over the idea of democracy is that since the early part of the 20th century high-minded Americans began to take on the old and well-failed mid-1700s idea of Jean Jacques Rousseau, that democracy is some kind of natural political condition of man – natural in the sense that if it were not for the corruptions of a bad culture or a corrupt government, people everywhere would live freely, lovingly, on the basis of a deeply instinctive desire to live peacefully in fellowship with each other as equals. That is, they would live democratically. They needed no autocratic authority to force them into social compliance. They could live together freely, strictly on the basis of their own personal instincts towards social harmony.

For Rousseau, the reason we did not find man presently living in such state of natural bliss was because of the corrupting influence on human behavior of societies built on wealth and power. As we have just noted, Rousseau felt that the solution was to tear down the artificial structure of European civilization and go back to nature, where we would then live naturally in blissful harmony.

So, according to Rousseau – and most utopian Western intellectuals since then, including a growing number of American Progressivists (and virtually all 20th century American hippies!) – democracy is supposed to be instinctive to man. And one day, through our evangelical efforts to spread democracy to the world, we will be able to bring our world to a state of perpetual peace by having everyone living democratically – that is, freely. It was and is a beautiful, utopian dream.

But it was and is a dangerous dream because it is built on an entirely naive understanding of human nature. It is an idea built on a great illusion.

Man is, by all natural instinct, self-preserving and self-promoting. This is how all people start out life as babies, highly demanding of attention to their personal needs. Their survival demands that. And that same sense of selfishness is vital to the process of socialization. Man is able to live or function socially only because he is taught (as he grows up) that by living in cooperation with others, he will actually improve the benefits he personally draws from life. Thus as he matures, he is taught by social authority how to cooperate with larger society in order to draw its tremendous benefits for himself.

The teaching process begins at an early age (the terrible twos), in his very first social context, that of the family (a family presided over by an authoritative mother and father). He then continues to learn through schooling to extend this realm of social self-interest by cultivating a deeper sense of social self-discipline.

If any part of this process fails to take place, the individual will have a hard time coping with the demands of social life and will not know how to "do adult" and find a productive place in society. Tragically, he might even fall into what society terms criminal behavior.

In short, the Rousseauian ideal if actually undertaken will result not in democracy but in anarchy, an anarchy however which will in no way resemble the beautiful anarchy dreamed of by the utopian anarchists!

A reprise: The original intent of America's Founding Fathers. Indeed, it is important to note that the Framers of the Constitution were definitely not intending to create a democracy. For whatever reasons – partly historical (remembering how the Athenian democracy had been manipulated by Sophist demagogues who could move the gullible Athenians to support self-destructive policies and actions), partly Puritan, partly Aristotelian – they were not believers that pure democracy was possible ... or even desirable. The earlier Puritan understanding of man's inherent selfishness or sinfulness – and Aristotle's teaching about the susceptibility to tyranny of any kind of government, including democracies – made the Framers very cautious about turning all power over directly to the people.

They had built on the developing British parliamentary system of the 1600s and 1700s, one that the French political philosopher Montesquieu had pointed out (and Madison reaffirmed in *The Federalist Papers*) afforded all sorts of checks and balances against any one particular kind of political impulse (rule of one, of the few, or of the many) securing a dominant or controlling – or tyrannical position – in the governing program. Power was cautiously allotted to this and to that part of the governing system, without it being concentrated in any one particular position. Power was purposefully spread widely across all these various political impulses to ensure that no power holder, not a presidential monarch, not a Congressional oligarchy, not an enlightened Federal judge, but especially not a democratic mob, could establish a controlling grip over the system. To allow that to happen would be to allow tyranny to develop. No indeed. This was no democracy – nor for that matter an oligarchy or certainly even a monarchy that they had created but instead was a mixed-system Republic, one designed to best serve the whole society, present and future – for hopefully a very long time.

Representative government (as close as they got to democracy) was really provided for originally only in the House of Representatives, where the citizens were allowed a direct vote for their representatives in Congress. The Senate was understood to represent the states and their governments, the two Senate seats each state was to receive generally being appointed by the state governors or elected by members of the state legislatures (the original Constitution did not specify how the states were to come up with their two senatorial representatives). In any case the U.S. senators were not originally intended to be elected by the people (the Seventeenth Amendment ratified in 1913, "democratizing" the Senate, would change that). Likewise the Chief Executive officer, the president, was not to be elected directly by the people, but by the states, each state awarded special electors in the same number of their senators and representatives in Congress. These electors would be the ones who would elect the president (how the states were to choose their electors was also originally left up to the states to decide). And the federal judges were not elected by the people but were appointed by the president, subject to a confirming vote of the U.S. Senate.

Furthermore, the national officers were given only very limited jurisdiction – that is, they were permitted to govern only in very specific areas. All other government functions were left to the state legislatures as their exclusive right to perform. Thus originally America's national democracy was quite limited in scope and subject to the checks and balances of the other branches and levels of the federal government, "federal" originally meaning the whole plan, including the huge governmental role reserved to the states as part of the federal system.

It must be remembered that the government set up by the Framers was actually a military-political alliance among thirteen independent-minded states, unifying them in the face of a threatening world outside of their own, such as the British wanting to come back to retake them, one by one – or even by greedy French or Spanish monarchs hoping to do the same. It was never conceived as a government that would rule over the internal affairs of the thirteen states, as the Tenth Amendment states quite clearly. The Framers neither desired nor needed such a government. They were very determined on that matter, having just gone through a huge war against the British King George III who had in mind to bring the thirteen colonies under his direct rule as their enlightened lord and master.

And yet this would always be the temptation of the powerful, to bring the less enlightened ones of society under the better rule of their natural superiors. Such is always the temptation of the Enlightened Ones, who have fed themselves on the fruit of the Tree of the Knowledge of Good and Evil. Such self-awarded enlightenment is the worst of all human sins, for it gives the Enlightened Ones the false impression of being sacred and all-powerful, like gods.

The "democratic" impulse at the heart of American Progressivism. However, the original American caution concerning unchecked democracy began to be set aside in the early part of the 20th century. In part this development was the outgrowth of the Progressivist Movement, as America became very self-critical of the many corruptions in American government and society, and always on the lookout for improved ways to bring to the surrounding society.

Rather naturally, it was to the national government that reformers ultimately looked, in the hope that wise legislators might remedy America's various social problems. And indeed the national government did just that, at least to the extent of stepping into the game of laissez-faire capitalism in order to referee the behavior of capitalism's prime players in the market place – thus the government's trust-busting of the financial monopolies that had come into ownership of huge sectors of the American economy. But governmental reforms also included the safeguarding of the lives of America's workers, and the inspection and enforcement of standards of quality of the agricultural and industrial products sold to the public.

The Rationalizing of Western Culture 419

The government also began to put pressure on urban bosses to be open and fair about how elections and political business were conducted in American cities. The party candidates for public office were usually selected behind the scenes by party bosses. But in a move state by state over a period starting in 1902 and involving all the states by 1915, candidates for office came to be selected through the primary system, where the voters themselves were given the right to select (vote for) the candidates of their parties. To this key democratic reform was added the ideas of popular recall of corrupt public officials. And finally, to move urban government to work along more professional lines was added the idea of hiring a professional city manager who would supposedly be neutral in the realm of party politics, and simply supervise the functions of urban government on scientific principles!

And in early 1913, two new Amendments to the American Constitution went into effect, ones designed to give both the voter and Congress new powers, thus enhancing democracy. However, these Amendments would also lessen greatly the effect of the checks and balances of the original Constitution.

The Sixteenth Amendment to the Constitution (1913): direct taxation. The Sixteenth Amendment gave Congress the right to expand its ability to function on its own by allowing Congress to tax directly the incomes of Americans. This would give Washington a new independence of operation from the states, which were viewed as too dependent on party machines and thus supposedly (supposedly by the Progressivists anyway) more susceptible than Washington to political corruption.

The power to tax is of course a great power – and the Progressivists had just given the government in Washington extensive powers not previously possessed. What they did not realize was that they had not solved the problem of corruption but had simply transferred the potential for that problem from the states to Washington – for they failed to understand that corruption always finds a path to wherever power is located.

The Seventeenth Amendment (1913): popular election of senators. The Seventeenth Amendment also diminished the power of the states by democratizing the U.S. Senate, making it now a body of government officials elected directly by the people rather than directly by the States. Again the supposition was that it would operate more responsibly if it were answerable directly to the people rather than to the states and their political machines.

This was widely understood at the time to be an excellent idea – this idea of democratizing further the operation of American government, discarding the suspicions of the original Framers of the American Constitution who held no particular form of government, including democracy, to be ideal.

And certainly democracy was ideal – as long as the people themselves were sophisticated in their understanding of the process of national government, remained vigilant with a detailed following of national politics, and were not easily manipulated by clever voices that could spin ideas and turn hearts easily. The Progressivists were confident that a well-educated electorate – under proper guidance (namely that of the Progressivists themselves) – could meet all these high standards.

The support of ever-centralizing power. But in doing this, this changed the very constitutional nature of American government from being a federal union of states (as in the United States) and instead a democratic republic (as in all modern dictatorial Socialist or Communist systems claiming to be People's Democratic Republics). This would remove one of the key pieces in the Constitution put there by the very wise Framers of the Constitution to check the growth of accumulating central power founded on democratic political instincts, well known in history to be so very easily manipulated by demagogues. Indeed, the French soon (1789) clearly – and violently – demonstrated this problem inherent in pure democracy.

This Seventeenth Amendment now opened the way for the Washington government step by step to override the states' role in governing the internal affairs of the country, which indeed was the purpose of this Amendment. And justified by supposedly the more Progressivist political professionalism found in a political bureaucracy which could now take its place in the nation's capital in Washington, D.C., this amendment would gradually take real government from the hands of the people themselves, instead, leaving the democratic masses increasingly dependent on the political favors coming their way from the Washington political professionals.

Thus the irony of "democracy," repeated so often in the coming 20th century: Lenin and Stalin's Russia, Hitler's Germany, Mao's China, Castro's Cuba, Kim's North Korea for instance, "enlightened" dictatorships claiming to best serve the interests of the people!

✶ ✶ ✶

WOODROW WILSON, THE DEMOCRATIC IDEALIST[104]

Certainly the most important person to shift America into a full devotion to the Democratic Idealism that was finding its way into the heart of the Progressivist Movement was Woodrow Wilson – Princeton professor (1890-1902), Princeton President (1902-1910), Governor of the State of New

The Rationalizing of Western Culture   421

Jersey (1911-1913), and finally President of the United States (1913-1921). He combined all the traits, positive and negative, of a Democratic Idealist: he detested corruption or imperfection of any kind in society, had very clear ideas of what needed to be done in order to promote democracy, had no patience for the art of compromise, and was very intolerant of anyone who did not support his views.

His early years. Wilson was born in 1856 to a Scots-Irish Protestant family, his father having moved from Ohio to the South to pastor Presbyterian churches in Georgia and South Carolina. Wilson was just four when the Civil War broke out, and his slave-owning father became a key leader in the Southern breakaway from the national Presbyterian Church (his father would lead the Southern Presbyterian church as its Stated Clerk from 1865 to 1898). After the war, Wilson lived in Columbia, South Carolina, where his father was a professor at the Columbia Theological Seminary.

Schooling. Wilson's schooling started late (perhaps from a problem of dyslexia) but he disciplined himself to compensate and developed strong academic skills as a result. Wilson started his college studies at Davidson College in North Carolina (his father taking up a pastorate there in the meantime), but had to drop out because of illness. He transferred the next year to Princeton, taking up the study of political philosophy and history, also becoming deeply involved in collegiate debate. After graduation from Princeton in 1879 he took up law studies at the University of Virginia. But again, health issues forced him to return home to North Carolina. There he continued his law studies, took and passed the Georgia bar exam, but after a year of law practice found the work uninteresting and decided in 1883 to pursue doctoral studies in political science and history at Johns Hopkins University.

Doctoral studies.   Here he wrote his doctoral dissertation, revealing himself to be a Democratic Idealist who could find no good reason for the American Constitutional checks and balances system. In his doctoral dissertation, *Congressional Government* (1885), he judged the checks and balances system as . . .

> manifestly a radical defect in our federal system that it parcels out power and confuses responsibility as it does. The main purpose of the Convention of 1787 seems to have been to accomplish this grievous mistake. The "literary theory" of checks and balances is simply a consistent account of what our Constitution makers tried to do; and those checks and balances

> have proved mischievous just to the extent which they have succeeded in establishing themselves. [p. 186-187]

He made it clear in his study that he preferred the parliamentary system of the British, which had a more "responsible" form of political authority in command of the political system. He viewed the American Constitution as terribly pre-modern and its checks and balances system as a formula designed merely to produce political stagnation and corruption. What modern Constitutional government required, he believed, was a strong hand at the helm of state.

In this, Wilson's thinking followed closely the line of other democratic idealists (including Marx and Lenin) who advocated revolutionary change to a system in which strong but enlightened leadership would serve as the people's advocate, thus qualifying it as very effective democracy. The fact that this easily opened the doors to popular dictatorship somehow escaped the understanding of these political scientists.

Professor Wilson. After marrying the very artistic Ellen Axson (daughter also of a Presbyterian minister) the Wilsons moved to New York for Wilson to teach history at Cornell University (1886-1887) and then Bryn Mawr College (1887-1888), then Connecticut Wesleyan University, until 1890 when he was offered the Chair of Jurisprudence and Political Economy at Princeton.

"Democratic politics would work better under a greatly empowered national leader." By this time he had eased up a little in his negative view of the legacy of the Founding Fathers. But he never seemed to back down on his view that American politics should be more like the British Parliamentary system in that it should be directly under the control of the national leader, through his command of the dominant political party dedicated to supporting the high principles set forth by that leader (Wilson's *Constitutional Government of the United States* - 1908). This lofty view of government by a principled leader would always remain at the heart of his idea of how politics should work, a position he himself eventually would take as American president, when he attempted to govern the country from just such a lofty position.

He was in fact a strong advocate of an activist government empowered to correct the ills of society, and published a number of articles and books over the next dozen years (actually at the time quite well received in intellectual circles) advocating exactly just such a government.

Princeton president. His writings had attracted the interest of other universities, the University of Illinois (1892) and the University of Virginia (1901) asking him to serve as their president, offers which he declined. But when Princeton asked him to serve as their new president in 1902, he accepted the offer. As Princeton president, he proved himself to be an active developer – programs, buildings and endowments developing rapidly under his leadership. He also worked hard to broaden the religious view of Princeton from beyond mere Presbyterian theological conservatism – and the student body from being a community of young gentlemen gliding through with a C average to being instead a community of serious scholars. He demanded more, much more of the school, cutting way back on the traditional religious activities expected of the students and introducing instead broader, more humanistic studies for them to focus on. Needless to say, he got some pushback from some of the professors for his reforms.

Nonetheless, In 1905 he represented Princeton at a huge gathering in New York City of various Christian leaders interested in promoting and formalizing inter-denominational cooperation in their conduct of world missions, both at home and abroad (this conference would lead three years later to the creation of the Federal Council of Churches). Wilson himself spoke of the need to make "the United States a mighty Christian nation, and to Christianize the world."

But ultimately he would take up the path not of Christianity's personal salvation mission but instead a more Progressivist or "democratic" social mission to the world – something by this time that had come to be known as the "Social Gospel." Ironically this "democratic mission" would come to be directed by a man (himself) with a very autocratic personality!

In fact it was this autocratic personality that ultimately found him opposed by various faculty and board members in his reform efforts at Princeton. A crisis developed because he was just not a person cut out to find a way to win people to his ideas through diplomacy. Wilson would not accept anything less than full compliance with his ideas of reform.

New Jersey Governor. Finding increasing opposition in academia, his thoughts began to turn to the idea of public office. And, oddly enough, New Jersey political bosses began to look with interest in Wilson as someone they might want to run for the 1910 state race for governor. He agreed to run, and they agreed to get him nominated as the Democratic Party candidate for governor (which they easily delivered to Wilson). Thus he resigned his position as Princeton president in October, just shortly before the November elections. And in November he easily won the election over his Republican rival.

Now as New Jersey Governor, he was in a position to pursue political reform – exactly according to his own ideas of what needed to be done. He was bold and unyielding in his attack on the party bosses of New Jersey, the same ones who had brought him to power! He instituted the primary system which allowed the ordinary voter to bypass the urban bosses in selecting electoral candidates themselves for public office – striking a blow for democracy.

Wilson elected U.S. president (1912). Thus after only a short term in office as governor his work was recognized sufficiently for his name to be put forward as a possible Democratic Party presidential candidate for the 1912 national elections. After much campaigning for the office himself, plus some critical last-minute support from Bryan at the convention – and after forty-six ballots – he was nominated as presidential candidate by his Democratic Party.

There was actually very little chance that this lofty Princeton professor turned New Jersey political reformer would have ever been elected American president – except that Teddy Roosevelt's decision to run as a third-party candidate changed entirely the political landscape. As already noted, this action consequently split the large Republican Party electorate, and allowed Wilson to win the presidency with a simple plurality of the votes.

But the election also brought large Democratic Party majorities in both houses of Congress, thus helping the new president get much of his legislative program moved forward.

As president, Wilson stuck closely to his strongly Progressivist principles of low tariffs, taxes on the wealthy, and antitrust reforms in the banking and industrial world. He turned trust-busting from Congressional legislation to regulation by a new Federal Trade Commission, empowered to guard against the development of large trusts and monopolistic buyouts, which now were permitted only with federal approval. He moved quickly to reform the nation's erratic banking system (which suffered so easily from the panics that struck the nation at regular intervals) by setting up a Federal Reserve System to help expand or contract the nation's money supply in order to offset both inflations and deflations. By 1915 the new system was ready to go to work, just in time to help the nation face the troubles going on in Europe.

But in the world of Black-White race relations he proved himself to still be a Southerner at heart, calling for the segregation of government workplaces and facilities, claiming that segregation removed the possibilities of racial tensions affecting government work (although both Roosevelt and Taft had undertaken something of a similar policy).

His reelection in 1916. Coming up for reelection, Wilson campaigned on the basis of the many reform measures passed under his presidency (which seemed connected to an obvious prosperity the nation was experiencing at the time), and the fact that he had artfully kept the nation out of the war going on in Europe, one that was clearly grinding down civilized life on that continent.

But events would soon change that picture. But that story belongs in the next chapter.

✳ ✳ ✳

AMERICAN LIBERALISM

Liberalism as a rising worldview (cosmology) or religion. At the same time that the concept of democracy was beginning to take hold of the American political imagination, a new term, Liberalism, was also coming into vogue. The term was borrowed in part from the British Liberal Party which had recently switched its classical anti state-position into a very activist or Progressivist position in English political life. Liberalism, as a political social ideal (even ideology), crossed the Atlantic and began to substitute itself for the term Progressivism assigned to American political activism since the turn into the 20th century.

Liberalism was a much more comprehensive idea than Progressivism. Progressivism had identified a number of programs that reformers sought to have instituted in order to bring the nation closer to utopian standards. Although Liberalism was also just such an idea and action, it was more than that ... much more than that. Like the term democracy (with which it identified itself closely) it was more a worldview, a new understanding about life and how it was supposed to work. It was in fact (like its cousin democracy) an ideology bordering on being a religion held in faith by a growing number of true believers. But whereas democracy tended to focus more on the idea of governmental reform, Liberalism took on for reform all aspects of social life – cultural, social, economic as well as political. In this it offered an even deeper challenge to the Christian worldview that had formed the ideological and spiritual foundation of America since its founding three centuries earlier.

The instinctive goodness of man. The Liberal ideology or cosmology (worldview) was typically Humanist in that it was built on the certainty that man was fully capable of knowing the difference between right and wrong, and – given the political power to do so – would instinctively want to correct the wrongs he saw in life, to bring about the right. Liberals, as Humanists or Idealists, had little doubt about the basic goodness of man – if given the right opportunities. This was a key part of the Liberal doctrine which gathered support as the early 20th century developed.

To Liberals, religion* was viewed as a private or personal matter – rather than as a vital instrument of social and political action. God was growing more distant – still lofty, but removed from the day to day affairs of man, which increasingly were seen solely as man's jurisdiction.

Liberalism was based on the ennobling of the idea of man – to the point of man being considered to be like God himself, the only significant sovereign over life on this planet (the heart of the Liberals' religion). Many Liberals (who also were Darwinists or Marxists) were in fact even acknowledged atheists (a religion without a personal god).

"Sin" as environmental rather than internal to man. As far as the problem of human sin, Liberals certainly recognized that there were sinners in the world. But they viewed these not as Christians did, as a matter of intrinsic sinful human nature manifesting itself, but rather as the impact of environmental factors that undermined the noble human spirit. Hunger, poverty, disease, alcohol, illiteracy, and, most importantly, oppression by others who had indeed fallen into the grips of evil (usually considered the rich and powerful), were factors external to the spirit of common man. These external or environmental factors however could and should be corrected (by the reformers themselves) to bring about the conditions that would allow fully the human powers of goodness to manifest themselves.

Thus democracy and Liberalism grew up together. Anything that would promote the dignity of man was considered democracy. Liberals looked forward eagerly to the day when common man would be freed from the shackles of antiquated social and cultural systems – to usher in a bright, new era of human wisdom, equality, prosperity and peace, all summed up in the highly emotional word "democracy."

Democracy from above. In this, Jefferson served as something of a patron saint to American Liberals. A century earlier Jefferson had expressed much the same expectations resulting from on-going and truly revolutionary social reform, always directed from above by more enlightened individuals like himself. Indeed, reform directed from above – from above because the unwashed masses were not considered by Liberal reformers competent enough to figure out on their own the path to utopia, and although directed from above done in the name of democracy – would always be one of the strange ironies of American Liberalism.†

---

*Meaning "Christianity" – although a religious mix of Christianity, Buddhism, Hinduism etc. was becoming increasingly popular among the more "sophisticated" cultural elite of the Western world.

†In continental Europe – this same philosophy was/is known as Socialism.

Liberalism as a rising Humanist religion. Liberalism was moving itself in America into an even stronger position as a rising religion, one entirely Humanist and Secular (thus "Secular Humanism"). At one point, Liberalism – or Humanism as it also would sometimes call itself – did acknowledge itself to be a new religion (as for instance in the 1933 *Humanist Manifesto*). But it would later step away from that confession of Humanism being a new religion (the 1973 *Humanist Manifesto II*), because it discovered that by denying that it was a religion, but claiming for itself the status as purely "scientific" Truth, and by pointing out at the same time that Christianity in the public arena violated the Constitutional principle of the separation of Church and State, it could – through the intervention of the Federal Courts – force Christianity out of the public life of America. It could then position its own supposed "non-religion" religion of Liberalism (or Secular Humanism) in Christianity's former position as America's foundational cosmology or belief system, thus monopolizing American public life – intellectually, morally and spiritually (much as the Soviets did in Communist Russia).

* * *

JOHN DEWEY AS A FOUNDING FATHER
OF AMERICAN LIBERALISM[105]

A major contributor to this Liberal sense of human confidence was John Dewey. This American educator and philosopher truly believed in man's natural ability to do the good and true – if he were merely educated properly to these higher standards. His optimism concerning human nature ultimately had not only a tremendous impact on the way America looked at the process of democratic education, it helped move America toward a general Democratic Idealism, one that would eventually become the basis of American Liberalism or Secular Humanism.

Dewey grew up in a typical middle-class Vermont family in a largely unremarkable manner. He attended and graduated with distinction (Phi Beta Kappa) from the University of Vermont in the field of education, and found a job teaching high school for two years in Pennsylvania and then a year closer to home at a primary school in Vermont. But he was not sufficiently challenged by the work and enrolled in a Ph.D. program at Johns Hopkins University in Baltimore. He then took a teaching job at the University of Michigan in 1884, and then ten years later moved on to Chicago to join the faculty of the new University of Chicago. This innovative Baptist school was set up with major Rockefeller funding designated for research, also serving as the intellectual centerpiece for a number of affiliated colleges spread across the country. Here he often found himself working with children alongside Jane Addams, as the University was an important supporter of her Hull House.

The rationalist atmosphere of the university fit well with Dewey's growing secular rationalism, labeled Pragmatism (or Instrumentalism) as a rising philosophical movement. Here he undertook experiments in early education, in accordance with his belief that early social education could produce (by way of the pragmatic example set by the excellent teacher) the type of rational adult that Dewey believed would usher in a brave new world of enlightenment. Ultimately however disagreements with the university's directors caused him to resign in 1904, and take a position in New York City at Columbia University, where he would remain for the next quarter of a century (except for his two sabbatical years spent in China, 1919-1921) until his retirement in 1930. Here at Columbia he continued his experiments in early education, and his publications in support of his educational theories (he published some 40 books and over 700 articles in his lifetime).

His philosophy was standard Liberal theory:[106] social environment determines human behavior; reform the environment in very practical ways and you will reform human behavior. He also, like so many intellectuals of his generation, believed that democracy was the proper formula for solving society's problems (though critics were quick to point out that he never really explained how democracy was supposed to work in a mass society). He might not have stood out from the intellectual crowd, except that his massive number of publications made him a well-recognized leader in the rising Humanist movement underway in America.

After retiring from Columbia, Dewey continued over the next twenty years to be very active in promoting his Secular (even atheistic) Humanist philosophy, taking a position in 1929 on the board of the Humanist Society of New York, then being one of the composers of the 1933 *Humanist Manifesto*, and an avid writer and lecturer on the subject thereafter.

And he (and his legacy) would continue after him to help direct the country's rising Liberal intellectualism in its battle against America's long-standing moral-spiritual foundations in the Christian faith.

✳ ✳ ✳

SUPREME COURT JUSTICE OLIVER WENDELL HOLMES, Jr.

The very scholarly Supreme Court Justice Oliver Wendell Homes, Jr., was another major contributor to the Progressivist Movement, who supported strongly the idea that the supreme law of the land, the fundamental order of society, was not to be found in some abstract set of rules put in place long ago as an absolute standard to be followed by each and every subsequent generation. Holmes was strongly opposed to such a fixed sense of the law ... especially laws that were supposedly required by some kind of unseen deity. He viewed such a legal philosophy as being no more than "Legal Formalism." Today we term this view "Legal Originalism."

To Holmes, a society's foundational legal order was instead to be understood as an ever-developing foundation, a natural byproduct of constant social development or change. Constant changes in social circumstances by very necessity required even the most fundamental laws to be revised according to quite practical needs of the times ... as these new social circumstances and thus social needs came into being. In other words, the law – even the most fundamental of all laws – ought to be whatever the political authorities should deem it to be by the sheer necessity of the times. And that held true especially of judges – who were given the critical responsibility of deciding what the rightful rules and conduct and the legal duties of all citizens should be ... given the particular circumstances that the society faced at the time. Holmes termed his personal view of the law as "Legal Realism" ... sometimes also termed "Legal Positivism."

As with all Progressivists, Holmes was certain that common sense – at least the "common sense" of those properly enlightened to the wiser ways of life – better served the needs of a constantly changing world. And certainly Holmes felt that he personally possessed all the right qualifications to understand and thus the wisdom to decide as to which were the more "realistic" lines and rules that a society should try to follow ... and be judged by.

Holmes was born of the right circumstances, his father (Holmes, Sr.) a well-known Boston writer and physician, with the family also close friends with the Transcendentalist Emerson and the famous writers Henry James, Jr. and his brother William James. Holmes followed in his father's footsteps to Harvard, where (like his father) he was a member of the Hasty Pudding writers' group and the prestigious Porcellian Club. He graduated Phi Beta Kappa in 1861 ... just in time to join the Massachusetts militia and become deeply involved in the Civil War ... in the Peninsula Campaign, at Fredericksburg, the Wilderness, Antietam, and Chancellorsville, among other battles ... being wounded on numerous occasions.

Overall, the experience determined his view of how duty in service to society – in all its needs, but especially its most critical needs – required a careful marshalling by those given the responsibilities of social oversight (society's leaders). This understanding would become the basis of Holmes's Legal Realism.

Not surprisingly, given his mindset, he chose to go into the practice of the law (Harvard Law School and then private practice in commercial and admiralty law), remaining a philosophical writer at the same time, in 1881 publishing a collection of his lectures and writings as *The Common Law*. It was here that the legal world would learn of Holmes's Legal Realism ... underscoring how judges had to make decisions on the basis of numerous factors – in a way that made Legal Originalism "unpractical," even unserviceable.

In 1902 Roosevelt appointed Holmes to the U.S. Supreme Court ... where he got the opportunity to put his ideas to work. But here is where Legal Realism ran into some difficulties. Even Holmes contradicted himself as he moved from cases to cases over the years, his "realism" inclining him first in this direction and then later in an even opposing direction. Thus in his famous *Schenck v. United States* (1919) opinion he took a stronger line in defense of the state's rights to censor behavior than he had earlier in his dissent in the *Baltzer v. United States* (1918) case when he opposed the court in its conviction of an anti-war socialist who had been distributing pamphlets in violation of Wilson's Espionage Act of 1917 and Sedition Act of 1918. In the Schenck case, Holmes came down strongly in support of state censorship, citing the state's rights in this famous comment that he First Amendment would not protect a person "falsely shouting fire in a theater and causing a panic." But in that same year, in the *Abrams v. United States* (1919) case, Holmes now dissented from the view that the state had the right to persecute those demonstrating sympathies with the Russian Revolution then underway ... and who had opposed Wilson's decision to intervene in the subsequent Russian Civil War.

So where exactly did Holmes stand with respect to the Espionage and Sedition Acts? That seemed to depend on whatever Holmes was inclined to find himself at the moment. In other words, under Legal Realism, the law was simply whatever the judges decided it to be ... under merely the immediate circumstances. Thus the law was not really the law until the society was able to find out what the Supreme Court justices themselves felt about matters at the time. That's a lot of power ... that answers to no one but the justices themselves.

* * *

CHRISTIANITY RESPONDS

This trend of American intellectuals to go down the road of Human Reason did not mean that there was a widespread mood growing in America to get rid of the idea of a God presiding over the nation, or Christ as the designer of the moral-spiritual ideals guiding the nation. For most of the people in the pews of the American churches, the personal relationship with God that they held individually had not changed substantially with all of this "higher" intellectual inquiry into the nature and meaning of life. If anything, that relationship had deepened as a result of the pain of going through a vicious Civil War.

However for the more intellectually inclined, the post-Civil-War era appeared as an age of wealth, security and leisure. For such Americans the idea of God did not seem to have a compelling place in the new, highly energetic, even highly competitive, social dynamic driving the country. Science and technology seemed to offer a better path to what faith once secured. In fact, science – not religion – was the key identifier that Humanists applied to this rising Secular Liberal-Democratic faith.

Science worked rationally, openly, no miracles, just hard work with predictable results. This seemed to be a vastly better way of going at life than expecting some peculiar intervention from a world beyond to clear away life's hurdles. And as science was clearly leading the country to unprecedented human progress, in the lives of the more intellectually inclined, Christianity simply seemed to shift to the sidelines.

A rising question of the reliability or "inerrancy" of Biblical Scripture. Ultimately, the Liberal challenge once again raised the age-old question (since at least the late 1600s) of the reliability of Scripture as foundational Truth. Stories that seemed to contradict what science, or just modern common sense, would dictate came again under attack by the more enlightened minds.

But Scripture was the bedrock of American Protestantism. Scripture was the final arbiter on what was Absolutely True and what was just merely human Rationalism. It was the foundation of all that Christian Americans held as moral absolutes. And ultimately, to Christians, it defined the very purpose of human life itself.

Liberals, whose faith was built now on the bedrock of secular science, naturally raised questions (and sneers) about Scripture's tales of changing water into wine, walking on water, raising the dead, stopping the sun in its path, etc. Biblical miracle stories and the rules of science clashed terribly, forcing Americans to choose on which side of the rising controversy they stood: for the Bible of God, Christ, and the Church – or for Science (and 20th century commonsense).

Defenders of the faith. But such attacks on Biblical faith did not occur without defenders of that faith trying to halt or even reverse this development. Given the serious challenge that the rising faith in science made to the old faith in God and Christ, some Christian apologetics (written and spoken defenses of the faith) tried to take on some of the new ideas and attitudes to create a more comfortable fit between the old faith and the rising world of modern science. But these ideas, however, would trouble the Christian community itself deeply. These new ideas and attitudes were not just a matter of new style versus old style – like the earlier battles (during America's Christian Awakenings) between the New Lights and the Old Lights concerning the spectacle of outdoor revival campaigns.

Even during the days of the Civil War, Darwin's challenge to the idea of life's divine origins as described in the Bible were finding a strong response in numerous Christian circles. One very notable individual in this regard was Charles Hodge, the dominant personality at the Presbyterian seminary in Princeton all the way up to 1878. He proudly boasted that he had held the line firmly against the kind of theological innovation that was infecting fellow seminarians elsewhere.

Others responded by simply by taking some kind of middle road between Christian traditionalism and rising Christian Liberalism. One of these was Crawford H. Toy, a professor at the Southern Baptist Seminary, who won hearts by simply focusing on the spirit of love that stood at the heart of Christianity – rather than theological doctrine. Unfortunately even that proved to be too much of a compromise for the otherwise creedless Baptists, whose Convention in 1879 forced him to resign his position at the seminary.

More successful in advocating a "middling" approach was Henry Ward Beecher,[107] son of the conservative Presbyterian preacher Lyman Beecher and brother of fellow Abolitionist Harriet Beecher Stowe (author of *Uncle Tom's Cabin*). As a popular pastor and circuit preacher, Beecher sidestepped the controversial intellectual issues of evolution and Biblical reliability, even stating at one point that he saw no problem with the theory of evolution – as long as it understood God to be at the heart of the process. He preached a very upbeat message of love, and a willing accommodation to the changing industrial culture developed around the Christian community. And he proved to be quite successful in developing a stable Middle-Class message in the face of Darwinism's intellectual challenge, all the way up until his death in 1887.

Another individual to take something of a middling approach to the issue of traditional theological correctness and the rising new cultural norm of industrial/scientific Rationalism was Dwight L. Moody, circuit preacher and simple but straightforward evangelist. Moody preached to crowds of mostly middle-class Americans, who were simply trying to make sense of the social changes underway in their once-familiar America. Moody was far from being an intellectual Progressivist with a moral program designed to make the world a better place. Nor did he have any strong views on the burning issues of the Christian seminaries, such as evolution or Biblical inerrancy. He was a classic premillennial who simply looked to Jesus's second coming to clean up the mess that human sin had made of creation. And that approach to life's challenges at the end of the 1800s made sense to thousands of people who flocked to hear what he had to say at his various urban rallies held around the country.

Charles Briggs and Biblical "higher criticism." Yet while a number of preachers were trying to find some kind of a middle road for the "average" Christian to go down, the battle at the higher realm of Christian intellectualism only hardened. A major contributor to his hardening was Union Theological Seminary's professor Charles Briggs. He even succeeded in getting himself excommunicated from the Presbyterian denomination in 1893* because of his teachings that text-criticism or literary analysis amply proved among other things that Moses did not actually write the first five books of Scripture but that these writings were the result of the much later collection of at least four different narrative traditions, and that Isaiah did not write the entire work given under his name but that later disciples of the Isaiah school had written the second half of the work. Although for any who might have understood that the Jewish Scriptures were community narrative (not "science"), such a revelation should have come as no surprise. Biblical narrative was about finding the path to Truth through divine inspiration, and was not assembled anciently by those with a modern scientific worldview.

But Briggs went further, even claiming that the Old Testament was morally inferior to the moral development of modern times. This so enraged the Presbyterian denomination that it not only excommunicated him but moved to block Briggs' professorial appointment to the faculty of the Union Seminary in New York City. But the seminary refused to dismiss Briggs, and instead the seminary withdrew from the Presbyterian denomination.

Asuza Street Pentecostalism.[108] Then, while all of this intellectual warfare was going on within the higher reaches of Christian leadership, a strange revival (but all revivals start out as strange events!) which exploded at the beginning of the 20th century across the Atlantic in Wales, deeply transforming Welsh society, made its way to America – thanks to a number of Holiness evangelists who brought the event to American shores. It dug in deeply in California in early 1906 when strange physical healings and "speaking in tongues" broke out at a home – when guest speaker William J. Seymour was kicked out of church after bringing his

---

*Commentators have noted that part of his difficulty with the denomination occurred in part also because of Briggs' abrasive manner when challenged.

Pentecostal message there, and simply moved his activities to this home. The event soon drew crowds to witness and then participate in this strange behavior, until it became literally an on-going twenty-four-hour-a-day phenomenon. When the crowds collapsed the porch to the house, the revival moved its operations to a Black Apostolic Faith Mission building on Asuza Street, making it quite inter-racial in nature as well as inter-ethnic (Hispanics also attending), even bringing women forward to take leading roles in the revival. Hundreds, then over a thousand individuals would soon be attending the meetings.

Thus pentecostalism or the Charismatic Movement came to America. But eventually the Azusa Street Revival would burn itself out, although it would leave behind rather permanently a strong spiritual legacy – occasionally picked up again here and there in 20th century America.

Most notable was the large Assemblies of God Christian denomination formed in 1914 out of the Asuza Street Revival. The Assemblies of God or AG Church would continue to develop pentecostalism or the charismatic movement all way to the point today in which the denomination has around 370 thousand congregations with over seventy million members worldwide.

The Social Gospel. At the same time, Christian Liberals busied themselves trying to find, through their Social Gospel, a middle ground in the science-versus-Christianity controversy, explaining that fact and faith were two different things. Science dealt with fact. But faith dealt with the question about how you handled fact. Christianity was ultimately what you did with your life, the moral quality of the decisions you made, especially in the social context of family, community, nation and even the world.

Key voices in this approach to Christianity were the economist and founder of the American Economic Association and also founder and secretary of the Christian Social Union, Richard Ely; the Congregational pastor, writer and ardent social reformer Washington Gladden (considered the Father of the Social Gospel Movement of the late1800s/early 1900s); and Baptist pastor and seminary professor, Walter Rauschenbusch. All three of these men were very active in their support of Progressivist economic programming, designed to help lift the American working class out of poverty – a very noble enterprise.

But all of this fine work had little to do with personal salvation, the individual "born-again" experience that comes with stepping back from the world and its ways in order to embrace a more personal relationship with God. Rauschenbusch was in fact very dismissive of such an approach to Christianity, seeing the true sin that needed to be addressed by the Christian as that of society and its cruelties.

In short, Christian Liberalism, with its Social Gospel, was largely a

The Rationalizing of Western Culture 435

matter of high social morality, the value of which one did not need to be a Christian to appreciate. Indeed, as Liberal America opened itself to the larger world around it, it encountered Hinduism, Buddhism, Confucianism, all of which had different ideas about the place of God in nature, but all of which held pretty much the same moral views on social behavior.

Universalism. Indeed, a number of intellectuals even proposed simply to create some kind of universal religion, combining the moral features of Christianity, Buddhism, etc.   Theosophy was just such an example – cultivated outside America by such Humanists as the Russian occultist and author Helena Blavatsky, her British disciple Annie Besant, and the Austrian educator Rudolf Steiner – that was taken up in America by intellectuals seeking to combine science and the mysticism of the world's great religions, as a form of personal development (also very popular later in the 20th century among very self-focused American hippies!). Thus science could continue to pursue fact and Progressive Liberals could pursue through private faith some kind of universal moral code, even some kind of personal mysticism.

Humanism. All of this of course was simply another version of the age-old philosophy of Humanism (the self-sufficient enlightened individual) – pursued at various times in history with mixed results. It was idealized during the Renaissance, leading eventually to the corruption and ultimately splintering of the medieval Church, and then after that the rise of fully sovereign monarchs pursuing greedily their own dynastic fortunes, which produced exhausting wars that accomplished nothing, until another attempt to humanize a bankrupt monarchy in France brought forth a very violent Revolution, and subsequently the bullying Napoleonic Empire required to save France from its self-destructive ways (by focusing those destructive instincts abroad). On and on it went – from one age to the next, enlightened man about to bring the world to utopia through clever human design and effort – ending up instead destroying huge sections of that world.

But at the time, these memories had faded from the minds of America's (and Europe's) rising group of Humanists, who as they stepped into the 20th century were unaware of how close they were coming, in the name of idealistic nationalism (and in America, its democratic Idealism), to the huge moral accounting known as the "Great War" (World War One: 1914-1918).

CHAPTER FOUR

NATIONALISM, IMPERIALISM, AND THE GREAT WAR (WORLD WAR ONE)

✳ ✳ ✳

EUROPEAN IMPERIALISM[109]

It is hard today to understand that in the late 1800s and early 1900s imperialism was generally (though there were exceptions) not considered to be some kind of great evil, but was quite the opposite, something able to bring patriotic tears to the eyes of Europeans as they reviewed the blessings brought to the world through their political, economic, cultural or even religious undertakings abroad. As with all aggressive dominators, their ability to rationalize such aggression with high sounding moral logic was truly amazing. But keep in mind that it was the age of Darwin and Social Progress. Darwinism, with its survival of the fittest mentality, made the justification of imperial aggression very natural, even laudable.

National interest at the heart of European imperialism. Actually imperialism, as practiced in the 1800s and early 1900s, involved simply the transferring away from European and American – or Western – society the naturally aggressive (tribal) tendencies of the West's new, rising and highly ambitious national political actors. This redirection of competitive instincts abroad would help immensely to keep peace within the West itself, for a while – that is until there were no more unclaimed overseas territories available for these hungry empires to grab up. When that happened, Europe fell into suicidal self-destruction: the Great War or World War One.

No two nations explained the blessings of imperialism exactly the same way. But that is because each of these dominators understood themselves in unique ways, and therefore moralized their imperialism in unique ways. In other words, there was no one standard thing called imperialism. It was simply nationalism written large, nation by nation.

The Portuguese. The Portuguese got an early start on (commercial) imperialism in the 1400s, setting out from their Atlantic ports and slowly advancing south down the West African coast, establishing Portuguese trading posts along the way – actually also crossing the Atlantic once the discovery of America occurred and establishing a base point there (Brazil) from which they could then take advantage of the Atlantic currents and sweep back again eastward towards Southern Africa – either way finally reaching the southern tip, the Cape of South Africa. Once around South Africa, the Portuguese then headed toward India, again establishing trading posts – the most notable and enduring being Goa on India's Western coast – and then heading on around India toward the valuable Spice Islands of Southeast Asia. From there they would by the mid-1500s even head north to China, establishing another port along the southern Chinese coast at Macao. They would later lose some of these holdings to the Dutch, but hold on to others, such as Goa and Macao, and their positions in Africa at Angola and Mozambique – well into the 20th century.

The Spanish. The Spanish found their way to the wealth of the Far East blocked by the Portuguese, so at the end of the 1400s they headed west across the Atlantic, and in doing so stumbled into the Americas – and a vast amount of gold they were able to acquire in plundering the Aztec and Inca Empires. The wealth was so vast that they had to – and were able to – build a huge navy to protect the transfer of that wealth from the pirates that lurked in the Caribbean waters, where their American empire was headquartered.

But their thirst for increasing the number of Catholic souls at a time that Protestantism was driving Catholicism from its religious monopoly in Europe became another key motif of Spanish imperialism. Huge numbers of Catholic priests were sent to establish missions among the new Indian subjects of the Spanish kings, thus bringing Spanish America emotionally as well as materially into the realm of Spanish feudalism. This feudal social-cultural legacy became so well-established that even when these colonies broke free from their Spanish (and closely related Portuguese) sovereigns in the early 1800s, the cultural patterns established through this imperialism remained firmly in place.

Indeed, by the late 1800s a romantic revival of Spanish nationalism was taking place in Spain, looking to Spanish America to rebuild the Spanish-Catholic cultural ties that once existed between Spain and America.

But Yankee Americans had other ideas. They wanted to democratize this feudal culture, and thus found themselves intervening frequently in the affairs of their neighbors to the south, under the principle of the Monroe Doctrine. These interventions (usually by the U.S. marines) helped support U.S. economic interests in Latin America, but had little impact on the political culture of the region, producing instead a lot of anti-Yankee resentment.

The Dutch. While the Portuguese and Spanish were busy setting their overseas empires in place, the Protestant Dutch were busy fending off the very-Catholic Spanish kings trying to force the Dutch provinces back into submission to Catholic Spain. The effort drained Spanish power considerably*, and instead strengthened Dutch power and resolve all the more. When Spanish power became feeble enough in the early 1600s, the Dutch then headed out on their own to explore the larger world – mostly following the Portuguese imperial route, seizing Portuguese ports along the way: notably South Africa and the Spice Islands (modern Indonesia). The Dutch also established trading posts in North America at the mouth of the Hudson River and the land behind it, on various islands in the Caribbean, and on the northeastern coast of South America at Suriname.

Like the Portuguese, the Dutch Empire was largely commercial (trading in valuable goods) in nature, which included a vast number of Africans sold into slavery in order to work the highly valuable sugar plantations in the Caribbean and at Suriname.

The British. Early British imperialism followed the pattern of the Portuguese and the Dutch, especially the Dutch with whom the English found themselves in deep commercial competition – with several wars fought in the process. Like the Dutch, the English were early capitalists, forming joint-stock corporations to amass the amount of investment money needed to pay for very expensive private business operations (meaning, not funded by the monarchy). A number of companies reached great size, such as the Muscovy Company in 1555, trying unsuccessfully to reach China by way of a Northeast passage across the arctic, or at least across Russia. And there was the East India Company, though as with all business enterprises, it had its ups and downs.

The British East India Company reached such enormous size that it became almost a government in itself, securing political as well as economic dominance over most of India and parts of China. After American independence – achieved through a rebellion sparked in part by the British king's attempt to establish an East India Company monopoly in the tea trade with the American colonies – the British Empire and the East India Company became almost one and the same.

The focus of the Company's activities was India, a huge sub-continent

---

*The disastrous attempt at about the same time (1588) to do the same thing to Protestant England by sending their mighty Spanish Armada (army and navy) against the English also drained Spanish power considerably.

Nationalism, Imperialism, and the Great War 439

over which the Company secured political control through an array of separate agreements with various local Indian lords or rajas. In essence the Indian rajas agreed to place themselves under the Company's protection in order to facilitate the all-important trade of tea, cotton, indigo and salt from India in exchange for the finished textiles of England. Backing up this arrangement was the Company's own private army made up of local Hindu and Muslim mercenaries – or sepoys – commanded locally by some of the rajas, but ultimately by Company officers themselves. It was all quite a noble arrangement for many Indians and Englishmen.

The Company and its army was an aggressive player in the international theater, fighting wars here and there in Asia, such as the one waged against the Chinese Emperor – who tried (unsuccessfully) to stop the Company from selling its highly profitable opium to his Chinese subjects. In essence the Company was the world's first major drug cartel!

But troubles with its own Indian sepoys developed over the thoughtlessness of some of its English officers, and a huge rebellion resulted (1857-1859) – involving the death of large numbers of English officials and their families serving in India. When the rebellion was finally put down, British Parliament liquidated the Company and took over its affairs directly, creating officially the British Empire – with Victoria now serving as the Empress of India as well Queen of England, Scotland and Ireland (along with many other titles).

These were the glory days of British imperialism. And the British Empire stood at the very heart of the whole European imperial system as its proudest symbol.

The French. Not to be outdone by the English, the French sought a similar imperial status during the mid-1800s under the new French Emperor, Louis Napoleon or Napoleon III (nephew of the famous Napoleon of the earlier 1800s). The French were having a hard time emotionally with the fact that French culture had once (during the 1700s and much of the 1800s) been a central part of the culture of Europe's ruling classes, and that its decline in the face of rising linguistic nationalism in Europe was a major blow to French pride. France's imperial mission therefore seemed to be to compensate for this loss by taking French culture abroad, trying now to plant French culture among the ruling elite in French Indochina of Cochin China (Vietnam), Cambodia and Laos and at various points along the African coast.

The scramble for European imperial territory in Africa and the Middle East. Then when in the latter part of the 1800s the Europeans began to take an interest in laying claim to the material wealth (and the souls of the people) in the dark unknown of interior Africa, the French made a huge effort to plant widely the French imperial flag there. Also Egypt – at least since Napoleon's invasion there in the early 1800s (an unsuccessful effort to block Britain's passage from the Mediterranean to India) – had long held French interest, and the French worked out a deal with the local king to build a canal at Suez, which then stirred British interest in the project. The British eventually bought out the king's interest in the Suez Canal, making European imperialism in Egypt at the very heart of the world of Islam a matter of cooperation between both the French and the English.

Also interested in Africa were the recent arrivals on the European national scene, the Germans and the Italians. The many Italian city-states and regional kingdoms had finally united into a single Italian state in 1860, and much the same was the case for Germany in 1870. Now fully national as Italy and Germany, both new countries wanted a piece of the imperial action in Africa – because that was about the only part of the earth that had not already been laid claim to by European imperialists.

The Portuguese, of course, were already in Africa (coastal Angola, Mozambique and other small positions along the coast being under Portuguese control since the 1400s and 1500s). And Spain was interested in the North African land across the Straits of Gibraltar (and British-held Gibraltar itself) in Morocco. And America had protectorate responsibilities over the tiny country of Liberia, set up as an independent country to receive American Blacks freed from slavery and returned to the African "homeland" earlier in the 1800s.

Then at the same time there was the matter of the Ottoman or Turkish Empire, a great Islamic domain at the eastern end of the Mediterranean and in Southeastern Europe (the huge, multi-ethnic Balkan Peninsula). The Ottoman Empire had lost considerable energy since its glory days in the 1500s, and like old Christendom, it was falling apart. Thus various newly emerging national groups, principally the Bulgarians, the Greeks and the Serbs – once part of the Ottoman empire – were moving to grab chunks of the Ottoman holdings in the Balkan Peninsula in order to establish their own national independence. Meanwhile the English and French busied themselves attempting to grab the rest of the Ottoman Empire – from Egypt to Syria – with the Russians coming at the Turks along the northern coast of the Black Sea at Crimea and Southeastern Ukraine (with the British actually attempting to help the Turks hold off this Russian expansion).

The Berlin conferences (1878 and 1884-1885). All this activity – focused on the dying Ottoman "Sick Man of Europe" plus the opening up of Africa – threatened to bring the aggressiveness of European imperialism much too close to home for the comfort of the major European players.

Something needed to be done to head off this growing danger to the peace of Europe itself.

Indeed, since the days of Napoleon's defeat in 1815, there had been a rather high level of diplomatic cooperation among Europe's imperial contenders, sort of a gentlemanly sharing of the spoils of imperialism. The ruling dynasties understood the importance of being somewhat cooperative in their aggressions. They had learned some hard lessons from the Napoleonic wars and had devised a system (the Concert of Europe) to bring their mutual tensions under discussion in order to keep those tensions from pushing them to war, and thus having to call on their people once again to come rescue their thrones from their enemies.

And thus it was that they gathered in Berlin in 1878 to come to an agreement as to how they wanted to divide up the dying Ottoman Empire, and assign Ottoman land to the various European participants, notably the Greeks, Bulgarians and Serbs. Everyone was mostly happy with the results – except the Turks, of course, whose nationalist fever began to rise in the face of this assault on their long-standing Empire.

Then in 1884-1885 the Europeans met again in Berlin, this time to get out a map of Africa and assign pieces of the continent to the conference's various European participants. Everyone was a winner (except the Africans, who were not consulted on the matter). The Portuguese were simply confirmed in their old African holdings. The French received major pieces of West Africa (interspersed with English holdings). The Belgian King Leopold was awarded the rich center-piece of Africa, the Congo, as a personal feudal domain, serving somewhat like Belgium itself as a buffer territory designed to keep any one of the major European powers from establishing a single line of dominance across the continent. The English were accorded vast pieces of the rest of Africa, most importantly from the Cape Province in the South – taken from the Dutch during the Napoleonic Wars – north through the Central part of Africa (with Leopold's Congo being the exception), all the way up through the Sudan to Egypt. The Germans finally got lands in Central Africa to the east (Tanganyika) and the west (Kamerun) of the Belgian Congo. And the Italians got a section of Somaliland at the vital juncture between the Indian Ocean and the Red Sea.

Under Bismarck's skillful leadership this business had all been conducted in a fairly rational fashion. For Bismarck and for Germany this was all part of the German nation's new birth, but also its growing sense of importance within the realm of European political affairs.

AMERICAN IMPERIALISM

Americans generally identified imperialism only in terms of direct governmental control of one people over another, the very thing America had revolted against when King George tried to pull that on America. Thus it was that at a time when European powers (but also some American politicians) were bragging about the human benefits of their particular brand of imperialism, "imperialism" in the American lexicon generally had become a very sinister word, something to be resisted at all costs – like Satan himself.

However, America actually had its own imperialist agenda, although it would have a very hard time recognizing this agenda as imperialism. For America, as was the case for everyone else, its version of imperialism too would be merely reflective of the social priorities and moral imperatives of the nation – such as it held in late 1800s and early 1900s – extended outward to the larger world as part of its naturally expanding power.

There were a number of facets to American imperialism. But basically, there were three paths that this imperialist agenda took: Christianity, American business, and democracy. Just like every other nation, America saw these as entirely noble enterprises, and thus tended to identify none of these as imperialism.

The Christian mission impetus. The swing of America from the 1800s into the 1900s was a very heady time, unprecedented material progress evident everywhere, the likes of which were more than just spectacular – they were totally unprecedented. Thus it was easy for Christian Americans (and many Christian Europeans) to believe strongly that the End Times (the Second Coming and Final Judgment of the Lord Jesus Christ) was at hand. But was the world ready for such divine judgment?

A rush was on, supported by missionary societies of all Christian varieties, to send out workers to reap the harvest of souls in anticipation of the approaching millennium. Especially prominent in this was the Student Volunteer Movement (Protestant, but not belonging to any particular Protestant denomination) which inspired thousands of fired-up students to leave their American college campuses and head out into the world to save souls. Soon supporting them was an equally highly motivated Laymen's Missionary Movement made up of Americans at home willing to support financially this massive missionary effort.

And thus, out Americans went, not only bringing the Christian gospel to Latin American neighbors to the South but also Africans and Asians to the East and West across the great oceans. With this supreme effort to be a Light to the Nations, America was finally fulfilling its long-standing covenant with God.

The democratic mission.[110] Closely accompanying this sense of Christian mission was the idea or doctrine of "democracy for all," related to America's long-held belief in grass-roots self-government – increasingly identified as democracy. Democracy certainly appeared to be the natural political accompaniment to the Christian life (as indeed something like that had been since Puritan days).

But Humanists were quick to point out that the political ideal of democracy did not depend on the gospel as its primary foundation. Indeed, the effort to spread democracy abroad would soon be carried out quite apart from the Christian missionary effort – as Humanists attempted to demonstrate in taking up the cause of building (Secular) democratic societies abroad wherever, and by whatever means necessary.

The Humanist procedure was quite simple: overthrow the authoritarian rule of the traditionalist ruling classes of the various societies abroad, call representatives of the newly freed people into consultation, develop a new constitution (modeled largely after the American Constitution), and hold elections to fill the offices of the new democratic government. With this new democracy in place, America could then take its leave as mentor and supervisor, and head home, leaving the new society to enjoy the bliss of democracy.

Again, the American desire to spread democracy abroad would supposedly put Americans in opposition to the imperialist practices of the other members of the imperial circle, because the imperialism of the others was so "imperialistic" (meaning, non-democratic). But it never occurred to an aggressive America that its desire to liberate the rest of the world (such as Cuba and the Philippines liberated from the Spanish Empire in 1898) in order for it to plant there enlightened American constitutional practices, was just as imperialistic as the behavior of the other, self-acknowledged, imperialists.*

In any case, as official government policy, America did not really have much of an overseas agenda during the first half of the 1800s, the nation

---

*Interestingly, it still has not occurred to Americans, who even today are in the habit of overthrowing foreign governments with the hope of instituting new governments in their place, ones that mirror the supposed American constitutional or democratic model – which even America has moved away from as it has come increasingly under the governance of an ever-expanding care-taker bureaucracy and activist judiciary. Vietnam, Iran, Russia, Iraq, Afghanistan, Libya, Syria and probably even China, have taught Americans nothing about democracy's dim possibilities in other unreformed cultures, even as violent – and unsuccessful – as the effort to institute democracy in these other countries has generally proven to be. On the other hand, the democratizing of Germany, Japan and South Korea has taken deep root – but required huge expenditures of American social assets (brutal war) and a rather deep and lengthy American occupation to bring about the necessary cultural transformation that democracy requires for it to be able to exist at all.

being so completely absorbed in its aggressive (imperialist) movement at home against the Indian tribes and against Mexico, and then being caught up in its own Civil War. But it would certainly find itself taking up a broader, more global cause, towards the end of that century and into the next.

The expansion of the Monroe Doctrine. Americans are generally well aware of the policy put in place in the early 1800s known as the Monroe Doctrine, declaring that anywhere in the Americas (central or south) was off-limits to European imperialism. Of course when the doctrine was announced, America had no way of enforcing the doctrine, Europe's armies and navies being much stronger that America's. In fact, America barely had either an army or a navy when U.S. President Monroe announced the doctrine bearing his name.

But actually the policy worked because the British – who did have the power (which other Europeans well understood) to enforce the doctrine – wanted to keep the door of Central and South America open to British trade, and opposed the kind of colonialism practiced by Spain, and France. The Spanish and French brand of colonialism allowed trade of their colonies in America with only the mother country in Europe (a practice called "mercantilism"). Both the British and the Americans were in agreement about keeping Spain – or any other European power – from retaking the former Spanish colonies. These new states had just secured independence from the mother country. The British for economic reasons and the Americans for reasons of political ideology – although later, like the British, for economic reasons as well – intended to "protect" that independence.

Americans did not consider the huge intervention of British business in Latin America as being in violation of the Monroe Doctrine, because they viewed imperialism almost completely in terms of the legal matter of who or what officially governed the country, not who did business with it. British business was just that, business, not government, and good business at that. In fact, Americans saw the opportunity to do the same – involve themselves deeply in the economic affairs of their neighbors to the south – without feeling that they were engaged in imperialism any more than were the British.

The "opening" of Japan. Back in the 1500s Jesuit missionaries had been so effective in making Japanese converts to Catholic Christianity that the Tokugawa Shogun seized control in Japan in 1604 in order to block and reverse this process of Westernization. The country had been closed to outsiders ever since. Then in 1852 American naval officer Commodore Perry was instructed to open up Japan to trade and diplomatic relations with the Americans. The following year, Perry's ships blasted their way into Tokyo harbor, signaling the seriousness of their intent to force negotiations. To the great shock of the Japanese, the Emperor agreed (though the Shogun did not) to the opening up of the country to Western trade and diplomatic relations, and Western Christian missionary activity. This put the Japanese in a state of major crisis. But the Japanese authorities realized that they had no recourse but to accept this intrusion, at least for a while.

An eventual effort to expel the Western barbarians was a dismal failure, and then the mysterious death of the Emperor in 1867 brought forward a young Emperor who was determined to begin the transformation of Japan, along Western industrial – and military – lines. The Meiji Restoration had begun.

Alaska. The Russians had been moving eastward across Asian Siberia from their base in Moscow since the 1500s, and may have reached all the way to Alaska with a small settlement by the mid-1600s. By the 1700s Russians were fishing the region, trading for the highly sought-after sea otter pelts, and placing more settlements in the coastal region. The Spanish also sent explorers to the region in the late 1700s to defend (largely unsuccessfully) their claims to the entire Pacific northwest of the American continent. Some Russian settlement continued into the 1800s, though slowly because the region did not seem to be a very profitable enterprise for the Russians.

In 1867, shortly after America's Civil War was brought to an end, U.S. Secretary of State William Seward negotiated the purchase of Alaska from the Russians for $7.2 million, mostly just for strategic reasons: to block further Russian or British expansion in the Pacific that could affect the American position in its own Northwest. But when the Dominion of Canada brought British Columbia into its confederation in 1871, hopes to link Alaska directly to the United States were blocked permanently.

Then in the 1890s a gold rush brought Americans to Alaska in the thousands, leading Alaska to become an American territory in 1912.

Hawaii. Meanwhile American expansion across the Pacific to the Hawaiian Islands was stirring American political interests ... and controversy. Protestant missionaries (also some Catholics and Mormons) had come to the islands in large numbers in the early 1800s, to bring to the islands the Christian religion as well as Western ways – with the cooperation of King Kamehameha II who looked to the missionaries for diplomatic counsel. The opportunities that the climate afforded for the development of the sugar industry became obvious, and soon new generations born of the missionary families, termed the Missionary Party, became very influential in Hawaiian social and political affairs. Workers were brought in from Asia to help work the sugar farms, helping to change drastically the demographic character of the islands.

When Kamehameha V died in 1874, the dynasty ended and strife hit the island as disputes arose over the succession. This brought both American and British troops to the islands to settle things down – and David Kalakaua to the throne. But the new king attempted to rule as an absolute monarch, at a time when the sugar economy was undergoing a global recession. His spendthrift ways and his love of global travel had also helped put the Hawaiian economy in trouble, and there were growing demands for him to cut back on his arbitrary powers.

His refusal led to a revolt in 1887, which he was unable to bring under control. At this point Hawaiian politics moved under the patronage of the Hawaiian League, an elite group of wealthy White-American sugar plantation owners and the core of the Missionary party. They forced on the king a new constitution which created an assembly, but also a House of Nobles, which they controlled and which now dominated Hawaiian politics.

When King Kalakaua died in 1891 his sister Liliuokalani took the throne as Queen of Hawaii. She immediately set aside the 1887 Constitution in order to restore full powers to the throne, setting off a revolt in 1893. The Missionary Party requested U.S. marines to intervene, thus bringing the revolt to an end, and the monarchy as well. A Hawaiian Republic was declared and a Provisional Government was set up in 1894, with Sanford Dole serving as the Hawaiian president. The new government then sent a request to the U.S. Congress that the islands be annexed to the U.S. as an official U.S. Territory.

There was much debate in Congress about the legitimacy of such an imperialistic move on the part of the United States, and when a Treaty of Annexation was sent to the Senate for ratification it failed to gain the two-thirds vote necessary for approval. Thus the pro-annexation group in Congress re-authorized the move as simply a resolution, requiring only a majority approval in both houses of Congress. Thus in 1898 Congress approved (barely) and McKinley signed the resolution annexing Hawaii, which took effect officially in August of 1898, at about the time that a conflict was breaking out with Spain over its actions in Cuba.

The Spanish-American War (1898).[111] We have already introduced discussion of this event in terms of Roosevelt's part in it. To elaborate a bit, it is necessary to put the event in terms of the social-cultural-political context of the day. We are of course talking about imperialist fever, which was actually beginning to infect many Americans as much as the Europeans. Since the publication in 1890 of U.S. Admiral Alfred Thayer Mahan's, *The Influence of Sea Power upon History, 1660-1783*, interest in American involvement on the larger world stage had been growing quickly.

After all, it was the age of Darwin and aggressive progress. In his book, Mahan laid out a very compelling argument stating how sea power would be the determining factor in the ultimate success of any nation's imperial strategy. Consequently, in the thinking of the growing imperialist party in America (which would include Roosevelt), America needed to get into the act as a victor in the imperialist game, lest it become a victim instead.

Meanwhile, just offshore from Florida, the Cubans were fighting for their independence from Spain, and the Spanish were absolutely determined to give up no more Spanish territory in the Americas. The violence between the two groups thus grew ugly. It was also affecting the huge sugar industry, largely under American domination (almost 90 percent of Cuba's huge sugar exports went to the U.S.). A large number of Americans began to call for U.S. intervention in the Spanish-Cuban conflict. President McKinley however, aware of the complexity of the crisis, instead sought to work with the Spanish government to see how a compromise could settle things down in Cuba.

Also, the increasing talk of intervening in the Cuban question was stirring much opposition, coming from the Anti-Imperialist League – including such individuals as Andrew Carnegie, Grover Cleveland, John Dewey, William Graham Sumner, and Samuel Clemens (Mark Twain).

In the midst of this controversy were the Hearst and Pulitzer newspapers, hyping the issue of the cruel Spanish actions in Cuba against the freedom-fighting Cubans, to increase their New York readership.

Consequently, the American warship U.S.S. *Maine* was sent in January of 1898 to Havana to put a chill on the violence. But then when the next month the *Maine* blew up and sunk in Havana harbor, the newspapers went wild with outrage at the Spanish government for having committed this vile act. A quick official investigation into the tragedy concluded that this was an act of perfidy on the part of the Spanish government.* With the publication of the findings at the end of March, Americans demanded war with Spain. Less than a month later both sides had declared war on each other.

The war in Cuba was of very brief duration, but of great consequence. With the capture of Santiago (via the Battle of San Juan Hill) and the destruction of both the Spanish fleet and army based there at the beginning of July, the Spanish quickly lost their hold over Cuba.

But the action also reached all the way across the Pacific to the Spanish Philippine Islands and the Pacific island of Guam. In the Philippines, over

---

*The actual evidence itself was very inconclusive, and is still under debate even today, although most researchers now think that the explosion occurred from within the ship, possibly from a coal fume (methane gas) buildup, and not from a Spanish mine outside the ship.

300 years of Spanish rule had been under challenge (much like events in Cuba) since 1896 by a liberal party of Filipinos demanding independence. Thus the position of Spain in the Philippines was very shaky at the time war between America and Spain was declared.

Even before action in Cuba had taken place, Americans made their move on the Spanish Philippines. The decision to do so itself was another huge moral stretch, it too being strongly opposed by the Anti-Imperialism League. Thus in late April 1898, as tensions mounted between America and Spain, McKinley spent an evening in prayer, before announcing the next morning that he perceived that it was God's will for America to "educate the Filipinos, and uplift and Christianize them." (But the Filipinos were already heavily Catholic. So what did "Christianize them" actually mean?) Standing in agreement with McKinley was the leading voice of the Imperialist party, Senator Albert Beveridge, who saw the taking of the Philippines as the call of the Divine Father himself on a noble and favored America to take up this mission, this sacred duty in the Philippines.

With such a divine duty having fallen on America, on May 1st Admiral George Dewey's fleet moved on the Spanish fleet based in Manila, quickly destroying the Spanish fleet in a single day's action.

Troubles then developed when warships from Britain, France, Germany, and Japan showed up at Manila, expecting to participate in the opening of the Philippines. Most aggressive were the Germans who sent numerous warships, having previously expected the Americans to be defeated by the Spanish and thus giving Germany the opportunity to take over the islands. But the Americans were quick to gain control of the islands, finally seizing the capital Manila itself on August 13th – a day after a peace agreement had already been worked out between Spain and America in which Spain simply turned control of the Philippines over to America.

Then American cooperation with the Filipino rebels abruptly ceased when American commanders refused to let the rebels enter Manila with the victorious American troops. Resentment flared, beginning a conflict between the Americans and Filipino rebels, who immediately declared a Philippine Republic. The Americans, however, were unwilling to surrender their role as "protectors" of the Philippines, claiming that without American protection, Spain or some other European power would soon drag the Philippines back under European imperial control. Besides, America wanted to make the Philippines a model of democratic creativity – under American tutelage (of course).

But the Filipinos didn't see things this way. And thus the Philippine-American War broke out in February of 1899, a war that would drag on until 1902 (although guerrilla action would continue sporadically in the Philippine provinces for ten more years after that). This war would tragically become much more deadly (the loss of much civilian life through disease and starvation) than had been the brief war with the Spanish during the summer of 1898.

The 1902 Philippine Organic Act helped settle things a bit, giving the Filipinos limited self-government in the form of a Philippine Assembly, elected by a select section of Philippine society. Eventually, under the urging of President Wilson, the Filipinos were promised future independence with the 1916 Philippine Autonomy Act.

The Boxer Rebellion (1898-1901) and its aftermath. From the early 1800s on, the British East India Company had begun the process of opening China to the West, to British trade, in particular the highly profitable and highly corrupting trade in opium. The Company had resorted to this trade in order to recover vast amount of silver coinage that had made its way to China to buy China's valuable porcelain ware (its china!), its silks, its teas, etc., a one-way trade because the British seemed to have no product – except opium – that interested the Chinese in exchange.

The Chinese emperor attempted to put a halt to this corrupting opium business, and the company fought back, resulting in two Opium Wars (1839-1842 and 1856-1860) which worked to the advantage only of the British and to the increasing political humiliation of the Chinese emperor and his people. The second war resulted even in the forced opening of a large number of Chinese coastal ports to European (and American) trade. It also opened all of China to Christian missionary activity, which previously had been limited only to the assigned open ports.

Numerous Chinese rose in popular revolt in 1850 against the weakened Manchu or Qing Dynasty, commencing the 14-year Taiping Rebellion, actually a civil war originally between the followers of a quasi-Christian Hong Xiuquan and the failing Manchus. The war savaged China horribly from end to end (somewhere between twenty and thirty million Chinese died in the war, mostly due to the famine and plague that broke out within this greatly weakened society). The Manchus were finally able to regain control of the country in 1864, although rebel armies continued to hold out until the last one was defeated in 1871.

A greatly weakened China had no real defenses against the Europeans and Americans who now flocked to China to participate in its trade, its industries, and its religion and education. Little by little the urban areas of coastal China began to take on Western appearances, to the distress of Chinese traditionalists in the interior of China.

Cooperation continued to be the general rule in the continuing opening of China by the European imperialists, joined by America, and now also by Japan, which had developed its own modern army and navy and a modern industrial economy to support its modern military.

Toward the end of the 1800s, Chinese resentment flared over this increasing domination of their society by these outsiders, especially by the Japanese, who humiliated the Chinese in the Chinese-Japanese (or Sino-Japanese) War of 1894-1895, fought largely over the matter of control of Korea. This humiliation led to a demand by both Chinese modernizers for more reform of the country along Western lines, and by traditionalists – members of the Boxer movement – pressing for a return of China to the greatness of its glorious past.

The Boxers were the first to act, breaking out in rebellion in 1899 against the Manchu Dynasty and against Westerners, but especially against fellow Chinese who had taken up Western ways – whom they murdered in vast numbers. Joint action by the English, Germans, French, Americans, and Japanese (among others) finally crushed the rebellion (1901). This was followed by the execution (by Japanese swords) of thousands of rebels and the permanent stationing of foreign troops in the Manchu capital at Beijing. It also included the agreement by the Manchu government to send annual indemnity payments to members of the eight-nation coalition, in the amount of virtually the entire annual Chinese governmental budget, over the next thirty-nine years.

But at least China was not divided up like Africa and the Ottoman Empire, because of an Open Door Policy put forward in 1899 by the American Secretary of State John Hay – a policy importantly supported by the British. This enabled tradesmen to operate anywhere in China rather than only in designated zones. It also served to preserve the unity of China, pleasing somewhat the anti-imperialist party in the U.S. Congress.

Nonetheless the Manchus could not deliver on the agreed indemnity payments, and their government, despite efforts at Western-style reform, finally collapsed, with local warlords now taking over different regions of China. China thus found itself again involved in chaotic civil strife.

This in turn moved the Chinese modernizers or Nationalists (the *Kuomintang*) in 1911 to depose the last of the Manchu emperors in an effort to establish a Chinese Republic. However a political mishap occurred along the pathway towards republican government when, in the process of trying to bring Chinese warlords under control of the new republican government, Nationalist Army General Yuan Shikai came close to establishing a personal dictatorship. He died however in 1916, ending this problem, but increasing the ability of the warlords to operate even more independently of the republican government.

It would take a massive effort on the part of the Kuomintang and the skillful leadership of Dr. Sun Yat-sen almost ten more years to bring the warlords under some degree of control by the Chinese Republic, although even then not fully so.

Teddy Roosevelt's heavy involvement in foreign affairs.[112] It was Roosevelt that truly brought America into the game of international diplomacy as a major power broker. In 1905 he hosted in New Hampshire a peace conference to help the Russians and Japanese work out a settlement ending their war fought along the Eastern coast of the Pacific (it had cost the Russian army and navy dearly and the Russian Tsar his standing in the hearts of his own people). The skillful diplomatic negotiator Roosevelt balanced the interests of both sides in such a way that a final settlement would cause Russia the least amount of loss of face, yet give Japan the recognition as a rising power that it so eagerly sought.

Roosevelt had no idealistic cause of his or America's own to pursue in this matter. Yet the action brought notice to the world that America was actually much more sophisticated politically than they had previously believed (America was still believed by Europeans to be merely a land of cowboys and Indians).   And it also brought Roosevelt in 1906 the Nobel Peace Prize for his mediation ending the Russo-Japanese War.

Also Roosevelt was personally present at the Algeciras Conference in southern Spain which was called (also in 1906) to resolve a growing naval confrontation between Germany on the one hand and Britain and France on the other over the status of the still somewhat independent Sultanate of Morocco on the North African coast just opposite Spain. Roosevelt threw America's weight to the British and French side, helping to force Germany to back away from a needless confrontation, one that looked as if it might lead to all-out war if allowed to continue.*

The Panama Canal. America had long looked at the necessity of connecting the Atlantic and Pacific Oceans in the narrow strip of land constituting the southern portion of Central America. The French jumped at the opportunity first, signing an expensive deal with the Colombian government to build a canal across the Isthmus of Panama – but had to drop the project because of the way malaria kept striking down their workers. Politicians in Washington in the meantime had been looking at the possibility of building a canal across the wider, but flatter expanse at Nicaragua. The French anticipated this move by offering to sell their Panama Canal rights cheap, and helped to move things along politically (Panamanian independence) when the Colombian Senate refused to accept the transfer.

---

*Unfortunately, the settlement only postponed the conflict; it reappeared in 1911 – which again was negotiated to a standoff – and then in 1914, at which point all parties involved lost complete control over events (the startup of World War One).

Thus America took up the project in 1904 with the newly independent government of Panama, first solving the malaria problem (mosquito control and vaccinations) and then putting their heart and soul into the massive digging involved. For Roosevelt, this became a chief project of his, however not being able personally to complete the project during his presidency (ending in 1908) but following closely the progress on the project until its completion in 1914.

The sending of the U.S. Great White Fleet around the world (1907-1909).[113] Roosevelt, who was entranced with naval power as the underpinning of national greatness, decided in the very last year of his presidency that it was time for America to demonstrate that greatness* by sending sixteen new battleships of the U.S. Navy around the world. There were many hurdles that had to be crossed to get this operation underway: the lack of coaling stations needed to refuel the ships' engines, the fact that the Panama Canal was not yet completed, and the opposition to the plan by congressmen who thought this all to be a needless government expense. But Roosevelt forged ahead anyway, had the hulls of the ships painted white (thus the name for the fleet), and sent them on their way.

They would complete the voyage a year later, just as Roosevelt was leaving the White House. It had been indeed an impressive display of American power, and Roosevelt was well satisfied that it had achieved the results he so deeply desired. It certainly marked America as a rising world power.

* * *

THE CLOUDS OF WAR BEGIN TO GATHER

The mounting dangers of nationalist diplomacy. The royalty and aristocracy (and their upper-middle-class associates) of Europe had long treated wars and diplomacy as a private or personal game of the members of their class. This was a most amazing class – with a good number of the European royalty in the early years of the 20th century being direct descendants of Queen Victoria of England and thus being first cousins, as for instance her grandsons English King George, German Emperor Wilhelm, and Russian Tsar Nicholas! Wars and diplomacy were considered the private business of their class alone. Involving the masses of peasants, townsmen

---

*Not just to the great European powers but also the Japanese who, having just humiliated Russia in their naval war in East Asia, seemed to pose something of a challenge to America and its position in Asia achieved through the Spanish-American War.

Nationalism, Imperialism, and the Great War 453

and industrial workers in this game was considered inappropriate – even highly dangerous – as the Napoleonic Wars at the beginning of the 1800s had clearly demonstrated. Armies and envoys were understood to be the tools of the ruling classes, to be used solely to promote the interests of the reigning kings and emperors and their personal dynasties.

But the rising spirit of nationalism was drawing the "democratic" masses into this game – clearly enhancing the powers of the ruling class players, but also drawing the European heads of state forward toward a conflict that they would soon discover was beyond their ability to manage or control. The passions of a fully armed society (and not just the ruling class and its private armies) once mobilized would move in the direction that tribal passion – and not diplomatic good sense – would take the nations of Europe.

Germany's new Emperor Wilhelm was becoming an increasing source of concern to the other players. Wilhelm demanded a greater share in the imperialist game than had previously been alotted to Germany. Also, despite the efforts at the Berlin conferences by European envoys to put some order to the redistribution in Southeastern Europe of pieces of the crumbling Turkish or Ottoman Empire, the Balkan peninsula continued to offer dangerous opportunities for trouble. The land-locked Austrian-Hungarian Empire had been looking for expansion into that area (and the possibility of finally acquiring a place to plant a naval base of its own on the Adriatic and thus the Mediterranean Sea), as had been its chief competitor in that region, Russia (for roughly the same reasons) – but also Bulgaria, Greece and Serbia. This potential for growing conflict among these interested powers drew the other European players (Great Britain, France, Italy, Germany, etc.) into the Balkan game as well – and soon formal alliances were drawn up to buttress the interests of one side or the other.

Thus by the early 1900s, the unifying ideal of the Concert of Europe had been replaced by a deeply divided Europe. On the one side of this division were the powers of the Triple Entente: Britain, France and Russia. This alliance was formed to check the growth of another new alliance, that of the Central Powers: the German and Austro-Hungarian Empires and, for a while anyway, Italy.

The first Moroccan crisis (1905-1906). Wilhelm was very unhappy about Germany's lack of a grand overseas empire such as the French and British possessed. He felt that it was in part the result of a conspiracy of the French and British to keep Germany from its place in the sun. He resented especially deeply the 1904 agreement by which France recognized Britain's dominance in Egypt in exchange for Britain's recognition of French dominance in Morocco (supported by Italy and Spain). Germany had been part of the 1881 agreement on Morocco, but had not been included in this new agreement. Wilhelm fumed.

Thus in 1905 Wilhelm sailed to Morocco to meet with the Moroccan sultan and offer German protection in defense of Moroccan sovereignty. A huge diplomatic crisis thus resulted. To avoid a mounting confrontation, all parties finally agreed to a conference to be held the following year. The conference confirmed the sovereignty of Morocco, but in fact allowed for both Spain and France (not Germany) to serve as the "protectors" of that sovereignty. Germany was still excluded from a role there.

Bosnia-Herzegovina (1908). Then with no warning, Austria-Hungary simply annexed the Balkan territory of Bosnia-Herzegovina (part of the weakening Turkish Empire), infuriating the Serbs who had a huge interest in the same region as an addition to their Greater Serbia, and as a path of access to the sea (Serbia also was landlocked). Serbs burned with a deep bitterness against the Austrians over this land grab. But this land grab also widened the divide between Austria and Russia, the latter being a strong supporter of Serbia. It also caused some consternation with Austria's ally Germany, which had not been consulted prior to the event. And it forced France and Britain – both neither in a position to help Serbia nor willing yet to help Russia – to stand off, very unhappy over the event. Turkey however seemed content to receive monetary compensation for its loss of another two of its provinces. But in general, feelings were running very raw in Europe's capitals.

The second Moroccan crisis (1911). Morocco was not doing well under French and Spanish protection. The sultan's finances were in crisis mode and unrest among the Moroccans was building. The French decided to send French troops into Morocco "to protect the lives of foreigners," upsetting greatly Wilhelm who saw this as simply a ploy for the French to add Morocco to their North African empire. He countered the French move by sending a German gunboat to Morocco to protect German citizens, and another crisis erupted. But France (and Britain, backing France) refused to be intimidated. Wilhelm backed down.

War fever refused to cool down however. Nationalists of all the major European countries seemed to want a street fight of some kind to finally settle the matter of Europe's power alignment. But what they failed to realize was that such a fight was not destined to be merely an afternoon sporting event. The powers seemed so evenly balanced at this point that once underway such a conflict would simply stalemate itself into a long, unrelenting slaughter – the kind that could result only in a huge loss of political strength by all parties, the kind that would in the end (should there ever be an end) resolve nothing. But passions at this point had greatly overridden cool logic. A war now seemed inevitable.

* * *

1914 – WAR FINALLY BREAKS OUT[114]

The assassination of the Austrian Archduke Franz Ferdinand (June 28, 1914). The absorption of Bosnia-Herzegovina by Austria was by no means a finished matter. Serbia was in no mood to accept this development and Austria knew it had work to do to complete the absorption of these Balkan provinces. When in June it was announced that the Austrian Archduke Franz Ferdinand – acting on behalf of his eighty-four-year-old uncle, the Emperor Franz Joseph – would be visiting Sarajevo, the capital of Bosnia, Serbian nationalists (including even some members of the Serbian government) planned his assassination. They wished to disrupt Austria's plan to create a new Triple-Monarchy (Austria, Hungary and now also a Slavonic state) under the Austrian emperor's authority. Austria's plan would have ended the Serbian dream of an independent Greater Serbia. Somehow Austria needed to be stopped.

Austria-Hungary's declaration of war on Serbia. Tragically, despite a number of blunders, the assassination succeeded, throwing Europe into diplomatic chaos. At this point Austria wanted to destroy Serbia, but needed German backing. Wilhelm was reluctant to get involved in such a tangle but also knew that German support was vital in keeping the Austrian-Hungarian empire from falling apart. He had to support Austria. Aware of this backing, the Austrian cabinet placed extremely heavy demands on Serbia to allow Austria to take over the search in Serbia for the Serbian criminals – presuming a Serbian refusal, and thus in effect precipitating the war sought by Austria. Surprisingly most of the demands were agreed on by the Serbian authorities. But Austria insisted that not most – but all – of the demands be met by Serbia. When Serbia stalled, Austria felt it had the justification it needed and on July 28 declared war on Serbia.

Austria supposed that this would remain a quick, local war, as most of the wars in the Balkans had been. But Austria foolishly had failed to take note of the fact that things were very different in the European diplomatic world at this point.

Russia joins in. It was now Russia's turn to decide what to do. Russia was not only the protector of Serbia, it saw in this outbreak of war the opportunity to take advantage of the crisis to seize Constantinople and complete its dream of possessing its own port with direct access to the Mediterranean. But Russia was not really prepared for a major war – and Tsar Nicholas was well aware of this fact. Yet he could not hold back his own ministers who wanted war nonetheless. They demanded a general mobilization. Nicholas knew well that this would constitute a declaration of war against Austria, and that by the terms of the Dual Alliance this would automatically bring Germany into the war as well. But he finally gave in to his ministers. On July 29 the Russian cabinet called for mobilization. A few hours later he received a conciliatory letter from his German cousin Wilhelm. But it was too late to call off the mobilization. Russia was at war.

Germany and France join in. Germany reacted immediately to the news of the Russian mobilization with a demand that the Russians immediately back down, and declared war (August 1) on Russia when Russia failed to do so. Germany then sent a letter to France demanding to know whether or not France was intending to stay out of the conflict, received an ambiguous reply, and thus most unwisely declared war on France (August 3).

The German invasion of Belgium, and Britain's entry into the war. Following an older plan laid out by General Von Schlieffen back in the late 1800s – a strategy that worked well for the Germans when they quickly crushed France during the Franco-Prussian War of 1870 – the German intent was to immediately march on France and quickly seize Paris, leaving the French largely unable to remain in the conflict that was fast unfolding.

But to do so German troops would have to pass through Belgium, whose steadfast neutrality during any European conflict had been guaranteed by treaty not only by Britain and France – but also by Germany. Thus Germany sent a request to Belgium (August 2) for permission to pass through the country in order to attack France. But Belgium refused permission. On August 4th, Germany crossed the border into Belgium anyway. This then led Britain to declare war on Germany for having broken the neutrality treaty. Britain claimed to be acting to protect that guarantee (and its ally France).

Italy, however, refused to support its allies Germany and Austria, claiming that it had agreed to support them only in a defensive war, not a war of aggression. Italy thus at this point remained neutral.

Turkey joins the German-Austrian side. After some indecision on the matter (the British had, after all, been supporters of the Turks in their troubles with the Russians and the Austrians) the Turks, impressed by German military professionalism, decided to come into the war on the side

Nationalism, Imperialism, and the Great War 457

of Germany. Whether or not this would add much to the joint German-Austrian effort was at this point somewhat debatable. But in any case, it put Turkey squarely into the war.

A murderous stalemate quickly sets in on the Western Front, and the slaughter is terrible to behold.[115] In the first month (August) of this long-developing war, things took pretty much the shape in Belgium and France that it would maintain for the next four years.

The Germans had expected to swing through a relatively defenseless Belgium and descend directly on Paris before the French could get organized. Without Paris, France was defenseless. Thus the march through Belgium – which Germany expected would bring a hostile British response. But the action was supposed to be so swift that, by the time the British got moving in defense of Belgium, and France also got itself mobilized, Paris would be in the hands of Germany and the war effectively would be over.

But Germany was not expecting such stiff resistance from the Belgians, which slowed the surprise move down greatly. The Germans were furious at the audacity of the Belgians and poured their wrath out onto the population of this small country, civilians included. So savage was the behavior of the Germans that the label "Huns" came to mind to those watching the German action. This would later come to haunt greatly the German national image.

Also, Britain was indeed able to get some of its small army (the British Expeditionary Force or BEF as it would be termed during the war) in place in Belgium, at least sufficient in number to help slow down the momentum. And France frantically mobilized whatever resources it could, and though being forced to fall back in the face of the much better prepared German army, was able to slow down and then grind to a halt the German offensive, just north of the Paris suburbs.

This halting of the German offensive was much the same along a line that curved eastward and then north through northern France, from the Rhine River in the East to the Belgian border (and into Western Belgium) along the North Sea in the West. Here a well dug-in battle line would hold rather permanently, barely moving but a few miles back and forth from its original position laid out in the first month of the war, despite four years of ferocious assault and counter assault. Millions of men would be sacrificed in the process, all without any seeming effect in breaking the murderous stalemate that settled in along this long line of battle.

The Eastern Front. Another long but more changeable line of battle ran through Eastern Europe from the Baltic Sea in the North to the Balkan Mountains of Serbia in the South. Russia and Germany were engaged against each other in the north, Russia and Austria in the middle portions of the line and Serbia and Austria in the south.

Russia had a huge (but ill-equipped and poorly trained) army to throw at Germany – and chose to initiate the action. However, Russia's attack failed, despite Germany's initial focus on the war in the West with France. Worse, Russia immediately found itself in trouble when one of its large field armies was skillfully surrounded and forced to surrender to the Germans.

Russia still had more men to bring into the war. But this initial defeat would be merely the beginning of many troubles the Russians would experience in continuing a war they now had no idea of how to pull out of without a huge loss of national pride.

In the central part of the line of engagement, the Russians were facing an Austrian army of equally inferior quality, largely because of the latter's multinational character. Here the war bogged down along a line that reached from the Carpathian Mountains in the south to Silesia in the north, and efforts of both sides to move the line proved to be dismal failures.

In the south, Russia's Serbian allies were able, for the time being, to hold back the Austrians. But they had much smaller resources at their command and thus time was not on their side.

* * *

1915/1916 – THE EXTREMELY UGLY WAR SEEMS TO HAVE NO END IN SIGHT

As Christmas 1914 came and went, so with it went the idea that the war would be "over by Christmas." Along the entire Western Front soldiers had dug deep trenches and settled into a life of moving back and forth between the rear and forward trenches, going into action, and then falling back to recover (whatever was left of a unit anyway) in the rear. The routine never varied. At the front the soldiers awaited the pounding of the enemy lines by heavy artillery before being ordered up out of the trenches in order to cross thick lines of barbed wire and a no-man's land filled with shell holes and dead and decaying bodies – facing enemy rifle and machine gun fire as they went – until the remaining soldiers were ordered to retreat after having failed to dislodge the enemy from their trenches. On and on it went.

The Germans got the brilliant idea of introducing poisonous gas with the hope of clearing the enemy trenches before their assaults. But while this proved deadly it did not prove as effective as they had hoped in clearing the enemy lines, and soon the British and French were attempting the same tactic, now also employing gas masks to protect themselves in the process.

Between the gas attacks and the constant barrage by enemy artillery,

Nationalism, Imperialism, and the Great War 459

life on the front was a person's worst nightmare, one that refused to go away. There was no escaping the slaughter. The casualty lists soon numbered in the millions on both sides.

Other countries join in. It seems strange that with the horrifying experience of the Great War (as it was coming to be called) by this point a year old, any other countries would want to get involved. But political folly is not unknown in high political places.

For Bulgaria there was in fact a good reason for joining the war: to get back the lands that it had lost to Serbia and Greece in the Balkan wars. In this they largely succeeded – until the war turned against their German allies in 1918.

Italy, however, was another story. Italians were deeply divided about the war. In one of the many secret treaties being issued during the war, the British and French in April of 1915 promised the Italian government lands taken from Austria along the upper Adriatic Sea coast and along the southern slopes of the Alps, plus the possibility of picking up colonial territory from the Germans in Africa. And although many Italians were adamantly opposed to getting involved in the war for any reason, pro-war enthusiasts, led especially by the fiery D'Annunzio, finally got most of Italy worked up for war. Finally in May, Italy declared war, coming in on the side of the British and French against Italy's former allies Germany and Austria. Not all Italians would be happy about this.

Italy was really not prepared mentally or physically for such a war. As it turned out, the Italians were unable to dislodge the Austrians from the mountainous Italian province of Trentino, despite repeated efforts. Finally they would find themselves in a humiliating retreat in the face of an advancing Austrian army in late 1917 after the fall of the Italian forward position at Caporetto.

Rumania also decided to enter the war (August 1916) after promises by Britain and France for territorial compensation were made to it similar to those made to Italy. When in September Rumania invaded Hungarian Transylvania to collect on those promises they were only briefly successful in holding that territory before they were thrown back by a joint attack of Austria and Bulgaria. Before the year was out Rumania had to yield not only its capital city Bucharest but most of its land to the invading Bulgarian and Austro-Hungarian forces. Rumania was effectively knocked out of the war.

Serbia is crushed. In the fall of 1915 Austria-Hungary and its allies Germany and Bulgaria joined forces to hit the Serbians hard. The Serbians were forced to retreat, leaving their capital Belgrade in enemy hands, even falling back into the Albanian mountains, and finally being chased down even there. Remnants of the Serbian army were finally, with British and French help, able to escape to Greece. In all, the Serbs lost over a million men (more than a quarter of its population and over half of its male population).

The 1916 Brusilov Offensive. The year 1915 did not go well for Russia. The Germans pushed the Russians out of Warsaw as well as the Polish lands further to the east. But the Russians planned to open up an offensive in June of 1916 (the Brusilov Offensive) against the Austrians in the hope not only of relieving the German-Austrian pressure on the Russian Ukraine region but also in the hope of retaking some of the lost Polish territory. The offensive was designed also to relieve pressure on the French at Verdun, where the Germans had earlier that year opened a major offensive on the Western Front.

The Brusilov offensive came to an end in September when both armies faced total exhaustion, and when Russian troops had to be withdrawn to try to help the retreating Rumanians. The net result of this massive encounter between the two sides was the smashing of the Austro-Hungarian army, which subsequently would have to rely increasingly on German support to conduct its campaigns. But the offensive had also been very costly to the Russian army, in equipment as well as men. This would mark the high point of the Russian role in the war.

The battles of Verdun and the Somme (1916). In the late winter (February) of 1916 the Germans opened up a massive offensive against the French line at the fortress city of Verdun. They literally reduced to rubble the complex fortifications of Verdun, hoping to annihilate completely the French troops gathered there. It was expected that this would open such a huge hole in the French line that the French would be thrown in disarray and the Germans could then move on the French capital and end the war. Massive amounts of German power would be thrown into this operation.

But the Germans had not counted on the stiff resistance that the French offered even amidst the rubble, and the French line held as more French divisions were brought into position by the determined French General Pétain. By July it was obvious to the Germans that their plan was not working. Verdun had been a gamble, which failed to yield any significant gains for the Germans despite the heavy costs involved (with somewhere between a third and a half a million casualties on both sides).

By July much of the action now moved north to the Somme River valley when on the first of the month the British opened up a major summer offensive against the German line. The goal was both to take pressure off the French at Verdun (which it did) and do what the Germans had attempted to do at Verdun: open up a gap in the enemy lines (which, as at Verdun, it did not do). Massed attacks on German lines failed to dislodge the Germans and hundreds of thousands of allied British and French troops died in the attempt. The attacks continued through August, September (growing even heavier) and October, until finally in November the rains turned the devastated land into knee-deep mud and the offensive ground to a halt.

An interesting new item of war was introduced at the Somme: the British tank. But the British had not yet learned to maximize its use with ground troops, and at this point it did little to impact trench warfare.

* * *

REVOLUTION IN RUSSIA (1917)[116]

Although Russia's army greatly outnumbered its enemies, it lacked the supplies necessary to make it an effective fighting force. Weapons and ammunition were always in short supply, demoralizing the Russian soldier who was expected to fight on empty-handed. Russian civilians were well aware of these problems and were quick to blame the Tsar and his government for these scandalous shortcomings.

Very unwisely, in September of 1915 the Tsar decided that he personally must lead the military from the front and left the governing of Russia to his wife. And the Tsarina in turn left matters to the nasty-smelling and crude mystic monk Rasputin, who made and unmade governments with his own personal appointments, further scandalizing the Russians in their dwindling respect for their imperial government.

By the beginning of 1917 wartime shortages had hit the civilian population as cruelly as it had the military. Food in the cities was very difficult to obtain, and grumbling turned into a full-scale protest by Petrograd (St. Petersburg) workers (the Russian "February Revolution"),* joined by masses of women. The protest built strength over the next days, and soldiers sent to restore order began to join the protesters.

Word reached the Tsar at the front that even his own bodyguard had joined the revolt, and under advisement of his generals, Nicholas simply abdicated his throne (March 15). When his brother Grand Duke Michael refused to take the throne, no other Romanovs stepped forward to take the reins of government, thus bringing 300 years of Romanov imperial government to an end in Russia.

---

*Occurring in early March on our Western calendar.

The Russian National Legislature (the Duma) tried to bring order to the chaos by setting up a Provisional Government – on the same day that a Soviet (Council) of Workers was established in Petrograd. At first under the presidency of Prince Lvov, the Duma set about decreeing a variety of social reforms and called for a national election for a national assembly specifically assigned the task of designing a new Russian constitution.

All this activity now gave the outward appearance that Russia had just become a democracy. Actually what it had become was hardly decided at that point. However, from a certain vantage point, it could be claimed that now the war had taken on the character of being a great moral matter of democracy (Britain, France, Italy – and now Russia) against autocracy (the empires of Germany, Austria-Hungary, and Turkey).

Seeing Russian developments in this light was, very importantly, Woodrow Wilson, the president of the United States.

Eventually heading up the new Provisional Government was Alexander Kerensky, leader of the Social Revolutionary party, but also vice-Chairman of the powerful Petrograd Council or Soviet. However, understanding the dynamic of this war no more than had the Tsar, Kerensky made the fateful decision to keep Russia in the war, to pursue Russia's new "democratic" cause (and redeem Russia's tarnished honor).

But Kerensky proved no more able to keep Russia together in the face of the demands of war than the Tsar, and the Russian soldiers now begin to protest against the new government

This gave the Bolshevik leader Lenin the opportunity to seize power (the Russian "October Revolution")[*] in both Petrograd[†] and Moscow, on the promise of taking Russia out of the War. This clever move made him instantly more popular among the Russian commoners than their new democratic champion, Kerensky. Lenin soon made good on his promise, and – with a Russian-German armistice in December – took Russia out of the war.

Russia was at this point finally out of the war, but tragically only to face now a new one – an internal civil war among various Russian groups, one that would prove to be even more devastating to Russia than had been the Great War that they had just dropped out of.

* * *

---

[*]Occurring in early November on Western calendars.

[†]St. Petersburg was renamed "Petrograd" during the War to give it a more Russian sound. Soon it would be renamed yet again as "Leningrad," in honor of the leader of the Communist Revolution in Russia. And then with the fall of the Communist system in Russia at the beginning of the 1990s, it would retake its original name, St. Petersburg.

AMERICA ENTERS THE WAR (1917)

Wilson was American president when World War One broke out in 1914. He correctly understood that this war was merely an ego battle among European empires and that the United States had absolutely no reason to get involved. In 1916 he ran for reelection as president in part on the position that "he kept us out of war."

The one-sidedness of American 'neutrality.'[117] It had never been easy trying to stay neutral in a war that affected America's vital business in trade with Europe, as European enemies attempted to isolate each other from resupply by America on the high seas. The British effectively put in place a naval blockade against Germany which prevented the Germans from receiving much-needed shipments of even food coming from America, both from the United States and from South American countries such as Argentina, which were also major exporters of food products. Americans complained bitterly about the way the British prevented neutral America from conducting trade with Germany in non-war goods. But the British ignored these complaints. Eventually the Americans responded by simply devoting their trade as a "neutral" nation to Britain and its ally France, which rewarded American businesses richly by purchasing everything America could send them. Germany was thus left out in the cold as its people drew closer to starvation.

The Germans countered by attempting to establish a blockade of their own around Great Britain, using submarines as the effective instrument. But submarines were viewed as inhuman instruments of war because they could not rescue the sailors of ships they had sunk. Thus the British blockade took on a legitimacy that the German blockade failed to receive in the eyes of Americans (although actually the German sinking of American shipping was quite light).

This played into the hands of the English propaganda machine operating very effectively in America with the American press (the Germans never really learned how to shape the narrative of events in Europe that could draw the sympathy of Americans).

The sinking of the *Lusitania*. In May of 1915 a German U-boat sank the massive English luxury liner *Lusitania* just off the coast of Ireland, with nearly 1200 people drowned, over a hundred of whom were Americans, including some very prominent citizens. The Germans had warned ahead of the dangers of bringing a luxury liner into the war zone, especially with huge amounts of contraband war materials in the ship's hold. Indeed, what the *Lusitania* had been doing was very illegal under the international rules of war as they stood in those days.

Nonetheless American fury was immense, and the Germans backed down by promising that no more civilian liners would be targeted.

For the moment the crisis passed and America maintained its neutrality, as lopsided as it was in the way it favored only Britain and France. But the Germans could do little about it, unless they wanted to make an enemy of America.

The Germans resume submarine warfare. But pushed to total frustration by a starving Germany, the Kaiser in early 1917 made the fateful decision to resume U-boat attacks on shipping, hoping to force the Americans to take a truly neutral side in the war. This resumption of U-boat attacks on American shipping heading to Great Britain and France instead served only to outrage the Americans, an outrage so great that it easily pushed America towards a readiness to go to war with Germany over this matter.

Then there was the incident of an incredibly stupid telegram sent around this same time by the Germans to the Mexicans – and intercepted by the British (and purposely placed in American hands) – inviting the Mexicans to go to war against America under the promise that the Germans would help them recover territory previously lost to the U.S. if they joined the Germans in this struggle. The Mexicans of course were not that foolish, and the telegram was ignored. But its exposure had helped immensely to stir up the demand of angry Americans for war against Germany.

But were these sufficient reasons in themselves to now take America into the War? Was the situation for America any different than it was in 1915 when Wilson was able to use diplomacy to keep heads cool and America out of the war?

But it was actually events in Russia that would tip the balance for Wilson towards the decision to finally take America into the European war.

The impact of the Russian Revolution on Wilson's thinking. Subsequent to the February Revolution – which occurred just as Wilson was being installed for his second term in office – Wilson no longer viewed the European conflict as a mere brawl among European powers. The collapse of the Tsar's imperial government in Russia in early 1917 and its replacement by a democratic Provisional Government certainly to Wilson gave the war a new look. Now on one side were the democracies – Great Britain, France, Italy and, complements of the recent Revolution in Russia, that country as well. Opposing them were the imperial governments ("autocracies" as Wilson termed them) of Germany, Austria-Hungary, and Ottoman Turkey. To Wilson the war now took on the appearance of being the good guys versus the bad guys. Now the war seemed to Wilson to have a moral cause worthy of American involvement. Thus on April 2nd (1917) he called Congress together to request a declaration of war.

America's crusade for democracy, against evil autocracy. In his speech delivered before Congress,[118] Wilson waxed eloquent (and amazingly wrong) in his appraisal of how recent Russian events had changed the game:

> *Does not every American feel that assurance has been added to our hope for the future peace of the world by the wonderful and heartening things that have been happening within the last few weeks in Russia? Russia was known by those who knew it best to have been always in fact democratic at heart, in all the vital habits of her thought, in all the intimate relationships of her people that spoke their natural instinct, their habitual attitude towards life. The autocracy that crowned the summit of her political structure, long as it had stood and terrible as was the reality of its power, was not in fact Russian in origin, character, or purpose; and now it has been shaken off and the great, generous Russian people have been added in all their naive majesty and might to the forces that are fighting for freedom in the world, for justice, and for peace. Here is a fit partner for a league of honour.*

This was an amazing misrepresentation of Russia in every way possible. It was also very characteristic of the Romantic view of human nature held by very privileged members of the American intellectual class – the class that Wilson himself belonged to – members of which tended to be far, far removed from the harsh realities of life lived by the vast majority of people on this planet.

These were harsh realities (soon to be encountered with America's entry into the pointless war) that sadly not only Wilson was about to encounter but also the American people as well. Instead of serving some great cause of democracy, America would end up serving only the grim imperial interests of Britain and France, and little else. And ultimately, soon coming face to face with this unpleasant reality, it would break the spirit (and health) of Wilson ... and, in odd ways, that of the American people.

"To make the world safe for democracy." In any case, Wilson represented the war as the opportunity to engage America in another one of the crusades of political reform that so captivated the imagination of this autocratic reformer. To the American people he now proclaimed that the war was an historical struggle between the forces of world democracy and the tyranny of autocracy – and that America needed to get involved on the side of democracy, "to make the world safe for democracy." He and the American people (their sons, brothers and husbands) needed to take up the challenge of defeating evil autocracy and bringing democracy – and consequently full political freedom, prosperity and justice – to the world.

Wilson's Idealism was boundless. And his mind was made up on this matter.* He was going to sell the war to the American people not only on how this was going to spread democracy everywhere in the world – but that in doing so this would finally bring a lasting peace to the world.

To Wilson, democracies were always presumed to be reasonable societies – not grasping, not bullying and brawling like European autocracies of the Old World. According to Wilson (and other American and European Idealists or Humanists), by natural instinct democracies used calm reason in pursuing their national politics – and sought merely for international understanding in their engagement in the world of international relations and diplomacy. Wilson thus fashioned the idea that the war which broke out in 1914 had been nothing more than the result of the disastrous policies of the ruling classes of the autocracies – rather than the passionate nationalist urge of the masses or commoners of nearly all European nations.

Also, of such an autocratic personality himself, Wilson did not bother to truly check out his claims that Germany was the autocracy and Britain (and now Russia!) the world's true democracies. He had simply made up his mind himself on the subject. End of discussion. However, not only were Germany and Britain governed in a fairly similar manner by cousin kings, Germany had enacted some of the most socially progressive legislation at a time that Britain's treatment of its own industrial workers was still a major problem in that country.

In any case, in his speech before Congress Wilson outlined clearly his lofty cause he was asking young Americans to give their lives for:

> *We are glad, now that we see the facts with no veil of false pretence about them, to fight thus for the ultimate peace of the world and for the liberation of its peoples, the German peoples included: for the rights of nations great and small and the privilege of men everywhere to choose their way of life and of obedience. The world must be made safe for democracy. Its peace must be planted upon the tested foundations of political*

---

*But like Wilson, ironically (or maybe not), the reformist American Progressives (with the strong exception of Wisconsin Senator Robert M. La Follette) were the ones who had for years taken the position that America needed join the war. It was the conservatives who had long held out in opposition to such involvement.

liberty. We have no selfish ends to serve. We desire no conquest, no dominion. We seek no indemnities for ourselves, no material compensation for the sacrifices we shall freely make. We are but one of the champions of the rights of mankind. We shall be satisfied when those rights have been made as secure as the faith and the freedom of nations can make them.

"To make the world itself at last free." According to Wilson, in the bright new world that would unfold with democratic victory, people everywhere would be ruled by unselfish reason rather than by greedy, brute force. Once freed from the tyranny of power and power holders (the imperialistic autocrats), mankind would live by the higher moral power of logic and Truth. Thus this last great wartime struggle, no matter how violent it might become (and how many young Americans it might kill), would be well worth the terrible sacrifice – for it would "make the world itself at last free." His concluding remarks state the matter clearly:

There are, it may be, many months of fiery trial and sacrifice ahead of us. It is a fearful thing to lead this great peaceful people into war, into the most terrible and disastrous of all wars, civilization itself seeming to be in the balance. But the right is more precious than peace, and we shall fight for the things which we have always carried nearest our hearts – for democracy, for the right of those who submit to authority to have a voice in their own governments, for the rights and liberties of small nations, for a universal dominion of right by such a concert of free peoples as shall bring peace and safety to all nations and make the world itself at last free. To such a task we can dedicate our lives and our fortunes, everything that we are and everything that we have, with the pride of those who know that the day has come when America is privileged to spend her blood and her might for the principles that gave her birth and happiness and the peace which she has treasured. God helping her, she can do no other.

America's democratic allies have a different agenda. Tragically, Wilson's take on the war was not exactly how America's new allies Great Britain and France saw the war. At their home front, in their national capitals, they were indeed democracies. Actually they were empires too, with both Britain and France controlling vast empires in Africa and Asia – and with clear intentions of extending their imperial grip into the Muslim Middle East once the Ottoman Turks were knocked out of the way. But they played along with Wilson. They were certainly glad to get American help in crushing their "autocratic" enemies, and thus played along with Wilson's crusading Idealism. American assistance would likely break the terrible stalemate that had set in on the war and finally bring their side to victory in this long and deadly (and largely pointless) struggle.

Gearing up. In any case, America was not immediately ready to go to war. The U.S. Army was very small in size, there having been since the end of the Civil War (and the American-Indian wars) no apparent need of a large force, except to fight nationalist insurgents in the Philippines (early 1900s) and Mexican raiders set loose to do damage along the Mexican-American border (Pancho Villa was still conducting raids along the border at the time of America's entry into the Great War in Europe). General Pershing was sent to Europe in June of 1917, at the head of a small American military force, to give tangible evidence of America's commitment to the war cause there. But before America could get seriously involved, millions of troops would have to be trained for battle. It would not be until the late spring of the next year, 1918, before the Americans would arrive in strength in Europe.

The Americans join the fight. The French and English attempted to direct American troops into their own ranks as replacement troops for their exhausted armies. But American commanding General Pershing refused to use American troops as mere replacements in the ranks of the French and British armies. He demanded that they be given their own sector along the long line of battle, where they could fight under their own flag as a fully American army. The allies reluctantly agreed, having no basis on which to refuse this American demand. And thus in early 1918 Americans began taking their position at the Belleau Wood and St. Mihiel sector near Verdun.

Having helped to push back the German lines in those sectors in the late summer they then took on the Germans dug in within the Argonne Forest, which proved to be much slower going and more murderous for the Americans. But the soldiers conducted themselves well.

Wilson's Fourteen Points. In January of 1918 Wilson went before Congress to outline what he expected to be the specific terms of the peace that America was fighting to secure. The terms were presented as Fourteen Points, including the end to secret treaties (which Wilson supposed were the primary cause of the war in the first place); the guarantee of full freedom of all navigation on the high seas (a major source of American annoyance with both the Germans and the English); the adjustment of territories such as would restore Russia, revive Poland and return to France

Nationalism, Imperialism, and the Great War

territory lost to Germany in 1871; the opportunity for independence of nations part of the Austro-Hungarian and Turkish Ottoman Empires; and most importantly (in Wilson's eyes), the creation of a general association of nations to guarantee the political independence and territorial integrity to all states, large or small. This last point was the intellectual foundation for what would become the first truly international diplomatic organization: the League of Nations.

He made it clear that even for the Germans he sought only a fair or equitable peace – though he would negotiate such a peace with only a German delegation representing the majority members of the Reichstag (the German National Assembly) and not the "military party and the men whose creed is imperial domination." This was a clear indication that America would not deal with the Kaiser but instead with only a German group representing supposedly the broader interests of the people of Germany.

In theory, this was all very noble. But it would leave the Germans at the negotiating table facing very hostile adversaries – at the same time having to operate from a position of incredible political weakness. Because of Wilson's requirements, Germany's national interests would be defended by a group of negotiators possessing very little German political or emotional support by their own German people to work from. Consequently, Germany would be walked over by France and Britain – despite Wilson's protests – and ultimately leave Germany in the future itching for a rematch to readjust the unfair outcome of the peace talks. Hitler would soon play big on this German understanding of what happened under Wilson's Armistice.

German troubles. Meanwhile the Germans were having tremendous difficulties keeping up their end of the war. This two-front war was draining down Germany's economic and spiritual strengths to a dangerous low.

In December of 1917 the Germans signed at Brest-Litovsk a treaty with Lenin's Communist government in Russia, in which the Germans agreed to halt their assault on Russian territory – thus freeing the Russian Communist Red Army to focus its efforts completely on defeating the Russian White Armies made up of a poorly united coalition of pro-Tsarists, Cossacks, ethnic minorities and pro-republicans. Part of the payoff for the Germans was the huge German territorial gains in Eastern Europe given up by the Russian Communists. But the main reason the Germans had agreed to this treaty was that they would then be free to rush the vast number of German troops massed in the Russian Front back to the Western Front. With this new concentration of German troops on the Western Front they could then break through the French and British lines and grab Paris, thus collapsing French resistance and ultimately ending the war itself before the

Americans could arrive in number in Europe in the spring of 1918.

Indeed, that next spring of 1918 the French and British lines initially were pushed back heavily in the face of Germany's new offensive (begun in March), but then held firm, so that overall the Germans failed in reaching their objective: Paris. By July the Germans found themselves merely exhausted all the more through this desperate effort. Meanwhile back in Germany, the population was finding itself on the brink of starvation, and movements to pull Germany out of the war were starting to form in opposition to the Kaiser's determination to fight the war to the finish.

* * *

THE TROUBLED PEACE[119]

Armistice (November 11, 1918) ends the war. Ultimately Wilson's offer of a fair and just peace was heard in Germany, now wavering in its loyalty to the Kaiser. Inquiries were sent to Wilson at the beginning of October 1918 about the possibility of a cease fire. Then when around the same time the Allied armies broke through Germany's heavily defended line of defense, the Hindenburg Line, the Germans realized that the war was finally truly over for them. But Wilson's requirement that the Kaiser abdicate was a major sticking point.

Then, inspired by the Russian Revolution of the previous year, in late October first sailors, then soldiers, then workers joined a growing revolt and simply took command and set up Soviet-style councils in various cities across Germany. Political chaos resulted, especially when the two wings of the large Social Democratic (Marxist) Party fell into fighting over whether or not to accept Wilson's peace offering – and then move quickly to set up a Soviet style Communist government in Germany – or instead redesign Germany as a parliamentary republic.

Ultimately most of the soldiers and workers threw their support to the pro-parliament Social Democrats (led by Friedrich Ebert), who took control of Germany's government on the 9th of November after Prince Max announced the end of the German monarchy. Realizing that he had lost all political support, the next day Kaiser Wilhelm went into exile in the neutral Netherlands.

Meanwhile Germans had taken up discussions with Wilson about an Armistice, which they were now willing to accept – on the basis of his Fourteen Points. Wilson agreed.

However, America's allies, Great Britain and France, had no intentions whatsoever of honoring Wilson's peace terms, as they sought unconditional surrender of Germany and nothing less. They had gone along with Wilson's

Nationalism, Imperialism, and the Great War 471

Fourteen Points only because they needed American aid and because they had recognized the propaganda value these had in undermining the Kaiser's political authority in Germany.

Unaware of what was actually going on politically within the camp of its adversaries, the Germans complied with Wilson's demands and declared at Weimar the creation of a German republic (thus known as the Weimar Republic) and announced their willingness to accept an Armistice based on Wilson's Fourteen Points. Thus at the eleventh hour of the eleventh day of the eleventh month of the year (November 11th 1918) the guns finally fell silent in Europe for the first time in over four years. The war was over.

Meanwhile tragedy continues in a new form: The 1918 Spanish flu epidemic. Whereas the war had caused approximately sixteen million deaths, a flu which struck broad sections of the world (including America) in 1918 within mere months killed three times as many people. The flu hit in the spring of 1918 – but involved few deaths. But when the disease reappeared in the fall of 1918 – it was devastating. Age, health, city or country-living made no difference in its attacks. Half a million Americans died from this flu. And those it did not kill, it produced permanent effects for approximately a quarter of the US population. In a few short months it lowered life expectancy in the US by twelve years.

And thus it was that as 1919 came into view, it was with much hope that the Western world greeted the first year since the end of the war – and the devastating Spanish flu. Hopefully much, much better days lay ahead.

The Peace of Versailles.[120] But tragically, reality would soon deliver a huge, disappointing blow to such hopes, and especially to the expectations of a triumphant Wilson, when all the warring parties sat down together to work out the specific terms of the peace that had looked so promising as 1918 came to a close.

Being the Idealistic Humanist that he was, Wilson failed to connect American power with American diplomacy (much less even attempt to understand the dynamics of international power), and thus the English and French took the opportunity to pounce upon the exhausted Germans to wreak an expensive revenge – despite Wilson's protests. Probably no English or French politician who failed to bring home to his people some major exaction of retribution against the Germans would have had a political future. But Wilson had power to use to move things more in the direction he wanted to see them go. But caught up in his utopian world, he failed to see the diplomatic opportunities he actually possessed in order to direct negotiations along the lines he had desired.

Wilson was deeply troubled at the bullying behavior at the peace table of his democratic allies Great Britain and France – quite in violation of his much-cherished notion that democracies will automatically behave only in the most enlightened way. His fellow democracies instead were determined to force crushing peace terms on Germany and to confiscate the Arab lands of the Ottoman Turks – very much in violation of the equitable peace terms which Wilson had announced to lure everyone to the peace table in the first place.

Then Wilson found himself shocked as he discovered that the English and French were not interested at all in assisting him in spreading his idea of the "rights of national self-determination of people everywhere." They were not about to do that because that would have meant having to give up their own multi-ethnic or multi-national empires.

Also, to Wilson's great distress, things were not doing well in Russia – because not blissful democratic peace but instead a violent civil war had accompanied Russia's move to democracy. And this civil war had Russia's democrats lined up on the same side with the old Russian autocrats (the Whites) in a ferocious battle against Marxist-Leninist Communist insurrectionists (the Reds).

Wilson's proposed League of Nations. On the other hand, Wilson was able to get his allies at least to accept the fourteenth and final point of his Fourteen Points: the idea of a world assembly (the League of Nations) where he hoped cooler heads could eventually come together once the fever of war had subsided and then reasonably right the wrongs of the abominable peace treaties foisted by the democracies on their defeated enemies.

But his plan was greatly foiled by his own United States Senate's refusal to go along with his grand international project, and more importantly, by his own personal intransigence. The extensive commitment required of membership in the League alarmed American senators when Wilson's League of Nations idea was put before them as a treaty requiring senatorial ratification. Senators demanded some compromises that permitted Congress to still control American foreign policy, in particular the Constitutional rule that Congress must be the one, not an international organization, to take America to war. The Senate (whose approval was necessary for all treaties to be fully ratified) was willing to cooperate with this new international government, but with a few key reservations.

Wilson's advisors begged Wilson to accept some compromise with Congress concerning these quite reasonable demands. But Wilson was an autocratic purist for whom compromise was an ugly and inadmissible concept. He would have the treaty bringing America into membership in his new international organization only on his terms, and no other. Thus the venture came to nothing in the United States when in late 1919 the Senate failed by only a few votes to ratify the treaty – even while most of the rest of the world went ahead with Wilson's project and joined the League of Nations. Irony of ironies, America was the only nation of note not to join.

Wilson incapacitated by a stroke (July 1919).[121] Not only was treaty ratification crippled by Wilson's intransigence, but so was his health, when during a tour of the country to gain support for ratification of the Versailles Treaty (and thus entrance into the League of Nations) Wilson suffered a crippling stroke. The seriousness of his disability was kept from the American public, who remained unaware during his last two years in office of how feeble Wilson had become (his more ambitious wife basically took care of what little presidential business there was during this time period.)

The larger impact on the international status quo. The betrayal of Wilson's promise of an equitable peace, to which the Germans thought they were agreeing when they laid down their arms, would become the source of German ideological opportunity for Hitler and his Nazis. They skillfully exploited this sense of betrayal (*Dolchstoss* or Stab in the Back) by the weak new German Weimar Republic, which had agreed to the grand humiliation forced on Germany at Versailles by the so-called democracies. The Nazis played the Dolchstoss idea so effectively that they were eventually able to overthrow the Republic and institute a *Neuordnung* (New Order) in Germany, one built on German tribal power – not on democratic virtues such as Wilson had believed would soon save the world. They sneered at the weakness of all such democracies and readied themselves to demonstrate exactly what the Neuordnung was to mean to the rest of the world. In short, the peace of 1919 merely set the scene for a return engagement twenty years later of a new round of war: World War Two.

In those peace treaties, the German and Austro-Hungarian Empires had large slices of land taken away from them, to be awarded to the newly reconstituted Poland and the newly invented Yugoslavia and Czechoslovakia. The latter, Czechoslovakia, was founded on an uncomfortable union between the Westward-oriented Czechs or Bohemians and the Eastward-oriented Slovaks – and contained a huge number of Germans along the Czech borders with Germany (Sudetenland).

Poland was restored (after having disappeared previously for a century) out of the territorial loss of Russia, Germany and Austria – with no tradition of democracy to guide it into the new era of "Polish democracy." This reconstituted Poland also contained vast numbers of ethnic Germans – which would make for a very uncomfortable situation facing the new Polish

Government, leaving Poland as a vulnerable target should its neighbors recover strength enough to grab back their lost territory (which they would do in 1939 – starting another World War in Europe).

Austria-Hungary was split into two separate nations, losing a lot of territory in the process, and like Germany acquiring democratic governments in order to make them members in good standing of the new democratic world.

The Serbs, who had been allies of the Big Four, were awarded the central or commanding position in the newly constituted nation of Yugoslavia (South Slavia) – also an uncomfortable union among Serbs, Croats, Slovenians, Bosnians, Albanians and Macedonians.

A large section of Hungary was awarded to another ally, Rumania (Romania), a recently independent nation split off in 1877 from the Ottoman Turkish Empire; this too would make for a very uncomfortable Romanian union between ethnic Hungarians and ethnic Romanians.

Bulgaria, an Ottoman province until it achieved full independence in 1908, had been an ally of Germany and Austria and thus suffered accordingly with the loss of territory along the strategically vital coast of the Aegean Sea awarded to its newly formed or reformed democratic neighbors.

The autocracy to suffer undoubtedly the largest territorial and thus political loss was the Turkish Ottoman Empire. This empire had its vast (but quite loose) Middle East Muslim holdings carved up into a number of newly independent nations – leaving the ethnic Turks themselves only a small remnant of an independent state in the center of Asia Minor.

The English and French took for themselves big slices of the Ottoman Empire, awarding themselves control over the newly formed Arab states under the Mandate system. The idea of the Mandate system was that these new Arab states were not ready for self-rule – and thus though independent, were to be carefully supervised by the holders of these mandates: Britain and France. Thus it was that Mesopotamia (Iraq), Palestine, and Transjordan were put under the "protection" of the British, and Syria and Lebanon were placed under the French.

These new states had some ancient historical claim to political existence, though hardly as true nations. Although mostly Arab in culture, these former provinces of the Ottoman Empire were made up of a mix of various contending Muslim sub-communities and even a mix of ancient Christian communities. They had lived side by side in some degree of peace under the enforcement of the Ottoman Turks. But with the Turkish authority removed these new states were forced to try to find a spirit of national unity on their own – a virtually impossible task. Western imposed democracy instead offered these many sub-communities the opportunity to revive ancient and bitter ethnic rivalries – which only strong-handed monarchies (backed by British or French power) seemed able to bring forcefully to some semblance of national peace. Indeed as democracies, these new states were pure fictions.

Germany suffered the loss of its African colonies (Great Britain and France held on to theirs for another forty years), these too being turned over to the English, the French and their Belgian and South African allies – also as "mandates." German colonies in the Pacific were awarded to Great Britain, Australia, New Zealand – and even Japan as mandates.

Italy, for its pitiful contribution to the winning of the Great War for democracy, was awarded German-speaking Austrian lands on the southern side of the Alps (South Tyrol).

Russia, meanwhile, was plunged into a long and bloody civil war (1918–1923) between Lenin's Communist Reds and the coalition of Kerensky's and the Tsarists' Whites. Ultimately, more soldiers and civilians died from this civil war than had died during their participation in the Great War.

In the end it was Lenin's Communists and the Red Army that won the day in Russia. But interestingly, in finally achieving some degree of control, Lenin backed away from some of his original ideas about moving directly to a Communist economy and society. Instead, with the new Russian or Soviet economy in shambles, Lenin introduced (1921) his New Economic Policy (NEP) allowing small-scale farming and light industry to operate on a moneyed or capitalist basis, which indeed soon brought some stability back to the Russian economy.

Moral-spiritual disillusionment among the victors. In general, the victorious democracies – America, Britain, France and Italy – were badly stung by the death and destruction that had ultimately produced no real progress in world civilization. Consequently, the democracies suffered a deep drop in moral nerve after the war. The aggressive instinct that marked the West's presence in the larger world before the war was largely lost, replaced among a number of the West's political leaders by a tired, timid spirit – a spirit which hoped that future conflicts could be avoided by a new attitude of mutual appeasement.

Indeed, America came quickly to the conclusion that it had been deceived in taking up arms to fight for the cause of democracy. The results of the peace were not at all what Wilson had promised that the sacrifices of the war would produce. Americans quickly became cynical about Wilson's great crusade – and determined never again to be smooth-talked into getting involved in a European war.

CHAPTER FIVE

THE "ROARING TWENTIES"

* * *

AMERICA DOES INDEED ROAR AFTER THE WAR[122]

The fast-paced life in Americas cities and towns. The war had brought a massive economic boom to a rapidly expanding American economy, with the huge demand for war goods: everything from the food products produced on vast numbers of American farms, to the uniforms, guns and munitions, even eventually tanks, airplanes, and battleships produced in American factories. But the war-time boom continued right on into the 1920s (at least for urban America) as businesses turned to the manufacture of radios, cars and home appliances – to meet a huge demand of a prospering urban society. Material goods abounded as never before for the great American urban middle class, imparting to urban culture a decidedly materialist flavor.

Some statistics clearly demonstrate the impact of materialism in American life. For instance, the radio, the wonderful invention that instantly connected the average American living room to the vast world of news, entertainment and even thoughtful ideas, went from sixty thousand radios owned by Americans in 1922, to a point only eight years later when American radios reached 13.8 million in number. Likewise, the automobile helped broaden that same world, allowing vast personal mobility never dreamed of during the horse and buggy days (although the development of the railroad in the 1800s had certainly pointed the way to such a possibility). So rapid was the expansion of the American automobile culture that by 1927, when Ford's Model-T was replaced by the Model A, the Ford Motor Company could brag that it had produced over fifteen million of its Model-T Fords. And to meet the needs of the rapidly expanding automobile culture, the number of gas stations exploded exponentially; for instance, Standard Oil of New Jersey had increased the number of its gas stations from twelve in 1920 to around 1,000 by 1929.

But it was not merely a world of expanded horizons. Average

The "Roaring Twenties" 477

middle-class Americans lived at a level of material wealth characteristic previously only of Europe's very upper classes. The wealth in available food, clothing, housing and furnishings, as well as the mechanical gadgets designed to ease the task of housekeeping, was truly amazing. In the period 1920 to 1929, Woolworth's 5-and-10-cent stores (founded back in the 1880s) went from over a thousand in number to nearly twice that number; the J.C. Penney department store chain went from over 300 in number to nearly five times that size; and grocery stores exploded in number, A&P numbering over 15,000 stores by 1929, with other grocery stores such as Safeway and Piggly Wiggly each expanding to over 2,500 stores in number; even Western Auto parts stores went from three in number in 1920 to over fifty in number during that same period.

The new culture of personal freedom. The new wealth allowed the more adventuresome set, America's youth, to experiment with exciting new clothing, dance, and general social styles, ones quite distinct from their parents' very traditional ways. Girls had their hair bobbed or cut very short (to the shock of their mothers and grandmothers), skirt hemlines were raised, feminine beach attire became much scantier in its body covering (getting young ladies in trouble with the beach patrols). Likewise, the young men also freed themselves, like the women, with their love of the latest in music trends, clothing styles, fast cars, booze and cigarettes, and sex in all varieties. And, of course, there was the excitement of drinking their alcoholic beverages now forbidden by Federal law under the Constitution's Eighteenth Amendment that had so recently gone into effect. In short, it looked as if youthful urban America was dedicated to the principle of party, party, party, to drink away the memories of a tragic world they had just left behind.

And along with the Eighteenth Amendment was the Nineteenth Amendment, going into effect in August of 1920 giving all American women the right to vote, just in time for the national elections scheduled for that November. Women no longer needed to rely on their husbands to defend the interests of the American family. Women could also do that as well, or simply defend their own personal interests quite apart from family concerns. The 1920s, after all, marked the rapid growth in the sense of personal rather than community interest, in part due to the reaction to the hyped patriotism the country had gone through in its war to make the world safe for democracy, and in part due simply to the fact that the American family was no longer the key support system that Americans needed to thrive. Under the newly rising culture, Americans were invited to try to undertake life entirely on their own.

The big disappointment: The Interchurch World Movement. Caught in the changing mood of the times was a major project of Christian America, started up by the Foreign Missions Board of the Presbyterian Church just one month after the end of the war. Operating under the enthusiasm and the grand idealism that had the world looking forward to its entrance into a whole new post-war era (Wilson's age of universal democratic peace), the idea was birthed of combining the efforts of a wide range of Protestant churches in their work abroad. The idea was that they all wanted the same thing, the world to be brought to Christ. So why not work together on this venture?

The response to the invitation was amazing. Huge amounts of money towards the effort were pledged by the denominations, with the Methodists and the Baptists pledging ultimately to contribute around $100 million each toward the Fund. But sadly the shine on this highly idealistic post-war period quickly faded (even just by 1920), due to a number of factors, not only including the way the post-war world was cynically negotiated at Versailles but also because of a serious post-war recession that set in on the American economy. Only half of the pledged amount was actually raised, leaving the project vastly overextended and thus being forced to cut back deeply in its planning.

But this coincided also with a general drop in Christian support across the nation, resulting in a loss of church attendance that gathered momentum as the 1920s advanced, which ran all the way into the 1930s. America was experiencing a deep existential challenge on all sorts of fronts, as the rather millennial expectations for a new world of universal peace, prosperity and cultural-spiritual dynamism faded from view. The 1920s rather quickly was proving itself to be quite something other than what the optimists, the progressivists, the idealists had been expecting.

* * *

TRADITIONALIST AMERICA
DOES NOT WARM UP TO THIS NEW CULTURE

The onset of a deep rural depression (early 1920s). It must be noted that although the 1920s is regarded as the materialist age of the radio, the automobile, the home appliances, etc. that made American life so rich – these riches were concentrated largely in urban, and to a lesser extent in small-town America. They were largely lacking on the farms of rural America, where generally electricity had not yet reached. But that was the least of the problems faced by rural America during the 1920s.

From the onset of the Great War in Europe in 1914 the demand for

American farm goods skyrocketed as European farmers were taken away from their fields and put into uniform to fight in the trenches. Prices for American farm goods rose accordingly and the American farmer found himself to be something of a very successful businessman. Life was full of promise on the American farm. So, the farmer mortgaged his home and farm to buy more land – and machinery to work the land – in order to greatly expand his business. The profits rolled in – while the war lasted.

When the Great War ended in late 1918, the good times of the American farmer ended as well. With European soldiers returning to their farms, Europe no longer needed American farm products, at least not in anywhere near the quantity that it needed them during the war. But the Americans had greatly expanded their operations and now a glut in the agricultural market appeared, and agricultural prices dropped away to nothing.

Thus for example: wheat prices in 1919 were at $2.15 a bushel. The farmers were doing very well! But by the fall of 1920 the price had fallen to $1.44 a bushel. And by 1922 the price was down to 88 cents a bushel!

Indeed, in his sales the American farmer hardly recovered the cost of producing his products much less make a profit or income for him and his family. But even worse, he owed huge amounts of money to the local banks that had lent him the money to buy all this additional land and machinery during the war. And he now had no way to pay back those loans or mortgages. One by one, farmers lost their land to the banks.

But banks were not in the business of farming. Instead of money returning to them as payments for the loans and mortgages, the banks received in default the title to these failed farms. To recover their money, they could sell these farms – but to whom? And when they did it was always for far less than the money that they themselves had originally invested in the mortgages and loans to the farmers. So it was that the farmers' troubles were simply passed on to the banks. Thus in the early 1920s, the rural banks began also to fail one by one. Deep misery set in on rural America.

The growing American rural-urban cultural divide. And to further deepen the misery, watching the wealth and fun gravitate to urban America in the 1920s only made spirits worse in rural America.

This economic divide unfortunately also happened to coincide with a growing cultural divide between rural and urban America. The rural side of this cultural divide was well-founded on the traditional, White Anglo-Saxon Protestant (WASP) population and ethic that had been at the core of American culture since the nation's founding in the early

1600s as a group of English colonies. On the urban side of the divide was a smaller, but growing ethic of immigrant cultures, Catholic, Jewish and secular Socialist, accompanying recently arriving immigrants from Europe – joined by Blacks migrating to northern cities from the rural American South. By the 1920s WASPs felt out of place in the American city, foreigners in their own land.

While the American countryside felt most comfortable and consoled itself with tradition, the cities were bubbling with a sense of change. This sense of change, of new possibilities, is what also brought WASPish intellectual Idealists to the cities, where they felt that they had greater freedom to explore social ideas that were considered largely taboo in the traditional countryside that they had been born and grew up in. A rather condescending attitude toward rural America began to register itself among these liberated intellectuals – adding considerably to the growing American cultural divide.

Prohibition.[123] Then there was this matter of the issue of the prevention or prohibition of the drinking of alcoholic beverages, an issue that divided America deeply. Perhaps most galling to rural America was the proliferation in urban America of the speakeasies (illegal bars), operating in brazen defiance of the new Eighteenth Amendment to the Constitution outlawing alcoholic beverages.

WASPish rural and small-town America, especially the feminine portion of it, had actually for quite some time taken up arms against one of the great sins of men, the excessive drinking of alcoholic beverages. WASPish Christian morality had always been negative about alcohol, especially its easy ability to lead to drunkenness and alcoholism, which were most definitely great sins. But immigrants coming from Europe – Irish, Germans, Italians, Polish, etc. – seemed not to have this anti-alcohol ethic, alcohol being part of their daily diet.

These immigrants for the most part upon their arrival were consigned to urban or industrial slums, farmland no longer being free for the taking from the Indians (the frontier had finally closed with the last Indian lands claimed by White frontiersmen farmers in the late 1800s). These immigrants were forced to find jobs in mines and factories where there was a great need for unskilled labor. But working conditions were terrible, the wages minimal, and life (to quote Hobbes) nasty, brutish and short. Men looked forward to payday when they could stop at the corner tavern on their way home from work and drown their sorrows in the bliss of alcohol. Their wives of course were upset that with things as troubled as they were, to have that money go to a drunken spree was heartbreaking. This whole scenario was one of deep tragedy.

Thus it was that the Women's Christian Temperance Union (WCTU) was formed in order to combat this social disgrace. The WCTU certainly fit the profile of the Progressive Movement as one of its main branches of social reform. But it also carried undertones of other political forces working in American society. One of these was the women's suffragist movement – and the women's demand to have their voices heard in American politics. The other was the growing irritation of WASPish rural America about the indecent lifestyle of urban-industrial America where the problem seemed to be largely located.

Temperance (moderation) easily turned into total prohibition as the best solution to the problem. And so a movement began to actually place this reform of total prohibition of the drinking of alcoholic into the Constitution as one of its amendments. And indeed, in early 1919 Prohibition took effect with the passing of the Eighteenth Amendment.

Urban Resistance to Prohibition. But urban-industrial culture did not take well to this imposed reform. It was understood (probably correctly) as simply a slap in the face of urban America by rural America – and urban America decided to strike back with a loud and very visible defiance of this law. Indeed, the culture that Prohibition was aimed at, urban America, seemed to actually increase its alcoholic consumption behind the closed doors of the speakeasy bars, which everyone (including the police) knew about quite readily.

The fast, easy money to be earned by the sale of illegal liquor (and other social services!) naturally led to the growth of a large, wealthy and very violent social structure: the "mob," constructed heavily along the lines of the Italian (actually Sicilian) Mafia, although the Irish and others also had their versions of the mob. Police and judges were paid to look the other way, and in general urban America turned into an even greater affront to the moral sensitivities of WASPish America. And the cities loved the pained outcries of rural America. Prohibition had become the gauntlet thrown down in the growing urban-rural cultural divide impacting the nation.

American Xenophobia. Along similar lines, immigrants in general become a target of traditionalist America after the war, being by this time mostly:
1) ethnically – Southern and Eastern European
2) religiously – Roman Catholic or Eastern Orthodox
3) politically – often sympathetic to one or another of the disgruntled European workers movements of Socialism, Communism, or even Anarchism

The Great 'Red Scare' in America. Relating closely to this mood of xenophobia was the huge Red Scare that captured the imaginations of Americans (urban as well as rural) after the war, and into the first part of the 1920s. This was not without cause, however. Not only was this fear inspired by the spectacle of European societies caught up in class warfare – inspired by a spreading Communist urge of an angry European working class as well as an equally aggressive spirit of anarchism, the close cousin of Communism – but also by a similar social agitation which seemed to be brewing in America itself, especially among recent immigrants to America's cities from Southern and Eastern Europe.

It was no secret that from Southern Italy came a large number of followers of the Italian anarchist Luigi Galleani, who brought with them their radical political instincts.

Also, numerous package bombs mailed to important American political and economic leaders thankfully were being intercepted before they could do their horrible damage. This too naturally put America on edge.

At the forefront of the movement to stop such radical violence was Wilson's Attorney General, Mitchell Palmer. Although he started out cautiously in his campaign against foreign agitators, he turned savagely against immigrants suspected of radical views after his home was blown up (along with the bomber himself, the Galleanist, Carlo Valdinoci).

Palmer hired 24-year-old J. Edgar Hoover to gather evidence and lead raids against such radicals. Files were gathered on 60,000 people and thousands were actually arrested in the period between November 1919 and February 1920. However, Palmer's plans for a presidential bid (his activity was making him a popular public figure) crumbled when a major Red uprising he predicted for May 1, 1920 failed to materialize.*

Then on September 16, 1920 a massive bomb exploded in the busy street in front of the Wall Street offices of the J.P. Morgan bank, killing 30 people and injuring 150 others (8 of whom would also die of their wounds). Although there was no precise evidence identifying the perpetrator of this vile event, suspicions were directed toward an Italian Galleanist anarchist, Mario Buda (verified as indeed the culprit 35 years later by a fellow anarchist and by Buda's nephew) who soon returned to Naples and thus was never apprehended.† Americans were shocked.

The Sacco and Vanzetti trial.[124] Another event was to rock the nation,

---

*May Day had long been the chief holiday of the Socialist Labor Movement in Europe.

†This was apparently a Galleanist retaliation (the first of many to follow) for the arrests of Sacco and Vanzetti.

not just in 1920 when the event occurred, but over the next seven years as the nation – and even the world – debated the event and the way it was handled by the American justice system. On April 15, 1920 robbers held up and killed one of two men transporting the company payroll of the Slater Morrill Shoe Company in Braintree, Massachusetts. Suspicions went immediately to a group of local Galleanist anarchists, of whom Nicola Sacco and Bartolomeo Vanzetti were arrested and charged with the crime.

The only real evidence to work with were the casings of bullets used in the attack. Testimonies by witnesses were confused and claims were made that the police had manipulated the evidence. Also there was a rush to judgment by the presiding judge, which later would become a major point of those who claimed that the two men were unfairly tried and sentenced for the murder the following summer (July 1921).

Almost immediately the court case became something of the case of the century. Writers, academics and even artists got into the act, protesting the probable innocence of the two Italians, citing the growing xenophobia (fear/hatred of foreigners) of Americans as the only driving force behind the conviction.

For the next six years the case was debated widely as the case was appealed through the American court system. Even the world got in on the act. Americans were widely understood to be cowboys when it came to justice, and the assumption arose that this was all nothing more than a typical vigilante lynching for which Americans were famous. Even the Pope intervened on Sacco and Vanzetti's behalf, asking Americans to check their motives. Then when finally in 1927 the sentence of death was issued for the two accused, protests (even riots) broke out in a number of the world's major cities. Nonetheless in August of 1927 the two were put to death in the electric chair.*

The Scopes Monkey Trial, Dayton, Tennessee – 1925.[125] But undoubtedly the most dramatic confrontation of the decade between the two cultures occurred over the issue of the teaching of Darwin's theory of evolution in the public schools.

In 1925 the two sides, liberal urban America and conservative rural

---

*The case continued however to draw the interest of journalists, artists and political activists over the decades that followed. In 1977 the liberal Massachusetts Governor Michel Dukakis issued a formal proclamation that the case was clearly unjust and that Sacco and Vanzetti's names should be cleared of the crime. However subsequent statements (most recently in 2005) by Italian colleagues of both men made it fairly clear that Sacco had indeed done the shooting and Vanzetti had been involved ... though only in the robbery portion of the event.

America met for something of a showdown in Dayton, Tennessee, over the question of teaching Darwinism in Tennessee's public schools. The battle was over the fundamental question: was man descended, as Darwin stated, through the evolutionary process of natural selection ("survival of the fittest") from some early version of a primate (something of an early "monkey" specie) – or was he, as the Bible states, created fully as a man by God in a single event?

The confrontation came to pass when in May of 1925, a group of Dayton civic leaders met at F.E. Robinson's Drugstore and decided to challenge Tennessee's new statute forbidding the teaching of Darwinist evolution. One motivation for holding the trial in Dayton was to revive the town's flagging economy. They knew that this would somehow put Dayton on everyone's map (and indeed it did!).

The mastermind behind this event was George Washington Rappleyea, an engineer and geologist who managed the Cumberland Coal and Iron Company. Rappleyea was widely credited with suggesting that Dayton challenge the new anti-evolution statute. Cooperating in this venture was the twenty-four-year-old John Thomas Scopes. He was teaching at the local high school, his first job after graduating from the University of Kentucky in 1924. He taught algebra and physics, served as athletic coach, and occasionally substituted in biology classes at the Rhea County High School. The idea was that he would teach Darwinist biology – at least once – in violation of the state's law prohibiting the teaching of Darwinism. This act would then set up the opportunity for the legal world in Tennessee to decide whether such a law was indeed constitutional.

During the extremely hot summer of 1925 the "Scopes Monkey Trial" riveted the attention of the nation as newspapermen from all around the country crowded into the steaming courthouse to follow the trial.

The old political warhorse, William Jennings Bryan, represented WASPish America, with its fervent dislike of Darwinism. Representing the Darwinists was Clarence Darrow, the celebrity New York lawyer who had dazzled the nation with his clever defense of two society boys who had killed a young fourteen-year-old neighbor in order to see what it would be like to commit the ultimate crime and to prove their Darwinian superiority (Darrow blamed their actions on the extravagantly wealthy socio-economic circumstances that had distorted their moral sensitivities). Darrow also represented the fast-rising urban, secular culture which ridiculed the superstition of the traditional Christian culture. Backing up Darrow was the American Civil Liberties Union (ACLU), which was to become the leading voice behind a movement to replace WASPish Christianity with Secular-Humanism as America's cultural-religious underpinning.

Which side actually won the 1925 contest depended on the natural sympathies of the person giving answer to the question. From pulpits, anti-Darwinism seemed vindicated by the fact that the judge decided to support the law prohibiting the teaching of Darwinism in the Tennessee public schools. But the up-East urban newspapers celebrated the quite obvious (obvious to them anyway) intellectual victory of the scientific Darwinists over the superstitious, backwoods fantasies of the anti-Darwinists.

Closing arguments were not allowed (defense attorney Darrow refused and thus prosecuting attorney Bryan was not permitted to do so either) and the sentence of guilty was quickly decided in matters of only minutes on July 21. But Bryan published his proposed closing argument subsequently. It is well worth the read because it is actually prophetic:

Science is a magnificent force, but it is not a teacher of morals. It can perfect machinery, but it adds no moral restraints to protect society from the misuse of the machine. It can also build gigantic intellectual ships, but it constructs no moral rudders for the control of storm-tossed human vessel. It not only fails to supply the spiritual element needed but some of its unproven hypotheses rob the ship of its compass and thus endanger its cargo. In war, science has proven itself an evil genius; it has made war more terrible than it ever was before. Man used to be content to slaughter his fellowmen on a single plane, the earth's surface. Science has taught him to go down into the water and shoot up from below and to go up into the clouds and shoot down from above, thus making the battlefield three times as bloody as it was before; but science does not teach brotherly love. Science has made war so hellish that civilization was about to commit suicide; and now we are told that newly discovered instruments of destruction will make the cruelties of the late war seem trivial in comparison with the cruelties of wars that may come in the future. If civilization is to be saved from the wreckage threatened by intelligence not consecrated by love, it must be saved by the moral code of the meek and lowly Nazarene. His teachings, and His teachings alone, can solve the problems that vex the heart and perplex the world.

Five days after the verdict, Bryan – back on the speaking tour – died quietly in his sleep. Ultimately the case itself decided nothing. But it considerably clarified the WASPish and anti-WASPish split in American culture.

Christian Fundamentalism vs. Christian Liberalism. This deep urban-rural cultural divide also registered itself as a deepening split within the Christian community itself. There were a number of issues that were behind this split, though one, the matter of biblical inerrancy, was definitely the most important. Almost everything else about the Liberal-Fundamentalist split followed from the ongoing issue of biblical inerrancy.

In the early 1900s the question of biblical inerrancy gathered force as a divisive issue, first within the Presbyterian denomination and then soon within the other mainline denominations. Heresy trials abounded as theologians and pastors lined up on one side or the other of the issue. For a time the Presbyterian denomination favored the Conservative view, demanding that all pastors adhere to five basic doctrines in order for their ordination to be in good standing with the denomination. But Liberals or "modernists" were gathering strength within the denomination. And with the unification with the Cumberland Presbyterian denomination, the Presbyterian Church shifted strongly toward the Liberal side of the debate.

Meanwhile, Presbyterian layman, Lyman Stewart, sponsored a new series of publications entitled *The Fundamentals* published between 1910 and 1915. This would become a rallying point for a number of Conservative theologians of a wide number of Christian denominations. In 1915 the Conservative journal, *The Presbyterian*, finally published a declaration entitled "Back to Fundamentals." And thus the term '"Fundamentalist" was brought into greater use to describe Conservative Christian theology.

At the same time the Liberal side of Christianity was taking a broader (Conservatives claimed shallower) approach to the faith, admitting that there was more than one road to God, that God's love extended to the saved and unsaved alike, and that Christians ought to be more ecumenical among themselves (ignoring doctrinal differences among Christians of all types) and more accommodating in their outreach to other cultures.

The gauntlet was thrown down in 1922 when the Liberal preacher Harry Emerson Fosdick presented a sermon at the First Presbyterian Church of New York City entitled "Shall the Fundamentalists Win?" So incensed was the General Assembly (sort of a Presbyterian Congress) at what it considered an attack on the fundamentals of the faith that it considered removing Fosdick from the pulpit (he was defended by the New York Lawyer, John Foster Dulles, who would serve as America's secretary of state during the Eisenhower presidency in the 1950s). But Fosdick instead simply resigned his position (John D. Rockefeller would subsequently select Fosdick to pastor the prestigious Riverside Church that he personally had funded!).

On the other hand, one of the foremost of the believers in the Christian Fundamentals and thus a major opponent of Christian Liberalism was J. Gresham Machen, New Testament professor at Princeton Seminary. Among the several books he published was *Christianity and Liberalism* (1923), in which he claimed that Christian Liberalism was not even Christianity, but some other religion. He was distressed that Christian Liberals believed (like Unitarians) that Christ was not primarily a personal savior but instead a personal teacher, setting moral examples which all, Christian and non-Christian, ought to follow. And Liberalism tended to view Christianity as simply one of many ways that led to the Fatherhood of God.

But the Liberal-Conservative balance of power was shifting within the Presbyterian denomination during the 1920s. When in 1928 the Presbyterian General Assembly voted to move Princeton from a traditionally Conservative theology to a more Liberal position, Machen and two other Princeton professors withdrew from the seminary to start a new one in nearby Philadelphia: Westminster Seminary.

✳ ✳ ✳

IN URBAN AMERICA A STRONG SENSE OF CYNICISM AFFLICTS THE ROAR OF THE ROARING TWENTIES

Actually, all this fascination with the exciting world of massive materialism and unlimited personal freedom seemed at times even to urban America to exist simply to cover over a darker suspicion about life, a suspicion that lurked just below the surface of all this hoopla.

The Great War – and its inevitable outcome of nothingness – had shaken the moral foundations of the American nation (as it did with every other participating nation) to the very core of what the society understood as being right and wrong. A form of cultural cynicism set in following the collapse of the Wilsonian dream in America. Many Americans (and Europeans) took the attitude that you had better enjoy life while you had it. "Eat, drink and be merry today because tomorrow you may die." Further, be wary of the high Idealism of those who want to invite you into some kind of higher world. Their world is only a fiction. The only world that really exists – or matters – is the one immediately in front of you. Such an attitude was considered being truly "realistic," and sophisticated.

In keeping with this mood of rampant cynicism, the general understanding was that there were no rights and wrongs, only just human impulses that people needed to be socially free to follow out. Whether these impulses were right or wrong (unless they were obviously self-destructive) was a matter that no one was supposed to be in a position to be a judge, either of themselves or of others.

Thus free-thinking artists and intellectuals boasted of their escape from the intellectual tyrannies of excessive patriotism and superstitious piety. They proudly professed belief in nothing except the immediacy of their own personal existence – and were quick to mock those who held higher ideals, whether founded on the past or the future. Philosophically they referred to themselves sometimes as Humanists, sometimes as Existentialists – but always as scientific.

But actually, as pure secularists (believing only in the reality of the immediately surrounding material order), they tended to be simply hedonistic cynics. They supported no causes – nor did they pay much attention to the social requirements of the larger social order. Those expected to lead the post-war societies got little or no support from this self-indulgent social group.

The "Lost Generation." Thus it was that despite all this freedom, despite the material glitz and glamor of the 1920s, there was beneath it all a spiritual emptiness, one that led Gertrude Stein – the grand patroness of the large number of American authors and poets who gathered in Paris to search for meaning to life – to call her literary flock gathered there the "Lost Generation." This group included such Americans as Ernest Hemingway, F. Scott Fitzgerald, John Dos Passos, E.E. Cummings, and Dorothy Parker.

The pointless brutality of the war had stolen from this generation the optimism that had characterized Western culture during the Progressivist Era. True, the material level that the people were able to live at was unparalleled in history. But this now seemed to be very small comfort to these intellectuals, who felt the necessity to plumb the depths of the human soul for some kind of new direction that would be worthy of the kind of commitment to life that they had felt before the war. But mostly they found no such direction or worth.

The spirit of these lost souls was summed up in such works as Hemmingway's *The Sun Also Rises* (1926) and Fitzgerald's *This Side of Paradise* (1920), *The Beautiful and Damned* (1922) and *The Great Gatsby* (1925).[126] This last-mentioned novel was highly representative of this Jazz Age mood: behind all the wealth, the fast life, the visible material achievements was a spiritual emptiness and social confusion that results in the murder of the gifted but corrupt young Gatsby and the collapse of the small social group that had once surrounded the Great Gatsby. Likewise, Hemmingway's novels seem to turn on the issue of hopes that lead nowhere because of life's complex, countering circumstances that the human will seems unable to overcome.

Meanwhile other intellectuals, repulsed by the failure of American

Progressivism to deliver on its promises, turned to other philosophies in the hope that they might find something more substantial to build their social hopes on. Marxism proved to be particularly popular, as the news coming out of Red Communist Russia (tainted by careful manipulation of that news by the Communists themselves) seemed to be working quite well once the Russian Civil War was over and Lenin's Communists had full mastery over the Russian situation, moving the country from feudal backwardness into something quite modern – and quite humane because it was supposedly so very communal. To a group of socially empty intellectual Westerners, this certainly was bound to have a very, very strong appeal.

Freudian psychology explains and justifies the American mood.
Then there was the degree of comforting logic that seemingly could be found in the psychological theories of the Austrian doctor Sigmund Freud. Though none of his theories were derived through the exacting rigors of the scientific method by which the rest of science accepted or rejected new truths, Freud's theories went unquestioned in much of urban America – and in fact were widely accepted as absolute Truth, because they made sense (when little else did)! That is to say, Freud's speculations about the motives and behaviors of humans seemed to offer an explanation to a culture, to a lifestyle, to a worldview that otherwise seemed shallow and mindless and beneath the dignity of human reason. Freud revived some element of hope that what the post-war, post-Christian culture was doing was actually logical.

Basically, Freud explained that we humans did things that made no sense because we were driven by even deeper, unexplored urges that ran beneath the level of what our conscious minds were capable of understanding and thus directing our actions in a logical manner. Freud speculated that these subconscious urges were formed in our early childhood out of sexual urges that had to be repressed in order to form us into reasonably well-functioning social creatures – that is, responsible members of society. Freud held to the idea that by going back in our earliest memories and revisiting the events of our early childhood that were part of this repressive experience, we might be freed from such repression, and find indeed fuller, more rewarding lives socially than the ones we were typically experiencing during the Roaring Twenties!

Freud mocked the idea of there being any ultimate truths that directed human existence, only socially useful ideas by which we humans were indoctrinated into society. Religion was chief among these socially useful ideas. Religion in itself could not be said to be true, for in exploring the many religious beliefs around the world it became clear to Freud (and most other intellectuals of those days) that the truths of religion were simply cultural explanations offered as comfort (such as Santa Claus and the Easter Bunny) to societies trying to make logical sense of an existence that otherwise had no particular logic to it. In short, to Freud, religion was a neurosis, or a useful illusion we fed ourselves in order to comfort ourselves in the face of a very difficult existence. To Freud, and to the hundreds of thousands of hip (cool) Freudian followers that believed Freud to be the supreme prophet of modern times, religion in itself was completely unrelated to Truth, and indeed was the source of some of the most illogical and cruel of human acts in history.*

However the followers of Freud failed to observe the fact that Freudian psychology itself was valued so highly by them only because "it made sense," ... which thus put Freudianism in the same category as the religions Freud mocked because they could be said to be true only because they too made sense to their religious followers. Freud himself made it clear that just because something made sense did not make it true. It merely made it socially useful.

And thus it was that Freudian followers followed Freud religiously! Indeed, in all this, Freud and his Freudian followers were helping to construct a new cultural Truth, contributing greatly to a new post-Christian religion within Western society, the Secular Humanism that was sweeping the intellectual circles of Europe and America.

* * *

THE AMERICAN QUEST FOR MORAL GROUNDING AND SOCIAL STABILITY[127]

The decline of moral vision in the nation's political leadership. Back in America, the Republicans were deadlocked in their effort to pick a presidential candidate for the upcoming elections of 1920, and finally settled on the supreme nice guy, Senator Warren G. Harding of Ohio, as a compromise candidate. He campaigned on the idea that as president he would do everything possible to promote a "return to normalcy" of life in America. With all of the wartime disruption of life and the post war political agitation that seemed to abound everywhere, this idea of a "return to normalcy" was so compelling to the American voter that in the

---

*Certainly to the followers of Freud, the experience of the recent "Great War" exposed such dangerous religious folly, in that each of the contending parties in the war claimed "Gott mit uns" (God is with us). Surely God was with no one during the war, unless God was indeed some kind of cruel monster delighting in watching "God-fearing" soldiers slaughter other "God-fearing" soldiers in vast numbers.

The "Roaring Twenties" 491

November elections, Harding received a huge 60 percent of the popular vote – against the Democratic candidate James Cox's mere 34 percent of the popular vote, the most lopsided presidential vote in American history.

Harding's post-war presidency (1921-1923).[128] As president, Harding surrounded himself with a set of personal advisors (drawn mostly from his home state of Ohio) to help him manage the federal budget and continue to advance social reforms in favor of American women, immigrants and Blacks.

But when it came to the personal behavior of many of these "Ohio Gang" advisors, Harding seemed to exercise little or no control. The results were embarrassing to the president (it would have been even more embarrassing had he lived a few more years to see his friends get what was due them)! In fact, Harding died as a result of a heart attack he experienced following a trip across the country in which he had set out to give answer to the growing rumors about the corruption of his presidential team.

One of the most outrageous examples of the corruption of the Harding Administration was the behavior of Harding's secretary of the interior, the elderly Albert Fall. He had secretly leased public oil lands to private companies to his own profit. Most scandalous were the Elk Reserve lease to Edward Doheny and the Teapot Dome Reserve lease to Harry Sinclair, earning Fall $105,000 and $304,000 respectively. This all came to light several years after the end of the Harding Administration as a result of investigations led by Senator Thomas Walsh (Montana).

Then there was Harry M. Daugherty, Harding's Attorney General, or top cop, in charge of the Department of Justice. Daugherty earned the nickname "The Fixer" for his role in arranging connections, such as the one that led to the Teapot Dome scandal. But there were others, including the corrupt Assistant Attorney General, Jess Smith, who committed suicide (or was he murdered?) when it was apparent that a Congressional investigation on corruption in the Justice Department was closing in on him (Smith's death occurred just before Harding's ill-fated trip).

But Coolidge (president: 1923-1929) is focused on bringing back to the White House a sense of the old Puritan values.[129] Calvin Coolidge was Harding's vice president – though not part of the corrupt Ohio Gang (nor was Harding's secretary of commerce, and future president, Herbert Hoover). Upon Harding's death in 1923 Coolidge was automatically elevated to the U.S. presidency.

To almost the same extreme that Harding was the picture of loose personal standards, Coolidge was the opposite: the picture of authentic

Puritan morality!

Coolidge grew up in Vermont, a descendant of a long line of Coolidges who had migrated to Massachusetts with the very first Puritans in 1630, and whose genealogy included officers of the American War of Independence and members of the Vermont House of Representatives. His ancestors tended to be farmers – very active in local politics.

Coolidge graduated as an honor student from Amherst College and then went on to clerk and study law in a Massachusetts law firm, eventually being admitted to the bar and setting up his own practice in Northampton, Massachusetts. He married a Vermont school teacher, Grace, and the two of them built a diplomatic marriage, reflective of the quiet and cautious way they both approached life.

He soon entered politics and performed decently in the elective offices he pursued, first as representative to the Massachusetts state assembly (the General Court), then as mayor of Northampton, then as state Senator, where he became noted for his moderately progressive positions on a number of issues. In 1915 he was elected Lieutenant Governor of Massachusetts and then in 1918 the state's Governor. He conducted himself as a moderate-progressive, and a reluctant spender of the state treasury – nothing that would have brought any particular notice to him nationally.

What brought him to national attention was the 1919 Boston police strike over the issue of a police union, pitting the state against the rising power of the labor unions. Coolidge took a strong position in support of the Boston mayor, calling out the national guard and answering the union that "there is no right to strike against the public safety by anyone, anywhere, any time." That indeed brought Coolidge national attention, at a time that America was undergoing a serious Red Scare.

And thus it was that in the Republican National Convention in which Harding was nominated as the party's presidential candidate, Coolidge was chosen as Harding's vice-presidential running mate. And from there – with Harding's unexpected death in 1923 – Coolidge found himself in the White House as the nation's president.

As president his attitude conformed nicely to the old adage: "the government that governs least governs best." Although Coolidge was deeply supportive of civil rights for Blacks (speaking out on their behalf in a time of extensive KKK activity across the nation, and appointing them to Federal positions) and Indians (pushing for full American citizenship of all American Indians), when it came to government programs and spending he was strongly opposed. He worked to cut back federal spending and move the budget to a balance instead of a spending deficit. As far as he was concerned the business of business was not the business of the government, but instead a matter of the private or capitalist sector (which was doing quite well during his presidency).

In 1924 he was returned to the White House on his own merits. He did quite well in the vote despite his very low-key candidacy (low key in great part due to the death of his sixteen-year-old son that July) and despite a third-party run of Progressive politician La Follette, which the Democratic Party opposition hoped would split the Republican vote and give the Democrats the victory – much as Teddy Roosevelts third-party run opened the way for the Democratic candidate Wilson to gain the presidency in 1912 on a mere plurality rather than a clear majority of the votes. But given the hugely upbeat mood of the country during the Roaring Twenties, Coolidge actually received 54 percent of the popular vote and 72 percent of the electoral vote.

He finished out his four years in office with no major programs of note (he believed that those matters belonged to the states, not the federal government) and no scandals. As there were no major foreign policy issues burning at the time, American foreign policy during his presidency was also quite low key. But that was the way Americans wanted things. They had other things personally to focus on, like getting rich fast.

And in 1928, as his term approached a close, Coolidge made it clear that he would not take on another term, although many expected him to do so. He was tired and ready to go home. Little did he know that by doing so he saved himself from being the one identified as "responsible" for the country's economic catastrophe, the Great Depression.

Herbert Hoover (U.S. president 1929-1933).[130] That horrible crisis would be dumped in the lap of the next president, Herbert Hoover, less than one year into his presidential term. And quite unfairly, he would naturally be the one that confused and angry Americans would take out their wrath on, for this is one of the perils of being the leader of any society.

Hoover was born in 1874 to a Quaker family in Iowa, his father dying when he was six and then his mother a few years later – leaving him and an older brother and younger sister orphans at a very early age. After changing hands among relatives, he finally ended up in the care of an uncle living in Oregon, settling in to work for his uncle and attend night school. At 17 he entered with the first class of the new Stanford University in California where he majored in geology.

After graduation from Stanford in 1895, he went to work for a mining engineering firm in California, moving two years later to work in the goldfields of Western Australia. Desert conditions there were harsh, but he worked hard and soon became a very young manager of a gold mine. Rivalry between himself and a higher official in the company led Hoover to move his operations to China (in 1899 marrying a Stanford college sweetheart, Lou, along the way), where he became the chief engineer for the Chinese Bureau of Mines and general manager of the Chinese Engineering and Mining Corporation.

Along with his rise in professional importance he seemed to pay close attention to the status of his workers, whether the Italians who were brought in to work under him in Australia or the Chinese who worked for him. He (and also his wife) would always have a strong humanitarian interest accompanying his extensive work in the mining profession.

He and his wife Lou held their own in Tianjin during a month-long siege (1900), part of the Chinese Boxer Rebellion, but soon after it was put down opened new operations in Australia (1901). At this point he became part owner of the gold mining company that was responsible for half the gold production in Australia, and thus found himself at a very early age on his way to enormous personal wealth.

Soon his operations expanded to South African gold mines, to Burmese silver mines, to Russian copper mines, and now also to Australian zinc mining. By 1908 he had established his own mining consultancy business, traveling the world from his offices in San Francisco, New York City, London, Paris and St. Petersburg (Russia). He soon found himself lecturing at various universities and writing what quickly became standard texts in his field of metallurgical engineering.

With the outbreak of the Great War in 1914, Hoover put aside his work to focus on getting Americans trapped in Europe back to the States, covering their travel expenses in the process. This was the beginning of the turn of his primary interest away from making money, to organizing operations (and money) needed to help people hurt by the ravages of the war that now consumed the Europeans. Basically, he undertook to feed the Belgian population, whose economy was devastated by the war. He did this for the next two years, heading up the Commission for Relief in Belgium, negotiating the arrangement with the German, Belgian, Dutch, French and British governments in order to be able to import massive amounts of food – and make sure it got delivered to the Belgian civilian population (over ten million individuals per day at the height of its operations) rather than the German troops occupying Belgium.

Then with the entry of the U.S. in the war his position as a neutral was ended and he returned to the States, newly appointed by President Wilson to head up the U.S. Food Administration, to avoid having to put the nation on rationing but nonetheless some kind of discipline in order to bring food to the American troops serving in Europe.

With the war's end in 1918 Hoover headed up the American Relief Administration, sending food to the starving population of Central Europe, including Germany, and even Russia (where the civil war was raging). Although some 6 million Russians died in the period immediately following the war, that number would have been more likely 20 million, had it not been for Hoover's relief work – a fact acknowledged even by the Bolshevik (Communist) government securing its hold over Russia at the time.

In the meantime, Hoover had not lost his interest in scholarship and left a huge endowment to his alma mater, Stanford, for the purpose of gathering important documents relating to the war. This effort led to the founding of the Hoover War Library, subsequently known as the Hoover Institution.

Now the 1920 presidential election was coming up, and Hoover announced himself as a candidate – with the Republican Party. But he did not do well early in the primaries and thus did not impress the national party greatly, which instead turned to Harding as its candidate. But Hoover supported the choice, Harding was elected, and Hoover was then asked by Harding to be his secretary of commerce (a fairly new cabinet position, whose exact function was not yet well established).

As secretary of commerce, Hoover went about organizing the operations of the department of commerce, finding new areas of responsibility for the department in – as he understood matters – improving the efficiency of the American economy. This of course put his hands in a wide range of government activity, so much so that at times (given the general restraint of the Republicans with their narrow view of the responsibilities of the federal government) Hoover seemed to be more central to governmental matters than the president! His goal was not to fight American industry (as trust-busting Progressives tended to do) but to work in close association with that industry, in order to get the very best out of it – with his activities in the field of electrical power generation, rural water management (and flood control), automobile and highway safety, aviation, radio broadcasting, and a sincere concern for the lives of sharecroppers, especially Black sharecroppers.

Sensing in 1928 that he now had a better chance at the U.S. presidency (Coolidge had announced that he would not run again), Hoover once again announced his candidacy, this time his wide popularity opening the door to the candidacy quite easily. And in the general election that November he easily carried both the popular vote – 58 percent against his Democratic Party opponent, the Roman Catholic and "wet" New Yorker (strongly opposed to the 18th Amendment prohibiting the consumption of alcohol), Al Smith with only 41 percent – and 444 electoral votes to

Smith's 87 electoral votes.

Thus when Hoover took office in 1929, America was expecting to see the fabulous economic journey that the country found itself embarked on expanded even more. Little did the country realize that the very opposite was soon to occur.

But in any case, that's how the country finished out the Roaring Twenties politically.

* * *

AMERICA CONFRONTS THE WORLD DURING THE 1920s

The League of Nations: Wilson's Utopian project. There had been a number of voluntary diplomatic councils in Europe's recent history (the Congress of Vienna in the early 1800s, the various Geneva Conventions on the rules of war during the 1800s and early 1900s, an Inter-Parliamentary Union in the late 1800s) – but Wilson's dream of having the major countries of the world joined in a permanent, on-going diplomatic union was quite a dramatic development. Wilson's hope had been that the world was ready to enter into a whole new era of diplomatic reason – in strong distinction to the uncontrolled passions that had so recently driven much of the world into the Great War. Wilson's hope was that nations would instead first seek international understanding through negotiations, before letting the heat of national hurt propel them to take up war against another nation. It seemed like a very good idea – very sensible and logical. But as things soon demonstrated it was a quite unrealistic dream.

The concept of collective security. It was hoped that reason would bring national disputes to settlement. But failing that, it was assumed that collective security would force war-prone nations to back down and behave, thus preserving the international status quo or world order. The supposition was that all nations loved world peace – and would by instinct come together to gang up on a would-be violator of that peace. That was the heart of the idea of collective security. But in fact, the instincts of nations, the way they viewed the international status quo or world order from their own particular point of view or national interest, varied quite widely from country to country. As it turned out there was nothing automatic about how collective security worked – especially when one or another of the world's major powers was involved. Nations always tended to decide on the basis of their own sense of national sovereignty how they wanted to approach a particular dispute.

By no means was there some single rational point of view that all nations automatically came to hold when faced with a dispute. Thus the idea did not work – except in a few minor cases in the early years of the League when the national interests of the members were not deeply affected by the dispute. But as international politics headed into the 1930s things got very tense – and the League not only was not able to resolve disputes that arose during that period, in attempting to do so the League nearly always drove one or another major power to resign from the League.*

The organization itself. The League of Nations was based in Geneva (Switzerland) and consisted of a number of diplomatic organizations, the most important of which were the League Assembly and the League Council. The Assembly was made up of a voting representative of each of the (50+) members. It could take up for consideration any issue it chose – and Assembly decisions required only a simple majority for passage of a League resolution. The League Council however was expected to be more the enforcer of the peace and was a smaller body at first with four permanent members (Britain, France, Italy and Japan); it had been expected that America would be the fifth – but America never joined the League. Eventually Germany was added to League membership and became the fifth permanent member. Non-permanent members elected by the Assembly were at first four in number and eventually expanded to ten in number, each serving for a three-year term. Decisions of the Council were understood to be weightier matters and thus a resolution required the affirming vote of all the members (a unanimous decision) unless one of the Council members was a party to a dispute – and then that nation was not entitled to vote.

There was also a Permanent Court of International Justice set up in The Hague (Netherlands) where cases could be put before highly trained international judges as a way of settling disputes. This recourse was used frequently during the 1920s. But as international disputes took on a more warlike nature the PCIJ was used less and less in the 1930s. (The PCIJ was nonetheless highly respected and was one of the several League organizations that was carried over as part of the new United Nations when it was set up in 1945).

There were also other organizations set up as part of the League – bureaucracies that were supposed to tackle a number of distinct problems

---

*A number of major powers party to disputes, in finding decisions going against their national interests, simply resigned: Japan (1933), Germany (1933), and Italy (1937). Soviet Russia was expelled by the League in 1939 when it refused to call off its invasion of Finland.

in the area of labor, health, education, women's rights, drug trade, slavery and other social conditions and issues. This idea of government action undertaken by technical specialists was in keeping with the rising spirit of Progressivism in America and Socialism in Europe in the early 1900s.

American isolationism with respect to entangling alliances. America had refused to join Wilson's League of Nations. Americans in general had come to feel that there had been a huge betrayal at the end of the Great War by the Wilson government and by their English and French allies. Both Wilson and America's allies had failed to make good the promise of the spread of democracy to the whole world – and thus of world peace (for why else indeed had Americans gone to Europe to die?). Consequently, there was virtually an immoveable resolve of Americans never to get involved again in the dangerous hypocrisies of another European conflict. This isolationist sentiment with respect to the events in the European Old World seemed unshakeable.

However ... a participant in the world disarmament movement. Americans *per se* were not opposed to peace itself – only to entangling alliances that would compromise the freedom of the nation. This mood therefore did not mean that America would not participate at all in the matter of securing a peaceful world. In the post-war 1920s America in fact was quite active in this regard.

The horrors of the Great War had been so terrible that a widespread sentiment among many of the victor nations was that henceforth – except for very dire defensive reasons – war was virtually unthinkable. This encouraged the utopian reasoning of European and American Idealists who sincerely believed that indeed the Great War had ended up being the war to end all wars. Supposedly peaceful reasoning had developed within world culture to the extent that passionate militarism was a dead thing of the past. "International understanding" was now the driving force within the new diplomacy.

Accompanying this general hope was the widely-held view of the times, both in America and Europe, that the greatest danger to the peace that the world craved so deeply was to be found in the heavy militarization of the nations. "Take the weapons away and the nations will be forced to act peacefully with each other." Thus the word of the day was *disarmament*.

When Germany was forced to agree to a huge cutback in its military as required by the Versailles Treaty, the Germans were led to believe that this was not intended as punishment but instead as the first step in a larger disarmament of all nations. On that basis the German negotiators

The "Roaring Twenties" 499

seemed to be accepting of the disarmament terms imposed on them.

The Washington Naval Conference (1921–1922). Seeking the same goal, America during the winter of 1921–1922 hosted a great disarmament conference at its capital. This conference was designed to set international standards and limits on the size and functioning of the navies of the major powers involved in the politics and diplomacy in East Asia and the Pacific Ocean, and also other subjects designed to reduce the horrors of war, such as the outlawing of the use of poison gas. Importantly the conference was designed both to recognize the role of the Japanese navy in this region while at the same time to set limits to just that role. It also set out to prevent any kind of naval arms race from developing among any of these powers, thus agreeing to limit the building of naval vessels at a ratio of 5:5:3 for Britain, America and Japan, these numbers reflecting the relative size of each nation's maritime activity.

But beyond this naval accord the powers were not able or willing to go in reducing the size of their military forces, France being especially nervous about reducing its military in the face of a Germany that would surely one day rebuild. Subsequent protests from the Germans that no serious moves were being made to bring other countries in line with Germany's level of forced disarmament ultimately fell on deaf ears.

The Locarno Agreement (1925). Instead another approach was made to the ideal of world peace. In 1925 Germany was admitted to the League of Nations – recognizing it as a major power with a permanent seat on the League Council. And in that same year Germany was a major participant at a diplomatic conference held in the Swiss Alpine city of Locarno. The Locarno Agreement contained the promise of France, Britain, Germany, Italy and Belgium that they would not resort to war in their relations with each other, but would resolve their conflicts only by peaceful means. Locarno thus gave hope that Europeans might be ready to move to more serious thoughts on military disarmament.

The Kellogg Briand Pact (1928). In 1928 American Secretary of State Frank Kellogg met with French Foreign Minister Aristide Briand and signed a pact agreeing to renounce war as a means of settling conflicts and to use peaceful means instead. Soon the Kellogg-Briand Pact was joined by fifty-nine other nations (including Germany, Italy and Japan) – seemingly indicating that the world was finally coming to its senses. Never again would a war such as what the world had gone through ten years earlier ever have to happen again.

Even Italy's worshiper of aggressive strength, Mussolini, pledged his country's support of the ideal – though it would not be long before Italian, German, Japanese and other supporters of Fascism were ridiculing the feebleness of such democratic idealism.

The grand illusion. In any case, the pact did nothing to stop or even slow down the Fascist aggressions that in the 1930s again moved the world closer to general war. Rather, it was a dazzling piece of Utopian Idealism: countries pledging to renounce war as a policy – except in instances of necessary self-defense (but when in war do countries not believe that they are fighting in defense of essential national principles?). Unfortunately, all of this was simply humanistic illusion, as events would soon prove. Serious conflicts of interest (such as contested boundaries and revanchist dreams of gathering nationals scattered in neighboring countries) were never really dealt with, nor could they be by peaceful means in any case. Too much was at stake for nation-states not to attempt the use of physical force if push came to shove. And it soon did.

But in the meantime, those still shocked by the trauma of the Great War were happy to believe that they had solved rationally one of life's most critical problems, forever.

The court-martial of General Billy Mitchell (1925).[131]   It is understandable when a people draw a lesson from a pointless war and thus find themselves very suspicious of anything that might soon draw them into another. What is not understandable is when professional military men do not also draw lessons from a fierce war they have just been through. When an army General Billy Mitchell himself drew a key lesson from the war, namely that air power was a major new weapon that needed to be developed by the U.S. military establishment, he found his urgings ignored. So, he made his case more demonstrably. In 1921 he had four obsolete battleships put to sea – and then attacked from the air. The ships were easily sunk by bombs from his airplanes.

He was told to cease his pressuring of the military higher ups. But Mitchell was not able to let the matter simply die quietly – and began to go public with his arguments. By doing so he courted the wrath of the old guard military. Being subsequently brought before a court martial, he was found guilty of undisciplined behavior and suspended from active duty (1925). He resigned his commission the following year to be able to pursue his air power crusade undeterred by military protocol.

The effort did indirectly make some headway eventually when America developed a naval air wing complete with aircraft carriers and fighter planes able to take off and land on the decks of these massive ships. This would prove to be a huge factor later in 1941–1942 when

America was attacked by the Japanese. It is what not only brought America back from the Pearl Harbor disaster but also delivered a blow to the Japanese navy so stunning (the Battle of Midway, June 1942) that the Japanese navy was never able to recover fully.

Meanwhile, Europe also struggles to find its way forward. Despite the Idealism of many of the European leaders, especially those of Great Britain and France, the mood of the average European was not all that different from the average American, rural or urban.

For Europeans, who had suffered greatly through the four years of war, the post-war period was troubled with the thought that all of the war's high-sounding nationalist spirit had produced in the end only mindless death and destruction. A spirit of disillusionment with politicians and cynicism with respect to their ideas and programs set in, much as it did in America.

This cynical spirit stirred a sense of political opportunity among a number of extremist political factions and their leaders: Communists and Social Democrats on the Left and Fascists on the Right. They found their appeal strongest among the social classes that had suffered most from the crumbling of the older social order.

European soldiers coming out of the war found that with the war over and war-time industry cutting back, jobs were scarce, and the ones that did exist paid very poorly. They were deeply resentful of the way their personal sacrifices were so poorly rewarded – while fat-cat wartime industrialist owners or capitalists still seemed to be doing fairly well for themselves. This group of industrial workers was thus easily manipulated by leaders who urged the workers to rise up against the wealthy industrial property owners, seize their property and make it communally their own. This was the basis of the Communist appeal which produced workers' uprisings all across Europe in the 1920s (and the huge Red Scare in early 1920s America).

Other European soldiers, upon a return to their farms, found that they had been left behind economically and culturally by developments brought on by the war. With international farm prices running at a new low, farmers found it difficult to sustain a living for themselves and their families. They watched with resentment as a fast-growing urban industrial order appeared to be enjoying many of the new economic opportunities of the post-war world. This agrarian/small-townsmen group was easily manipulated by leaders who stressed the importance of restoring a largely romanticized traditional agrarian social order. They promised to bring the glories of a mythical past back to existence – if the people simply surrendered their hopes and dreams to the total management by their great leaders. This appeal is the basis for what will come to be called Fascism.

Italian Fascism. European Fascism actually had its roots in Italy when post-war Italy seemed literally to have fallen apart politically. Although Italy had finally joined the war in 1915 on the "victorious" side in the Great War, there had been nothing at all about Italy's performance in the war to indicate to the average Italian that they had achieved anything at all of what might be classed as victory. Instead, coming out of the war, the Italians generally considered their former leaders as grand failures – which the Italian leaders themselves understood was their political standing in Italy. Thus they tended to lay low. And thus also a power vacuum existed in Italy after the war.

And into that vacuum had stepped Benito Mussolini, the bombastic editor of a Milan newspaper. Mussolini had started out as a Socialist propagandist – who turned against Socialism when it refused to support the Italian entry into the Great War. Mussolini saw the war as a means of bringing Italy to a new strength and prominence: strength through collective struggle (Fascism). Mussolini became bitterly opposed to Marxist Socialism, with its call to European workers to resist taking up arms on behalf of capitalist war profiteers – a call which Europe's fiercely nationalist workers had largely ignored ... and then had paid a huge price for their patriotism.

But Mussolini was opposed not only to Socialist pacifism, he was as opposed to Liberal Idealism with its hopes to build an international order of peace through a new spirit of international democratic cooperation. Mussolini accused such philosophies of peace as merely weakening human strength and producing effete societies. He exalted strength – strength through conflict, strength through struggle – which would produce a warlike character among a people. This in turn would bring them to greatness – greatness such as the ancient Romans had once exemplified. The key to this process was achieving an absolute unity of the people through unswerving loyalty to a great leader, a Duce (Italian simply for "Leader") such as Mussolini himself proposed to become. He promised Italians (notably Italy's industrial leaders) to bring unity to Italy through a policy of strict enforcement of social conformity through the use of his street toughs (the Fascist Blackshirts) – who stood ready to strike total fear in the hearts of labor agitators and anarchists through whatever means necessary to do so.

At a time when Italy seemed to be threatened internally by the same forces tearing Russia and Germany apart, this Fascist call of Mussolini's to enforced unity had a very strong appeal. Thus it was

The "Roaring Twenties"

that in October of 1922 a small group of Mussolini's Fascists marched on Rome – facing virtually no resistance. The Italian king responded by asking Mussolini to save the nation by becoming its leader. Italy now began to head down the path of Fascism – forced national unity under the domination of the Duce, who was to do the thinking and direct all the actions of the Italian nation. Any resistance to his program, actively or even just verbally, was met with stiff repression.

Stalin takes command of Soviet Russia. Slowly and painfully the Communist "Red" Army of Lenin and his close associate Trotsky gained ground against the "White" Armies of Kerensky and the Tsarists* – and by 1923 the horrendous Russian civil war was finally over. Lenin's Bolsheviks or Communists ruled Russia – and much of its former empire among surrounding non-Russian ethnic groups. But Lenin was a sick man, and died the following year (1924).

Power was supposedly held jointly by the Bolsheviks serving on the Communist Party's Central Committee – though most observers supposed that Lenin's closest colleague Trotsky would emerge as the supreme leader. But Trotsky was more interested in spreading the Communist revolution to the rest of Europe, treating the Russian Revolution simply as a staging ground for continuing revolution.

Working behind the scenes was the mysterious Joseph Stalin, who had been assigned the less glorious task of overseeing personnel issues (recruitment and promotion of regular members) at the lower levels of the Party hierarchy. But Stalin had been using his position to place and promote individuals presumably loyal to himself personally – thereby building up a personal power base within the Party, a development that the Bolshevik intellectuals directing the Party at its highest levels had not been paying much attention to. Toward the end of the 1920s Stalin was ready to make his move: he impressed (or intimidated) his fellow Bolsheviks into agreeing to the need to focus on "revolution in one country" (Russia), to stand behind his Five-Year Plan for the rapid industrialization of Russia (at the expense of the Russian countryside and its people), and to oust Trotsky whose internationalism threatened the security of the revolution in Russia (or so said Stalin anyway).

With the introduction of his Five-Year Plan in 1928, Stalin took

---

*At the end of the war, Wilson had sent American soldiers into Russia to join with other pro-democracy troops (everything from fellow British, to Czechs and Japanese) in supporting the Whites in the early stages of that civil war. It was supposedly a most noble effort – in support of democracy – to intervene in Russia's civil war for such a grand purpose. Ultimately seeing that this would achieve nothing except to make the situation worse, Wilson brought the troops home. At least he got that part right.

complete control of the wealth, the productivity, the very life of the nation – and completely reoriented its culture to his industrial agenda. Millions of lives would be lost in this transition, millions more permanently shattered as Stalin forcibly made the shift of the Russian economy away from agriculture to heavy industry. Anyone who complained, anyone he even suspected of complaining, he simply destroyed. There was no way to offer resistance to Stalin.

And so, the Soviet Russian economy and culture began its move in the new Stalinist direction.

* * *

THE 1920s COME TO A CRASHING END[132]

The stock market crash. Suddenly, without any apparent warning, the fun in urban America stopped abruptly toward the end of October 1929 when the great Wall Street Stock Market came crashing down – and with it the fortunes of countless Americans (and ultimately also Europeans). Overnight the boisterous optimism of industrial America turned into fear and panic – and then sad resignation as the national economy at the beginning of the 1930s collapsed into a long and deep Depression.

Consumer frenzy in the world of capitalism. During the 1920s businesses that made radios, vacuum sweepers, washing machines, cars, etc. reaped huge fortunes from the sale of these goods to eager American buyers or consumers who wanted to have the latest new thing that came onto the market. Such ownership signified arrival at the good life. Thus the markets for such goods were hot, driven by consumer desires to own all these new things. And so consumers bought these things – in droves.

And thus also the businesses that made them were busy. And workers had jobs. Companies were making great profits. Investors were getting fine dividends on their investments in these companies. And everyone was happy.

In the capitalist system, the profits made by these companies (the profits anyway that were not plowed back into production expansion of the companies) were distributed as dividends to the owners of the company in accordance with the number of stocks or shares of the company that an investor owned. You bought these stocks or shares on the open stock market (Wall Street's stock market being a favorite). Anyone with money could buy a share or two, or twenty, or a hundred or many hundreds, depending on how much money you had to invest in these stocks.

Speculative fever.[133] Thus throughout the 1920s, the stock markets were busy buying and trading shares as people everywhere wanted to get in on the profits. People started frantically bidding higher and higher prices for each of those stocks or shares – not for the size of the dividends they would receive as shareholders, which in terms of what they now had to pay for a share was minuscule, but because they figured that they could turn around in short order and sell these shares on the fast-rising stock exchange or stock market to someone else for far more than they had paid for them, pocketing a huge profit in the exchange. This is called speculation.

Toward the end of the 1920s speculation fever was running hot. People cashed in their life savings to get into the stock market. They even borrowed huge amounts from banks on margin (just putting up themselves personally a small percentage of the money needed to buy these stocks and borrowing the rest of the needed money from banks) so that these mom and pop investors found themselves deeply in debt. But they all figured, oh why not? ... I can turn around and sell these stocks in a few months for much more than I paid for them. I can pay back the bank, and pocket the large amount still remaining. That was a marvelous idea – as long as the speculative fever continued to drive stock prices up at this continuing frenetic rate.

Market saturation. But toward the end of the 1920s, the economic picture in American industry was beginning to change. People were still buying radios, home appliances, cars – though not at the same rate as in the early and mid-1920s, because most of the people in a position to buy these things (the urban middle class) possessed most of these things by the late 1920s. There were fewer new purchasers of these goods coming into the economic marketplace. As a result sales slowed down. Profits declined, production slowed, and workers were let go in small numbers. And the bloom on the economic picture faded a bit.

The crash itself. The smart money boys decided it was time to sell their stocks. Moms and pops were still rushing to get into the market. But the big money boys were becoming cautious. Then other investors started to take notice of what the smart money was doing, and began to step back. Quickly rumors of the step back began to spread and uneasiness set in as people became less confident that the easy money was going to continue. Concern resulted – especially because many people were heavily indebted to the banks and a slowing stock market could mean trouble for them. As people started to sell stocks, they were willing to do so at a lower price, just to get out. Soon prices started to drop rather seriously. By the end of October of 1929, they were dropping precipitously. Suddenly people who just a month or two before were incredibly rich now found themselves in such massive debt that they were not now just poor. They were totally bankrupt.*

The sobering effect of the crash. What a tragic end to a decade that started out with such material promise (at least in the cities). But such tragedy would have a wonderfully disciplining effect on Americans as they faced a new decade (the 1930s) which required of them morally and spiritually much greater effort than they had employed during the Roaring Twenties.

It was just as well, because Americans were going to have to be much leaner and hungrier than they were in the 1920s in order to face successfully the challenges to their civilization that events of the thirties (the Great Depression) and first half of the forties (World War Two) would throw in front of them.

---

*Actually, the Stock Market decline would continue all the way downward into the early 1930s. The Dow Jones Industrial Average (an index that measures the level of general wealth of the world of corporate stocks) reached its highest level in early September of 1929 at a little over 380 points. But by late October it had dropped to 230 points, having dropped nearly 70 points on just the 28th and 29th of October (a loss of around $30 billion in 1929 dollar value on just those two days alone). By mid-November it dropped below 200 points – and then began a slow rally, reaching a secondary peak of nearly 300 points in mid-April of 1930. Then it began another slide the next year (1931) – reaching its all-time low of a little over 40 points in July of 1932. It would not recover its 1929 high until 1954.

CHAPTER SIXTEEN

THE GREAT DEPRESSION (THE 1930s)[134]

* * *

EARLY ATTEMPTS TO ANSWER THE ECONOMIC CRISIS

Hoover's indecision. The October 1929 crash occurred during the first year of the presidency of the Republican Herbert Hoover, the famous philanthropist who at the end of the Great War had organized a huge relief effort for the starving people of war-torn Belgium. Now it was his turn to do something about a worsening economic picture in America.

In the face of this massive shock to the American stock market, Hoover tended to follow the common wisdom of the Republican Party (which had long dominated American politics) which was simply to follow the central principle of capitalism and let the market correct itself; it was not the government's job to meddle with the nation's economy.

Hoover looked especially to his Secretary of the Treasury Mellon for encouragement and advice. But Mellon's approach to the depression was not only Republican but even rather Darwinian: government should not intervene, but instead allow a natural liquidation or shake out of weak or poor business factors (notably labor, farmers, and small businesses) in the market mechanism. But ultimately this philosophy helped no one, not even the big capitalists who depended on an affluent society to sell their products to. Enforced poverty helped no one. The economy worsened. Eventually Mellon was dismissed by Hoover – though only when his failure to pay federal income taxes was discovered.

Congress at one point attempted to help the economy – through the erecting of a new trade barrier (the infamous Hawley Smoot Tariff) designed to protect struggling American producers. But it only made the situation far worse. It stirred up a trade war with America's trade partners – who in retaliation against American protectionism moved to protect their own industries from American competition. Ultimately this merely helped to pass the depression on to the rest of the Western world.

Belated government efforts to support the economy. Finally and belatedly, as the economy continued to fail to revive (one fourth of American workers were unemployed), Hoover began to propose government measures to try to help out the worst parts of the economy. The 1932 Emergency Relief and Construction Act attempted to start up public works programs to put the unemployed to work and to provide government-secured capital to help start up industries. But these measures came too late to swing the country back in support of Hoover's presidency. Besides, the Democrats smelled political victory in the November 1932 elections and were not in a mood to be very cooperative with the Hoover presidency, which they were pleased to blame as the cause of the depression.

The Bonus Army (1932). One sad incident that happened toward the end of Hoover's presidency was the march on Washington of the Bonus Army in the summer of 1932. The marchers came to Washington, D.C., to demand their veterans' bonus payments early from Congress, a bonus that had been promised them for their service in the Great War. But the payments were not due to begin until 1945. The veterans wanted them now – even if it meant they would be receiving these bonuses at a lower rate. They and their families needed the money now in order to survive. After several months of camping near the Anacostia River, and after several confrontations with police, federal troops (commanded by Douglas MacArthur and his staff assistant Dwight D. Eisenhower, aided by George Patton), upon orders by Hoover drove the marchers from the city. The roughness of the police and troops on these war veterans shocked the nation – and further alienated the people from the Hoover administration.

* * *
ROOSEVELT'S NEW DEAL

The election of 1932. Hoover was an easy target for his opponent, Franklin D. Roosevelt, in the 1932 presidential race. Roosevelt took Hoover to task for his many failures as president in dealing with this national crisis. Ironically one of his favorite lines of attack during the campaign was Hoover's extravagant spending in order to buy the country out of the economic crisis – and how Hoover wanted to turn Washington into the control center of the American economy. Roosevelt's Vice-presidential running mate, Nance Garner, even accused Hoover of advancing the cause of Socialism in America. How ironic, for the incoming Roosevelt Administration would not only undertake exactly these same kind of Washington-directed measures – but would do so in massive proportion!

Blaming Capitalism for the Depression. No one really understood

The Great Depression (the 1930s) 509

the actual dynamic that had caused the Depression: the fanciful belief that reached down to very ordinary Americans that somehow the fast path to wealth offered through Wall Street investment was destined to go on forever and the presumption that the hot consumer market that kept millions employed was also a permanent feature of American life. The 1920s economy was all so new that there was bound to be little perspective available to the average American as to how economics actually worked. And when the dream came crashing down, confusion, then bitterness, naturally took over. Worse, Americans grasped ahold of easy explanations, simple portrayals of evil behind this whole catastrophe.

And history reveals that there is nothing uglier to behold than a society's treatment of a respected prophet, whose prophecies have failed to come to pass. And in the case of early 1930s America those failed prophets would be the capitalists, once worshiped as gods, and now despised as the very devils themselves.

And Roosevelt picked up on this opportunity to use exactly just that imagery in this run against the heavily pro-capitalist Republican Party. Using Christian religious imagery quite familiar to the American people, in his acceptance speech as the Democratic Party's presidential candidate he blamed the depression on those among the American people who had "made obeisance to Mammon" (worshiped wealth and the providers of just such wealth). This attack on the prophets of capitalism played well, for to the average American it was the only thing that made sense as they faced a surrounding world of economic disaster. The capitalists themselves had caused this through their own greediness. What Americans now needed was a nation run by compassion, directed not by capitalism but by a government in Washington sensitive to the needs of the people. And Roosevelt promised to be exactly that sensitive caretaker if elected. During his campaign he regularly employed Christian ideals and language that had been at the heart of the older Social Gospel, promising the people in so many words that the Democratic party would do the "Christian thing," unlike the insensitive pro-capitalist Republicans. And of course the tactic worked beautifully, because the Republicans had no countering ideas to offer. Clearly the god Capitalism had failed.

The November elections were extremely sad for Hoover and elating for Roosevelt. Roosevelt had received 57.4 percent of the popular vote to only 39.7 percent for Hoover. And the electoral vote went 472 for Roosevelt and 52 for Hoover.

And just to drive home this anti-capitalist message, in his inauguration address delivered in early 1933, he not only issued his famous "firm belief that the only thing we have to fear is, fear itself" he went on to attack the legacy that greedy capitalism had left Americans with. Again, using familiar Christian terminology to bash the greedy agents of capitalism, whom he referred to as "the money changers," he stated:

> ...rulers of the exchange of mankind's goods have failed through their own stubbornness and their own incompetence, have admitted their failure, and have abdicated. Practices of the unscrupulous money changers stand indicted in the court of public opinion, rejected by the hearts and minds of men.
>
> The money changers have fled from their high seats in the temple of our civilization. We may now restore that temple to the ancient truths. The measure of the restoration lies in the extent to which we apply social values more noble than mere monetary profit.

His promise to the American people was that his administration would now take over the matter, and undertake *action*, such as capitalism had failed to do in the face of this national tragedy.

> *I am prepared under my constitutional duty to recommend the measures that a stricken Nation in the midst of a stricken world may require. These measures, or such other measures as the Congress may build out of its experience and wisdom, I shall seek, within my constitutional authority, to bring to speedy adoption.*

And thus it was that Americans now hungrily looked to Washington – not Wall Street – to move their lives forward. None dared call this Socialism (except a group of Humanists that year who were proud to do so) because in a still highly individualistic America, Socialism remained largely a taboo concept. Thus the Roosevelt program was never assigned any other label except "New Deal," although Roosevelt's actions would come to look amazingly like that which was going on in a number of European countries faced with the same problem. Many Americans were quick to point this out. But it was not wise to speak out too much about what was happening to an American society increasingly dependent on the good intentions of political authorities gathered in Washington. The election had made it quite clear: the majority of the Americans had just given Roosevelt full authorization to fix the problem any way he saw fit to do so.

Roosevelt the Christian. It is important to note however that behind this carefully chosen anti-capitalist political stance there existed a very strong personal faith that moved Roosevelt, one which actually guided him very strongly as he made his way through the challenges before him. He had

The Great Depression (the 1930s)

been raised a believing Episcopalian and had been directed in key times of his life by strong Christian counsel, and called on that faith when he was stricken in the prime of his professional life by crippling polio. But he was an overcomer by character, amazingly confident that all challenges could be met simply by seeking to do the right thing. He believed strongly in a God of justice and fairness, and a sense that despite – or even because of – his crippling affliction he had been chosen by God to show the world how to overcome life's worst challenges. He was therefore incredibly optimistic, a personal trait that would attract many to this man of enormous moral and spiritual strength, including a nation that would somehow have to keep moving forward even in the darkest of times. That was his understanding of his Christian faith, a matter of enormous importance to him, and as he saw it, to America and the world as well.

The making of the president.[135] Roosevelt was born in 1882 in the Hudson River Valley town of Hyde Park to a very prominent New York family, was raised as an only child in considerable privilege, and was watched over carefully by a doting mother, Sara. Sara, who was of Massachusetts stock, directed him to spend his summers in her home state (when not in Europe, which the family also visited every year) and had him enrolled in the prestigious Groton Academy in northern Massachusetts. Most significantly, here under the direction of the Episcopal priest and school headmaster Endicott Peabody,* he was taught the importance of those raised to privilege in developing a commitment to public service – but also the importance of a strong Christian sense of responsibility toward those less fortunate than they. This effort of Peabody's would not be lost on Roosevelt.

As was generally expected of a Groton boy, he then went on to study at Harvard, where he continued his standing as an average student. But while at Harvard he began to develop political ambitions, particularly with his uncle Theodore (Teddy Roosevelt) becoming U.S. president at that time. He now had a political role model to follow – however as a Democrat, unlike his Republican uncle (nearly all those around him, even since he had entered Groton, were also Republicans).

With the death of his father James at the end of 1900, Roosevelt's mother Sara became even more directly engaged in her son's life (she had even followed him to Boston when he was at Harvard). But Franklin finally found that a relationship which developed in 1902 with Eleanor Roosevelt (Teddy's niece and thus a distant cousin of Franklin's) allowed him to free himself considerably from his mother's domineering ways (Sara was very opposed to Franklin's and Eleanor's relationship).

---

*Roosevelt became very close to Peabody, having him preside at his wedding with Eleanor and at the weddings of his children.

The next year he graduated from Harvard and entered Columbia Law School in New York City, and a year and a half later (March 1905) married Eleanor. Then soon, having passed the New York State Bar exam, he could see no reason for continuing his law studies and dropped out of Columbia in 1907. The next year he took a job with a New York City Wall Street firm, where he specialized in corporate law.

His marriage with Eleanor was not an easy one for either of the two. They had six children in fairly short order between 1906 and 1916, although the third child died soon after birth. They both took the child's death very hard. Also in moving after their marriage to the Roosevelt estate (Springwood), Sara moved in with them, a constant source of irritation for Eleanor.

Also, Franklin had a fascination with a number of other women, producing scandals – especially his affair with Eleanor's social secretary, Lucy Mercer. Divorce was considered – but Lucy was not interested in a marriage with Franklin (too many complications). His marriage with Eleanor thus somehow survived, after he promised not ever to see Lucy again (a promise he did not keep). But it was a cold marriage, mostly thereafter just an arrangement of some small degree of social and political convenience. Eleanor found herself busied elsewhere with a number of social causes that kept her away from her husband.[136]

In 1910 Roosevelt ran for the position as New York State senator, the local Democrat Party glad to have a Roosevelt name to put forward in a district that had been solidly Republican since before the Civil War, and shocked when he was actually elected to the position. In the New York Senate he found himself in opposition to the New York Tammany Hall political machine, and consequently developed considerable experience in the art of political maneuvering – which helped him be reelected to the Senate position in 1912 as something of a distinct social reformer or progressivist. But that same year he had also thrown personal support to the reformist Democratic Party presidential candidate, Woodrow Wilson (who also was running against Franklin's uncle), earning Franklin a cabinet appointment as the assistant secretary of the navy – a position he would hold for the next seven years, (ironically, the same position that also his uncle had held in the early years of his national political career). Also, like his uncle, the younger Roosevelt actually had long been interested in naval affairs, was very well read-up on the subject, and was fully capable of being an excellent contributor to American naval policy. He would continue to serve in this capacity through the years of the Great War.

In 1920, the Democratic National Convention picked Roosevelt, only thirty-eight at the time, to run as the party's vice-presidential candidate, serving alongside the party's presidential candidate, Ohio Governor James

Cox. But the election turned into a landslide for the Republican ticket of Warren G. Harding and Calvin Coolidge. After the election Roosevelt returned to his law practice in New York.

But tragedy struck in August of the next year (1921). He contracted polio while vacationing at Campobello Island in Canada, the polio leaving him permanently paralyzed from the waist down. A man of iron will, he refused to admit defeat by the disease and maintained his law practice, while at the same time attempting various therapies. In 1926 he purchased a resort at Warm Spring, Georgia, not only for his own treatment, but for others also afflicted with the disease. His disease in fact had become for him something of a cause, and two years later he created the organization that would eventually become the famous March of Dimes, dedicated to fighting the scourge of polio. He also developed immense upper body strength and the ability to walk (short distances) with the aid of iron braces, often also leaning on the arms of an assistant – so as not to have to appear in public in a wheelchair.

In the meantime, he kept up with New York Democratic Party politics, improving his relations with Tammany Hall, and supporting Alfred E. Smith in the New York race for governor in 1922 and again in 1924 (which Smith won), then for U.S. president in 1928 (which Smith lost). At the same time Smith encouraged and supported Roosevelt's candidacy for New York governor in 1928, which Roosevelt won (twice) making him the state's governor from 1929 to 1932, when he chose to run for the U.S. presidency.

And in 1932, with the country caught in the depths of the Great Depression his win over his Republican opponent Hoover (naturally blamed for the tragedy) was fairly easy: Roosevelt was elected to the U.S. presidency with one of Americas widest margins of victory (14 percent) over his Republican opponent.

The 'New Deal.'[137] As can be seen in the way Roosevelt attacked Hoover for his new government-spending programs – which is exactly what Roosevelt would come quickly to advocate early on in office – Roosevelt really did not have a specific set of plans in mind to deal with the Depression as he took office in early 1933. In his acceptance speech at the Democratic nominating convention in 1932 Roosevelt had talked about a "new deal" for the American people, though he had not given any details as to what that might specifically be all about. The idea new deal soon became the program New Deal (a term he chose which sounded quite similar to his uncle Theodore's Square Deal) – and it meant whatever Roosevelt chose for it to mean as he struggled forward to put policies into play that might solve the problem of the Depression.

Roosevelt's Brain Trust. Whatever it meant specifically, it meant generally that the national government was going to have to step into the realm of the economy and take the lead in getting things moving again. Roosevelt assembled an advisory council made up of a number of intellectuals (originally a small group of Columbia University professors, soon joined by a number of lawyers), that would come to be known as Roosevelt's Brain Trust. These economic and legal experts would advise Roosevelt in ways to program the country out of the economic mess it found itself in. They would be the ones to put actual substance to Roosevelt's New Deal idealism.

The First 100 Days. One of the early projects during the Roosevelt Administration's First-100-Days push was the National Recovery Administration (NRA) set up in 1933. It was a voluntary program that employers were supposed to engage in, promising that they would observe certain minimum pricing schedules for their products (to stop the competitive lowering of prices designed to drive the competition out of business) – and help their workers by offering at least minimum wages and maximum working hours. Those businesses which signed on with the program were permitted to display the Blue Eagle poster. But those that did not were often boycotted – and thus the voluntary nature of the program was compromised. There were complaints about this.

Roosevelt also in those First 100 Days created the CCC (Civilian Conservation Corps) to provide three million jobs for young family men, building 800 national or state parks and planting three billion trees. He put some price-control policies in place (the Agricultural Adjustment Act of 1933) to help raise the incomes of the American farmer, essentially by taking land and thus crops out of production, thus raising the farmers' prices for their crops (but also making food more expensive for everyone else). Also in 1933 he set up the Tennessee Valley Authority (TVA) to control the Tennessee River flowing through the heart of the American South, offering not only flood control but also electrical generation and transmission to the entire region, which previously had no electrical service.

Supporting and regulating the banking and finance industry. In accordance with the Glass Steagall Act of 1933, Roosevelt set up the Federal Deposit Insurance Corporation (FDIC) as a guarantee to Americans that their bank accounts were protected by a Federal insurance guarantee against bank failure – thus putting confidence back into the American banking system (the FDIC is still in operation today). The Act also prevented commercial banks (which receive checking and savings deposits and extend loans to individual Americans) from involvement in the realm of investment banks (which buy and sell stocks, bonds and other securities). The next

The Great Depression (the 1930s)

year, 1934, he set up the Securities and Exchange Commission (SEC) to put the stock markets under federal regulation, to curb the excesses of speculation that appeared to have caused the problems in the first place – and to put confidence back into the American stock markets (the SEC is also still in operation today). He also in 1934 created the Federal Housing Administration (FHA also still in operation today) to insure home mortgages and thereby stabilize the mortgage market.*

The growth of government as industrialist. He also, through the Works Progress Administration or WPA of 1935, had the government move into the new realm of state-directed industry: the building of national highways, new libraries, government buildings, special camp and park facilities, even hydroelectric power generating dams. He hired artists to paint murals in public buildings and musicians and playwrights to compose new music and plays. His program even paid women to sew.

Roosevelt also moved to strengthen labor's position in the bargaining with the owners of Americas major businesses (The National Labor Relations Act or Wagner Act of 1935). This gave a tremendous boost to the American labor movement ... and made the labor unions very loyal to the Democratic Party after that.

Social Security. And the New Deal set up a program of basic social security for the elderly in their years of retirement (the Social Security Act of 1935). The program also included unemployment insurance and welfare support for the poor and handicapped.

"Roosevelt's New Deal brought us out of the Depression." Actually, no! Not at all! It is common among most Americans today to refer to how "Roosevelt's New Deal brought us out of the Depression" when contemplating what to do in the face of a new round of economic difficulties facing the nation. This popular myth however is quite untrue. Certainly, the New Deal helped many idle workers find work. It certainly built highways, dams, municipal buildings, national parks, rural electrification, new rail services, etc. Government projects were truly a blessing to many Americans desperate to find work. But these projects did not solve the problem of the Depression itself.

---

*Unfortunately, much of the regulatory work of the SEC and FHA was most unwisely cut back by the Bush, Jr. administration in the opening years of the 2000s – presumably to help free up a slowing economy. Actually, what it did was to help produce, through the so-called "shadow banking system," the subprime mortgage crisis which started in early 2007 and reached the level of a major financial meltdown in September of 2008.

The American Free Market or 'consumer' economy. America has long been a grass-roots democracy not only in the area of government or politics, but also in the very nature of its economy. Unlike most societies of the world which throughout history have traditionally been driven by the economic wants or goals of the rich and powerful – emperors, kings, aristocrats and priests – the American economy has been built, since its origins in the early 1600s, on the interests of very ordinary people. There have been of course exceptions to this picture: the slave-holding South prior to 1865 and the Gilded Age of the late 1800s dominated by the captains of industry – or, as some would say, the industrial robber barons. But in general, the American economic system has been built on the labor, the product, and the economic desires of very ordinary citizens.

The personal or private consumer is king. What determines what actually gets made in America are the simple interests of the average American – known simply as the American consumer. These interests of the American consumer register themselves in what is termed the market place or free market. The matter of what gets made, how much gets made, and what it will cost, are all determined simply by how much interest the American consumer has in a product when it goes to market. If it is a really hot item, drawing strong consumer interest, it will enter the market place quite pricey – and highly profitable to the producer. But other producers with a typical American entrepreneurial spirit will want to get into the act and also begin producing this highly profitable product (or – under copyright laws – something somewhat like it) and bring it to market – and themselves share in the blessings of high profits. But this entrepreneurial urge will eventually be met with a declining consumer interest – as most of the people who wanted these hot items now are in possession of them (radios, cars, tractors, washing machines, etc.). Unsold items will begin to pile up on the market shelves. To move these items to sale, producers will attempt to make these same products continue to be attractive – thus the American advertising industry – but ultimately attractive through lower pricing. Lower prices will help bring some additional consumers to the market – but not at the rate that they were there when the item was hot.

At this point the producer has to make some decisions. He can continue to make the product, though at a slower rate – which means he is going to have to cut back on production and let some workers go. He does not need their labor, and anyway, because his products are not selling well and profits are way down, he cannot afford to pay them.

Or – he can switch to a new product, even a new line of products, simply to keep his business going. This means he has to be inventive, imaginative – and a natural risk taker. He needs to listen to the market,

The Great Depression (the 1930s) 517

to the consumer, to sound the consumer out in terms of possible interest in new products. He can also go to advertising in an attempt to create consumer interest – by letting the consumer know in written or broadcast advertising, in words, song, or even drama, how wonderful life would be if the consumer only had his new product!

But this is how the Free Market works. The consumer is king. It's all very democratic. There is no political authority dictating production or distribution or pricing according to official decrees. In fact, the American free market system has traditionally been highly suspicious of such governmental interventions into the economic system (commonly termed a "Command Economy") and tolerates only the slightest of such interventions under very special circumstances, and only for a limited time.

For government intervention to go beyond that would be to undermine the whole idea of the Free Market system – and instead produce an economic system in which "enlightened" social authorities decide for the people themselves what they are going to get from the economy and how they are going to get it. This latter economic system is termed "Socialism" or "Communism" (although Fascism has many of the same characteristics.)

Dealing with the business cycle. Of course, as with all social systems, this Free Market economic system is not without its problems. Market saturation such as described above, when most consumers have these products and therefore show a declining interest in them, is one of these problems. This is a big part of what was happening to the American economy at the end of the Roaring 20s. The market for consumer products stopped roaring.

Because of this tendency of the market to heat up as new products are brought to market – and then cool down as the market becomes saturated – industrial production, and the economy in general, tends to move in cycles of growth, maturity and decline. Economists call this the business cycle. Economists have long attempted to find ways to smooth out the peaks and valleys of the business cycle, make the economy steadier in its movement. But the very nature of the Free Market system itself seems to make it immune from such efforts.

The famous English economist John Maynard Keynes put forth the idea in the 1930s that the business cycle could be modulated or smoothed by the government's interventions as the economy goes through the various phases of a business cycle. He advocated a governmental strategy of loosening money supply (creating more money for the market to work with) during the cooling phase of the business cycle and then tightening that money supply during period of a hot market.

This Keynesian theory seemed to make a lot of sense to a lot of economists – and to a lot of government officials. In a sense Roosevelt's New Deal moved in accordance with this theory. But whether it actually contributed to – or simply slowed down – the recovery of the market economies in the 1930s remains even to this day a matter of great debate.

What is not debatable is the fact that what a Free Market truly needs to keep going or get back going if it has slumped and fallen into idleness is new products. New products are what bring the consumer back to the market place to do business.

In a sense the New Deal produced new products – but products desired not by the individual consumer, but collectively by the society, sometimes termed infrastructure items. These items are vital to the society as a whole ... but beyond the scope of any individual or even group of individuals to produce or sell (or even finance). The New Deal produced highways, parks, public buildings, etc., social items certainly desired by the average American – but products that no one single consumer would have ever been able to buy. So in that sense the New Deal worked. Government-funded projects certainly met important infrastructure needs of American society.

"Market saturation" for government products (roads, dams, parks, etc.). But even here part of the problem was that the New Deal suffered from its own version of market saturation. Under the New Deal a great number of national highways were built. But once built, Americans did not need new ones to replace them right away. Highway building slowed down. New dams were built at the most likely spots where energy could be cheaply generated. After that, dam building became much less cost effective. Dam building slowed to a halt. Parks were built – until the need for park building was greatly reduced. In short the government as producer was facing the same problem that the private producer had faced at the end of the 1920s: market saturation for government or social products. By the late 1930s, with the government forced to slow up in its building projects, unemployment began to rise again in America.

Government intervention into the economy certainly had taken up some of the slack in an idle American economy during a good part of the 1930s. And it had brought good things to America. But it had not solved the basic problem of the Depression. The American economy simply seemed to have no urge to take off again on its own. That's because new personal consumer products were needed to bring the American consumer, the bedrock of the American economic system, back to market.

But coming up with a new line of products to go to market with is not easy. It takes discovery, new technologies, changing circumstances – many things that are not automatically brought into being. And during the entire 1930s there really was no such development of new product lines by

The Great Depression (the 1930s) 519

private industry.

Some blame the New Deal itself for the failure of new products, new technologies, to develop during the 1930s. They claim that scarce investment funds were all used up by the government to push its own economic agendas. Financial capital that was needed to back up new inventions and new production was simply not available to the private entrepreneur because it was all flowing to the government. Perhaps this was true. But perhaps not. Clearly there was another factor involved that unquestionably shaped the way the private industrial system was to behave in the 1930s.

Consumer confidence. The New Deal put money in the pockets of the workers that built all these New Deal products. But what did the worker do with this money? In general, the worker put it away in a safe place (the old adage is that he put it under his mattress!). Actually, he most likely put it in a savings bank. Thanks to Roosevelt's FDIC insurance of bank deposits, a savings bank was finally a safe place to put one's money. In any case he was not going to put it in the stock market any time soon. He was still too frightened about what might happen if he put his money there. So, workers' wages were of little help in producing a revival of the capital market which financed the business ventures of private manufacturers.

The banks where he deposited his money were of no help to the capital market either. And it was not just because banks too had been scared away from involvement in that market. Actually because of the Glass Steagall Act of 1933 it was illegal for such commercial or depository banks to enter the capital market. Only banks licensed as investment banks were permitted to trade in the capital market. These were not the banks where the worker placed his savings. Investment banks were not permitted to do this simple kind of business. They were the banks you went to if you wanted to buy or sell (or borrow – though with new limits) corporate stocks, bonds or other kinds of corporate securities. Thus it was that workers' wages did not usually translate themselves into new inputs into the capital markets vital to the recovery of private industry.

In short, the average American wage earner now suffered from the economic disease of lacking consumer confidence in the market place. He earned his money – and then put it away, where it would go unused in stimulating new market demands. And thus the market continued to sit quietly while little happened in the private economic sector.

The New Deal runs into serious problems. Roosevelt's first term in office, especially his First Hundred Days, saw the coming into existence of a massive number of government economic programs. Roosevelt seemed the master of the situation – and encountered relatively little opposition. But towards the end of his first term, and in the early part of his second term, Roosevelt found his programs coming under a lot of criticism – and even determined opposition.

Criticism began to build about how his New Deal was becoming simply creeping Socialism. There was also mounting criticism about how many of these make-work programs were a waste of taxpayers' money. Jokes and sneers arose about all the standing around that seemed to accompany many of these work projects.

Problems with the Supreme Court. The biggest problem however was the Supreme Court. By 1935 the Supreme Court was knocking down one program after another of Roosevelt's New Deal for being unconstitutional. According to the Supreme Court, there was no constitutional basis for the national government to be meddling in the affairs that were clearly reserved to the states as part of their jurisdiction.

The worst blow came on Black Monday (May 27, 1935) when the Supreme Court pronounced unanimously on three cases – all of them going against Roosevelt's New Deal. The hardest of them for Roosevelt to swallow was the *Schechter Poultry Corp. v. United States* case in which the Court declared that the NRA was unconstitutional. The NRA, in violation of the constitution's design of the separation of powers, had assigned legislative powers to the Presidency that belonged alone to Congress. But also Congress's use of the interstate commerce clause to justify the creation of the NRA program was clearly in excess of the powers allotted Congress by the Constitution. But more such anti-New-Deal decisions were to be handed down during the next year.

The Court-packing scheme. Roosevelt was so upset by this personal rebuff by the Supreme Court that he decided to remake the ideological character of the Supreme Court. In early 1937 he announced that he would be introducing into Congress a new Judiciary Reorganization Bill, expanding the number of the Court's justices. The political intent was clear to all: he was looking to pack the Court, through the presidential power of appointment, with enough new justices to swing the Supreme Court rulings in his favor politically.

The public reaction was negative, despite Roosevelt's many efforts during the spring of 1937 to enlist popular support for his idea. To the contrary. Opposition to the idea grew with the passage of time. Opposition in the House of Representatives was apparent from the outset, so Roosevelt introduced the bill into the Senate instead. But the Senate dragged on in debate. Eventually a split began to open up between the president and

The Great Depression (the 1930s) 521

the senators of his own Democratic Party. Roosevelt was losing political ground fast.

But in the meantime, a switch of votes in the Supreme Court had occurred, with one of the justices changing sides from anti to pro New Deal, and another justice retiring, thus giving Roosevelt the opportunity to make a new appointment. He now had a voting majority without having to pack the Court. Roosevelt backed down on his court-packing scheme. But he had lost a lot of political standing in the process. Many Americans felt that Roosevelt was taking notes from the highhanded ways of the European dictators, Stalin, Hitler and Mussolini. Roosevelt not only had gambled personally and lost in this contest, his attack on the Supreme Court also greatly weakened his ability to continue the political reforms he felt the country needed to undergo in order to get back to sound economic health.

Bad economic news continues. This event was also timed with another slowdown in the American economy which hit in 1937, resulting in the growth again in the number of unemployed Americans. 1938 was not any better economically – and 1939 saw only a very slight economic recovery. There seemed to be little that Roosevelt could do to get the economy back on track again.

The Midwestern Dust Bowl.[138] To make matters worse, during the entire 1930s, but becoming incredibly intense in the mid-1930s, a deep and persistent drought hit the Midwest states, worst in the Panhandle area of Texas and Oklahoma, northwestern New Mexico, western Kansas, and eastern Colorado – but extending all the way from central Texas in the south to the Dakotas in the North. The topsoil was simply blown away by hot winds which turned the air into black clouds of choking dust. Farms were simply abandoned as destitute farmers headed west to California to look for work – any work. Most of them ended up living in migrant workers' camps under the worst conditions imaginable. People survived – but only by toughening up tremendously.

With all of this happening to America, Roosevelt found his popularity slipping during the latter part of the 1930s. He would not regain the popularity he had in the first of his terms in office until the entrance of America into World War Two in late 1941.

World War Two finally brought America out of the Depression. In the end what brought America out of the Depression was not the New Deal – but was World War Two, which the country embarked upon only at the very end of 1941. The war, and the war alone, proved to be the factor that would put America back to work. New products (uniforms, guns, fighter planes, bombers, tanks, trucks, canons, battleships, carriers, submarines, etc.) would be needed in vast, virtually unlimited quantity. Every American that was not in uniform would be needed to support the war on the home front – in particular even young women working in the production and assembly plants where these products were manufactured.

And there was no danger of market saturation – at least until the war was over. Such products were quickly destroyed in the action of war and thus immediately called forth replacement products.

In the American economic system, the government did not make these products. Private industrial manufacturers did. Of course, the finished product did not need to go to market. The government was the market – under contract to buy the product as soon as it came off the assembly line. But as with the New Deal economy, the average American was the financial underwriter of the war economy. Part of this support was in the form of taxes paid to the government – which Americans were quick to offer because this was their war – not just their government's.

But taxes were not sufficient to cover the huge government expenditures involved in this business of war. The government needed to go into deficit spending – borrowing money now with the promise to pay it back later, when the emergency of the war was over. And who was the lender to the government? The American people themselves. They lent to the government huge amounts of their personal industrial earnings (created by war production) – in the form of war bonds: contracts or certificates issued by the government which promised the American lenders that they would be repaid in the future, with nice interest earnings added. Purchasing war bonds turned the average American into a capital financier lending to the government. The possibility of guaranteed interest earnings was part of the motivation. Besides, what was a person to spend his or her money on anyway? Automobile manufacturers had turned to the business of making army trucks and tanks. No automobiles were manufactured during the war. Except for war goods there wasn't much of anything to spend your money on anyway. Everyone was under rationing so you couldn't even go on a food-spending splurge. So putting your money away in the form of war bonds made natural sense. Besides, it seemed to be one's patriotic duty.

And that's how the American economy came back to life. World War Two, not the New Deal, brought America finally out of the Great Depression.

A SHIFT IN THE AMERICAN SENSE OF ORDER

Bringing down the High Priests of Wall Street. With the failure of

The Great Depression (the 1930s)

the former god Capitalism to make any kind of a comeback, a toughening American spirit turned itself into a vindictiveness against those responsible for the Depression. For instance, the elderly inventor and business tycoon Samuel Insull fled to France when the Stock Market collapsed, moved from country to country until he was arrested in 1934 by the Turkish government and sent back to America. Here he was sent to jail for a brief period. Actually, at his trial, the jury could not find him guilty of violating any particular law or laws, although he certainly was guilty of the moral sin of selling worthless stocks to people who trusted him because of his high position in Wall Street. Also the collapse of his holding company had wiped out the life savings of some 600,000 shareholders.

Also, in 1938 a jury convicted and imprisoned Richard Whitney, former president of the New York Stock Exchange (1930-1935), after he pleaded guilty to two charges of grand larceny, having embezzled funds from the Stock Exchange Gratuity Fund (and elsewhere) to cover huge personal and corporate financial losses.

Going after the mob. At the same time, Americans became much less tolerant of the colorful doings of Americas urban bosses and the corruption and violence of the American mobsters. Hot on their trail was the Bureau of Prohibition agent, Eliot Ness – leader of the Untouchables, agents who would not accept bribes.[139]

And bringing many of them (at least the New York operations) to court was New York's Special Prosecutor, Thomas Dewey, who from 1935 to 1937 won seventy-two convictions in seventy-three of his cases (including Whitney's). So outraged by Dewey's relentlessness was New York mobster Dutch Schultz that he had scheduled a hit on Dewey in 1935 – but was himself gunned down by a rival gang in a Newark, New Jersey, restaurant just a few days before the scheduled event – which thus never took place! Dewey also ended the career of the New York mob fixer James J. Hines – a Tammany Hall ward heeler who had long protected the likes of Lucky Luciano, Dutch Schultz, Frank Costello and Joe Adonis by bribing police and judges – Dewey gaining a conviction and prison sentence for Hines in 1939.

The American labor movement toughens up.[140] The failure of the high priests of capitalism was also met with the rise in labor militancy, demanding better wages and working conditions – and displaying a readiness to shut down American businesses that did not meet these demands. Labor unions were not waiting around to see what economic wonders might come their way. They were quick to move to safeguard and extend their economic position wherever they could. And of course there was a degree, at times quite high, of ideology involved in this dynamic, inspired in part by the

American Communist Party, in part simply by the ambitions of labor leaders themselves, and by the continuing infusion in the ranks of American labor by immigrants with European political attitudes – at least Socialist if not even Communist.

Likewise on the business side of the conflict there was an equal ideological-philosophical concern. Capitalists had not only lost their former place of glory, they had become the object of wrath, for having "caused" the Depression. But they themselves had lost whole fortunes, were struggling to keep business operations going, and were confused and angry – hungry for some kind of idea or philosophy that could restore for them a sense of social pride rather than scorn.

Tensions even beyond FDR's New Deal operating out of Washington were running hot in the rest of the nation. In May of 1934 a massive general strike called by the dockworkers of the entire West Coast (joined by merchant sailors) succeeded in shutting down the ports that fed the West Coast. Working conditions at the docks were tough (as they were also in the mines and factories of America), and the striking workers were demanding $1 an hour wages – and no more than six hours of work per day or 120 hours per month. And in shutting down the ports, they had a strangle-hold on the cities lining the coast, most violently San Francisco and Seattle where the strike dragged on and in early July turned violent.

Roosevelt tried arbitration, but the strikers were not interested in any compromise. Police and then troops were brought in and two workers were killed. At the same time, sailors refused to dock their ships to unload their cargos, and truckers refused to pick up and ship inland goods that had been unloaded – in sympathy with the striking workers. But eventually no one was gaining much in all this. Finally in October a compromise was reached in which the workers made almost the $1 per hour wage, the promise of safer working conditions, and shorter working hours.

Leading the way through all this was the very charismatic labor union leader John L. Lewis – not only willing to take on big-business (actually not so big at this point) but also the Republican Party, which traditionally had stood so strongly in support of American capitalism. A favorite target of Lewis was Kansas governor Alf Landon, running as the Republican presidential candidate in the 1936 elections, whom Lewis accused of being a mere puppet of the steel industry.

There were, of course, still many unemployed men out there eager to find jobs. And when union members went on shutdown strikes against their employers their employers were more than happy to offer the positions of the absentee workers to newcomers – or "scabs," as striking workers called them. The hatred of the two groups, strikers and scabs, became very violent, as for instance during the 1937 Republic Steel strike in Cleveland,

The Great Depression (the 1930s)

in which a battle between the two groups (and police) resulted in eighteen deaths.

America's home-grown variety of Fascism.[141] While the country seemed to be falling apart in a desperate scramble of Americans simply to find work, feed a family and stay alive, Germany clearly had its act together. The contrast between the precise order of Germany and the listless wandering of America was quite upsetting to many Americans.

Indeed, it even seemed in America to be a very bad time for democracy – and for its cousin, free market economics or capitalism. State-managed (even dictated) life seemed to work better in providing the people a much better life than a free market capitalist economic system and a democratic government representing directly the clear voice and will of the people themselves. Strong leaders (such as the German Führer, Hitler; the Italian Duce, Mussolini; the Soviet First Secretary, Stalin; etc.) seemed to know better what would work best for the people than the people themselves. Political elitism seemed to be the better way to embrace the future.

Indeed, America (as also other countries such as Great Britain and France and Spain) seemed to be producing their own varieties of Fascist or Communist or Populist leaders. The times seemed to demand bold leadership. And there were a number of American candidates willing to put themselves forward as just the answer to the nation's problems.

Father Charles E. Coughlin. Through his radio reach to forty-five million regular listeners, this powerful Catholic priest put forth stinging social commentary on the times. He could be really biting in his attack on the flaws of the country. Eventually he moved more and more to the ultra-Conservative Right, becoming increasingly anti-Semitic and anti-New-Deal – even pro-Fascist with respect to events in Europe.

The 'Kingfish' Louisiana Governor Huey Long. Quite a different style was forthcoming from this ambitious Southern Populist, who talked about taking the money from the rich and giving it to the poor so that there could be a chicken in every American pot. Statistically that made no sense, because confiscating the wealth of the rich would have made little financial difference to the millions of poor Americans. But the rhetoric sold well – until an irate medical doctor shot and killed this little Führer wannabe.

"Roosevelt actually saved capitalism." A thesis argued back and forth is the idea that Roosevelt's New Deal actually saved capitalism. There is no way actually to prove or disprove what exactly it was that were Roosevelt's true thoughts and actual intentions concerning capitalism. He certainly picked up much of the language of the radical Left in attacking capitalism as an insensitive, deficient economic philosophy, although it has been argued that he did so only to steal the thunder of a small but growing American Communist Party, the American Labor Party, and the Farmer-Labor Party, rising political movements which advocated all-out Socialism as the policy that America must turn to in order to save itself. Roosevelt purposely opened the ranks of his New Deal organization to rising leaders within those Leftist movements, to undercut the possibility of them becoming third-party movements which would steal millions of votes from the Democratic Party, thus preventing these parties from inadvertently (as third-party movements always do) advancing the Congressional position of the Republican Party opposition.

Certainly, given the rising anger of impoverished Americans – on the farms and in the industrial cities – Roosevelt helped head off the political urge of millions of Americans (perhaps as much as a quarter of the citizens) to want to push America toward the National Socialism (Italian Fascism or German Nazism) on the one hand or the Workers' Socialism (Russian Communism) on the other that seemed to be working so well in Europe. But exactly how Roosevelt's politics saved capitalism is not quite clear, because throughout the rest of the 1930s – until World War Two when American capitalists were called on to rebuild a huge wartime economy – capitalism itself remained the bad boy in popular thinking.

Liberal Humanism vs. Traditional Christianity. Meanwhile, all this economic stress was also shaking the very spiritual foundations of the country. What had happened to America? It seemed almost as if America's God had failed the country. In fact, who exactly was at fault? And what exactly at this point could be done to get the country up and moving again?

The very popular early 20th century American philosopher John Dewey, who more than anyone else shaped modern American Liberal views on education and social reform, was a self-avowed Humanist who believed completely in the power of human logic and in man's basic goodness. There was no place in his worldview for God – though he did not attack the idea directly. He simply moved on past the idea of God to build his ideas of secular Liberal reform entirely around the notion of man's instinctive logic and good intentions. In this he was very typical of a growing segment of intellectual America

To Dewey's way of thinking, Christianity needed to be pushed out of its central position as the foundational worldview of Western society and culture in order that the way could be made for the birth of a new religion, a secular religion originally identified as Humanism (referred to more often today as Secular Humanism, or just simply Secularism).

The Great Depression (the 1930s) 527

The 1933 *Humanist Manifesto* calls for a new religion. In 1933, thirty-four individuals well-placed in the world of academics, the publishing industry, and Unitarian ministry, published a *Humanist Manifesto* – calling for a new religion and an accompanying social order focusing on the powers of man. Among those signers was, unsurprisingly, John Dewey.

The goal of the *Humanist Manifesto* was to take up the responsibility of restoring a bright light of human optimism in the midst of a very gloomy Great Depression America. The Manifesto declared that that the time had passed for "mere revision of traditional attitudes." It was time to come to terms with "new conditions created by a vastly increased knowledge and experience." Thus:

> . . . *any religion that can hope to be a synthesizing and dynamic force for today must be shaped for the needs of this age. To establish such a religion is a major necessity of the present.*

The Manifesto's fifteen affirmations made clear the specifics of this necessary new religion ("Religious Humanism"). Its beliefs were: no creation but simply self-existent creation; man as an evolved natural creature; truth only through scientific study; the end to theistic (God based) religion; social concern and service to replace the self-serving profit motive of capitalism; the need to embrace life rather than flee from it (seeing traditional religion, as the famous psychiatrist Freud claimed it to be, as escapist in nature). Of particular interest are several of the Manifesto's affirmations.

In the Ninth Affirmation it claims that humanists will replace "old attitudes involved in worship and prayer" with "a heightened sense of personal life" and "a cooperative effort to promote social well-being."

In the Tenth Affirmation the Humanists proclaim that in their Humanism "there will be no uniquely religious emotions and attitudes of the kind hitherto associated with belief in the supernatural."

In the Eleventh Affirmation they claim that in approaching life's crises, employing "reasonable and manly attitudes" – acquired through education (their version of education, of course) – that their Religious Humanism "will take the path of social and mental hygiene and discourage sentimental and unreal hopes and wishful thinking."

In the Thirteenth Affirmation, they make it very clear that the intent of Religious Humanism is to remake the religious life of the nation around their modern religious ideals and to see that particular traditional church practices and activities "be reconstituted as rapidly as experience allows, in order to function effectively in the modern world."

It is very important to note that the Humanists of the 1930s were well aware that in their fervor for Humanism they were pushing for the establishment of a new religion in America. They intended at that time to do so simply by appealing to the common sense of a greatly distressed American people (thanks to the Depression) to see that the old days were gone. It was time to go modern.

But things did not ultimately go that way. World War Two came, the Depression consequently disappeared, America came out of that war victorious and ever stronger in its Christian faith. This was not the way the Humanists wanted to see things go and did not give up their battle. But instead of appealing to the American people, they eventually went to the federal courts, complaining that Christianity's central place in American culture was in violation of the Constitution's "separation of church and state" – their own (and Jefferson's) interpretation of the words of the First Amendment.* And therefore something "not religious" – like supposedly their "secular" Humanism – should properly be the only foundational cultural principle supported and defended by the federal courts.

In this quest, the Humanists got the Supreme Court finally to bow to the Humanist viewpoint in the 1971 case of *Lemon v. Kurtzman*. In that case the idea that secular Humanism was itself a fundamental worldview or religion was not mentioned (of course not). The embarrassing 1933 *Humanist Manifesto* (which would have made a complete lie of the Humanists' position in the case) was conveniently overlooked. And the Humanists were quick in 1973 to come out with *Humanist Manifesto II*, which drops the affirmation that what the Humanists are doing is pure religion, and instead recasts Humanism as simply "scientific Truth." But all religions are about what a community sees as fundamental Truth, the kind of Truth that everything else about their society's norms and laws flow from faithfully.

But anyway, there it is, the 1933 *Humanist Manifesto*, admitting that it is seeking avidly to bring America to a new religion.

The growing Liberal-Conservative split within the Church itself.
Meanwhile the mainline churches continued to plunge deeper into Liberal-Fundamentalist infighting. In 1933 J. Gresham Machen, who had left Princeton Seminary and had founded Westminster Seminary in order to keep a more traditional evangelical Presbyterian theology alive and well, was finally forced by more progressive Presbyterians out of the Presbyterian denomination itself. He subsequently helped found the Conservative Orthodox Presbyterian Church, contributing to the movement of a number of individuals and congregations out of membership in the old mainline

---

*"Congress shall make no law respecting an establishment of religion, or prohibiting the free exercise thereof; or abridging the freedom of speech, or of the press; or the right of the people peaceably to assemble, and to petition the Government for a redress of grievances."

The Great Depression (the 1930s)

denomination. But it was a departure that gladdened the hearts of mainline Christians – who tended to be major supporters of the Social Gospel of good works as Christianity's central message to the country and the world. Furthermore, this departure of the Conservatives left the old mainstream Christian churches all the more clearly in the hands of Christian Liberals.

Within the American church in general, Conservatives everywhere sensed that they were fighting a rear-guard action similar to the Presbyterians. And of course Liberals likewise felt that history and time were on their side – and that soon all reasonable people would be joining them in their modernizing religious camp. To forward-thinking Americans, their nation was entering enthusiastically another Age of Reason.

Sadly, the more Liberal the churches became, the more they sounded like the Secular Humanists in the way they approached life. And as the mainline churches drifted further and further in this direction, they increasingly lost their strong, clear moral voice – once the moral bedrock of American politics. The churches were fast making themselves irrelevant. How ironic: it was their claim that by making themselves look more like the world they would enhance their influence in the world's affairs. But in fact, the end result was quite the opposite of what they were hoping for!

This cultural movement would not occur as rapidly in America as it had in Hitler's Germany. But the nature of the movement would remain much the same: man, not God, would be looked to as the Savior of the rising world.

In the midst of this religious transition one of Americas greatest theologians, H. Richard Niebuhr, so tellingly described what was happening to the message of the American church:

> *A God without wrath brought men without sin into a kingdom without judgment through the ministrations of a Christ without a cross.*
> Niebuhr, *The Kingdom of God in America* (1937)

Fifield's Spiritual Mobilization movement. Yet outside of the world of theological academics there was some serious action underway to get the country back on course with God, and away from an increasing dependence on salvation by social design coming from FDR's Washington experts. Los Angeles Congregational pastor James W. Fifield, Jr. – who had some of the same bold instincts as did once the greatest of the American capitalists. In the mid-1930s he founded Spiritual Mobilization, a grass-roots movement dedicated to getting the gospel of personal independence out to the nation, through the sermons preached from the pulpits of the movement's extensive pastoral membership. Fifield was able to gain enormous financial backing from key business leaders so as to hold conferences, bring in speakers and publish materials to enlighten America's clergy as to the role they needed to play in bringing the country out of its drift towards Socialism and back to America's tradition of personal freedom, one that prompted personal initiative and responsibility, and ultimately personal success, something they were certain was mandated by God himself. This broad mix of Christianity with conservative political values during the last half of the 1930s (continuing through the 1940s and into the 1950s) brought thousands of pastors (and hundreds of businessmen) to active support of Spiritual Mobilization.

Vereide's prayer breakfast movement. On another front, and also originating in the American West, was Norwegian-born Methodist minister Abraham Vereide's City Chapel program, bringing businessmen and local political officials (across the broadest religious and political spectrum possible, although basically Protestant in character) to "breakfasts" where extensive prayer would be offered – for the local community, the nation and the world. Vereide had earlier founded and led the Seattle operations of Goodwill Industries, a company focused on offering employment to those who had such disabilities that they would not likely find employment elsewhere. Vereide proved to be an outstanding organizational leader, building up the Seattle operation to involve tens of thousands of workers and supporters. But gradually he grew disillusioned with the failure of charity to change people's circumstances for the better, and resigned – to look for life's answers elsewhere. He too was a strong believer in personal initiative rather than governmental dependency.

His next direction in life came when he visited San Francisco during the violent longshoremen's strike of 1934, and found himself invited to lead the local businessmen's association in prayer during those dark times. Then when he returned to Seattle (where the strike was also ongoing) he deliberately set up an early morning breakfast prayer meeting at his City Chapel for some of Seattle's business leaders, soon joined as well by some local politicians.

These prayer breakfasts proved so encouraging to Seattle's demoralized business class that they continued their existence year after year, growing all the while. Here too in the early 1940s the war would only amplify the sense of need of such prayer gatherings, spreading Vereide's movement from city to city across the nation so that they would eventually become a key part of the American national religious and political scene, eventually including the president's annual Prayer Breakfast, started up in 1952.

BIBLIOGRAPHY AND ENDNOTES

Important reads of a general, but religious, historical nature:

Bennett, William J. *America: The Last Best Hope; Volume I: From the Age of Discovery to a World at War, 1492-1914*. Nashville, TN: Nelson Current, 2006.

Corrigan, John and Hudson, Winthrop S. *Religion in America*. 9th Edition. New York: Routledge, 2018.

Gaustad, Edwin S. and Noll, Mark A., eds. *A Documentary History of Religion in America to 1877*. 3rd Edition. Grand Rapids, Michigan: Wm. B. Eerdmans, 2003.

Hudson, Winthrop S. *Religion in America: An Historical Account of the Development of American Religious Life.* 3rd Edition. New York: Charles Scribner's Sons, 1981.

Noll, Mark A. *A History of Christianity in the United States and Canada.* Grand Rapids, Michigan: Wm. B. Eerdmans, 1992.

Noll, Mark A. *America's God: From Jonathan Edwards to Abraham Lincoln.* New York: Oxford University Press, 2002.

Marshall, Peter and Manuel, David. *The Light and the Glory: Did God Have a Plan for America?* Old Tappan, NJ: Fleming H. Revell Company, 1977. (basically covering the period 1492 to 1793)

Marshall, Peter and Manuel, David. *From Sea to Shining Sea: God's Plan for America Unfolds*. Grand Rapids, MI: Fleming H. Revell, 1986. (basically covering the period 1787 to 1837)

Marshall, Peter and Manuel, David. *Sounding Forth the Trumpet: God's Plan for America in Peril – 1837-1860*. Grand Rapids, MI: Revell, 1998.

Meacham, Jon. *American Gospel: God, The Founding Fathers, and the Making of a Nation*. New York: Random House, 2006.

The Oxford History of the United States series:

Middlekauff, Robert. *The Glorious Cause: The American Revolution, 1763-1789.* Oxford History of the United States. New York: Oxford University Press, 2007.

Wood, Gordon S. *Empire of Liberty: A History of the Early Republic, 1789 -1815.* Oxford History of the United States. New York: Oxford University Press, 2009.

Howe, Daniel Walker. *What Hath God Wrought: The Transformation of America, 1815-1848.* Oxford History of the United States. New York: Oxford University Press, 2007.

McPherson, James M. *Battle Cry of Freedom: The Civil War Era, 1848 -1865.* Oxford History of the United States. New York: Oxford University Press, 1988.

White, Richard. *The Republic for Which It Stands: The United States during Reconstruction and the Gilded Age, 1865-1896.* Oxford History of the United States. New York: Oxford University Press, 2017.

Herring, George. *Years of Peril and Ambition: U.S. Foreign Relations, 1776-1921.* Oxford History of the United States. New York: Oxford University Press, 2007.

Other key works of a general nature:

Furnas, J.C. *The Americans: A Social History of the United States, 1587-1914.* New York: B.P. Putnam's Sons, 1969.

James, Edward T., ed. *The American Plutarch: 18 Lives Selected from the Dictionary of American Biography, with an Introduction by Howard Mumford Jones.* New York: Charles Scribner's Sons, for American Council for Learned Societies, 1964, renewing numerous copyrights going back to 1929.

Morison, Samuel Eliot. *The Oxford History of the American People.* New York: Oxford University Press, 1965.

Morison, Samuel Eliot and Commager, Henry Steele. *The Growth of the American Republic.* 5th edition, Volume One. New York: Oxford University Press, 1962.

Schweikart, Larry and Allen, Michael. *A Patriot's History of the United States: From Columbus's Great Discovery to the War on Terror.* New York: Penguin Sentinel, 2007.

Tindall, George Brown. *America: A Narrative History.* Volume 1. New York: W.W. Norton & Company, 1984.

Introduction: On Being a Covenant People

[1]Winthrop, John. A Modell of Christian Charity. *Collections of the Massachusetts Historical Society.* Boston, 1838. 3rd series 7:46-47. (history.hanover.edu/texts/winthmod.html)

Chapter 1. Colonial Foundations: The Two Americas

[2]Hundersmarck, Lawrence H. Martin Luther, in Ian P. McGreal's *Great Thinkers*

Bibliography and Endnotes 533

of the Western World (New York: Harper Collins, 1992) pp. 150–154; Sabine, George H. and Thorson, Thomas L. *A History of Political Theory* 4th edition (Hinsdale, IL: Dryden Press, 1973), pp. 336-339.

[3]Allen, Wl. Loyd, John Calvin, in Ian P. McGreal's *Great Thinkers of the Western World* pp. 155–158; Sabine and Thorson, *A History of Political Theory*, pp. 339-344.

[4]Calvin, John. *Institutes of the Christian Religion.* Translated from the 1541 French edition by Elsie Anne McKee. Grand Rapids, Michigan, William B. Eerdmans, 2009.

[5]Rolfe's very touching letter to the Virginia Governor, requesting marriage to Pocahontas in 1614, is to be found in Gaustand and Noll's *A Documentary History of Religion in American to 1877*, pp. 54-57.

[6]Billings, Warren M. *Sir William Berkeley and the Forging of Colonial Virginia.* Baton Rouge: Louisiana State University Press, 2004.

[7]Austin, Beth. *1619: Virginia's First Africans.* Hampton VA: Hampton History Museum, 2019. www.HamptonHistoryMuseum.org/1619.

[8]An excellent re-edition (in modern English) of the Pilgrim leader Bradford's own memoires was produced by Samuel Eliot Morison, *Of Plymouth Plantation 1620–1647 by William Bradford* (New York: Alfred A. Knopf, 1991); an old but insightful study is George F. Willison's *Saints and Strangers: Being the Lives of the Pilgrim Fathers & Their Families, with their Friends & Foes (*Orleans MA: Parnassus Imprints, Inc., 1945).

[9]Morison's *Of Plymouth Plantation 1620–1647 by William Bradford*, pp. 75-76.

[10]Brown, John. *The Pilgrim Fathers of New England and the Puritan Successors* (London: The Religious Tract Society, 1906) reprinted by Pilgrim Publications, Pasadena, Texas, 1970, p. 203.
(archive.org/details/pilgrimfathersof00browuoft)

[11]An excellent collection of various writings on a full range of social issues – and just personal reflections, offering great insight as to what motivated this community of Puritans, is to be found in Perry Miller and Thomas H. Johnson's *The Puritans: A Sourcebook of Their Writings.* 2 Volumes Bound as One (Mineola, NY: Dover Publications, Inc., 2001).

[12]A great read on the life of Winthrop is to be found in Francis J. Bremer's *John Winthrop: America's Forgotten Founding Father* (Oxford University Press, 2003).

[13]Heimart, Alan and Delbanco, Andrew, eds. *The Puritans in America: A Narrative Anthology* (Cambridge, Massachusetts: Harvard University Press, 1985) pp. 157–161.

Chapter 2. The Colonies Mature

[14] Airy, Anthony. Cooper, Anthony Ashley (1621–1683) *The Dictionary of National Biography* (Smith, Elder & Co., 1887) Vol 12. pp. 111–130. (en.wikisource.org/wiki/Cooper,_Anthony_Ashley_(1621–1683)_(DNB00))

[15] Marty. *Pilgrims in Their Own Land*, p. 66-67.

[16] Fantel, Hans. *William Penn: Apostle of Dissent*. William Morrow & Co., New York, 1974.

[17] Mora witch trial, Wikipedia.

[18] Locke, John. *Two Treatises of Government. Treatise II: An Essay Concerning the Original, Extent, and End, of Civil Government. From The Works of John Locke, A New Edition, Corrected*. Vol. V. London: Thomas Tegg, 1823. (yorku.ca/comninel/courses/3025pdf/Locke.pdf)

[19] Woolhouse, Roger. *John Locke: An Essay Concerning Human Understanding*. Penguin Classic. London: Penguin Books, 1997.

[20] Toland, John. *Christianity not Mysterious: Or A Treatise Shewing, That there is nothing in the Gospel Contrary to Reason Nor Above it: And that no Christian Doctrine can be properly call'd a Mystery*. London: Dolphin, 1696. (books.google.com/books/about/Christianity_Not_Mysterious.html?id=fHhOAAAAcAAJ)

[21] Tindal, Matthew. *Christianity As Old As The Creation, Or The Gospel, A Republication of the Religion of Nature*. London: 1731. (books.google.com/books?id=-khhAAAAcAAJ&source= gbs_similarbooks)

[22] William Byrd (1674–1744) *Encyclopedia Virginia*. Virginia Humanities; Byrd II, William (1674–1744) Encyclopedia.com

[23] Murray, Iain H. *Johnathan Edwards: A New Biography*. Edinburgh: The Banner of Truth Trust, 1987.

[24] Dallimore, Arnold A. *George Whitefield: God's Anointed Servant in the Great Revival of the Eighteenth Century*. Wheaton, Illinois: Crossway Books, 1990.

[25] Foster, Rebecca Lunceford. The Preacher and the Printer. In Sidwell, Mark. ed. *Faith of Our Fathers: Scenes from American Church History* (Greenville, SC: BJU Press, 1991) 44-49. Also, Benjamin Franklin on the Great Awakening, from His Autobiography Digital History ID 1278 (2019) (digitalhistory.uh.edu/disp_textbook.cfm?smtID=3&psid=1278)

Chapter 3. Independence

Norman Cousins provides valuable biographical insight into ten of America's Founding Fathers in his *"In God We Trust": The Religious Beliefs and Ideas of the American Founding Fathers* (Kingsport, TN: Kingsport Press, 1958). Also,

Bibliography and Endnotes 535

a huge work on this event is Page Smith's *A New Age Now Begins: A People's History of the American Revolution*. 2 vols. (New York: McGraw Hill Book Company, 1976). And an easy read, of almost a novel-like character, is Bill O'Reilly and Martin Dugard's *Killing England: The Brutal Struggle for American Independence* (New York: Henry Holt and Company, 2017).

[26] Jensen, Merrill. *The Founding of a Nation: A History of the American Revolution, 1763–1776* (New York: Oxford University Press, 1968) pp. 671-704.

[27] Of course there are multitudes of biographies written about Washington. An excellent one that describes his early years is by Thomas A. Lewis, *For King and Country: The Maturing of George Washington 1748–1760* (Edison, NJ: Castle Books, 2006). A Pulitzer prize-winning biography of Washington is by Ron Chernow, *Washington: A Life* (New York: Penguin Press, 2010). And an interesting comparison of the differing personalities of America's two most powerful generals of the day was written by a former Superintendent of West Point, Dave R. Palmer, *George Washington and Benedict Arnold: A Tale of Two Patriots* [with a subheading: One became the father of our country; the other became a man without a country] (Washington, D.C.: Regnery Publishing, Inc., 2006).

[28] From *Washington in Prayer*, presenting a 1945 article, "Prayer of Valley Forge May Be Legend or Tradition or a Fact, Yet It Remains Symbol of Faith" written by Gilbert Starling Jones and published by the Valley Forge Historical Society, April, 1945, No, 9. The article discusses in depth whether the later recollection of an elderly Potts could be accurate or not, a typical issue that Christians and Secularists were already debating. The article concludes with a strong argument in favor of the truth of the Potts legend. (ushistory.org/valleyforge/washington/prayer.html)

[29] From the opening lines of Thomas Paine's first of sixteen pamphlets of *The American Crisis* series that he published over the period 1776 to 1783, most of them in the first year. This one was published with the *Pennsylvania Journal* on December 19, 1776 under the author's pseudonym "Common Sense"!

Chapter 4. The Birth of the American Republic

[30] Beeman, Richard R. *Perspective on the Constitution: A Republic, If You Can Keep It*, Philadelphia, National Constitutional Center [no date].

[31] Hunt, Gaillard, ed. *James Madison, The Writings of James Madison*. Vol. 3, 1787, The Journal of the Constitutional Convention, Part I. Thursday, June 28th. New York: G.P. Putnam's Sons, 1902.
(oll.libertyfund.org/titles/madison-the-writings-vol-3-1787)

[32] Faÿ, Bernard. *Franklin, The Apostle of Modern Times, With Illustrations*. Boston: Little, Brown and Company, 1929. An old, but excellent read.

[33] Jacob E. Cooke wrote an article debating this quote, Alexander Hamilton's Authorship of the Caesar Letters, *The William and Mary Quarterly*, Vol. 17, No. 1 (January 1960), pp. 78-85. This quote had been published under the

pseudonym of Caesar in the October 15th 1787 *New York Daily Advertiser*. Paul Leicester Ford, in his Introduction to *The Federalist: A Commentary on the Constitution of the United States* (1898) pp. xxi-xxiii, had claimed that Caesar was Hamilton, and – justifiably – this had been the American understanding on this matter since then.

[34] Query XVIII, Notes on the State of Virginia (1781–1782), p. 173.

Chapter 5. The Young Republic

[35] An outstanding biography on Hamilton is Ron Chernow's *Alexander Hamilton* (New York: The Penguin Press, 2004).

[36] An interesting biography on Jefferson is Joseph J. Ellis National Book Award-winning, *American Sphinx: The Character of Thomas Jefferson* (New York: Alfred A. Knopf, 1997). He describes the sometime wise, sometimes naïve Jefferson, with his often-contradictory positions that Jefferson took over the course of his life, the most complex being the matter of slavery.

[37] In his book, *John Adams* (New York: Simon & Schuster, 2001), David McCullough explores the genius, dedication, and often enormous bravery, of the ambitious Adams – at the same time his foibles, and his dramatically evolving relationship with Jefferson.

[38] *Fletcher v. Peck*, 10 U.S. 87 (1810).

[39] *McCulloch v. Maryland*, 17 US 316 (1819).

[40] *Cohens v. Virginia*, 19 US 264 (1821).

[41] A short but excellent study of the complexities of Madison – and all that he had to deal with as the political match-maker – is Garry Wills *James Madison* [part of Schlesinger's American President Series] New York: Henry Holt and Company, 2002.

[42] An excellent book by Merrill D. Peterson is *The Great Triumvirate: Webster, Clay, and Calhoun* (New York: Oxford University Press, 1987). This work describes their relationship beginning in early 1813 – but especially from the point of uniting in 1832 in the Senate against Jackson – to eventually the point of going their separate ways, just as the country itself was headed off in different, increasingly opposing directions.

Chapter 6. The Shaping of a Nation

[43] Nagel, Paul C. *John Quincy Adams: A Public Life, A Private Life*. New York: Alfred A. Knopf, 1997.

[44] An excellent analysis of the Jacksonian Era was presented by the scholarly, but politically sophisticated (future Kennedy advisor) Arthur M. Schlesinger, Jr. in his Pulitzer prize-winning *The Age of Jackson* (Boston: Little, Brown and

Company, 1945). Another excellent but more recent study of Jackson himself is Jon Meacham's *American Lion: Andrew Jackson in the White House* (New York: Random House, 2008).

[45] An excellent study of the political dynamics that shaped the modernization of the Cherokee nation, and then forced it to have to vacate its lands in the East anyway and head to new Indian Territory west of the Mississippi is John Ehle's *Trail of Tears: The Rise and Fall of the Cherokee Nation* (New York: Random House, 1988).

[46] *The Cherokee Nation v. The State of Georgia*, 30 US 1 (1831).

[47] *Worchester v. Georgia*, 31 US 515 (1832).

[48] Goldhammer, Arthur, trans. *Tocqueville: Democracy in America*. New York: Literary Classics of the United States, Inc./Penguin Putnam Inc., 2004.

[49] To Dr. Benjamin Waterhouse Monticello, June 26, 1822 *The Letters of Thomas Jefferson 1743–1826*. American History: From Revolution to Reconstruction and Beyond. (let.rug.nl/usa/presidents/thomas-jefferson/ letters-of-thomas-jefferson/jefl268.php)

[50] Thoreau, Henry David. *Walden: Or, Life in the Woods*. Dover Thrift Editions, [date varies].

[51] An excellent investigation into the many facets of Emerson's complex life was written by Gay Wilson Allen, *Waldo Emerson* (New York: Viking Press, 1981).

[52] For a general overview of the period see Barry Hankins, *The Second Great Awakening and the Transcendentalists,* "Greenwood Guides to Historic Events 1500–1900" (Westport, CT: Greenwood Press, 2004).

[53] Two excellent works focusing on Asbury and how he shaped the development of Methodism in America are LC. Rudolph's *Francis Asbury: The Apostle Whose Only Home Was His Saddle, His Parish – The Continent*. (Ashville, TN: Abingdon Press, 1966) and John Wigger's *American Saint: Francis Asbury and the Methodists* (New York: Oxford University Press, 2012).

[54] An excellent narrative of the spiritual empowerment of America's bold circuit riders is found in Rimi Xhemajli's *The Supernatural and the Circuit Riders: The Rise of Early American Methodism*. Eugene, OR: Pickwick Publications, 2021.

[55] The organization and colorful character of the early rural camp meetings (the period roughly 1800-1830) is detailed in Hudson's, *Religion in America*, pp. 137-140

[56] Wessel, Helen, ed. *The Autobiography of Charles G. Finney: The Life Story of America's Greatest Evangelist in His Own Words* (Minneapolis, Minnesota: Bethany House, 1977).

[57] Barnes, Howard A. *Horace Bushnell and the Virtuous Republic*. ATLA Monograph Series, No. 27 (Metuchen, NJ: The American Theological Library Association, 1991).

[58] Bushnell's *Christian Nurture* can be downloaded from the Christian Classics Ethereal Library at: ccel.org/ccel/bushnell/nurture.html.

[59] Hudson, *Religion in America*, pp. 178-179.

Chapter 7. Expansion, and Division

[60] Encyclopedia Britannica's article on "Manifest Destiny" cites two of O'Sullivan's articles, "Annexation" published in his own *The United States Magazine and Democratic Review*, in the July-August 1845 edition, and another article, published in *The New York Morning News* on December 27, 1845, as generating the term. (britannica.com/event/Manifest-Destiny).

[61] Hardin, Stephen L. *Lust for Glory: An Epic Story of Early Texas and the Sacrifice That Defined a Nation*. Oxford: Osprey Publishing, 2005.

[62] Eisenhower, John S.D. *So Far From God: The U.S. War with Mexico, 1846-1848*. New York: Random House, 1989.

[63] McNeese, Tim. *The Abolitionist Movement: Ending Slavery. Reform Movements in American History*. New York: Chelsea House Publishers, 2008.

Chapter 8. The Gathering Clouds of War

[64] Etcheson, Nicole. B*leeding Kansas: Contested Liberty in the Civil War Era*. Lawrence: the University Press of Kansas, 2004; Sutton, Robert K. *Stark Mad Abolitionists: Lawrence, Kansas, and the Battle over Slavery in the Civil War Era*. Foreword by Bob Dole. New York: Skyhorse Publishing, 2017.

[65] Finkelman, Paul. *Dred Scott v. Sandford: A Brief History with Documents*. Boston: Bedford, 1997.

[66] The works on Lincoln are virtually endless. But some stand out among the pack. Classic, of course, is the poet Carl Sandburg's six-volume set, *Abraham Lincoln: The Prairie Years & the War Years* (New York: Charles Scribner's Sons, 1939) or his summary Reader's Digest Illustrated Edition. Also outstanding is Doris Kearns Goodwin's prize-winning *Team of Rivals: The Political Genius of Abraham Lincoln* (New York: Simon & Schuster, 2005). And William Lee Miller contributed two excellent studies on Lincoln: *Lincoln's Virtues: An Ethical Biography* (New York: Alfred A. Knopf, 2002) and *President Lincoln: The Duty of a Statesman* (New York: Alfred A. Knopf, 2008), the former focusing on Lincoln's formative years and the latter on his years in office as president.

Chapter 9. Civil War

[67] The books published on the Civil War are also endless. But Bruce Catton

Bibliography and Endnotes 539

distinguished himself as an authority on the subject with his *This Hallowed Ground: The Story of the Union Side of the Civil War* (Garden City, New York: Doubleday & Company, 1956), along with a number of other works of his on the Civil War. His *American Heritage Picture History of the Civil War* (New York: American Heritage, 1988), is a wonderful pictorial supplement to his other works. Also highly distinguished is Shelby Foote's classic three-volume series on the Civil War: Vol. 1: *Fort Sumter to Perryville*; Vol. 2: *Fredericksburg to Meridian*; Vol. 3: *Red River to Appomattox* (New York: Random House Vintage Books, 1986). Biographies of 24 American generals, South and North, is to be found in Alan Axelrod's *Generals South, Generals North: The Commanders of the Civil War Reconsidered* (Guilford, CT: Globe Pequot Press, 2011).

[68] Davis, William C. *Crucible of Command: Ulysses S. Grant and Robert E. Lee – The War They Fought, the Peace They Forged*. Philadelphia: Da Capo Press, 2014.

[69] Again, like Lincoln, there are multitudes of books on Grant. Besides the Davis book, *Crucible of Command*, there is H.W. Brands' *The Man Who Saved the Union: Ulysses Grant in War and Peace* (New York: Doubleday, 2012); Edward G. Longacre's *General Ulysses S. Grant: The Soldier and the Man* (Cambridge, Mass.: Da Capo Press, 2006). Also very important is the reprint of the two volumes (in one) of the 1885 *Personal Memoires of U.S. Grant* (Old Saybrook, CT: Konecky & Konecky).

10. America Recovers

[70] In addition to Richard White's *The Republic for Which It Stands*, excellent coverage of the individuals who shaped America into something quite new in the post-war period is James Robertson's *After the Civil War: The Heroes, Villains, Soldiers, and Civilians Who Changed America* (Washington, DC: The National Geographic Society, 2015). Some 70 short biographies (each 4 to 5 pages) of an array of individuals – well-known and not-so-well-known today. Also an excellent study of this time period (also heroes and villains alike!) is H.W. Brands' *American Colossus: The Triumph of Capitalism, 1865-1900* (New York: Doubleday, 2010).

[71] Milton, George Fort. *The Age of Hate: Andrew Johnson and the Radicals*. New York: Coward-McCann Company, 1930.

[72] Foner, Eric. *Reconstruction: America's Unfinished Revolution, 1863-1877*. Updated Edition. New York: Harper Perennial, 2014. Foner seeks to merge different historical interpretations or revisions concerning the social-moral character of post-war Reconstruction.

[73] Smith, Jean Edward. *Grant*. New York: Simon & Schuster, 2001, an enormous volume covering Grant, not only as a soldier and general but Grant as U.S. president.

[74] Two excellent narratives on the Battle for the West are Dee Brown's, *The American West* (New York: Touchstone, 1994) and Bill Yenne's *Indian Wars: The Campaign for the Indian West* (Yardley, PA: Westholme Publishing, 2006).

Chapter 11. The "Gilded Aged" of American Capitalism

[75] An excellent study of the Captains of Industry (or Robber Barons as other termed them) who took the lead in shaping strongly the character of post-Civil-War America is found in H.W. Brands' *American Colossus: The Triumph of Capitalism, 1865-1900* (New York: Doubleday, 2010). Along those same lines is James Robertson's biographical collection, *After the Civil War: The Heroes, Villains, Soldiers, and Civilians Who Changed America* (Washington, D.C.: The National Geographic Society, 2015) is Richard White's *The Republic for Which It Stands: The United States during Reconstruction and the Gilded Age, 1865-1896*, "Oxford History of the United States" (New York: Oxford University Press, 2017); also the classic: Matthew Josephson's *The Robber Barons: The Great American Capitalists: 1861-1901* (New York: Harcourt, Brace, 1934.

[76] Andrew Carnegie, *Autobiography of Andrew Carnegy* (Boston: Northeastern University Press, 1986).

[77] Ron Chernow, *The House of Morgan: An American Banking Dynasty and the Rise of Modern Finance* (New York: Simon & Schuster, 1990); Andrew Sinclair, *Corsair: The Life of J. Pierpont Morgan* (Boston: Little, Brown, 1981).

[78] Ron Chernow, *Titan: The Life of John D. Rockefeller, Sr.* (New York: Random House, 1998).

[79] Robert W. Cherny, *American Politics in the Gilded Age, 1868-1900* (Wheeling, IL: Harlan-Davidson, 1997).

[80] Alan Nevins, *Grover Cleveland: A Study in Courage* (New York: Dodd, Mead, 1966).

[81] Karl Rove, extremely knowledgeable himself about electoral campaigns, demonstrates how William McKinleys close ally, Mark Hanna, conducted for McKinley one of the first modern presidential campaigns. See: *The Triumph of William McKinley: Why the Election of 1896 Still Matters* (New York: Simon & Schuster, 2015).

[82] H. Wayne Morgan, *William McKinley and His America* (Syracuse: Syracuse University Press, 1963); Lewis L. Gould, *The Presidency of William McKinley* (Lawrence: Regents Press of Kansas, 1980).

Chapter 12. American Progressivism

[83] An old but highly insightful study of the reformist age of Progressivism, especially in the early years of the 20th century is Eric F. Goldman's *Rendezvous with Destiny: A History of Modern American Reform* (New York: Vintage Books, 1956). Also excellent in its coverage of the Progressivist Era is Michael McGerr's *A Fierce Discontent: The Rise and Fall of the Progressive Movement in America* (New York: Oxford University Press, 2003). A classic is Richard Hofstadter, ed., *The Progressive Movement, 1900-1913*. Englewood Cliffs, N.J.: Prentice-Hall, 1963. Another excellent source of selected writings and speeches of the Progressivists themselves is Ronald J. Pestritto and William J. Atto, eds.,

Bibliography and Endnotes 541

American Progressivism: A Reader (Lanham, MD: Lexington Books, 2008.)

[84] John C. Farell, *Beloved Lady: A History of Jane Addams Ideas on Reform and Peace* (Baltimore: Johns Hopkins University Press, 1967).

[85] Michael Kazin, *A Godly Hero: The Life of William Jennings Bryan* (New York: Alfred A. Knopf, 2006); LeRoy Ashby, *William Jennings Bryan: Champion of Democracy* (Boston: Twayne Publishers, 1987); Robert W. Cherny, *A Righteous Cause: The Life of William Jennings Bryan* (Glenview, IL: Scott, Foresman and Co., 1985).

[86] David McCullough, *Mornings on Horseback: The Story of an Extraordinary Family, a Vanished Way of Life and the Unique Child Who Became Theodore Roosevelt* (New York: Simon & Schuster, 2001); George E. Mowry, *The Era of Theodore Roosevelt and the Birth of Modern America, 1900-1912* (New York: Harper Torchbooks, 1958); Joshua David Hawley, *Theodore Roosevelt: Preacher of Righteousness,* Foreword by David M. Kennedy (New Haven, CT: Yale University Press, 2008).

[87] Michael L. Bromley, *William Howard Taft and the First Motoring Presidency, 1909-1913* (Jefferson, NC: McFarland & Company, 2003).

Chapter 13. The Rationalizing of Western Culture

[88] Much of this chapter is drawn from the 3rd edition (1961) of George H. Sabine's classic text, *A History of Political Theory* and the more recent 4th edition issued through the efforts of Thomas Thorson (Hinsdale, IL: Dryden Press, 1973) [Sabine died the year of the publication of the 3rd edition].

Also Bertrand Russell's *A History of Western Philosophy: And Its Connection with Political and Social Circumstances from the Earliest Times to the Present Day* (New York: Simon and Schuster, 1945) form a big part of the foundation for this chapter. A much more summarized version of Russell's work is his *Wisdom of the West* (New York: Crescent Books, 1959, reprinted many times since then).

An outstanding reference work on this same subject can be found in Ian P. McGreal, ed. *Great Thinkers of the Western World: The Major Ideas and Classic Works of More Than 100 Outstanding Western Philosophers, Physical and Social Scientists, Psychologists, Religious Writers and Theologians* (New York: Harper Collins, 1992), some 35 scholars (themselves outstanding in their fields!) contributing short biographies and intellectual summaries of these 100 builders of Western thought and understanding.

[89] Russell, *A History of Western Philosophy*, pp. 557-568; Bowman L Clarke, "René Descartes" in McGreal, *Great Thinkers of the Western World*, pp. 195-199.

[90] Donald E. Hall, "Isaac Newton" in McGreal, *Great Thinkers of the Western World*, pp. 232-236.

[91] Russell, *A History of Western Philosophy*, pp. 581-596; Richard Muller, "Gottfried Wilhelm Leibniz" in McGreal, *Great Thinkers of the Western World*, pp. 237-242.

[92] Russell, *A History of Western Philosophy*, pp. 604-647; Sabine and Thorson, *A History of Political Theory*, pp. 483-499; Burton M. Leiser, John Locke" in McGreal, *Great Thinkers of the Western World*, pp. 223-227.

[93] Sabine and Thorson, *A History of Political Theory*, pp. 529-548; Russell, *A History of Western Philosophy*, pp. 684-701; Constance Creede, "Jean-Jacques Rousseau," in McGreal, *Great Thinkers of the Western World*, pp. 271-274.

[94] Russell, *A History of Western Philosophy*, pp. 659-674; Sabine and Thorson, *A History of Political Theory*, pp. 549-557; Oliver A. Johnson, "David Hume," in McGreal, *Great Thinkers of the Western World*, pp. 266-270.

[95] Adam Smith, *The Wealth of Nations* (New York: Alfred A. Knopf, 1991); Don Thomas Dugi, "Adam Smith," in McGreal, *Great Thinkers of the Western World*, pp. 275-280.

[96] Russell, *A History of Western Philosophy*, pp. 701-718; Oliver A. Johnson, "Immanuel Kant," in McGreal, *Great Thinkers of the Western World*, pp. 281-285.

[97] Sabine and Thorson, *A History of Political Theory*, pp. 570-607; Russell, *A History of Western Philosophy*, pp. 730-746; Clark K. Kucheman, "Georg Wilhelm Friedrich Hegel" in McGreal, *Great Thinkers of the Western World*, pp. 311-336.

[98] Mark T. Riley, "Thomas Robert Malthus," in McGreal, *Great Thinkers of the Western World*, pp. 328-330.

[99] Mark T. Riley, "Charles Darwin," in McGreal, *Great Thinkers of the Western World*, pp. 364-368.

[100] Herbert Spencer, *Social Statistics; Or The Conditions Essential to Human Happiness Specified and the First of Them Developed* (New York: A.M. Kelley, 1969.); Robert C. Bannister, *Social Darwinism: Science and Myth in Anglo-American Social Thought* (Philadelphia: Temple University Press, 1988); Richard Hofstadter, *Social Darwinism in American Thought*. Boston: Beacon Press, 1992); James Gettier Kennedy, *Herbert Spencer* (Boston: Twayne Publishers, 1978); Don Thomas Dugi, "Herbert Spencer," in McGreal, *Great Thinkers of the Western World*, pp. 382-387.

[101] Russell, *A History of Western Philosophy*, pp. 760-773; John K. Roth, "Friedrich Nietzsche," in McGreal, *Great Thinkers of the Western World*, pp. 408-413.

[102] Sabine and Thorson, *A History of Political Theory*, pp. 681-723; Russell, *A History of Western Philosophy*, pp. 782-790; Terry Kershaw, "Karl Marx," in McGreal, *Great Thinkers of the Western World*, pp. 378-381.

[103] Sabine and Thorson, *A History of Political Theory*, pp. 724-773.

Bibliography and Endnotes 543

[104] Arthur S. Link, *Woodrow Wilson: A Brief Biography* (Cleveland: World Publishing, 1963); Ronald J. Pestritto, *Woodrow Wilson and the Roots of Modern Liberalism* (Lanham, MD: Rowan & Littlefield Publishers, Inc., 2005); H.W. Brands, *Woodrow Wilson* (Henry Holt and Co., 2003).

[105] Russell, A History of Western Philosophy, pp. 819-828; Paul E. Hurley, "John Dewey," in McGreal, Great Thinkers of the Western World, pp. 434-440.

[106] John Dewey, *Liberalism and Social Action* (New York: Capricorn Books, 1935); John Dewey, *A Common Faith* (New Haven: Yale University Press, 1934).

[107] Marty, *Pilgrims in Their Own Land*, pp. 311-313.

[108] Robert R. Owens, *Speak to the Rock: The Asuza Street Revival and Its Message* (Lanham, MD: University Press of America, 1998).

Chapter 14. Nationalism, Imperialism and the Great War

[109] E.J. Hobsbawm, *The Age of Empire, 1875-1914* (New York: Vintage Books, 1989).

[110] Ernest May, *Imperial Democracy: The Emergence of America as a Great Power* (New York: Harcourt, Brace & World, 1961).

[111] Lewis L. Gould, *The Spanish-American War and President McKinley* (Lawrence: University Press of Kansas, 1982); Ivan Musicant, *Empire by Default: The Spanish-American War and the Dawn of the American Century* (New York: Henry Holt, 1998).

[112] Lewis L. Gould *The Presidency of Theodore Roosevelt* (Lawrence: University Press of Kansas, 1991).

[113] James R. Reckner, *Teddy Roosevelt's Great White Fleet* (Annapolis: Naval Institute Press, 1988).

[114] Without a doubt, an outstanding presentation of the causes and start-up of World War One is found in Barbara W. Tuchman's *The Guns of August* (New York: Macmillan, 1962). Also very important is Winton Churchill's *The Great War* (London: G. Newnes, 1934) and Vincent J. Esposito, Ed. *A Concise History of World War I* (New York: Praeger, 1964). And an outstanding pictorial history of the war is S.L.A. Marshall's *American Heritage of World War One* (New York: Simon and Schuster, 1964).

[115] J.H. Johnson, *Stalemate! The Great Trench Warfare Battles of 1915-1917* (New York: Arms and Armour, 1995).

[116] Richard Pipes *The Russian Revolution* (New York: Alfred A. Knopf, 1990).

[117] Ernest R. May, *The World War and American Isolation, 1914-1917* (Cambridge: Harvard University Press, 1959).

[118] www.ourdocuments.gov/doc.php?flash=false&doc=61&page=transcript.

[119] Thomas Fleming hits hard at Wilson's unique world with his *The Illusion of Victory: America in World War I* (New York: Basic Books, 2003); also Thomas J. Knock, *To End All Wars: Woodrow Wilson and the Quest for a New World Order* (New York: Oxford University Press, 1992).

[120] Theodore P. Greene, *Wilson at Versailles* "Problems in American Civilization: Readings Selected by the Department of American Studies, Amherst College (Boston: D.C. Heath and Company, 1957); Charles L. Mee, Jr., *The End of Order: Versailles, 1919* (New York: E.P. Dutton, 1948); Arthur Walsworth, *Wilson and His Peacemakers: American Diplomacy at the Paris Peace Conference, 1919* (New York: Norton, 1986); Thomas A. Bailey, *Woodrow Wilson and the Lost Peace* (New York: Macmillan, 1944).

[121] Gene Smith, *When the Cheering Stopped: The Last Years of Woodrow Wilson* (New York: Simon and Schuster, 1968).

Chapter 15. The 'Roaring Twenties'

[122] Frederick Lewis Allen, *Only Yesterday: An Informal History of the Nineteen-Twenties* (New York: Harper & Row, 1964); Geoffrey Perrett, *America in the Twenties: A History* (New York: Simon and Schuster, 1982); William E. Leuchtenburg, *The Perils of Prosperity - 1914-1932* (Chicago: The University of Chicago Press, 1958).

[123] Edward Behr, *Prohibition: Thirteen Years That Changed America* (New York: Arcade Publishers, 1996); Kenneth Allsop, *The Bootleggers: The Story of Chicago's Prohibition Era* (New Rochelle, NY: Arlington House, 1968); John Kobler, *Ardent Spirits: The Rise and Fall of Prohibition* (New York: Da Capo Press, 1993).

[124] David Felix, *Protest: Sacco-Vanzetti and the Intellectuals* (Bloomington: Indiana University Press, 1965).

[125] Lawrence W. Levine, *Defender of the Faith: William Jennings Bryan, the Last Decade, 1915-1925* (Cambridge: Harvard University Press, 1987); Michael Kazin, *A Godly Hero: The Life of William Jennings Bryan* (New York: Alfred A. Knopf, 2006); Kevin Tierney, *Darrow: A Biography* (New York: Thomas Y. Crowell, 1979).

[126] F. Scott Fitzgerald, *The Great Gatsby* (New York: Scribners, 1981).

[127] Robert K. Murray, *The Politics of Normalcy: Governmental Theory and Practice in the Harding-Coolidge Era* (New York: Norton, 1973).

[128] Robert K. Murray, *The Harding Era: Warren G. Harding and His Administration* (Minneapolis: University of Minnesota Press, 1969).

[129] William Allen White, *A Puritan in Babylon: The Story of Calvin Coolidge* (New York: Capricorn Books, 1965).

[130] Richard Norton Smith, *An Uncommon Man: The Triumph of Herbert Hoover* (New York: Simon and Schuster, 1984); George H. Nash, *The Life of Herbert Hoover* (New York: W.W. Norton, 1983).

[131] Burke Davis, *The Billy Mitchell Affair* (New York: Random House, 1967).

[132] John Kenneth Galbraith, *The Great Crash - 1929* (Boston: Houghton Mifflin Company, 1961)

[133] Robert Sobel, *The Great Bull Market: Wall Street in the 1920s* (New York: W.W. Norton, 1968).

Chapter 16. The Great Depression

[134] Charles P. Kindleberger, *The World in Depression, 1929-1939* (Berkeley, University of California Press, 1986); Robert S. McElvaine, *The Great Depression: America, 1929-1941* (New York: Times Books, 1993).

[135] Jean Edward Smith, *FDR* (New York: Random House, 2008); James MacGregor Burns, *Roosevelt: The Lion and the Fox* (New York: Harcourt Brace Jovanovich, 1984); Frank Freidel, *Franklin D. Roosevelt: A Rendez-Vous with Destiny* (Boston: Little, Brown, 1990).

[136] Eleanor Roosevelt, *This I Remember* (New York: Harper, 1949).

[137] Paul K. Conkin, *FDR and the Origins of the Welfare State* (New York: Crowell, 1967); Burton Folsom, Jr., *New Deal or Raw Deal? How FDR's Economic Legacy Has Damaged America* (New York: Simon and Schuster, 2008); Kenneth S. Davis, *FDR: The New Deal Years, 1933-1937* (New York: Random House, 198); Albert U. Romasco, *The Politics of Recovery: Roosevelt's New Deal* (New York: Oxford University Press, 1983); Matthew J. Dickinson, *Bitter Harvest: FDR, Presidential Power, and the Growth of the Presidential Branch* (New York: Cambridge University Press, 1997).

[138] Hurt, R. Douglas. *The Dust Bowl: An Agricultural and Social History*. Chicago: Nelson-Hall, 1981.

[139] Eliot Ness with Oscar Frale. *The Untouchables* (New York: Pocket Books, 1985).

[140] Robert H. Zieger, *John L. Lewis: Labor Leader* (Boston: Twayne Publishers, 1988); Irving Bernstein, *Turbulent Years: A History of the American Worker, 1933-1941* (Boston: Houghton Mifflin, 1970).

[141] Alan Brinkley, *Voices of Protest: Huey Long, Father Coughlin and the Great Depression* (New York: Vintage Books, 1983).

INDEX

A

Abolition/Abolitionists 262, 263, 265, 271, 273, 275, 276, 281, 284, 302
  Abolitionism and the 2nd Great Awakening 262
  Christian Abolitionists 261
  Early Abolitionists 263
    Elijah Parish Lovejoy 263
    Frederick Douglass 264
    Grimké sisters, Angelina and Sarah 263
    Harriet Beecher Stowe 263, 274
    Harriet Tubman 263
    Horace Greeley 263
    John Quincy Adams 264
    Lucretia Mott 263
    Sojourner Truth 263
    William Lloyd Garrison 263
  Europe's example 262
  The slave-holders' moral response "Bible says 'Sons of Ham' (Blacks) must always serve others" 264
Acadia/Acadian/'Cajun' 108, 110
Act of Settlement of 1701 - excluding Catholic Stuarts 91
Adam and Eve eat from the Tree of the Knowledge of Good and Evil 153, 154, 233, 336
Adams, John 114, 153, 155, 157, 181, 185
  1776 - Adams heads effort to draft a Declaration of Independence 119
  1778 - Adams sent to Europe to represent America in France and the Netherlands 187
  1783 - Adams joins Franklin and Jay in finalizing the Treaty of Paris with the British 138
  1797-1801 - U.S. President 185
  Adams' background and personal character 185, 186, 187
Adams, John Quincy 186, 213, 215, 216, 217, 254, 259, 264, 275
  1810s - Adams a young Republican Party nationalists 202
  1817-1825 - Secretary of State under Monroe 213
  1825-1829 - U.S. President 216
  1831-1848 - In Congress as Massachusetts Representative 251
  1837-1845 - Adams leads debate opposing admission of Texas as a slave state 251
  1846-1848 - Adams opposes American war with Mexico over Texas 258
Adams, Samuel 115, 157
Addams, Jane 371, 428
Adventurers (corporate investors) 72
African Methodist Episcopal (AME) Church 241
African Methodist Episcopal Zion (AME Zion) Church 241
Age of Reason 37
Albany Plan (1754) to unite the colonies 112
Alcott, Amos Bronson 236, 237
Alexander Graham Bell 349
Alexander the Great 4
Alien and Sedition Acts (1798) 189
Allen, Richard 242
Amendments to the Constitution
  10th Amendment 418
  16th Amendment (1913) 419
  17th Amendment (1913) 419
  Direct election of the Senators by the people (not the States) 417

American Anti-Slavery Society 246, 263
American Board of Commissioners for Foreign Missions (ABDFM) Created in 1810 234, 246
American Federation of Labor 370
American Sunday School Union 246
American Tract Society 246
A Modell of Christian Charity 16
Anarchist/Anarchism/Anarchy 344, 360, 414, 416, 481, 482
Andros, Governor Sir Edmund 90, 99
An Essay Concerning Human Understanding (1690) by John Locke 95
Anglican/Anglicans/Episcopalian 48, 52, 74, 81, 86, 102, 114, 148, 239
Anglo-Dutch War
  First (1664) 84
  Second (1665-1667) 85
  Third (1673-1674) 85
Anthony, Susan B. 263
Anti-Federalists 157, 172
Appalachian Mountains 48, 98, 107, 114, 157, 193, 194, 232

Index 547

Argall, Samuel 46
Aristotle 4, 144, 417
Arnold, Benedict 116, 117, 118, 122, 126, 127, 132, 137, 181
  1775-1776 - Arnold fails to gain Canada 118
  1777-10 - Arnold leads the charge at Saratoga 132
  1780-07 - Secretely switches from Patriot to British command 127
  1780-09 - Nearly caught trying to turn West Point over to the British 127
  1781 - Leads British attacks in Northern Virginia 127
Arthur, Chester A. 352, 353, 378
Articles of Confederation 121, 122, 129, 142, 158, 201
Asbury, Bishop (Superintendent) Francis 103
Asuza Street Revival 433, 434
Atheist/Atheism 405, 408
Atheist/Atheists/Atheism 97
Athens, Ancient city of 1, 144, 145, 146, 168, 170
Austin, Stephen 249

B

Babcock, Orville E.
  Grant's corrupt personal secretary 328
Bacon, Francis 391
Bacon, Nathaniel
  1676 - Bacon's rebellion in Virginia 49
Baird, Mary Elizabeth 374
Baltimore and Ohio Railroad
  1828 - First section of rails completed 231
  1852 - Reaches to the Ohio River 231
Bank of the United States (BUS) 209, 212, 225, 228, 229, 252
Baptist/Baptists 64, 83, 86, 87, 147, 167, 239, 242, 262
Bashaw of Tripoli 192
Bates, Edward
  Lincoln's Attorney General 287
Battle Hymn of the Republic
  1862-02 - Composed by Julia Ward Howe 290
Beauregard, Confederate General P.G.T. 297
Benz, Karl Friedrich 361
Berkeley, Lord John 49
  1665 - Berkeley (brother of William) received proprietorship of West Jersey 85
  1764 - Berkeley sells his West Jersey proprietorship of a group of Quaker leaders (including William Penn) 86
Berkeley, Sir William 47, 48, 49, 50, 77, 85
  1642-1652 and 1660-1677 - Governor of the Virginia Colony 47
  1663 - Named co-proprietor of the new Carolina Colony 77
Berlin conferences (1878 and 1884-1885) 440
Biblical inerrancy 376, 431, 433, 486
Bill of Rights (American)
  First Amendment 18, 165
Bill of Rights - English (1689) 90
Bingham, George 238
Bison/Buffalo herds 335, 336
Black Hawk, Chief of Sauk and Fox Indians 227
Blaine, James 353, 378
Bland-Allison Act (1878) 355
Bloomer, Amelia 263
Bonus Bill of 1817 209
Boone, Daniel 114
Booth, John Wilkes
  1865-04 - Kills Lincoln 317
Boston Massacre (1770) 114
Boston Tea Party (1773) 115
Boxer Rebellion (1898-1901) 449
Bradford, William 54
Brainerd, David 104
Briggs, Charles 433
Brooks, Preston - South Carolina Representative
  1856 - Nearly canes to death Massachusetts Senator Charles Sumner 280
Brown, John
  1856-05 ('Pottawatomie Massacre') - Border Ruffians attack his home in Osawatomie, Kansas, killing two sons and some neighbors 281
  1859-10 Brown's unsuccesful attempt at Harpers Ferry to spark slave revolt 284
Bryan, William Jennings
  1860-1881 - Early years and schooling 373
  1881-1884 - Law school and marriage 374
  1891-1895 - Served in Congress (Nebraska Representative) 374
  1894 - Loss in Senate race sends him on a lecture tour attacking the $

gold standard 374
1896 - Democratic Party presidential candidate 358, 374
1898 - Opposed to the imperialism of the Spanish-American War 375
1900 - Democratic Party presidential candidate 360, 375
1908 - Democratic Party presidential candidate 376
1913-1915 - Wilson's Secretary of State 376
1925 - Defends Christian world-view at the 'Scopes Monkey Trial' 485
Buchanan, James 253, 260, 281, 282, 285, 292, 332
   1857-1861 - U.S. President 281
Buda, Mario (Galleanist) 482
Burgoyne, General John 132
Burke, Edmund 397
Burnside, Union General Ambrose 302, 309
Burr, Aaron 195, 199
Bushnell, Horace 247
Bustamante, Anastasio 249
Butler, Edward 361
Butler, South Carolina Senator Andrew 280
Byrd, William II 98, 99, 100

C

Caldwell, James 128
Calhoun, John C. 223, 251, 264, 271, 273
   1810s - A young Republican 'War Hawk" 202
   1817 - Secretary of War Calhoun orders Jackson to take action against Seminole raids 213
   1829-1833 - Jackson's Vice President 221
   1837-1845 - Insistent that Texas be admitted to the Union as a slave state 223
   1850 - Dies - while opposing Abolitionism - and even Clay's 'Compromise of 1850' 275
California Gold Rush
   1848 - Gold discovered at Sutter's Mill 260
   1849 - 'Forty-Niners' rush to California 260
   1855 - 300,000 Americans now in California 260
Calverts (Lords Baltimore) 73, 74
   Cecil (Son) 74, 75
   George (Father) 74

Calvinist/Calvinists/Calvinism 35, 36, 37, 41, 53, 69, 75, 78, 83, 84, 89, 102, 235, 239, 245, 247
   Dutch Reformed 36, 83, 101, 167, 245, 246
   German Reformed 36, 167
   Huguenots 36, 37, 88, 89
   Presbyterians 36, 75, 78, 147, 167, 239, 242, 245, 262
   Puritans 7, 12, 14, 15, 16, 17, 36, 38, 39, 48, 53, 56, 57, 58, 59, 60, 61, 63, 68, 69, 74, 75, 78, 88, 91, 92, 95, 96, 167, 170, 230, 232, 246, 332
   Separatists 36, 53, 54, 91
Calvin, John 35, 38
   Institutes of the Christian Religion 35
Camp meetings 242
Canaanites 219
Capitalist/Capitalists/Capitalism 341, 370, 395, 407, 408, 410, 411, 412, 475, 525
Carnegie, Andrew 343, 344, 346, 347, 349, 447, 540
Carroll, Charles 129
Carroll, Daniel 129
Carroll, Father John, S.J. (Jesuit) 129
Carson, Kit 330, 331
Carteret, George 77, 85
Cass, Lewis 265
Castro, Fidel 420
Catherine de Médicis, Queen of France 36
Catholic/Catholics/Catholicism 10, 27, 28, 33, 36, 37, 38, 39, 51, 53, 56, 74, 75, 76, 77, 78, 81, 83, 89, 91, 107, 108, 114, 129, 130, 147, 148, 249
Cattleman versus farmer 333
Charismatic Movement 434
Charlemagne 29
Charles II, King of England and Scotland 48, 75, 76, 77, 79, 82, 84, 87, 92
Charles I, King of England and Scotland 39, 48, 56, 57, 75, 76
Charles V, Holy Roman Emperor and King of Spain 33, 34, 38, 39
Chase, Salmon P. 287
   1861 - Former Ohio Governor; served as Lincoln's Secretary of the Treasury 287
   1864-12 - Lincoln appoints Chase Chief Justice of the Supreme Court ... to remove a constant annoyance 287

Index

Chauncy, Charles 104
Checks and Balances 169
Christendom/Imperial Christianity 24, 26
Christian 'Awakenings' 432
Christian colleges 246
Christian Realism 170
Church of England 15, 39, 47, 48, 51, 53, 64, 103, 104, 128, 147, 201, 239
Circuit riders (Methodist) 103, 241, 242
'Citizen'Genet, French Ambassador 183
Civil War (1861-1865)
  1861-00 The war strategies of both North and South 294
  1861-04-05 - Southern States secede from the Union 292
  1861-04 - Southerners fire on Fort Sumter (Charleston) - officially starting the war 292
  1861-06 - 1st Battle of Manassas / Bull Run 296
    McDowell v. Beauregard and Johnston 296
  1861-08 - Battle of Wilson's Creek (Missouri) 298
  1861-11 - Battle of Belmont 298
  1861-11 Mason-Slidell or Trent Affair 299
  1862-03 - Hampton Roads ... or the 'Battle of the Ironclads'
    Virginia (or Merrimac) versus Monitor 299
  1862-04 - Farragut captures New Orleans 300
  1862-05-07 - McClellan's Peninsula Campaign and the Seven Days Battles
    McClellan v. Johnston, then Lee 300
  1862-08 - 2nd Battle of Manassas / Bull Run
    Pope v. Lee 301
  1862-09a - Jackson captures 12,000 Union troops at Harpers Ferry 302
  1862-09b - Battle of Antietam / Sharpsburg 302
  1862-09 - Lincoln issues the Emancipation Proclamation
    Frees slaves in those states in rebellion against the Union 302
  1862-11 - Lincoln replaces McClellan with Burnside 302
  1862-12 - Burnside fails to take Fredericksburg 303
  1862-12 - Grant begins his campaign against Vicksburg 300
  1863-01 - Burnside fails at 2nd attempt at Fredericksburg
    Lincoln replaces Burnsde with 'Fighting Joe' Hooker 304
  1863-05 - Grant brings town of Jackson (Mississippi) to surrender 307
  1863-05 - Vallandigham arrested for leading 'Copperheads' to call for Northerners to support the Confederate agenda 305
  1863-07 - Battle of Gettysburg
    General Meade (replacing Hooker) v. Lee; Union wins ... but Meade does not pursue a defeated Lee 306
  1863-07 - Grant brings Vicksburg to defeat 307
  1863-07 - New York City anti-draft riots by Irish immigrants 305
  1863-11 - Battle of Chattanooga
    Confederation position at this strategic position crushed 308
  1864-05-09 - Sherman's March on Atlanta 310
  1864-07 - Grant's siege of Petersburg (Virginia) begins 310
  1864-08-10 Shenandoah Valley Campaign
    Sheridan v. Early; Union victorious 312
  1864-08 - Battle of Mobile Bay
    Farragut order advance of fleet despite 'torpidoes' (mines) 311
  1864-09 - Hood pulls out of Atlanta; Sherman's troops take control; Atlanta burns (November) 311
  1864-11-12 - Sherman's 'March to the Sea' from Atlanta to Savannah 313
  1865-04a - Lincoln's 2nd Inaugural Address
    Calls on the nation to live by God's judgment - not man's 314
  1865-04b - Fall of Petersburg and Richmond 316
  1865-04c - Lee surrenders to Grant at Appomattox 317
  1865-04d - Lincoln is assassinated 317
Clarendon Code 79
Clark, William 194
Clay, Henry 252, 253, 258, 264, 265, 270, 271, 272, 275, 276
  1806-1852 - U.S. Senator from Kentucky during different periods

252
   1810's - A young Repubican Party 'War Hawk' 202
   1811-1825 - Member of House of Representatives off and on during this period 202
   1820 - Authorizes the 'Missouri Compromise' legislation 214
   1824 - Throws support of House of Representatives behind J.Q. Adams for President 214
   1825-1829 - Secretary of State under J.Q. Adams 216
   1840s (early) - Clay and President Tyler battle over the BUS 252
   1850 - Exhausted Clay has Douglas run his Compromise proposal through Congress 273
Clemens, Samuel (Mark Twain) 447
Cleveland, Grover 345, 353, 354, 355, 356, 357, 358, 374, 378, 447
Clinton, British General Henry 5, 133, 134, 136, 137, 138, 231
Coke, Bishop Thomas 103
Coker, Daniel 242
Cole, Thomas 238
College of New Jersey (Princeton University) 105, 128, 247
Columbus, Christopher 39
Compromise of 1850 275, 276
   California a 'free soil' state; other new states given free choice; South promised return of all fugitive slaves 270
   Clay offers the 'Compromise' 270
   Followed up by the 150 Fugutive Slave Act 270
   Weakened Calhoun opposes Clay's 'Compromise' 271
Comstock Lode (Nevada Gold) 332
Congregationalist/Congregationalists 102, 128, 146, 233, 234, 239, 245, 246
Congressional elections of 1854
   Democratic Party loses heavily in the North; 6 parties now competing in Congress 279
   Republican Party (new) soon suceeds in absorbing the other Northern parties (including Whigs) 280
Conkling, 'Boss' Roscoe 352, 353
Constitution/Constitutional Convention (summer 1787)
   Comparing American and French efforts at Republic-building 155
   Connecticut Compromise 159
   Example of Ancient Athens 144

Example of Ancient Israel 146
Example of Ancient Rome 144
Framers acknowledge the role of religion in shaping the Constitution 154
Framers' original intentions 140
Franklin answering - "A Republic - if you can keep it" 139
Franklin's call for daily prayer 150
"In God We Trust" 169
Madison records discussions 150
Mechanical system of 'checks and balances' 169
President - Duties and Powers 161
Ratification - 1787-1788 171
Rule of Law rather than Rule of Human Will 163
Supreme Court - Duties and Powers 162
The people's 'Divine Rights' 166
The strong Christian component in the discussions 146
The Ten Amendments (Bill of Rights) 164
Virginia Plan introduced by Madison 158
Continental Congress (First)
   1774-09-10 Meet at Carpenter's Hall - Philadelphia 115
Continental Congress (Second) 117, 119, 120, 121, 122, 125, 126, 129, 142, 153, 159, 160, 176, 180, 181, 187, 201, 213, 220
   1775-05 - Formed in Philadelphia after events in Lexington and Concord 117
Coolidge, Calvin
   1872-1923 Early life and career 491
   1923-1929 - U.S. President 492
Cooper, Anthony Ashley, Earl of Shaftesbury 77, 78, 79, 80, 81, 238
Cooper, James Fenimore 238
Copperheads - Vallandigham's pro-Confederacy Northerners 305
Cornwallis, British General Charles 134, 136, 137, 138, 181
Coughlin, Father Charles E. 525
Covenant 7, 8, 14, 16, 17, 18, 19, 54, 91, 92, 105, 170, 262
   Moses explains the Covenant to Israel 170
   Winthrop explains the Covenant to the Massachusetts Puritans 16
Covenant Society/Nation 19, 57
Coxey, Jacob 358
Crawford, William 216

Index 551

Cromwell, Oliver 'Lord Protector' of English Commonwealth 75, 76, 78, 86

D

Darwin, Charles 402, 403, 404, 406, 408, 436, 447, 483
Darwin, Erasmus 403
Darwinist/Darwinism 340, 341, 376, 377, 389, 404, 405, 407, 409, 426, 436, 485, 507
Davenport, James 104
Davies, Samuel 104
Davis, Jefferson
  1861-1865 - President of the Southern Confederacy 296
Dawes Severalty Act (1887)
  Restricts Indians to particular reservations 338
Debs, Eugene 358
Declaration of Independence 119, 121, 129, 141, 153, 167, 181, 250
Deist/Deists/Deism 97, 151, 233, 234
De La Warr (Delaware), Lord Thomas 44
Democracy 415, 416, 426, 443
Democratic Idealism 420, 427
Depression
  1920 - Onset of the 1920s Rural Depression 478
  1930s 'Dust Bowl' only makes matters much worse 521
  1933-1937 - FDR's 'New Deal' attempts to revive the deonomy with government projects 514
  1937-1941 - The U.S. economy slides back into the Depression 521
  1941-1945 - World war Two economy ends the Depression finally 521
Descartes, René 37, 391
Deus vult ("God wills it") 167
Dewey, John 427, 428, 447, 448, 523
Dewey, Thomas
  N.Y. Special Prosecutor wins 72 of 73 cases against mobsters 523
Dialectic 401, 406, 408, 411
Dingley Tariff (1897) 359
Divine Rights 96, 146, 167
Dix, Dorthea 263
Douglass, Frederick 264
Drake, Sir Francis 42
Dred Scott Case (1857) 282
'Dust Bowl' in the Mid-West - 1930s 521
Dutch West Indies Company 84
Dwight, Timothy 234

E

Economic Panic of 1819-1821 210
Economic Panic of 1837-1841 228, 229
Economic Panic of 1857-1859 283
Economic Panic of 1873-1877 326
Economic Panic of 1893 344, 356, 357, 370, 374
Economic Panic of 1907 381, 384
Edison, Thomas Alva 350, 351, 362
Edwards, Jonathan 101, 102, 103, 104, 105, 534
Eisenhower, Dwight D. 508
Elizabeth I, Queen of England 38, 53
Ellen G. White 243
Ely, Richard 434
Emancipation Proclamation (September 22, 1862) 302, 320
Emerson, Ralph Waldo 236, 237
  Background and personal character 236
Empiricism 389, 394, 395, 396
Empresario 249
Endecott, John 57
English Civil War (1642-1649) 75
'Enlightened' Christianity
  Matthew Tindal - Christianity as Old as the Creation (1731) 98
Enlightenment 390, 391, 392, 394, 398
Enlightenment/Human Enlightenment 37, 80, 89, 95, 139, 182, 199, 201, 233
Episcopal/Episcopalian 10, 25, 103, 239, 241, 242
Episcopos (Greek: 'bishop') 25
'Era of Good Feeling' 210, 212
Erie Canal
  1825 - Completed between Albany and Lake Erie 231
Exclusion Bill against the Stuarts (1679) 81

F

Farragut, Captain David 300
Federal Council of Churches 423
Federalists 157, 172, 174, 180, 183, 184, 185, 189, 190, 191, 195, 196, 198, 199, 202, 203, 208, 212, 249, 254, 255
Ferdinand of Aragon and Isabella of Castile 39
Feudal system 20, 21, 29, 30, 31, 32, 35, 36, 47, 51, 62, 73, 98, 224, 290, 294
  Lords and vassals 30
Fillmore, Millard 276, 281, 282

1849-1850 - Vice President under
    Zachary Taylor 265
1850-07 - Becomes President upon
    Taylor's death 272
1850-1853 - U.S. President 276
1856 - Know-Nothing candidate
    for Presidency; not elected
    (Northern vote split) 281
Finney, Charles Grandison 242
Fisk, James 342, 343
Fitzgerald, F. Scott 488
Ford, Henry 351, 361, 362, 363, 364,
    388
Forrest, Confederate General Nathan
    Bedford
    Heads KKK after the war 322
Fort Christina' (Wilmington) 84
Founding Fathers 7, 14, 18, 61, 259,
    286
Fourteenth Amendment (1868)
    'Equal protection' of all under the
    law; no removal of rights except
    under 'due process' 320
Fox, George 86
Franklin, Benjamin
    1733 - Franklin begins publication of
        Poor Richard's Almanack 152
    1750s-mid-1770s - Franklin sent
        often to London on behalf of
        Pennsylvania 152
    1753-1755 - Franklin establishes
        a 'New Model' College in
        Philadelphia 152
    1776-1785 - Franklin sent to Paris on
        behalf of the new United States
        153
    1783 - Franklin, Adams and Jay
        negotiate peace with Britain in
        Paris 138
    Franklin publishes 40 of the sermons
        of Whitefield 105
    Franklin's background and personal
        character 152
Franz Ferdinand, Austrian Archduke
    455
Frederick'the Great of Prussia 109
Freedman/Freedmen 320, 321
Free Soil/Free Soilers 258, 265, 270,
    271, 273, 278, 285
Free Soil Party 265
Frémont, General John C. 255, 256,
    281, 282
    1845 - Polk orders Frémont to
        'explore' Northern California and
        Oregon 255
    1846 - Frémont invites California's
        'Bear Flag Revolt' against Mexico
        256
    1854 - 1st Republican Party candidate
        for Presidency; not elected
        (Northern vote split) 281
French and Indian War/Seven Years'
    War (1754 1763) 110, 111
    1754 - Washington builds Fort
        Necessity (1754) 110
    1755 - Massive deportation of French
        Acadians begins 110
    1757 - Huron Indians slaughter
        surrendered English at Fort
        William Henry 110
    1759 - Quebec falls to the English
        111
    1760 - The war comes to an end in
        North America 111
French Reign of Terror (1793-1794)
    156, 182, 183
French Revolution 390, 395, 396, 397,
    399, 400, 435
Freud, Sigmund 489
Freylinghuysen, Theodore 101
Frick, Henry Clay 344
Fugitive Slave Act of 1850 273, 274,
    275, 276
Fundamentalist/Fundamentalism 528

G

Gadsden Purchase (1853) 277
Gallatin, Albert 191
Garfield, James A. 352, 353
Garrison, William Lloyd 263
Gates, Patriot General Horatio 122,
    126, 127, 132, 136
Generations
    1st Generation 2, 4, 6, 8
    2nd Generation 3, 4
    3rd Generation 4, 6, 8
    4th (and final) Generation 5, 8
George II, British King 91, 100, 106,
    112
George III, British King 111, 112, 114,
    138, 148, 157, 166, 167
George I of Brunswick Lüneburg/British
    King 91, 106
Geronimo - and his Apache Raiders 331
Gilded Age 340
Gladden, Washington 434
Glorious Revolution (1688-1689) 89
God/'Providence' 2, 7, 8, 10, 12, 13,
    14, 15, 16, 17, 18, 19, 21, 22,
    23, 25, 26, 27, 34, 35, 37, 51,
    53, 54, 56, 57, 58, 59, 60, 61,
    62, 64, 66, 67, 68, 86, 92, 94,
    95, 96, 97, 101, 103, 104, 105,

Index 553

118, 122, 123, 124, 125, 126, 131, 138, 146, 147, 148, 149, 150, 151, 153, 154, 155, 157, 159, 167, 168, 169, 170, 171, 186, 198, 217, 219, 225, 233, 234, 235, 237, 238, 240, 241, 242, 244, 245, 247, 248, 262, 264, 265, 272, 285, 289, 290, 291, 295, 315, 316, 336
Goethe, Johann Wolfgang von 400, 401
Gospel 10, 239
Gould, Jay 342, 343, 378
Grand Model, designed for the Carolina Colony by John Locke 79, 80, 95
Grant, Ulysses S. 298
  1861-11 - Grant's resolve at the Battle of Belmont impresses Lincoln 298
  1863-10 - Grant assigned command over all Western and Central Union armies
  Grant takes command at Chattanooga 308
  1864-03 - Grant promoted to head of all Union armies 309
  1864-05 - Grant engages Lee relentlessly in a number of battles in Virginia 309
  1864-07 to 1865-03 - Grant engaged in the siege of Petersburg 310
  1865-04 - Petersburg and Richmond fall to Grant ... and Lee surrenders at Appomattox 316
  1867 - Radicals prevent Johnson from replacing Stanton with Grant as Secretary of War 320
  1869-1877 - U.S. President 323
  1873-1877 - Economic Panic 326
  National political-economic scandals
    Boss Tweed of Tammany Hall 325
    Crédit Mobilier scandal 324
    Fisk-Gould gold scandal 323
    Grant's corrupt personal secretary Babcock 328
    'Whiskey Ring' owing $ millions in taxes 328
Grasse, French Admiral François Joseph Paul de 137
'Great Awakenings' 7, 8
  First 'Great Awakening' 101, 103, 105, 239
    George Whitefield 101, 102, 103, 105
    Jonathan Edwards 101, 102, 103, 104, 105
    'New Light' vs. 'Old Light' Congregationalists 104
    'New Side' vs. 'Old Side' Presbyterians 105
    Theodore Freylinghuysen 101
    William and Gilbert Tennent 102
  Second 'Great Awakening' 103, 238, 244, 246, 248
    Camp meetings 242
    Charles Grandison Finney 242, 243
    Francis Asbury 103, 241
    Methodist circuit riders 103, 241, 242
    Millenialists 239
'Great Migration' of English Puritans to America (c. 1630-1642) 61
'Great Triumvirate'
  John Calhoun, Henry Clay, Daniel Webster 275
Great White Fleet (1907-1909) 452
Greeley, Horace 263, 326
Grimké sisters, Angelina and Sarah 263
Guadalupe Hidalgo Treaty (1848) 259
  U.S. offers Mexico $15 million for land taken from Mexico during the war 258

H

Habsburg Dynasty 1, 33, 34, 36, 38, 39, 41, 83, 107, 109
Halfway Covenant of 1662 91, 92
Hamilton, Alexander 3, 138, 150, 154, 157, 172, 175, 176, 177, 182, 183, 185, 188, 189, 191, 193, 195, 198, 199, 200, 201, 209
  1781 - Hamilton leads American charge at Yorktown 138
  1789-1797 - Washington's Secretary of the Treasury 177
  Hamilton's debt-assumption program 177
  Author of many of the Federalist Papers 172
  Hamilton's background and personal character 175, 176, 177
Hancock, General Winfield Scott 352
Hanna, Mark 359
Harding, Warren G.
  1921-1923 - U.S. President 491
Harrison, Benjamin 355, 356, 357, 378, 382, 383
Harrison, William Henry
  1811 - Defeated Tecumseh's and the 'Prophet's' warriors at the Battle of Tippecanoe 202
  1812 - Commander of America's Northwestern troops 204
  1841-03/04 - U.S. President (only one

month) 252
Harvard College - est. 1636 58
Hawaii 445
  King David Kalakaua 446
  King Kamehamaha II 445
  King Kamehamaha V 446
  Queen Liliuokalani 446
  Sanford Dole 446
  The 'Missionary Party' 445
Hawthorne, Nathaniel 238
Hayes, Rutherford B. 350, 352
  1877-1881 - U.S. President 328
Haymarket Square Riot (1886) 370
Hayne, Robert 224
Hegel, Georg Wilhelm Friedrich 401
Hegelian 406, 407
Henry, Patrick 113, 157, 172
Henry VIII, King of England 32, 36, 38, 39
Henry VII, King of England 32
Herder, Johann Gottfried 400, 401
Historical narrative 8, 11, 12, 13, 14, 23, 25, 233
Hitler, Adolph 420, 473, 521, 525, 529
Hodge, Charles 432
Hood, Confederate General John Bell 311, 313
Hooker, Thomas 68
Hoover, Herbert
  1874-1895 - Early life and schooling 493
  1895-1908 - Mining engineer in California, China, Australia and elsewhere 494
  1908-1914 - global mining consultant 494
  1914-1917 - Heads Belgium relief program 494
  1918-1921 - Heads the American Relief Administration 495
  1929-1933 - U.S. President 496
  1932 Emergency Relief and Construction Act
  Democrats accuse Hoover of practicing 'Socialism' 508
  1932 - Hoover dismisses brutally 'Bonus Army' protesters 508
Hoover, J. Edgar 482
Horseshoe Bend, Battle of (1814) 205, 213
House of Burgesses 46, 52, 99, 180
House of Representatives 159, 160, 161, 168, 195, 216, 222, 251, 254, 264, 275, 276, 285, 317, 320, 327
Houston, Texas General Sam 250
Howe, British General William 132, 133

Howe, Julia Ward
  1862-02 - wrote the Battle Hymn of the Republic 290
Hudson, Henry 82
Hull, General William 203
Hull House 372, 428
Humanist/Humanists/Humanism 8, 63, 94, 151, 165, 233, 234, 235, 237, 238, 336, 368, 373, 425, 427, 428, 443, 471, 527
Humanist Manifesto (1933) 428, 527, 528
Human Reason 8, 10, 37, 38, 233, 265, 390, 399
Hume, David 394, 395, 396, 397, 542
Hundred Years' War (mid-1300s - mid 1400s) 31
Hus, Jan 129
Hussey, Obed
  1833 - invents an improved reaper 232
Hutchinson, Anne 61, 65, 66, 67, 87
Hyde, Edward, Earl of Clarendon 77, 79

I

Imperialism 359, 360, 375, 380, 399, 436, 437, 439, 440, 441, 442, 443, 444
  American 442
    Annexation of Hawaii (1898) 445, 446
    Expansion of the 'Monroe Doctrine' 444
    The Christian mission impetus 442
    The 'opening' of Japan (1853) 444
    The Philippine 'protectorate'
    1916 - Philippine Autonomy Act 449
    The purchase of Alaska (1867) 445
  British 438
    The British East India Company 438, 439
  Dutch 438
  French 439
  Portuguese 436, 437
  Spanish 437
  The Berlin Conferences (1878 & 1884-1885) 440
  The carving up of the Ottoman or Turkish Empire 440
  The 'opening' of Africa 439, 441
Indenture 50
Indian Removal/'Trail of Tears' (1830s)
  1830 - Indian Removal Act 226
  1831 - Choctaw 227
  1832 - Seminole 227

Index

1834 - Creek 227
1837 - Chickasaw 227
1838 - Cherokee 227
Indian Tribes 219, 220
  Apache 257, 330, 331, 335
  Arapaho 330, 337
  Cherokee 205, 217, 226, 227, 246, 337
  Cheyenne 330
  Comanche 249, 257, 331
  Creek 204, 205
  Dakota (or Lakota/Sioux) 330
  Fox 227
  Hopi 335
  Huron 110
  Iroquois 108
  Kiowa 331
  Mohawks 71
  Mohegan 69
  Narragansett 64, 69, 219
  Natick 69
  Navajo 330, 331, 335
  Pequot 68, 69
  Potawatomi 204
  Powhatan 44, 45, 46
  Sauk 227
  Seminole 213
  Shawnee 202, 203
  Wampanoag 55
Indian Wars 329
  1862 - New Ulm/Hutchinson (Minnesota) massacres of German immigrants by Dakota (or Sioux) warriors 330
  1864-11 - Battle of Adobe Walls Carson v. Kiowas and Comanches 331
  1864-11 - U.S. troop massacre of Cheyenne and Arapaho families at Sand Creek 330
  1887 - Dawes Severalty Act restricts Indians to particular reservations 338
  1890a - Ghost Dance craze incites Indian rebellion under Sitting Bull 338
  1890b - Battle of Wounded Knee 338
  Chief Sitting Bull - last of the Indian leaders 337, 338, 339
  Geronimo and his Apache Raiders 331
  Kit Carson - Indian fighter 330, 331
Institutes of the Christian Religion - by John Calvin 35
Insull, Samuel 523
Isolationism - American 498

J

Jackson, Andrew 205, 208, 213, 216, 217, 220, 221, 222, 223, 225, 226, 227, 228, 229, 230, 254, 264
  1814 - Jackson's troops defeat the Red Stick Indians at Horseshhoe Bend 205
  1818 - Jackson's troops defeat the Seminole Indians in Florida 213
  1824 - Jackson gains the largest popular vote by loses the Presidential election to Adams 216
  1828 - Jackson finally elected President 220
  1829-1837 - U.S. President 221
  1832 - Jackson refuses to bow to Supreme Court decision on Indian Removal 227
  1833 - Jackson undercuts the BUS 225
Jackson, Confederate General Thomas
  1861-07 - Jackson stands like a 'Stone Wall' at the Battle of Bull Run 297
  1862-09 - Jackson captures 12,000 Union troops at Harpers Ferry just prior to the Battle at Antietam 302
  1863-05 - Jackson mistakenly shot by one of his own men at Chancellorsville 306
Jackson, Confederate General Thomas 'Stonewall' 297
Jacksonian Democrats 220, 228, 248
James II, Duke of York/King of England 74, 81, 82, 84, 89, 95, 96, 147
James I, King of England and Scotland 39, 53, 56
Jamestown 20, 43, 44, 45, 46, 47, 49, 60, 98
Jay, John 138, 172, 184
  1783 - Negotiated the Treaty of Paris alongside Franklin and Adams 138
  1787-1789 - Author of some of the Federalist Papers 172
  1789-1795 - First Chief Justice of the Supreme Court 184
  1794 - Negotiated 'Jay Treaty' with Britain 183
Jay's Treaty (1794) 183
Jeffersonian Republicans 190, 196, 199, 203, 221
Jefferson, Thomas 5, 120, 121, 129,

153, 156, 164, 165, 168, 180, 181, 182, 183, 184, 185, 187, 188, 189, 190, 191, 192, 193, 194, 195, 198, 199, 200, 201, 202, 203, 208, 209, 210, 221, 224, 234, 235, 261, 277, 288, 291, 296, 392, 397, 426
1776 - Drafts the Declaration of Independence 120
1779-1781 - Virginia's governor 181
1781 - Notes on the State of Virginia 168
1785-1789 - Minister (Ambassador) to France 156, 181
1789-1793 - Washington's Secretary of State) 180
1793 - Jefferson steps down as Secretary of State over opposition to Hamilton and Washington 183
1793 - Letter to William Short supporting the French Reign of Terror 182
1801-1809 - U.S. President 191
1803 - Jefferson authorizes Livingston and Monroe to negotiate the purchase of New Orleans 193
Jefferson's background and personal character 180, 181, 182, 183
Jesuit priests 129
Jesus Christ 368, 389, 402, 405, 430, 431, 442, 529
Jesus/Christ 10, 14, 16, 22, 23, 24, 25, 26, 27, 38, 66, 67, 86, 97, 98, 101, 104, 219, 233, 235, 237, 239, 240, 243, 244, 245, 260, 262
Jew/Jews/Jewish/Judaism 11, 12, 22, 26, 77, 83, 88, 151, 244
Johnson, Andrew
  1864-11 - Elected as Lincoln's Vice President 312
  1865-1869 - U.S. President 319
  1868-03-35 - Impeached (House) and almost convicted (Senate) 320
Judiciary Act of 1801 190

K

Kansas Crisis ('Bleeding Kansas')
  1854 - Kansas-Nebraska Act - Kansans themselves to vote to determine status on slavery 278
  1854 - Pro-slavery Kansans ('Border Ruffians') keep Kansas capital at Lecompton 280
  1856-06 Border Ruffians attack home of John Brown at Osawatomie ('Pottawatomie Massacre') 281
  1856 - Civil War already started in Kansas 281
Kant, Immanuel 395, 396, 400
Kellogg Briand Pact (1928) 499
Kentucky Question (1791-1792)
  Problem of admitting a new slave state 180
Kieft, Willem 83
King George's War/War of Austrian Succession (1744-1748) 109
  Treaty of Aix la Chapelle 109
King Philip's (Metacom's) War (1675-1676) 70
Knights of Labor 370
Ku Klux Klan 322, 327
  Created in 1866; headed by Nathan Bedford Forrest 322

L

Lafayette, French General Gilbert du Moitierm Marquis de 137
Lamarck, Jean-Baptiste 403, 404
'Lame duck' 190
Laplace, Pierre Simon de 398
Laud, English Archbishop William 56
League of Nations 386, 469, 472, 473, 496, 497, 498
Lee, Confederate General Robert E. 296, 301, 302, 306, 307, 309, 310, 312, 313, 316, 317
Lee, Patriot General Charles 126, 134
Leibniz, Gottfried Wilhelm 392, 396, 541
Leisler, Jacob 90
Lenin, Vladimir Ilyich Ulyanov 410, 411, 412, 413, 420, 422, 462, 469, 475, 489, 503
  'Vanguard of the Industrial Proletariat' 411, 412, 413, 414
Lewis and Clark Expedition (1804-1806) 194
Lewis, Meriwether 194
Liberal/Liberalism 425, 426, 427, 428, 431, 486, 526, 528, 529, 543
Lincoln, Abraham 3, 78, 136, 227, 285, 286, 287, 288, 289, 290, 291, 292, 293, 295, 296, 298, 300, 301, 302, 303, 304, 305, 306, 307, 308, 309, 312, 313, 314, 316, 317, 318, 319, 320, 321, 323, 330
  1830s - rose out of poverty by training himself in the law 285
  1832 - served as a captain in the

Index 557

Black Hawk War 285
1834-1836 - Served as a Whig in the Illinois House of Representatives 285
1847-1849 - Illinois Whig member of the U.S. House of Representatives 285
1858-08-10 - The Lincoln-Douglas debates 286
1860-02 - The Cooper Union speech 286
1860-05 - Nominated for President by the new Republican Party 287
1861-1865 - U.S. President 287
1861 - A 'Team of Rivals' appointed to his Cabinet 287
1861 - Works out war strategy with General Winfield Scott 288
1862-09 - Issues the Emancipation Proclamation 302
1864-11 - Lincoln elected to a 2nd term 312
1865-03 - 2nd Inaugural Address Calling on the nation to live by God's judgments - not man's 314
1865-04 - Lincoln is assassinated 317
Background and personal character 285, 286, 287, 288, 289
Livingston, Robert 193
Locarno Agreement (1925) 499
Locke, John 79, 80, 95, 96, 120, 391, 392, 403
   An Essay Concerning Human Understanding (1690) 95
   Two Treatises of Government 95
Lodge, Henry Cabot 380
Log College (Princeton Seminary) 105
Longstreet, Confederate General James 308, 309
Long, the 'Kingfish' Louisiana Governor Huey 525
Longworth, Alice Roosevelt 378
'Lost Generation' 488
   Ernest Hemingway 488
   F. Scott Fitzgerald 488
Louisbourg, French Canadian fortress 109, 110
Louisiana Purchase (1803) 193
Louis XIV, King of France 85, 89, 90, 107, 166
Lovejoy, Elijah Parish 263
Lusitania 463
Lutheran/Lutherans 83, 84, 129, 235, 306
Luther, Martin 33, 34, 35

M

MacArthur, General Douglas 508
Machen, J. Gresham 528
Madison, James 150, 155, 157, 158, 172, 183, 189, 200, 201, 202, 203, 206, 208, 209, 210, 221, 224, 291
   1787-1788 - Author of many of the Federalist Papers 172
   1801-1809 - Secretary of State under Jefferson 202
   1809-1817 - U.S. President 200
   Background and personal character 200, 201, 202
Mahan, Admiral Alfred Thayer 446
Malthus, Robert 403, 404, 405, 542
Manifest Destiny 248, 249
Mao Tse-tung (Zedong) 420
Maria Theresa of Habsburg 109
Marion, Francis ('Swamp Fox') 136
Marshall, George C. 543
Marshall, John 190, 196, 197, 227
Marxism/Communism 406, 408, 409, 410, 412, 413, 414, 462, 469, 470, 472, 475, 481, 489, 495, 503, 525, 526
Marx, Karl 405, 406, 407, 408, 409, 410, 411, 412, 422
Mary II, Queen of England/co-regent with William III 90
Mary, Mother of Jesus 24, 25
Mason, James 299
Massachusetts Bay Colony
   General Court 62, 69
   Massachusetts Bay Company 57, 72
Massasoit 55, 56, 70
Mayflower Compact 54
Mayhew, Jonathan 113
McClellan, Union General George 300
McCormick, Cyrus
   1831 - McCormick demonstrates new reaper 232
McKinley Tariff 356, 357, 359
McKinley, William 356, 357, 359, 360, 374, 375, 380, 382, 383, 414, 446, 447
   'Full Dinner Pail' - 1900 electoral theme 375
Metacom ('King Philip') 70, 71
Methodist/Methodists/Wesleyan 102, 103, 147, 239, 241, 242, 245, 246, 247, 290
Mexican-American War (1846-1848)
   1845 - President Polk sends troops under Taylor to Texas and troops under Frémont to California 255
   1845 - Texas admitted to the Union as 28th state - over Whig opposition

(December) 253
1846-05 - Mexico declares war against the U.S. 255
1846-06 - Frémont gets California to join the revolt against Mexico 256
1846-09 - Taylor negotiates a 'win' against the Mexicans at Monterey 256
1847-01 - California fully independent 256
1847-03 - Commodore Perry and General Scott capture Veracruz on the Gulf coast 257
1847-09 - Scott's troops sieze Mexico City 257
1848 - Negotiations at Guadalupe Hidalgo produce Treaty - offering $15 million for land taken from Mexico 258
'Midnight' judicial appointments 190
Millennialist/Millennialists/Millennialiism 239
Millennium/Millennialist/Millennialism 368, 408
  Postmillennial
    Christ will come only after all the world has been converted 368
  Premillennial
    A 'Great Tribulation' will take place prior to the coming of Christ 368
Millerites 244
  1833 - William Miller predicts 'second coming' within ten years 243
  1844 - Jesus fails to show up on schedule 243
Missouri Compromise (1820) 213
Mitchell , General Billy (Court-martial - 1925) 500
Model T Ford 361, 362, 363
Mohammad 27
Monck, General George 76, 79
Monroe Doctrine 437, 444
'Monroe Doctrine' (1823) 215, 277
Monroe, James 193, 210, 213, 215, 221, 263, 277
  1803 - Monroe helps negotiate the Louisiana Purchase 193
  1817-1825 - U.S. President 210
  1823 - Monroe announces the 'Monroe Doctrine' 215
Montcalm, French General Louis Joseph de 110, 111
Montgomery, Richard 118
Moravian/Moravians 103, 129, 130
Morgan, John Pierpont (J.P.) 344, 345, 347, 350, 351, 358, 382, 384, 482
Mormon/Mormons/Mormonism 244, 245, 332
  1827 - Smith's vision of a visit by the angel Moroni 244
  1830s - Mormons migrating to Missouri 332
  1838 - Mormons driven from Missoouri to Illinois 245
  1844-06 - Smith and his brother killed by an angry mob 245
  1847 - Brigham Young leads Mormons to Utah Territory 245
  1857-1858 - 'Mormon War/Rebellion' - U.S. troops v Mormons over polygamy 332
  1857 - Mountain Meadows massacre of 'Gentile' families by Mormons 332
Moroccan crisis
  First Moroccan Crisis (1905-1906) 453
  Second Moroccan Crisis (1911) 454
Morse, Samuel 349
Mott, Lucretia 263
Müntzer, Thomas 34
Mussolini, Benito 502, 503, 521, 525

N

Napoleon 155, 193, 199, 200, 203, 205, 206, 262, 397, 398, 399, 439, 440, 441
Natural Philosophers/Natural Philosophy (Modern Science) 97
Natural philosophy 37, 95, 96
New Deal 359, 513, 514, 515, 518, 519, 520, 521, 522, 525, 526
New England Confederation 63
New England - Protestant foundations 21
New Harmony (Indiana) Project 235
New Netherland 42, 67, 82, 83, 84, 85
Newton, Isaac 392, 398
New York, James' proprietary colony 84
Niebuhr, H. Richard 529
Nietzsche, Friedrich 404, 405
Nobel Peace Prize 373, 451
North, Prime Minister Frederick Lord North 138
Northwest Territory 213, 220
Nullification, Doctrine of 189, 224

O

Oglethorpe, General James 100
Oldfield, Barney 362

Index 559

'Omnibus' Bill 272, 273
  Various measures lumped together as a single issue 272
Opechancanough, Powhatan chief 46
Oregon Question
  1842 - Dispute arises with Britain over the Western territory 259
  1846 - Oregon Treaty ratified by the U.S. Senate (June) 260
Oregon Trail 260
Ostend Manifesto (1854)
  Meeting of American Southerners in Belgium to plan the takeover of Cuba 277
O'Sullivan, John L. 248
Owen, Robert
  'New Harmony' communitarian project in Indiana 235

P

Paine, Thomas 131
Panama Canal 383, 451, 452
Patrick of Ireland 28
Patriots (American - 1770s-1780s) 74, 116, 125, 128, 135, 136, 137, 142, 535
Patton, General George S. 508
Peabody, Endicott 511
Peace of Utrecht (1713) 107
Pearl Harbor 501
Penn, William 86, 87, 88, 89, 152, 534
Pentecostal/Pentecostalism 434
  Asuza Street Revival 433
Pequot War (1636) 69
Perfectionism 239, 240
Perry, Commodore Oliver Hazzard 205
Philip II, King of Spain 36, 38, 39, 147
Philip II of Macedon 4
Pierce, Franklin
  1853-1857 - U.S. President 276
Pike, Zebulon 194, 204
Pilgrim Separatists / Plymouth Plantation 20, 43, 53, 54, 55, 56, 57, 60, 63, 64, 70, 71, 72, 73, 533
  1606-1620 - Pilgrims in Leiden 53
  1620-11 - Arrive at Cape Cod 54
  1620-11 - Mayflower Compact 54
  1621 - 50 Pilgrims celebrate a Thanksgiving feast to God with 90 Wampanoag Indians 55
Pinckney, Henry 225
Platt, 'Boss' Thomas 360, 378
Pocahontas 45
Poe, Edgar Allan 238
Polk, James
  1845-1849 - U.S. President 253
Pope - Roman Catholic 29
  Leo X 34
Pope, Union General John 301
Praying Indians 69
Presbyterian/Presbyterians 12, 13, 36, 75, 78, 81, 102, 104, 105, 123, 128, 129, 147, 148, 167, 201, 239, 242, 245, 246, 262, 263, 288
Privy Council 79
Progressive Party ('Bullmoose Party') 1912 385
Progressivist/Progressivists/Progressivism 80, 366, 367, 368, 369, 370, 371, 372, 373, 376, 377, 378, 382, 387, 388, 418, 420, 424, 425, 488, 489, 498
Prohibition 480, 481, 523
Protestant/Protestants/Protestantism 21, 27, 35, 36, 37, 38, 39, 41, 42, 48, 53, 56, 74, 75, 77, 83, 84, 87, 88, 89, 91, 129, 146, 147, 148, 167, 249, 267
Protestant Reformation 27, 37, 38, 83
Providence Colony (Rhode Island) 20, 63, 64, 65, 67, 68, 71, 123, 148, 219, 248
Pure Food and Drug Act (1906) 381
Puritan 368, 413, 417, 443, 491, 492
Puritan Commonwealth (1649-1659) 48, 76, 78
Puritan/Puritans/Puritanism 7, 17, 18, 48, 52, 57, 58, 60, 61, 62, 63, 64, 65, 68, 69, 74, 75, 76, 78, 86, 91, 92, 93, 94, 95, 101, 147, 169, 171, 186, 197, 230, 261
  The 'Great Migration' (ca. 1630-1642) 57, 61

Q

Quaker/Quakers 65, 83, 86, 87, 88, 123, 147, 151, 167, 244
Queen Anne's War/War of Spanish Succession (1701-1713) 107
  Treaty (or 'Peace') of Utrecht (1713) 107, 108

R

Rapp, George 235
Rationalists/Rationalism 392, 394, 395, 396, 397, 398, 400, 431
Rauschenbusch, Walter 434
Realist/Realists/Realism 10, 151
Realpolitik 10

Reconstruction - Post-Civil-War (1865-1877) 323, 326, 327, 329, 537
  1865 - Johnson attempts to continue Lincoln's agenda 319
  1865 - Northern Radicals demand serious remake of Southern society 320
  1866 - Civil Rights Act 320
  1866 - former Confederate General Forrest heads up KKK 322
  1867 - Military Reconstruction Act Places the South under U.S. military command 322
  1867 - Tenure of Office Act Designed to prevent Johnson from assembling his own cabinet 320
  1868-03-05 - Johnson impeached (House) and nearly convicted (Senate) 320
  1868-07 - 14th Amendment 'Equal protection' of all under the law; no removal or rights except under 'due process' 320
  1870s (early) - Rise of the 'Bourbon' or 'Redeemer' Democrats in the South
  Taking away Black civil rights 327
  1877 - Reconstruction ended when miliitary pulled from the South to fight the Indian wars in the West 329
Red Scare 413, 414, 482, 492
Res publica (Latin: 'Republic') 22
Restoration of the Stuart Kings 77, 79
Rise of the American farme 334
Roanoke - The 'Lost Colony' 43
Rochambeau, French General/Count Jean-Baptist Donatiene de Vimeur 137
Rockefeller Foundation 347
Rockefeller, John D. 343, 345, 346, 347, 427
Rolfe, John 44, 45
Romanticism 392, 394, 398, 399, 400, 401
Rome - Republic and Empire 1, 22, 23, 24, 25, 27, 28, 29, 38, 109, 144, 145
Roosevelt, Franklin D.
  1882-1903 - Early years and schooling 511
  1903-1907 - Attends Columbia Law School - but does not finish Marries distant cousin Eleanor in 1905 511
  1911-1913 - New York State Senator in Albany 512
  1913-1920 - Assistant Secretary of the Navy 512
  1920 - runs (unsuccessfully) as Democratic Party Vice-Presidential candidate 512
  1921 - Hit by polio; paralyzed from the waist down 513
  1926 - Purchases Warm Spring, Georgia, spa for polio therapy for himself and others 513
  1928-1932 - New York Governor 513
  1932-11 - FDR is elected President 508, 513
  1933 - Creates numerous government social programs during the 'First 100 Days' as basis for hiis 'New Deal' 513
  1935 - Supreme Court shutting down FDR's programs 520
  1937 - Congress refuses to 'pack' the Supreme Court with new FDR appointees 520
  1937 - US economy slids back into post-New-Deal Depression 521
Roosevelt, Theodore ('Teddy')
  1858-1882 - Early years and schooling: Harvard and Columbia Law School 377
  1882 - Publishes study of War of 1812 and enters New York Republican politics 377
  1884 - His wife and mother die on the same day 378
  1885-1887 - The 'Dakota' cowboy in North Dakota 378
  1888-1894 - Civil Service Commissioner in Washington 378
  1894-1897 - NY City Police Commissioner 378
  1898-06 - Organizes and leads the 'Rough Riders' in the Spanish-American War 380
  1898-11 - Elected New York Governor 380
  1900 - Elected Vice-President under McKinley 380, 454
  1901-1909 - Expands greatly the Federal role in national economic management 381
  1904 - Starts up the Panama Canal project 452
  1905 - Hosts the Peace conference between Russia and Japan 451
  1907-1909 - Send the 'Great White Fleet' sailing around the world ... to announce America's entry into

Index 561

'Big Power' status 452
1908 - Does not run for reelection ... and quickly regrets the decision 383
1912 - Sets up the Progressive ('Bullmoose') Party in an unsuccessful presidential run against his former ally Taft 385
Rothschild bankers of Paris 344, 358
Rousseau, Jean Jacques 391, 392, 393, 394, 396, 415, 416
Rousseau, Jean-Jacques 336
  Civilization has corrupted the human spirit 260
Rousseauian Idealism 336
Royal Absolutism 81
Rump Parliament' 76
Russian Revolution (1917-1922) 414, 464, 470, 503

S

Sacajawea 194
Sacco and Vanzetti trial
  1920-04 - Payroll holdup and killing in Braintree, Mass. 483
  1920-05 - Nicola Sacco and Bertolomeo Vanzetti (Galleanists) arrested 483
  1921 - Sacco and Vanzetti tried and found guilty of murder 483
  1927-08 - Both are executed (electric chair) 483
Salem Witch Trials (1692-1693) 92, 93, 94
Samuel Morse 349
Santa Anna, Antonio Lopez de 250, 251, 257
Scopes 'Monkey Trial' (summer 1925) 483
Scott, General Winfield 227, 257, 295, 296
Second Great Awakening 103, 244, 246, 248, 262, 537
Secular Humanism 165
Secular/Secularist/Secularists/ Secularism 8, 94, 95, 96, 155, 165
Secular/Secularists/Secularism 368, 373, 393, 427, 431, 480, 490, 526, 529
Separatists 36, 53, 54, 91
Seventh Day Adventists
  Ellen G. White - Prophet 243
Seward, William H. 281, 287, 288, 317, 445
  1850 - New York Senator and anti-slavery Seward speaks against Clay's 'Compromise' 272
  1861-1869 - serves Lincoln and Johnson as U.S. Secretary of State 287
  1865-04 - Seward stabbed in same plot that killed Lincoln 317
Shays, Daniel 143
Shay's Rebellion (1786-1787) 143
Sherman Antitrust Act (1890) 346, 356
Sherman, Roger 159
Sherman, Senator John 356
Sherman Silver Purchase Act (1890) 356, 357, 374
Sherman, Union General William Tecumseh 308, 309, 310, 311, 313, 314, 316, 321
  1864-03 - Lincoln turn's Grant's Central and Western Command over to Sherman 308
  1864-05 - Under Grant's orders - Sherman begin his march toward Atlanta from Chattanooga 309
  1864-07 - Hood's Confederate troops pull out of Atlanta afte six weeks of battle with Sherman's troops
  1964-11 - Atlanta burns badly 310
  1864-11-12 - Sherman turns his troops Southeast from Atlanta to Savannah (Sherman's 'March to the Sea') 313
  1865-01-04 - Sherman marches north from Savannah through the Carolinas 313
Silverite/Silverites 358
Sitting Bull, Sioux (or Lakota) Chief 337
Slater, Samuel 197
Slaves/Slavery 50, 51, 69, 71, 75, 83, 98, 99, 104, 108, 120, 130, 138, 159, 160, 168, 171, 180, 181, 183, 192, 198, 204, 205, 213, 214, 223, 224, 228, 230, 240, 241, 242, 248, 249, 251, 254, 257, 258, 259, 261, 262, 263, 264, 265, 266, 267, 268, 269, 270, 271, 272, 273, 274, 275, 276, 279, 280, 281, 282, 283, 284, 285, 286, 287, 288, 289, 291, 294, 295, 298, 302, 303, 304, 305, 312, 315, 317, 318, 319, 321, 322
Slidell, John 299
Smith, Adam 395
Smith, Captain John 44
Smith, Joseph Jr. 244
Social Gospel 434

Socialist/Socialists/Socialism 211, 212, 235, 326
Society for the Propagation of the Gospel 239
Sojourner Truth 263, 264
Spanish-American War (1898) 375, 378, 379, 382, 446, 447, 452
Spanish Armada - defeat in 1588 42, 43, 147
Spanish Flu Epidemic of 1918 471
Spencer, Herbert 404, 542
'Spoils system' 216, 222
Squanto 55
Stalin, Joseph 420, 503, 521, 525
Stamp Act of 1765 113, 152, 186
Standard Oil Company 346
Stanton, Edwin
  Lincoln's Secretary of War 320
St. Bartholomew's Day Massacre (1572) 36
Stevens, Thaddeus 320
Stewart, Lyman 486
Stone, Lucy 263
Stowe, Harriet Beecher 263, 274
  1851-1852 - Uncle Tom's Cabin 274
Stuyvesant, Peter 83, 84
Sumner, Massachusetts Senator Charles
  1856 - Sumner nearly beaten to death by South Carolina Representative Preston Brooks 280
  Leading post-war Northern 'Radical' 280, 281, 320
Sumner, William Graham 447
Supreme Court 162, 163, 165, 190, 196, 197, 227, 279, 282, 283, 288, 293
  1810 - Fletcher v. Peck 197, 536
  1819 - McCulloch v. Maryland 197, 536
  1821 - Cohens v. Virginia 197, 536
  1831 - The Cherokee Nation v. Georgia 227
  1832 - Worcester v. Georgia 227

T

Taft, President William Howard 376, 382, 383, 384, 385, 386, 424
Tammany Hall 356, 378, 512, 513, 523
Taney, Chief Justice Roger B. 282, 283, 293
'Tariff of Abominations' (1828) 223
Tarleton, Colonel 'Bloody' Banastre 136, 137
Taylor, Zachary
  1845-1846 - Leads U.S. troops into Texas and Northern Mexico 255
  1849-1850 - U.S. President 265
Tecumseh 202, 205, 308
Tennent, Gilbert (Son) 102, 103, 105
Tennent, William (Father) 102
Texas Independence 249
  1822 - Austin brings in 300 Americans to settle along the Brazos River 249
  1830 - Mexican government tries to block further American settlement in Texas 249
  1835 - Battle of Gonzales 249
  1835 - The Consultation 249
  1836-03 - Mexican massacres of Americans at the Alamo and at Goliad 250
  1836-03 - Texas declared an independent Republic 250
  1836-04 - Houston's troops defeat Santa Anna's troops at San Jacinto 250
  1845 - Texas admitted to the Union as a new (slave) state 253
Text-Criticism 433
Theosophy 435
  Annie Besant 435
  Helena Blavatsky 435
  Rudolf Steiner 435
Thirty Years' War (1618-1648)
  Treaty or 'Peace' of Westphalia (1648) 37, 83
Thomas, Union General George 'Rock of Chicamauga' 308
Thoreau, Henry David 236
Tidewater Virginia and Maryland 46, 51, 98
Tilden, Samuel J. 328
Tillman Act (1907)
  Outlawed corporate contributions to electoral campaigns 381
Tippecanoe, Battle of (1811) 202
Tocqueville, Alexis de
  Democracy in America 230
Tories - American 'Loyalists' 90, 128, 134, 135, 176, 183, 239
Tories - English 81, 113
Toy, Crawford H. 432
Toynbee Hall 372
Transcendentalist/Transcendentalists/ Transcendentalism 236, 237, 238, 247, 537
Treaty or 'Peace' of Versailles 471, 472, 473, 474, 475
Trinity/Trinitarian Christianity 25, 26, 27, 28, 58, 234, 247
Trotsky, Leon 413, 503
Tubman, Harriet 263

Index 563

Tweed, William M. 'Boss'
  New York Tammany Hall Boss 305
Two Treatises of Government (1689) by John Locke 95
Tyler, John
  1841-1845 - U.S. President 252
  1845 - runs through a 'Lame Duck' Congress the admission of Texas into the Union 253

U

Übermensch 404, 405
Ulfilas (Wulfila) 28
Underground Railroad 264, 274
Unitarian/Unitarians/Unitarianism 26, 27, 28, 233, 234, 235, 236, 247
  Christian Unitarians
    Channing, William Ellery 234
    Jefferson, Thomas 234
    Ware, Henry 233
United Nations Organization 497
Universalism 435
Utopia 396, 407, 411, 426

V

Vail, Alfred 349
Vallandigham, Clement 305
Van Buren, Martin 221, 222, 223, 226, 228, 229, 230, 251, 253, 265
  1828 - Van Buren organizes the 'Jackson Democrats' 220
  1829-1833 - Secretary of State under Jackson 228
  1833-1837 - Jackson's Vice President 228
  1837-1841 - U.S. President 228
Vanderbilt, Cornelius 'Commodore' 342, 343, 347
Vereide, Abraham 530
Virginia Company 44, 46, 72, 73
Virginia - feudal foundations 20, 42, 51
Virginia Governor's Council 46, 47, 49, 52, 99, 201
Virginia's Tidewater Region 46, 51, 98

W

War Hawks 202
War of 1812
  1812-06 - War is declared 203
  1812-08 - Potawatomi Indians slaughter surrendered Americans at Fort Dearborn (Chicago) 204
  1813-01 - Americans defeated (and slaughtered) at Detroit 204
  1813-04 - Americans burn York (Toronto) to the ground 204
  1813-08 - 'Red Stick' Creek Indians slaughter Americans at Fort Mims (Alabama) 204
  1814-04 - General Jackson's troops and Indian allies destroy Red Sticks at Horseshoe Bend 203
  1814-08 British burn Washington 206
  1814-09 - British advance stopped at Fort McHenry (Baltimore) 207
  1814-09 - British defeated on Lake Champlain 207
  1814-12 - Treaty of Ghent officially ends the war 207
  1815-01 - Jackson's forces annihilate the British at the Battle of New Orleans 207
War of American Independence (1775-1783) 114
  1770-02 - Boston Massacre 114
  1773-12 - Boston Tea Party 115
  1774 - 'Coercive' or 'Intolerable Acts' 115
  1775-04 - Battles of Lexington and Concord 116
  1775-05 - 2nd Continental Congress convenes in Philadelphia 117
  1775-06 - Battle of Bunker (and Breed's Hill) 116
  1776-02 - Tory Loyalists badly defeated at Moore's Creek Bridge (North Carolina) 135
  1776-03 - British vacate Boston 119
  1776-06 - Arnold fails to gain Canada 118
  1776-06 - British fail to take Charleston at Sullivan's Island 135
  1776-06 - Virginia Resolution 120
  1776-07 - Declaration of Independence 119
  1776-12 - Battle of Trenton 131
  1777-01 - Battle of Princeton 131
  1777-09-10 - Battle of Saratoga 132
  1777-10 - British under Howe take Philadelphia 133
  1777-11 - Articles of Confederation 121
  1777-1778 - Wintering at Valley Forge 115
  1778-06 - Battle of Monmouth 133
  1780-03-05 - Clinton and Cornwallis force Charleston to surrender 136
  1780-05 - At Waxhaws, 'Bloody Tarleton' cuts down surrendered

Americans 136
1780-08 - Gates defeated at Camden 136
1780-10 - Patriots defeat Loyalists at King's Mountain 136
1781-01 - Morgan destroys Tarleton at Cowpens 136
1781-05 - Guilford Court House - Greene's Patriot Army defeated / But Cornwallis' troops exhausted 137
1781-09-10 - Siege of Cornwallis' troops at Yorktown; Cornwallis surrenders 137
1783- 09 - Treaty of Paris 138
War of Austrian Succession/King George's War (1744-1748) 109
Treaty of Aix la Chapelle 109
War of Jenkins' Ear (1739 1742) 108
War of Spanish Succession/Queen Anne's War (1701-1713) 107
Treaty (or 'Peace') of Utrecht (1713) 107, 108
War of the Roses (1455-1487) 31
War with the Barbary pirates (1801-1807) 192
Washington, George 3, 19, 110, 117, 119, 122, 123, 124, 125, 126, 127, 128, 129, 130, 131, 132, 133, 134, 137, 138, 142, 143, 154, 157, 158, 169, 170, 174, 175, 176, 177, 180, 182, 183, 184, 185, 187, 190, 191, 192, 199, 201, 210
1750s - Washington as a young Virginia officer 110
1775 - Washington placed in command of the Continental Army 117
1776-08 - Washington barely escapes British encirclement in New York 130
1776-12 Washington's troops defeat Britain's Hessian troops at Trenton 130
1777-01 - Washington's troops defeat British at Princeton 132
1777-1778 - Wintering with the troops at Valley Forge 133
1778-06 - Lee messes up Washington's chance for a victory at Monmouth 134
1781 - Defeats Cornwallis at Yorktown 137
1787 - Washington quietly presides over the Constitutional debates 142
1787 - Washington stops Shay's Rebellion 143
1789-1797 - U.S. President 174
1789 - Inauguration speech acknowledging the nation's debt to the Almighty Being ('God') 169
1793 - Washington and Jefferson split over French-English dispute 183
1796 - Washington refuses a third term as President 185
Washington's background and personal character 122
Ethical troubles behind Washington's back 125
Washington at Prayer (viewed by Isaac Potts) 123, 124
Washington's war goals and strategy 124
Waterhouse, Benjamin 234, 537
Webster, Daniel 271, 272, 276, 536
1813-1827 - Member of the House of Representatives (New Hampshire, then Massachusetts) during two different periods 224
1827-1841 and 1845-1850 - Senator from Massachusetts 224
1830 - Webster-Hayne debate 224
1841-1843 and 1850-1852 - Secretary of State under Harrison, Tyler and Fillmore 276
1842 - Webster-Ashburton Treaty Sets Canadian-American border 253
1848 - Declines Harrison's offer to run as his Vice President (but Harrison dies one year later) 265
1848 - Webster argues against accepting the Guadalupe Hidalgo Treaty 259
1850 - Webster strongly supports Clay's 'Compromise' Bill 271
Wellington, Arthur 206
Wesley, John 102, 103, 130, 241, 242
Westinghouse, George 351, 362
Westphalia, Treaty or 'Peace' of (1648) 37, 83
West's Cattle Kingdoms (1860s-1880s) 333
Whig Party (American) 248, 252, 254, 257, 258, 259, 265, 276, 277, 278, 280
1834 - Formation of the party 228
Whigs - American 'Patriots' 116, 134
Whigs - English 81, 90, 96, 112, 113,

Index 565

147
Whiskey Ring
  Owing $ millions in taxes during Grant Administration 328
Whitefield, George 101, 102, 103, 105
Whitney, Eli 197
William of Orange/William III, King of England 89, 90, 91
Williams, Roger 61, 63, 65, 86, 219
Wilmot, David
  1846 - ' Wilmot Provison' bans slavery in lands taken from Mexico 258
Wilson, Woodrow
  1856-1879 - Early Years and schooling 420
  1879-1883 - Law studies and law practice 421
  1883-1890 - Doctoral studies, writer and young professor 421
  1890-1902 - Princeton Professor 422
  1902-1910 - President of Princeton 422
  1911-1913 - New Jersey Governor 423
  1913 - Elected U.S. President 424
  1914-1917 - Keeps America 'neutral' in the 'Great War' 463
  1916 - Re-elected U.S. President 424
  1917 - Decides to take America into the war … to bring 'democracy' to the world 465
  1918 - Offers the 'Autocracies' an Armistice based on his 14 Points 468
  1919-01-06 - Betrayed by his 'democratic' allies at the Versailles Peace talks 471
  1919-07 - Incapacitated by a serious stroke 473
  1919-11 - The U.S. Senate refuses to accept entry into Wilson's League of Nations 472, 498
Winthrop, John 3, 15, 16, 17, 18, 19, 57, 58, 59, 60, 61, 63, 65, 66, 67, 68, 69, 170
Witches/Witchcraft 92, 93, 94
Witherspoon, John 128, 201
Wobblies - Industrial Workers of the World 371
Wolfe, General James 111
Women's Christian Temperance Union (WCTU) 371, 481
Woolman, John 214
World War One/'The Great War' (1914-1918)
  1908 - Austria-Hungary annexes Bosnia-Herzegovina 454
  1914-06 - Assassination of Austrian Archduke Franz Ferdinand and his wife 455
  1914-07-08 The European powers declare war 455
  1914-09 - A bloody statemate sets in in the West 457
  1916 - The Battles of Verdun and the Somme 460
  1917-03 - Russia's 'February Revolution' 461
  1917-04 - Wilson Takes America into the War 463
  1917-12 - Bolshevik 'Reds' take Russia out of the war in order to fight the 'Whites' 469
  1918-01 - Wilson Announces his 'Fourteen Points' 468
  1918-03-07 - A German 'Spring Offensive' fails, exhausting Germany 469
  1918-11 The Germans agree to an Armistice on Wilson's 14-point terms 470
  1919 - But peace negotiations at Versailles go in a very anti-German direction 471
  1919 - France and Britain carve up the German, Austro-Hungarian and Turkish Empires 473
  1919 - Wilson hopes a 'League of Nations' will be able to renegotiate a fairer 'Peace' 472
  1920s - Post-war moral/spiritual loss 487
Wright Brothers, Orville & Wilbur 364

X

X, Y, Z Affair 188

Y

Yankee culture 198
Young, Brigham 245

Z

Zinzendorf, Count Nikolaus von 129

www.ingramcontent.com/pod-product-compliance
Lightning Source LLC
Chambersburg PA
CBHW071800080526
44589CB00012B/625